# HTTP
## *The Definitive Guide*

# HTTP
## *The Definitive Guide*

*David Gourley and Brian Totty*

*with Marjorie Sayer, Sailu Reddy, and Anshu Aggarwal*

O'REILLY®

Beijing · Cambridge · Farnham · Köln · Sebastopol · Taipei · Tokyo

**HTTP: The Definitive Guide**
by David Gourley and Brian Totty
with Marjorie Sayer, Sailu Reddy, and Anshu Aggarwal

Published by O'Reilly Media, Inc., 1005 Gravenstein Highway North, Sebastopol, CA 95472.

O'Reilly Media, Inc. books may be purchased for educational, business, or sales promotional use. On-line editions are also available for most titles (*safari.oreilly.com*). For more information, contact our corporate/institutional sales department: (800) 998-9938 or *corporate@oreilly.com*.

| | |
|---|---|
| **Editor:** | Linda Mui |
| **Production Editor:** | Rachel Wheeler |
| **Cover Designer:** | Ellie Volckhausen |
| **Interior Designers:** | David Futato and Melanie Wang |

**Printing History:**

| | |
|---|---|
| September 2002: | First Edition. |

 This book uses RepKover™, a durable and flexible lay-flat binding.

ISBN: 978-1-56592-509-0
[C]                                                                                         [12/09]

# Table of Contents

**Part I.   HTTP: The Web's Foundation**

## Part III.  Identification, Authorization, and Security

## Part VI. Appendixes

# Preface

The Hypertext Transfer Protocol (HTTP) is the protocol programs use to communicate over the World Wide Web. There are many applications of HTTP, but HTTP is most famous for two-way conversation between web browsers and web servers.

HTTP began as a simple protocol, so you might think there really isn't that much to say about it. And yet here you stand, with a two-pound book in your hands. If you're wondering how we could have written 650 pages on HTTP, take a look at the Table of Contents. This book isn't just an HTTP header reference manual; it's a veritable bible of web architecture.

In this book, we try to tease apart HTTP's interrelated and often misunderstood rules, and we offer you a series of topic-based chapters that explain all the aspects of HTTP. Throughout the book, we are careful to explain the "why" of HTTP, not just the "how." And to save you time chasing references, we explain many of the critical non-HTTP technologies that are required to make HTTP applications work. You can find the alphabetical header reference (which forms the basis of most conventional HTTP texts) in a conveniently organized appendix. We hope this conceptual design makes it easy for you to work with HTTP.

This book is written for anyone who wants to understand HTTP and the underlying architecture of the Web. Software and hardware engineers can use this book as a coherent reference for HTTP and related web technologies. Systems architects and network administrators can use this book to better understand how to design, deploy, and manage complicated web architectures. Performance engineers and analysts can benefit from the sections on caching and performance optimization. Marketing and consulting professionals will be able to use the conceptual orientation to better understand the landscape of web technologies.

This book illustrates common misconceptions, advises on "tricks of the trade," provides convenient reference material, and serves as a readable introduction to dry and confusing standards specifications. In a single book, we detail the essential and interrelated technologies that make the Web work.

This book is the result of a tremendous amount of work by many people who share an enthusiasm for Internet technologies. We hope you find it useful.

## Running Example: Joe's Hardware Store

Many of our chapters include a running example of a hypothetical online hardware and home-improvement store called "Joe's Hardware" to demonstrate technology concepts. We have set up a real web site for the store (*http://www.joes-hardware. com*) for you to test some of the examples in the book. We will maintain this web site while this book remains in print.

## Chapter-by-Chapter Guide

This book contains 21 chapters, divided into 5 logical parts (each with a technology theme), and 8 useful appendixes containing reference data and surveys of related technologies:

> Part I, *HTTP: The Web's Foundation*
> Part II, *HTTP Architecture*
> Part III, *Identification, Authorization, and Security*
> Part IV, *Entities, Encodings, and Internationalization*
> Part V, *Content Publishing and Distribution*
> Part VI, *Appendixes*

Part I, *HTTP: The Web's Foundation*, describes the core technology of HTTP, the foundation of the Web, in four chapters:

- Chapter 1, *Overview of HTTP*, is a rapid-paced overview of HTTP.
- Chapter 2, *URLs and Resources*, details the formats of uniform resource locators (URLs) and the various types of resources that URLs name across the Internet. It also outlines the evolution to uniform resource names (URNs).
- Chapter 3, *HTTP Messages*, details how HTTP messages transport web content.
- Chapter 4, *Connection Management*, explains the commonly misunderstood and poorly documented rules and behavior for managing HTTP connections.

Part II, *HTTP Architecture*, highlights the HTTP server, proxy, cache, gateway, and robot applications that are the architectural building blocks of web systems. (Web browsers are another building block, of course, but browsers already were covered thoroughly in Part I of the book.) Part II contains the following six chapters:

- Chapter 5, *Web Servers*, gives an overview of web server architectures.
- Chapter 6, *Proxies*, explores HTTP proxy servers, which are intermediary servers that act as platforms for HTTP services and controls.
- Chapter 7, *Caching*, delves into the science of web caches—devices that improve performance and reduce traffic by making local copies of popular documents.

- Chapter 8, *Integration Points: Gateways, Tunnels, and Relays*, explains gateways and application servers that allow HTTP to work with software that speaks different protocols, including Secure Sockets Layer (SSL) encrypted protocols.

- Chapter 9, *Web Robots*, describes the various types of clients that pervade the Web, including the ubiquitous browsers, robots and spiders, and search engines.

- Chapter 10, *HTTP-NG*, talks about HTTP developments still in the works: the HTTP-NG protocol.

Part III, *Identification, Authorization, and Security*, presents a suite of techniques and technologies to track identity, enforce security, and control access to content. It contains the following four chapters:

- Chapter 11, *Client Identification and Cookies*, talks about techniques to identify users so that content can be personalized to the user audience.

- Chapter 12, *Basic Authentication*, highlights the basic mechanisms to verify user identity. The chapter also examines how HTTP authentication interfaces with databases.

- Chapter 13, *Digest Authentication*, explains digest authentication, a complex proposed enhancement to HTTP that provides significantly enhanced security.

- Chapter 14, *Secure HTTP*, is a detailed overview of Internet cryptography, digital certificates, and SSL.

Part IV, *Entities, Encodings, and Internationalization*, focuses on the bodies of HTTP messages (which contain the actual web content) and on the web standards that describe and manipulate content stored in the message bodies. Part IV contains three chapters:

- Chapter 15, *Entities and Encodings*, describes the structure of HTTP content.

- Chapter 16, *Internationalization*, surveys the web standards that allow users around the globe to exchange content in different languages and character sets.

- Chapter 17, *Content Negotiation and Transcoding*, explains mechanisms for negotiating acceptable content.

Part V, *Content Publishing and Distribution*, discusses the technology for publishing and disseminating web content. It contains four chapters:

- Chapter 18, *Web Hosting*, discusses the ways people deploy servers in modern web hosting environments and HTTP support for virtual web hosting.

- Chapter 19, *Publishing Systems*, discusses the technologies for creating web content and installing it onto web servers.

- Chapter 20, *Redirection and Load Balancing*, surveys the tools and techniques for distributing incoming web traffic among a collection of servers.

- Chapter 21, *Logging and Usage Tracking*, covers log formats and common questions.

Part VI, *Appendixes*, contains helpful reference appendixes and tutorials in related technologies:

- Appendix A, *URI Schemes*, summarizes the protocols supported through uniform resource identifier (URI) schemes.
- Appendix B, *HTTP Status Codes*, conveniently lists the HTTP response codes.
- Appendix C, *HTTP Header Reference*, provides a reference list of HTTP header fields.
- Appendix D, *MIME Types*, provides an extensive list of MIME types and explains how MIME types are registered.
- Appendix E, *Base-64 Encoding*, explains base-64 encoding, used by HTTP authentication.
- Appendix F, *Digest Authentication*, gives details on how to implement various authentication schemes in HTTP.
- Appendix G, *Language Tags*, defines language tag values for HTTP language headers.
- Appendix H, *MIME Charset Registry*, provides a detailed list of character encodings, used for HTTP internationalization support.

Each chapter contains many examples and pointers to additional reference material.

## Typographic Conventions

In this book, we use the following typographic conventions:

*Italic*
>  Used for URLs, C functions, command names, MIME types, new terms where they are defined, and emphasis

Constant width
>  Used for computer output, code, and any literal text

**Constant width bold**
>  Used for user input

## Comments and Questions

Please address comments and questions concerning this book to the publisher:

>  O'Reilly & Associates, Inc.
>  1005 Gravenstein Highway North
>  Sebastopol, CA 95472
>  (800) 998-9938 (in the United States or Canada)
>  (707) 829-0515 (international/local)
>  (707) 829-0104 (fax)

There is a web page for this book, which lists errata, examples, or any additional information. You can access this page at:

*http://www.oreilly.com/catalog/httptdg/*

To comment or ask technical questions about this book, send email to:

*bookquestions@oreilly.com*

For more information about books, conferences, Resource Centers, and the O'Reilly Network, see the O'Reilly web site at:

*http://www.oreilly.com*

# Acknowledgments

This book is the labor of many. The five authors would like to hold up a few people in thanks for their significant contributions to this project.

To start, we'd like to thank Linda Mui, our editor at O'Reilly. Linda first met with David and Brian way back in 1996, and she refined and steered several concepts into the book you hold today. Linda also helped keep our wandering gang of first-time book authors moving in a coherent direction and on a progressing (if not rapid) timeline. Most of all, Linda gave us the chance to create this book. We're very grateful.

We'd also like to thank several tremendously bright, knowledgeable, and kind souls who devoted noteworthy energy to reviewing, commenting on, and correcting drafts of this book. These include Tony Bourke, Sean Burke, Mike Chowla, Shernaz Daver, Fred Douglis, Paula Ferguson, Vikas Jha, Yves Lafon, Peter Mattis, Chuck Neerdaels, Luis Tavera, Duane Wessels, Dave Wu, and Marco Zagha. Their viewpoints and suggestions have improved the book tremendously.

Rob Romano from O'Reilly created most of the amazing artwork you'll find in this book. The book contains an unusually large number of detailed illustrations that make subtle concepts very clear. Many of these illustrations were painstakingly created and revised numerous times. If a picture is worth a thousand words, Rob added hundreds of pages of value to this book.

Brian would like to personally thank all of the authors for their dedication to this project. A tremendous amount of time was invested by the authors in a challenge to make the first detailed but accessible treatment of HTTP. Weddings, childbirths, killer work projects, startup companies, and graduate schools intervened, but the authors held together to bring this project to a successful completion. We believe the result is worthy of everyone's hard work and, most importantly, that it provides a valuable service. Brian also would like to thank the employees of Inktomi for their enthusiasm and support and for their deep insights about the use of HTTP in real-world applications. Also, thanks to the fine folks at Cajun-shop.com for allowing us to use their site for some of the examples in this book.

David would like to thank his family, particularly his mother and grandfather for their ongoing support. He'd like to thank those that have put up with his erratic schedule over the years writing the book. He'd also like to thank Slurp, Orctomi, and Norma for everything they've done, and his fellow authors for all their hard work. Finally, he would like to thank Brian for roping him into yet another adventure.

Marjorie would like to thank her husband, Alan Liu, for technical insight, familial support and understanding. Marjorie thanks her fellow authors for many insights and inspirations. She is grateful for the experience of working together on this book.

Sailu would like to thank David and Brian for the opportunity to work on this book, and Chuck Neerdaels for introducing him to HTTP.

Anshu would like to thank his wife, Rashi, and his parents for their patience, support, and encouragement during the long years spent writing this book.

Finally, the authors collectively thank the famous and nameless Internet pioneers, whose research, development, and evangelism over the past four decades contributed so much to our scientific, social, and economic community. Without these labors, there would be no subject for this book.

# PART I

# HTTP: The Web's Foundation

This section is an introduction to the HTTP protocol. The next four chapters describe the core technology of HTTP, the foundation of the Web:

- Chapter 1, *Overview of HTTP*, is a rapid-paced overview of HTTP.

- Chapter 2, *URLs and Resources*, details the formats of URLs and the various types of resources that URLs name across the Internet. We also outline the evolution to URNs.

- Chapter 3, *HTTP Messages*, details the HTTP messages that transport web content.

- Chapter 4, *Connection Management*, discusses the commonly misunderstood and poorly documented rules and behavior for managing TCP connections by HTTP.

# CHAPTER 1

# Overview of HTTP

The world's web browsers, servers, and related web applications all talk to each other through HTTP, the Hypertext Transfer Protocol. HTTP is the common language of the modern global Internet.

This chapter is a concise overview of HTTP. You'll see how web applications use HTTP to communicate, and you'll get a rough idea of how HTTP does its job. In particular, we talk about:

- How web clients and servers communicate
- Where resources (web content) come from
- How web transactions work
- The format of the messages used for HTTP communication
- The underlying TCP network transport
- The different variations of the HTTP protocol
- Some of the many HTTP architectural components installed around the Internet

We've got a lot of ground to cover, so let's get started on our tour of HTTP.

## HTTP: The Internet's Multimedia Courier

Billions of JPEG images, HTML pages, text files, MPEG movies, WAV audio files, Java applets, and more cruise through the Internet each and every day. HTTP moves the bulk of this information quickly, conveniently, and reliably from web servers all around the world to web browsers on people's desktops.

Because HTTP uses reliable data-transmission protocols, it guarantees that your data will not be damaged or scrambled in transit, even when it comes from the other side of the globe. This is good for you as a user, because you can access information without worrying about its integrity. Reliable transmission is also good for you as an Internet application developer, because you don't have to worry about HTTP communications being destroyed, duplicated, or distorted in transit. You can focus on programming the distinguishing details of your application, without worrying about the flaws and foibles of the Internet.

Let's look more closely at how HTTP transports the Web's traffic.

## Web Clients and Servers

Web content lives on web servers. Web servers speak the HTTP protocol, so they are often called HTTP servers. These HTTP servers store the Internet's data and provide the data when it is requested by HTTP clients. The clients send HTTP requests to servers, and servers return the requested data in HTTP responses, as sketched in Figure 1-1. Together, HTTP clients and HTTP servers make up the basic components of the World Wide Web.

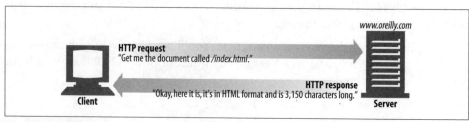

*Figure 1-1. Web clients and servers*

You probably use HTTP clients every day. The most common client is a web browser, such as Microsoft Internet Explorer or Netscape Navigator. Web browsers request HTTP objects from servers and display the objects on your screen.

When you browse to a page, such as "http://www.oreilly.com/index.html," your browser sends an HTTP request to the server *www.oreilly.com* (see Figure 1-1). The server tries to find the desired object (in this case, "/index.html") and, if successful, sends the object to the client in an HTTP response, along with the type of the object, the length of the object, and other information.

## Resources

Web servers host *web resources*. A web resource is the source of web content. The simplest kind of web resource is a static file on the web server's filesystem. These files can contain anything: they might be text files, HTML files, Microsoft Word files, Adobe Acrobat files, JPEG image files, AVI movie files, or any other format you can think of.

However, resources don't have to be static files. Resources can also be software programs that generate content on demand. These dynamic content resources can generate content based on your identity, on what information you've requested, or on the time of day. They can show you a live image from a camera, or let you trade stocks, search real estate databases, or buy gifts from online stores (see Figure 1-2).

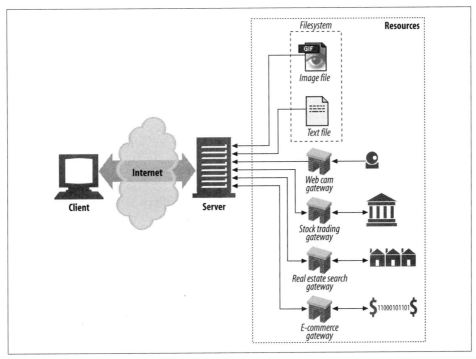

*Figure 1-2. A web resource is anything that provides web content*

In summary, a resource is any kind of content source. A file containing your company's sales forecast spreadsheet is a resource. A web gateway to scan your local public library's shelves is a resource. An Internet search engine is a resource.

## Media Types

Because the Internet hosts many thousands of different data types, HTTP carefully tags each object being transported through the Web with a data format label called a *MIME type*. MIME (Multipurpose Internet Mail Extensions) was originally designed to solve problems encountered in moving messages between different electronic mail systems. MIME worked so well for email that HTTP adopted it to describe and label its own multimedia content.

Web servers attach a MIME type to all HTTP object data (see Figure 1-3). When a web browser gets an object back from a server, it looks at the associated MIME type to see if it knows how to handle the object. Most browsers can handle hundreds of popular object types: displaying image files, parsing and formatting HTML files, playing audio files through the computer's speakers, or launching external plug-in software to handle special formats.

*Figure 1-3. MIME types are sent back with the data content*

A MIME type is a textual label, represented as a primary object type and a specific subtype, separated by a slash. For example:

- An HTML-formatted text document would be labeled with type text/html.
- A plain ASCII text document would be labeled with type text/plain.
- A JPEG version of an image would be image/jpeg.
- A GIF-format image would be image/gif.
- An Apple QuickTime movie would be video/quicktime.
- A Microsoft PowerPoint presentation would be application/vnd.ms-powerpoint.

There are hundreds of popular MIME types, and many more experimental or limited-use types. A very thorough MIME type list is provided in Appendix D.

## URIs

Each web server resource has a name, so clients can point out what resources they are interested in. The server resource name is called a *uniform resource identifier*, or URI. URIs are like the postal addresses of the Internet, uniquely identifying and locating information resources around the world.

Here's a URI for an image resource on Joe's Hardware store's web server:

```
http://www.joes-hardware.com/specials/saw-blade.gif
```

Figure 1-4 shows how the URI specifies the HTTP protocol to access the saw-blade GIF resource on Joe's store's server. Given the URI, HTTP can retrieve the object. URIs come in two flavors, called URLs and URNs. Let's take a peek at each of these types of resource identifiers now.

## URLs

The *uniform resource locator* (URL) is the most common form of resource identifier. URLs describe the specific location of a resource on a particular server. They tell you exactly how to fetch a resource from a precise, fixed location. Figure 1-4 shows how a URL tells precisely where a resource is located and how to access it. Table 1-1 shows a few examples of URLs.

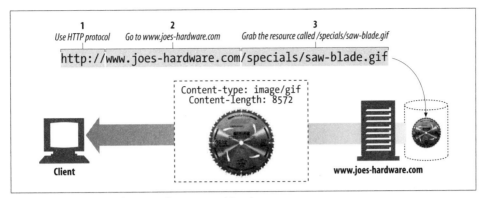

*Figure 1-4. URLs specify protocol, server, and local resource*

*Table 1-1. Example URLs*

| URL | Description |
|---|---|
| *http://www.oreilly.com/index.html* | The home URL for O'Reilly & Associates, Inc. |
| *http://www.yahoo.com/images/logo.gif* | The URL for the Yahoo! web site's logo |
| *http://www.joes-hardware.com/inventory-check.cgi?item=12731* | The URL for a program that checks if inventory item #12731 is in stock |
| *ftp://joe:tools4u@ftp.joes-hardware.com/locking-pliers.gif* | The URL for the *locking-pliers.gif* image file, using password-protected FTP as the access protocol |

Most URLs follow a standardized format of three main parts:

- The first part of the URL is called the *scheme*, and it describes the protocol used to access the resource. This is usually the HTTP protocol (*http://*).
- The second part gives the server Internet address (e.g., *www.joes-hardware.com*).
- The rest names a resource on the web server (e.g., */specials/saw-blade.gif*).

Today, almost every URI is a URL.

## URNs

The second flavor of URI is the *uniform resource name*, or URN. A URN serves as a unique name for a particular piece of content, independent of where the resource currently resides. These location-independent URNs allow resources to move from place to place. URNs also allow resources to be accessed by multiple network access protocols while maintaining the same name.

For example, the following URN might be used to name the Internet standards document "RFC 2141" regardless of where it resides (it may even be copied in several places):

   *urn:ietf:rfc:2141*

URNs are still experimental and not yet widely adopted. To work effectively, URNs need a supporting infrastructure to resolve resource locations; the lack of such an infrastructure has also slowed their adoption. But URNs do hold some exciting promise for the future. We'll discuss URNs in a bit more detail in Chapter 2, but most of the remainder of this book focuses almost exclusively on URLs.

Unless stated otherwise, we adopt the conventional terminology and use URI and URL interchangeably for the remainder of this book.

# Transactions

Let's look in more detail how clients use HTTP to transact with web servers and their resources. An HTTP transaction consists of a request command (sent from client to server), and a response result (sent from the server back to the client). This communication happens with formatted blocks of data called *HTTP messages*, as illustrated in Figure 1-5.

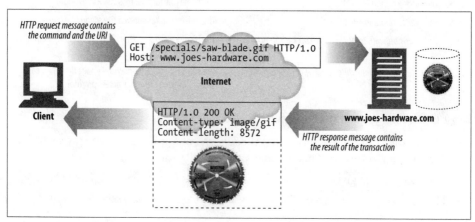

*Figure 1-5. HTTP transactions consist of request and response messages*

## Methods

HTTP supports several different request commands, called *HTTP methods*. Every HTTP request message has a method. The method tells the server what action to perform (fetch a web page, run a gateway program, delete a file, etc.). Table 1-2 lists five common HTTP methods.

*Table 1-2. Some common HTTP methods*

| HTTP method | Description |
| --- | --- |
| GET | Send named resource from the server to the client. |
| PUT | Store data from client into a named server resource. |

*Table 1-2. Some common HTTP methods (continued)*

| HTTP method | Description |
|---|---|
| DELETE | Delete the named resource from a server. |
| POST | Send client data into a server gateway application. |
| HEAD | Send just the HTTP headers from the response for the named resource. |

We'll discuss HTTP methods in detail in Chapter 3.

## Status Codes

Every HTTP response message comes back with a status code. The status code is a three-digit numeric code that tells the client if the request succeeded, or if other actions are required. A few common status codes are shown in Table 1-3.

*Table 1-3. Some common HTTP status codes*

| HTTP status code | Description |
|---|---|
| 200 | OK. Document returned correctly. |
| 302 | Redirect. Go someplace else to get the resource. |
| 404 | Not Found. Can't find this resource. |

HTTP also sends an explanatory textual "reason phrase" with each numeric status code (see the response message in Figure 1-5). The textual phrase is included only for descriptive purposes; the numeric code is used for all processing.

The following status codes and reason phrases are treated identically by HTTP software:

```
200 OK
200 Document attached
200 Success
200 All's cool, dude
```

HTTP status codes are explained in detail in Chapter 3.

## Web Pages Can Consist of Multiple Objects

An application often issues multiple HTTP transactions to accomplish a task. For example, a web browser issues a cascade of HTTP transactions to fetch and display a graphics-rich web page. The browser performs one transaction to fetch the HTML "skeleton" that describes the page layout, then issues additional HTTP transactions for each embedded image, graphics pane, Java applet, etc. These embedded resources might even reside on different servers, as shown in Figure 1-6. Thus, a "web page" often is a collection of resources, not a single resource.

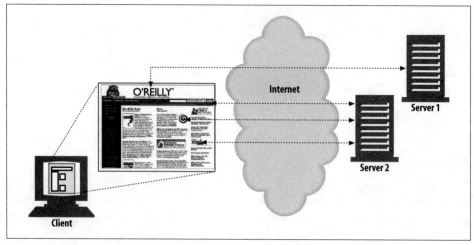

Figure 1-6. Composite web pages require separate HTTP transactions for each embedded resource

## Messages

Now let's take a quick look at the structure of HTTP request and response messages. We'll study HTTP messages in exquisite detail in Chapter 3.

HTTP messages are simple, line-oriented sequences of characters. Because they are plain text, not binary, they are easy for humans to read and write.* Figure 1-7 shows the HTTP messages for a simple transaction.

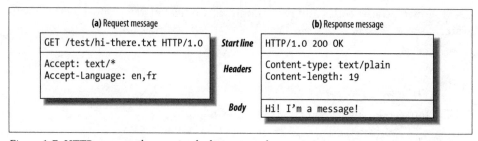

Figure 1-7. HTTP messages have a simple, line-oriented text structure

HTTP messages sent from web clients to web servers are called *request messages*. Messages from servers to clients are called *response messages*. There are no other kinds of HTTP messages. The formats of HTTP request and response messages are very similar.

---

* Some programmers complain about the difficulty of HTTP parsing, which can be tricky and error-prone, especially when designing high-speed software. A binary format or a more restricted text format might have been simpler to process, but most HTTP programmers appreciate HTTP's extensibility and debuggability.

HTTP messages consist of three parts:

*Start line*
> The first line of the message is the start line, indicating what to do for a request or what happened for a response.

*Header fields*
> Zero or more header fields follow the start line. Each header field consists of a name and a value, separated by a colon (:) for easy parsing. The headers end with a blank line. Adding a header field is as easy as adding another line.

*Body*
> After the blank line is an optional message body containing any kind of data. Request bodies carry data to the web server; response bodies carry data back to the client. Unlike the start lines and headers, which are textual and structured, the body can contain arbitrary binary data (e.g., images, videos, audio tracks, software applications). Of course, the body can also contain text.

## Simple Message Example

Figure 1-8 shows the HTTP messages that might be sent as part of a simple transaction. The browser requests the resource http://www.joes-hardware.com/tools.html.

In Figure 1-8, the browser sends an HTTP request message. The request has a GET method in the start line, and the local resource is */tools.html*. The request indicates it is speaking Version 1.0 of the HTTP protocol. The request message has no body, because no request data is needed to GET a simple document from a server.

The server sends back an HTTP response message. The response contains the HTTP version number (HTTP/1.0), a success status code (200), a descriptive reason phrase (OK), and a block of response header fields, all followed by the response body containing the requested document. The response body length is noted in the Content-Length header, and the document's MIME type is noted in the Content-Type header.

# Connections

Now that we've sketched what HTTP's messages look like, let's talk for a moment about how messages move from place to place, across Transmission Control Protocol (TCP) connections.

## TCP/IP

HTTP is an application layer protocol. HTTP doesn't worry about the nitty-gritty details of network communication; instead, it leaves the details of networking to TCP/IP, the popular reliable Internet transport protocol.

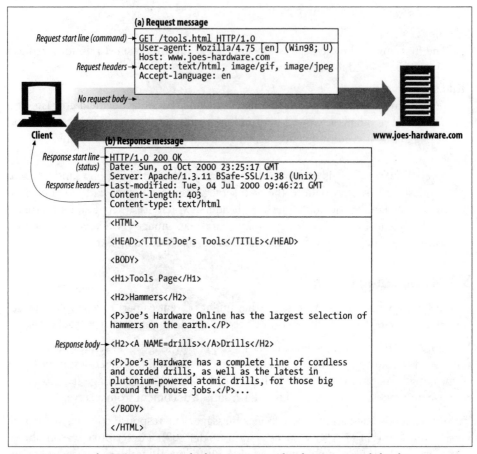

*Figure 1-8. Example GET transaction for http://www.joes-hardware.com/tools.html*

TCP provides:

- Error-free data transportation
- In-order delivery (data will always arrive in the order in which it was sent)
- Unsegmented data stream (can dribble out data in any size at any time)

The Internet itself is based on TCP/IP, a popular layered set of packet-switched network protocols spoken by computers and network devices around the world. TCP/IP hides the peculiarities and foibles of individual networks and hardware, letting computers and networks of any type talk together reliably.

Once a TCP connection is established, messages exchanged between the client and server computers will never be lost, damaged, or received out of order.

In networking terms, the HTTP protocol is *layered* over TCP. HTTP uses TCP to transport its message data. Likewise, TCP is layered over IP (see Figure 1-9).

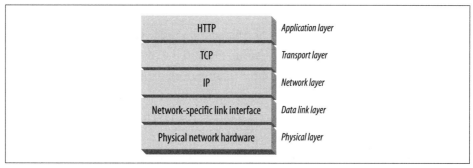

| | |
|---|---|
| HTTP | *Application layer* |
| TCP | *Transport layer* |
| IP | *Network layer* |
| Network-specific link interface | *Data link layer* |
| Physical network hardware | *Physical layer* |

*Figure 1-9. HTTP network protocol stack*

## Connections, IP Addresses, and Port Numbers

Before an HTTP client can send a message to a server, it needs to establish a TCP/IP connection between the client and server using Internet protocol (IP) addresses and port numbers.

Setting up a TCP connection is sort of like calling someone at a corporate office. First, you dial the company's phone number. This gets you to the right organization. Then, you dial the specific extension of the person you're trying to reach.

In TCP, you need the IP address of the server computer and the TCP port number associated with the specific software program running on the server.

This is all well and good, but how do you get the IP address and port number of the HTTP server in the first place? Why, the URL, of course! We mentioned before that URLs are the addresses for resources, so naturally enough they can provide us with the IP address for the machine that has the resource. Let's take a look at a few URLs:

```
http://207.200.83.29:80/index.html
http://www.netscape.com:80/index.html
http://www.netscape.com/index.html
```

The first URL has the machine's IP address, "207.200.83.29", and port number, "80".

The second URL doesn't have a numeric IP address; it has a textual domain name, or *hostname* ("www.netscape.com"). The hostname is just a human-friendly alias for an IP address. Hostnames can easily be converted into IP addresses through a facility called the Domain Name Service (DNS), so we're all set here, too. We will talk much more about DNS and URLs in Chapter 2.

The final URL has no port number. When the port number is missing from an HTTP URL, you can assume the default value of port 80.

With the IP address and port number, a client can easily communicate via TCP/IP. Figure 1-10 shows how a browser uses HTTP to display a simple HTML resource that resides on a distant server.

Here are the steps:

*(a)* The browser extracts the server's hostname from the URL.

*(b)* The browser converts the server's hostname into the server's IP address.

*(c)* The browser extracts the port number (if any) from the URL.

*(d)* The browser establishes a TCP connection with the web server.

*(e)* The browser sends an HTTP request message to the server.

*(f)* The server sends an HTTP response back to the browser.

*(g)* The connection is closed, and the browser displays the document.

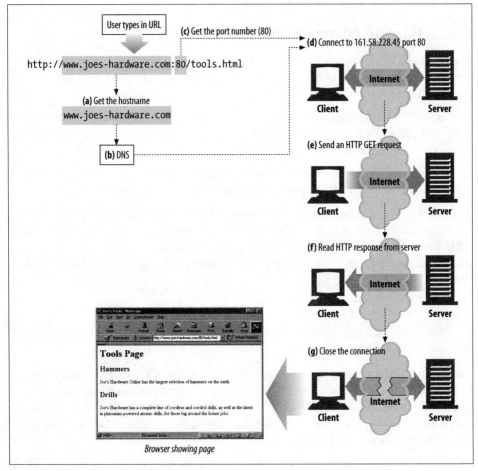

*Figure 1-10. Basic browser connection process*

## A Real Example Using Telnet

Because HTTP uses TCP/IP, and is text-based, as opposed to using some obscure binary format, it is simple to talk directly to a web server.

The Telnet utility connects your keyboard to a destination TCP port and connects the TCP port output back to your display screen. Telnet is commonly used for remote terminal sessions, but it can generally connect to any TCP server, including HTTP servers.

You can use the Telnet utility to talk directly to web servers. Telnet lets you open a TCP connection to a port on a machine and type characters directly into the port. The web server treats you as a web client, and any data sent back on the TCP connection is displayed onscreen.

Let's use Telnet to interact with a real web server. We will use Telnet to fetch the document pointed to by the URL *http://www.joes-hardware.com:80/tools.html* (you can try this example yourself).

Let's review what should happen:

- First, we need to look up the IP address of *www.joes-hardware.com* and open a TCP connection to port 80 on that machine. Telnet does this legwork for us.
- Once the TCP connection is open, we need to type in the HTTP request.
- When the request is complete (indicated by a blank line), the server should send back the content in an HTTP response and close the connection.

Our example HTTP request for *http://www.joes-hardware.com:80/tools.html* is shown in Example 1-1. What we typed is shown in boldface.

*Example 1-1. An HTTP transaction using telnet*

```
% telnet www.joes-hardware.com 80
Trying 161.58.228.45...
Connected to joes-hardware.com.
Escape character is '^]'.
GET /tools.html HTTP/1.1
Host: www.joes-hardware.com

HTTP/1.1 200 OK
Date: Sun, 01 Oct 2000 23:25:17 GMT
Server: Apache/1.3.11 BSafe-SSL/1.38 (Unix) FrontPage/4.0.4.3
Last-Modified: Tue, 04 Jul 2000 09:46:21 GMT
ETag: "373979-193-3961b26d"
Accept-Ranges: bytes
Content-Length: 403
Connection: close
Content-Type: text/html
```

*Example 1-1. An HTTP transaction using telnet (continued)*

```
<HTML>
<HEAD><TITLE>Joe's Tools</TITLE></HEAD>
<BODY>
<H1>Tools Page</H1>
<H2>Hammers</H2>
<P>Joe's Hardware Online has the largest selection of hammers on the earth.</P>
<H2><A NAME=drills></A>Drills</H2>
<P>Joe's Hardware has a complete line of cordless and corded drills, as well as the latest
in plutonium-powered atomic drills, for those big around the house jobs.</P> ...
</BODY>
</HTML>
Connection closed by foreign host.
```

Telnet looks up the hostname and opens a connection to the *www.joes-hardware.com* web server, which is listening on port 80. The three lines after the command are output from Telnet, telling us it has established a connection.

We then type in our basic request command, "GET /tools.html HTTP/1.1", and send a Host header providing the original hostname, followed by a blank line, asking the server to GET us the resource "/tools.html" from the server *www.joes-hardware.com*. After that, the server responds with a response line, several response headers, a blank line, and finally the body of the HTML document.

Beware that Telnet mimics HTTP clients well but doesn't work well as a server. And automated Telnet scripting is no fun at all. For a more flexible tool, you might want to check out nc (netcat). The nc tool lets you easily manipulate and script UDP- and TCP-based traffic, including HTTP. See *http://netcat. sourceforge.net* for details.

# Protocol Versions

There are several versions of the HTTP protocol in use today. HTTP applications need to work hard to robustly handle different variations of the HTTP protocol. The versions in use are:

*HTTP/0.9*

> The 1991 prototype version of HTTP is known as HTTP/0.9. This protocol contains many serious design flaws and should be used only to interoperate with legacy clients. HTTP/0.9 supports only the GET method, and it does not support MIME typing of multimedia content, HTTP headers, or version numbers. HTTP/0.9 was originally defined to fetch simple HTML objects. It was soon replaced with HTTP/1.0.

*HTTP/1.0*

> 1.0 was the first version of HTTP that was widely deployed. HTTP/1.0 added version numbers, HTTP headers, additional methods, and multimedia object handling. HTTP/1.0 made it practical to support graphically appealing web

pages and interactive forms, which helped promote the wide-scale adoption of the World Wide Web. This specification was never well specified. It represented a collection of best practices in a time of rapid commercial and academic evolution of the protocol.

*HTTP/1.0+*

Many popular web clients and servers rapidly added features to HTTP in the mid-1990s to meet the demands of a rapidly expanding, commercially successful World Wide Web. Many of these features, including long-lasting "keep-alive" connections, virtual hosting support, and proxy connection support, were added to HTTP and became unofficial, de facto standards. This informal, extended version of HTTP is often referred to as HTTP/1.0+.

*HTTP/1.1*

HTTP/1.1 focused on correcting architectural flaws in the design of HTTP, specifying semantics, introducing significant performance optimizations, and removing mis-features. HTTP/1.1 also included support for the more sophisticated web applications and deployments that were under way in the late 1990s. HTTP/1.1 is the current version of HTTP.

*HTTP-NG (a.k.a. HTTP/2.0)*

HTTP-NG is a prototype proposal for an architectural successor to HTTP/1.1 that focuses on significant performance optimizations and a more powerful framework for remote execution of server logic. The HTTP-NG research effort concluded in 1998, and at the time of this writing, there are no plans to advance this proposal as a replacement for HTTP/1.1. See Chapter 10 for more information.

# Architectural Components of the Web

In this overview chapter, we've focused on how two web applications (web browsers and web servers) send messages back and forth to implement basic transactions. There are many other web applications that you interact with on the Internet. In this section, we'll outline several other important applications, including:

*Proxies*

HTTP intermediaries that sit between clients and servers

*Caches*

HTTP storehouses that keep copies of popular web pages close to clients

*Gateways*

Special web servers that connect to other applications

*Tunnels*

Special proxies that blindly forward HTTP communications

*Agents*

Semi-intelligent web clients that make automated HTTP requests

## Proxies

Let's start by looking at HTTP *proxy servers*, important building blocks for web security, application integration, and performance optimization.

As shown in Figure 1-11, a proxy sits between a client and a server, receiving all of the client's HTTP requests and relaying the requests to the server (perhaps after modifying the requests). These applications act as a proxy for the user, accessing the server on the user's behalf.

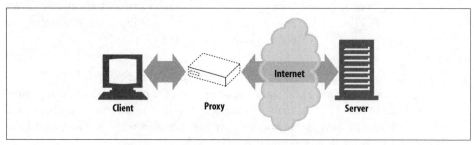

*Figure 1-11. Proxies relay traffic between client and server*

Proxies are often used for security, acting as trusted intermediaries through which all web traffic flows. Proxies can also filter requests and responses; for example, to detect application viruses in corporate downloads or to filter adult content away from elementary-school students. We'll talk about proxies in detail in Chapter 6.

## Caches

A *web cache* or *caching proxy* is a special type of HTTP proxy server that keeps copies of popular documents that pass through the proxy. The next client requesting the same document can be served from the cache's personal copy (see Figure 1-12).

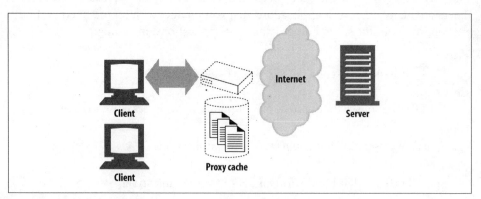

*Figure 1-12. Caching proxies keep local copies of popular documents to improve performance*

A client may be able to download a document much more quickly from a nearby cache than from a distant web server. HTTP defines many facilities to make caching more effective and to regulate the freshness and privacy of cached content. We cover caching technology in Chapter 7.

## Gateways

*Gateways* are special servers that act as intermediaries for other servers. They are often used to convert HTTP traffic to another protocol. A gateway always receives requests as if it was the origin server for the resource. The client may not be aware it is communicating with a gateway.

For example, an HTTP/FTP gateway receives requests for FTP URIs via HTTP requests but fetches the documents using the FTP protocol (see Figure 1-13). The resulting document is packed into an HTTP message and sent to the client. We discuss gateways in Chapter 8.

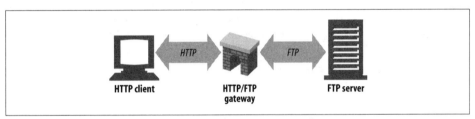

*Figure 1-13. HTTP/FTP gateway*

## Tunnels

*Tunnels* are HTTP applications that, after setup, blindly relay raw data between two connections. HTTP tunnels are often used to transport non-HTTP data over one or more HTTP connections, without looking at the data.

One popular use of HTTP tunnels is to carry encrypted Secure Sockets Layer (SSL) traffic through an HTTP connection, allowing SSL traffic through corporate firewalls that permit only web traffic. As sketched in Figure 1-14, an HTTP/SSL tunnel receives an HTTP request to establish an outgoing connection to a destination address and port, then proceeds to tunnel the encrypted SSL traffic over the HTTP channel so that it can be blindly relayed to the destination server.

## Agents

User agents (or just *agents*) are client programs that make HTTP requests on the user's behalf. Any application that issues web requests is an HTTP agent. So far, we've talked about only one kind of HTTP agent: web browsers. But there are many other kinds of user agents.

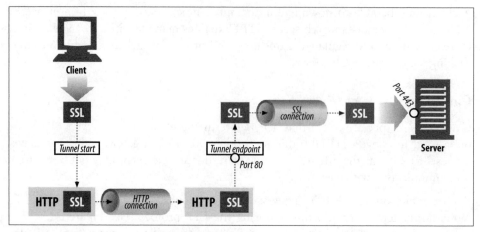

*Figure 1-14. Tunnels forward data across non-HTTP networks (HTTP/SSL tunnel shown)*

For example, there are machine-automated user agents that autonomously wander the Web, issuing HTTP transactions and fetching content, without human supervision. These automated agents often have colorful names, such as "spiders" or "web robots" (see Figure 1-15). Spiders wander the Web to build useful archives of web content, such as a search engine's database or a product catalog for a comparison-shopping robot. See Chapter 9 for more information.

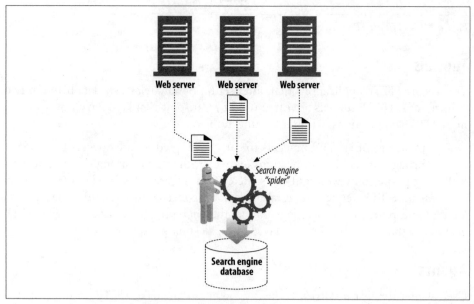

*Figure 1-15. Automated search engine "spiders" are agents, fetching web pages around the world*

# The End of the Beginning

That's it for our quick introduction to HTTP. In this chapter, we highlighted HTTP's role as a multimedia transport protocol. We outlined how HTTP uses URIs to name multimedia resources on remote servers, we sketched how HTTP request and response messages are used to manipulate multimedia resources on remote servers, and we finished by surveying a few of the web applications that use HTTP.

The remaining chapters explain the technical machinery of the HTTP protocol, applications, and resources in much more detail.

# For More Information

Later chapters of this book will explore HTTP in much more detail, but you might find that some of the following sources contain useful background about particular topics we covered in this chapter.

## HTTP Protocol Information

*HTTP Pocket Reference*
> Clinton Wong, O'Reilly & Associates, Inc. This little book provides a concise introduction to HTTP and a quick reference to each of the headers and status codes that compose HTTP transactions.

*http://www.w3.org/Protocols/*
> This W3C web page contains many great links about the HTTP protocol.

*http://www.ietf.org/rfc/rfc2616.txt*
> RFC 2616, "Hypertext Transfer Protocol—HTTP/1.1," is the official specification for HTTP/1.1, the current version of the HTTP protocol. The specification is a well-written, well-organized, detailed reference for HTTP, but it isn't ideal for readers who want to learn the underlying concepts and motivations of HTTP or the differences between theory and practice. We hope that this book fills in the underlying concepts, so you can make better use of the specification.

*http://www.ietf.org/rfc/rfc1945.txt*
> RFC 1945, "Hypertext Transfer Protocol—HTTP/1.0," is an informational RFC that describes the modern foundation for HTTP. It details the officially sanctioned and "best-practice" behavior of web applications at the time the specification was written. It also contains some useful descriptions about behavior that is deprecated in HTTP/1.1 but still widely implemented by legacy applications.

*http://www.w3.org/Protocols/HTTP/AsImplemented.html*
> This web page contains a description of the 1991 HTTP/0.9 protocol, which implements only GET requests and has no content typing.

# Historical Perspective

*http://www.w3.org/Protocols/WhyHTTP.html*
> This brief web page from 1991, from the author of HTTP, highlights some of the original, minimalist goals of HTTP.

*http://www.w3.org/History.html*
> "A Little History of the World Wide Web" gives a short but interesting perspective on some of the early goals and foundations of the World Wide Web and HTTP.

*http://www.w3.org/DesignIssues/Architecture.html*
> "Web Architecture from 50,000 Feet" paints a broad, ambitious view of the World Wide Web and the design principles that affect HTTP and related web technologies.

# Other World Wide Web Information

*http://www.w3.org*
> The World Wide Web Consortium (W3C) is the technology steering team for the Web. The W3C develops interoperable technologies (specifications, guidelines, software, and tools) for the evolving Web. The W3C site is a treasure trove of introductory and detailed documentation about web technologies.

*http://www.ietf.org/rfc/rfc2396.txt*
> RFC 2396, "Uniform Resource Identifiers (URI): Generic Syntax," is the detailed reference for URIs and URLs.

*http://www.ietf.org/rfc/rfc2141.txt*
> RFC 2141, "URN Syntax," is a 1997 specification describing URN syntax.

*http://www.ietf.org/rfc/rfc2046.txt*
> RFC 2046, "MIME Part 2: Media Types," is the second in a suite of five Internet specifications defining the Multipurpose Internet Mail Extensions standard for multimedia content management.

*http://www.wrec.org/Drafts/draft-ietf-wrec-taxonomy-06.txt*
> This Internet draft, "Internet Web Replication and Caching Taxonomy," specifies standard terminology for web architectural components.

# CHAPTER 2

# URLs and Resources

Think of the Internet as a giant, expanding city, full of places to see and things to do. You and the other residents and tourists of this booming community would use standard naming conventions for the city's vast attractions and services. You'd use street addresses for museums, restaurants, and people's homes. You'd use phone numbers for the fire department, the boss's secretary, and your mother, who says you don't call enough.

Everything has a standardized name, to help sort out the city's resources. Books have ISBN numbers, buses have route numbers, bank accounts have account numbers, and people have social security numbers. Tomorrow you will meet your business partners at gate 31 of the airport. Every morning you take a Red-line train and exit at Kendall Square station.

And because everyone agreed on standards for these different names, we can easily share the city's treasures with each other. You can tell the cab driver to take you to 246 McAllister Street, and he'll know what you mean (even if he takes the long way).

Uniform resource locators (URLs) are the standardized names for the Internet's resources. URLs point to pieces of electronic information, telling you where they are located and how to interact with them.

In this chapter, we'll cover:

- URL syntax and what the various URL components mean and do
- URL shortcuts that many web clients support, including relative URLs and expandomatic URLs
- URL encoding and character rules
- Common URL schemes that support a variety of Internet information systems
- The future of URLs, including uniform resource names (URNs)—a framework to support objects that move from place to place while retaining stable names

# Navigating the Internet's Resources

URLs are the resource locations that your browser needs to find information. They let people and applications find, use, and share the billions of data resources on the Internet. URLs are the usual human access point to HTTP and other protocols: a person points a browser at a URL and, behind the scenes, the browser sends the appropriate protocol messages to get the resource that the person wants.

URLs actually are a subset of a more general class of resource identifier called a uniform resource identifier, or URI. URIs are a general concept comprised of two main subsets, URLs and URNs. URLs identify resources by describing where resources are located, whereas URNs (which we'll cover later in this chapter) identify resources by name, regardless of where they currently reside.

The HTTP specification uses the more general concept of URIs as its resource identifiers; in practice, however, HTTP applications deal only with the URL subset of URIs. Throughout this book, we'll sometimes refer to URIs and URLs interchangeably, but we're almost always talking about URLs.

Say you want to fetch the URL *http://www.joes-hardware.com/seasonal/index-fall.html*:

- The first part of the URL (*http*) is the *URL scheme*. The scheme tells a web client *how* to access the resource. In this case, the URL says to use the HTTP protocol.
- The second part of the URL (*www.joes-hardware.com*) is the server location. This tells the web client *where* the resource is hosted.
- The third part of the URL (*/seasonal/index-fall.html*) is the resource path. The path tells *what* particular local resource on the server is being requested.

See Figure 2-1 for an illustration.

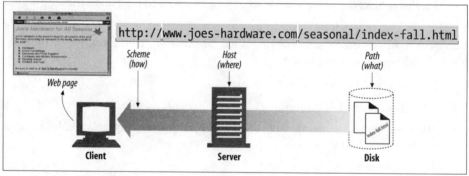

*Figure 2-1. How URLs relate to browser, machine, server, and location on the server's filesystem*

URLs can direct you to resources available through protocols other than HTTP. They can point you to any resource on the Internet, from a person's email account:

```
mailto:president@whitehouse.gov
```

to files that are available through other protocols, such as the File Transfer Protocol (FTP):

```
ftp://ftp.lots-o-books.com/pub/complete-price-list.xls
```

to movies hosted off of streaming video servers:

```
rtsp://www.joes-hardware.com:554/interview/cto_video
```

URLs provide a way to uniformly name resources. Most URLs have the same "scheme://server location/path" structure. So, for every resource out there and every way to get those resources, you have a single way to name each resource so that anyone can use that name to find it. However, this wasn't always the case.

## The Dark Days Before URLs

Before the Web and URLs, people relied on a rag-tag assortment of applications to access data distributed throughout the Net. Most people were not lucky enough to have all the right applications or were not savvy and patient enough to use them.

Before URLs came along, if you wanted to share the *complete-catalog.xls* file with a friend, you would have had to say something like this: "Use FTP to connect to *ftp. joes-hardware.com*. Log in as *anonymous*. Then type your username as the password. Change to the *pub* directory. Switch to binary mode. Now download the file named *complete-catalog.xls* to your local filesystem and view it there."

Today, browsers such as Netscape Navigator and Microsoft Internet Explorer bundle much of this functionality into one convenient package. Using URLs, these applications are able to access many resources in a uniform way, through one interface. Instead of the complicated instructions above, you could just say "Point your browser at *ftp://ftp.lots-o-books.com/pub/complete-catalog.xls*."

URLs have provided a means for applications to be aware of how to access a resource. In fact, many users are probably unaware of the protocols and access methods their browsers use to get the resources they are requesting.

With web browsers, you no longer need a news reader to read Internet news or an FTP client to access files on FTP servers. You don't need an electronic mail program to send and receive email messages. URLs have helped to simplify the online world, by allowing the browser to be smart about how to access and handle resources.[*] Applications can use URLs to simplify access to information.

URLs give you and your browser all you need to find a piece of information. They define the particular resource you want, where it is located, and how to get it.

---

[*] Browsers often use other applications to handle specific resources. For example, Internet Explorer launches an email application to handle URLs that identify email resources.

# URL Syntax

URLs provide a means of locating any resource on the Internet, but these resources can be accessed by different schemes (e.g., HTTP, FTP, SMTP), and URL syntax varies from scheme to scheme.

Does this mean that each different URL scheme has a radically different syntax? In practice, no. Most URLs adhere to a general URL syntax, and there is significant overlap in the style and syntax between different URL schemes.

Most URL schemes base their URL syntax on this nine-part general format:

```
<scheme>://<user>:<password>@<host>:<port>/<path>;<params>?<query>#<frag>
```

Almost no URLs contain all these components. The three most important parts of a URL are the *scheme*, the *host*, and the *path*. Table 2-1 summarizes the various components.

*Table 2-1. General URL components*

| Component | Description | Default value |
|---|---|---|
| scheme | Which protocol to use when accessing a server to get a resource. | None |
| user | The username some schemes require to access a resource. | anonymous |
| password | The password that may be included after the username, separated by a colon (:). | &lt;Email address&gt; |
| host | The hostname or dotted IP address of the server hosting the resource. | None |
| port | The port number on which the server hosting the resource is listening. Many schemes have default port numbers (the default port number for HTTP is 80). | Scheme-specific |
| path | The local name for the resource on the server, separated from the previous URL components by a slash (/). The syntax of the path component is server- and scheme-specific. (We will see later in this chapter that a URL's path can be divided into segments, and each segment can have its own components specific to that segment.) | None |
| params | Used by some schemes to specify input parameters. Params are name/value pairs. A URL can contain multiple params fields, separated from themselves and the rest of the path by semicolons (;). | None |
| query | Used by some schemes to pass parameters to active applications (such as databases, bulletin boards, search engines, and other Internet gateways). There is no common format for the contents of the query component. It is separated from the rest of the URL by the "?" character. | None |
| frag | A name for a piece or part of the resource. The frag field is not passed to the server when referencing the object; it is used internally by the client. It is separated from the rest of the URL by the "#" character. | None |

For example, consider the URL *http://www.joes-hardware.com:80/index.html*. The scheme is "http", the host is "www.joes-hardware.com", the port is "80", and the path is "/index.html".

## Schemes: What Protocol to Use

The *scheme* is really the main identifier of how to access a given resource; it tells the application interpreting the URL what protocol it needs to speak. In our simple HTTP URL, the scheme is simply "http".

The scheme component must start with an alphabetic character, and it is separated from the rest of the URL by the first ":" character. Scheme names are case-insensitive, so the URLs "http://www.joes-hardware.com" and "HTTP://www.joes-hardware.com" are equivalent.

## Hosts and Ports

To find a resource on the Internet, an application needs to know what machine is hosting the resource and where on that machine it can find the server that has access to the desired resource. The *host* and *port* components of the URL provide these two pieces of information.

The host component identifies the host machine on the Internet that has access to the resource. The name can be provided as a hostname, as above ("www.joes-hardware.com") or as an IP address. For example, the following two URLs point to the same resource—the first refers to the server by its hostname and the second by its IP address:

```
http://www.joes-hardware.com:80/index.html
http://161.58.228.45:80/index.html
```

The port component identifies the network port on which the server is listening. For HTTP, which uses the underlying TCP protocol, the default port is 80.

## Usernames and Passwords

More interesting components are the *user* and *password* components. Many servers require a username and password before you can access data through them. FTP servers are a common example of this. Here are a few examples:

```
ftp://ftp.prep.ai.mit.edu/pub/gnu
ftp://anonymous@ftp.prep.ai.mit.edu/pub/gnu
ftp://anonymous:my_passwd@ftp.prep.ai.mit.edu/pub/gnu
http://joe:joespasswd@www.joes-hardware.com/sales_info.txt
```

The first example has no user or password component, just our standard scheme, host, and path. If an application is using a URL scheme that requires a username and password, such as FTP, it generally will insert a default username and password if they aren't supplied. For example, if you hand your browser an FTP URL without specifying a username and password, it will insert "anonymous" for your username and send a default password (Internet Explorer sends "IEUser", while Netscape Navigator sends "mozilla").

The second example shows a username being specified as "anonymous". This username, combined with the host component, looks just like an email address. The "@" character separates the user and password components from the rest of the URL.

In the third example, both a username ("anonymous") and password ("my_passwd") are specified, separated by the ":" character.

## Paths

The *path* component of the URL specifies where on the server machine the resource lives. The path often resembles a hierarchical filesystem path. For example:

```
http://www.joes-hardware.com:80/seasonal/index-fall.html
```

The path in this URL is "/seasonal/index-fall.html", which resembles a filesystem path on a Unix filesystem. The path is the information that the server needs to locate the resource.* The path component for HTTP URLs can be divided into *path segments* separated by "/" characters (again, as in a file path on a Unix filesystem). Each path segment can have its own *params* component.

## Parameters

For many schemes, a simple host and path to the object just aren't enough. Aside from what port the server is listening to and even whether or not you have access to the resource with a username and password, many protocols require more information to work.

Applications interpreting URLs need these protocol parameters to access the resource. Otherwise, the server on the other side might not service the request or, worse yet, might service it wrong. For example, take a protocol like FTP, which has two modes of transfer, binary and text. You wouldn't want your binary image transferred in text mode, because the binary image could be scrambled.

To give applications the input parameters they need in order to talk to the server correctly, URLs have a *params* component. This component is just a list of name/value pairs in the URL, separated from the rest of the URL (and from each other) by ";" characters. They provide applications with any additional information that they need to access the resource. For example:

```
ftp://prep.ai.mit.edu/pub/gnu;type=d
```

In this example, there is one param, type=d, where the name of the param is "type" and its value is "d".

---

* This is a bit of a simplification. In "Virtual Hosting" in Chapter 18, we will see that the path is not always enough information to locate a resource. Sometimes a server needs additional information.

As we mentioned earlier, the path component for HTTP URLs can be broken into path segments. Each segment can have its own params. For example:

```
http://www.joes-hardware.com/hammers;sale=false/index.html;graphics=true
```

In this example there are two path segments, hammers and index.html. The hammers path segment has the param sale, and its value is false. The index.html segment has the param graphics, and its value is true.

## Query Strings

Some resources, such as database services, can be asked questions or queries to narrow down the type of resource being requested.

Let's say Joe's Hardware store maintains a list of unsold inventory in a database and allows the inventory to be queried, to see whether products are in stock. The following URL might be used to query a web database gateway to see if item number 12731 is available:

```
http://www.joes-hardware.com/inventory-check.cgi?item=12731
```

For the most part, this resembles the other URLs we have looked at. What is new is everything to the right of the question mark (?). This is called the *query* component. The query component of the URL is passed along to a gateway resource, with the path component of the URL identifying the gateway resource. Basically, gateways can be thought of as access points to other applications (we discuss gateways in detail in Chapter 8).

Figure 2-2 shows an example of a query component being passed to a server that is acting as a gateway to Joe's Hardware's inventory-checking application. The query is checking whether a particular item, 12731, is in inventory in size large and color blue.

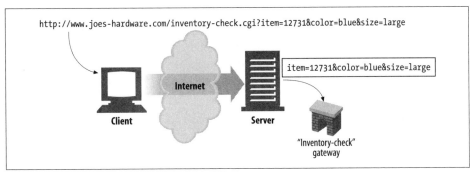

*Figure 2-2. The URL query component is sent along to the gateway application*

There is no requirement for the format of the query component, except that some characters are illegal, as we'll see later in this chapter. By convention, many gateways expect the query string to be formatted as a series of "name=value" pairs, separated by "&" characters:

```
http://www.joes-hardware.com/inventory-check.cgi?item=12731&color=blue
```

In this example, there are two name/value pairs in the query component: `item=12731` and `color=blue`.

## Fragments

Some resource types, such as HTML, can be divided further than just the resource level. For example, for a single, large text document with sections in it, the URL for the resource would point to the entire text document, but ideally you could specify the sections within the resource.

To allow referencing of parts or fragments of a resource, URLs support a *frag* component to identify pieces within a resource. For example, a URL could point to a particular image or section within an HTML document.

A fragment dangles off the right-hand side of a URL, preceded by a # character. For example:

```
http://www.joes-hardware.com/tools.html#drills
```

In this example, the fragment `drills` references a portion of the */tools.html* web page located on the Joe's Hardware web server. The portion is named "drills".

Because HTTP servers generally deal only with entire objects,* not with fragments of objects, clients don't pass fragments along to servers (see Figure 2-3). After your browser gets the *entire* resource from the server, it then uses the fragment to display the part of the resource in which you are interested.

# URL Shortcuts

Web clients understand and use a few URL shortcuts. Relative URLs are a convenient shorthand for specifying a resource within a resource. Many browsers also support "automatic expansion" of URLs, where the user can type in a key (memorable) part of a URL, and the browser fills in the rest. This is explained in "Expandomatic URLs."

## Relative URLs

URLs come in two flavors: *absolute* and *relative*. So far, we have looked only at absolute URLs. With an absolute URL, you have all the information you need to access a resource.

---

* In "Range Requests" in Chapter 15, we will see that HTTP agents may request byte ranges of objects. However, in the context of URL fragments, the server sends the entire object and the agent applies the fragment identifier to the resource.

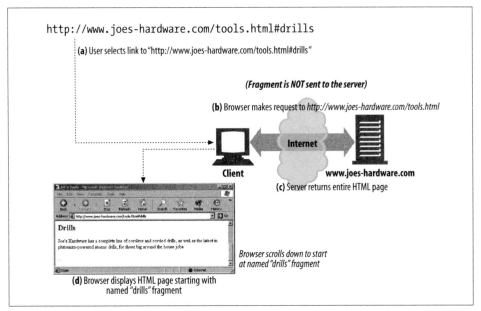

```
http://www.joes-hardware.com/tools.html#drills
```
(a) User selects link to "http://www.joes-hardware.com/tools.html#drills"

*(Fragment is NOT sent to the server)*

(b) Browser makes request to *http://www.joes-hardware.com/tools.html*

**Client**

**Internet**

**www.joes-hardware.com**

(c) Server returns entire HTML page

**Drills**

Joe's Hardware has a complete line of cordless and corded drills, as well as the latest in plutonium-powered atomic drills, for those big around the house jobs

*Browser scrolls down to start at named "drills" fragment*

(d) Browser displays HTML page starting with named "drills" fragment

*Figure 2-3. The URL fragment is used only by the client, because the server deals with entire objects*

On the other hand, relative URLs are incomplete. To get all the information needed to access a resource from a relative URL, you must interpret it relative to another URL, called its *base*.

Relative URLs are a convenient shorthand notation for URLs. If you have ever written HTML by hand, you have probably found them to be a great shortcut. Example 2-1 contains an example HTML document with an embedded relative URL.

*Example 2-1. HTML snippet with relative URLs*

```
<HTML>
<HEAD><TITLE>Joe's Tools</TITLE></HEAD>
<BODY>
<H1> Tools Page </H1>
<H2> Hammers <H2>
<P> Joe's Hardware Online has the largest selection of <A HREF="./hammers.html">hammers
</A> on earth.
</BODY>
</HTML>
```

In Example 2-1, we have an HTML document for the resource:

> http://www.joes-hardware.com/tools.html

In the HTML document, there is a hyperlink containing the URL *./hammers.html*. This URL seems incomplete, but it is a legal relative URL. It can be interpreted relative to the URL of the document in which it is found; in this case, relative to the resource */tools.html* on the Joe's Hardware web server.

The abbreviated relative URL syntax lets HTML authors omit from URLs the scheme, host, and other components. These components can be inferred by the *base* URL of the resource they are in. URLs for other resources also can be specified in this shorthand.

In Example 2-1, our base URL is:

```
http://www.joes-hardware.com/tools.html
```

Using this URL as a base, we can infer the missing information. We know the resource is *./hammers.html*, but we don't know the scheme or host. Using the base URL, we can infer that the scheme is *http* and the host is *www.joes-hardware.com*. Figure 2-4 illustrates this.

*Figure 2-4. Using a base URL*

Relative URLs are only fragments or pieces of URLs. Applications that process URLs (such as your browser) need to be able to convert between relative and absolute URLs.

It is also worth noting that relative URLs provide a convenient way to keep a set of resources (such as HTML pages) portable. If you use relative URLs, you can move a set of documents around and still have their links work, because they will be interpreted relative to the new base. This allows for things like mirroring content on other servers.

## Base URLs

The first step in the conversion process is to find a base URL. The base URL serves as a point of reference for the relative URL. It can come from a few places:

*Explicitly provided in the resource*
    Some resources explicitly specify the base URL. An HTML document, for example, may include a <BASE> HTML tag defining the base URL by which to convert all relative URLs in that HTML document.

*Base URL of the encapsulating resource*
    If a relative URL is found in a resource that does not explicitly specify a base URL, as in Example 2-1, it can use the URL of the resource in which it is embedded as a base (as we did in our example).

*No base URL*

In some instances, there is no base URL. This often means that you have an absolute URL; however, sometimes you may just have an incomplete or broken URL.

### Resolving relative references

Previously, we showed the basic components and syntax of URLs. The next step in converting a relative URL into an absolute one is to break up both the relative and base URLs into their component pieces.

In effect, you are just parsing the URL, but this is often called *decomposing* the URL, because you are breaking it up into its components. Once you have broken the base and relative URLs into their components, you can then apply the algorithm pictured in Figure 2-5 to finish the conversion.

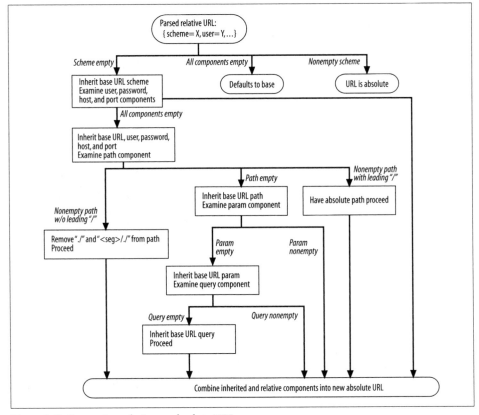

*Figure 2-5. Converting relative to absolute URLs*

This algorithm converts a relative URL to its absolute form, which can then be used to reference the resource. This algorithm was originally specified in RFC 1808 and later incorporated into RFC 2396.

With our *./hammers.html* example from Example 2-1, we can apply the algorithm depicted in Figure 2-5:

1. Path is *./hammers.html*; base URL is *http://www.joes-hardware.com/tools.html*.

2. Scheme is empty; proceed down left half of chart and inherit the base URL scheme (HTTP).

3. At least one component is non-empty; proceed to bottom, inheriting host and port components.

4. Combining the components we have from the relative URL (path: *./hammers.html*) with what we have inherited (scheme: *http*, host: *www.joes-hardware.com*, port: *80*), we get our new absolute URL: *http://www.joes-hardware.com/hammers.html*.

## Expandomatic URLs

Some browsers try to expand URLs automatically, either after you submit the URL or while you're typing. This provides users with a shortcut: they don't have to type in the complete URL, because it automatically expands itself.

These "expandomatic" features come in two flavors:

*Hostname expansion*

In hostname expansion, the browser can often expand the hostname you type in into the full hostname without your help, just by using some simple heuristics.

For example if you type "yahoo" in the address box, your browser can automatically insert "www." and ".com" onto the hostname, creating "www.yahoo.com". Some browsers will try this if they are unable to find a site that matches "yahoo", trying a few expansions before giving up. Browsers apply these simple tricks to save you some time and frustration.

However, these expansion tricks on hostnames can cause problems for other HTTP applications, such as proxies. In Chapter 6, we will discuss these problems in more detail.

*History expansion*

Another technique that browsers use to save you time typing URLs is to store a history of the URLs that you have visited in the past. As you type in the URL, they can offer you completed choices to select from by matching what you type to the prefixes of the URLs in your history. So, if you were typing in the start of a URL that you had visited previously, such as *http://www.joes-*, your browser could suggest *http://www.joes-hardware.com*. You could then select that instead of typing out the complete URL.

Be aware that URL auto-expansion may behave differently when used with proxies. We discuss this further in "URI Client Auto-Expansion and Hostname Resolution" in Chapter 6.

# Shady Characters

URLs were designed to be *portable*. They were also designed to uniformly name all the resources on the Internet, which means that they will be transmitted through various protocols. Because all of these protocols have different mechanisms for transmitting their data, it was important for URLs to be designed so that they could be transmitted safely through any Internet protocol.

Safe transmission means that URLs can be transmitted without the risk of losing information. Some protocols, such as the Simple Mail Transfer Protocol (SMTP) for electronic mail, use transmission methods that can strip off certain characters.[*] To get around this, URLs are permitted to contain only characters from a relatively small, universally safe alphabet.

In addition to wanting URLs to be transportable by all Internet protocols, designers wanted them to be *readable* by people. So invisible, nonprinting characters also are prohibited in URLs, even though these characters may pass through mailers and otherwise be portable.[†]

To complicate matters further, URLs also need to be *complete*. URL designers realized there would be times when people would want URLs to contain binary data or characters outside of the universally safe alphabet. So, an escape mechanism was added, allowing unsafe characters to be encoded into safe characters for transport.

This section summarizes the universal alphabet and encoding rules for URLs.

## The URL Character Set

Default computer system character sets often have an Anglocentric bias. Historically, many computer applications have used the US-ASCII character set. US-ASCII uses 7 bits to represent most keys available on an English typewriter and a few non-printing control characters for text formatting and hardware signalling.

US-ASCII is very portable, due to its long legacy. But while it's convenient to citizens of the U.S., it doesn't support the inflected characters common in European languages or the hundreds of non-Romanic languages read by billions of people around the world.

---

[*] This is caused by the use of a 7-bit encoding for messages; this can strip off information if the source is encoded in 8 bits or more.

[†] Nonprinting characters include whitespace (note that RFC 2396 recommends that applications ignore whitespace).

Furthermore, some URLs may need to contain arbitrary binary data. Recognizing the need for completeness, the URL designers have incorporated *escape sequences*. Escape sequences allow the encoding of arbitrary character values or data using a restricted subset of the US-ASCII character set, yielding portability and completeness.

## Encoding Mechanisms

To get around the limitations of a safe character set representation, an encoding scheme was devised to represent characters in a URL that are not safe. The encoding simply represents the unsafe character by an "escape" notation, consisting of a percent sign (%) followed by two hexadecimal digits that represent the ASCII code of the character.

Table 2-2 shows a few examples.

*Table 2-2. Some encoded character examples*

| Character | ASCII code | Example URL |
|-----------|-----------|-------------|
| ~ | 126 (0x7E) | *http://www.joes-hardware.com/%7Ejoe* |
| SPACE | 32 (0x20) | *http://www.joes-hardware.com/more%20tools.html* |
| % | 37 (0x25) | *http://www.joes-hardware.com/100%25satisfaction.html* |

## Character Restrictions

Several characters have been reserved to have special meaning inside of a URL. Others are not in the defined US-ASCII printable set. And still others are known to confuse some Internet gateways and protocols, so their use is discouraged.

Table 2-3 lists characters that should be encoded in a URL before you use them for anything other than their reserved purposes.

*Table 2-3. Reserved and restricted characters*

| Character | Reservation/Restriction |
|-----------|------------------------|
| % | Reserved as escape token for encoded characters |
| / | Reserved for delimiting splitting up path segments in the path component |
| . | Reserved in the path component |
| .. | Reserved in the path component |
| # | Reserved as the fragment delimiter |
| ? | Reserved as the query-string delimiter |
| ; | Reserved as the params delimiter |
| : | Reserved to delimit the scheme, user/password, and host/port components |
| $ , + | Reserved |
| @ & = | Reserved because they have special meaning in the context of some schemes |

*Table 2-3. Reserved and restricted characters (continued)*

| Character | Reservation/Restriction |
|---|---|
| {} \ ^ ~ [ ] ' | Restricted because of unsafe handling by various transport agents, such as gateways |
| < > " | Unsafe; should be encoded because these characters often have meaning outside the scope of the URL, such as delimiting the URL itself in a document (e.g., "http://www.joes-hardware.com") |
| 0x00–0x1F, 0x7F | Restricted; characters within these hex ranges fall within the nonprintable section of the US-ASCII character set |
| > 0x7F | Restricted; characters whose hex values fall within this range do not fall within the 7-bit range of the US-ASCII character set |

# A Bit More

You might be wondering why nothing bad has happened when you have used characters that are unsafe. For instance, you can visit Joe's home page at:

```
http://www.joes-hardware.com/~joe
```

and not encode the "~" character. For some transport protocols this is not an issue, but it is still unwise for application developers not to encode unsafe characters.

Applications need to walk a fine line. It is best for client applications to convert any unsafe or restricted characters before sending any URL to any other application.* Once all the unsafe characters have been encoded, the URL is in a *canonical form* that can be shared between applications; there is no need to worry about the other application getting confused by any of the characters' special meanings.

The original application that gets the URL from the user is best fit to determine which characters need to be encoded. Because each component of the URL may have its own safe/unsafe characters, and which characters are safe/unsafe is scheme-dependent, only the application receiving the URL from the user really is in a position to determine what needs to be encoded.

Of course, the other extreme is for the application to encode all characters. While this is not recommended, there is no hard and fast rule against encoding characters that are considered safe already; however, in practice this can lead to odd and broken behavior, because some applications may assume that safe characters will not be encoded.

Sometimes, malicious folks encode extra characters in an attempt to get around applications that are doing pattern matching on URLs—for example, web filtering applications. Encoding safe URL components can cause pattern-matching applications to fail to recognize the patterns for which they are searching. In general, applications interpreting URLs must decode the URLs before processing them.

---

* Here we are specifically talking about client applications, not other HTTP intermediaries, like proxies. In "In-Flight URI Modification" in Chapter 6, we discuss some of the problems that can arise when proxies or other intermediary HTTP applications attempt to change (e.g., encode) URLs on the behalf of a client.

Some URL components, such as the scheme, need to be recognized readily and are required to start with an alphabetic character. Refer back to "URL Syntax" for more guidelines on the use of reserved and unsafe characters within different URL components.[*]

## A Sea of Schemes

In this section, we'll take a look at the more common scheme formats on the Web. Appendix A gives a fairly exhaustive list of schemes and references to their individual documentation.

Table 2-4 summarizes some of the most popular schemes. Reviewing "URL Syntax" will make the syntax portion of the table a little more familiar.

*Table 2-4. Common scheme formats*

| Scheme | Description |
|---|---|
| http | The Hypertext Transfer Protocol scheme conforms to the general URL format, except that there is no username or password. The port defaults to 80 if omitted. |
| | Basic form: |
| | *http://<host>:<port>/<path>?<query>#<frag>* |
| | Examples: |
| | *http://www.joes-hardware.com/index.html* |
| | *http://www.joes-hardware.com:80/index.html* |
| https | The https scheme is a twin to the http scheme. The only difference is that the https scheme uses Netscape's Secure Sockets Layer (SSL), which provides end-to-end encryption of HTTP connections. Its syntax is identical to that of HTTP, with a default port of 443. |
| | Basic form: |
| | *https://<host>:<port>/<path>?<query>#<frag>* |
| | Example: |
| | *https://www.joes-hardware.com/secure.html* |
| mailto | Mailto URLs refer to email addresses. Because email behaves differently from other schemes (it does not refer to objects that can be accessed directly), the format of a mailto URL differs from that of the standard URL. The syntax for Internet email addresses is documented in Internet RFC 822. |
| | Basic form: |
| | *mailto:<RFC-822-addr-spec>* |
| | Example: |
| | *mailto:joe@joes-hardware.com* |

[*] Table 2-3 lists reserved characters for the various URL components. In general, encoding should be limited to those characters that are unsafe for transport.

*Table 2-4. Common scheme formats (continued)*

| Scheme | Description |
|---|---|
| ftp | File Transfer Protocol URLs can be used to download and upload files on an FTP server and to obtain listings of the contents of a directory structure on an FTP server. |
| | FTP has been around since before the advent of the Web and URLs. Web applications have assimilated FTP as a data-access scheme. The URL syntax follows the general form. |
| | Basic form: |
| | *ftp://<user>:<password>@<host>:<port>/<path>;<params>* |
| | Example: |
| | *ftp://anonymous:joe%40joes-hardware.com@prep.ai.mit.edu:21/pub/gnu/* |
| rtsp, rtspu | RTSP URLs are identifiers for audio and video media resources that can be retrieved through the Real Time Streaming Protocol. |
| | The "u" in the rtspu scheme denotes that the UDP protocol is used to retrieve the resource. |
| | Basic forms: |
| | *rtsp://<user>:<password>@<host>:<port>/<path>* |
| | *rtspu://<user>:<password>@<host>:<port>/<path>* |
| | Example: |
| | *rtsp://www.joes-hardware.com:554/interview/cto_video* |
| file | The file scheme denotes files directly accessible on a given host machine (by local disk, a network filesystem, or some other file-sharing system). The fields follow the general form. If the host is omitted, it defaults to the local host from which the URL is being used. |
| | Basic form: |
| | *file://<host>/<path>* |
| | Example: |
| | *file://OFFICE-FS/policies/casual-fridays.doc* |
| news | The news scheme is used to access specific articles or newsgroups, as defined by RFC 1036. It has the unusual property that a news URL in itself does not contain sufficient information to locate the resource. |
| | The news URL is missing information about where to acquire the resource—no hostname or machine name is supplied. It is the interpreting application's job to acquire this information from the user. For example, in your Netscape browser, under the Options menu, you can specify your NNTP (news) server. This tells your browser what server to use when it has a news URL. |
| | News resources can be accessed from multiple servers. They are said to be location-independent, as they are not dependent on any one source for access. |
| | The "@" character is reserved within a news URL and is used to distinguish between news URLs that refer to newsgroups and news URLs that refer to specific news articles. |
| | Basic forms: |
| | *news:<newsgroup>* |
| | *news:<news-article-id>* |
| | Example: |
| | *news:rec.arts.startrek* |

*Table 2-4. Common scheme formats (continued)*

| Scheme | Description |
|--------|-------------|
| telnet | The telnet scheme is used to access interactive services. It does not represent an object per se, but an interactive application (resource) accessible via the telnet protocol. |
|        | Basic form: |
|        | *telnet://<user>:<password>@<host>:<port>/* |
|        | Example: |
|        | *telnet://slurp:webhound@joes-hardware.com:23/* |

# The Future

URLs are a powerful tool. Their design allows them to name all existing objects and easily encompass new formats. They provide a uniform naming mechanism that can be shared between Internet protocols.

However, they are not perfect. URLs are really addresses, not true names. This means that a URL tells you where something is located, for the moment. It provides you with the name of a specific server on a specific port, where you can find the resource. The downfall of this scheme is that if the resource is moved, the URL is no longer valid. And at that point, it provides no way to locate the object.

What would be ideal is if you had the real name of an object, which you could use to look up that object regardless of its location. As with a person, given the name of the resource and a few other facts, you could track down that resource, regardless of where it moved.

The Internet Engineering Task Force (IETF) has been working on a new standard, uniform resource names (URNs), for some time now, to address just this issue. URNs provide a stable name for an object, regardless of where that object moves (either inside a web server or across web servers).

*Persistent uniform resource locators* (PURLs) are an example of how URN functionality can be achieved using URLs. The concept is to introduce another level of indirection in looking up a resource, using an intermediary *resource locator* server that catalogues and tracks the actual URL of a resource. A client can request a persistent URL from the locator, which can then respond with a resource that redirects the client to the actual and current URL for the resource (see Figure 2-6). For more information on PURLs, visit *http://purl.oclc.org*.

## If Not Now, When?

The ideas behind URNs have been around for some time. Indeed, if you look at the publication dates for some of their specifications, you might ask yourself why they have yet to be adopted.

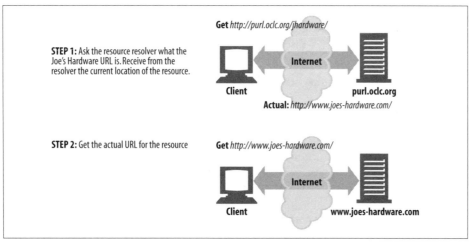

*Figure 2-6. PURLs use a resource locator server to name the current location of a resource*

The change from URLs to URNs is an enormous task. Standardization is a slow process, often for good reason. Support for URNs will require many changes—consensus from the standards bodies, modifications to various HTTP applications, etc. A tremendous amount of critical mass is required to make such changes, and unfortunately (or perhaps fortunately), there is so much momentum behind URLs that it will be some time before all the stars align to make such a conversion possible.

Throughout the explosive growth of the Web, Internet users—everyone from computer scientists to the average Internet user—have been taught to use URLs. While they suffer from clumsy syntax (for the novice) and persistence problems, people have learned how to use them and how to deal with their drawbacks. URLs have some limitations, but they're not the web development community's most pressing problem.

Currently, and for the foreseeable future, URLs are the way to name resources on the Internet. They are everywhere, and they have proven to be a very important part of the Web's success. It will be a while before any other naming scheme unseats URLs. However, URLs do have their limitations, and it is likely that new standards (possibly URNs) will emerge and be deployed to address some of these limitations.

# For More Information

For more information on URLs, refer to:

*http://www.w3.org/Addressing/*
    The W3C web page about naming and addressing URIs and URLs.

*http://www.ietf.org/rfc/rfc1738*
    RFC 1738, "Uniform Resource Locators (URL)," by T. Berners-Lee, L. Masinter, and M. McCahill.

*http://www.ietf.org/rfc/rfc2396.txt*

RFC 2396, "Uniform Resource Identifiers (URI): Generic Syntax," by T. Berners-Lee, R. Fielding, and L. Masinter.

*http://www.ietf.org/rfc/rfc2141.txt*

RFC 2141, "URN Syntax," by R. Moats.

*http://purl.oclc.org*

The persistent uniform resource locator web site.

*http://www.ietf.org/rfc/rfc1808.txt*

RFC 1808, "Relative Uniform Resource Locators," by R. Fielding.

# CHAPTER 3

# HTTP Messages

If HTTP is the Internet's courier, HTTP messages are the packages it uses to move things around. In Chapter 1, we showed how HTTP programs send each other messages to get work done. This chapter tells you all about HTTP messages—how to create them and how to understand them. After reading this chapter, you'll know most of what you need to know to write your own HTTP applications. In particular, you'll understand:

- How messages flow
- The three parts of HTTP messages (start line, headers, and entity body)
- The differences between request and response messages
- The various functions (methods) that request messages support
- The various status codes that are returned with response messages
- What the various HTTP headers do

## The Flow of Messages

HTTP messages are the blocks of data sent between HTTP applications. These blocks of data begin with some text *meta-information* describing the message contents and meaning, followed by optional data. These messages flow between clients, servers, and proxies. The terms "inbound," "outbound," "upstream," and "downstream" describe message direction.

### Messages Commute Inbound to the Origin Server

HTTP uses the terms *inbound* and *outbound* to describe *transactional* direction. Messages travel inbound to the origin server, and when their work is done, they travel outbound back to the user agent (see Figure 3-1).

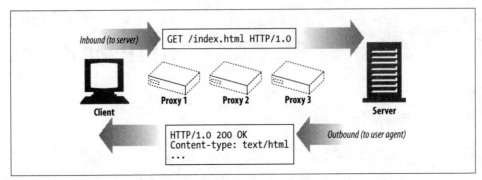

*Figure 3-1. Messages travel inbound to the origin server and outbound back to the client*

## Messages Flow Downstream

HTTP messages flow like rivers. All messages flow *downstream*, regardless of whether they are request messages or response messages (see Figure 3-2). The sender of any message is *upstream* of the receiver. In Figure 3-2, proxy 1 is upstream of proxy 3 for the request but downstream of proxy 3 for the response.[*]

# The Parts of a Message

HTTP messages are simple, formatted blocks of data. Take a peek at Figure 3-3 for an example. Each message contains either a request from a client or a response from a server. They consist of three parts: a *start line* describing the message, a block of *headers* containing attributes, and an optional *body* containing data.

The start line and headers are just ASCII text, broken up by lines. Each line ends with a two-character end-of-line sequence, consisting of a carriage return (ASCII 13) and a line-feed character (ASCII 10). This end-of-line sequence is written "CRLF." It is worth pointing out that while the HTTP specification for terminating lines is CRLF, robust applications also should accept just a line-feed character. Some older or broken HTTP applications do not always send both the carriage return and line feed.

The entity body or message body (or just plain "body") is simply an optional chunk of data. Unlike the start line and headers, the body can contain text or binary data or can be empty.

In the example in Figure 3-3, the headers give you a bit of information about the body. The Content-Type line tells you what the body is—in this example, it is a plain-text document. The Content-Length line tells you how big the body is; here it is a meager 19 bytes.

---

[*] The terms "upstream" and "downstream" relate only to the sender and receiver. We can't tell whether a message is heading to the origin server or the client, because both are downstream.

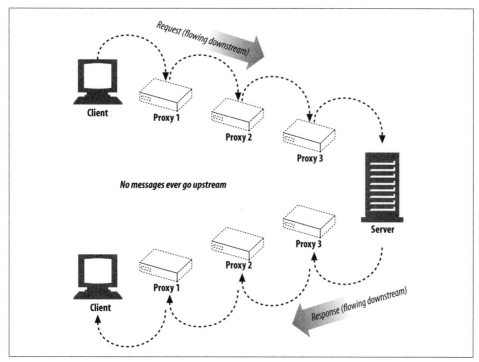

Figure 3-2. All messages flow downstream

Figure 3-3. Three parts of an HTTP message

## Message Syntax

All HTTP messages fall into two types: *request messages* and *response messages.* Request messages request an action from a web server. Response messages carry results of a request back to a client. Both request and response messages have the same basic message structure. Figure 3-4 shows request and response messages to get a GIF image.

Here's the format for a request message:

```
<method> <request-URL> <version>
<headers>

<entity-body>
```

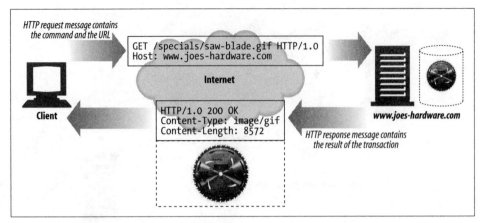

*Figure 3-4. An HTTP transaction has request and response messages*

Here's the format for a response message (note that the syntax differs only in the start line):

```
<version> <status> <reason-phrase>
<headers>

<entity-body>
```

Here's a quick description of the various parts:

*method*

The action that the client wants the server to perform on the resource. It is a single word, like "GET," "HEAD," or "POST". We cover the method in detail later in this chapter.

*request-URL*

A complete URL naming the requested resource, or the *path* component of the URL. If you are talking directly to the server, the path component of the URL is usually okay as long as it is the absolute path to the resource—the server can assume itself as the host/port of the URL. Chapter 2 covers URL syntax in detail.

*version*

The version of HTTP that the message is using. Its format looks like:

```
HTTP/<major>.<minor>
```

where *major* and *minor* both are integers. We discuss HTTP versioning a bit more later in this chapter.

*status-code*

A three-digit number describing what happened during the request. The first digit of each code describes the general class of status ("success," "error," etc.). An exhaustive list of status codes defined in the HTTP specification and their meanings is provided later in this chapter.

*reason-phrase*

A human-readable version of the numeric status code, consisting of all the text until the end-of-line sequence. Example reason phrases for all the status codes defined in the HTTP specification are provided later in this chapter. The reason phrase is meant solely for human consumption, so, for example, response lines containing "HTTP/1.0 200 NOT OK" and "HTTP/1.0 200 OK" should be treated as equivalent success indications, despite the reason phrases suggesting otherwise.

*headers*

Zero or more headers, each of which is a name, followed by a colon (:), followed by optional whitespace, followed by a value, followed by a CRLF. The headers are terminated by a blank line (CRLF), marking the end of the list of headers and the beginning of the entity body. Some versions of HTTP, such as HTTP/1.1, require certain headers to be present for the request or response message to be valid. The various HTTP headers are covered later in this chapter.

*entity-body*

The entity body contains a block of arbitrary data. Not all messages contain entity bodies, so sometimes a message terminates with a bare CRLF. We discuss entities in detail in Chapter 15.

Figure 3-5 demonstrates hypothetical request and response messages.

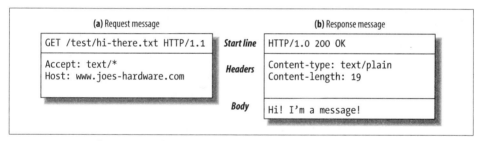

*Figure 3-5. Example request and response messages*

Note that a set of HTTP headers should always end in a blank line (bare CRLF), even if there are no headers and even if there is no entity body. Historically, however, many clients and servers (mistakenly) omitted the final CRLF if there was no entity body. To interoperate with these popular but noncompliant implementations, clients and servers should accept messages that end without the final CRLF.

## Start Lines

All HTTP messages begin with a start line. The start line for a request message says *what to do*. The start line for a response message says *what happened*.

## Request line

Request messages ask servers to do something to a resource. The start line for a request message, or *request line*, contains a method describing what operation the server should perform and a request URL describing the resource on which to perform the method. The request line also includes an HTTP *version* which tells the server what dialect of HTTP the client is speaking.

All of these fields are separated by whitespace. In Figure 3-5a, the request method is GET, the request URL is */test/hi-there.txt*, and the version is HTTP/1.1. Prior to HTTP/1.0, request lines were not required to contain an HTTP version.

## Response line

Response messages carry status information and any resulting data from an operation back to a client. The start line for a response message, or *response line*, contains the HTTP version that the response message is using, a numeric status code, and a textual reason phrase describing the status of the operation.

All these fields are separated by whitespace. In Figure 3-5b, the HTTP version is HTTP/1.0, the status code is 200 (indicating success), and the reason phrase is OK, meaning the document was returned successfully. Prior to HTTP/1.0, responses were not required to contain a response line.

## Methods

The method begins the start line of requests, telling the server what to do. For example, in the line "GET /specials/saw-blade.gif HTTP/1.0," the method is GET.

The HTTP specifications have defined a set of common request methods. For example, the GET method gets a document from a server, the POST method sends data to a server for processing, and the OPTIONS method determines the general capabilities of a web server or the capabilities of a web server for a specific resource.

Table 3-1 describes seven of these methods. Note that some methods have a body in the request message, and other methods have bodyless requests.

*Table 3-1. Common HTTP methods*

| Method | Description | Message body? |
| --- | --- | --- |
| GET | Get a document from the server. | No |
| HEAD | Get just the headers for a document from the server. | No |
| POST | Send data to the server for processing. | Yes |
| PUT | Store the body of the request on the server. | Yes |
| TRACE | Trace the message through proxy servers to the server. | No |
| OPTIONS | Determine what methods can operate on a server. | No |
| DELETE | Remove a document from the server. | No |

Not all servers implement all seven of the methods in Table 3-1. Furthermore, because HTTP was designed to be easily extensible, other servers may implement their own request methods in addition to these. These additional methods are called *extension methods*, because they extend the HTTP specification.

### Status codes

As methods tell the server what to do, status codes tell the client what happened. Status codes live in the start lines of responses. For example, in the line "HTTP/1.0 200 OK," the status code is 200.

When clients send request messages to an HTTP server, many things can happen. If you are fortunate, the request will complete successfully. You might not always be so lucky. The server may tell you that the resource you requested could not be found, that you don't have permission to access the resource, or perhaps that the resource has moved someplace else.

Status codes are returned in the start line of each response message. Both a numeric and a human-readable status are returned. The numeric code makes error processing easy for programs, while the reason phrase is easily understood by humans.

The different status codes are grouped into classes by their three-digit numeric codes. Status codes between 200 and 299 represent success. Codes between 300 and 399 indicate that the resource has been moved. Codes between 400 and 499 mean that the client did something wrong in the request. Codes between 500 and 599 mean something went awry on the server.

The status code classes are shown in Table 3-2.

*Table 3-2. Status code classes*

| Overall range | Defined range | Category |
| --- | --- | --- |
| 100-199 | 100-101 | Informational |
| 200-299 | 200-206 | Successful |
| 300-399 | 300-305 | Redirection |
| 400-499 | 400-415 | Client error |
| 500-599 | 500-505 | Server error |

Current versions of HTTP define only a few codes for each status category. As the protocol evolves, more status codes will be defined officially in the HTTP specification. If you receive a status code that you don't recognize, chances are someone has defined it as an extension to the current protocol. You should treat it as a general member of the class whose range it falls into.

For example, if you receive status code 515 (which is outside of the defined range for 5XX codes listed in Table 3-2), you should treat the response as indicating a server error, which is the general class of 5XX messages.

Table 3-3 lists some of the most common status codes that you will see. We will explain all the current HTTP status codes in detail later in this chapter.

*Table 3-3. Common status codes*

| Status code | Reason phrase | Meaning |
|-------------|---------------|---------|
| 200 | OK | Success! Any requested data is in the response body. |
| 401 | Unauthorized | You need to enter a username and password. |
| 404 | Not Found | The server cannot find a resource for the requested URL. |

### Reason phrases

The reason phrase is the last component of the start line of the response. It provides a textual explanation of the status code. For example, in the line "HTTP/1.0 200 OK," the reason phrase is OK.

Reason phrases are paired one-to-one with status codes. The reason phrase provides a human-readable version of the status code that application developers can pass along to their users to indicate what happened during the request.

The HTTP specification does not provide any hard and fast rules for what reason phrases should look like. Later in this chapter, we list the status codes and some suggested reason phrases.

### Version numbers

Version numbers appear in both request and response message start lines in the format HTTP/x.y. They provide a means for HTTP applications to tell each other what version of the protocol they conform to.

Version numbers are intended to provide applications speaking HTTP with a clue about each other's capabilities and the format of the message. An HTTP Version 1.2 application communicating with an HTTP Version 1.1 application should know that it should not use any new 1.2 features, as they likely are not implemented by the application speaking the older version of the protocol.

The version number indicates the highest version of HTTP that an application supports. In some cases this leads to confusion between applications,[*] because HTTP/1.0 applications interpret a response with HTTP/1.1 in it to indicate that the response is a 1.1 response, when in fact that's just the level of protocol used by the responding application.

Note that version numbers are not treated as fractional numbers. Each number in the version (for example, the "1" and "0" in HTTP/1.0) is treated as a separate number. So, when comparing HTTP versions, each number must be compared separately in

---

[*] See *http://httpd.apache.org/docs-2.0/misc/known_client_problems.html* for more on cases in which Apache has run into this problem with clients.

order to determine which is the higher version. For example, HTTP/2.22 is a higher version than HTTP/2.3, because 22 is a larger number than 3.

# Headers

The previous section focused on the first line of request and response messages (methods, status codes, reason phrases, and version numbers). Following the start line comes a list of zero, one, or many HTTP header fields (see Figure 3-5).

HTTP header fields add additional information to request and response messages. They are basically just lists of name/value pairs. For example, the following header line assigns the value 19 to the Content-Length header field:

```
Content-length: 19
```

### Header classifications

The HTTP specification defines several header fields. Applications also are free to invent their own home-brewed headers. HTTP headers are classified into:

*General headers*
> Can appear in both request and response messages

*Request headers*
> Provide more information about the request

*Response headers*
> Provide more information about the response

*Entity headers*
> Describe body size and contents, or the resource itself

*Extension headers*
> New headers that are not defined in the specification

Each HTTP header has a simple syntax: a name, followed by a colon (:), followed by optional whitespace, followed by the field value, followed by a CRLF. Table 3-4 lists some common header examples.

*Table 3-4. Common header examples*

| Header example | Description |
| --- | --- |
| Date: Tue, 3 Oct 1997 02:16:03 GMT | The date the server generated the response |
| Content-length: 15040 | The entity body contains 15,040 bytes of data |
| Content-type: image/gif | The entity body is a GIF image |
| Accept: image/gif, image/jpeg, text/html | The client accepts GIF and JPEG images and HTML |

### Header continuation lines

Long header lines can be made more readable by breaking them into multiple lines, preceding each extra line with at least one space or tab character.

For example:

```
HTTP/1.0 200 OK
Content-Type: image/gif
Content-Length: 8572
Server: Test Server
     Version 1.0
```

In this example, the response message contains a Server header whose value is broken into continuation lines. The complete value of the header is "Test Server Version 1.0".

We'll briefly describe all the HTTP headers later in this chapter. We also provide a more detailed reference summary of all the headers in Appendix C.

## Entity Bodies

The third part of an HTTP message is the optional entity body. Entity bodies are the payload of HTTP messages. They are the things that HTTP was designed to transport.

HTTP messages can carry many kinds of digital data: images, video, HTML documents, software applications, credit card transactions, electronic mail, and so on.

## Version 0.9 Messages

HTTP Version 0.9 was an early version of the HTTP protocol. It was the starting point for the request and response messages that HTTP has today, but with a far simpler protocol (see Figure 3-6).

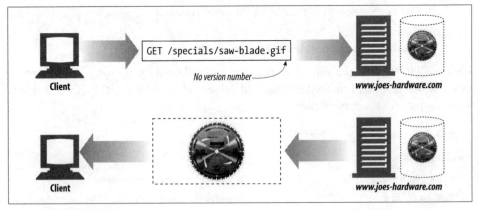

*Figure 3-6. HTTP/0.9 transaction*

HTTP/0.9 messages also consisted of requests and responses, but the request contained merely the *method* and the *request URL*, and the response contained only the *entity*. No version information (it was the first and only version at the time), no status code or reason phrase, and no headers were included.

However, this simplicity did not allow for much flexibility or the implementation of most of the HTTP features and applications described in this book. We briefly describe it here because there are still clients, servers, and other applications that use it, and application writers should be aware of its limitations.

# Methods

Let's talk in more detail about some of the basic HTTP methods, listed earlier in Table 3-1. Note that not all methods are implemented by every server. To be compliant with HTTP Version 1.1, a server need implement only the GET and HEAD methods for its resources.

Even when servers do implement all of these methods, the methods most likely have restricted uses. For example, servers that support DELETE or PUT (described later in this section) would not want just anyone to be able to delete or store resources. These restrictions generally are set up in the server's configuration, so they vary from site to site and from server to server.

## Safe Methods

HTTP defines a set of methods that are called *safe* methods. The GET and HEAD methods are said to be safe, meaning that no action should occur as a result of an HTTP request that uses either the GET or HEAD method.

By no action, we mean that nothing will happen on the server as a result of the HTTP request. For example, consider when you are shopping online at Joe's Hardware and you click on the "submit purchase" button. Clicking on the button submits a POST request (discussed later) with your credit card information, and an action is performed on the server on your behalf. In this case, the action is your credit card being charged for your purchase.

There is no guarantee that a safe method won't cause an action to be performed (in practice, that is up to the web developers). Safe methods are meant to allow HTTP application developers to let users know when an unsafe method that may cause some action to be performed is being used. In our Joe's Hardware example, your web browser may pop up a warning message letting you know that you are making a request with an unsafe method and that, as a result, something might happen on the server (e.g., your credit card being charged).

## GET

GET is the most common method. It usually is used to ask a server to send a resource. HTTP/1.1 requires servers to implement this method. Figure 3-7 shows an example of a client making an HTTP request with the GET method.

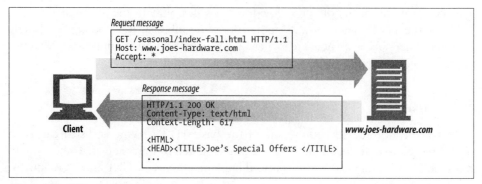

Figure 3-7. GET example

## HEAD

The HEAD method behaves exactly like the GET method, but the server returns only the headers in the response. No entity body is ever returned. This allows a client to inspect the headers for a resource without having to actually get the resource. Using HEAD, you can:

- Find out about a resource (e.g., determine its type) without getting it.
- See if an object exists, by looking at the status code of the response.
- Test if the resource has been modified, by looking at the headers.

Server developers must ensure that the headers returned are exactly those that a GET request would return. The HEAD method also is required for HTTP/1.1 compliance. Figure 3-8 shows the HEAD method in action.

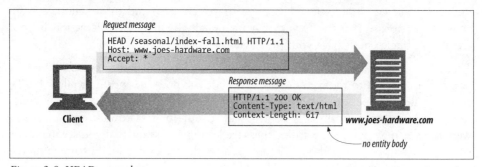

Figure 3-8. HEAD example

## PUT

The PUT method writes documents to a server, in the inverse of the way that GET reads documents from a server. Some publishing systems let you create web pages and install them directly on a web server using PUT (see Figure 3-9).

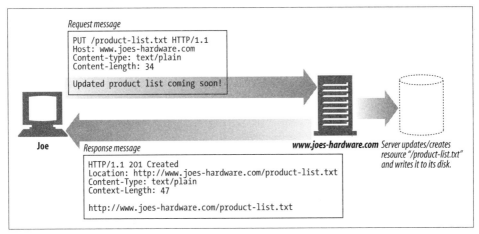

Request message

```
PUT /product-list.txt HTTP/1.1
Host: www.joes-hardware.com
Content-type: text/plain
Content-length: 34

Updated product list coming soon!
```

Joe

Response message

```
HTTP/1.1 201 Created
Location: http://www.joes-hardware.com/product-list.txt
Content-Type: text/plain
Context-Length: 47

http://www.joes-hardware.com/product-list.txt
```

www.joes-hardware.com    Server updates/creates
resource "/product-list.txt"
and writes it to its disk.

*Figure 3-9. PUT example*

The semantics of the PUT method are for the server to take the body of the request and either use it to create a new document named by the requested URL or, if that URL already exists, use the body to replace it.

Because PUT allows you to change content, many web servers require you to log in with a password before you can perform a PUT. You can read more about password authentication in Chapter 12.

## POST

The POST method was designed to send input data to the server.* In practice, it is often used to support HTML forms. The data from a filled-in form typically is sent to the server, which then marshals it off to where it needs to go (e.g., to a server gateway program, which then processes it). Figure 3-10 shows a client making an HTTP request—sending form data to a server—with the POST method.

## TRACE

When a client makes a request, that request may have to travel through firewalls, proxies, gateways, or other applications. Each of these has the opportunity to modify the original HTTP request. The TRACE method allows clients to see how its request looks when it finally makes it to the server.

A TRACE request initiates a "loopback" diagnostic at the destination server. The server at the final leg of the trip bounces back a TRACE response, with the virgin

---

* POST is used to send data to a server. PUT is used to deposit data into a resource on the server (e.g., a file).

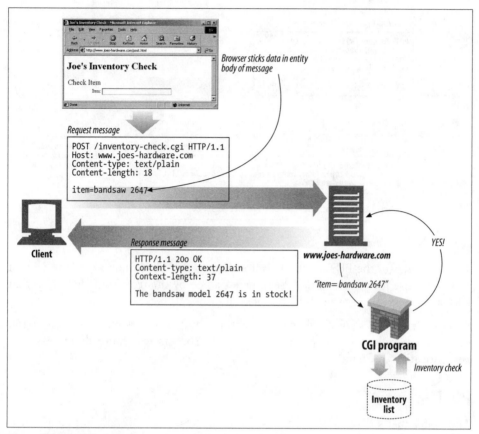

*Figure 3-10. POST example*

request message it received in the body of its response. A client can then see how, or if, its original message was munged or modified along the request/response chain of any intervening HTTP applications (see Figure 3-11).

The TRACE method is used primarily for diagnostics; i.e., verifying that requests are going through the request/response chain as intended. It's also a good tool for seeing the effects of proxies and other applications on your requests.

As good as TRACE is for diagnostics, it does have the drawback of assuming that intervening applications will treat different types of requests (different methods— GET, HEAD, POST, etc.) the same. Many HTTP applications do different things depending on the method—for example, a proxy might pass a POST request directly to the server but attempt to send a GET request to another HTTP application (such as a web cache). TRACE does not provide a mechanism to distinguish methods. Generally, intervening applications make the call as to how they process a TRACE request.

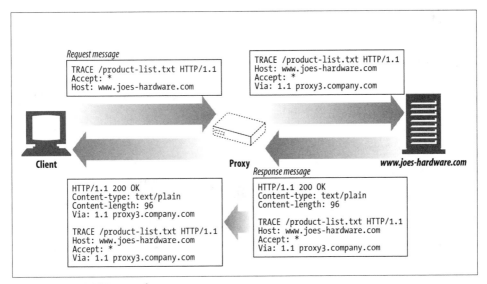

*Figure 3-11. TRACE example*

No entity body can be sent with a TRACE request. The entity body of the TRACE response contains, verbatim, the request that the responding server received.

## OPTIONS

The OPTIONS method asks the server to tell us about the various supported capabilities of the web server. You can ask a server about what methods it supports in general or for particular resources. (Some servers may support particular operations only on particular kinds of objects).

This provides a means for client applications to determine how best to access various resources without actually having to access them. Figure 3-12 shows a request scenario using the OPTIONS method.

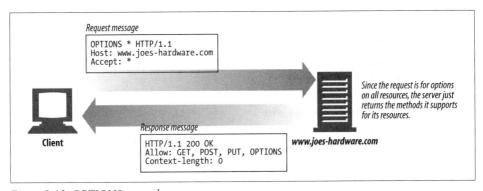

*Figure 3-12. OPTIONS example*

# DELETE

The DELETE method does just what you would think—it asks the server to delete the resources specified by the request URL. However, the client application is not guaranteed that the delete is carried out. This is because the HTTP specification allows the server to override the request without telling the client. Figure 3-13 shows an example of the DELETE method.

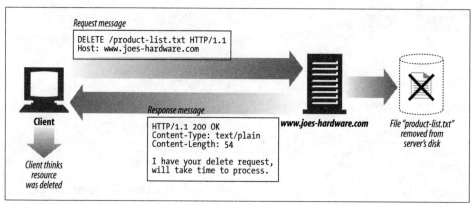

*Figure 3-13. DELETE example*

## Extension Methods

HTTP was designed to be field-extensible, so new features wouldn't cause older software to fail. Extension methods are methods that are not defined in the HTTP/1.1 specification. They provide developers with a means of extending the capabilities of the HTTP services their servers implement on the resources that the servers manage. Some common examples of extension methods are listed in Table 3-5. These methods are all part of the WebDAV HTTP extension (see Chapter 19) that helps support publishing of web content to web servers over HTTP.

*Table 3-5. Example web publishing extension methods*

| Method | Description |
| --- | --- |
| LOCK | Allows a user to "lock" a resource—for example, you could lock a resource while you are editing it to prevent others from editing it at the same time |
| MKCOL | Allows a user to create a resource |
| COPY | Facilitates copying resources on a server |
| MOVE | Moves a resource on a server |

It's important to note that not all extension methods are defined in a formal specification. If you define an extension method, it's likely not to be understood by most HTTP applications. Likewise, it's possible that your HTTP applications could run into extension methods being used by other applications that it does not understand.

In these cases, it is best to be tolerant of extension methods. Proxies should try to relay messages with unknown methods through to downstream servers if they are capable of doing that without breaking end-to-end behavior. Otherwise, they should respond with a 501 Not Implemented status code. Dealing with extension methods (and HTTP extensions in general) is best done with the old rule, "be conservative in what you send, be liberal in what you accept."

# Status Codes

HTTP status codes are classified into five broad categories, as shown earlier in Table 3-2. This section summarizes the HTTP status codes for each of the five classes.

The status codes provide an easy way for clients to understand the results of their transactions. In this section, we also list example reason phrases, though there is no real guidance on the exact text for reason phrases. We include the recommended reason phrases from the HTTP/1.1 specification.

## 100–199: Informational Status Codes

HTTP/1.1 introduced the informational status codes to the protocol. They are relatively new and subject to a bit of controversy about their complexity and perceived value. Table 3-6 lists the defined informational status codes.

*Table 3-6. Informational status codes and reason phrases*

| Status code | Reason phrase | Meaning |
| --- | --- | --- |
| 100 | Continue | Indicates that an initial part of the request was received and the client should continue. After sending this, the server must respond after receiving the request. See the Expect header in Appendix C for more information. |
| 101 | Switching Protocols | Indicates that the server is changing protocols, as specified by the client, to one listed in the Upgrade header. |

The 100 Continue status code, in particular, is a bit confusing. It's intended to optimize the case where an HTTP client application has an entity body to send to a server but wants to check that the server will accept the entity before it sends it. We discuss it here in a bit more detail (how it interacts with clients, servers, and proxies) because it tends to confuse HTTP programmers.

### Clients and 100 Continue

If a client is sending an entity to a server and is willing to wait for a 100 Continue response before it sends the entity, the client needs to send an Expect request header (see Appendix C) with the value 100-continue. If the client is not sending an entity, it shouldn't send a 100-continue Expect header, because this will only confuse the server into thinking that the client might be sending an entity.

100-continue, in many ways, is an optimization. A client application should really use 100-continue only to avoid sending a server a large entity that the server will not be able to handle or use.

Because of the initial confusion around the 100 Continue status (and given some of the older implementations out there), clients that send an Expect header for 100-continue should not wait forever for the server to send a 100 Continue response. After some timeout, the client should just send the entity.

In practice, client implementors also should be prepared to deal with unexpected 100 Continue responses (annoying, but true). Some errant HTTP applications send this code inappropriately.

### Servers and 100 Continue

If a server receives a request with the Expect header and 100-continue value, it should respond with either the 100 Continue response or an error code (see Table 3-9). Servers should never send a 100 Continue status code to clients that do not send the 100-continue expectation. However, as we noted above, some errant servers do this.

If for some reason the server receives some (or all) of the entity before it has had a chance to send a 100 Continue response, it does not need to send this status code, because the client already has decided to continue. When the server is done reading the request, however, it still needs to send a final status code for the request (it can just skip the 100 Continue status).

Finally, if a server receives a request with a 100-continue expectation and it decides to end the request before it has read the entity body (e.g., because an error has occurred), it should not just send a response and close the connection, as this can prevent the client from receiving the response (see "TCP close and reset errors" in Chapter 4).

### Proxies and 100 Continue

A proxy that receives from a client a request that contains the 100-continue expectation needs to do a few things. If the proxy either knows that the next-hop server (discussed in Chapter 6) is HTTP/1.1-compliant or does not know what version the next-hop server is compliant with, it should forward the request with the Expect header in it. If it knows that the next-hop server is compliant with a version of HTTP earlier than 1.1, it should respond with the 417 Expectation Failed error.

If a proxy decides to include an Expect header and 100-continue value in its request on behalf of a client that is compliant with HTTP/1.0 or earlier, it should not forward the 100 Continue response (if it receives one from the server) to the client, because the client won't know what to make of it.

It can pay for proxies to maintain some state about next-hop servers and the versions of HTTP they support (at least for servers that have received recent requests), so they can better handle requests received with a 100-continue expectation.

## 200–299: Success Status Codes

When clients make requests, the requests usually are successful. Servers have an array of status codes to indicate success, matched up with different types of requests. Table 3-7 lists the defined success status codes.

*Table 3-7. Success status codes and reason phrases*

| Status code | Reason phrase | Meaning |
|---|---|---|
| 200 | OK | Request is okay, entity body contains requested resource. |
| 201 | Created | For requests that create server objects (e.g., PUT). The entity body of the response should contain the various URLs for referencing the created resource, with the Location header containing the most specific reference. See Table 3-21 for more on the Location header. |
| | | The server must have created the object prior to sending this status code. |
| 202 | Accepted | The request was accepted, but the server has not yet performed any action with it. There are no guarantees that the server will complete the request; this just means that the request looked valid when accepted. |
| | | The server should include an entity body with a description indicating the status of the request and possibly an estimate for when it will be completed (or a pointer to where this information can be obtained). |
| 203 | Non-Authoritative Information | The information contained in the entity headers (see "Entity Headers" for more information on entity headers) came not from the origin server but from a copy of the resource. This could happen if an intermediary had a copy of a resource but could not or did not validate the meta-information (headers) it sent about the resource. |
| | | This response code is not required to be used; it is an option for applications that have a response that would be a 200 status if the entity headers had come from the origin server. |
| 204 | No Content | The response message contains headers and a status line, but no entity body. Primarily used to update browsers without having them move to a new document (e.g., refreshing a form page). |
| 205 | Reset Content | Another code primarily for browsers. Tells the browser to clear any HTML form elements on the current page. |
| 206 | Partial Content | A partial or *range* request was successful. Later, we will see that clients can request part or a range of a document by using special headers—this status code indicates that the range request was successful. See "Range Requests" in Chapter 15 for more on the Range header. |
| | | A 206 response must include a Content-Range, Date, and either ETag or Content-Location header. |

## 300–399: Redirection Status Codes

The redirection status codes either tell clients to use alternate locations for the resources they're interested in or provide an alternate response instead of the content. If a resource has moved, a redirection status code and an optional Location header can be sent to tell the client that the resource has moved and where it can now be found (see Figure 3-14). This allows browsers to go to the new location transparently, without bothering their human users.

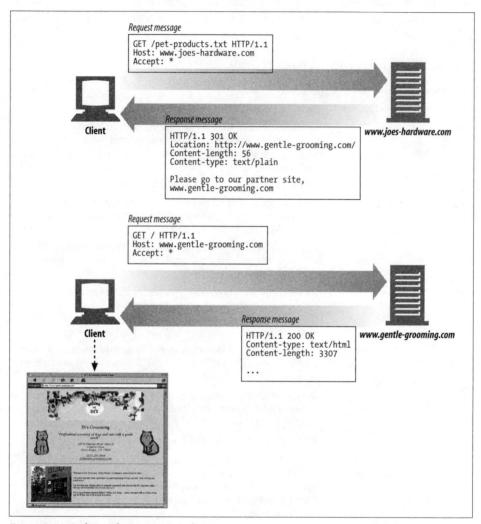

*Figure 3-14. Redirected request to new location*

Some of the redirection status codes can be used to validate an application's local copy of a resource with the origin server. For example, an HTTP application can check if the local copy of its resource is still up-to-date or if the resource has been modified on the origin server. Figure 3-15 shows an example of this. The client sends a special If-Modified-Since header saying to get the document only if it has been modified since October 1997. The document has not changed since this date, so the server replies with a 304 status code instead of the contents.

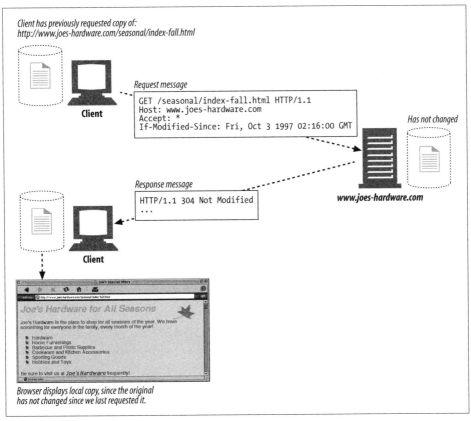

Client has previously requested copy of:
http://www.joes-hardware.com/seasonal/index-fall.html

**Client**

Request message

```
GET /seasonal/index-fall.html HTTP/1.1
Host: www.joes-hardware.com
Accept: *
If-Modified-Since: Fri, Oct 3 1997 02:16:00 GMT
```

Has not changed

**www.joes-hardware.com**

Response message

```
HTTP/1.1 304 Not Modified
...
```

**Client**

Joe's Hardware for All Seasons

Joe's Hardware is the place to shop for all seasons of the year. We have something for everyone in the family, every month of the year!

- Hardware
- Home Furnishings
- Barbecue and Picnic Supplies
- Cookware and Kitchen Accessories
- Sporting Goods
- Hobbies and Toys

Be sure to visit us at *Joe's Hardware* frequently!

Browser displays local copy, since the original
has not changed since we last requested it.

*Figure 3-15. Request redirected to use local copy*

In general, it's good practice for responses to non-HEAD requests that include a redirection status code to include an entity with a description and links to the redirected URL(s)—see the first response message in Figure 3-14. Table 3-8 lists the defined redirection status codes.

*Table 3-8. Redirection status codes and reason phrases*

| Status code | Reason phrase | Meaning |
|---|---|---|
| 300 | Multiple Choices | Returned when a client has requested a URL that actually refers to multiple resources, such as a server hosting an English and French version of an HTML document. This code is returned along with a list of options; the user can then select which one he wants. See Chapter 17 for more on clients negotiating when there are multiple versions. The server can include the preferred URL in the Location header. |
| 301 | Moved Permanently | Used when the requested URL has been moved. The response should contain in the Location header the URL where the resource now resides. |
| 302 | Found | Like the 301 status code; however, the client should use the URL given in the Location header to locate the resource temporarily. Future requests should use the old URL. |

*Table 3-8. Redirection status codes and reason phrases (continued)*

| Status code | Reason phrase | Meaning |
|---|---|---|
| 303 | See Other | Used to tell the client that the resource should be fetched using a different URL. This new URL is in the Location header of the response message. Its main purpose is to allow responses to POST requests to direct a client to a resource. |
| 304 | Not Modified | Clients can make their requests conditional by the request headers they include. See Table 3-15 for more on conditional headers. If a client makes a conditional request, such as a GET if the resource has not been changed recently, this code is used to indicate that the resource has not changed. Responses with this status code should not contain an entity body. |
| 305 | Use Proxy | Used to indicate that the resource must be accessed through a proxy; the location of the proxy is given in the Location header. It's important that clients interpret this response relative to a specific resource and do not assume that this proxy should be used for all requests or even all requests to the server holding the requested resource. This could lead to broken behavior if the proxy mistakenly interfered with a request, and it poses a security hole. |
| 306 | (Unused) | Not currently used. |
| 307 | Temporary Redirect | Like the 301 status code; however, the client should use the URL given in the Location header to locate the resource temporarily. Future requests should use the old URL. |

From Table 3-8, you may have noticed a bit of overlap between the 302, 303, and 307 status codes. There is some nuance to how these status codes are used, most of which stems from differences in the ways that HTTP/1.0 and HTTP/1.1 applications treat these status codes.

When an HTTP/1.0 client makes a POST request and receives a 302 redirect status code in response, it will follow the redirect URL in the Location header with a GET request to that URL (instead of making a POST request, as it did in the original request).

HTTP/1.0 servers expect HTTP/1.0 clients to do this—when an HTTP/1.0 server sends a 302 status code after receiving a POST request from an HTTP/1.0 client, the server expects that client to follow the redirect with a GET request to the redirected URL.

The confusion comes in with HTTP/1.1. The HTTP/1.1 specification uses the 303 status code to get this same behavior (servers send the 303 status code to redirect a client's POST request to be followed with a GET request).

To get around the confusion, the HTTP/1.1 specification says to use the 307 status code in place of the 302 status code for temporary redirects to HTTP/1.1 clients. Servers can then save the 302 status code for use with HTTP/1.0 clients.

What this all boils down to is that servers need to check a client's HTTP version to properly select which redirect status code to send in a redirect response.

# 400–499: Client Error Status Codes

Sometimes a client sends something that a server just can't handle, such as a badly formed request message or, most often, a request for a URL that does not exist.

We've all seen the infamous 404 Not Found error code while browsing—this is just the server telling us that we have requested a resource about which it knows nothing.

Many of the client errors are dealt with by your browser, without it ever bothering you. A few, like 404, might still pass through. Table 3-9 shows the various client error status codes.

*Table 3-9. Client error status codes and reason phrases*

| Status code | Reason phrase | Meaning |
| --- | --- | --- |
| 400 | Bad Request | Used to tell the client that it has sent a malformed request. |
| 401 | Unauthorized | Returned along with appropriate headers that ask the client to authenticate itself before it can gain access to the resource. See Chapter 12 for more on authentication. |
| 402 | Payment Required | Currently this status code is not used, but it has been set aside for future use. |
| 403 | Forbidden | Used to indicate that the request was refused by the server. If the server wants to indicate why the request was denied, it can include an entity body describing the reason. However, this code usually is used when the server does not want to reveal the reason for the refusal. |
| 404 | Not Found | Used to indicate that the server cannot find the requested URL. Often, an entity is included for the client application to display to the user. |
| 405 | Method Not Allowed | Used when a request is made with a method that is not supported for the requested URL. The Allow header should be included in the response to tell the client what methods are allowed on the requested resource. See "Entity Headers" for more on the Allow header. |
| 406 | Not Acceptable | Clients can specify parameters about what types of entities they are willing to accept. This code is used when the server has no resource matching the URL that is acceptable for the client. Often, servers include headers that allow the client to figure out why the request could not be satisfied. See "Content Negotiation and Transcoding" in Chapter 17 for more information. |
| 407 | Proxy Authentication Required | Like the 401 status code, but used for proxy servers that require authentication for a resource. |
| 408 | Request Timeout | If a client takes too long to complete its request, a server can send back this status code and close down the connection. The length of this timeout varies from server to server but generally is long enough to accommodate any legitimate request. |
| 409 | Conflict | Used to indicate some conflict that the request may be causing on a resource. Servers might send this code when they fear that a request could cause a conflict. The response should contain a body describing the conflict. |
| 410 | Gone | Similar to 404, except that the server once held the resource. Used mostly for web site maintenance, so a server's administrator can notify clients when a resource has been removed. |

*Table 3-9. Client error status codes and reason phrases (continued)*

| Status code | Reason phrase | Meaning |
|---|---|---|
| 411 | Length Required | Used when the server requires a Content-Length header in the request message. See "Content headers" for more on the Content-Length header. |
| 412 | Precondition Failed | Used if a client makes a conditional request and one of the conditions fails. Conditional requests occur when a client includes an Expect header. See Appendix C for more on the Expect header. |
| 413 | Request Entity Too Large | Used when a client sends an entity body that is larger than the server can or wants to process. |
| 414 | Request URI Too Long | Used when a client sends a request with a request URL that is larger than the server can or wants to process. |
| 415 | Unsupported Media Type | Used when a client sends an entity of a content type that the server does not understand or support. |
| 416 | Requested Range Not Satisfiable | Used when the request message requested a range of a given resource and that range either was invalid or could not be met. |
| 417 | Expectation Failed | Used when the request contained an expectation in the Expect request header that the server could not satisfy. See Appendix C for more on the Expect header. |
|  |  | A proxy or other intermediary application can send this response code if it has unambiguous evidence that the origin server will generate a failed expectation for the request. |

# 500–599: Server Error Status Codes

Sometimes a client sends a valid request, but the server itself has an error. This could be a client running into a limitation of the server or an error in one of the server's subcomponents, such as a gateway resource.

Proxies often run into problems when trying to talk to servers on a client's behalf. Proxies issue 5XX server error status codes to describe the problem (Chapter 6 covers this in detail). Table 3-10 lists the defined server error status codes.

*Table 3-10. Server error status codes and reason phrases*

| Status code | Reason phrase | Meaning |
|---|---|---|
| 500 | Internal Server Error | Used when the server encounters an error that prevents it from servicing the request. |
| 501 | Not Implemented | Used when a client makes a request that is beyond the server's capabilities (e.g., using a request method that the server does not support). |
| 502 | Bad Gateway | Used when a server acting as a proxy or gateway encounters a bogus response from the next link in the request response chain (e.g., if it is unable to connect to its parent gateway). |
| 503 | Service Unavailable | Used to indicate that the server currently cannot service the request but will be able to in the future. If the server knows when the resource will become available, it can include a Retry-After header in the response. See "Response Headers" for more on the Retry-After header. |

*Table 3-10. Server error status codes and reason phrases (continued)*

| Status code | Reason phrase | Meaning |
| --- | --- | --- |
| 504 | Gateway Timeout | Similar to status code 408, except that the response is coming from a gateway or proxy that has timed out waiting for a response to its request from another server. |
| 505 | HTTP Version Not Supported | Used when a server receives a request in a version of the protocol that it can't or won't support. Some server applications elect not to support older versions of the protocol. |

# Headers

Headers and methods work together to determine what clients and servers do. This section quickly sketches the purposes of the standard HTTP headers and some headers that are not explicitly defined in the HTTP/1.1 specification (RFC 2616). Appendix C summarizes all these headers in more detail.

There are headers that are specific for each type of message and headers that are more general in purpose, providing information in both request and response messages. Headers fall into five main classes:

*General headers*

These are generic headers used by both clients and servers. They serve general purposes that are useful for clients, servers, and other applications to supply to one another. For example, the Date header is a general-purpose header that allows both sides to indicate the time and date at which the message was constructed:

```
Date: Tue, 3 Oct 1974 02:16:00 GMT
```

*Request headers*

As the name implies, request headers are specific to request messages. They provide extra information to servers, such as what type of data the client is willing to receive. For example, the following Accept header tells the server that the client will accept any media type that matches its request:

```
Accept: */*
```

*Response headers*

Response messages have their own set of headers that provide information to the client (e.g., what type of server the client is talking to). For example, the following Server header tells the client that it is talking to a Version 1.0 Tiki-Hut server:

```
Server: Tiki-Hut/1.0
```

*Entity headers*

Entity headers refer to headers that deal with the entity body. For instance, entity headers can tell the type of the data in the entity body. For example, the following Content-Type header lets the application know that the data is an HTML document in the iso-latin-1 character set:

```
Content-Type: text/html; charset=iso-latin-1
```

*Extension headers*

> Extension headers are nonstandard headers that have been created by application developers but not yet added to the sanctioned HTTP specification. HTTP programs need to tolerate and forward extension headers, even if they don't know what the headers mean.

## General Headers

Some headers provide very basic information about a message. These headers are called general headers. They are the fence straddlers, supplying useful information about a message regardless of its type.

For example, whether you are constructing a request message or a response message, the date and time the message is created means the same thing, so the header that provides this kind of information is general to both types of messages. Table 3-11 lists the general informational headers.

*Table 3-11. General informational headers*

| Header | Description |
| --- | --- |
| Connection | Allows clients and servers to specify options about the request/response connection |
| Date[a] | Provides a date and time stamp telling when the message was created |
| MIME-Version | Gives the version of MIME that the sender is using |
| Trailer | Lists the set of headers that are in the trailer of a message encoded with the chunked transfer encoding[b] |
| Transfer-Encoding | Tells the receiver what encoding was performed on the message in order for it to be transported safely |
| Upgrade | Gives a new version or protocol that the sender would like to "upgrade" to using |
| Via | Shows what intermediaries (proxies, gateways) the message has gone through |

[a] Appendix C lists the acceptable date formats for the Date header.
[b] Chunked transfer codings are discussed further in "Chunking and persistent connections" in Chapter 15.

### General caching headers

HTTP/1.0 introduced the first headers that allowed HTTP applications to cache local copies of objects instead of always fetching them directly from the origin server. The latest version of HTTP has a very rich set of cache parameters. In Chapter 7, we cover caching in depth. Table 3-12 lists the basic caching headers.

*Table 3-12. General caching headers*

| Header | Description |
| --- | --- |
| Cache-Control | Used to pass caching directions along with the message |
| Pragma[a] | Another way to pass directions along with the message, though not specific to caching |

[a] Pragma technically is a request header. It was never specified for use in responses. Because of its common misuse as a response header, many clients and proxies will interpret Pragma as a response header, but the precise semantics are not well defined. In any case, Pragma is deprecated in favor of Cache-Control.

# Request Headers

Request headers are headers that make sense only in a request message. They give information about who or what is sending the request, where the request originated, or what the preferences and capabilities of the client are. Servers can use the information the request headers give them about the client to try to give the client a better response. Table 3-13 lists the request informational headers.

*Table 3-13. Request informational headers*

| Header | Description |
|---|---|
| Client-IP[a] | Provides the IP address of the machine on which the client is running |
| From | Provides the email address of the client's user[b] |
| Host | Gives the hostname and port of the server to which the request is being sent |
| Referer | Provides the URL of the document that contains the current request URI |
| UA-Color | Provides information about the color capabilities of the client machine's display |
| UA-CPU[c] | Gives the type or manufacturer of the client's CPU |
| UA-Disp | Provides information about the client's display (screen) capabilities |
| UA-OS | Gives the name and version of operating system running on the client machine |
| UA-Pixels | Provides pixel information about the client machine's display |
| User-Agent | Tells the server the name of the application making the request |

[a] Client-IP and the UA-* headers are not defined in RFC 2616 but are implemented by many HTTP client applications.
[b] An RFC 822 email address format.
[c] While implemented by some clients, the UA-* headers can be considered harmful. Content, specifically HTML, should not be targeted at specific client configurations.

## Accept headers

Accept headers give the client a way to tell servers their preferences and capabilities: what they want, what they can use, and, most importantly, what they don't want. Servers can then use this extra information to make more intelligent decisions about what to send. Accept headers benefit both sides of the connection. Clients get what they want, and servers don't waste their time and bandwidth sending something the client can't use. Table 3-14 lists the various accept headers.

*Table 3-14. Accept headers*

| Header | Description |
|---|---|
| Accept | Tells the server what media types are okay to send |
| Accept-Charset | Tells the server what charsets are okay to send |
| Accept-Encoding | Tells the server what encodings are okay to send |
| Accept-Language | Tells the server what languages are okay to send |
| TE[a] | Tells the server what extension transfer codings are okay to use |

[a] See "Transfer-Encoding Headers" in Chapter 15 for more on the TE header.

## Conditional request headers

Sometimes, clients want to put some restrictions on a request. For instance, if the client already has a copy of a document, it might want to ask a server to send the document only if it is different from the copy the client already has. Using conditional request headers, clients can put such restrictions on requests, requiring the server to make sure that the conditions are true before satisfying the request. Table 3-15 lists the various conditional request headers.

*Table 3-15. Conditional request headers*

| Header | Description |
| --- | --- |
| Expect | Allows a client to list server behaviors that it requires for a request |
| If-Match | Gets the document if the entity tag matches the current entity tag for the document[a] |
| If-Modified-Since | Restricts the request unless the resource has been modified since the specified date |
| If-None-Match | Gets the document if the entity tags supplied do not match those of the current document |
| If-Range | Allows a conditional request for a range of a document |
| If-Unmodified-Since | Restricts the request unless the resource has *not* been modified since the specified date |
| Range | Requests a specific range of a resource, if the server supports range requests[b] |

[a] See Chapter 7 for more on entity tags. The tag is basically an identifier for a version of the resource.
[b] See "Range Requests" in Chapter 15 for more on the Range header.

## Request security headers

HTTP natively supports a simple challenge/response authentication scheme for requests. It attempts to make transactions slightly more secure by requiring clients to authenticate themselves before getting access to certain resources. We discuss this challenge/response scheme in Chapter 14, along with other security schemes that have been implemented on top of HTTP. Table 3-16 lists the request security headers.

*Table 3-16. Request security headers*

| Header | Description |
| --- | --- |
| Authorization | Contains the data the client is supplying to the server to authenticate itself |
| Cookie | Used by clients to pass a token to the server—not a true security header, but it does have security implications[a] |
| Cookie2 | Used to note the version of cookies a requestor supports; see "Version 1 (RFC 2965) Cookies" in Chapter 11 |

[a] The Cookie header is not defined in RFC 2616; it is discussed in detail in Chapter 11.

## Proxy request headers

As proxies become increasingly common on the Internet, a few headers have been defined to help them function better. In Chapter 6, we discuss these headers in detail. Table 3-17 lists the proxy request headers.

*Table 3-17. Proxy request headers*

| Header | Description |
|---|---|
| Max-Forwards | The maximum number of times a request should be forwarded to another proxy or gateway on its way to the origin server—used with the TRACE method[a] |
| Proxy-Authorization | Same as Authorization, but used when authenticating with a proxy |
| Proxy-Connection | Same as Connection, but used when establishing connections with a proxy |

[a] See "Max-Forwards" in Chapter 6.

## Response Headers

Response messages have their own set of response headers. Response headers provide clients with extra information, such as who is sending the response, the capabilities of the responder, or even special instructions regarding the response. These headers help the client deal with the response and make better requests in the future. Table 3-18 lists the response informational headers.

*Table 3-18. Response informational headers*

| Header | Description |
|---|---|
| Age | How old the response is[a] |
| Public[b] | A list of request methods the server supports for its resources |
| Retry-After | A date or time to try back, if a resource is unavailable |
| Server | The name and version of the server's application software |
| Title[c] | For HTML documents, the title as given by the HTML document source |
| Warning | A more detailed warning message than what is in the reason phrase |

[a] Implies that the response has traveled through an intermediary, possibly from a proxy cache.
[b] The Public header is defined in RFC 2068 but does not appear in the latest HTTP definition (RFC 2616).
[c] The Title header is not defined in RFC 2616; see the original HTTP/1.0 draft definition (*http://www.w3.org/Protocols/HTTP/HTTP2.html*).

### Negotiation headers

HTTP/1.1 provides servers and clients with the ability to negotiate for a resource if multiple representations are available—for instance, when there are both French and German translations of an HTML document on a server. Chapter 17 walks through negotiation in detail. Here are a few headers servers use to convey information about resources that are negotiable. Table 3-19 lists the negotiation headers.

*Table 3-19. Negotiation headers*

| Header | Description |
|---|---|
| Accept-Ranges | The type of ranges that a server will accept for this resource |
| Vary | A list of other headers that the server looks at and that may cause the response to vary; i.e., a list of headers the server looks at to pick which is the best version of a resource to send the client |

### Response security headers

You've already seen the request security headers, which are basically the *response* side of HTTP's challenge/response authentication scheme. We talk about security in detail in Chapter 14. For now, here are the basic *challenge* headers. Table 3-20 lists the response security headers.

*Table 3-20. Response security headers*

| Header | Description |
| --- | --- |
| Proxy-Authenticate | A list of challenges for the client from the proxy |
| Set-Cookie | Not a true security header, but it has security implications; used to set a token on the client side that the server can use to identify the client[a] |
| Set-Cookie2 | Similar to Set-Cookie, RFC 2965 Cookie definition; see "Version 1 (RFC 2965) Cookies" in Chapter 11 |
| WWW-Authenticate | A list of challenges for the client from the server |

[a] Set-Cookie and Set-Cookie2 are extension headers that are also covered in Chapter 11.

## Entity Headers

There are many headers to describe the payload of HTTP messages. Because both request and response messages can contain entities, these headers can appear in either type of message.

Entity headers provide a broad range of information about the entity and its content, from information about the type of the object to valid request methods that can be made on the resource. In general, entity headers tell the receiver of the message what it's dealing with. Table 3-21 lists the entity informational headers.

*Table 3-21. Entity informational headers*

| Header | Description |
| --- | --- |
| Allow | Lists the request methods that can be performed on this entity |
| Location | Tells the client where the entity really is located; used in directing the receiver to a (possibly new) location (URL) for the resource |

### Content headers

The content headers provide specific information about the content of the entity, revealing its type, size, and other information useful for processing it. For instance, a web browser can look at the content type returned and know how to display the object. Table 3-22 lists the various content headers.

*Table 3-22. Content headers*

| Header | Description |
| --- | --- |
| Content-Base[a] | The base URL for resolving relative URLs within the body |
| Content-Encoding | Any encoding that was performed on the body |

*Table 3-22. Content headers (continued)*

| Header | Description |
|---|---|
| Content-Language | The natural language that is best used to understand the body |
| Content-Length | The length or size of the body |
| Content-Location | Where the resource actually is located |
| Content-MD5 | An MD5 checksum of the body |
| Content-Range | The range of bytes that this entity represents from the entire resource |
| Content-Type | The type of object that this body is |

[a] The Content-Base header is not defined in RFC 2616.

### Entity caching headers

The general caching headers provide directives about how or when to cache. The entity caching headers provide information about the entity being cached—for example, information needed to validate whether a cached copy of the resource is still valid and hints about how better to estimate when a cached resource may no longer be valid.

In Chapter 7, we dive deep into the heart of caching HTTP requests and responses. We will see these headers again there. Table 3-23 lists the entity caching headers.

*Table 3-23. Entity caching headers*

| Header | Description |
|---|---|
| ETag | The entity tag associated with this entity[a] |
| Expires | The date and time at which this entity will no longer be valid and will need to be fetched from the original source |
| Last-Modified | The last date and time when this entity changed |

[a] Entity tags are basically identifiers for a particular version of a resource.

# For More Information

For more information, refer to:

*http://www.w3.org/Protocols/rfc2616/rfc2616.txt*
> RFC 2616, "Hypertext Transfer Protocol," by R. Fielding, J. Gettys, J. Mogul, H. Frystyk, L. Mastinter, P. Leach, and T. Berners-Lee.

*HTTP Pocket Reference*
> Clintin Wong, O'Reilly & Associates, Inc.

*http://www.w3.org/Protocols/*
> The W3C architecture page for HTTP.

## CHAPTER 4

# Connection Management

The HTTP specifications explain HTTP messages fairly well, but they don't talk much about HTTP connections, the critical plumbing that HTTP messages flow through. If you're a programmer writing HTTP applications, you need to understand the ins and outs of HTTP connections and how to use them.

HTTP connection management has been a bit of a black art, learned as much from experimentation and apprenticeship as from published literature. In this chapter, you'll learn about:

- How HTTP uses TCP connections
- Delays, bottlenecks and clogs in TCP connections
- HTTP optimizations, including parallel, keep-alive, and pipelined connections
- Dos and don'ts for managing connections

## TCP Connections

Just about all of the world's HTTP communication is carried over TCP/IP, a popular layered set of packet-switched network protocols spoken by computers and network devices around the globe. A client application can open a TCP/IP connection to a server application, running just about anywhere in the world. Once the connection is established, messages exchanged between the client's and server's computers will never be lost, damaged, or received out of order.*

Say you want the latest power tools price list from Joe's Hardware store:

*http://www.joes-hardware.com:80/power-tools.html*

When given this URL, your browser performs the steps shown in Figure 4-1. In Steps 1–3, the IP address and port number of the server are pulled from the URL. A TCP

---

* Though messages won't be lost or corrupted, communication between client and server can be severed if a computer or network breaks. In this case, the client and server are notified of the communication breakdown.

connection is made to the web server in Step 4, and a request message is sent across the connection in Step 5. The response is read in Step 6, and the connection is closed in Step 7.

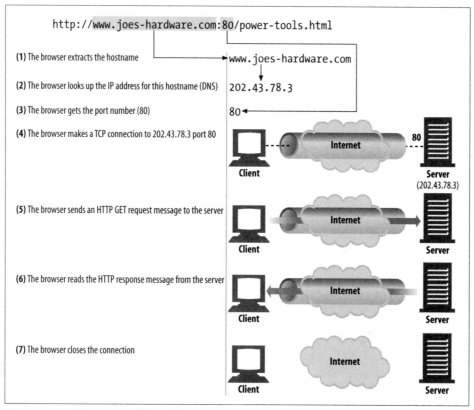

Figure 4-1. Web browsers talk to web servers over TCP connections

## TCP Reliable Data Pipes

HTTP connections really are nothing more than TCP connections, plus a few rules about how to use them. TCP connections are the reliable connections of the Internet. To send data accurately and quickly, you need to know the basics of TCP.*

TCP gives HTTP a *reliable bit pipe*. Bytes stuffed in one side of a TCP connection come out the other side correctly, and in the right order (see Figure 4-2).

---

* If you are trying to write sophisticated HTTP applications, and especially if you want them to be fast, you'll want to learn a lot more about the internals and performance of TCP than we discuss in this chapter. We recommend the "TCP/IP Illustrated" books by W. Richard Stevens (Addison Wesley).

Figure 4-2. TCP carries HTTP data in order, and without corruption

## TCP Streams Are Segmented and Shipped by IP Packets

TCP sends its data in little chunks called *IP packets* (or *IP datagrams*). In this way, HTTP is the top layer in a "protocol stack" of "HTTP over TCP over IP," as depicted in Figure 4-3a. A secure variant, HTTPS, inserts a cryptographic encryption layer (called TLS or SSL) between HTTP and TCP (Figure 4-3b).

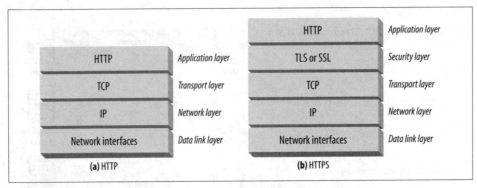

Figure 4-3. HTTP and HTTPS network protocol stacks

When HTTP wants to transmit a message, it streams the contents of the message data, in order, through an open TCP connection. TCP takes the stream of data, chops up the data stream into chunks called segments, and transports the segments across the Internet inside envelopes called IP packets (see Figure 4-4). This is all handled by the TCP/IP software; the HTTP programmer sees none of it.

Each TCP segment is carried by an IP packet from one IP address to another IP address. Each of these IP packets contains:

- An IP packet header (usually 20 bytes)
- A TCP segment header (usually 20 bytes)
- A chunk of TCP data (0 or more bytes)

The IP header contains the source and destination IP addresses, the size, and other flags. The TCP segment header contains TCP port numbers, TCP control flags, and numeric values used for data ordering and integrity checking.

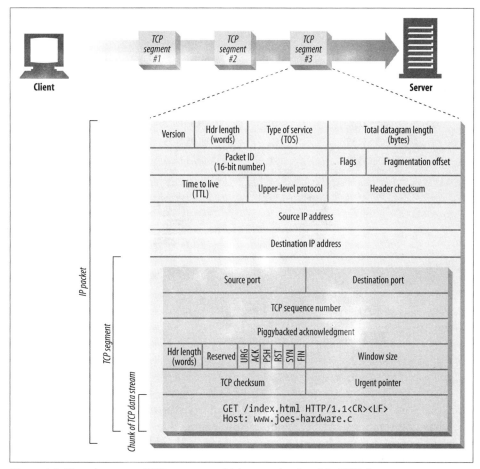

Figure 4-4. IP packets carry TCP segments, which carry chunks of the TCP data stream

## Keeping TCP Connections Straight

A computer might have several TCP connections open at any one time. TCP keeps all these connections straight through *port numbers*.

Port numbers are like employees' phone extensions. Just as a company's main phone number gets you to the front desk and the extension gets you to the right employee, the IP address gets you to the right computer and the port number gets you to the right application. A TCP connection is distinguished by four values:

```
<source-IP-address, source-port, destination-IP-address, destination-port>
```

Together, these four values uniquely define a connection. Two different TCP connections are not allowed to have the same values for all four address components (but different connections can have the same values for some of the components).

In Figure 4-5, there are four connections: A, B, C and D. The relevant information for each port is listed in Table 4-1.

*Table 4-1. TCP connection values*

| Connection | Source IP address | Source port | Destination IP address | Destination port |
|---|---|---|---|---|
| A | 209.1.32.34 | 2034 | 204.62.128.58 | 4133 |
| B | 209.1.32.35 | 3227 | 204.62.128.58 | 4140 |
| C | 209.1.32.35 | 3105 | 207.25.71.25 | 80 |
| D | 209.1.33.89 | 5100 | 207.25.71.25 | 80 |

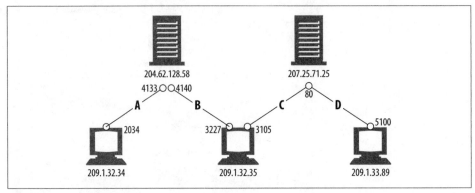

*Figure 4-5. Four distinct TCP connections*

Note that some of the connections share the same destination port number (C and D both have destination port 80). Some of the connections have the same source IP address (B and C). Some have the same destination IP address (A and B, and C and D). But no two different connections share all four identical values.

## Programming with TCP Sockets

Operating systems provide different facilities for manipulating their TCP connections. Let's take a quick look at one TCP programming interface, to make things concrete. Table 4-2 shows some of the primary interfaces provided by the sockets API. This sockets API hides all the details of TCP and IP from the HTTP programmer. The sockets API was first developed for the Unix operating system, but variants are now available for almost every operating system and language.

*Table 4-2. Common socket interface functions for programming TCP connections*

| Sockets API call | Description |
|---|---|
| s = socket(<parameters>) | Creates a new, unnamed, unattached socket. |
| bind(s, <local IP:port>) | Assigns a local port number and interface to the socket. |

*Table 4-2. Common socket interface functions for programming TCP connections (continued)*

| Sockets API call | Description |
| --- | --- |
| connect(s, <remote IP:port>) | Establishes a TCP connection to a local socket and a remote host and port. |
| listen(s,...) | Marks a local socket as legal to accept connections. |
| s2 = accept(s) | Waits for someone to establish a connection to a local port. |
| n = read(s,buffer,n) | Tries to read n bytes from the socket into the buffer. |
| n = write(s,buffer,n) | Tries to write n bytes from the buffer into the socket. |
| close(s) | Completely closes the TCP connection. |
| shutdown(s,<side>) | Closes just the input or the output of the TCP connection. |
| getsockopt(s, ...) | Reads the value of an internal socket configuration option. |
| setsockopt(s, ...) | Changes the value of an internal socket configuration option. |

The sockets API lets you create TCP endpoint data structures, connect these end-points to remote server TCP endpoints, and read and write data streams. The TCP API hides all the details of the underlying network protocol handshaking and the segmentation and reassembly of the TCP data stream to and from IP packets.

In Figure 4-1, we showed how a web browser could download the *power-tools.html* web page from Joe's Hardware store using HTTP. The pseudocode in Figure 4-6 sketches how we might use the sockets API to highlight the steps the client and server could perform to implement this HTTP transaction.

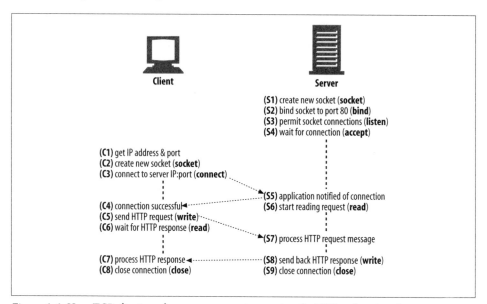

*Figure 4-6. How TCP clients and servers communicate using the TCP sockets interface*

We begin with the web server waiting for a connection (Figure 4-6, S4). The client determines the IP address and port number from the URL and proceeds to establish a TCP connection to the server (Figure 4-6, C3). Establishing a connection can take a while, depending on how far away the server is, the load on the server, and the congestion of the Internet.

Once the connection is set up, the client sends the HTTP request (Figure 4-6, C5) and the server reads it (Figure 4-6, S6). Once the server gets the entire request message, it processes the request, performs the requested action (Figure 4-6, S7), and writes the data back to the client. The client reads it (Figure 4-6, C6) and processes the response data (Figure 4-6, C7).

# TCP Performance Considerations

Because HTTP is layered directly on TCP, the performance of HTTP transactions depends critically on the performance of the underlying TCP plumbing. This section highlights some significant performance considerations of these TCP connections. By understanding some of the basic performance characteristics of TCP, you'll better appreciate HTTP's connection optimization features, and you'll be able to design and implement higher-performance HTTP applications.

This section requires some understanding of the internal details of the TCP protocol. If you are not interested in (or are comfortable with) the details of TCP performance considerations, feel free to skip ahead to "HTTP Connection Handling." Because TCP is a complex topic, we can provide only a brief overview of TCP performance here. Refer to the section "For More Information" at the end of this chapter for a list of excellent TCP references.

## HTTP Transaction Delays

Let's start our TCP performance tour by reviewing what networking delays occur in the course of an HTTP request. Figure 4-7 depicts the major connect, transfer, and processing delays for an HTTP transaction.

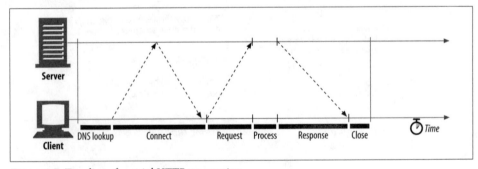

*Figure 4-7. Timeline of a serial HTTP transaction*

Notice that the transaction processing time can be quite small compared to the time required to set up TCP connections and transfer the request and response messages. Unless the client or server is overloaded or executing complex dynamic resources, most HTTP delays are caused by TCP network delays.

There are several possible causes of delay in an HTTP transaction:

1. A client first needs to determine the IP address and port number of the web server from the URI. If the hostname in the URI was not recently visited, it may take tens of seconds to convert the hostname from a URI into an IP address using the DNS resolution infrastructure.[*]

2. Next, the client sends a TCP connection request to the server and waits for the server to send back a connection acceptance reply. Connection setup delay occurs for every new TCP connection. This usually takes at most a second or two, but it can add up quickly when hundreds of HTTP transactions are made.

3. Once the connection is established, the client sends the HTTP request over the newly established TCP pipe. The web server reads the request message from the TCP connection as the data arrives and processes the request. It takes time for the request message to travel over the Internet and get processed by the server.

4. The web server then writes back the HTTP response, which also takes time.

The magnitude of these TCP network delays depends on hardware speed, the load of the network and server, the size of the request and response messages, and the distance between client and server. The delays also are significantly affected by technical intricacies of the TCP protocol.

## Performance Focus Areas

The remainder of this section outlines some of the most common TCP-related delays affecting HTTP programmers, including the causes and performance impacts of:

- The TCP connection setup handshake
- TCP slow-start congestion control
- Nagle's algorithm for data aggregation
- TCP's delayed acknowledgment algorithm for piggybacked acknowledgments
- TIME_WAIT delays and port exhaustion

If you are writing high-performance HTTP software, you should understand each of these factors. If you don't need this level of performance optimization, feel free to skip ahead.

---

[*] Luckily, most HTTP clients keep a small DNS cache of IP addresses for recently accessed sites. When the IP address is already "cached" (recorded) locally, the lookup is instantaneous. Because most web browsing is to a small number of popular sites, hostnames usually are resolved very quickly.

## TCP Connection Handshake Delays

When you set up a new TCP connection, even before you send any data, the TCP software exchanges a series of IP packets to negotiate the terms of the connection (see Figure 4-8). These exchanges can significantly degrade HTTP performance if the connections are used for small data transfers.

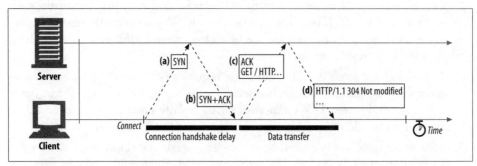

*Figure 4-8. TCP requires two packet transfers to set up the connection before it can send data*

Here are the steps in the TCP connection handshake:

1. To request a new TCP connection, the client sends a small TCP packet (usually 40–60 bytes) to the server. The packet has a special "SYN" flag set, which means it's a connection request. This is shown in Figure 4-8a.

2. If the server accepts the connection, it computes some connection parameters and sends a TCP packet back to the client, with both the "SYN" and "ACK" flags set, indicating that the connection request is accepted (see Figure 4-8b).

3. Finally, the client sends an acknowledgment back to the server, letting it know that the connection was established successfully (see Figure 4-8c). Modern TCP stacks let the client send data in this acknowledgment packet.

The HTTP programmer never sees these packets—they are managed invisibly by the TCP/IP software. All the HTTP programmer sees is a delay when creating a new TCP connection.

The SYN/SYN+ACK handshake (Figure 4-8a and b) creates a measurable delay when HTTP transactions do not exchange much data, as is commonly the case. The TCP connect ACK packet (Figure 4-8c) often is large enough to carry the entire HTTP request message,* and many HTTP server response messages fit into a single IP packet (e.g., when the response is a small HTML file of a decorative graphic, or a 304 Not Modified response to a browser cache request).

---

* IP packets are usually a few hundred bytes for Internet traffic and around 1,500 bytes for local traffic.

---

The end result is that small HTTP transactions may spend 50% or more of their time doing TCP setup. Later sections will discuss how HTTP allows reuse of existing connections to eliminate the impact of this TCP setup delay.

## Delayed Acknowledgments

Because the Internet itself does not guarantee reliable packet delivery (Internet routers are free to destroy packets at will if they are overloaded), TCP implements its own acknowledgment scheme to guarantee successful data delivery.

Each TCP segment gets a sequence number and a data-integrity checksum. The receiver of each segment returns small acknowledgment packets back to the sender when segments have been received intact. If a sender does not receive an acknowledgment within a specified window of time, the sender concludes the packet was destroyed or corrupted and resends the data.

Because acknowledgments are small, TCP allows them to "piggyback" on outgoing data packets heading in the same direction. By combining returning acknowledgments with outgoing data packets, TCP can make more efficient use of the network. To increase the chances that an acknowledgment will find a data packet headed in the same direction, many TCP stacks implement a "delayed acknowledgment" algorithm. Delayed acknowledgments hold outgoing acknowledgments in a buffer for a certain window of time (usually 100–200 milliseconds), looking for an outgoing data packet on which to piggyback. If no outgoing data packet arrives in that time, the acknowledgment is sent in its own packet.

Unfortunately, the bimodal request-reply behavior of HTTP reduces the chances that piggybacking can occur. There just aren't many packets heading in the reverse direction when you want them. Frequently, the delayed acknowledgment algorithms introduce significant delays. Depending on your operating system, you may be able to adjust or disable the delayed acknowledgment algorithm.

Before you modify any parameters of your TCP stack, be sure you know what you are doing. Algorithms inside TCP were introduced to protect the Internet from poorly designed applications. If you modify any TCP configurations, be absolutely sure your application will not create the problems the algorithms were designed to avoid.

## TCP Slow Start

The performance of TCP data transfer also depends on the *age* of the TCP connection. TCP connections "tune" themselves over time, initially limiting the maximum speed of the connection and increasing the speed over time as data is transmitted successfully. This tuning is called *TCP slow start*, and it is used to prevent sudden overloading and congestion of the Internet.

TCP slow start throttles the number of packets a TCP endpoint can have in flight at any one time. Put simply, each time a packet is received successfully, the sender gets permission to send two more packets. If an HTTP transaction has a large amount of data to send, it cannot send all the packets at once. It must send one packet and wait for an acknowledgment; then it can send two packets, each of which must be acknowledged, which allows four packets, etc. This is called "opening the congestion window."

Because of this congestion-control feature, new connections are slower than "tuned" connections that already have exchanged a modest amount of data. Because tuned connections are faster, HTTP includes facilities that let you reuse existing connections. We'll talk about these HTTP "persistent connections" later in this chapter.

## Nagle's Algorithm and TCP_NODELAY

TCP has a data stream interface that permits applications to stream data of any size to the TCP stack—even a single byte at a time! But because each TCP segment carries at least 40 bytes of flags and headers, network performance can be degraded severely if TCP sends large numbers of packets containing small amounts of data.*

Nagle's algorithm (named for its creator, John Nagle) attempts to bundle up a large amount of TCP data before sending a packet, aiding network efficiency. The algorithm is described in RFC 896, "Congestion Control in IP/TCP Internetworks."

Nagle's algorithm discourages the sending of segments that are not full-size (a maximum-size packet is around 1,500 bytes on a LAN, or a few hundred bytes across the Internet). Nagle's algorithm lets you send a non-full-size packet only if all other packets have been acknowledged. If other packets are still in flight, the partial data is buffered. This buffered data is sent only when pending packets are acknowledged or when the buffer has accumulated enough data to send a full packet.†

Nagle's algorithm causes several HTTP performance problems. First, small HTTP messages may not fill a packet, so they may be delayed waiting for additional data that will never arrive. Second, Nagle's algorithm interacts poorly with delayed acknowledgments—Nagle's algorithm will hold up the sending of data until an acknowledgment arrives, but the acknowledgment itself will be delayed 100–200 milliseconds by the delayed acknowledgment algorithm.‡

HTTP applications often disable Nagle's algorithm to improve performance, by setting the TCP_NODELAY parameter on their stacks. If you do this, you must ensure that you write large chunks of data to TCP so you don't create a flurry of small packets.

---

* Sending a storm of single-byte packets is called "sender silly window syndrome." This is inefficient, antisocial, and can be disruptive to other Internet traffic.

† Several variations of this algorithm exist, including timeouts and acknowledgment logic changes, but the basic algorithm causes buffering of data smaller than a TCP segment.

‡ These problems can become worse when using pipelined connections (described later in this chapter), because clients may have several messages to send to the same server and do not want delays.

---

# TIME_WAIT Accumulation and Port Exhaustion

TIME_WAIT port exhaustion is a serious performance problem that affects performance benchmarking but is relatively uncommon in real deployments. It warrants special attention because most people involved in performance benchmarking eventually run into this problem and get unexpectedly poor performance.

When a TCP endpoint closes a TCP connection, it maintains in memory a small control block recording the IP addresses and port numbers of the recently closed connection. This information is maintained for a short time, typically around twice the estimated maximum segment lifetime (called "2MSL"; often two minutes*), to make sure a new TCP connection with the same addresses and port numbers is not created during this time. This prevents any stray duplicate packets from the previous connection from accidentally being injected into a new connection that has the same addresses and port numbers. In practice, this algorithm prevents two connections with the exact same IP addresses and port numbers from being created, closed, and recreated within two minutes.

Today's higher-speed routers make it extremely unlikely that a duplicate packet will show up on a server's doorstep minutes after a connection closes. Some operating systems set 2MSL to a smaller value, but be careful about overriding this value. Packets do get duplicated, and TCP data will be corrupted if a duplicate packet from a past connection gets inserted into a new stream with the same connection values.

The 2MSL connection close delay normally is not a problem, but in benchmarking situations, it can be. It's common that only one or a few test load-generation computers are connecting to a system under benchmark test, which limits the number of client IP addresses that connect to the server. Furthermore, the server typically is listening on HTTP's default TCP port, 80. These circumstances limit the available combinations of connection values, at a time when port numbers are blocked from reuse by TIME_WAIT.

In a pathological situation with one client and one web server, of the four values that make up a TCP connection:

        <source-IP-address, source-port, destination-IP-address, destination-port>

three of them are fixed—only the source port is free to change:

        <client-IP, source-port, server-IP, 80>

Each time the client connects to the server, it gets a new source port in order to have a unique connection. But because a limited number of source ports are available (say, 60,000) and no connection can be reused for 2MSL seconds (say, 120 seconds), this limits the connect rate to 60,000 / 120 = 500 transactions/sec. If you keep

---

* The 2MSL value of two minutes is historical. Long ago, when routers were much slower, it was estimated that a duplicate copy of a packet might be able to remain queued in the Internet for up to a minute before being destroyed. Today, the maximum segment lifetime is much smaller.

making optimizations, and your server doesn't get faster than about 500 transactions/sec, make sure you are not experiencing TIME_WAIT port exhaustion. You can fix this problem by using more client load-generator machines or making sure the client and server rotate through several virtual IP addresses to add more connection combinations.

Even if you do not suffer port exhaustion problems, be careful about having large numbers of open connections or large numbers of control blocks allocated for connection in wait states. Some operating systems slow down dramatically when there are numerous open connections or control blocks.

# HTTP Connection Handling

The first two sections of this chapter provided a fire-hose tour of TCP connections and their performance implications. If you'd like to learn more about TCP networking, check out the resources listed at the end of the chapter.

We're going to switch gears now and get squarely back to HTTP. The rest of this chapter explains the HTTP technology for manipulating and optimizing connections. We'll start with the HTTP Connection header, an often misunderstood but important part of HTTP connection management. Then we'll talk about HTTP's connection optimization techniques.

## The Oft-Misunderstood Connection Header

HTTP allows a chain of HTTP intermediaries between the client and the ultimate origin server (proxies, caches, etc.). HTTP messages are forwarded hop by hop from the client, through intermediary devices, to the origin server (or the reverse).

In some cases, two adjacent HTTP applications may want to apply a set of options to their shared connection. The HTTP Connection header field has a comma-separated list of *connection tokens* that specify options for the connection that aren't propagated to other connections. For example, a connection that must be closed after sending the next message can be indicated by Connection: close.

The Connection header sometimes is confusing, because it can carry three different types of tokens:

- HTTP header field names, listing headers relevant for only this connection
- Arbitrary token values, describing nonstandard options for this connection
- The value close, indicating the persistent connection will be closed when done

If a connection token contains the name of an HTTP header field, that header field contains connection-specific information and must not be forwarded. Any header fields listed in the Connection header must be deleted before the message is forwarded. Placing a hop-by-hop header name in a Connection header is known as "protecting the header," because the Connection header protects against accidental forwarding of the local header. An example is shown in Figure 4-9.

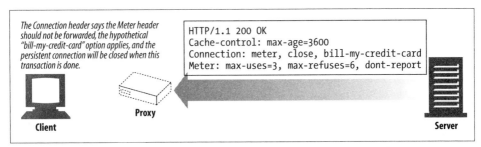

*Figure 4-9. The Connection header allows the sender to specify connection-specific options*

When an HTTP application receives a message with a Connection header, the receiver parses and applies all options requested by the sender. It then deletes the Connection header and all headers listed in the Connection header before forwarding the message to the next hop. In addition, there are a few hop-by-hop headers that might not be listed as values of a Connection header, but must not be proxied. These include Proxy-Authenticate, Proxy-Connection, Transfer-Encoding, and Upgrade. For more about the Connection header, see Appendix C.

## Serial Transaction Delays

TCP performance delays can add up if the connections are managed naively. For example, suppose you have a web page with three embedded images. Your browser needs to issue four HTTP transactions to display this page: one for the top-level HTML and three for the embedded images. If each transaction requires a new connection, the connection and slow-start delays can add up (see Figure 4-10).*

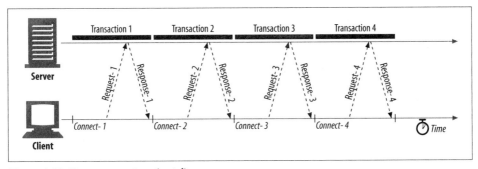

*Figure 4-10. Four transactions (serial)*

---

\* For the purpose of this example, assume all objects are roughly the same size and are hosted from the same server, and that the DNS entry is cached, eliminating the DNS lookup time.

In addition to the real delay imposed by serial loading, there is also a psychological perception of slowness when a single image is loading and nothing is happening on the rest of the page. Users prefer multiple images to load at the same time.*

Another disadvantage of serial loading is that some browsers are unable to display anything onscreen until enough objects are loaded, because they don't know the sizes of the objects until they are loaded, and they may need the size information to decide where to position the objects on the screen. In this situation, the browser may be making good progress loading objects serially, but the user may be faced with a blank white screen, unaware that any progress is being made at all.†

Several current and emerging techniques are available to improve HTTP connection performance. The next several sections discuss four such techniques:

*Parallel connections*
> Concurrent HTTP requests across multiple TCP connections

*Persistent connections*
> Reusing TCP connections to eliminate connect/close delays

*Pipelined connections*
> Concurrent HTTP requests across a shared TCP connection

*Multiplexed connections*
> Interleaving chunks of requests and responses (experimental)

# Parallel Connections

As we mentioned previously, a browser could naively process each embedded object serially by completely requesting the original HTML page, then the first embedded object, then the second embedded object, etc. But this is too slow!

HTTP allows clients to open multiple connections and perform multiple HTTP transactions in parallel, as sketched in Figure 4-11. In this example, four embedded images are loaded in parallel, with each transaction getting its own TCP connection.‡

## Parallel Connections May Make Pages Load Faster

Composite pages consisting of embedded objects may load faster if they take advantage of the dead time and bandwidth limits of a single connection. The delays can be

---

* This is true even if loading multiple images at the same time is *slower* than loading images one at a time! Users often perceive multiple-image loading as faster.

† HTML designers can help eliminate this "layout delay" by explicitly adding width and height attributes to HTML tags for embedded objects such as images. Explicitly providing the width and height of the embedded image allows the browser to make graphical layout decisions before it receives the objects from the server.

‡ The embedded components do not all need to be hosted on the same web server, so the parallel connections can be established to multiple servers.

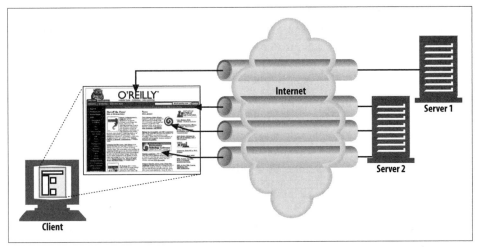

Figure 4-11. Each component of a page involves a separate HTTP transaction

overlapped, and if a single connection does not saturate the client's Internet bandwidth, the unused bandwidth can be allocated to loading additional objects.

Figure 4-12 shows a timeline for parallel connections, which is significantly faster than Figure 4-10. The enclosing HTML page is loaded first, and then the remaining three transactions are processed concurrently, each with their own connection.* Because the images are loaded in parallel, the connection delays are overlapped.

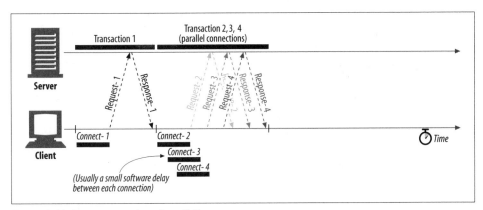

Figure 4-12. Four transactions (parallel)

## Parallel Connections Are Not Always Faster

Even though parallel connections may be faster, however, they are not *always* faster. When the client's network bandwidth is scarce (for example, a browser connected to

---

* There will generally still be a small delay between each connection request due to software overheads, but the connection requests and transfer times are mostly overlapped.

the Internet through a 28.8-Kbps modem), most of the time might be spent just transferring data. In this situation, a single HTTP transaction to a fast server could easily consume all of the available modem bandwidth. If multiple objects are loaded in parallel, each object will just compete for this limited bandwidth, so each object will load proportionally slower, yielding little or no performance advantage.*

Also, a large number of open connections can consume a lot of memory and cause performance problems of their own. Complex web pages may have tens or hundreds of embedded objects. Clients might be able to open hundreds of connections, but few web servers will want to do that, because they often are processing requests for many other users at the same time. A hundred simultaneous users, each opening 100 connections, will put the burden of 10,000 connections on the server. This can cause significant server slowdown. The same situation is true for high-load proxies.

In practice, browsers do use parallel connections, but they limit the total number of parallel connections to a small number (often four). Servers are free to close excessive connections from a particular client.

## Parallel Connections May "Feel" Faster

Okay, so parallel connections don't always make pages load faster. But even if they don't actually speed up the page transfer, as we said earlier, parallel connections often make users *feel* that the page loads faster, because they can see progress being made as multiple component objects appear onscreen in parallel.† Human beings perceive that web pages load faster if there's lots of action all over the screen, even if a stopwatch actually shows the aggregate page download time to be slower!

# Persistent Connections

Web clients often open connections to the same site. For example, most of the embedded images in a web page often come from the same web site, and a significant number of hyperlinks to other objects often point to the same site. Thus, an application that initiates an HTTP request to a server likely will make more requests to that server in the near future (to fetch the inline images, for example). This property is called *site locality*.

For this reason, HTTP/1.1 (and enhanced versions of HTTP/1.0) allows HTTP devices to keep TCP connections open after transactions complete and to reuse the preexisting connections for future HTTP requests. TCP connections that are kept

---

* In fact, because of the extra overhead from multiple connections, it's quite possible that parallel connections could take longer to load the entire page than serial downloads.

† This effect is amplified by the increasing use of progressive images that produce low-resolution approximations of images first and gradually increase the resolution.

open after transactions complete are called *persistent* connections. Nonpersistent connections are closed after each transaction. Persistent connections stay open across transactions, until either the client or the server decides to close them.

By reusing an idle, persistent connection that is already open to the target server, you can avoid the slow connection setup. In addition, the already open connection can avoid the slow-start congestion adaptation phase, allowing faster data transfers.

## Persistent Versus Parallel Connections

As we've seen, parallel connections can speed up the transfer of composite pages. But parallel connections have some disadvantages:

- Each transaction opens/closes a new connection, costing time and bandwidth.
- Each new connection has reduced performance because of TCP slow start.
- There is a practical limit on the number of open parallel connections.

Persistent connections offer some advantages over parallel connections. They reduce the delay and overhead of connection establishment, keep the connections in a tuned state, and reduce the potential number of open connections. However, persistent connections need to be managed with care, or you may end up accumulating a large number of idle connections, consuming local resources and resources on remote clients and servers.

Persistent connections can be most effective when used in conjunction with parallel connections. Today, many web applications open a small number of parallel connections, each persistent. There are two types of persistent connections: the older HTTP/1.0+ "keep-alive" connections and the modern HTTP/1.1 "persistent" connections. We'll look at both flavors in the next few sections.

## HTTP/1.0+ Keep-Alive Connections

Many HTTP/1.0 browsers and servers were extended (starting around 1996) to support an early, experimental type of persistent connections called *keep-alive connections*. These early persistent connections suffered from some interoperability design problems that were rectified in later revisions of HTTP/1.1, but many clients and servers still use these earlier keep-alive connections.

Some of the performance advantages of keep-alive connections are visible in Figure 4-13, which compares the timeline for four HTTP transactions over serial connections against the same transactions over a single persistent connection. The timeline is compressed because the connect and close overheads are removed.*

---

* Additionally, the request and response time might also be reduced because of elimination of the slow-start phase. This performance benefit is not depicted in the figure.

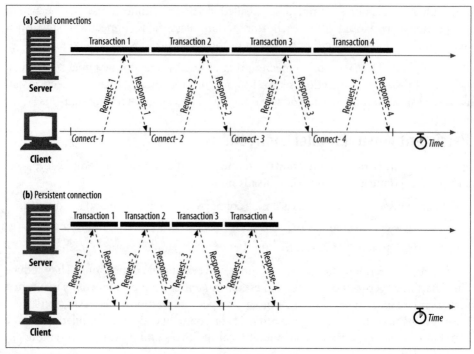

*Figure 4-13. Four transactions (serial versus persistent)*

## Keep-Alive Operation

Keep-alive is deprecated and no longer documented in the current HTTP/1.1 specification. However, keep-alive handshaking is still in relatively common use by browsers and servers, so HTTP implementors should be prepared to interoperate with it. We'll take a quick look at keep-alive operation now. Refer to older versions of the HTTP/1.1 specification (such as RFC 2068) for a more complete explanation of keep-alive handshaking.

Clients implementing HTTP/1.0 keep-alive connections can request that a connection be kept open by including the Connection: Keep-Alive request header.

If the server is willing to keep the connection open for the next request, it will respond with the same header in the response (see Figure 4-14). If there is no Connection: keep-alive header in the response, the client assumes that the server does not support keep-alive and that the server will close the connection when the response message is sent back.

## Keep-Alive Options

Note that the keep-alive headers are just requests to keep the connection alive. Clients and servers do not need to agree to a keep-alive session if it is requested. They

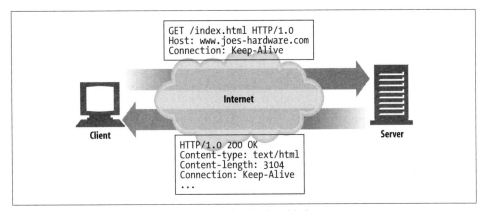

```
GET /index.html HTTP/1.0
Host: www.joes-hardware.com
Connection: Keep-Alive
```

Internet

Client

Server

```
HTTP/1.0 200 OK
Content-type: text/html
Content-length: 3104
Connection: Keep-Alive
...
```

*Figure 4-14. HTTP/1.0 keep-alive transaction header handshake*

can close idle keep-alive connections at any time and are free to limit the number of transactions processed on a keep-alive connection.

The keep-alive behavior can be tuned by comma-separated options specified in the Keep-Alive general header:

- The timeout parameter is sent in a Keep-Alive response header. It estimates how long the server is likely to keep the connection alive for. This is not a guarantee.

- The max parameter is sent in a Keep-Alive response header. It estimates how many more HTTP transactions the server is likely to keep the connection alive for. This is not a guarantee.

- The Keep-Alive header also supports arbitrary unprocessed attributes, primarily for diagnostic and debugging purposes. The syntax is *name* [= *value*].

The Keep-Alive header is completely optional but is permitted only when Connection: Keep-Alive also is present. Here's an example of a Keep-Alive response header indicating that the server intends to keep the connection open for at most five more transactions, or until it has sat idle for two minutes:

```
Connection: Keep-Alive
Keep-Alive: max=5, timeout=120
```

## Keep-Alive Connection Restrictions and Rules

Here are some restrictions and clarifications regarding the use of keep-alive connections:

- Keep-alive does not happen by default in HTTP/1.0. The client must send a Connection: Keep-Alive request header to activate keep-alive connections.

- The Connection: Keep-Alive header must be sent with all messages that want to continue the persistence. If the client does not send a Connection: Keep-Alive header, the server will close the connection after that request.

- Clients can tell if the server will close the connection after the response by detecting the absence of the Connection: Keep-Alive response header.

- The connection can be kept open only if the length of the message's entity body can be determined without sensing a connection close—this means that the entity body must have a correct Content-Length, have a multipart media type, or be encoded with the chunked transfer encoding. Sending the wrong Content-Length back on a keep-alive channel is bad, because the other end of the transaction will not be able to accurately detect the end of one message and the start of another.

- Proxies and gateways must enforce the rules of the Connection header; the proxy or gateway must remove any header fields named in the Connection header, and the Connection header itself, before forwarding or caching the message.

- Formally, keep-alive connections should not be established with a proxy server that isn't guaranteed to support the Connection header, to prevent the problem with dumb proxies described below. This is not always possible in practice.

- Technically, any Connection header fields (including Connection: Keep-Alive) received from an HTTP/1.0 device should be ignored, because they may have been forwarded mistakenly by an older proxy server. In practice, some clients and servers bend this rule, although they run the risk of hanging on older proxies.

- Clients must be prepared to retry requests if the connection closes before they receive the entire response, unless the request could have side effects if repeated.

## Keep-Alive and Dumb Proxies

Let's take a closer look at the subtle problem with keep-alive and dumb proxies. A web client's Connection: Keep-Alive header is intended to affect just the single TCP link leaving the client. This is why it is named the "connection" header. If the client is talking to a web server, the client sends a Connection: Keep-Alive header to tell the server it wants keep-alive. The server sends a Connection: Keep-Alive header back if it supports keep-alive and doesn't send it if it doesn't.

### The Connection header and blind relays

The problem comes with proxies—in particular, proxies that don't understand the Connection header and don't know that they need to remove the header before proxying it down the chain. Many older or simple proxies act as *blind relays*, tunneling bytes from one connection to another, without specially processing the Connection header.

Imagine a web client talking to a web server through a dumb proxy that is acting as a blind relay. This situation is depicted in Figure 4-15.

Here's what's going on in this figure:

1. In Figure 4-15a, a web client sends a message to the proxy, including the Connection: Keep-Alive header, requesting a keep-alive connection if possible. The client waits for a response to learn if its request for a keep-alive channel was granted.

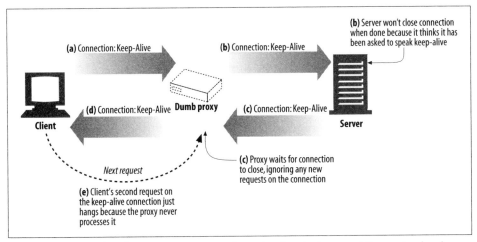

*Figure 4-15. Keep-alive doesn't interoperate with proxies that don't support Connection headers*

2. The dumb proxy gets the HTTP request, but it doesn't understand the Connection header (it just treats it as an extension header). The proxy has no idea what keep-alive is, so it passes the message verbatim down the chain to the server (Figure 4-15b). But the Connection header is a hop-by-hop header; it applies to only a single transport link and shouldn't be passed down the chain. Bad things are about to happen.

3. In Figure 4-15b, the relayed HTTP request arrives at the web server. When the web server receives the proxied Connection: Keep-Alive header, it mistakenly concludes that the proxy (which looks like any other client to the server) wants to speak keep-alive! That's fine with the web server—it agrees to speak keep-alive and sends a Connection: Keep-Alive response header back in Figure 4-15c. So, at this point, the web server thinks it is speaking keep-alive with the proxy and will adhere to rules of keep-alive. But the proxy doesn't know the first thing about keep-alive. Uh-oh.

4. In Figure 4-15d, the dumb proxy relays the web server's response message back to the client, passing along the Connection: Keep-Alive header from the web server. The client sees this header and assumes the proxy has agreed to speak keep-alive. So at this point, both the client and server believe they are speaking keep-alive, but the proxy they are talking to doesn't know anything about keep-alive.

5. Because the proxy doesn't know anything about keep-alive, it reflects all the data it receives back to the client and then waits for the origin server to close the connection. But the origin server will not close the connection, because it believes the proxy explicitly asked the server to keep the connection open. So the proxy will hang waiting for the connection to close.

6. When the client gets the response message back in Figure 4-15d, it moves right along to the next request, sending another request to the proxy on the keep-alive connection (see Figure 4-15e). Because the proxy never expects another request

on the same connection, the request is ignored and the browser just spins, making no progress.

7. This miscommunication causes the browser to hang until the client or server times out the connection and closes it.[*]

### Proxies and hop-by-hop headers

To avoid this kind of proxy miscommunication, modern proxies must never proxy the Connection header or any headers whose names appear inside the Connection values. So if a proxy receives a Connection: Keep-Alive header, it shouldn't proxy either the Connection header or any headers named Keep-Alive.

In addition, there are a few hop-by-hop headers that might not be listed as values of a Connection header, but must not be proxied or served as a cache response either. These include Proxy-Authenticate, Proxy-Connection, Transfer-Encoding, and Upgrade. For more information, refer back to "The Oft-Misunderstood Connection Header."

## The Proxy-Connection Hack

Browser and proxy implementors at Netscape proposed a clever workaround to the blind relay problem that didn't require all web applications to support advanced versions of HTTP. The workaround introduced a new header called Proxy-Connection and solved the problem of a single blind relay interposed directly after the client— but not all other situations. Proxy-Connection is implemented by modern browsers when proxies are explicitly configured and is understood by many proxies.

The idea is that dumb proxies get into trouble because they blindly forward hop-by-hop headers such as Connection: Keep-Alive. Hop-by-hop headers are relevant only for that single, particular connection and must not be forwarded. This causes trouble when the forwarded headers are misinterpreted by downstream servers as requests from the proxy itself to control its connection.

In the Netscape workaround, browsers send nonstandard Proxy-Connection extension headers to proxies, instead of officially supported and well-known Connection headers. If the proxy is a blind relay, it relays the nonsense Proxy-Connection header to the web server, which harmlessly ignores the header. But if the proxy is a smart proxy (capable of understanding persistent connection handshaking), it replaces the nonsense Proxy-Connection header with a Connection header, which is then sent to the server, having the desired effect.

Figure 4-16a–d shows how a blind relay harmlessly forwards Proxy-Connection headers to the web server, which ignores the header, causing no keep-alive connection to

---

[*] There are many similar scenarios where failures occur due to blind relays and forwarded handshaking.

be established between the client and proxy or the proxy and server. The smart proxy in Figure 4-16e–h understands the Proxy-Connection header as a request to speak keep-alive, and it sends out its own Connection: Keep-Alive headers to establish keep-alive connections.

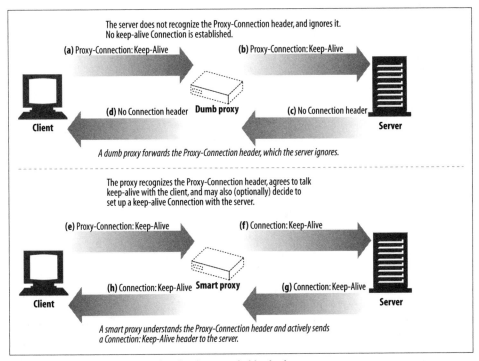

*Figure 4-16. Proxy-Connection header fixes single blind relay*

This scheme works around situations where there is only one proxy between the client and server. But if there is a smart proxy on either side of the dumb proxy, the problem will rear its ugly head again, as shown in Figure 4-17.

Furthermore, it is becoming quite common for "invisible" proxies to appear in networks, either as firewalls, intercepting caches, or reverse proxy server accelerators. Because these devices are invisible to the browser, the browser will not send them Proxy-Connection headers. It is critical that transparent web applications implement persistent connections correctly.

## HTTP/1.1 Persistent Connections

HTTP/1.1 phased out support for keep-alive connections, replacing them with an improved design called *persistent connections*. The goals of persistent connections are the same as those of keep-alive connections, but the mechanisms behave better.

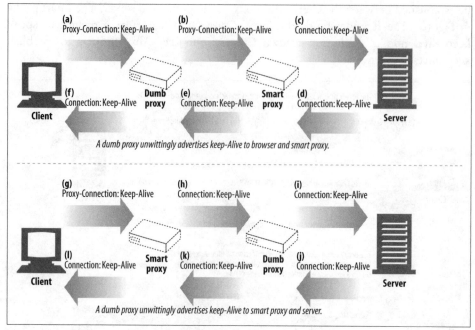

*Figure 4-17. Proxy-Connection still fails for deeper hierarchies of proxies*

Unlike HTTP/1.0+ keep-alive connections, HTTP/1.1 persistent connections are active by default. HTTP/1.1 assumes *all* connections are persistent unless otherwise indicated. HTTP/1.1 applications have to explicitly add a Connection: close header to a message to indicate that a connection should close after the transaction is complete. This is a significant difference from previous versions of the HTTP protocol, where keep-alive connections were either optional or completely unsupported.

An HTTP/1.1 client assumes an HTTP/1.1 connection will remain open after a response, unless the response contains a Connection: close header. However, clients and servers still can close idle connections at any time. Not sending Connection: close does not mean that the server promises to keep the connection open forever.

## Persistent Connection Restrictions and Rules

Here are the restrictions and clarifications regarding the use of persistent connections:

- After sending a Connection: close request header, the client can't send more requests on that connection.
- If a client does not want to send another request on the connection, it should send a Connection: close request header in the final request.
- The connection can be kept persistent only if all messages on the connection have a correct, self-defined message length—i.e., the entity bodies must have correct Content-Lengths or be encoded with the chunked transfer encoding.

- HTTP/1.1 proxies must manage persistent connections separately with clients and servers—each persistent connection applies to a single transport hop.

- HTTP/1.1 proxy servers should not establish persistent connections with an HTTP/1.0 client (because of the problems of older proxies forwarding Connection headers) unless they know something about the capabilities of the client. This is, in practice, difficult, and many vendors bend this rule.

- Regardless of the values of Connection headers, HTTP/1.1 devices may close the connection at any time, though servers should try not to close in the middle of transmitting a message and should always respond to at least one request before closing.

- HTTP/1.1 applications must be able to recover from asynchronous closes. Clients should retry the requests as long as they don't have side effects that could accumulate.

- Clients must be prepared to retry requests if the connection closes before they receive the entire response, unless the request could have side effects if repeated.

- A single user client should maintain at most two persistent connections to any server or proxy, to prevent the server from being overloaded. Because proxies may need more connections to a server to support concurrent users, a proxy should maintain at most 2N connections to any server or parent proxy, if there are N users trying to access the servers.

## Pipelined Connections

HTTP/1.1 permits optional *request pipelining* over persistent connections. This is a further performance optimization over keep-alive connections. Multiple requests can be enqueued before the responses arrive. While the first request is streaming across the network to a server on the other side of the globe, the second and third requests can get underway. This can improve performance in high-latency network conditions, by reducing network round trips.

Figure 4-18a-c shows how persistent connections can eliminate TCP connection delays and how pipelined requests (Figure 4-18c) can eliminate transfer latencies.

There are several restrictions for pipelining:

- HTTP clients should not pipeline until they are sure the connection is persistent.

- HTTP responses must be returned in the same order as the requests. HTTP messages are not tagged with sequence numbers, so there is no way to match responses with requests if the responses are received out of order.

- HTTP clients must be prepared for the connection to close at any time and be prepared to redo any pipelined requests that did not finish. If the client opens a persistent connection and immediately issues 10 requests, the server is free to close the connection after processing only, say, 5 requests. The remaining 5

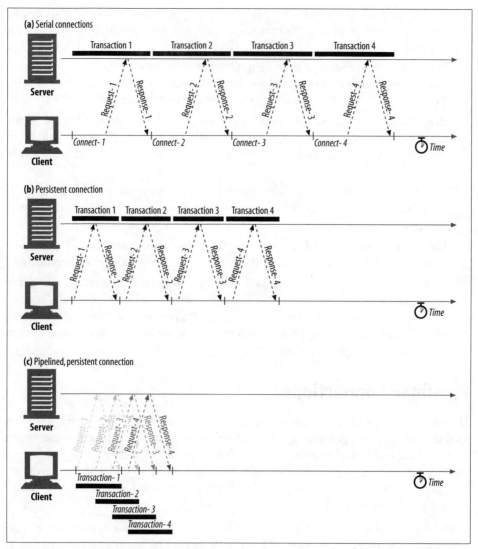

*Figure 4-18. Four transactions (pipelined connections)*

requests will fail, and the client must be willing to handle these premature closes and reissue the requests.

- HTTP clients should not pipeline requests that have side effects (such as POSTs). In general, on error, pipelining prevents clients from knowing which of a series of pipelined requests were executed by the server. Because nonidempotent requests such as POSTs cannot safely be retried, you run the risk of some methods never being executed in error conditions.

# The Mysteries of Connection Close

Connection management—particularly knowing when and how to close connections—is one of the practical black arts of HTTP. This issue is more subtle than many developers first realize, and little has been written on the subject.

## "At Will" Disconnection

Any HTTP client, server, or proxy can close a TCP transport connection at any time. The connections normally are closed at the end of a message,* but during error conditions, the connection may be closed in the middle of a header line or in other strange places.

This situation is common with pipelined persistent connections. HTTP applications are free to close persistent connections after any period of time. For example, after a persistent connection has been idle for a while, a server may decide to shut it down.

However, the server can never know for sure that the client on the other end of the line wasn't about to send data at the same time that the "idle" connection was being shut down by the server. If this happens, the client sees a connection error in the middle of writing its request message.

## Content-Length and Truncation

Each HTTP response should have an accurate Content-Length header to describe the size of the response body. Some older HTTP servers omit the Content-Length header or include an erroneous length, depending on a server connection close to signify the actual end of data.

When a client or proxy receives an HTTP response terminating in connection close, and the actual transferred entity length doesn't match the Content-Length (or there is no Content-Length), the receiver should question the correctness of the length.

If the receiver is a caching proxy, the receiver should not cache the response (to minimize future compounding of a potential error). The proxy should forward the questionable message intact, without attempting to "correct" the Content-Length, to maintain semantic transparency.

## Connection Close Tolerance, Retries, and Idempotency

Connections can close at any time, even in non-error conditions. HTTP applications have to be ready to properly handle unexpected closes. If a transport connection closes while the client is performing a transaction, the client should reopen the

---

* Servers shouldn't close a connection in the middle of a response unless client or network failure is suspected.

connection and retry one time, unless the transaction has side effects. The situation is worse for pipelined connections. The client can enqueue a large number of requests, but the origin server can close the connection, leaving numerous requests unprocessed and in need of rescheduling.

Side effects are important. When a connection closes after some request data was sent but before the response is returned, the client cannot be 100% sure how much of the transaction actually was invoked by the server. Some transactions, such as GETting a static HTML page, can be repeated again and again without changing anything. Other transactions, such as POSTing an order to an online book store, shouldn't be repeated, or you may risk multiple orders.

A transaction is *idempotent* if it yields the same result regardless of whether it is executed once or many times. Implementors can assume the GET, HEAD, PUT, DELETE, TRACE, and OPTIONS methods share this property.* Clients shouldn't pipeline nonidempotent requests (such as POSTs). Otherwise, a premature termination of the transport connection could lead to indeterminate results. If you want to send a nonidempotent request, you should wait for the response status for the previous request.

Nonidempotent methods or sequences must not be retried automatically, although user agents may offer a human operator the choice of retrying the request. For example, most browsers will offer a dialog box when reloading a cached POST response, asking if you want to post the transaction again.

## Graceful Connection Close

TCP connections are bidirectional, as shown in Figure 4-19. Each side of a TCP connection has an input queue and an output queue, for data being read or written. Data placed in the output of one side will eventually show up on the input of the other side.

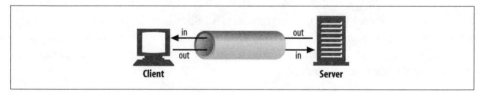

*Figure 4-19. TCP connections are bidirectional*

### Full and half closes

An application can close either or both of the TCP input and output channels. A close( ) sockets call closes both the input and output channels of a TCP connection.

---

*Administrators who use GET-based dynamic forms should make sure the forms are idempotent.

This is called a "full close" and is depicted in Figure 4-20a. You can use the shutdown( ) sockets call to close either the input or output channel individually. This is called a "half close" and is depicted in Figure 4-20b.

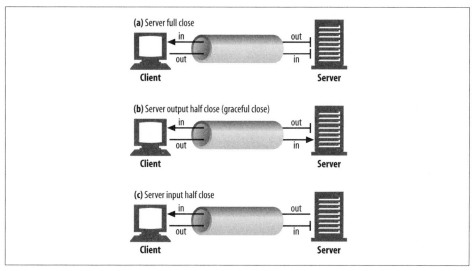

Figure 4-20. Full and half close

### TCP close and reset errors

Simple HTTP applications can use only full closes. But when applications start talking to many other types of HTTP clients, servers, and proxies, and when they start using pipelined persistent connections, it becomes important for them to use half closes to prevent peers from getting unexpected write errors.

In general, closing the output channel of your connection is always safe. The peer on the other side of the connection will be notified that you closed the connection by getting an end-of-stream notification once all the data has been read from its buffer.

Closing the input channel of your connection is riskier, unless you know the other side doesn't plan to send any more data. If the other side sends data to your closed input channel, the operating system will issue a TCP "connection reset by peer" message back to the other side's machine, as shown in Figure 4-21. Most operating systems treat this as a serious error and erase any buffered data the other side has not read yet. This is very bad for pipelined connections.

Say you have sent 10 pipelined requests on a persistent connection, and the responses already have arrived and are sitting in your operating system's buffer (but the application hasn't read them yet). Now say you send request #11, but the server decides you've used this connection long enough, and closes it. Your request #11 will arrive at a closed connection and will reflect a reset back to you. This reset will erase your input buffers.

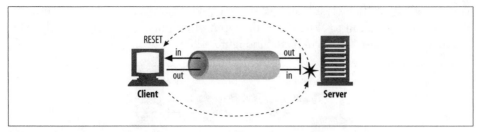

*Figure 4-21. Data arriving at closed connection generates "connection reset by peer" error*

When you finally get to reading data, you will get a connection reset by peer error, and the buffered, unread response data will be lost, even though much of it successfully arrived at your machine.

### Graceful close

The HTTP specification counsels that when clients or servers want to close a connection unexpectedly, they should "issue a graceful close on the transport connection," but it doesn't describe how to do that.

In general, applications implementing graceful closes will first close their output channels and then wait for the peer on the other side of the connection to close *its* output channels. When both sides are done telling each other they won't be sending any more data (i.e., closing output channels), the connection can be closed fully, with no risk of reset.

Unfortunately, there is no guarantee that the peer implements or checks for half closes. For this reason, applications wanting to close gracefully should half close their output channels and periodically check the status of their input channels (looking for data or for the end of the stream). If the input channel isn't closed by the peer within some timeout period, the application may force connection close to save resources.

## For More Information

This completes our overview of the HTTP plumbing trade. Please refer to the following reference sources for more information about TCP performance and HTTP connection-management facilities.

## HTTP Connections

*http://www.ietf.org/rfc/rfc2616.txt*
> RFC 2616, "Hypertext Transfer Protocol—HTTP/1.1," is the official specification for HTTP/1.1; it explains the usage of and HTTP header fields for implementing

parallel, persistent, and pipelined HTTP connections. This document does not cover the proper use of the underlying TCP connections.

*http://www.ietf.org/rfc/rfc2068.txt*
RFC 2068 is the 1997 version of the HTTP/1.1 protocol. It contains explanation of the HTTP/1.0+ Keep-Alive connections that is missing from RFC 2616.

*http://www.ics.uci.edu/pub/ietf/http/draft-ietf-http-connection-00.txt*
This expired Internet draft, "HTTP Connection Management," has some good discussion of issues facing HTTP connection management.

## HTTP Performance Issues

*http://www.w3.org/Protocols/HTTP/Performance/*
This W3C web page, entitled "HTTP Performance Overview," contains a few papers and tools related to HTTP performance and connection management.

*http://www.w3.org/Protocols/HTTP/1.0/HTTPPerformance.html*
This short memo by Simon Spero, "Analysis of HTTP Performance Problems," is one of the earliest (1994) assessments of HTTP connection performance. The memo gives some early performance measurements of the effect of connection setup, slow start, and lack of connection sharing.

*ftp://gatekeeper.dec.com/pub/DEC/WRL/research-reports/WRL-TR-95.4.pdf*
"The Case for Persistent-Connection HTTP."

*http://www.isi.edu/lsam/publications/phttp_tcp_interactions/paper.html*
"Performance Interactions Between P-HTTP and TCP Implementations."

*http://www.sun.com/sun-on-net/performance/tcp.slowstart.html*
"TCP Slow Start Tuning for Solaris" is a web page from Sun Microsystems that talks about some of the practical implications of TCP slow start. It's a useful read, even if you are working with different operating systems.

## TCP/IP

The following three books by W. Richard Stevens are excellent, detailed engineering texts on TCP/IP. These are extremely useful for anyone using TCP:

*TCP Illustrated, Volume I: The Protocols*
W. Richard Stevens, Addison Wesley

*UNIX Network Programming, Volume 1: Networking APIs*
W. Richard Stevens, Prentice-Hall

*UNIX Network Programming, Volume 2: The Implementation*
W. Richard Stevens, Prentice-Hall

The following papers and specifications describe TCP/IP and features that affect its performance. Some of these specifications are over 20 years old and, given the world-wide success of TCP/IP, probably can be classified as historical treasures:

*http://www.acm.org/sigcomm/ccr/archive/2001/jan01/ccr-200101-mogul.pdf*
> In "Rethinking the TCP Nagle Algorithm," Jeff Mogul and Greg Minshall present a modern perspective on Nagle's algorithm, outline what applications should and should not use the algorithm, and propose several modifications.

*http://www.ietf.org/rfc/rfc2001.txt*
> RFC 2001, "TCP Slow Start, Congestion Avoidance, Fast Retransmit, and Fast Recovery Algorithms," defines the TCP slow-start algorithm.

*http://www.ietf.org/rfc/rfc1122.txt*
> RFC 1122, "Requirements for Internet Hosts—Communication Layers," discusses TCP acknowledgment and delayed acknowledgments.

*http://www.ietf.org/rfc/rfc896.txt*
> RFC 896, "Congestion Control in IP/TCP Internetworks," was released by John Nagle in 1984. It describes the need for TCP congestion control and introduces what is now called "Nagle's algorithm."

*http://www.ietf.org/rfc/rfc0813.txt*
> RFC 813, "Window and Acknowledgement Strategy in TCP," is a historical (1982) specification that describes TCP window and acknowledgment implementation strategies and provides an early description of the delayed acknowledgment technique.

*http://www.ietf.org/rfc/rfc0793.txt*
> RFC 793, "Transmission Control Protocol," is Jon Postel's classic 1981 definition of the TCP protocol.

# PART II

# HTTP Architecture

The six chapters of Part II highlight the HTTP server, proxy, cache, gateway, and robot applications, which are the building blocks of web systems architecture:

- Chapter 5, *Web Servers*, gives an overview of web server architectures.

- Chapter 6, *Proxies*, describes HTTP proxy servers, which are intermediary servers that connect HTTP clients and act as platforms for HTTP services and controls.

- Chapter 7, *Caching*, delves into the science of web caches—devices that improve performance and reduce traffic by making local copies of popular documents.

- Chapter 8, *Integration Points: Gateways, Tunnels, and Relays*, explains applications that allow HTTP to interoperate with software that speaks different protocols, including SSL encrypted protocols.

- Chapter 9, *Web Robots*, wraps up our tour of HTTP architecture with web clients.

- Chapter 10, *HTTP-NG*, covers future topics for HTTP—in particular, HTTP-NG.

# CHAPTER 5

# Web Servers

Web servers dish out billions of web pages a day. They tell you the weather, load up your online shopping carts, and let you find long-lost high-school buddies. Web servers are the workhorses of the World Wide Web. In this chapter, we:

- Survey the many different types of software and hardware web servers.
- Describe how to write a simple diagnostic web server in Perl.
- Explain how web servers process HTTP transactions, step by step.

Where it helps to make things concrete, our examples use the Apache web server and its configuration options.

## Web Servers Come in All Shapes and Sizes

A web server processes HTTP requests and serves responses. The term "web server" can refer either to web server software or to the particular device or computer dedicated to serving the web pages.

Web servers comes in all flavors, shapes, and sizes. There are trivial 10-line Perl script web servers, 50-MB secure commerce engines, and tiny servers-on-a-card. But whatever the functional differences, all web servers receive HTTP requests for resources and serve content back to the clients (look back to Figure 1-5).

### Web Server Implementations

Web servers implement HTTP and the related TCP connection handling. They also manage the resources served by the web server and provide administrative features to configure, control, and enhance the web server.

The web server logic implements the HTTP protocol, manages web resources, and provides web server administrative capabilities. The web server logic shares responsibilities for managing TCP connections with the operating system. The underlying operating system manages the hardware details of the underlying computer system and provides TCP/IP network support, filesystems to hold web resources, and process management to control current computing activities.

Web servers are available in many forms:

- You can install and run general-purpose software web servers on standard computer systems.

- If you don't want the hassle of installing software, you can purchase a web server appliance, in which the software comes preinstalled and preconfigured on a computer, often in a snazzy-looking chassis.

- Given the miracles of microprocessors, some companies even offer embedded web servers implemented in a small number of computer chips, making them perfect administration consoles for consumer devices.

Let's look at each of those types of implementations.

## General-Purpose Software Web Servers

General-purpose software web servers run on standard, network-enabled computer systems. You can choose open source software (such as Apache or W3C's Jigsaw) or commercial software (such as Microsoft's and iPlanet's web servers). Web server software is available for just about every computer and operating system.

While there are tens of thousands of different kinds of web server programs (including custom-crafted, special-purpose web servers), most web server software comes from a small number of organizations.

In February 2002, the Netcraft survey (*http://www.netcraft.com/survey/*) showed three vendors dominating the public Internet web server market (see Figure 5-1):

- The free Apache software powers nearly 60% of all Internet web servers.

- Microsoft web server makes up another 30%.

- Sun iPlanet servers comprise another 3%.

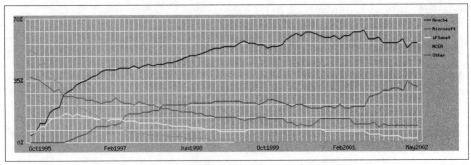

*Figure 5-1. Web server market share as estimated by Netcraft's automated survey*

Take these numbers with a few grains of salt, however, as the Netcraft survey is commonly believed to exaggerate the dominance of Apache software. First, the survey counts servers independent of server popularity. Proxy server access studies from large ISPs suggest that the amount of pages served from Apache servers is much less than 60% but still exceeds Microsoft and Sun iPlanet. Additionally, it is anecdotally believed that Microsoft and iPlanet servers are more popular than Apache inside corporate enterprises.

## Web Server Appliances

*Web server appliances* are prepackaged software/hardware solutions. The vendor preinstalls a software server onto a vendor-chosen computer platform and preconfigures the software. Some examples of web server appliances include:

- Sun/Cobalt RaQ web appliances (*http://www.cobalt.com*)
- Toshiba Magnia SG10 (*http://www.toshiba.com*)
- IBM Whistle web server appliance (*http://www.whistle.com*)

Appliance solutions remove the need to install and configure software and often greatly simplify administration. However, the web server often is less flexible and feature-rich, and the server hardware is not easily repurposeable or upgradable.

## Embedded Web Servers

*Embedded servers* are tiny web servers intended to be embedded into consumer products (e.g., printers or home appliances). Embedded web servers allow users to administer their consumer devices using a convenient web browser interface.

Some embedded web servers can even be implemented in less than one square inch, but they usually offer a minimal feature set. Two examples of very small embedded web servers are:

- IPic match-head sized web server (*http://www-ccs.cs.umass.edu/~shri/iPic.html*)
- NetMedia SitePlayer SP1 Ethernet Web Server (*http://www.siteplayer.com*)

# A Minimal Perl Web Server

If you want to build a full-featured HTTP server, you have some work to do. The core of the Apache web server has over 50,000 lines of code, and optional processing modules make that number much bigger.

All this software is needed to support HTTP/1.1 features: rich resource support, virtual hosting, access control, logging, configuration, monitoring, and performance features. That said, you can create a minimally functional HTTP server in under 30 lines of Perl. Let's take a look.

Example 5-1 shows a tiny Perl program called *type-o-serve*. This program is a useful diagnostic tool for testing interactions with clients and proxies. Like any web server, *type-o-serve* waits for an HTTP connection. As soon as *type-o-serve* gets the request message, it prints the message on the screen; then it waits for you to type (or paste) in a response message, which is sent back to the client. This way, *type-o-serve* pretends to be a web server, records the exact HTTP request messages, and allows you to send back any HTTP response message.

This simple *type-o-serve* utility doesn't implement most HTTP functionality, but it is a useful tool to generate server response messages the same way you can use Telnet to generate client request messages (refer back to Example 5-1). You can download the *type-o-serve* program from *http://www.http-guide.com/tools/type-o-serve.pl*.

*Example 5-1. type-o-serve—a minimal Perl web server used for HTTP debugging*

```perl
#!/usr/bin/perl

use Socket;
use Carp;
use FileHandle;

# (1) use port 8080 by default, unless overridden on command line
$port = (@ARGV ? $ARGV[0] : 8080);

# (2) create local TCP socket and set it to listen for connections
$proto = getprotobyname('tcp');
socket(S, PF_INET, SOCK_STREAM, $proto) || die;
setsockopt(S, SOL_SOCKET, SO_REUSEADDR, pack("l", 1)) || die;
bind(S, sockaddr_in($port, INADDR_ANY)) || die;
listen(S, SOMAXCONN) || die;

# (3) print a startup message
printf("   <<<Type-O-Serve Accepting on Port %d>>>\n\n",$port);

while (1)
{
    # (4) wait for a connection C
    $cport_caddr = accept(C, S);
    ($cport,$caddr) = sockaddr_in($cport_caddr);
    C->autoflush(1);

    # (5) print who the connection is from
    $cname = gethostbyaddr($caddr,AF_INET);
    printf("    <<<Request From '%s'>>>\n",$cname);

    # (6) read request msg until blank line, and print on screen
    while ($line = <C>)
    {
        print $line;
        if ($line =~ /^\r/) { last; }
    }
```

```
# (7) prompt for response message, and input response lines,
#     sending response lines to client, until solitary "."
printf("   <<<Type Response Followed by '.'>>>\n");

while ($line = <STDIN>)
{
    $line =~ s/\r//;
    $line =~ s/\n//;
    if ($line =~ /^\./) { last; }
    print C $line . "\r\n";
}
close(C);
}
```

Figure 5-2 shows how the administrator of Joe's Hardware store might use *type-o-serve* to test HTTP communication:

- First, the administrator starts the *type-o-serve* diagnostic server, listening on a particular port. Because Joe's Hardware store already has a production web server listing on port 80, the administrator starts the *type-o-serve* server on port 8080 (you can pick any unused port) with this command line:

      % type-o-serve.pl 8080

- Once *type-o-serve* is running, you can point a browser to this web server. In Figure 5-2, we browse to *http://www.joes-hardware.com:8080/foo/bar/blah.txt*.

- The *type-o-serve* program receives the HTTP request message from the browser and prints the contents of the HTTP request message on screen. The *type-o-serve* diagnostic tool then waits for the user to type in a simple response message, followed by a period on a blank line.

- *type-o-serve* sends the HTTP response message back to the browser, and the browser displays the body of the response message.

# What Real Web Servers Do

The Perl server we showed in Example 5-1 is a trivial example web server. State-of-the-art commercial web servers are much more complicated, but they do perform several common tasks, as shown in Figure 5-3:

1. Set up connection—accept a client connection, or close if the client is unwanted.
2. Receive request—read an HTTP request message from the network.
3. Process request—interpret the request message and take action.
4. Access resource—access the resource specified in the message.
5. Construct response—create the HTTP response message with the right headers.
6. Send response—send the response back to the client.
7. Log transaction—place notes about the completed transaction in a log file.

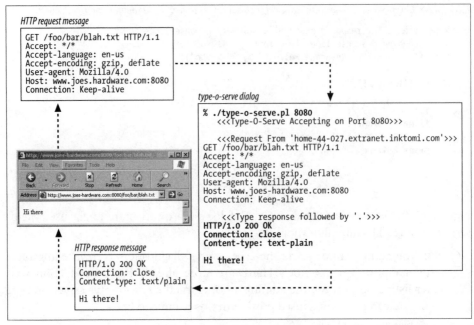

*Figure 5-2. The type-o-serve utility lets you type in server responses to send back to clients*

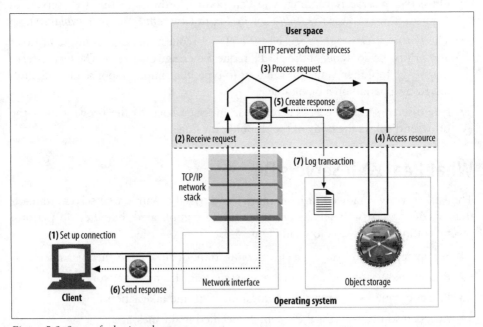

*Figure 5-3. Steps of a basic web server request*

The next seven sections highlight how web servers perform these basic tasks.

# Step 1: Accepting Client Connections

If a client already has a persistent connection open to the server, it can use that connection to send its request. Otherwise, the client needs to open a new connection to the server (refer back to Chapter 4 to review HTTP connection-management technology).

## Handling New Connections

When a client requests a TCP connection to the web server, the web server establishes the connection and determines which client is on the other side of the connection, extracting the IP address from the TCP connection.* Once a new connection is established and accepted, the server adds the new connection to its list of existing web server connections and prepares to watch for data on the connection.

The web server is free to reject and immediately close any connection. Some web servers close connections because the client IP address or hostname is unauthorized or is a known malicious client. Other identification techniques can also be used.

## Client Hostname Identification

Most web servers can be configured to convert client IP addresses into client hostnames, using "reverse DNS." Web servers can use the client hostname for detailed access control and logging. Be warned that hostname lookups can take a very long time, slowing down web transactions. Many high-capacity web servers either disable hostname resolution or enable it only for particular content.

You can enable hostname lookups in Apache with the *HostnameLookups* configuration directive. For example, the Apache configuration directives in Example 5-2 turn on hostname resolution for only HTML and CGI resources.

*Example 5-2. Configuring Apache to look up hostnames for HTML and CGI resources*

```
HostnameLookups off
<Files ~ "\.(html|htm|cgi)$">
    HostnameLookups on
</Files>
```

## Determining the Client User Through ident

Some web servers also support the IETF *ident* protocol. The *ident* protocol lets servers find out what username initiated an HTTP connection. This information is

---

* Different operating systems have different interfaces and data structures for manipulating TCP connections. In Unix environments, the TCP connection is represented by a *socket*, and the IP address of the client can be found from the socket using the *getpeername* call.

particularly useful for web server logging—the second field of the popular Common Log Format contains the *ident* username of each HTTP request.[*]

If a client supports the *ident* protocol, the client listens on TCP port 113 for *ident* requests. Figure 5-4 shows how the *ident* protocol works. In Figure 5-4a, the client opens an HTTP connection. The server then opens its own connection back to the client's *identd* server port (113), sends a simple request asking for the username corresponding to the new connection (specified by client and server port numbers), and retrieves from the client the response containing the username.

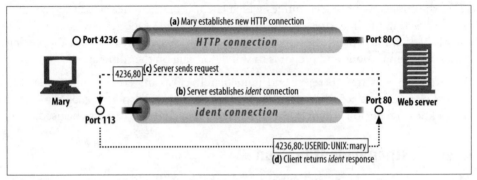

*Figure 5-4. Using the ident protocol to determine HTTP client username*

*ident* can work inside organizations, but it does not work well across the public Internet for many reasons, including:

- Many client PCs don't run the *identd* Identification Protocol daemon software.
- The *ident* protocol significantly delays HTTP transactions.
- Many firewalls won't permit incoming *ident* traffic.
- The *ident* protocol is insecure and easy to fabricate.
- The *ident* protocol doesn't support virtual IP addresses well.
- There are privacy concerns about exposing client usernames.

You can tell Apache web servers to use *ident* lookups with Apache's *IdentityCheck on* directive. If no *ident* information is available, Apache will fill *ident* log fields with hyphens (-). Common Log Format log files typically contain hyphens in the second field because no *ident* information is available.

## Step 2: Receiving Request Messages

As the data arrives on connections, the web server reads out the data from the network connection and parses out the pieces of the request message (Figure 5-5).

---

[*] This Common Log Format *ident* field is called "rfc931," after an outdated version of the RFC defining the *ident* protocol (the updated *ident* specification is documented by RFC 1413).

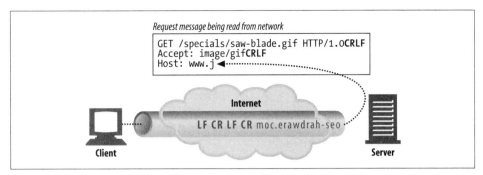

*Figure 5-5. Reading a request message from a connection*

When parsing the request message, the web server:

- Parses the request line looking for the request method, the specified resource identifier (URI), and the version number,* each separated by a single space, and ending with a carriage-return line-feed (CRLF) sequence†
- Reads the message headers, each ending in CRLF
- Detects the end-of-headers blank line, ending in CRLF (if present)
- Reads the request body, if any (length specified by the Content-Length header)

When parsing request messages, web servers receive input data erratically from the network. The network connection can stall at any point. The web server needs to read data from the network and temporarily store the partial message data in memory until it receives enough data to parse it and make sense of it.

## Internal Representations of Messages

Some web servers also store the request messages in internal data structures that make the message easy to manipulate. For example, the data structure might contain pointers and lengths of each piece of the request message, and the headers might be stored in a fast lookup table so the specific values of particular headers can be accessed quickly (Figure 5-6).

## Connection Input/Output Processing Architectures

High-performance web servers support thousands of simultaneous connections. These connections let the web server communicate with clients around the world, each with one or more connections open to the server. Some of these connections may be sending requests rapidly to the web server, while other connections trickle

---

* The initial version of HTTP, called HTTP/0.9, does not support version numbers. Some web servers support missing version numbers, interpreting the message as an HTTP/0.9 request.

† Many web servers support LF or CRLF as end-of-line sequences, because some clients mistakenly send LF as the end-of-line terminator.

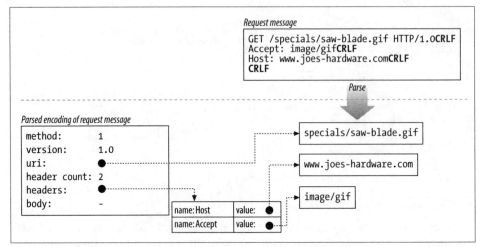

*Figure 5-6. Parsing a request message into a convenient internal representation*

requests slowly or infrequently, and still others are idle, waiting quietly for some future activity.

Web servers constantly watch for new web requests, because requests can arrive at any time. Different web server architectures service requests in different ways, as Figure 5-7 illustrates:

*Single-threaded web servers (Figure 5-7a)*

Single-threaded web servers process one request at a time until completion. When the transaction is complete, the next connection is processed. This architecture is simple to implement, but during processing, all the other connections are ignored. This creates serious performance problems and is appropriate only for low-load servers and diagnostic tools like *type-o-serve*.

*Multiprocess and multithreaded web servers (Figure 5-7b)*

Multiprocess and multithreaded web servers dedicate multiple processes or higher-efficiency threads to process requests simultaneously.* The threads/processes may be created on demand or in advance.† Some servers dedicate a thread/process for every connection, but when a server processes hundreds, thousands, or even tens of thousands of simultaneous connections, the resulting number of processes or threads may consume too much memory or system

---

* A process is an individual program flow of control, with its own set of variables. A thread is a faster, more efficient version of a process. Both threads and processes let a single program do multiple things at the same time. For simplicity of explanation, we treat processes and threads interchangeably. But, because of the performance differences, many high-performance servers are both multiprocess *and* multithreaded.

† Systems where threads are created in advance are called "worker pool" systems, because a set of threads waits in a pool for work to do.

resources. Thus, many multithreaded web servers put a limit on the maximum number of threads/processes.

*Multiplexed I/O servers (Figure 5-7c)*

To support large numbers of connections, many web servers adopt *multiplexed architectures*. In a multiplexed architecture, all the connections are simultaneously watched for activity. When a connection changes state (e.g., when data becomes available or an error condition occurs), a small amount of processing is performed on the connection; when that processing is complete, the connection is returned to the open connection list for the next change in state. Work is done on a connection only when there is something to be done; threads and processes are not tied up waiting on idle connections.

*Multiplexed multithreaded web servers (Figure 5-7d)*

Some systems combine multithreading and multiplexing to take advantage of multiple CPUs in the computer platform. Multiple threads (often one per physical processor) each watch the open connections (or a subset of the open connections) and perform a small amount of work on each connection.

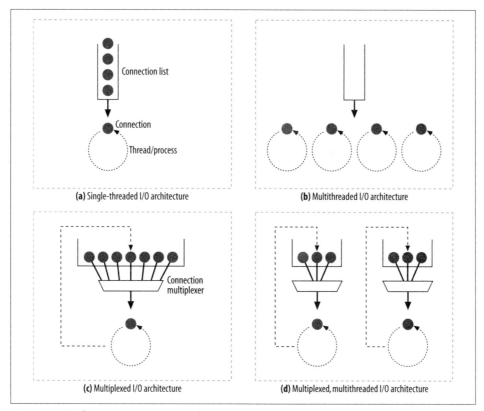

Figure 5-7. Web server input/output architectures

# Step 3: Processing Requests

Once the web server has received a request, it can process the request using the method, resource, headers, and optional body.

Some methods (e.g., POST) require entity body data in the request message. Other methods (e.g., OPTIONS) allow a request body but don't require one. A few methods (e.g., GET) forbid entity body data in request messages.

We won't talk about request processing here, because it's the subject of most of the chapters in the rest of this book!

# Step 4: Mapping and Accessing Resources

Web servers are resource servers. They deliver precreated content, such as HTML pages or JPEG images, as well as dynamic content from resource-generating applications running on the servers.

Before the web server can deliver content to the client, it needs to identify the source of the content, by mapping the URI from the request message to the proper content or content generator on the web server.

## Docroots

Web servers support different kinds of resource mapping, but the simplest form of resource mapping uses the request URI to name a file in the web server's filesystem. Typically, a special folder in the web server filesystem is reserved for web content. This folder is called the *document root*, or *docroot*. The web server takes the URI from the request message and appends it to the document root.

In Figure 5-8, a request arrives for */specials/saw-blade.gif*. The web server in this example has document root */usr/local/httpd/files*. The web server returns the file */usr/local/httpd/files/specials/saw-blade.gif*.

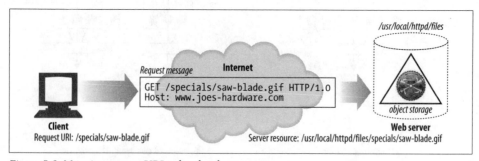

*Figure 5-8. Mapping request URI to local web server resource*

To set the document root for an Apache web server, add a *DocumentRoot* line to the *httpd.conf* configuration file:

```
DocumentRoot /usr/local/httpd/files
```

Servers are careful not to let relative URLs back up out of a docroot and expose other parts of the filesystem. For example, most mature web servers will not permit this URI to see files above the Joe's Hardware document root:

> *http://www.joes-hardware.com/../*

### Virtually hosted docroots

Virtually hosted web servers host multiple web sites on the same web server, giving each site its own distinct document root on the server. A virtually hosted web server identifies the correct document root to use from the IP address or hostname in the URI or the Host header. This way, two web sites hosted on the same web server can have completely distinct content, even if the request URIs are identical.

In Figure 5-9, the server hosts two sites: *www.joes-hardware.com* and *www.marys-antiques.com*. The server can distinguish the web sites using the HTTP Host header, or from distinct IP addresses.

- When request A arrives, the server fetches the file for */docs/joe/index.html*.
- When request B arrives, the server fetches the file for */docs/mary/index.html*.

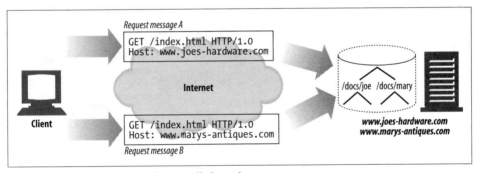

*Figure 5-9. Different docroots for virtually hosted requests*

Configuring virtually hosted docroots is simple for most web servers. For the popular Apache web server, you need to configure a *VirtualHost* block for each virtual web site, and include the *DocumentRoot* for each virtual server (Example 5-3).

*Example 5-3. Apache web server virtual host docroot configuration*

```
<VirtualHost www.joes-hardware.com>
  ServerName www.joes-hardware.com
  DocumentRoot /docs/joe
```

*Example 5-3. Apache web server virtual host docroot configuration (continued)*

```
  TransferLog /logs/joe.access_log
  ErrorLog /logs/joe.error_log
</VirtualHost>

<VirtualHost www.marys-antiques.com>
  ServerName www.marys-antiques.com
  DocumentRoot /docs/mary
  TransferLog /logs/mary.access_log
  ErrorLog /logs/mary.error_log
</VirtualHost>
    ...
```

Look forward to "Virtual Hosting" in Chapter 18 for much more detail about virtual hosting.

### User home directory docroots

Another common use of docroots gives people private web sites on a web server. A typical convention maps URIs whose paths begin with a slash and tilde (/~) followed by a username to a private document root for that user. The private docroot is often the folder called *public_html* inside that user's home directory, but it can be configured differently (Figure 5-10).

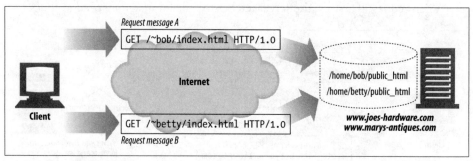

*Figure 5-10. Different docroots for different users*

## Directory Listings

A web server can receive requests for directory URLs, where the path resolves to a directory, not a file. Most web servers can be configured to take a few different actions when a client requests a directory URL:

- Return an error.
- Return a special, default, "index file" instead of the directory.
- Scan the directory, and return an HTML page containing the contents.

Most web servers look for a file named *index.html* or *index.htm* inside a directory to represent that directory. If a user requests a URL for a directory and the directory contains a file named *index.html* (or *index.htm*), the server will return the contents of that file.

In the Apache web server, you can configure the set of filenames that will be interpreted as default directory files using the *DirectoryIndex* configuration directive. The *DirectoryIndex* directive lists all filenames that serve as directory index files, in preferred order. The following configuration line causes Apache to search a directory for any of the listed files in response to a directory URL request:

```
DirectoryIndex index.html index.htm home.html home.htm index.cgi
```

If no default index file is present when a user requests a directory URI, and if directory indexes are not disabled, many web servers automatically return an HTML file listing the files in that directory, and the sizes and modification dates of each file, including URI links to each file. This file listing can be convenient, but it also allows nosy people to find files on a web server that they might not normally find.

You can disable the automatic generation of directory index files with the Apache directive:

```
Options -Indexes
```

## Dynamic Content Resource Mapping

Web servers also can map URIs to dynamic resources—that is, to programs that generate content on demand (Figure 5-11). In fact, a whole class of web servers called *application servers* connect web servers to sophisticated backend applications. The web server needs to be able to tell when a resource is a dynamic resource, where the dynamic content generator program is located, and how to run the program. Most web servers provide basic mechanisms to identify and map dynamic resources.

Apache lets you map URI pathname components into executable program directories. When a server receives a request for a URI with an executable path component, it attempts to execute a program in a corresponding server directory. For example, the following Apache configuration directive specifies that all URIs whose paths begin with */cgi-bin/* should execute corresponding programs found in the directory */usr/local/etc/httpd/cgi-programs/*:

```
ScriptAlias /cgi-bin/ /usr/local/etc/httpd/cgi-programs/
```

Apache also lets you mark executable files with a special file extension. This way, executable scripts can be placed in any directory. The following Apache configuration directive specifies that all web resources ending in *.cgi* should be executed:

```
AddHandler cgi-script .cgi
```

CGI is an early, simple, and popular interface for executing server-side applications. Modern application servers have more powerful and efficient server-side dynamic content support, including Microsoft's Active Server Pages and Java servlets.

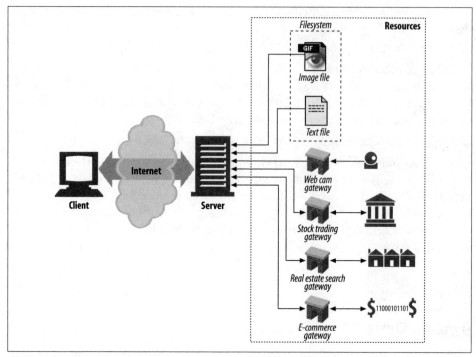

*Figure 5-11. A web server can serve static resources as well as dynamic resources*

## Server-Side Includes (SSI)

Many web servers also provide support for server-side includes. If a resource is flagged as containing server-side includes, the server processes the resource contents before sending them to the client.

The contents are scanned for certain special patterns (often contained inside special HTML comments), which can be variable names or embedded scripts. The special patterns are replaced with the values of variables or the output of executable scripts. This is an easy way to create dynamic content.

## Access Controls

Web servers also can assign access controls to particular resources. When a request arrives for an access-controlled resource, the web server can control access based on the IP address of the client, or it can issue a password challenge to get access to the resource.

Refer to Chapter 12 for more information about HTTP authentication.

# Step 5: Building Responses

Once the web server has identified the resource, it performs the action described in the request method and returns the response message. The response message contains a response status code, response headers, and a response body if one was generated. HTTP response codes were detailed in "Status Codes" in Chapter 3.

## Response Entities

If the transaction generated a response body, the content is sent back with the response message. If there was a body, the response message usually contains:

- A Content-Type header, describing the MIME type of the response body
- A Content-Length header, describing the size of the response body
- The actual message body content

## MIME Typing

The web server is responsible for determining the MIME type of the response body. There are many ways to configure servers to associate MIME types with resources:

*mime.types*
> The web server can use the extension of the filename to indicate MIME type. The web server scans a file containing MIME types for each extension to compute the MIME type for each resource. This extension-based type association is the most common; it is illustrated in Figure 5-12.

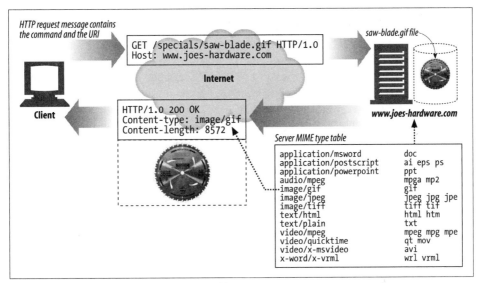

*Figure 5-12. A web server uses MIME types file to set outgoing Content-Type of resources*

*Magic typing*

> The Apache web server can scan the contents of each resource and pattern-match the content against a table of known patterns (called the *magic* file) to determine the MIME type for each file. This can be slow, but it is convenient, especially if the files are named without standard extensions.

*Explicit typing*

> Web servers can be configured to force particular files or directory contents to have a MIME type, regardless of the file extension or contents.

*Type negotiation*

> Some web servers can be configured to store a resource in multiple document formats. In this case, the web server can be configured to determine the "best" format to use (and the associated MIME type) by a negotiation process with the user. We'll discuss this in Chapter 17.

Web servers also can be configured to associate particular files with MIME types.

## Redirection

Web servers sometimes return redirection responses instead of success messages. A web server can redirect the browser to go elsewhere to perform the request. A redirection response is indicated by a 3XX return code. The Location response header contains a URI for the new or preferred location of the content. Redirects are useful for:

*Permanently moved resources*

> A resource might have been moved to a new location, or otherwise renamed, giving it a new URL. The web server can tell the client that the resource has been renamed, and the client can update any bookmarks, etc. before fetching the resource from its new location. The status code 301 Moved Permanently is used for this kind of redirect.

*Temporarily moved resources*

> If a resource is temporarily moved or renamed, the server may want to redirect the client to the new location. But, because the renaming is temporary, the server wants the client to come back with the old URL in the future and not to update any bookmarks. The status codes 303 See Other and 307 Temporary Redirect are used for this kind of redirect.

*URL augmentation*

> Servers often use redirects to rewrite URLs, often to embed context. When the request arrives, the server generates a new URL containing embedded state information and redirects the user to this new URL.* The client follows the redirect, reissuing the request, but now including the full, state-augmented URL. This is a

---

\* These extended, state-augmented URLs are sometimes called "fat URLs."

useful way of maintaining state across transactions. The status codes 303 See Other and 307 Temporary Redirect are used for this kind of redirect.

*Load balancing*
If an overloaded server gets a request, the server can redirect the client to a less heavily loaded server. The status codes 303 See Other and 307 Temporary Redirect are used for this kind of redirect.

*Server affinity*
Web servers may have local information for certain users; a server can redirect the client to a server that contains information about the client. The status codes 303 See Other and 307 Temporary Redirect are used for this kind of redirect.

*Canonicalizing directory names*
When a client requests a URI for a directory name without a trailing slash, most web servers redirect the client to a URI with the slash added, so that relative links work correctly.

# Step 6: Sending Responses

Web servers face similar issues sending data across connections as they do receiving. The server may have many connections to many clients, some idle, some sending data to the server, and some carrying response data back to the clients.

The server needs to keep track of the connection state and handle persistent connections with special care. For nonpersistent connections, the server is expected to close its side of the connection when the entire message is sent.

For persistent connections, the connection may stay open, in which case the server needs to be extra cautious to compute the Content-Length header correctly, or the client will have no way of knowing when a response ends (see Chapter 4).

# Step 7: Logging

Finally, when a transaction is complete, the web server notes an entry into a log file, describing the transaction performed. Most web servers provide several configurable forms of logging. Refer to Chapter 21 for more details.

# For More Information

For more information on Apache, Jigsaw, and *ident*, check out:

*Apache: The Definitive Guide*
Ben Laurie and Peter Laurie, O'Reilly & Associates, Inc.

*Professional Apache*
Peter Wainwright, Wrox Press.

*http://www.w3c.org/Jigsaw/*
   Jigsaw—W3C's Server W3C Consortium Web Site.

*http://www.ietf.org/rfc/rfc1413.txt*
   RFC 1413, "Identification Protocol," by M. St. Johns.

# CHAPTER 6

# Proxies

Web proxy servers are intermediaries. Proxies sit between clients and servers and act as "middlemen," shuffling HTTP messages back and forth between the parties. This chapter talks all about HTTP proxy servers, the special support for proxy features, and some of the tricky behaviors you'll see when you use proxy servers.

In this chapter, we:

- Explain HTTP proxies, contrasting them to web gateways and illustrating how proxies are deployed.
- Show some of the ways proxies are helpful.
- Describe how proxies are deployed in real networks and how traffic is directed to proxy servers.
- Show how to configure your browser to use a proxy.
- Demonstrate HTTP proxy requests, how they differ from server requests, and how proxies can subtly change the behavior of browsers.
- Explain how you can record the path of your messages through chains of proxy servers, using Via headers and the TRACE method.
- Describe proxy-based HTTP access control.
- Explain how proxies can interoperate between clients and servers, each of which may support different features and versions.

## Web Intermediaries

Web proxy servers are middlemen that fulfill transactions on the client's behalf. Without a web proxy, HTTP clients talk directly to HTTP servers. With a web proxy, the client instead talks to the proxy, which itself communicates with the server on the client's behalf. The client still completes the transaction, but through the good services of the proxy server.

HTTP proxy servers are both web servers and web clients. Because HTTP clients send request messages to proxies, the proxy server must properly handle the requests and the connections and return responses, just like a web server. At the same time, the proxy itself sends requests to servers, so it must also behave like a correct HTTP client, sending requests and receiving responses (see Figure 6-1). If you are creating your own HTTP proxy, you'll need to carefully follow the rules for both HTTP clients and HTTP servers.

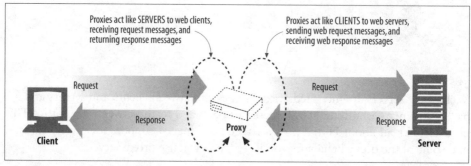

*Figure 6-1. A proxy must be both a server and a client*

## Private and Shared Proxies

A proxy server can be dedicated to a single client or shared among many clients. Proxies dedicated to a single client are called *private proxies*. Proxies shared among numerous clients are called *public proxies*.

*Public proxies*
> Most proxies are public, shared proxies. It's more cost effective and easier to administer a centralized proxy. And some proxy applications, such as caching proxy servers, become more useful as more users are funneled into the same proxy server, because they can take advantage of common requests between users.

*Private proxies*
> Dedicated private proxies are not as common, but they do have a place, especially when run directly on the client computer. Some browser assistant products, as well as some ISP services, run small proxies directly on the user's PC in order to extend browser features, improve performance, or host advertising for free ISP services.

## Proxies Versus Gateways

Strictly speaking, proxies connect two or more applications that speak the same protocol, while gateways hook up two or more parties that speak different protocols. A gateway acts as a "protocol converter," allowing a client to complete a transaction with a server, even when the client and server speak different protocols.

Figure 6-2 illustrates the difference between proxies and gateways:

- The intermediary device in Figure 6-2a is an HTTP proxy, because the proxy speaks HTTP to both the client and server.
- The intermediary device in Figure 6-2b is an HTTP/POP gateway, because it ties an HTTP frontend to a POP email backend. The gateway converts web transactions into the appropriate POP transactions, to allow the user to read email through HTTP. Web-based email programs such as Yahoo! Mail and MSN Hotmail are HTTP email gateways.

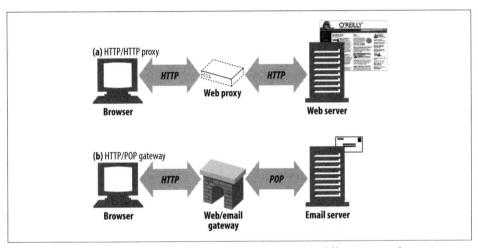

*Figure 6-2. Proxies speak the same protocol; gateways tie together different protocols*

In practice, the difference between proxies and gateways is blurry. Because browsers and servers implement different versions of HTTP, proxies often do some amount of protocol conversion. And commercial proxy servers implement gateway functionality to support SSL security protocols, SOCKS firewalls, FTP access, and web-based applications. We'll talk more about gateways in Chapter 8.

## Why Use Proxies?

Proxy servers can do all kinds of nifty and useful things. They can improve security, enhance performance, and save money. And because proxy servers can see and touch all the passing HTTP traffic, proxies can monitor and modify the traffic to implement many useful value-added web services. Here are examples of just a few of the ways proxies can be used:

*Child filter (Figure 6-3)*
 Elementary schools use filtering proxies to block access to adult content, while providing unhindered access to educational sites. As shown in Figure 6-3, the

proxy might permit unrestricted access to educational content but forcibly deny access to sites that are inappropriate for children.*

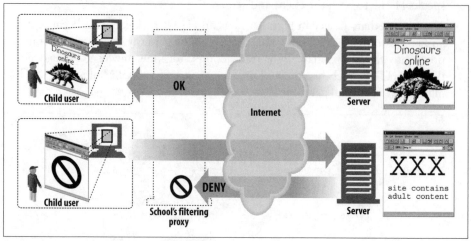

*Figure 6-3. Proxy application example: child-safe Internet filter*

*Document access controller (Figure 6-4)*

Proxy servers can be used to implement a uniform access-control strategy across a large set of web servers and web resources and to create an audit trail. This is useful in large corporate settings or other distributed bureaucracies.

All the access controls can be configured on the centralized proxy server, without requiring the access controls to be updated frequently on numerous web servers, of different makes and models, administered by different organizations.†

In Figure 6-4, the centralized access-control proxy:

- Permits client 1 to access news pages from server A without restriction
- Gives client 2 unrestricted access to Internet content
- Requires a password from client 3 before allowing access to server B

*Security firewall (Figure 6-5)*

Network security engineers often use proxy servers to enhance security. Proxy servers restrict which application-level protocols flow in and out of an organization, at a single secure point in the network. They also can provide hooks to scrutinize that traffic (Figure 6-5), as used by virus-eliminating web and email proxies.

---

* Several companies and nonprofit organizations provide filtering software and maintain "blacklists" in order to identify and restrict access to objectionable content.

† To prevent sophisticated users from willfully bypassing the control proxy, the web servers can be statically configured to accept requests only from the proxy servers.

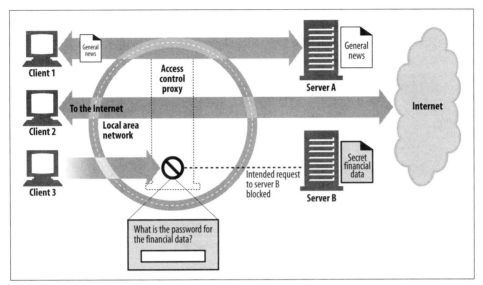

*Figure 6-4. Proxy application example: centralized document access control*

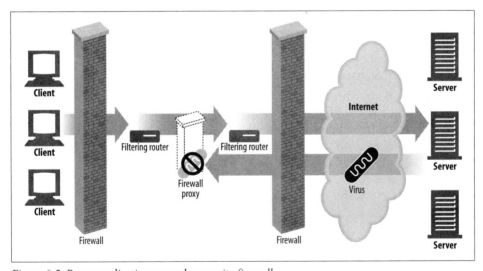

*Figure 6-5. Proxy application example: security firewall*

*Web cache (Figure 6-6)*

Proxy caches maintain local copies of popular documents and serve them on demand, reducing slow and costly Internet communication.

In Figure 6-6, clients 1 and 2 access object A from a nearby web cache, while clients 3 and 4 access the document from the origin server.

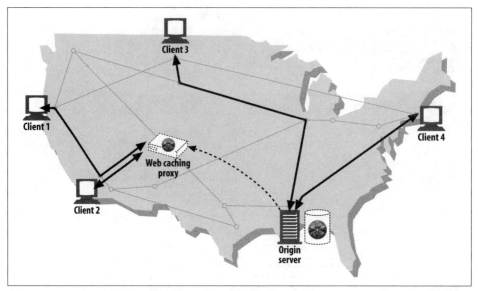

*Figure 6-6. Proxy application example: web cache*

*Surrogate (Figure 6-7)*

Proxies can masquerade as web servers. These so-called *surrogates* or *reverse proxies* receive real web server requests, but, unlike web servers, they may initiate communication with other servers to locate the requested content on demand.

Surrogates may be used to improve the performance of slow web servers for common content. In this configuration, the surrogates often are called *server accelerators* (Figure 6-7). Surrogates also can be used in conjunction with content-routing functionality to create distributed networks of on-demand replicated content.

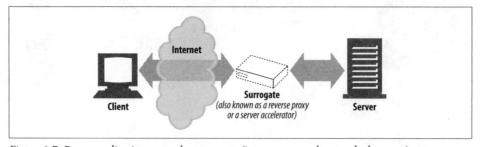

*Figure 6-7. Proxy application example: surrogate (in a server accelerator deployment)*

*Content router (Figure 6-8)*

Proxy servers can act as "content routers," vectoring requests to particular web servers based on Internet traffic conditions and type of content.

Content routers also can be used to implement various service-level offerings. For example, content routers can forward requests to nearby replica caches if the user or content provider has paid for higher performance (Figure 6-8), or route HTTP requests through filtering proxies if the user has signed up for a filtering service. Many interesting services can be constructed using adaptive content-routing proxies.

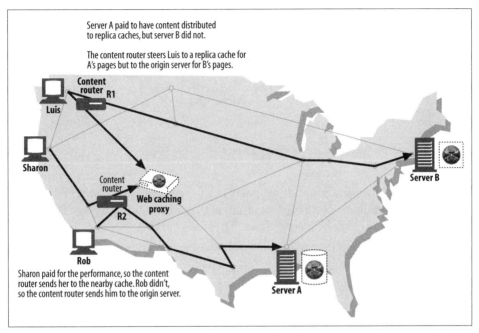

Figure 6-8. *Proxy application example: content routing*

*Transcoder (Figure 6-9)*

Proxy servers can modify the body format of content before delivering it to clients. This transparent translation between data representations is called *transcoding.*

Transcoding proxies can convert GIF images into JPEG images as they fly by, to reduce size. Images also can be shrunk and reduced in color intensity to be viewable on television sets. Likewise, text files can be compressed, and small text summaries of web pages can be generated for Internet-enabled pagers and smart phones. It's even possible for proxies to convert documents into foreign languages on the fly!

Figure 6-9 shows a transcoding proxy that converts English text into Spanish text and also reformats HTML pages into simpler text that can displayed on the small screen of a mobile phone.

---

* Some people distinguish "transcoding" and "translation," defining transcoding as relatively simple conversions of the encoding of the data (e.g., lossless compression) and translation as more significant reformatting or semantic changes of the data. We use the term transcoding to mean any intermediary-based modification of the content.

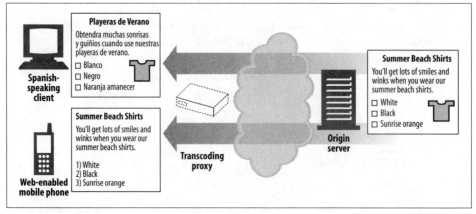

*Figure 6-9. Proxy application example: content transcoder*

## Anonymizer (Figure 6-10)

Anonymizer proxies provide heightened privacy and anonymity, by actively removing identifying characteristics from HTTP messages (e.g., client IP address, From header, Referer header, cookies, URI session IDs).*

In Figure 6-10, the anonymizing proxy makes the following changes to the user's messages to increase privacy:

- The user's computer and OS type is removed from the User-Agent header.
- The From header is removed to protect the user's email address.
- The Referer header is removed to obscure other sites the user has visited.
- The Cookie headers are removed to eliminate profiling and identity data.

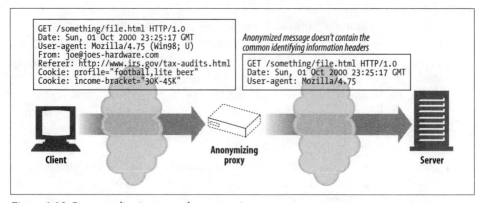

*Figure 6-10. Proxy application example: anonymizer*

---

* However, because identifying information is removed, the quality of the user's browsing experience may be diminished, and some web sites may not function properly.

---

# Where Do Proxies Go?

The previous section explained what proxies do. Now let's talk about where proxies sit when they are deployed into a network architecture. We'll cover:

- How proxies can be deployed into networks
- How proxies can chain together into hierarchies
- How traffic gets directed to a proxy server in the first place

## Proxy Server Deployment

You can place proxies in all kinds of places, depending on their intended uses. Figure 6-11 sketches a few ways proxy servers can be deployed.

*Egress proxy (Figure 6-11a)*
> You can stick proxies at the exit points of local networks to control the traffic flow between the local network and the greater Internet. You might use egress proxies in a corporation to offer firewall protection against malicious hackers outside the enterprise or to reduce bandwidth charges and improve performance of Internet traffic. An elementary school might use a filtering egress proxy to prevent precocious students from browsing inappropriate content.

*Access (ingress) proxy (Figure 6-11b)*
> Proxies are often placed at ISP access points, processing the aggregate requests from the customers. ISPs use caching proxies to store copies of popular documents, to improve the download speed for their users (especially those with high-speed connections) and reduce Internet bandwidth costs.

*Surrogates (Figure 6-11c)*
> Proxies frequently are deployed as surrogates (also commonly called reverse proxies) at the edge of the network, in front of web servers, where they can field all of the requests directed at the web server and ask the web server for resources only when necessary. Surrogates can add security features to web servers or improve performance by placing fast web server caches in front of slower web servers. Surrogates typically assume the name and IP address of the web server directly, so all requests go to the proxy instead of the server.

*Network exchange proxy (Figure 6-11d)*
> With sufficient horsepower, proxies can be placed in the Internet peering exchange points between networks, to alleviate congestion at Internet junctions through caching and to monitor traffic flows.[*]

---

[*] Core proxies often are deployed where Internet bandwidth is very expensive (especially in Europe). Some countries (such as the UK) also are evaluating controversial proxy deployments to monitor Internet traffic for national security concerns.

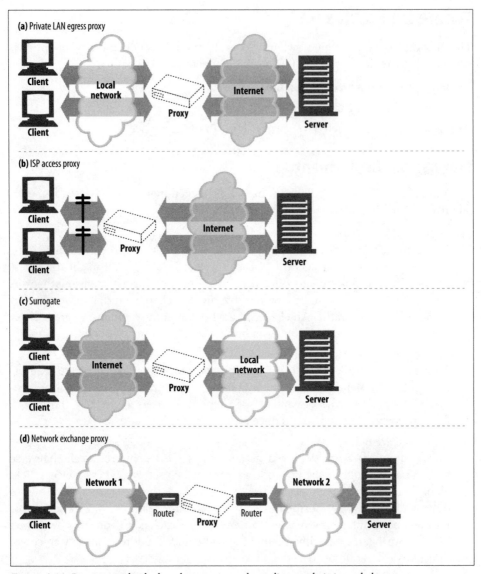

Figure 6-11. *Proxies can be deployed many ways, depending on their intended use*

## Proxy Hierarchies

Proxies can be cascaded in chains called *proxy hierarchies*. In a proxy hierarchy, messages are passed from proxy to proxy until they eventually reach the origin server (and then are passed back through the proxies to the client), as shown in Figure 6-12.

Proxy servers in a proxy hierarchy are assigned *parent* and *child* relationships. The next *inbound* proxy (closer to the server) is called the parent, and the next *outbound* proxy (closer to the client) is called the child. In Figure 6-12, proxy 1 is the child

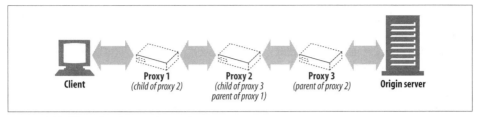

*Figure 6-12. Three-level proxy hierarchy*

proxy of proxy 2. Likewise, proxy 2 is the child proxy of proxy 3, and proxy 3 is the parent proxy of proxy 2.

### Proxy hierarchy content routing

The proxy hierarchy in Figure 6-12 is static—proxy 1 always forwards messages to proxy 2, and proxy 2 always forwards messages to proxy 3. However, hierarchies do not have to be static. A proxy server can forward messages to a varied and changing set of proxy servers and origin servers, based on many factors.

For example, in Figure 6-13, the access proxy routes to parent proxies or origin servers in different circumstances:

- If the requested object belongs to a web server that has paid for content distribution, the proxy could route the request to a nearby cache server that would either return the cached object or fetch it if it wasn't available.

- If the request was for a particular type of image, the access proxy might route the request to a dedicated compression proxy that would fetch the image and then compress it, so it would download faster across a slow modem to the client.

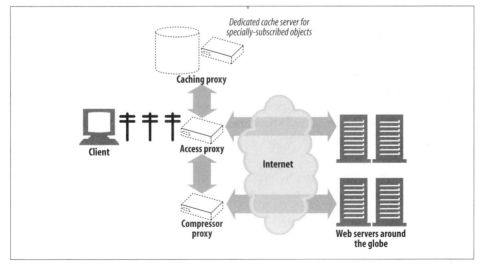

*Figure 6-13. Proxy hierarchies can be dynamic, changing for each request*

Here are a few other examples of dynamic parent selection:

*Load balancing*
>A child proxy might pick a parent proxy based on the current level of workload on the parents, to spread the load around.

*Geographic proximity routing*
>A child proxy might select a parent responsible for the origin server's geographic region.

*Protocol/type routing*
>A child proxy might route to different parents and origin servers based on the URI. Certain types of URIs might cause the requests to be transported through special proxy servers, for special protocol handling.

*Subscription-based routing*
>If publishers have paid extra money for high-performance service, their URIs might be routed to large caches or compression engines to improve performance.

Dynamic parenting routing logic is implemented differently in different products, including configuration files, scripting languages, and dynamic executable plug-ins.

## How Proxies Get Traffic

Because clients normally talk directly to web servers, we need to explain how HTTP traffic finds its way to a proxy in the first place. There are four common ways to cause client traffic to get to a proxy:

*Modify the client*
>Many web clients, including Netscape and Microsoft browsers, support both manual and automated proxy configuration. If a client is configured to use a proxy server, the client sends HTTP requests directly and intentionally to the proxy, instead of to the origin server (Figure 6-14a).

*Modify the network*
>There are several techniques where the network infrastructure intercepts and steers web traffic into a proxy, without the client's knowledge or participation. This interception typically relies on switching and routing devices that watch for HTTP traffic, intercept it, and shunt the traffic into a proxy, without the client's knowledge (Figure 6-14b). This is called an *intercepting* proxy.[*]

*Modify the DNS namespace*
>Surrogates, which are proxy servers placed in front of web servers, assume the name and IP address of the web server directly, so all requests go to them instead

---

[*] Intercepting proxies commonly are called "transparent proxies," because you connect to them without being aware of their presence. Because the term "transparency" already is used in the HTTP specifications to indicate functions that don't change semantic behavior, the standards community suggests using the term "interception" for traffic capture. We adopt this nomenclature here.

of to the server (Figure 6-14c). This can be arranged by manually editing the DNS naming tables or by using special dynamic DNS servers that compute the appropriate proxy or server to use on-demand. In some installations, the IP address and name of the real server is changed and the surrogate is given the former address and name.

*Modify the web server*
Some web servers also can be configured to redirect client requests to a proxy by sending an HTTP redirection command (response code 305) back to the client. Upon receiving the redirect, the client transacts with the proxy (Figure 6-14d).

The next section explains how to configure clients to send traffic to proxies. Chapter 20 will explain how to configure the network, DNS, and servers to redirect traffic to proxy servers.

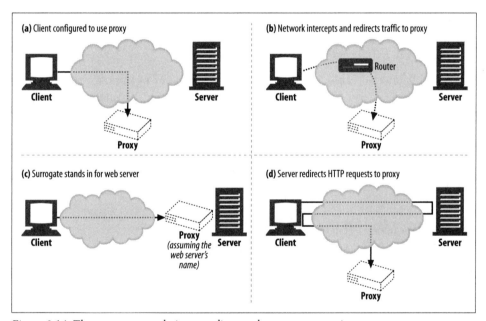

*Figure 6-14. There are many techniques to direct web requests to proxies*

# Client Proxy Settings

All modern web browsers let you configure the use of proxies. In fact, many browsers provide multiple ways of configuring proxies, including:

*Manual configuration*
You explicitly set a proxy to use.

*Browser preconfiguration*
The browser vendor or distributor manually preconfigures the proxy setting of the browser (or any other web client) before delivering it to customers.

*Proxy auto-configuration (PAC)*
> You provide a URI to a JavaScript *proxy auto-configuration* (PAC) file; the client fetches the JavaScript file and runs it to decide if it should use a proxy and, if so, which proxy server to use.

*WPAD proxy discovery*
> Some browsers support the Web Proxy Autodiscovery Protocol (WPAD), which automatically detects a "configuration server" from which the browser can download an auto-configuration file.*

## Client Proxy Configuration: Manual

Many web clients allow you to configure proxies manually. Both Netscape Navigator and Microsoft Internet Explorer have convenient support for proxy configuration.

In Netscape Navigator 6, you specify proxies through the menu selection Edit → Preferences → Advanced → Proxies and then selecting the "Manual proxy configuration" radio button.

In Microsoft Internet Explorer 5, you can manually specify proxies from the Tools → Internet Options menu, by selecting a connection, pressing "Settings," checking the "Use a proxy server" box, and clicking "Advanced."

Other browsers have different ways of making manual configuration changes, but the idea is the same: specifying the host and port for the proxy. Several ISPs ship customers preconfigured browsers, or customized operating systems, that redirect web traffic to proxy servers.

## Client Proxy Configuration: PAC Files

Manual proxy configuration is simple but inflexible. You can specify only one proxy server for all content, and there is no support for failover. Manual proxy configuration also leads to administrative problems for large organizations. With a large base of configured browsers, it's difficult or impossible to reconfigure every browser if you need to make changes.

Proxy auto-configuration (PAC) files are a more dynamic solution for proxy configuration, because they are small JavaScript programs that compute proxy settings on the fly. Each time a document is accessed, a JavaScript function selects the proper proxy server.

To use PAC files, configure your browser with the URI of the JavaScript PAC file (configuration is similar to manual configuration, but you provide a URI in an "automatic configuration" box). The browser will fetch the PAC file from this URI and use

---

* Currently supported only by Internet Explorer.

the JavaScript logic to compute the proper proxy server for each access. PAC files typically have a *.pac* suffix and the MIME type "application/x-ns-proxy-autoconfig."

Each PAC file must define a function called FindProxyForURL(url,host) that computes the proper proxy server to use for accessing the URI. The return value of the function can be any of the values in Table 6-1.

*Table 6-1. Proxy auto-configuration script return values*

| FindProxyForURL return value | Description |
| --- | --- |
| DIRECT | Connections should be made directly, without any proxies. |
| PROXY host:port | The specified proxy should be used. |
| SOCKS host:port | The specified SOCKS server should be used. |

The PAC file in Example 6-1 mandates one proxy for HTTP transactions, another proxy for FTP transactions, and direct connections for all other kinds of transactions.

*Example 6-1. Example proxy auto-configuration file*

```
function FindProxyForURL(url, host) {
    if (url.substring(0,5) == "http:") {
        return "PROXY http-proxy.mydomain.com:8080";
    } else if (url.substring(0,4) =="ftp:") {
        return "PROXY ftp-proxy.mydomain.com:8080";
    } else {
        return "DIRECT";
    }
}
```

For more details about PAC files, refer to Chapter 20.

## Client Proxy Configuration: WPAD

Another mechanism for browser configuration is the Web Proxy Autodiscovery Protocol (WPAD). WPAD is an algorithm that uses an escalating strategy of discovery mechanisms to find the appropriate PAC file for the browser automatically. A client that implements the WPAD protocol will:

- Use WPAD to find the PAC URI.
- Fetch the PAC file given the URI.
- Execute the PAC file to determine the proxy server.
- Use the proxy server for requests.

WPAD uses a series of resource-discovery techniques to determine the proper PAC file. Multiple discovery techniques are used, because not all organizations can use all techniques. WPAD attempts each technique, one by one, until it succeeds.

The current WPAD specification defines the following techniques, in order:

- Dynamic Host Discovery Protocol (DHCP)
- Service Location Protocol (SLP)
- DNS well-known hostnames
- DNS SRV records
- DNS service URIs in TXT records

For more information, consult Chapter 20.

# Tricky Things About Proxy Requests

This section explains some of the tricky and much misunderstood aspects of proxy server requests, including:

- How the URIs in proxy requests differ from server requests
- How intercepting and reverse proxies can obscure server host information
- The rules for URI modification
- How proxies impact a browser's clever URI auto-completion or hostname-expansion features

## Proxy URIs Differ from Server URIs

Web server and web proxy messages have the same syntax, with one exception. The URI in an HTTP request message differs when a client sends the request to a server instead of a proxy.

When a client sends a request to a web server, the request line contains only a partial URI (without a scheme, host, or port), as shown in the following example:

```
GET /index.html HTTP/1.0
User-Agent: SuperBrowserv1.3
```

When a client sends a request to a proxy, however, the request line contains the full URI. For example:

```
GET http://www.marys-antiques.com/index.html HTTP/1.0
User-Agent: SuperBrowser v1.3
```

Why have two different request formats, one for proxies and one for servers? In the original HTTP design, clients talked directly to a single server. Virtual hosting did not exist, and no provision was made for proxies. Because a single server knows its own hostname and port, to avoid sending redundant information, clients sent just the partial URI, without the scheme and host (and port).

When proxies emerged, the partial URIs became a problem. Proxies needed to know the name of the destination server, so they could establish their own connections to the server. And proxy-based gateways needed the scheme of the URI to connect to FTP resources and other schemes. HTTP/1.0 solved the problem by requiring the full URI for proxy requests, but it retained partial URIs for server requests (there were too many servers already deployed to change all of them to support full URIs).*

So we need to send partial URIs to servers, and full URIs to proxies. In the case of explicitly configured client proxy settings, the client knows what type of request to issue:

- When the client *is not* set to use a proxy, it sends the partial URI (Figure 6-15a).
- When the client *is* set to use a proxy, it sends the full URI (Figure 6-15b).

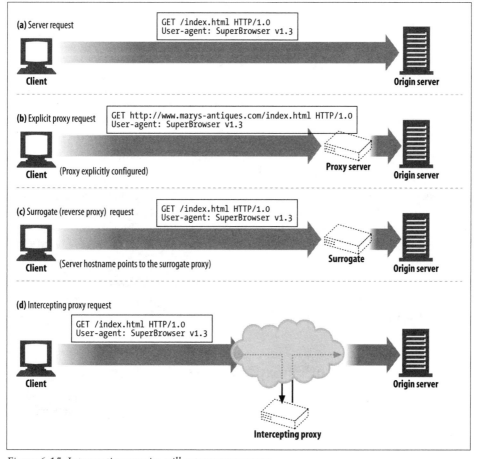

Figure 6-15. Intercepting proxies will get server requests

---

* HTTP/1.1 now requires servers to handle full URIs for both proxy and server requests, but in practice, many deployed servers still accept only partial URIs.

## The Same Problem with Virtual Hosting

The proxy "missing scheme/host/port" problem is the same problem faced by virtually hosted web servers. Virtually hosted web servers share the same physical web server among many web sites. When a request comes in for the partial URI /index.html, the virtually hosted web server needs to know the hostname of the intended web site (see "Virtually hosted docroots" in Chapter 5 and "Virtual Hosting" in Chapter 18 for more information).

In spite of the problems being similar, they were solved in different ways:

- Explicit proxies solve the problem by requiring a full URI in the request message.
- Virtually hosted web servers require a Host header to carry the host and port information.

## Intercepting Proxies Get Partial URIs

As long as the clients properly implement HTTP, they will send full URIs in requests to explicitly configured proxies. That solves part of the problem, but there's a catch: a client *will not always know* it's talking to a proxy, because some proxies may be invisible to the client. Even if the client is not configured to use a proxy, the client's traffic still may go through a surrogate or intercepting proxy. In both of these cases, the client will think it's talking to a web server and won't send the full URI:

- A *surrogate*, as described earlier, is a proxy server taking the place of the origin server, usually by assuming its hostname or IP address. It receives the web server request and may serve cached responses or proxy requests to the real server. A client cannot distinguish a surrogate from a web server, so it sends partial URIs (Figure 6-15c).
- An *intercepting proxy* is a proxy server in the network flow that hijacks traffic from the client to the server and either serves a cached response or proxies it. Because the intercepting proxy hijacks client-to-server traffic, it will receive partial URIs that are sent to web servers (Figure 6-15d).*

## Proxies Can Handle Both Proxy and Server Requests

Because of the different ways that traffic can be redirected into proxy servers, general-purpose proxy servers should support both full URIs and partial URIs in request messages. The proxy should use the full URI if it is an explicit proxy request or use the partial URI and the virtual Host header if it is a web server request.

---

\* Intercepting proxies also might intercept client-to-proxy traffic in some circumstances, in which case the intercepting proxy might get full URIs and need to handle them. This doesn't happen often, because explicit proxies normally communicate on a port different from that used by HTTP (usually 8080 instead of 80), and intercepting proxies usually intercept only port 80.

The rules for using full and partial URIs are:

- If a full URI is provided, the proxy should use it.
- If a partial URI is provided, and a Host header is present, the Host header should be used to determine the origin server name and port number.
- If a partial URI is provided, and there is no Host header, the origin server needs to be determined in some other way:
    — If the proxy is a surrogate, standing in for an origin server, the proxy can be configured with the real server's address and port number.
    — If the traffic was intercepted, and the interceptor makes the original IP address and port available, the proxy can use the IP address and port number from the interception technology (see Chapter 20).
    — If all else fails, the proxy doesn't have enough information to determine the origin server and must return an error message (often suggesting that the user upgrade to a modern browser that supports Host headers).*

## In-Flight URI Modification

Proxy servers need to be very careful about changing the request URI as they forward messages. Slight changes in the URI, even if they seem benign, may create interoperability problems with downstream servers.

In particular, some proxies have been known to "canonicalize" URIs into a standard form before forwarding them to the next hop. Seemingly benign transformations, such as replacing default HTTP ports with an explicit ":80", or correcting URIs by replacing illegal reserved characters with their properly escaped substitutions, can cause interoperation problems.

In general, proxy servers should strive to be as tolerant as possible. They should not aim to be "protocol policemen" looking to enforce strict protocol compliance, because this could involve significant disruption of previously functional services.

In particular, the HTTP specifications forbid general intercepting proxies from rewriting the absolute path parts of URIs when forwarding them. The only exception is that they can replace an empty path with "/".

## URI Client Auto-Expansion and Hostname Resolution

Browsers resolve request URIs differently, depending on whether or not a proxy is present. Without a proxy, the browser takes the URI you type in and tries to find a corresponding IP address. If the hostname is found, the browser tries the corresponding IP addresses until it gets a successful connection.

---

* This shouldn't be done casually. Users will receive cryptic error pages they never got before.

But if the host isn't found, many browsers attempt to provide some automatic "expansion" of hostnames, in case you typed in a "shorthand" abbreviation of the host (refer back to "Expandomatic URLs" in Chapter 2):*

- Many browsers attempt adding a "www." prefix and a ".com" suffix, in case you just entered the middle piece of a common web site name (e.g., to let people enter "yahoo" instead of "www.yahoo.com").

- Some browsers even pass your unresolvable URI to a third-party site, which attempts to correct spelling mistakes and suggest URIs you may have intended.

- In addition, the DNS configuration on most systems allows you to enter just the prefix of the hostname, and the DNS automatically searches the domain. If you are in the domain "oreilly.com" and type in the hostname "host7," the DNS automatically attempts to match "host7.oreilly.com". It's not a complete, valid hostname.

## URI Resolution Without a Proxy

Figure 6-16 shows an example of browser hostname auto-expansion without a proxy. In steps 2a–3c, the browser looks up variations of the hostname until a valid hostname is found.

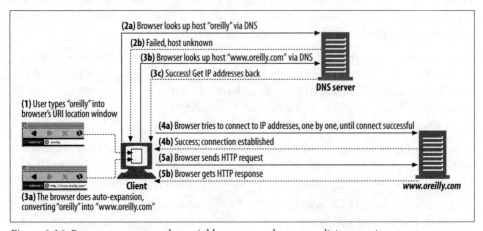

*Figure 6-16. Browser auto-expands partial hostnames when no explicit proxy is present*

Here's what's going on in this figure:

- In Step 1, the user types "oreilly" into the browser's URI window. The browser uses "oreilly" as the hostname and assumes a default scheme of "http://", a default port of "80", and a default path of "/".

- In Step 2a, the browser looks up host "oreilly." This fails.

---

* Most browsers let you type in "yahoo" and auto-expand that into "www.yahoo.com." Similarly, browsers let you omit the "http://" prefix and insert it if it's missing.

- In Step 3a, the browser auto-expands the hostname and asks the DNS to resolve "www.oreilly.com." This is successful.
- The browser then successfully connects to *www.oreilly.com*.

## URI Resolution with an Explicit Proxy

When you use an explicit proxy the browser no longer performs any of these convenience expansions, because the user's URI is passed directly to the proxy.

As shown in Figure 6-17, the browser does not auto-expand the partial hostname when there is an explicit proxy. As a result, when the user types "oreilly" into the browser's location window, the proxy is sent "http://oreilly/" (the browser adds the default scheme and path but leaves the hostname as entered).

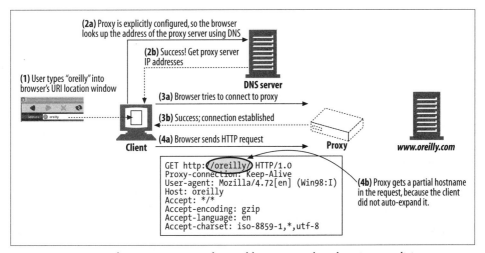

*Figure 6-17. Browser does not auto-expand partial hostnames when there is an explicit proxy*

For this reason, some proxies attempt to mimic as much as possible of the browser's convenience services as they can, including "www...com" auto-expansion and addition of local domain suffixes.[*]

## URI Resolution with an Intercepting Proxy

Hostname resolution is a little different with an invisible intercepting proxy, because as far as the client is concerned, there is no proxy! The behavior proceeds much like the server case, with the browser auto-expanding hostnames until DNS success. But a significant difference occurs when the connection to the server is made, as Figure 6-18 illustrates.

---

[*] But, for widely shared proxies, it may be impossible to know the proper domain suffix for individual users.

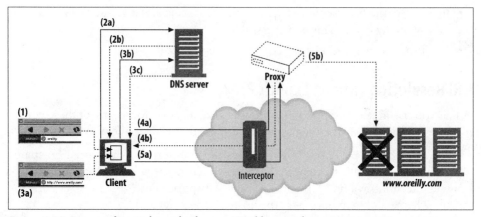

*Figure 6-18. Browser doesn't detect dead server IP addresses when using intercepting proxies*

Figure 6-18 demonstrates the following transaction:

- In Step 1, the user types "oreilly" into the browser's URI location window.

- In Step 2a, the browser looks up the host "oreilly" via DNS, but the DNS server fails and responds that the host is unknown, as shown in Step 2b.

- In Step 3a, the browser does auto-expansion, converting "oreilly" into "www. oreilly.com." In Step 3b, the browser looks up the host "www.oreilly.com" via DNS. This time, as shown in Step 3c, the DNS server is successful and returns IP addresses back to the browser.

- In Step 4a, the client already has successfully resolved the hostname and has a list of IP addresses. Normally, the client tries to connect to each IP address until it succeeds, because some of the IP addresses may be dead. But with an intercepting proxy, the first connection attempt is terminated by the proxy server, not the origin server. The client believes it is successfully talking to the web server, but the web server might not even be alive.

- When the proxy finally is ready to interact with the real origin server (Step 5b), the proxy may find that the IP address actually points to a down server. To provide the same level of fault tolerance provided by the browser, the proxy needs to try other IP addresses, either by reresolving the hostname in the Host header or by doing a reverse DNS lookup on the IP address. It is important that both intercepting and explicit proxy implementations support fault tolerance on DNS resolution to dead servers, because when browsers are configured to use an explicit proxy, they rely on the proxy for fault tolerance.

## Tracing Messages

Today, it's not uncommon for web requests to go through a chain of two or more proxies on their way from the client to the server (Figure 6-19). For example, many corporations use caching proxy servers to access the Internet, for security and cost savings, and many large ISPs use proxy caches to improve performance and implement features. A significant percentage of web requests today go through proxies. At the same time, it's becoming increasingly popular to replicate content on banks of surrogate caches scattered around the globe, for performance reasons.

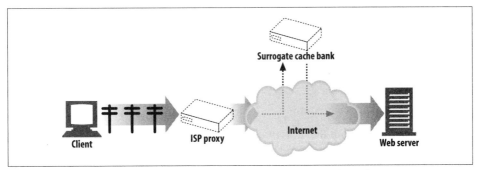

*Figure 6-19. Access proxies and CDN proxies create two-level proxy hierarchies*

Proxies are developed by different vendors. They have different features and bugs and are administrated by various organizations.

As proxies become more prevalent, you need to be able to trace the flow of messages across proxies and to detect any problems, just as it is important to trace the flow of IP packets across different switches and routers.

## The Via Header

The Via header field lists information about each intermediate node (proxy or gateway) through which a message passes. Each time a message goes through another node, the intermediate node must be added to the end of the Via list.

The following Via string tells us that the message traveled through two proxies. It indicates that the first proxy implemented the HTTP/1.1 protocol and was called *proxy-62.irenes-isp.net*, and that the second proxy implemented HTTP/1.0 and was called *cache.joes-hardware.com*:

```
Via: 1.1 proxy-62.irenes-isp.net, 1.0 cache.joes-hardware.com
```

The Via header field is used to track the forwarding of messages, diagnose message loops, and identify the protocol capabilities of all senders along the request/response chain (Figure 6-20).

Proxies also can use Via headers to detect routing loops in the network. A proxy should insert a unique string associated with itself in the Via header before sending out a request and should check for the presence of this string in incoming requests to detect routing loops in the network.

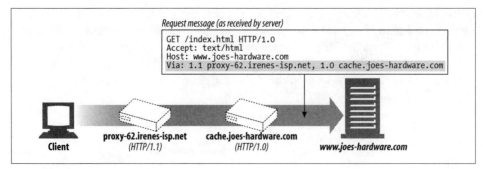

*Figure 6-20. Via header example*

### Via syntax

The Via header field contains a comma-separated list of *waypoints*. Each waypoint represents an individual proxy server or gateway hop and contains information about the protocol and address of that intermediate node. Here is an example of a Via header with two waypoints:

```
Via: 1.1 proxy-62.irenes-isp.net, 1.0 cache.joes-hardware.com
```

The formal syntax for a Via header is shown here:

```
Via               = "Via" ":" ( waypoint ) [", " ( waypoint )...]
waypoint          = ( received-protocol received-by [ comment ] )
received-protocol = [ protocol-name "/" ] protocol-version
received-by       = ( host [ ":" port ] ) | pseudonym
```

Note that each Via waypoint contains up to four components: an optional protocol name (defaults to HTTP), a required protocol version, a required node name, and an optional descriptive comment:

*Protocol name*

> The protocol received by an intermediary. The protocol name is optional if the protocol is HTTP. Otherwise, the protocol name is prepended to the version, separated by a "/". Non-HTTP protocols can occur when gateways connect HTTP requests for other protocols (HTTPS, FTP, etc.).

*Protocol version*

> The version of the message received. The format of the version depends on the protocol. For HTTP, the standard version numbers are used ("1.0", "1.1", etc.). The version is included in the Via field, so later applications will know the protocol capabilities of all previous intermediaries.

*Node name*

> The host and optional port number of the intermediary (if the port isn't included, you can assume the default port for the protocol). In some cases an organization might not want to give out the real hostname, for privacy reasons, in which case it may be replaced by a pseudonym.

*Node comment*

> An optional comment that further describes the intermediary node. It's common to include vendor and version information here, and some proxy servers also use the comment field to include diagnostic information about the events that occurred on that device.*

## Via request and response paths

Both request and response messages pass through proxies, so both request and response messages have Via headers.

Because requests and responses usually travel over the same TCP connection, response messages travel backward across the same path as the requests. If a request message goes through proxies A, B, and C, the corresponding response message travels through proxies C, B, then A. So, the Via header for responses is almost always the reverse of the Via header for responses (Figure 6-21).

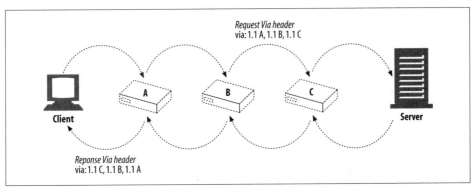

*Figure 6-21. The response Via is usually the reverse of the request Via*

## Via and gateways

Some proxies provide gateway functionality to servers that speak non-HTTP protocols. The Via header records these protocol conversions, so HTTP applications can be aware of protocol capabilities and conversions along the proxy chain. Figure 6-22 shows an HTTP client requesting an FTP URI through an HTTP/FTP gateway.

The client sends an HTTP request for *ftp://http-guide.com/pub/welcome.txt* to the gateway *proxy.irenes-isp.net*. The proxy, acting as a protocol gateway, retrieves the desired object from the FTP server, using the FTP protocol. The proxy then sends the object back to the client in an HTTP response, with this Via header field:

```
Via: FTP/1.0 proxy.irenes-isp.net (Traffic-Server/5.0.1-17882 [cMs f ])
```

---

* For example, caching proxy servers may include hit/miss information.

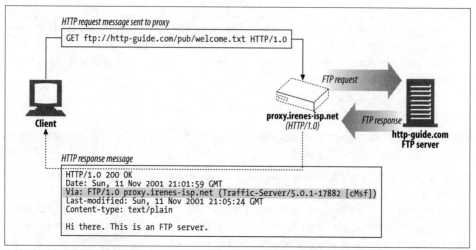

```
HTTP request message sent to proxy
    GET ftp://http-guide.com/pub/welcome.txt HTTP/1.0
```

```
HTTP response message
    HTTP/1.0 200 OK
    Date: Sun, 11 Nov 2001 21:01:59 GMT
    Via: FTP/1.0 proxy.irenes-isp.net (Traffic-Server/5.0.1-17882 [cMsf])
    Last-modified: Sun, 11 Nov 2001 21:05:24 GMT
    Content-type: text/plain

    Hi there. This is an FTP server.
```

*Figure 6-22. HTTP/FTP gateway generates Via headers, logging the received protocol (FTP)*

Notice the received protocol is FTP. The optional comment contains the brand and version number of the proxy server and some vendor diagnostic information. You can read all about gateways in Chapter 8.

### The Server and Via headers

The Server response header field describes the software used by the origin server. Here are a few examples:

```
Server: Apache/1.3.14 (Unix) PHP/4.0.4
Server: Netscape-Enterprise/4.1
Server: Microsoft-IIS/5.0
```

If a response message is being forwarded through a proxy, make sure the proxy does not modify the Server header. The Server header is meant for the origin server. Instead, the proxy should add a Via entry.

### Privacy and security implications of Via

There are some cases when we don't want exact hostnames in the Via string. In general, unless this behavior is explicitly enabled, when a proxy server is part of a network firewall it should not forward the names and ports of hosts behind the firewall, because knowledge of network architecture behind a firewall might be of use to a malicious party.*

---

* Malicious people can use the names of computers and version numbers to learn about the network architecture behind a security perimeter. This information might be helpful in security attacks. In addition, the names of computers might be clues to private projects within an organization.

If Via node-name forwarding is not enabled, proxies that are part of a security perimeter should replace the hostname with an appropriate pseudonym for that host. Generally, though, proxies should try to retain a Via waypoint entry for each proxy server, even if the real name is obscured.

For organizations that have very strong privacy requirements for obscuring the design and topology of internal network architectures, a proxy may combine an ordered sequence of Via waypoint entries (with identical received-protocol values) into a single, joined entry. For example:

```
Via: 1.0 foo, 1.1 devirus.company.com, 1.1 access-logger.company.com
```

could be collapsed to:

```
Via: 1.0 foo, 1.1 concealed-stuff
```

Don't combine multiple entries unless they all are under the same organizational control and the hosts already have been replaced by pseudonyms. Also, don't combine entries that have different received-protocol values.

## The TRACE Method

Proxy servers can change messages as the messages are forwarded. Headers are added, modified, and removed, and bodies can be converted to different formats. As proxies become more sophisticated, and more vendors deploy proxy products, interoperability problems increase. To easily diagnose proxy networks, we need a way to conveniently watch how messages change as they are forwarded, hop by hop, through the HTTP proxy network.

HTTP/1.1's TRACE method lets you trace a request message through a chain of proxies, observing what proxies the message passes through and how each proxy modifies the request message. TRACE is very useful for debugging proxy flows.*

When the TRACE request reaches the destination server,† the entire request message is reflected back to the sender, bundled up in the body of an HTTP response (see Figure 6-23). When the TRACE response arrives, the client can examine the exact message the server received and the list of proxies through which it passed (in the Via header). The TRACE response has Content-Type message/http and a 200 OK status.

### Max-Forwards

Normally, TRACE messages travel all the way to the destination server, regardless of the number of intervening proxies. You can use the Max-Forwards header to limit

---

* Unfortunately, it isn't widely implemented yet.

† The final recipient is either the origin server or the first proxy or gateway to receive a Max-Forwards value of zero (0) in the request.

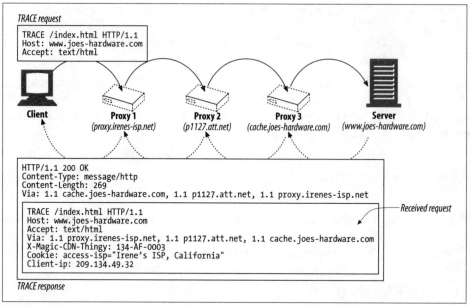

```
TRACE /index.html HTTP/1.1
Host: www.joes-hardware.com
Accept: text/html
```

**Client**  **Proxy 1**  **Proxy 2**  **Proxy 3**  **Server**
(*proxy.irenes-isp.net*)  (*p1127.att.net*)  (*cache.joes-hardware.com*)  (*www.joes-hardware.com*)

```
HTTP/1.1 200 OK
Content-Type: message/http
Content-Length: 269
Via: 1.1 cache.joes-hardware.com, 1.1 p1127.att.net, 1.1 proxy.irenes-isp.net
```

```
TRACE /index.html HTTP/1.1
Host: www.joes-hardware.com
Accept: text/html
Via: 1.1 proxy.irenes-isp.net, 1.1 p1127.att.net, 1.1 cache.joes-hardware.com
X-Magic-CDN-Thingy: 134-AF-0003
Cookie: access-isp="Irene's ISP, California"
Client-ip: 209.134.49.32
```
*Received request*

TRACE response

*Figure 6-23. TRACE response reflects back the received request message*

the number of proxy hops for TRACE and OPTIONS requests, which is useful for testing a chain of proxies forwarding messages in an infinite loop or for checking the effects of particular proxy servers in the middle of a chain. Max-Forwards also limits the forwarding of OPTIONS messages (see "Proxy Interoperation").

The Max-Forwards request header field contains a single integer indicating the remaining number of times this request message may be forwarded (Figure 6-24). If the Max-Forwards value is zero (Max-Forwards: 0), the receiver must reflect the TRACE message back toward the client without forwarding it further, even if the receiver is not the origin server.

If the received Max-Forwards value is greater than zero, the forwarded message must contain an updated Max-Forwards field with a value decremented by one. All proxies and gateways should support Max-Forwards. You can use Max-Forwards to view the request at any hop in a proxy chain.

## Proxy Authentication

Proxies can serve as access-control devices. HTTP defines a mechanism called *proxy authentication* that blocks requests for content until the user provides valid access-permission credentials to the proxy:

• When a request for restricted content arrives at a proxy server, the proxy server can return a 407 Proxy Authorization Required status code demanding access

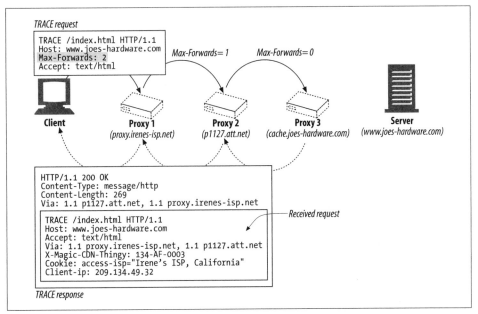

*Figure 6-24. You can limit the forwarding hop count with the Max-Forwards header field*

credentials, accompanied by a Proxy-Authenticate header field that describes how to provide those credentials (Figure 6-25b).

- When the client receives the 407 response, it attempts to gather the required credentials, either from a local database or by prompting the user.

- Once the credentials are obtained, the client resends the request, providing the required credentials in a Proxy-Authorization header field.

- If the credentials are valid, the proxy passes the original request along the chain (Figure 6-25c); otherwise, another 407 reply is sent.

Proxy authentication generally does not work well when there are multiple proxies in a chain, each participating in authentication. People have proposed enhancements to HTTP to associate authentication credentials with particular waypoints in a proxy chain, but those enhancements have not been widely implemented.

Be sure to read Chapter 12 for a detailed explanation of HTTP's authentication mechanisms.

## Proxy Interoperation

Clients, servers, and proxies are built by multiple vendors, to different versions of the HTTP specification. They support various features and have different bugs. Proxy servers need to intermediate between client-side and server-side devices, which may implement different protocols and have troublesome quirks.

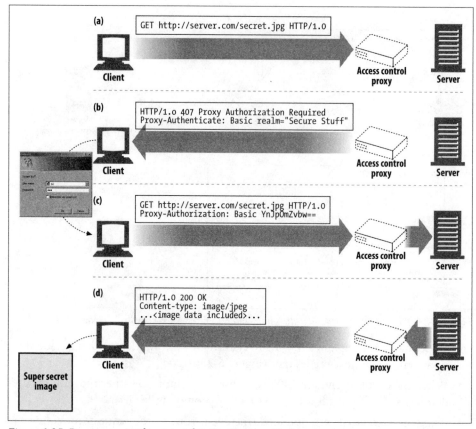

*Figure 6-25. Proxies can implement authentication to control access to content*

## Handling Unsupported Headers and Methods

The proxy server may not understand all the header fields that pass through it. Some headers may be newer than the proxy itself; others may be customized header fields unique to a particular application. Proxies must forward unrecognized header fields and must maintain the relative order of header fields with the same name.* Similarly, if a proxy is unfamiliar with a method, it should try to forward the message to the next hop, if possible.

Proxies that cannot tunnel unsupported methods may not be viable in most networks today, because Hotmail access through Microsoft Outlook makes extensive use of HTTP extension methods.

---

* Multiple message header fields with the same field name may be present in a message, but if they are, they must be able to be equivalently combined into a comma-separated list. The order in which header fields with the same field name are received is therefore significant to the interpretation of the combined field value, so a proxy can't change the relative order of these same-named field values when it forwards a message.

## OPTIONS: Discovering Optional Feature Support

The HTTP OPTIONS method lets a client (or proxy) discover the supported functionality (for example, supported methods) of a web server or of a particular resource on a web server (Figure 6-26). Clients can use OPTIONS to determine a server's capabilities before interacting with the server, making it easier to interoperate with proxies and servers of different feature levels.

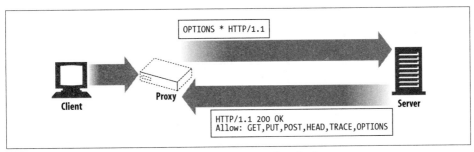

```
OPTIONS * HTTP/1.1
```

```
HTTP/1.1 200 OK
Allow: GET,PUT,POST,HEAD,TRACE,OPTIONS
```

Figure 6-26. Using OPTIONS to find a server's supported methods

If the URI of the OPTIONS request is an asterisk (*), the request pertains to the entire server's supported functionality. For example:

```
OPTIONS * HTTP/1.1
```

If the URI is a real resource, the OPTIONS request inquires about the features available to that particular resource:

```
OPTIONS http://www.joes-hardware.com/index.html HTTP/1.1
```

On success, the OPTIONS method returns a 200 OK response that includes various header fields that describe optional features that are supported on the server or available to the resource. The only header field that HTTP/1.1 specifies in the response is the Allow header, which describes what methods are supported by the server (or particular resource on the server).* OPTIONS allows an optional response body with more information, but this is undefined.

## The Allow Header

The Allow entity header field lists the set of methods supported by the resource identified by the request URI, or the entire server if the request URI is *. For example:

```
Allow: GET, HEAD, PUT
```

The Allow header can be used as a request header to recommend the methods to be supported by the new resource. The server is not required to support these methods

---

* Not all resources support every method. For example, a CGI script query may not support a file PUT, and a static HTML file wouldn't accept a POST method.

and should include an Allow header in the matching response, listing the actual supported methods.

A proxy can't modify the Allow header field even if it does not understand all the methods specified, because the client might have other paths to talk to the origin server.

# For More Information

For more information, refer to:

*http://www.w3.org/Protocols/rfc2616/rfc2616.txt*
  RFC 2616, "Hypertext Transfer Protocol," by R. Fielding, J. Gettys, J. Mogul, H. Frystyk, L. Mastinter, P. Leach, and T. Berners-Lee.

*http://search.ietf.org/rfc/rfc3040.txt*
  RFC 3040, "Internet Web Replication and Caching Taxonomy."

*Web Proxy Servers*
  Ari Luotonen, Prentice Hall Computer Books.

*http://search.ietf.org/rfc/rfc3143.txt*
  RFC 3143, "Known HTTP Proxy/Caching Problems."

*Web Caching*
  Duane Wessels, O'Reilly & Associates, Inc.

# CHAPTER 7

# Caching

Web caches are HTTP devices that automatically keep copies of popular documents. When a web request arrives at a cache, if a local "cached" copy is available, the document is served from the local storage instead of from the origin server. Caches have the following benefits:

- Caches *reduce redundant data transfers*, saving you money in network charges.
- Caches *reduce network bottlenecks*. Pages load faster without more bandwidth.
- Caches *reduce demand on origin servers*. Servers reply faster and avoid overload.
- Caches *reduce distance delays*, because pages load slower from farther away.

In this chapter, we explain how caches improve performance and reduce cost, how to measure their effectiveness, and where to place caches to maximize impact. We also explain how HTTP keeps cached copies fresh and how caches interact with other caches and servers.

## Redundant Data Transfers

When multiple clients access a popular origin server page, the server transmits the same document multiple times, once to each client. The same bytes travel across the network over and over again. These redundant data transfers eat up expensive network bandwidth, slow down transfers, and overload web servers. With caches, the cache keeps a copy of the first server response. Subsequent requests can be fulfilled from the cached copy, reducing wasteful, duplicate traffic to and from origin servers.

## Bandwidth Bottlenecks

Caches also can reduce network bottlenecks. Many networks provide more bandwidth to local network clients than to remote servers (Figure 7-1). Clients access servers at the speed of the slowest network on the way. If a client gets a copy from a cache on a fast LAN, caching can boost performance—especially for larger documents.

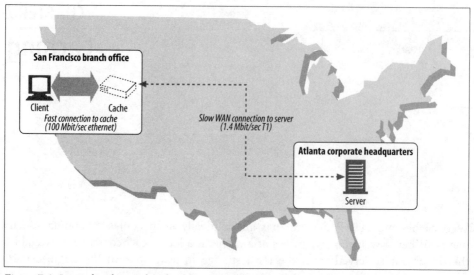

*Figure 7-1. Limited wide area bandwidth creates a bottleneck that caches can improve*

In Figure 7-1, it might take 30 seconds for a user in the San Francisco branch of Joe's Hardware, Inc. to download a 5-MB inventory file from the Atlanta headquarters, across the 1.4-Mbps T1 Internet connection. If the document was cached in the San Francisco office, a local user might be able to get the same document in less than a second across the Ethernet connection.

Table 7-1 shows how bandwidth affects transfer time for a few different network speeds and a few different sizes of documents. Bandwidth causes noticeable delays for larger documents, and the speed difference between different network types is dramatic.* A 56-Kbps modem would take 749 seconds (over 12 minutes) to transfer a 5-MB file that could be transported in under a second across a fast Ethernet LAN.

*Table 7-1. Bandwidth-imposed transfer time delays, idealized (time in seconds)*

|  | Large HTML (15 KB) | JPEG (40 KB) | Large JPEG (150 KB) | Large file (5 MB) |
|---|---|---|---|---|
| Dialup modem (56 Kbit/sec) | 2.19 | 5.85 | 21.94 | 748.98 |
| DSL (256 Kbit/sec) | .48 | 1.28 | 4.80 | 163.84 |
| T1 (1.4 Mbit/sec) | .09 | .23 | .85 | 29.13 |
| Slow Ethernet (10 Mbit/sec) | .01 | .03 | .12 | 4.19 |
| DS3 (45 Mbit/sec) | .00 | .01 | .03 | .93 |
| Fast Ethernet (100 Mbit/sec) | .00 | .00 | .01 | .42 |

---

* This table shows just the effect of network bandwidth on transfer time. It assumes 100% network efficiency and no network or application processing latencies. In this way, the delay is a lower bound. Real delays will be larger, and the delays for small objects will be dominated by non-bandwidth overheads.

# Flash Crowds

Caching is especially important to break up flash crowds. Flash crowds occur when a sudden event (such as breaking news, a bulk email announcement, or a celebrity event) causes many people to access a web document at nearly the same time (Figure 7-2). The resulting redundant traffic spike can cause a catastrophic collapse of networks and web servers.

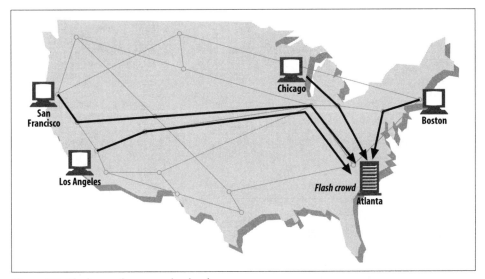

*Figure 7-2. Flash crowds can overload web servers*

When the "Starr Report" detailing Kenneth Starr's investigation of U.S. President Clinton was released to the Internet on September 11, 1998, the U.S. House of Representatives web servers received over 3 million requests per hour, 50 times the average server load. One news web site, CNN.com, reported an average of over 50,000 requests every second to its servers.

# Distance Delays

Even if bandwidth isn't a problem, distance might be. Every network router adds delays to Internet traffic. And even if there are not many routers between client and server, the speed of light alone can cause a significant delay.

The direct distance from Boston to San Francisco is about 2,700 miles. In the very best case, at the speed of light (186,000 miles/sec), a signal could travel from Boston to San Francisco in about 15 milliseconds and complete a round trip in 30 milliseconds.*

---

* In reality, signals travel at somewhat less than the speed of light, so distance delays are even worse.

Say a web page contains 20 small images, all located on a server in San Francisco. If a client in Boston opens four parallel connections to the server, and keeps the connections alive, the speed of light alone contributes almost 1/4 second (240 msec) to the download time (Figure 7-3). If the server is in Tokyo (6,700 miles from Boston), the delay grows to 600 msec. Moderately complicated web pages can incur several seconds of speed-of-light delays.

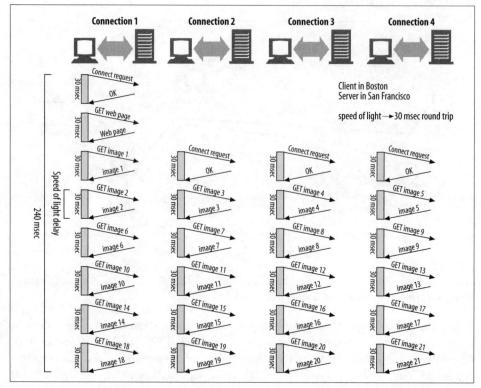

*Figure 7-3. Speed of light can cause significant delays, even with parallel, keep-alive connections*

Placing caches in nearby machine rooms can shrink document travel distance from thousands of miles to tens of yards.

## Hits and Misses

So caches can help. But a cache doesn't store a copy of *every* document in the world.*

---

\* Few folks can afford to buy a cache big enough to hold all the Web's documents. And even if you could afford gigantic "whole-Web caches," some documents change so frequently that they won't be fresh in many caches.

Some requests that arrive at a cache can be served from an available copy. This is called a *cache hit* (Figure 7-4a). Other requests arrive at a cache only to be forwarded to the origin server, because no copy is available. This is called a *cache miss* (Figure 7-4b).

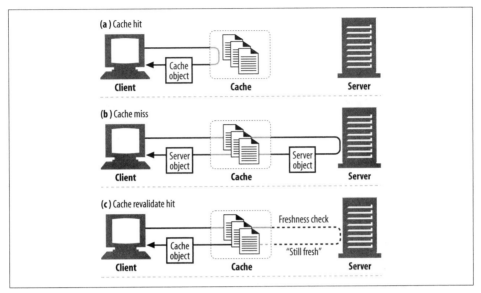

*Figure 7-4. Cache hits, misses, and revalidations*

## Revalidations

Because the origin server content can change, caches have to check every now and then that their copies are still up-to-date with the server. These "freshness checks" are called HTTP *revalidations* (Figure 7-4c). To make revalidations efficient, HTTP defines special requests that can quickly check if content is still fresh, without fetching the entire object from the server.

A cache can revalidate a copy any time it wants, and as often as it wants. But because caches often contain millions of documents, and because network bandwidth is scarce, most caches revalidate a copy only when it is requested by a client and when the copy is old enough to warrant a check. We'll explain the HTTP rules for freshness checking later in the chapter.

When a cache needs to revalidate a cached copy, it sends a small revalidation request to the origin server. If the content hasn't changed, the server responds with a tiny 304 Not Modified response. As soon as the cache learns the copy is still valid, it marks the copy temporarily fresh again and serves the copy to the client (Figure 7-5a). This is called a *revalidate hit* or a *slow hit*. It's slower than a pure cache hit, because it *does* need to check with the origin server, but it's faster than a cache miss, because no object data is retrieved from the server.

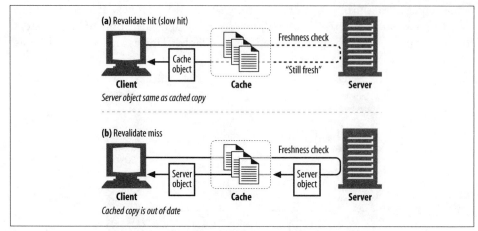

Figure 7-5. Successful revalidations are faster than cache misses; failed revalidations are nearly identical to misses

HTTP gives us a few tools to revalidate cached objects, but the most popular is the If-Modified-Since header. When added to a GET request, this header tells the server to send the object only if it has been modified since the time the copy was cached.

Here is what happens when a GET If-Modified-Since request arrives at the server in three circumstances—when the server content is not modified, when the server content has been changed, and when the object on the server is deleted:

*Revalidate hit*

> If the server object isn't modified, the server sends the client a small HTTP 304 Not Modified response. This is depicted in Figure 7-6.

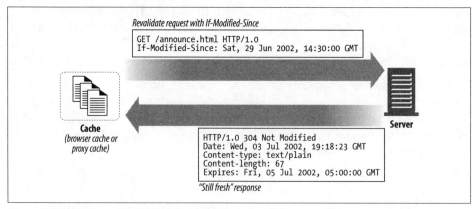

Figure 7-6. HTTP uses If-Modified-Since header for revalidation

*Revalidate miss*

> If the server object is different from the cached copy, the server sends the client a normal HTTP 200 OK response, with the full content.

*Object deleted*
> If the server object has been deleted, the server sends back a 404 Not Found response, and the cache deletes its copy.

## Hit Rate

The fraction of requests that are served from cache is called the *cache hit rate* (or cache hit ratio),[*] or sometimes the *document hit rate* (or document hit ratio). The hit rate ranges from 0 to 1 but is often described as a percentage, where 0% means that every request was a miss (had to get the document across the network), and 100% means every request was a hit (had a copy in the cache).[†]

Cache administrators would like the cache hit rate to approach 100%. The actual hit rate you get depends on how big your cache is, how similar the interests of the cache users are, how frequently the cached data is changing or personalized, and how the caches are configured. Hit rate is notoriously difficult to predict, but a hit rate of 40% is decent for a modest web cache today. The nice thing about caches is that even a modest-sized cache may contain enough popular documents to significantly improve performance and reduce traffic. Caches work hard to ensure that useful content stays in the cache.

## Byte Hit Rate

Document hit rate doesn't tell the whole story, though, because documents are not all the same size. Some large objects might be accessed less often but contribute more to overall data traffic, because of their size. For this reason, some people prefer the *byte hit rate* metric (especially those folks who are billed for each byte of traffic!).

The byte hit rate represents the fraction of all bytes transferred that were served from cache. This metric captures the degree of traffic savings. A byte hit rate of 100% means every byte came from the cache, and no traffic went out across the Internet.

Document hit rate and byte hit rate are both useful gauges of cache performance. Document hit rate describes how many web transactions are kept off the outgoing network. Because transactions have a fixed time component that can often be large (setting up a TCP connection to a server, for example), improving the document hit rate will optimize for overall latency (delay) reduction. Byte hit rate describes how many bytes are kept off the Internet. Improving the byte hit rate will optimize for bandwidth savings.

---

[*] The term "hit ratio" probably is better than "hit rate," because "hit rate" mistakenly suggests a time factor. However, "hit rate" is in common use, so we use it here.

[†] Sometimes people include revalidate hits in the hit rate, but other times hit rate and revalidate hit rate are measured separately. When you are examining hit rates, be sure you know what counts as a "hit."

## Distinguishing Hits and Misses

Unfortunately, HTTP provides no way for a client to tell if a response was a cache hit or an origin server access. In both cases, the response code will be 200 OK, indicating that the response has a body. Some commercial proxy caches attach additional information to Via headers to describe what happened in the cache.

One way that a client can usually detect if the response came from a cache is to use the Date header. By comparing the value of the Date header in the response to the current time, a client can often detect a cached response by its older date value. Another way a client can detect a cached response is the Age header, which tells how old the response is (see "Age" in Appendix C).

# Cache Topologies

Caches can be dedicated to a single user or shared between thousands of users. Dedicated caches are called *private caches*. Private caches are personal caches, containing popular pages for a single user (Figure 7-7a). Shared caches are called *public caches*. Public caches contain the pages popular in the user community (Figure 7-7b).

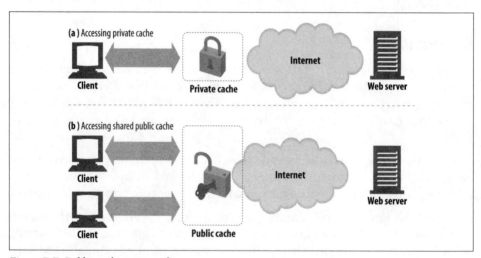

*Figure 7-7. Public and private caches*

## Private Caches

Private caches don't need much horsepower or storage space, so they can be made small and cheap. Web browsers have private caches built right in—most browsers cache popular documents in the disk and memory of your personal computer and allow you to configure the cache size and settings. You also can peek inside the browser caches to see what they contain. For example, with Microsoft Internet

Explorer, you can get the cache contents from the Tools → Internet Options... dialog box. MSIE calls the cached documents "Temporary Files" and lists them in a file display, along with the associated URLs and document expiration times. You can view Netscape Navigator's cache contents through the special URL *about:cache*, which gives you a "Disk Cache statistics" page showing the cache contents.

## Public Proxy Caches

Public caches are special, shared proxy servers called *caching proxy servers* or, more commonly, *proxy caches* (proxies were discussed in Chapter 6). Proxy caches serve documents from the local cache or contact the server on the user's behalf. Because a public cache receives accesses from multiple users, it has more opportunity to eliminate redundant traffic.[*]

In Figure 7-8a, each client redundantly accesses a new, "hot" document (not yet in the private cache). Each private cache fetches the same document, crossing the network multiple times. With a shared, public cache, as in Figure 7-8b, the cache needs to fetch the popular object only once, and it uses the shared copy to service all requests, reducing network traffic.

Proxy caches follow the rules for proxies described in Chapter 6. You can configure your browser to use a proxy cache by specifying a manual proxy or by configuring a proxy auto-configuration file (see "Client Proxy Configuration: Manual" in Chapter 6). You also can force HTTP requests through caches without configuring your browser by using intercepting proxies (see Chapter 20).

## Proxy Cache Hierarchies

In practice, it often makes sense to deploy *hierarchies* of caches, where cache misses in smaller caches are funneled to larger *parent caches* that service the leftover "distilled" traffic. Figure 7-9 shows a two-level cache hierarchy.[†] The idea is to use small, inexpensive caches near the clients and progressively larger, more powerful caches up the hierarchy to hold documents shared by many users.[‡]

Hopefully, most users will get cache hits on the nearby, level-1 caches (as shown in Figure 7-9a). If not, larger parent caches may be able to handle their requests (Figure 7-9b). For deep cache hierarchies it's possible to go through long chains of

---

[*] Because a public cache caches the diverse interests of the user community, it needs to be large enough to hold a set of popular documents, without being swept clean by individual user interests.

[†] If the clients are browsers with browser caches, Figure 7-9 technically shows a *three*-level cache hierarchy.

[‡] Parent caches may need to be larger, to hold the documents popular across more users, and higher-performance, because they receive the aggregate traffic of many children, whose interests may be diverse.

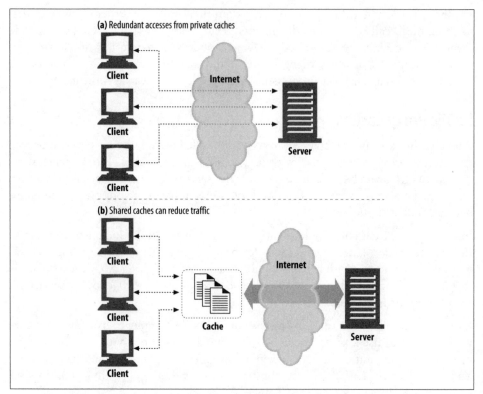

*Figure 7-8. Shared, public caches can decrease network traffic*

caches, but each intervening proxy does impose some performance penalty that can become noticeable as the proxy chain becomes long.[*]

## Cache Meshes, Content Routing, and Peering

Some network architects build complex *cache meshes* instead of simple cache hierarchies. Proxy caches in cache meshes talk to each other in more sophisticated ways, and make dynamic cache communication decisions, deciding which parent caches to talk to, or deciding to bypass caches entirely and direct themselves to the origin server. Such proxy caches can be described as *content routers*, because they make routing decisions about how to access, manage, and deliver content.

Caches designed for content routing within cache meshes may do all of the following (among other things):

- Select between a parent cache or origin server dynamically, based on the URL.

- Select a particular parent cache dynamically, based on the URL.

---

[*] In practice, network architects try to limit themselves to two or three proxies in a row. However, a new generation of high-performance proxy servers may make proxy-chain length less of an issue.

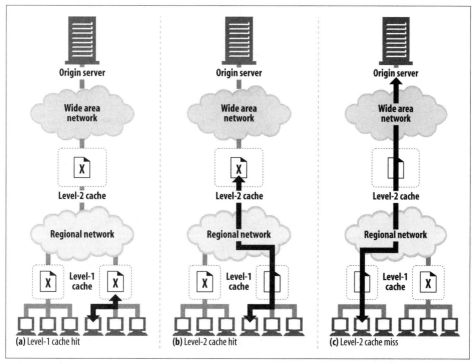

Figure 7-9. Accessing documents in a two-level cache hierarchy

- Search caches in the local area for a cached copy before going to a parent cache.
- Allow other caches to access portions of their cached content, but do not permit Internet transit through their cache.

These more complex relationships between caches allow different organizations to *peer* with each other, connecting their caches for mutual benefit. Caches that provide selective peering support are called *sibling caches* (Figure 7-10). Because HTTP doesn't provide sibling cache support, people have extended HTTP with protocols, such as the Internet Cache Protocol (ICP) and the HyperText Caching Protocol (HTCP). We'll talk about these protocols in Chapter 20.

## Cache Processing Steps

Modern commercial proxy caches are quite complicated. They are built to be very high-performance and to support advanced features of HTTP and other technologies. But, despite some subtle details, the basic workings of a web cache are mostly simple. A basic cache-processing sequence for an HTTP GET message consists of seven steps (illustrated in Figure 7-11):

1. Receiving—Cache reads the arriving request message from the network.
2. Parsing—Cache parses the message, extracting the URL and headers.

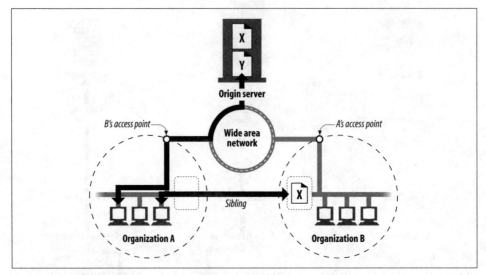

*Figure 7-10. Sibling caches*

3. Lookup—Cache checks if a local copy is available and, if not, fetches a copy (and stores it locally).

4. Freshness check—Cache checks if cached copy is fresh enough and, if not, asks server for any updates.

5. Response creation—Cache makes a response message with the new headers and cached body.

6. Sending—Cache sends the response back to the client over the network.

7. Logging—Optionally, cache creates a log file entry describing the transaction.

## Step 1: Receiving

In Step 1, the cache detects activity on a network connection and reads the incoming data. High-performance caches read data simultaneously from multiple incoming connections and begin processing the transaction before the entire message has arrived.

## Step 2: Parsing

Next, the cache parses the request message into pieces and places the header parts in easy-to-manipulate data structures. This makes it easier for the caching software to process the header fields and fiddle with them.*

---

* The parser also is responsible for normalizing the parts of the header so that unimportant differences, like capitalization or alternate date formats, all are viewed equivalently. Also, because some request messages contain a full absolute URL and other request messages contain a relative URL and Host header, the parser typically hides these details (see "Relative URLs" in Chapter 2).

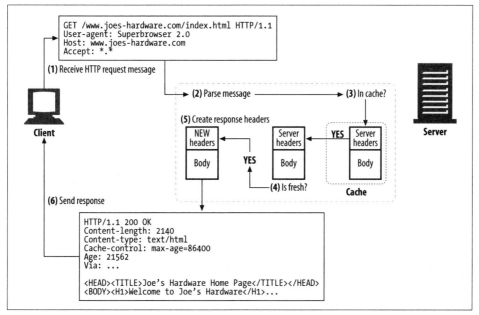

```
GET /www.joes-hardware.com/index.html HTTP/1.1
User-agent: Superbrowser 2.0
Host: www.joes-hardware.com
Accept: *.*
```

**(1)** Receive HTTP request message

**Client**

**(2)** Parse message ———————→ **(3)** In cache?

**(5)** Create response headers

NEW headers
Body

**YES**

Server headers
Body

**(4)** Is fresh?

**YES**

Server headers
Body

**Cache**

**Server**

**(6)** Send response

```
HTTP/1.1 200 OK
Content-length: 2140
Content-type: text/html
Cache-control: max-age=86400
Age: 21562
Via: ...

<HEAD><TITLE>Joe's Hardware Home Page</TITLE></HEAD>
<BODY><H1>Welcome to Joe's Hardware</H1>...
```

*Figure 7-11. Processing a fresh cache hit*

## Step 3: Lookup

In Step 3, the cache takes the URL and checks for a local copy. The local copy might be stored in memory, on a local disk, or even in another nearby computer. Professional-grade caches use fast algorithms to determine whether an object is available in the local cache. If the document is not available locally, it can be fetched from the origin server or a parent proxy, or return a failure, based on the situation and configuration.

The cached object contains the server response body and the original server response headers, so the correct server headers can be returned during a cache hit. The cached object also includes some *metadata*, used for bookkeeping how long the object has been sitting in the cache, how many times it was used, etc.*

## Step 4: Freshness Check

HTTP lets caches keep copies of server documents for a period of time. During this time, the document is considered "fresh" and the cache can serve the document without contacting the server. But once the cached copy has sat around for too long, past the document's *freshness limit*, the object is considered "stale," and the cache needs to

---

* Sophisticated caches also keep a copy of the original client response headers that yielded the server response, for use in HTTP/1.1 content negotiation (see Chapter 17).

revalidate with the server to check for any document changes before serving it. Complicating things further are any request headers that a client sends to a cache, which themselves can force the cache to either revalidate or avoid validation altogether.

HTTP has a set of very complicated rules for freshness checking, made worse by the large number of configuration options cache products support and by the need to interoperate with non-HTTP freshness standards. We'll devote most of the rest of this chapter to explaining freshness calculations.

## Step 5: Response Creation

Because we want the cached response to look like it came from the origin server, the cache uses the cached server response headers as the starting point for the response headers. These base headers are then modified and augmented by the cache.

The cache is responsible for adapting the headers to match the client. For example, the server may return an HTTP/1.0 response (or even an HTTP/0.9 response), while the client expects an HTTP/1.1 response, in which case the cache must translate the headers accordingly. Caches also insert cache freshness information (Cache-Control, Age, and Expires headers) and often include a Via header to note that a proxy cache served the request.

Note that the cache should *not* adjust the Date header. The Date header represents the date of the object when it was originally generated at the origin server.

## Step 6: Sending

Once the response headers are ready, the cache sends the response back to the client. Like all proxy servers, a proxy cache needs to manage the connection with the client. High-performance caches work hard to send the data efficiently, often avoiding copying the document content between the local storage and the network I/O buffers.

## Step 7: Logging

Most caches keep log files and statistics about cache usage. After each cache transaction is complete, the cache updates statistics counting the number of cache hits and misses (and other relevant metrics) and inserts an entry into a log file showing the request type, URL, and what happened.

The most popular cache log formats are the Squid log format and the Netscape extended common log format, but many cache products allow you to create custom log files. We discuss log file formats in detail in Chapter 21.

## Cache Processing Flowchart

Figure 7-12 shows, in simplified form, how a cache processes a request to GET a URL.*

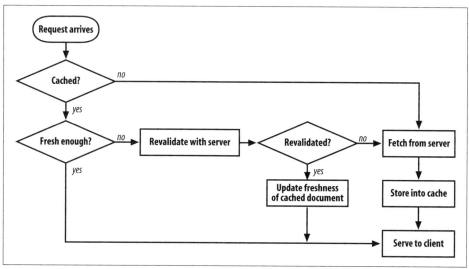

*Figure 7-12. Cache GET request flowchart*

# Keeping Copies Fresh

Cached copies might not all be consistent with the documents on the server. After all, documents do change over time. Reports might change monthly. Online newspapers change daily. Financial data may change every few seconds. Caches would be useless if they always served old data. Cached data needs to maintain some consistency with the server data.

HTTP includes simple mechanisms to keep cached data sufficiently consistent with servers, without requiring servers to remember which caches have copies of their documents. HTTP calls these simple mechanisms *document expiration* and *server revalidation*.

## Document Expiration

HTTP lets an origin server attach an "expiration date" to each document, using special HTTP Cache-Control and Expires headers (Figure 7-13). Like an expiration date on a quart of milk, these headers dictate how long content should be viewed as fresh.

---

* The revalidation and fetching of a resource as outlined in Figure 7-12 can be done in one step with a conditional request (see "Revalidation with Conditional Methods").

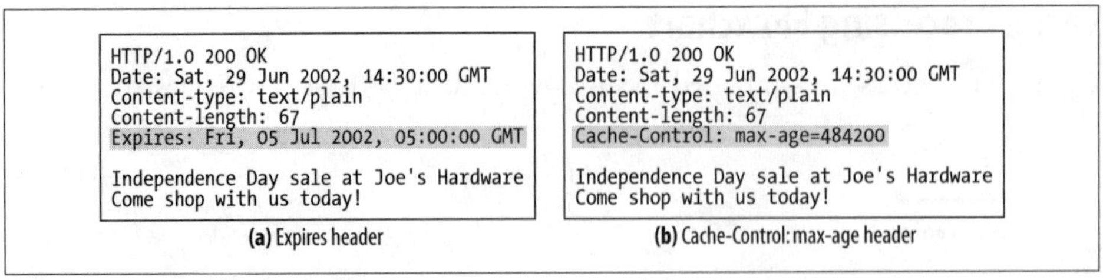

```
HTTP/1.0 200 OK
Date: Sat, 29 Jun 2002, 14:30:00 GMT
Content-type: text/plain
Content-length: 67
Expires: Fri, 05 Jul 2002, 05:00:00 GMT

Independence Day sale at Joe's Hardware
Come shop with us today!
```

```
HTTP/1.0 200 OK
Date: Sat, 29 Jun 2002, 14:30:00 GMT
Content-type: text/plain
Content-length: 67
Cache-Control: max-age=484200

Independence Day sale at Joe's Hardware
Come shop with us today!
```

**(a)** Expires header

**(b)** Cache-Control: max-age header

*Figure 7-13. Expires and Cache Control headers*

Until a cache document expires, the cache can serve the copy as often as it wants, without ever contacting the server—unless, of course, a client request includes headers that prevent serving a cached or unvalidated resource. But, once the cached document expires, the cache must check with the server to ask if the document has changed and, if so, get a fresh copy (with a new expiration date).

## Expiration Dates and Ages

Servers specify expiration dates using the HTTP/1.0+ Expires or the HTTP/1.1 Cache-Control: max-age response headers, which accompany a response body. The Expires and Cache-Control: max-age headers do basically the same thing, but the newer Cache-Control header is preferred, because it uses a relative time instead of an absolute date. Absolute dates depend on computer clocks being set correctly. Table 7-2 lists the expiration response headers.

*Table 7-2. Expiration response headers*

| Header | Description |
|---|---|
| Cache-Control: max-age | The max-age value defines the maximum age of the document—the maximum legal elapsed time (in seconds) from when a document is first generated to when it can no longer be considered fresh enough to serve. |
| | `Cache-Control: max-age=484200` |
| Expires | Specifies an absolute expiration date. If the expiration date is in the past, the document is no longer fresh. |
| | `Expires: Fri, 05 Jul 2002, 05:00:00 GMT` |

Let's say today is June 29, 2002 at 9:30 am Eastern Standard Time (EST), and Joe's Hardware store is getting ready for a Fourth of July sale (only five days away). Joe wants to put a special web page on his web server and set it to expire at midnight EST on the night of July 5, 2002. If Joe's server uses the older-style Expires headers, the server response message (Figure 7-13a) might include this header:[*]

```
Expires: Fri, 05 Jul 2002, 05:00:00 GMT
```

---

[*] Note that all HTTP dates and times are expressed in Greenwich Mean Time (GMT). GMT is the time at the prime meridian (0° longitude) that passes through Greenwich, UK. GMT is five hours ahead of U.S. Eastern Standard Time, so midnight EST is 05:00 GMT.

If Joe's server uses the newer Cache-Control: max-age headers, the server response message (Figure 7-13b) might contain this header:

```
Cache-Control: max-age=484200
```

In case that wasn't immediately obvious, 484,200 is the number of seconds between the current date, June 29, 2002 at 9:30 am EST, and the sale end date, July 5, 2002 at midnight. There are 134.5 hours (about 5 days) until the sale ends. With 3,600 seconds in each hour, that leaves 484,200 seconds until the sale ends.

## Server Revalidation

Just because a cached document has expired doesn't mean it is actually different from what's living on the origin server; it just means that it's time to check. This is called "server revalidation," meaning the cache needs to ask the origin server whether the document has changed:

- If revalidation shows the content *has changed*, the cache gets a new copy of the document, stores it in place of the old data, and sends the document to the client.
- If revalidation shows the content *has not changed*, the cache only gets new headers, including a new expiration date, and updates the headers in the cache.

This is a nice system. The cache doesn't have to verify a document's freshness for every request—it has to revalidate with the server only once the document has expired. This saves server traffic and provides better user response time, without serving stale content.

The HTTP protocol requires a correctly behaving cache to return one of the following:

- A cached copy that is "fresh enough"
- A cached copy that has been revalidated with the server to ensure it's still fresh
- An error message, if the origin server to revalidate with is down[*]
- A cached copy, with an attached warning that it might be incorrect

## Revalidation with Conditional Methods

HTTP's conditional methods make revalidation efficient. HTTP allows a cache to send a "conditional GET" to the origin server, asking the server to send back an object body only if the document is different from the copy currently in the cache. In this manner, the freshness check and the object fetch are combined into a single conditional GET. Conditional GETs are initiated by adding special conditional headers to GET request messages. The web server returns the object only if the condition is true.

---

[*] If the origin server is not accessible, but the cache needs to revalidate, the cache must return an error or a warning describing the communication failure. Otherwise, pages from a removed server may live in network caches for an arbitrary time into the future.

HTTP defines five conditional request headers. The two that are most useful for cache revalidation are If-Modified-Since and If-None-Match.* All conditional headers begin with the prefix "If-". Table 7-3 lists the conditional response headers used in cache revalidation.

*Table 7-3. Two conditional headers used in cache revalidation*

| Header | Description |
|--------|-------------|
| If-Modified-Since: <*date*> | Perform the requested method if the document has been modified since the specified date. This is used in conjunction with the Last-Modified server response header, to fetch content only if the content has been modified from the cached version. |
| If-None-Match: <*tags*> | Instead of matching on last-modified date, the server may provide special tags (see "ETag" in Appendix C) on the document that act like serial numbers. The If-None-Match header performs the requested method if the cached tags differ from the tags in the server's document. |

## If-Modified-Since: Date Revalidation

The most common cache revalidation header is If-Modified-Since. If-Modified-Since revalidation requests often are called "IMS" requests. IMS requests instruct a server to perform the request only if the resource has changed since a certain date:

- If the document was modified since the specified date, the If-Modified-Since condition is true, and the GET succeeds normally. The new document is returned to the cache, along with new headers containing, among other information, a new expiration date.

- If the document was not modified since the specified date, the condition is false, and a small 304 Not Modified response message is returned to the client, without a document body, for efficiency.† Headers are returned in the response; however, only the headers that need updating from the original need to be returned. For example, the Content-Type header does not usually need to be sent, since it usually has not changed. A new expiration date typically is sent.

The If-Modified-Since header works in conjunction with the Last-Modified server response header. The origin server attaches the last modification date to served documents. When a cache wants to revalidate a cached document, it includes an If-Modified-Since header with the date the cached copy was last modified:

```
If-Modified-Since: <cached last-modified date>
```

---

* Other conditional headers include If-Unmodified-Since (useful for partial document transfers, when you need to ensure the document is unchanged before you fetch another piece of it), If-Range (to support caching of incomplete documents), and If-Match (useful for concurrency control when dealing with web servers).

† If an old server that doesn't recognize the If-Modified-Since header gets the conditional request, it interprets it as a normal GET. In this case, the system will still work, but it will be less efficient due to unnecessary transmittal of unchanged document data.

If the content has changed in the meantime, the last modification date will be different, and the origin server will send back the new document. Otherwise, the server will note that the cache's last-modified date matches the server document's current last-modified date, and it will return a 304 Not Modified response.

For example, as shown in Figure 7-14, if your cache revalidates Joe's Hardware's Fourth of July sale announcement on July 3, you will receive back a Not Modified response (Figure 7-14a). But if your cache revalidates the document after the sale ends at midnight on July 5, the cache will receive a new document, because the server content has changed (Figure 7-14b).

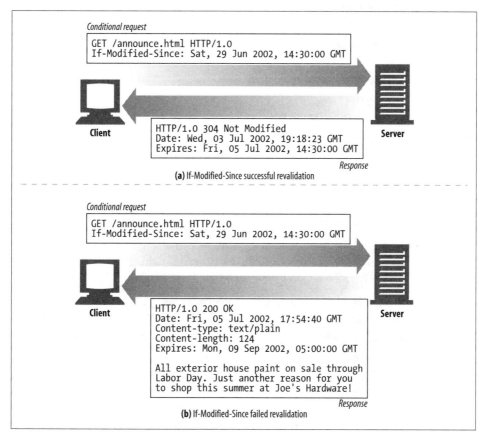

*Figure 7-14. If-Modified-Since revalidations return 304 if unchanged or 200 with new body if changed*

Note that some web servers don't implement If-Modified-Since as a true date comparison. Instead, they do a string match between the IMS date and the last-modified date. As such, the semantics behave as "if not last modified on this exact date" instead of "if modified since this date." This alternative semantic works fine for cache expiration, when you are using the last-modified date as a kind of serial number, but it prevents clients from using the If-Modified-Since header for true time-based purposes.

## If-None-Match: Entity Tag Revalidation

There are some situations when the last-modified date revalidation isn't adequate:

- Some documents may be rewritten periodically (e.g., from a background process) but actually often contain the same data. The modification dates will change, even though the content hasn't.

- Some documents may have changed, but only in ways that aren't important enough to warrant caches worldwide to reload the data (e.g., spelling or comment changes).

- Some servers cannot accurately determine the last modification dates of their pages.

- For servers that serve documents that change in sub-second intervals (e.g. real-time monitors), the one-second granularity of modification dates might not be adequate.

To get around these problems, HTTP allows you to compare document "version identifiers" called *entity tags* (ETags). Entity tags are arbitrary labels (quoted strings) attached to the document. They might contain a serial number or version name for the document, or a checksum or other fingerprint of the document content.

When the publisher makes a document change, he can change the document's entity tag to represent this new version. Caches can then use the If-None-Match conditional header to GET a new copy of the document if the entity tags have changed.

In Figure 7-15, the cache has a document with entity tag "v2.6". It revalidates with the origin server asking for a new object only if the tag "v2.6" no longer matches. In Figure 7-15, the tag still matches, so a 304 Not Modified response is returned.

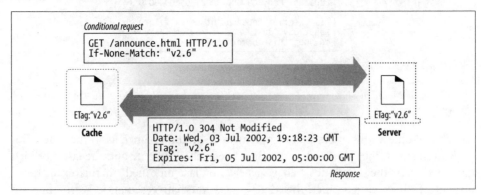

*Figure 7-15. If-None-Match revalidates because entity tag still matches*

If the entity tag on the server had changed (perhaps to "v3.0"), the server would return the new content in a 200 OK response, along with the content and new ETag.

Several entity tags can be included in an If-None-Match header, to tell the server that the cache already has copies of objects with those entity tags:

```
If-None-Match: "v2.6"
If-None-Match: "v2.4","v2.5","v2.6"
If-None-Match: "foobar","A34FAC0095","Profiles in Courage"
```

## Weak and Strong Validators

Caches use entity tags to determine whether the cached version is up-to-date with respect to the server (much like they use last-modified dates). In this way, entity tags and last-modified dates both are *cache validators*.

Servers may sometimes want to allow cosmetic or insignificant changes to documents without invalidating all cached copies. HTTP/1.1 supports "weak validators," which allow the server to claim "good enough" equivalence even if the contents have changed slightly.

Strong validators change any time the content changes. Weak validators allow some content change but generally change when the significant meaning of the content changes. Some operations cannot be performed using weak validators (such as conditional partial-range fetches), so servers identify validators that are weak with a "W/" prefix:

```
ETag: W/"v2.6"
If-None-Match: W/"v2.6"
```

A strong entity tag must change whenever the associated entity value changes in any way. A weak entity tag should change whenever the associated entity changes in a semantically significant way.

Note that an origin server must avoid reusing a specific strong entity tag value for two different entities, or reusing a specific weak entity tag value for two semantically different entities. Cache entries might persist for arbitrarily long periods, regardless of expiration times, so it might be inappropriate to expect that a cache will never again attempt to validate an entry using a validator that it obtained at some point in the past.

## When to Use Entity Tags and Last-Modified Dates

HTTP/1.1 clients must use an entity tag validator if a server sends back an entity tag. If the server sends back only a Last-Modified value, the client can use If-Modified-Since validation. If both an entity tag and a last-modified date are available, the client should use both revalidation schemes, allowing both HTTP/1.0 and HTTP/1.1 caches to respond appropriately.

HTTP/1.1 origin servers should send an entity tag validator unless it is not feasible to generate one, and it may be a weak entity tag instead of a strong entity tag, if there are benefits to weak validators. Also, it's preferred to also send a last-modified value.

If an HTTP/1.1 cache or server receives a request with both If-Modified-Since and entity tag conditional headers, it must not return a 304 Not Modified response unless doing so is consistent with all of the conditional header fields in the request.

# Controlling Cachability

HTTP defines several ways for a server to specify how long a document can be cached before it expires. In decreasing order of priority, the server can:

- Attach a Cache-Control: no-store header to the response.
- Attach a Cache-Control: no-cache header to the response.
- Attach a Cache-Control: must-revalidate header to the response.
- Attach a Cache-Control: max-age header to the response.
- Attach an Expires date header to the response.
- Attach no expiration information, letting the cache determine its own heuristic expiration date.

This section describes the cache controlling headers. The next section, "Setting Cache Controls," describes how to assign different cache information to different content.

## No-Cache and No-Store Response Headers

HTTP/1.1 offers several ways to limit the caching of objects, or the serving of cached objects, to maintain freshness. The no-store and no-cache headers prevent caches from serving unverified cached objects:

```
Cache-Control: no-store
Cache-Control: no-cache
Pragma: no-cache
```

A response that is marked "no-store" forbids a cache from making a copy of the response. A cache would typically forward a no-store response to the client, and then delete the object, as would a non-caching proxy server.

A response that is marked "no-cache" can actually be stored in the local cache storage. It just cannot be served from the cache to the client without first revalidating the freshness with the origin server. A better name for this header might be "do-not-serve-from-cache-without-revalidation."

The Pragma: no-cache header is included in HTTP/1.1 for backward compatibility with HTTP/1.0+. HTTP 1.1 applications should use Cache-Control: no-cache, except when dealing with HTTP 1.0 applications, which understand only Pragma: no-cache.*

## Max-Age Response Headers

The Cache-Control: max-age header indicates the number of seconds since it came from the server for which a document can be considered fresh. There is also an s-maxage header (note the absence of a hyphen in "maxage") that acts like max-age but applies only to shared (public) caches:

```
Cache-Control: max-age=3600
Cache-Control: s-maxage=3600
```

Servers can request that caches either not cache a document or refresh on every access by setting the maximum aging to zero:

```
Cache-Control: max-age=0
Cache-Control: s-maxage=0
```

## Expires Response Headers

The deprecated Expires header specifies an actual expiration date instead of a time in seconds. The HTTP designers later decided that, because many servers have unsynchronized or incorrect clocks, it would be better to represent expiration in elapsed seconds, rather than absolute time. An analogous freshness lifetime can be calculated by computing the number of seconds difference between the expires value and the date value:

```
Expires: Fri, 05 Jul 2002, 05:00:00 GMT
```

Some servers also send back an Expires: 0 response header to try to make documents always expire, but this syntax is illegal and can cause problems with some software. You should try to support this construct as input, but shouldn't generate it.

## Must-Revalidate Response Headers

Caches may be configured to serve stale (expired) objects, in order to improve performance. If an origin server wishes caches to strictly adhere to expiration information, it can attach a Cache-Control:

```
Cache-Control: must-revalidate
```

The Cache-Control: must-revalidate response header tells caches they cannot serve a stale copy of this object without first revalidating with the origin server. Caches are still free to serve fresh copies. If the origin server is unavailable when a cache attempts a must-revalidate freshness check, the cache must return a 504 Gateway Timeout error.

---

\* Pragma no-cache is technically valid only for HTTP requests, yet it is widely used as an extension header for both HTTP erquests and responses.

## Heuristic Expiration

If the response doesn't contain either a Cache-Control: max-age header or an Expires header, the cache may compute a heuristic maximum age. Any algorithm may be used, but if the resulting maximum age is greater than 24 hours, a Heuristic Expiration Warning (Warning 13) header should be added to the response headers. As far as we know, few browsers make this warning information available to users.

One popular heuristic expiration algorithm, the *LM-Factor* algorithm, can be used if the document contains a last-modified date. The LM-Factor algorithm uses the last-modified date as an estimate of how volatile a document is. Here's the logic:

- If a cached document was last changed in the distant past, it may be a stable document and less likely to change suddenly, so it is safer to keep it in the cache longer.

- If the cached document was modified just recently, it probably changes frequently, so we should cache it only a short while before revalidating with the server.

The actual LM-Factor algorithm computes the time between when the cache talked to the server and when the server said the document was last modified, takes some fraction of this intervening time, and uses this fraction as the freshness duration in the cache. Here is some Perl pseudocode for the LM-factor algorithm:

```
$time_since_modify = max(0, $server_Date - $server_Last_Modified);
$server_freshness_limit = int($time_since_modify * $lm_factor);
```

Figure 7-16 depicts the LM-factor freshness period graphically. The cross-hatched line indicates the freshness period, using an LM-factor of 0.2.

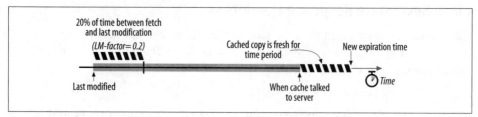

*Figure 7-16. Computing a freshness period using the LM-Factor algorithm*

Typically, people place upper bounds on heuristic freshness periods so they can't grow excessively large. A week is typical, though more conservative sites use a day.

Finally, if you don't have a last-modified date either, the cache doesn't have much information to go on. Caches typically assign a default freshness period (an hour or a day is typical) for documents without any freshness clues. More conservative caches sometimes choose freshness lifetimes of 0 for these heuristic documents, forcing the cache to validate that the data is still fresh before each time it is served to a client.

One last note about heuristic freshness calculations—they are more common than you might think. Many origin servers still don't generate Expires and max-age headers. Pick your cache's expiration defaults carefully!

## Client Freshness Constraints

Web browsers have a Refresh or Reload button to forcibly refresh content, which might be stale in the browser or proxy caches. The Refresh button issues a GET request with additional Cache-control request headers that force a revalidation or unconditional fetch from the server. The precise Refresh behavior depends on the particular browser, document, and intervening cache configurations.

Clients use Cache-Control request headers to tighten or loosen expiration constraints. Clients can use Cache-control headers to make the expiration more strict, for applications that need the very freshest documents (such as the manual Refresh button). On the other hand, clients might also want to relax the freshness requirements as a compromise to improve performance, reliability, or expenses. Table 7-4 summarizes the Cache-Control request directives.

*Table 7-4. Cache-Control request directives*

| Directive | Purpose |
| --- | --- |
| Cache-Control: max-stale<br>Cache-Control: max-stale = $<s>$ | The cache is free to serve a stale document. If the $<s>$ parameter is specified, the document must not be stale by more than this amount of time. This relaxes the caching rules. |
| Cache-Control: min-fresh = $<s>$ | The document must still be fresh for at least $<s>$ seconds in the future. This makes the caching rules more strict. |
| Cache-Control: max-age = $<s>$ | The cache cannot return a document that has been cached for longer than $<s>$ seconds. This directive makes the caching rules more strict, unless the max-stale directive also is set, in which case the age can exceed its expiration time. |
| Cache-Control: no-cache<br>Pragma: no-cache | This client won't accept a cached resource unless it has been revalidated. |
| Cache-Control: no-store | The cache should delete every trace of the document from storage as soon as possible, because it might contain sensitive information. |
| Cache-Control: only-if-cached | The client wants a copy only if it is in the cache. |

## Cautions

Document expiration isn't a perfect system. If a publisher accidentally assigns an expiration date too far in the future, any document changes she needs to make won't necessarily show up in all caches until the document has expired.* For this reason,

---

\* Document expiration is a form of "time to live" technique used in many Internet protocols, such as DNS. DNS, like HTTP, has trouble if you publish an expiration date far in the future and then find that you need to make a change. However, HTTP provides mechanisms for a client to override and force a reloading, unlike DNS.

many publishers don't use distant expiration dates. Also, many publishers don't even use expiration dates, making it tough for caches to know how long the document will be fresh.

# Setting Cache Controls

Different web servers provide different mechanisms for setting HTTP cache-control and expiration headers. In this section, we'll talk briefly about how the popular Apache web server supports cache controls. Refer to your web server documentation for specific details.

## Controlling HTTP Headers with Apache

The Apache web server provides several mechanisms for setting HTTP cache-controlling headers. Many of these mechanisms are not enabled by default—you have to enable them (in some cases first obtaining Apache extension modules). Here is a brief description of some of the Apache features:

*mod_headers*

> The mod_headers module lets you set individual headers. Once this module is loaded, you can augment the Apache configuration files with directives to set individual HTTP headers. You also can use these settings in combination with Apache's regular expressions and filters to associate headers with individual content. Here is an example of a configuration that could mark all HTML files in a directory as uncachable:
>
> ```
> <Files *.html>
>     Header set Cache-control no-cache
> </Files>
> ```

*mod_expires*

> The mod_expires module provides program logic to automatically generate Expires headers with the correct expiration dates. This module allows you to set expiration dates for some time period after a document was last accessed or after its last-modified date. The module also lets you assign different expiration dates to different file types and use convenient verbose descriptions, like "access plus 1 month," to describe cachability. Here are a few examples:
>
> ```
> ExpiresDefault A3600
> ExpiresDefault M86400
> ExpiresDefault "access plus 1 week"
> ExpiresByType text/html "modification plus 2 days 6 hours 12 minutes"
> ```

*mod_cern_meta*

> The mod_cern_meta module allows you to associate a file of HTTP headers with particular objects. When you enable this module, you create a set of "metafiles," one for each document you want to control, and add the desired headers to each metafile.

## Controlling HTML Caching Through HTTP-EQUIV

HTTP server response headers are used to carry back document expiration and cache-control information. Web servers interact with configuration files to assign the correct cache-control headers to served documents.

To make it easier for authors to assign HTTP header information to served HTML documents without interacting with web server configuration files, HTML 2.0 defined the <META HTTP-EQUIV> tag. This optional tag sits at the top of an HTML document and defines HTTP headers that should be associated with the document. Here is an example of a <META HTTP-EQUIV> tag set to mark the HTML document uncachable:

```
<HTML>
  <HEAD>
    <TITLE>My Document</TITLE>
    <META HTTP-EQUIV="Cache-control" CONTENT="no-cache">
  </HEAD>
    ...
```

This HTTP-EQUIV tag was originally intended to be used by web servers. Web servers were supposed to parse HTML for <META HTTP-EQUIV> tags and insert the prescribed headers into the HTTP response, as documented in HTML RFC 1866:

> An HTTP server may use this information to process the document. In particular, it may include a header field in the responses to requests for this document: the header name is taken from the HTTP-EQUIV attribute value, and the header value is taken from the value of the CONTENT attribute.

Unfortunately, few web servers and proxies support this optional feature because of the extra server load, the values being static, and the fact that it supports only HTML and not the many other file types.

However, some browsers do parse and adhere to HTTP-EQUIV tags in the HTML content, treating the embedded headers like real HTTP headers (Figure 7-17). This is unfortunate, because HTML browsers that do support HTTP-EQUIV may apply different cache-control rules than intervening proxy caches. This causes confusing cache expiration behavior.

In general, <META HTTP-EQUIV> tags are a poor way of controlling document cachability. The only sure-fire way to communicate cache-control requests for documents is through HTTP headers sent by a properly configured server.

# Detailed Algorithms

The HTTP specification provides a detailed, but slightly obscure and often confusing, algorithm for computing document aging and cache freshness. In this section, we'll discuss the HTTP freshness computation algorithms in detail (the "Fresh enough?" diamond in Figure 7-12) and explain the motivation behind them.

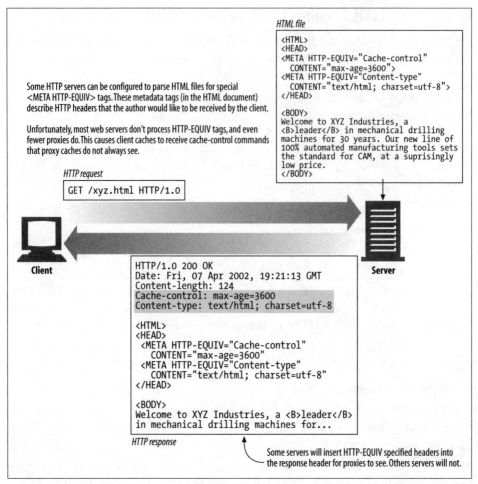

*Figure 7-17. HTTP-EQUIV tags cause problems, because most software ignores them*

This section will be most useful to readers working with cache internals. To help illustrate the wording in the HTTP specification, we will make use of Perl pseudocode. If you aren't interested in the gory details of cache expiration formulas, feel free to skip this section.

## Age and Freshness Lifetime

To tell whether a cached document is fresh enough to serve, a cache needs to compute only two values: the cached copy's *age* and the cached copy's *freshness lifetime*. If the age of a cached copy is less than the freshness lifetime, the copy is fresh enough to serve. In Perl:

```
$is_fresh_enough = ($age < $freshness_lifetime);
```

The age of the document is the total time the document has "aged" since it was sent from the server (or was last revalidated by the server).[*] Because a cache might not know if a document response is coming from an upstream cache or a server, it can't assume that the document is brand new. It must determine the document's age, either from an explicit Age header (preferred) or by processing the server-generated Date header.

The freshness lifetime of a document tells how old a cached copy can get before it is no longer fresh enough to serve to clients. The freshness lifetime takes into account the expiration date of the document and any freshness overrides the client might request.

Some clients may be willing to accept slightly stale documents (using the Cache-Control: max-stale header). Other clients may not accept documents that will become stale in the near future (using the Cache-Control: min-fresh header). The cache combines the server expiration information with the client freshness requirements to determine the maximum freshness lifetime.

## Age Computation

The age of the response is the total time since the response was issued from the server (or revalidated from the server). The age includes the time the response has floated around in the routers and gateways of the Internet, the time stored in intermediate caches, and the time the response has been resident in your cache. Example 7-1 provides pseudocode for the age calculation.

*Example 7-1. HTTP/1.1 age-calculation algorithm calculates the overall age of a cached document*

```
$apparent_age = max(0, $time_got_response - $Date_header_value);
$corrected_apparent_age = max($apparent_age, $Age_header_value);
$response_delay_estimate = ($time_got_response - $time_issued_request);
$age_when_document_arrived_at_our_cache =
    $corrected_apparent_age + $response_delay_estimate;
$how_long_copy_has_been_in_our_cache = $current_time - $time_got_response;

$age = $age_when_document_arrived_at_our_cache +
        $how_long_copy_has_been_in_our_cache;
```

The particulars of HTTP age calculation are a bit tricky, but the basic concept is simple. Caches can tell how old the response was when it arrived at the cache by examining the Date or Age headers. Caches also can note how long the document has been sitting in the local cache. Summed together, these values are the entire age of the response. HTTP throws in some magic to attempt to compensate for clock skew and network delays, but the basic computation is simple enough:

```
$age = $age_when_document_arrived_at_our_cache +
        $how_long_copy_has_been_in_our_cache;
```

---

[*] Remember that the server always has the most up-to-date version of any document.

A cache can pretty easily determine how long a cached copy has been cached locally (a matter of simple bookkeeping), but it is harder to determine the age of a response when it arrives at the cache, because not all servers have synchronized clocks and because we don't know where the response has been. The complete age-calculation algorithm tries to remedy this.

## Apparent age is based on the Date header

If all computers shared the same, exactly correct clock, the age of a cached document would simply be the "apparent age" of the document—the current time minus the time when the server sent the document. The server send time is simply the value of the Date header. The simplest initial age calculation would just use the apparent age:

```
$apparent_age = $time_got_response - $Date_header_value;
$age_when_document_arrived_at_our_cache = $apparent_age;
```

Unfortunately, not all clocks are well synchronized. The client and server clocks may differ by many minutes, or even by hours or days when clocks are set improperly.*

Web applications, especially caching proxies, have to be prepared to interact with servers with wildly differing clock values. The problem is called *clock skew*—the difference between two computers' clock settings. Because of clock skew, the apparent age sometimes is inaccurate and occasionally is negative.

If the age is ever negative, we just set it to zero. We also could sanity check that the apparent age isn't ridiculously large, but large apparent ages might actually be correct. We might be talking to a parent cache that has cached the document for a long time (the cache also stores the original Date header):

```
$apparent_age = max(0, $time_got_response - $Date_header_value);
$age_when_document_arrived_at_our_cache = $apparent_age;
```

Be aware that the Date header describes the original origin server date. Proxies and caches must *not* change this date!

## Hop-by-hop age calculations

So, we can eliminate negative ages caused by clock skew, but we can't do much about overall loss of accuracy due to clock skew. HTTP/1.1 attempts to work around the lack of universal synchronized clocks by asking each device to accumulate relative aging into an Age header, as a document passes through proxies and caches. This way, no cross-server, end-to-end clock comparisons are needed.

The Age header value increases as the document passes through proxies. HTTP/1.1-aware applications should augment the Age header value by the time the document

---

* The HTTP specification recommends that clients, servers, and proxies use a time synchronization protocol such as NTP to enforce a consistent time base.

sat in each application and in network transit. Each intermediate application can easily compute the document's resident time by using its local clock.

However, any non-HTTP/1.1 device in the response chain will not recognize the Age header and will either proxy the header unchanged or remove it. So, until HTTP/1.1 is universally adopted, the Age header will be an underestimate of the relative age.

The relative age values are used in addition to the Date-based age calculation, and the most conservative of the two age estimates is chosen, because either the cross-server Date value or the Age-computed value may be an underestimate (the most conservative is the oldest age). This way, HTTP tolerates errors in Age headers as well, while erring on the side of fresher content:

```
$apparent_age = max(0, $time_got_response - $Date_header_value);
$corrected_apparent_age = max($apparent_age, $Age_header_value);
$age_when_document_arrived_at_our_cache = $corrected_apparent_age;
```

### Compensating for network delays

Transactions can be slow. This is the major motivation for caching. But for very slow networks, or overloaded servers, the relative age calculation may significantly underestimate the age of documents if the documents spend a long time stuck in network or server traffic jams.

The Date header indicates when the document left the origin server,* but it doesn't say how long the document spent in transit on the way to the cache. If the document came through a long chain of proxies and parent caches, the network delay might be significant.†

There is no easy way to measure one-way network delay from server to cache, but it is easier to measure the round-trip delay. A cache knows when it requested the document and when it arrived. HTTP/1.1 conservatively corrects for these network delays by adding the entire round-trip delay. This cache-to-server-to-cache delay is an overestimate of the server-to-cache delay, but it is conservative. If it is in error, it will only make the documents appear older than they really are and cause unnecessary revalidations. Here's how the calculation is made:

```
$apparent_age = max(0, $time_got_response - $Date_header_value);
$corrected_apparent_age = max($apparent_age, $Age_header_value);
$response_delay_estimate = ($time_got_response - $time_issued_request);
$age_when_document_arrived_at_our_cache =
    $corrected_apparent_age + $response_delay_estimate;
```

---

* Note that if the document came from a parent cache and not from an origin server, the Date header will reflect the date of the origin server, not of the parent cache.

† In practice, this shouldn't be more than a few tens of seconds (or users will abort), but the HTTP designers wanted to try to support accurate expiration of even short-lifetime objects.

## Complete Age-Calculation Algorithm

The last section showed how to compute the age of an HTTP-carried document when it arrives at a cache. Once this response is stored in the cache, it ages further. When a request arrives for the document in the cache, we need to know how long the document has been resident in the cache, so we can compute the current document age:

```
$age = $age_when_document_arrived_at_our_cache +
       $how_long_copy_has_been_in_our_cache;
```

Ta-da! This gives us the complete HTTP/1.1 age-calculation algorithm we presented in Example 7-1. This is a matter of simple bookkeeping—we know when the document arrived at the cache ($time_got_response) and we know when the current request arrived (right now), so the resident time is just the difference. This is all shown graphically in Figure 7-18.

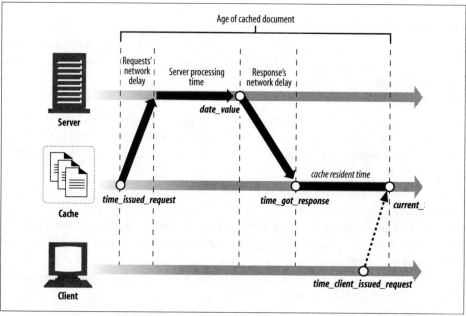

*Figure 7-18. The age of a cached document includes resident time in the network and cache*

## Freshness Lifetime Computation

Recall that we're trying to figure out whether a cached document is fresh enough to serve to a client. To answer this question, we must determine the age of the cached document and compute the freshness lifetime based on server and client constraints. We just explained how to compute the age; now let's move on to freshness lifetimes.

The freshness lifetime of a document tells how old a document is allowed to get before it is no longer fresh enough to serve to a particular client. The freshness lifetime depends on server and client constraints. The server may have information about the publication change rate of the document. Very stable, filed reports may stay fresh for years. Periodicals may be up-to-date only for the time remaining until the next scheduled publication—next week, or 6:00 am tomorrow.

Clients may have certain other guidelines. They may be willing to accept slightly stale content, if it is faster, or they might need the most up-to-date content possible. Caches serve the users. We must adhere to their requests.

## Complete Server-Freshness Algorithm

Example 7-2 shows a Perl algorithm to compute server freshness limits. It returns the maximum age that a document can reach and still be served by the server.

*Example 7-2. Server freshness constraint calculation*

```perl
sub server_freshness_limit
{
    local($heuristic,$server_freshness_limit,$time_since_last_modify);

    $heuristic = 0;

    if ($Max_Age_value_set)
    {
        $server_freshness_limit = $Max_Age_value;
    }
    elsif ($Expires_value_set)
    {
        $server_freshness_limit = $Expires_value - $Date_value;
    }
    elsif ($Last_Modified_value_set)
    {
        $time_since_last_modify = max(0, $Date_value - $Last_Modified_value);
        $server_freshness_limit = int($time_since_last_modify * $lm_factor);
        $heuristic = 1;
    }
    else
    {
        $server_freshness_limit = $default_cache_min_lifetime;
        $heuristic = 1;
    }

    if ($heuristic)
    {
        if ($server_freshness_limit > $default_cache_max_lifetime)
        { $server_freshness_limit = $default_cache_max_lifetime; }
        if ($server_freshness_limit < $default_cache_min_lifetime)
        { $server_freshness_limit = $default_cache_min_lifetime; }
    }

    return($server_freshness_limit);
}
```

Now let's look at how the client can override the document's server-specified age limit. Example 7-3 shows a Perl algorithm to take a server freshness limit and modify it by the client constraints. It returns the maximum age that a document can reach and still be served by the cache without revalidation.

*Example 7-3. Client freshness constraint calculation*

```
sub client_modified_freshness_limit
{
    $age_limit = server_freshness_limit();   ## From Example 7-2

    if ($Max_Stale_value_set)
    {
        if ($Max_Stale_value == $INT_MAX)
        { $age_limit = $INT_MAX; }
        else
        { $age_limit = server_freshness_limit() + $Max_Stale_value; }
    }

    if ($Min_Fresh_value_set)
    {
        $age_limit = min($age_limit, server_freshness_limit() - $Min_Fresh_value_set);
    }

    if ($Max_Age_value_set)
    {
        $age_limit = min($age_limit, $Max_Age_value);
    }
}
```

The whole process involves two variables: the document's age and its freshness limit. The document is "fresh enough" if the age is less than the freshness limit. The algorithm in Example 7-3 just takes the server freshness limit and slides it around based on additional client constraints. We hope this section made the subtle expiration algorithms described in the HTTP specifications a bit clearer.

# Caches and Advertising

If you've made it this far, you've realized that caches improve performance and reduce traffic. You know caches can help users and give them a better experience, and you know caches can help network operators reduce their traffic.

## The Advertiser's Dilemma

You might also expect content providers to like caches. After all, if caches were everywhere, content providers wouldn't have to buy big multiprocessor web servers to keep up with demand—and they wouldn't have to pay steep network service charges to feed the same data to their viewers over and over again. And better yet, caches make the flashy articles and advertisements show up even faster and look even better on the viewer's screens, encouraging them to consume more content and see more advertisements. And that's just what content providers want! More eyeballs and more advertisements!

But that's the rub. Many content providers are paid through advertising—in particular, they get paid every time an advertisement is shown to a user (maybe just a fraction of a penny or two, but they add up if you show a million ads a day!). And that's the problem with caches—they can hide the real access counts from the origin server. If caching was perfect, an origin server might not receive any HTTP accesses at all, because they would be absorbed by Internet caches. But, if you are paid on access counts, you won't be celebrating.

## The Publisher's Response

Today, advertisers use all sorts of "cache-busting" techniques to ensure that caches don't steal their hit stream. They slap no-cache headers on their content. They serve advertisements through CGI gateways. They rewrite advertisement URLs on each access.

And these cache-busting techniques aren't just for proxy caches. In fact, today they are targeted primarily at the cache that's enabled in every web browser. Unfortunately, while over-aggressively trying to maintain their hit stream, some content providers are reducing the positive effects of caching to their site.

In the ideal world, content providers would let caches absorb their traffic, and the caches would tell them how many hits they got. Today, there are a few ways caches can do this.

One solution is to configure caches to revalidate with the origin server on every access. This pushes a hit to the origin server for each access but usually does not transfer any body data. Of course, this slows down the transaction.*

## Log Migration

One ideal solution wouldn't require sending hits through to the server. After all, the cache can keep a log of all the hits. Caches could just distribute the hit logs to servers. In fact, some large cache providers have been known to manually process and hand-deliver cache logs to influential content providers to keep the content providers happy.

---

* Some caches support a variant of this revalidation, where they do a conditional GET or a HEAD request in the background. The user does not perceive the delay, but the request triggers an offline access to the origin server. This is an improvement, but it places more load on the caches and significantly increases traffic across the network.

Unfortunately, hit logs are large, which makes them tough to move. And cache logs are not standardized or organized to separate logs out to individual content providers. Also, there are authentication and privacy issues.

Proposals have been made for efficient (and less efficient) log-redistribution schemes. None are far enough developed to be adopted by web software vendors. Many are extremely complex and require joint business partnerships to succeed.* Several corporate ventures have been launched to develop supporting infrastructure for advertising revenue reclamation.

## Hit Metering and Usage Limiting

RFC 2227, "Simple Hit-Metering and Usage-Limiting for HTTP," defines a much simpler scheme. This protocol adds one new header to HTTP, called Meter, that periodically carries hit counts for particular URLs back to the servers. This way, servers get periodic updates from caches about the number of times cached documents were hit.

In addition, the server can control how many times documents can be served from cache, or a wall clock timeout, before the cache must report back to the server. This is called usage limiting; it allows servers to control how much a cached resource can be used before it needs to report back to the origin server.

We'll describe RFC 2227 in detail in Chapter 21.

# For More Information

For more information on caching, refer to:

*http://www.w3.org/Protocols/rfc2616/rfc2616.txt*
> RFC 2616, "Hypertext Transfer Protocol," by R. Fielding, J. Gettys, J. Mogul, H. Frystyk, L. Mastinter, P. Leach, and T. Berners-Lee.

*Web Caching*
> Duane Wessels, O'Reilly & Associates, Inc.

*http://search.ietf.org/rfc/rfc3040.txt*
> RFC 3040, "Internet Web Replication and Caching Taxonomy."

*Web Proxy Servers*
> Ari Luotonen, Prentice Hall Computer Books.

*http://search.ietf.org/rfc/rfc3143.txt*
> RFC 3143, "Known HTTP Proxy/Caching Problems."

*http://www.squid-cache.org*
> Squid Web Proxy Cache.

---

* Several businesses have launched trying to develop global solutions for integrated caching and logging.

# CHAPTER 8

# Integration Points: Gateways, Tunnels, and Relays

The Web has proven to be an incredible tool for disseminating content. Over time, people have moved from just wanting to put static documents online to wanting to share ever more complex resources, such as database content or dynamically generated HTML pages. HTTP applications, like web browsers, have provided users with a unified means of accessing content over the Internet.

HTTP also has come to be a fundamental building block for application developers, who piggyback other protocols on top of HTTP (for example, using HTTP to tunnel or relay other protocol traffic through corporate firewalls, by wrapping that traffic in HTTP). HTTP is used as a protocol for all of the Web's resources, and it's also a protocol that other applications and application protocols make use of to get their jobs done.

This chapter takes a general look at some of the methods that developers have come up with for using HTTP to access different resources and examines how developers use HTTP as a framework for enabling other protocols and application communication.

In this chapter, we discuss:

- Gateways, which interface HTTP with other protocols and applications
- Application interfaces, which allow different types of web applications to communicate with one another
- Tunnels, which let you send non-HTTP traffic over HTTP connections
- Relays, which are a type of simplified HTTP proxy used to forward data one hop at a time

## Gateways

The history behind HTTP extensions and interfaces was driven by people's needs. When the desire to put more complicated resources on the Web emerged, it rapidly became clear that no single application could handle all imaginable resources.

To get around this problem, developers came up with the notion of a *gateway* that could serve as a sort of interpreter, abstracting a way to get at the resource. A gateway is the glue between resources and applications. An application can ask (through HTTP or some other defined interface) a gateway to handle the request, and the gateway can provide a response. The gateway can speak the query language to the database or generate the dynamic content, acting like a portal: a request goes in, and a response comes out.

Figure 8-1 depicts a kind of resource gateway. Here, the Joe's Hardware server is acting as a gateway to database content—note that the client is simply asking for a resource through HTTP, and the Joe's Hardware server is interfacing with a gateway to get at the resource.

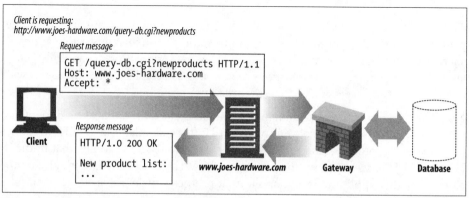

*Figure 8-1. Gateway magic*

Some gateways automatically translate HTTP traffic to other protocols, so HTTP clients can interface with other applications without the clients needing to know other protocols (Figure 8-2).

Figure 8-2 shows three examples of gateways:

- In Figure 8-2a, the gateway receives HTTP requests for FTP URLs. The gateway then opens FTP connections and issues the appropriate commands to the FTP server. The document is sent back through HTTP, along with the correct HTTP headers.

- In Figure 8-2b, the gateway receives an encrypted web request through SSL, decrypts the request,* and forwards a normal HTTP request to the destination server. These security accelerators can be placed directly in front of web servers (usually in the same premises) to provide high-performance encryption for origin servers.

---

* The gateway would need to have the proper server certificates installed.

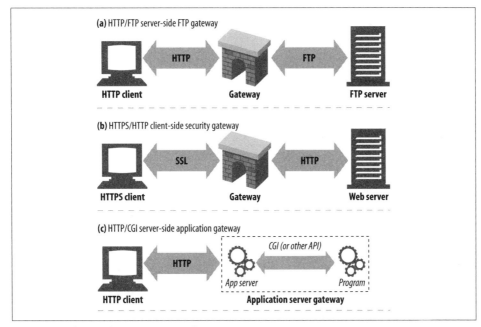

Figure 8-2. Three web gateway examples

- In Figure 8-2c, the gateway connects HTTP clients to server-side application programs, through an application server gateway API. When you purchase from e-commerce stores on the Web, check the weather forecast, or get stock quotes, you are visiting application server gateways.

## Client-Side and Server-Side Gateways

Web gateways speak HTTP on one side and a different protocol on the other side.* Gateways are described by their client- and server-side protocols, separated by a slash:

```
<client-protocol>/<server-protocol>
```

So a gateway joining HTTP clients to NNTP news servers is an *HTTP/NNTP gateway*. We use the terms "server-side gateway" and "client-side gateway" to describe what side of the gateway the conversion is done for:

- *Server-side gateways* speak HTTP with clients and a foreign protocol with servers (HTTP/*).
- *Client-side gateways* speak foreign protocols with clients and HTTP with servers (*/HTTP).

---

\* Web proxies that convert between different versions of HTTP are like gateways, because they perform sophisticated logic to negotiate between the parties. But because they speak HTTP on both sides, they are technically proxies.

# Protocol Gateways

You can direct HTTP traffic to gateways the same way you direct traffic to proxies. Most commonly, you explicitly configure browsers to use gateways, intercept traffic transparently, or configure gateways as surrogates (reverse proxies).

Figure 8-3 shows the dialog boxes used to configure a browser to use server-side FTP gateways. In the configuration shown, the browser is configured to use *gw1.joes-hardware.com* as an HTTP/FTP gateway for all FTP URLs. Instead of sending FTP commands to an FTP server, the browser will send HTTP commands to the HTTP/FTP gateway *gw1.joes-hardware.com* on port 8080.

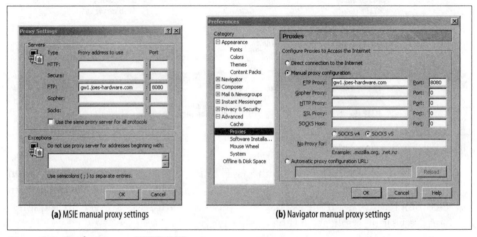

**(a)** MSIE manual proxy settings      **(b)** Navigator manual proxy settings

*Figure 8-3. Configuring an HTTP/FTP gateway*

The result of this gateway configuration is shown in Figure 8-4. Normal HTTP traffic is unaffected; it continues to flow directly to origin servers. But requests for FTP URLs are sent to the gateway *gw1.joes-hardware.com* within HTTP requests. The gateway performs the FTP transactions on the client's behalf and carries results back to the client by HTTP.

The following sections describe common kinds of gateways: server protocol converters, server-side security gateways, client-side security gateways, and application servers.

## HTTP/*: Server-Side Web Gateways

Server-side web gateways convert client-side HTTP requests into a foreign protocol, as the requests travel inbound to the origin server (see Figure 8-5).

In Figure 8-5, the gateway receives an HTTP request for an FTP resource:

```
ftp://ftp.irs.gov/pub/00-index.txt
```

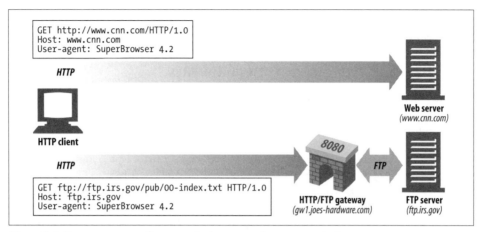

*Figure 8-4. Browsers can configure particular protocols to use particular gateways*

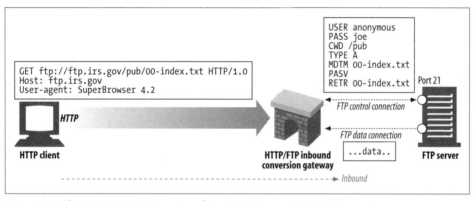

*Figure 8-5. The HTTP/FTP gateway translates HTTP request into FTP requests*

The gateway proceeds to open an FTP connection to the FTP port on the origin server (port 21) and speak the FTP protocol to fetch the object. The gateway does the following:

- Sends the USER and PASS commands to log in to the server
- Issues the CWD command to change to the proper directory on the server
- Sets the download type to ASCII
- Fetches the document's last modification time with MDTM
- Tells the server to expect a passive data retrieval request using PASV
- Requests the object retrieval using RETR
- Opens a data connection to the FTP server on a port returned on the control channel; as soon as the data channel is opened, the object content flows back to the gateway

When the retrieval is complete, the object will be sent to the client in an HTTP response.

## HTTP/HTTPS: Server-Side Security Gateways

Gateways can be used to provide extra privacy and security for an organization, by encrypting all inbound web requests. Clients can browse the Web using normal HTTP, but the gateway will automatically encrypt the user's sessions (Figure 8-6).

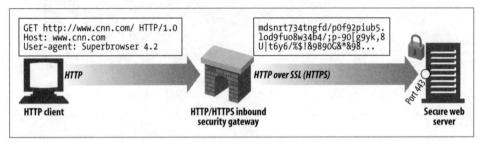

*Figure 8-6. Inbound HTTP/HTTPS security gateway*

## HTTPS/HTTP: Client-Side Security Accelerator Gateways

Recently, HTTPS/HTTP gateways have become popular as security accelerators. These HTTPS/HTTP gateways sit in front of the web server, usually as an invisible intercepting gateway or a reverse proxy. They receive secure HTTPS traffic, decrypt the secure traffic, and make normal HTTP requests to the web server (Figure 8-7).

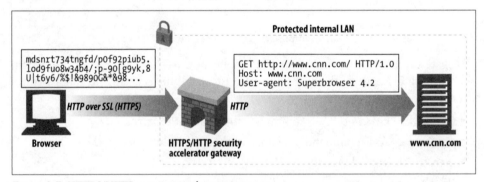

*Figure 8-7. HTTPS/HTTP security accelerator gateway*

These gateways often include special decryption hardware to decrypt secure traffic much more efficiently than the origin server, removing load from the origin server. Because these gateways send unencrypted traffic between the gateway and origin server, you need to use caution to make sure the network between the gateway and origin server is secure.

# Resource Gateways

So far, we've been talking about gateways that connect clients and servers across a network. However, the most common form of gateway, the application server, combines the destination server and gateway into a single server. Application servers are server-side gateways that speak HTTP with the client and connect to an application program on the server side (see Figure 8-8).

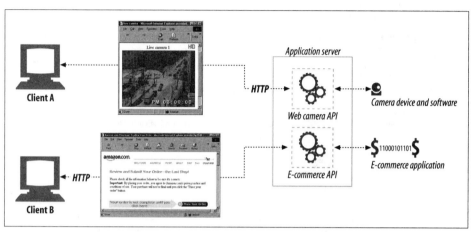

*Figure 8-8. An application server connects HTTP clients to arbitrary backend applications*

In Figure 8-8, two clients are connecting to an application server using HTTP. But, instead of sending back files from the server, the application server passes the requests through a gateway *application programming interface* (API) to applications running on the server:

- Client A's request is received and, based on the URI, is sent through an API to a digital camera application. The resulting camera image is bundled up into an HTTP response message and sent back to the client, for display in the client's browser.

- Client B's URI is for an e-commerce application. Client B's requests are sent through the server gateway API to the e-commerce software, and the results are sent back to the browser. The e-commerce software interacts with the client, walking the user through a sequence of HTML pages to complete a purchase.

The first popular API for application gateways was the *Common Gateway Interface* (CGI). CGI is a standardized set of interfaces that web servers use to launch programs in response to HTTP requests for special URLs, collect the program output, and send it back in HTTP responses. Over the past several years, commercial web servers have provided more sophisticated interfaces for connecting web servers to applications.

Early web servers were fairly simple creations, and the simple approach that was taken for implementing an interface for gateways has stuck to this day.

When a request comes in for a resource that needs a gateway, the server spawns the helper application to handle the request. The helper application is passed the data it needs. Often this is just the entire request or something like the query the user wants to run on the database (from the query string of the URL; see Chapter 2).

It then returns a response or response data to the server, which vectors it off to the client. The server and gateway are separate applications, so the lines of responsibility are kept clear. Figure 8-9 shows the basic mechanics behind server and gateway application interactions.

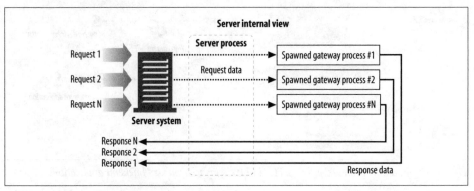

*Figure 8-9. Server gateway application mechanics*

This simple protocol (request in, hand off, and respond) is the essence behind the oldest and one of the most common server extension interfaces, CGI.

## Common Gateway Interface (CGI)

The Common Gateway Interface was the first and probably still is the most widely used server extension. It is used throughout the Web for things like dynamic HTML, credit card processing, and querying databases.

Since CGI applications are separate from the server, they can be implemented in almost any language, including Perl, Tcl, C, and various shell languages. And because CGI is simple, almost all HTTP servers support it. The basic mechanics of the CGI model are shown in Figure 8-9.

CGI processing is invisible to users. From the perspective of the client, it's just making a normal request. It is completely unaware of the hand-off procedure going on between the server and the CGI application. The client's only hint that a CGI application might be involved would be the presence of the letters "cgi" and maybe "?" in the URL.

So CGI is wonderful, right? Well, yes and no. It provides a simple, functional form of glue between servers and pretty much any type of resource, handling any translation that needs to occur. The interface also is elegant in protecting the server from buggy extensions (if the extension were glommed onto the server itself, it could cause an error that might end up crashing the server).

However, this separation incurs a cost in performance. The overhead to spawn a new process for every CGI request is quite high, limiting the performance of servers that use CGI and taxing the server machine's resources. To try to get around this problem, a new form of CGI—aptly dubbed *Fast CGI*—has been developed. This interface mimics CGI, but it runs as a persistent daemon, eliminating the performance penalty of setting up and tearing down a new process for each request.

## Server Extension APIs

The CGI protocol provides a clean way to interface external interpreters with stock HTTP servers, but what if you want to alter the behavior of the server itself, or you just want to eke every last drop of performance you can get out of your server? For these two needs, server developers have provided server extension APIs, which provide a powerful interface for web developers to interface their own modules with an HTTP server directly. Extension APIs allow programmers to graft their own code onto the server or completely swap out a component of the server and replace it with their own.

Most popular servers provide one or more extension APIs for developers. Since these extensions often are tied to the architecture of the server itself, most of them are specific to one server type. Microsoft, Netscape, Apache, and other server flavors all have API interfaces that allow developers to alter the behavior of the server or provide custom interfaces to different resources. These custom interfaces provide a powerful interface for developers.

One example of a server extension is Microsoft's FrontPage Server Extension (FPSE), which supports web publishing services for FrontPage authors. FPSE is able to interpret remote procedure call (RPC) commands sent by FrontPage clients. These commands are piggybacked on HTTP (specifically, overlaid on the HTTP POST method). For details, see "FrontPage Server Extensions for Publishing Support" in Chapter 19.

# Application Interfaces and Web Services

We've discussed resource gateways as ways for web servers to communicate with applications. More generally, with web applications providing ever more types of services, it becomes clear that HTTP can be part of a foundation for linking together applications. One of the trickier issues in wiring up applications is negotiating the protocol interface between the two applications so that they can exchange data— often this is done on an application-by-application basis.

To work together, applications usually need to exchange more complex information with one another than is expressible in HTTP headers. A couple of examples of extending HTTP or layering protocols on top of HTTP in order to exchange customized information are described in Chapter 19. "FrontPage Server Extensions for Publishing Support" in Chapter 19 talks about layering RPCs over HTTP POST messages, and "WebDAV and Collaborative Authoring" talks about adding XML to HTTP headers.

The Internet community has developed a set of standards and protocols that allow web applications to talk to each other. These standards are loosely referred to as *web services*, although the term can mean standalone web applications (building blocks) themselves. The premise of web services is not new, but they are a new mechanism for applications to share information. Web services are built on standard web technologies, such as HTTP.

Web services exchange information using XML over SOAP. The Extensible Markup Language (XML) provides a way to create and interpret customized information about a data object. The Simple Object Access Protocol (SOAP) is a standard for adding XML information to HTTP messages.[*]

# Tunnels

We've discussed different ways that HTTP can be used to enable access to various kinds of resources (through gateways) and to enable application-to-application communication. In this section, we'll take a look at another use of HTTP, *web tunnels*, which enable access to applications that speak non-HTTP protocols through HTTP applications.

Web tunnels let you send non-HTTP traffic through HTTP connections, allowing other protocols to piggyback on top of HTTP. The most common reason to use web tunnels is to embed non-HTTP traffic inside an HTTP connection, so it can be sent through firewalls that allow only web traffic.

## Establishing HTTP Tunnels with CONNECT

Web tunnels are established using HTTP's CONNECT method. The CONNECT protocol is not part of the core HTTP/1.1 specification,[†] but it is a widely implemented extension. Technical specifications can be found in Ari Luotonen's expired Internet draft specification, "Tunneling TCP based protocols through Web proxy servers," or in his book *Web Proxy Servers*, both of which are cited at the end of this chapter.

---

[*] For more information, see *http://www.w3.org/TR/2001/WD-soap12-part0-20011217/. Programming Web Services with SOAP*, by Doug Tidwell, James Snell, and Pavel Kulchenko (O'Reilly) is also an excellent source of information on the SOAP protocol.

[†] The HTTP/1.1 specification reserves the CONNECT method but does not describe its function.

The CONNECT method asks a tunnel gateway to create a TCP connection to an arbitrary destination server and port and to blindly relay subsequent data between client and server.

Figure 8-10 shows how the CONNECT method works to establish a tunnel to a gateway:

- In Figure 8-10a, the client sends a CONNECT request to the tunnel gateway. The client's CONNECT method asks the tunnel gateway to open a TCP connection (here, to the host named *orders.joes-hardware.com* on port 443, the normal SSL port).

- The TCP connection is created in Figure 8-10b and Figure 8-10c.

- Once the TCP connection is established, the gateway notifies the client (Figure 8-10d) by sending an HTTP 200 Connection Established response.

- At this point, the tunnel is set up. Any data sent by the client over the HTTP tunnel will be relayed directly to the outgoing TCP connection, and any data sent by the server will be relayed to the client over the HTTP tunnel.

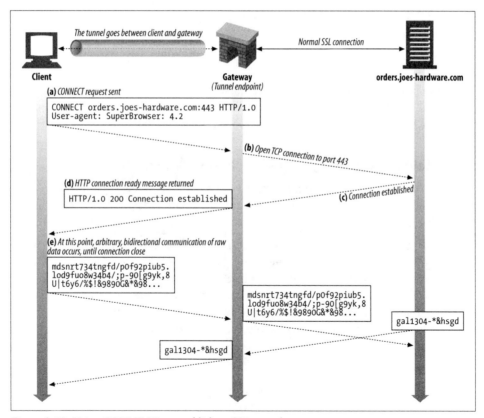

*Figure 8-10. Using CONNECT to establish an SSL tunnel*

The example in Figure 8-10 describes an SSL tunnel, where SSL traffic is sent over an HTTP connection, but the CONNECT method can be used to establish a TCP connection to any server using any protocol.

### CONNECT requests

The CONNECT syntax is identical in form to other HTTP methods, with the exception of the start line. The request URI is replaced by a hostname, followed by a colon, followed by a port number. Both the host and the port must be specified:

```
CONNECT home.netscape.com:443 HTTP/1.0
User-agent: Mozilla/4.0
```

After the start line, there are zero or more HTTP request header fields, as in other HTTP messages. As usual, the lines end in CRLFs, and the list of headers ends with a bare CRLF.

### CONNECT responses

After the request is sent, the client waits for a response from the gateway. As with normal HTTP messages, a 200 response code indicates success. By convention, the reason phrase in the response is normally set to "Connection Established":

```
HTTP/1.0 200 Connection Established
Proxy-agent: Netscape-Proxy/1.1
```

Unlike normal HTTP responses, the response does not need to include a Content-Type header. No content type is required* because the connection becomes a raw byte relay, instead of a message carrier.

## Data Tunneling, Timing, and Connection Management

Because the tunneled data is opaque to the gateway, the gateway cannot make any assumptions about the order and flow of packets. Once the tunnel is established, data is free to flow in any direction at any time.†

As a performance optimization, clients are allowed to send tunnel data after sending the CONNECT request but before receiving the response. This gets data to the server faster, but it means that the gateway must be able to handle data following the request properly. In particular, the gateway cannot assume that a network I/O request will return only header data, and the gateway must be sure to forward any data read with the header to the server, when the connection is ready. Clients that pipeline data

---

* Future specifications may define a media type for tunnels (e.g., application/tunnel), for uniformity.

† The two endpoints of the tunnel (the client and the gateway) must be prepared to accept packets from either of the connections at any time and must forward that data immediately. Because the tunneled protocol may include data dependencies, neither end of the tunnel can ignore input data. Lack of data consumption on one end of the tunnel may hang the producer on the other end of the tunnel, leading to deadlock.

---

after the request must be prepared to resend the request data if the response comes back as an authentication challenge or other non-200, nonfatal status. *

If at any point either one of the tunnel endpoints gets disconnected, any outstanding data that came from that endpoint will be passed to the other one, and after that also the other connection will be terminated by the proxy. If there is undelivered data for the closing endpoint, that data will be discarded.

## SSL Tunneling

Web tunnels were first developed to carry encrypted SSL traffic through firewalls. Many organizations funnel all traffic through packet-filtering routers and proxy servers to enhance security. But some protocols, such as encrypted SSL, cannot be proxied by traditional proxy servers, because the information is encrypted. Tunnels let the SSL traffic be carried through the port 80 HTTP firewall by transporting it through an HTTP connection (Figure 8-11).

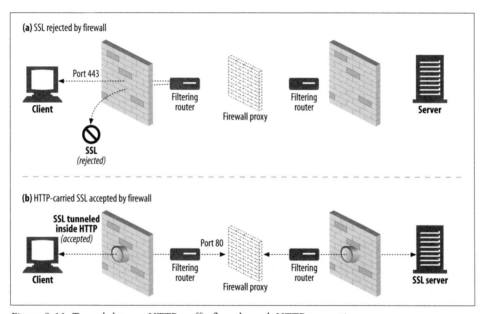

*Figure 8-11. Tunnels let non-HTTP traffic flow through HTTP connections*

To allow SSL traffic to flow through existing proxy firewalls, a tunneling feature was added to HTTP, in which raw, encrypted data is placed inside HTTP messages and sent through normal HTTP channels (Figure 8-12).

---

* Try not to pipeline more data than can fit into the remainder of the request's TCP packet. Pipelining more data can cause a client TCP reset if the gateway subsequently closes the connection before all pipelined TCP packets are received. A TCP reset can cause the client to lose the received gateway response, so the client won't be able to tell whether the failure was due to a network error, access control, or authentication challenge.

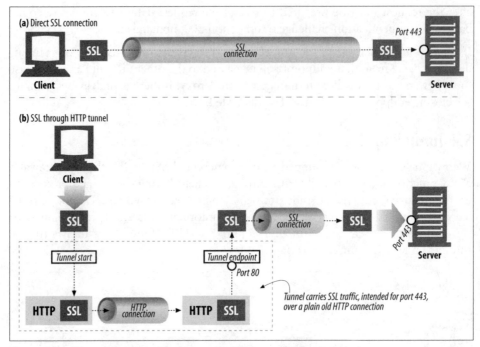

*Figure 8-12. Direct SSL connection vs. tunnelled SSL connection*

In Figure 8-12a, SSL traffic is sent directly to a secure web server (on SSL port 443). In Figure 8-12b, SSL traffic is encapsulated into HTTP messages and sent over HTTP port 80 connections, until it is decapsulated back into normal SSL connections.

Tunnels often are used to let non-HTTP traffic pass through port-filtering firewalls. This can be put to good use, for example, to allow secure SSL traffic to flow through firewalls. However, this feature can be abused, allowing malicious protocols to flow into an organization through the HTTP tunnel.

## SSL Tunneling Versus HTTP/HTTPS Gateways

The HTTPS protocol (HTTP over SSL) can alternatively be gatewayed in the same way as other protocols: having the gateway (instead of the client) initiate the SSL session with the remote HTTPS server and then perform the HTTPS transaction on the client's part. The response will be received and decrypted by the proxy and sent to the client over (insecure) HTTP. This is the way gateways handle FTP. However, this approach has several disadvantages:

- The client-to-gateway connection is normal, insecure HTTP.
- The client is not able to perform SSL client authentication (authentication based on X509 certificates) to the remote server, as the proxy is the authenticated party.
- The gateway needs to support a full SSL implementation.

Note that this mechanism, if used for SSL tunneling, does not require an implementation of SSL in the proxy. The SSL session is established between the client generating the request and the destination (secure) web server; the proxy server in between merely tunnels the encrypted data and does not take any other part in the secure transaction.

## Tunnel Authentication

Other features of HTTP can be used with tunnels where appropriate. In particular, the proxy authentication support can be used with tunnels to authenticate a client's right to use a tunnel (Figure 8-13).

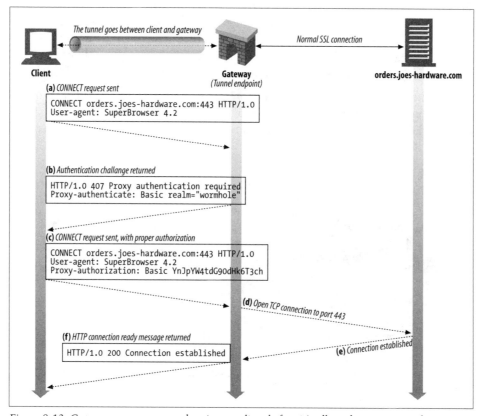

*Figure 8-13. Gateways can proxy-authenticate a client before it's allowed to use a tunnel*

## Tunnel Security Considerations

In general, the tunnel gateway cannot verify that the protocol being spoken is really what it is supposed to tunnel. Thus, for example, mischievous users might use tunnels intended for SSL to tunnel Internet gaming traffic through a corporate firewall, or malicious users might use tunnels to open Telnet sessions or to send email that bypasses corporate email scanners.

To minimize abuse of tunnels, the gateway should open tunnels only for particular well-known ports, such as 443 for HTTPS.

# Relays

HTTP *relays* are simple HTTP proxies that do not fully adhere to the HTTP specifications. Relays process enough HTTP to establish connections, then blindly forward bytes.

Because HTTP is complicated, it's sometimes useful to implement bare-bones proxies that just blindly forward traffic, without performing all of the header and method logic. Because blind relays are easy to implement, they sometimes are used to provide simple filtering, diagnostics, or content transformation. But they should be deployed with great caution, because of the serious potential for interoperability problems.

One of the more common (and infamous) problems with some implementations of simple blind relays relates to their potential to cause keep-alive connections to hang, because they don't properly process the Connection header. This situation is depicted in Figure 8-14.

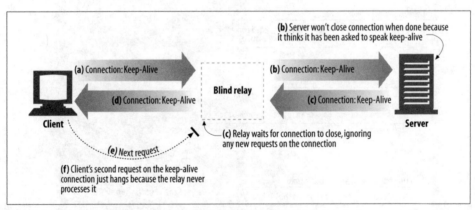

*Figure 8-14. Simple blind relays can hang if they are single-tasking and don't support the Connection header*

Here's what's going on in this figure:

- In Figure 8-14a, a web client sends a message to the relay, including the Connection: Keep-Alive header, requesting a keep-alive connection if possible. The client waits for a response to learn if its request for a keep-alive channel was granted.
- The relay gets the HTTP request, but it doesn't understand the Connection header, so it passes the message verbatim down the chain to the server (Figure 8-14b). However, the Connection header is a hop-by-hop header; it

applies only to a single transport link and shouldn't be passed down the chain. Bad things are about to start happening!

- In Figure 8-14b, the relayed HTTP request arrives at the web server. When the web server receives the proxied Connection: Keep-Alive header, it mistakenly concludes that the relay (which looks like any other client to the server) wants to speak keep-alive! That's fine with the web server—it agrees to speak keep-alive and sends a Connection: Keep-Alive response header back in Figure 8-14c. So, at this point, the web server thinks it is speaking keep-alive with the relay, and it will adhere to rules of keep-alive. But the relay doesn't know anything about keep-alive.

- In Figure 8-14d, the relay forwards the web server's response message back to the client, passing along the Connection: Keep-Alive header from the web server. The client sees this header and assumes the relay has agreed to speak keep-alive. At this point, both the client and server believe they are speaking keep-alive, but the relay to which they are talking doesn't know the first thing about keep-alive.

- Because the relay doesn't know anything about keepalive, it forwards all the data it receives back to the client, waiting for the origin server to close the connection. But the origin server will not close the connection, because it believes the relay asked the server to keep the connection open! So, the relay will hang waiting for the connection to close.

- When the client gets the response message back in Figure 8-14d, it moves right along to the next request, sending another request to the relay on the keep-alive connection (Figure 8-14e). Simple relays usually never expect another request on the same connection. The browser just spins, making no progress.

There are ways to make relays slightly smarter, to remove these risks, but any simplification of proxies runs the risk of interoperation problems. If you are building simple HTTP relays for a particular purpose, be cautious how you use them. For any wide-scale deployment, you should strongly consider using a real, HTTP-compliant proxy server instead.

For more information about relays and connection management, see "Keep-Alive and Dumb Proxies" in Chapter 4.

# For More Information

For more information, refer to:

*http://www.w3.org/Protocols/rfc2616/rfc2616.txt*
　　RFC 2616, "Hypertext Transfer Protocol," by R. Fielding, J. Gettys, J. Mogul, H. Frystyk, L. Mastinter, P. Leach, and T. Berners-Lee.

*Web Proxy Servers*
　　Ari Luotonen, Prentice Hall Computer Books.

*http://www.alternic.org/drafts/drafts-l-m/draft-luotonen-web-proxy-tunneling-01.txt*
   "Tunneling TCP based protocols through Web proxy servers," by Ari Luotonen.

*http://cgi-spec.golux.com*
   The Common Gateway Interface—RFC Project Page.

*http://www.w3.org/TR/2001/WD-soap12-part0-20011217/*
   W3C—SOAP Version 1.2 Working Draft.

*Programming Web Services with SOAP*
   James Snell, Doug Tidwell, and Pavel Kulchenko, O'Reilly & Associates, Inc.

*http://www.w3.org/TR/2002/WD-wsa-reqs-20020429*
   W3C—Web Services Architecture Requirements.

*Web Services Essentials*
   Ethan Cermai, O'Reilly & Associates, Inc.

# CHAPTER 9

# Web Robots

We continue our tour of HTTP architecture with a close look at the self-animating user agents called *web robots*.

Web robots are software programs that automate a series of web transactions without human interaction. Many robots wander from web site to web site, fetching content, following hyperlinks, and processing the data they find. These kinds of robots are given colorful names such as "crawlers," "spiders," "worms," and "bots" because of the way they automatically explore web sites, seemingly with minds of their own.

Here are a few examples of web robots:

- Stock-graphing robots issue HTTP GETs to stock market servers every few minutes and use the data to build stock price trend graphs.

- Web-census robots gather "census" information about the scale and evolution of the World Wide Web. They wander the Web counting the number of pages and recording the size, language, and media type of each page.*

- Search-engine robots collect all the documents they find to create search databases.

- Comparison-shopping robots gather web pages from online store catalogs to build databases of products and their prices.

## Crawlers and Crawling

Web crawlers are robots that recursively traverse information webs, fetching first one web page, then all the web pages to which that page points, then all the web pages to which those pages point, and so on. When a robot recursively follows web links, it is called a *crawler* or a *spider* because it "crawls" along the web created by HTML hyperlinks.

---

* *http://www.netcraft.com* collects great census metrics on what flavors of servers are being used by sites around the Web.

Internet search engines use crawlers to wander about the Web and pull back all the documents they encounter. These documents are then processed to create a searchable database, allowing users to find documents that contain particular words. With billions of web pages out there to find and bring back, these search-engine spiders necessarily are some of the most sophisticated robots. Let's look in more detail at how crawlers work.

## Where to Start: The "Root Set"

Before you can unleash your hungry crawler, you need to give it a starting point. The initial set of URLs that a crawler starts visiting is referred to as the *root set*. When picking a root set, you should choose URLs from enough different places that crawling all the links will eventually get you to most of the web pages that interest you.

What's a good root set to use for crawling the web in Figure 9-1? As in the real Web, there is no single document that eventually links to every document. If you start with document A in Figure 9-1, you can get to B, C, and D, then to E and F, then to J, and then to K. But there's no chain of links from A to G or from A to N.

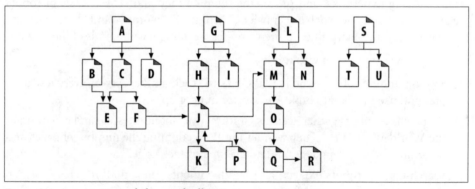

*Figure 9-1. A root set is needed to reach all pages*

Some web pages in this web, such as S, T, and U, are nearly stranded—isolated, without any links pointing at them. Perhaps these lonely pages are new, and no one has found them yet. Or perhaps they are really old or obscure.

In general, you don't need too many pages in the root set to cover a large portion of the web. In Figure 9-1, you need only A, G, and S in the root set to reach all pages.

Typically, a good root set consists of the big, popular web sites (for example, *http://www.yahoo.com*), a list of newly created pages, and a list of obscure pages that aren't often linked to. Many large-scale production crawlers, such as those used by Internet search engines, have a way for users to submit new or obscure pages into the root set. This root set grows over time and is the seed list for any fresh crawls.

## Extracting Links and Normalizing Relative Links

As a crawler moves through the Web, it is constantly retrieving HTML pages. It needs to parse out the URL links in each page it retrieves and add them to the list of pages that need to be crawled. While a crawl is progressing, this list often expands rapidly, as the crawler discovers new links that need to be explored.* Crawlers need to do some simple HTML parsing to extract these links and to convert relative URLs into their absolute form. "Relative URLs" in Chapter 2 discusses how to do this conversion.

## Cycle Avoidance

When a robot crawls a web, it must be very careful not to get stuck in a loop, or *cycle*. Look at the crawler in Figure 9-2:

- In Figure 9-2a, the robot fetches page A, sees that A links to B, and fetches page B.
- In Figure 9-2b, the robot fetches page B, sees that B links to C, and fetches page C.
- In Figure 9-2c, the robot fetches page C and sees that C links to A. If the robot fetches page A again, it will end up in a cycle, fetching A, B, C, A, B, C, A...

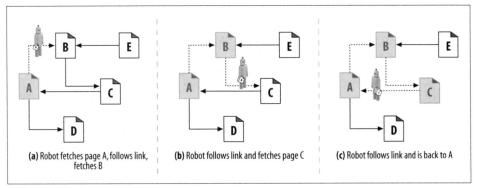

Figure 9-2. Crawling over a web of hyperlinks

Robots must know where they've been to avoid cycles. Cycles can lead to robot traps that can either halt or slow down a robot's progress.

## Loops and Dups

Cycles are bad for crawlers for at least three reasons:

- They get the crawler into a loop where it can get stuck. A loop can cause a poorly designed crawler to spin round and round, spending all its time fetching

---

* In "Cycle Avoidance," we begin to discuss the need for crawlers to remember where they have been. During a crawl, this list of *discovered* URLs grows until the web space has been explored thoroughly and the crawler reaches a point at which it is no longer discovering new links.

the same pages over and over again. The crawler can burn up lots of network bandwidth and may be completely unable to fetch any other pages.

- While the crawler is fetching the same pages repeatedly, the web server on the other side is getting pounded. If the crawler is well connected, it can overwhelm the web site and prevent any real users from accessing the site. Such denial of service can be grounds for legal claims.

- Even if the looping isn't a problem itself, the crawler is fetching a large number of duplicate pages (often called "dups," which rhymes with "loops"). The crawler's application will be flooded with duplicate content, which may make the application useless. An example of this is an Internet search engine that returns hundreds of matches of the exact same page.

## Trails of Breadcrumbs

Unfortunately, keeping track of where you've been isn't always so easy. At the time of this writing, there are billions of distinct web pages on the Internet, not counting content generated from dynamic gateways.

If you are going to crawl a big chunk of the world's web content, you need to be prepared to visit billions of URLs. Keeping track of which URLs have been visited can be quite challenging. Because of the huge number of URLs, you need to use sophisticated data structures to quickly determine which URLs you've visited. The data structures need to be efficient in speed and memory use.

Speed is important because hundreds of millions of URLs require fast search structures. Exhaustive searching of URL lists is out of the question. At the very least, a robot will need to use a search tree or hash table to be able to quickly determine whether a URL has been visited.

Hundreds of millions of URLs take up a lot of space, too. If the average URL is 40 characters long, and a web robot crawls 500 million URLs (just a small portion of the Web), a search data structure could require 20 GB or more of memory just to hold the URLs (40 bytes per URL × 500 million URLs = 20 GB)!

Here are some useful techniques that large-scale web crawlers use to manage where they visit:

*Trees and hash tables*
Sophisticated robots might use a search tree or a hash table to keep track of visited URLs. These are software data structures that make URL lookup much faster.

*Lossy presence bit maps*
To minimize space, some large-scale crawlers use lossy data structures such as presence bit arrays. Each URL is converted into a fixed size number by a hash function, and this number has an associated "presence bit" in an array. When a

URL is crawled, the corresponding presence bit is set. If the presence bit is already set, the crawler assumes the URL has already been crawled.*

*Checkpoints*

Be sure to save the list of visited URLs to disk, in case the robot program crashes.

*Partitioning*

As the Web grows, it may become impractical to complete a crawl with a single robot on a single computer. That computer may not have enough memory, disk space, computing power, or network bandwidth to complete a crawl.

Some large-scale web robots use "farms" of robots, each a separate computer, working in tandem. Each robot is assigned a particular "slice" of URLs, for which it is responsible. Together, the robots work to crawl the Web. The individual robots may need to communicate to pass URLs back and forth, to cover for malfunctioning peers, or to otherwise coordinate their efforts.

A good reference book for implementing huge data structures is *Managing Gigabytes: Compressing and Indexing Documents and Images*, by Witten, et. al (Morgan Kaufmann). This book is full of tricks and techniques for managing large amounts of data.

## Aliases and Robot Cycles

Even with the right data structures, it is sometimes difficult to tell if you have visited a page before, because of URL "aliasing." Two URLs are *aliases* if the URLs look different but really refer to the same resource.

Table 9-1 illustrates a few simple ways that different URLs can point to the same resource.

*Table 9-1. Different URLs that alias to the same documents*

|   | First URL | Second URL | When aliased |
|---|-----------|------------|--------------|
| a | http://www.foo.com/bar.html | http://www.foo.com:80/bar.html | Port is 80 by default |
| b | http://www.foo.com/~fred | http://www.foo.com/%7Ffred | %7F is same as ~ |
| c | http://www.foo.com/x.html#early | http://www.foo.com/x.html#middle | Tags don't change the page |
| d | http://www.foo.com/readme.htm | http://www.foo.com/README.HTM | Case-insensitive server |
| e | http://www.foo.com/ | http://www.foo.com/index.html | Default page is *index.html* |
| f | http://www.foo.com/index.html | http://209.231.87.45/index.html | *www.foo.com* has this IP address |

---

* Because there are a potentially infinite number of URLs and only a finite number of bits in the presence bit array, there is potential for collision—two URLs can map to the same presence bit. When this happens, the crawler mistakenly concludes that a page has been crawled when it hasn't. In practice, this situation can be made very unlikely by using a large number of presence bits. The penalty for collision is that a page will be omitted from a crawl.

## Canonicalizing URLs

Most web robots try to eliminate the obvious aliases up front by "canonicalizing" URLs into a standard form. A robot might first convert every URL into a canonical form, by:

1. Adding ":80" to the hostname, if the port isn't specified
2. Converting all %xx escaped characters into their character equivalents
3. Removing # tags

These steps can eliminate the aliasing problems shown in Table 9-1a–c. But, without knowing information about the particular web server, the robot doesn't have any good way of avoiding the duplicates from Table 9-1d–f:

- The robot would need to know whether the web server was case-insensitive to avoid the alias in Table 9-1d.
- The robot would need to know the web server's index-page configuration for this directory to know whether the URLs in Table 9-1e were aliases.
- The robot would need to know if the web server was configured to do virtual hosting (covered in Chapter 5) to know if the URLs in Table 9-1f were aliases, even if it knew the hostname and IP address referred to the same physical computer.

URL canonicalization can eliminate the basic syntactic aliases, but robots will encounter other URL aliases that can't be eliminated through converting URLs to standard forms.

## Filesystem Link Cycles

Symbolic links on a filesystem can cause a particularly insidious kind of cycle, because they can create an illusion of an infinitely deep directory hierarchy where none exists. Symbolic link cycles usually are the result of an unintentional error by the server administrator, but they also can be created by "evil webmasters" as a malicious trap for robots.

Figure 9-3 shows two filesystems. In Figure 9-3a, *subdir* is a normal directory. In Figure 9-3b, *subdir* is a symbolic link pointing back to /. In both figures, assume the file */index.html* contains a hyperlink to the file *subdir/index.html*.

Using Figure 9-3a's filesystem, a web crawler may take the following actions:

1. GET http://www.foo.com/index.html
   Get */index.html*, find link to *subdir/index.html*.
2. GET http://www.foo.com/subdir/index.html
   Get *subdir/index.html*, find link to *subdir/logo.gif*.
3. GET http://www.foo.com/subdir/logo.gif
   Get *subdir/logo.gif*, no more links, all done.

---

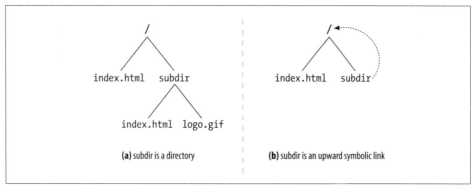

*Figure 9-3. Symbolic link cycles*

But in Figure 9-3b's filesystem, the following might happen:

1. GET `http://www.foo.com/index.html`

   Get */index.html*, find link to *subdir/index.html*.

2. GET `http://www.foo.com/subdir/index.html`

   Get *subdir/index.html*, but get back same *index.html*.

3. GET `http://www.foo.com/subdir/subdir/index.html`

   Get *subdir/subdir/index.html*.

4. GET `http://www.foo.com/subdir/subdir/subdir/index.html`

   Get *subdir/subdir/subdir/index.html*.

The problem with Figure 9-3b is that *subdir/* is a cycle back to /, but because the URLs look different, the robot doesn't know from the URL alone that the documents are identical. The unsuspecting robot runs the risk of getting into a loop. Without some kind of loop detection, this cycle will continue, often until the length of the URL exceeds the robot's or the server's limits.

## Dynamic Virtual Web Spaces

It's possible for malicious webmasters to intentionally create sophisticated crawler loops to trap innocent, unsuspecting robots. In particular, it's easy to publish a URL that looks like a normal file but really is a gateway application. This application can whip up HTML on the fly that contains links to imaginary URLs on the same server. When these imaginary URLs are requested, the nasty server fabricates a new HTML page with new imaginary URLs.

The malicious web server can take the poor robot on an Alice-in-Wonderland journey through an infinite virtual web space, even if the web server doesn't really contain any files. Even worse, it can make it very difficult for the robot to detect the cycle, because the URLs and HTML can look very different each time. Figure 9-4 shows an example of a malicious web server generating bogus content.

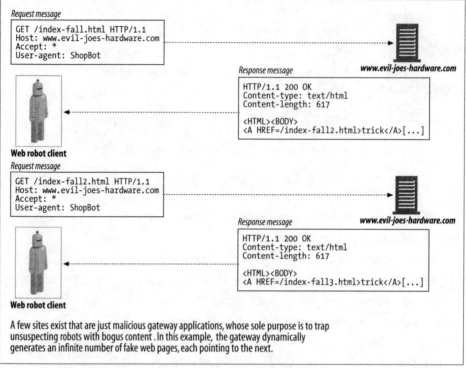

*Figure 9-4. Malicious dynamic web space example*

More commonly, well-intentioned webmasters may unwittingly create a crawler trap through symbolic links or dynamic content. For example, consider a CGI-based calendaring program that generates a monthly calendar and a link to the next month. A real user would not keep requesting the next-month link forever, but a robot that is unaware of the dynamic nature of the content might keep requesting these resources indefinitely.[*]

## Avoiding Loops and Dups

There is no foolproof way to avoid all cycles. In practice, well-designed robots need to include a set of heuristics to try to avoid cycles.

Generally, the more autonomous a crawler is (less human oversight), the more likely it is to get into trouble. There is a bit of a trade-off that robot implementors need to make—these heuristics can help avoid problems, but they also are somewhat "lossy," because you can end up skipping valid content that looks suspect.

---

[*] This is a real example mentioned on *http://www.searchtools.com/robots/robot-checklist.html* for the calendaring site at *http://cgi.umbc.edu/cgi-bin/WebEvent/webevent.cgi*. As a result of dynamic content like this, many robots refuse to crawl pages that have the substring "cgi" anywhere in the URL.

Some techniques that robots use to behave better in a web full of robot dangers are:

*Canonicalizing URLs*

Avoid syntactic aliases by converting URLs into standard form.

*Breadth-first crawling*

Crawlers have a large set of potential URLs to crawl at any one time. By scheduling the URLs to visit in a breadth-first manner, across web sites, you can minimize the impact of cycles. Even if you hit a robot trap, you still can fetch hundreds of thousands of pages from other web sites before returning to fetch a page from the cycle. If you operate depth-first, diving head-first into a single site, you may hit a cycle and never escape to other sites.*

*Throttling†*

Limit the number of pages the robot can fetch from a web site in a period of time. If the robot hits a cycle and continually tries to access aliases from a site, you can cap the total number of duplicates generated and the total number of accesses to the server by throttling.

*Limit URL size*

The robot may refuse to crawl URLs beyond a certain length (1KB is common). If a cycle causes the URL to grow in size, a length limit will eventually stop the cycle. Some web servers fail when given long URLs, and robots caught in a URL-increasing cycle can cause some web servers to crash. This may make webmasters misinterpret the robot as a denial-of-service attacker.

As a caution, this technique can certainly lead to missed content. Many sites today use URLs to help manage user state (for example, storing user IDs in the URLs referenced in a page). URL size can be a tricky way to limit a crawl; however, it can provide a great flag for a user to inspect what is happening on a particular site, by logging an error whenever requested URLs reach a certain size.

*URL/site blacklist*

Maintain a list of known sites and URLs that correspond to robot cycles and traps, and avoid them like the plague. As new problems are found, add them to the blacklist.

This requires human action. However, most large-scale crawlers in production today have some form of a blacklist, used to avoid certain sites because of inherent problems or something malicious in the sites. The blacklist also can be used to avoid certain sites that have made a fuss about being crawled.‡

---

* Breadth-first crawling is a good idea in general, so as to more evenly disperse requests and not overwhelm any one server. This can help keep the resources that a robot uses on a server to a minimum.

† Throttling of request rate is also discussed in "Robot Etiquette."

‡ "Excluding Robots" discusses how sites can avoid being crawled, but some users refuse to use this simple control mechanism and become quite irate when their sites are crawled.

*Pattern detection*

Cycles caused by filesystem symlinks and similar misconfigurations tend to follow patterns; for example, the URL may grow with components duplicated. Some robots view URLs with repeating components as potential cycles and refuse to crawl URLs with more than two or three repeated components.

Not all repetition is immediate (e.g., "/subdir/subdir/subdir..."). It's possible to have cycles of period 2 or other intervals, such as "/subdir/images/subdir/images/subdir/images/...". Some robots look for repeating patterns of a few different periods.

*Content fingerprinting*

Fingerprinting is a more direct way of detecting duplicates that is used by some of the more sophisticated web crawlers. Robots using content fingerprinting take the bytes in the content of the page and compute a *checksum*. This checksum is a compact representation of the content of the page. If a robot ever fetches a page whose checksum it has seen before, the page's links are not crawled—if the robot has seen the page's content before, it has already initiated the crawling of the page's links.

The checksum function must be chosen so that the odds of two different pages having the same checksum are small. Message digest functions such as MD5 are popular for fingerprinting.

Because some web servers dynamically modify pages on the fly, robots sometimes omit certain parts of the web page content, such as embedded links, from the checksum calculation. Still, dynamic server-side includes that customize arbitrary page content (adding dates, access counters, etc.) may prevent duplicate detection.

*Human monitoring*

The Web is a wild place. Your brave robot eventually will stumble into a problem that none of your techniques will catch. All production-quality robots must be designed with diagnostics and logging, so human beings can easily monitor the robot's progress and be warned quickly if something unusual is happening. In some cases, angry net citizens will highlight the problem for you by sending you nasty email.

Good spider heuristics for crawling datasets as vast as the Web are always works in progress. Rules are built over time and adapted as new types of resources are added to the Web. Good rules are always evolving.

Many smaller, more customized crawlers skirt some of these issues, as the resources (servers, network bandwidth, etc.) that are impacted by an errant crawler are manageable, or possibly even are under the control of the person performing the crawl (such as on an intranet site). These crawlers rely on more human monitoring to prevent problems.

# Robotic HTTP

Robots are no different from any other HTTP client program. They too need to abide by the rules of the HTTP specification. A robot that is making HTTP requests and advertising itself as an HTTP/1.1 client needs to use the appropriate HTTP request headers.

Many robots try to implement the minimum amount of HTTP needed to request the content they seek. This can lead to problems; however, it's unlikely that this behavior will change anytime soon. As a result, many robots make HTTP/1.0 requests, because that protocol has few requirements.

## Identifying Request Headers

Despite the minimum amount of HTTP that robots tend to support, most do implement and send some identification headers—most notably, the User-Agent HTTP header. It's recommended that robot implementors send some basic header information to notify the site of the capabilities of the robot, the robot's identity, and where it originated.

This is useful information both for tracking down the owner of an errant crawler and for giving the server some information about what types of content the robot can handle. Some of the basic identifying headers that robot implementors are encouraged to implement are:

*User-Agent*
> Tells the server the name of the robot making the request.

*From*
> Provides the email address of the robot's user/administrator.*

*Accept*
> Tells the server what media types are okay to send.† This can help ensure that the robot receives only content in which it's interested (text, images, etc.).

*Referer*
> Provides the URL of the document that contains the current request-URL.‡

## Virtual Hosting

Robot implementors need to support the Host header. Given the prevalence of virtual hosting (Chapter 5 discusses virtually hosted servers in more detail), not including the

---

\* An RFC 822 email address format.

† "Accept headers" in Chapter 3 lists all of the accept headers; robots may find it useful to send headers such as Accept-Charset if they are interested in particular versions.

‡ This can be very useful to site administrators that are trying to track down how a robot found links to their sites' content.

Host HTTP header in requests can lead to robots identifying the wrong content with a particular URL. HTTP/1.1 requires the use of the Host header for this reason.

Most servers are configured to serve a particular site by default. Thus, a crawler not including the Host header can make a request to a server serving two sites, like those in Figure 9-5 (*www.joes-hardware.com* and *www.foo.com*) and, if the server is configured to serve *www.joes-hardware.com* by default (and does not require the Host header), a request for a page on *www.foo.com* can result in the crawler getting content from the Joe's Hardware site. Worse yet, the crawler will actually think the content from Joe's Hardware was from *www.foo.com*. I am sure you can think of some more unfortunate situations if documents from two sites with polar political or other views were served from the same server.

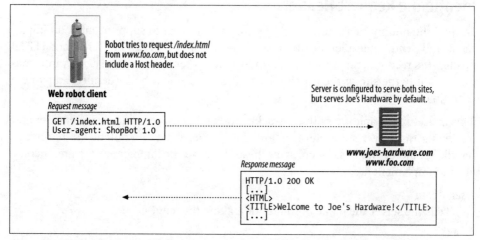

*Figure 9-5. Example of virtual docroots causing trouble if no Host header is sent with the request*

## Conditional Requests

Given the enormity of some robotic endeavors, it often makes sense to minimize the amount of content a robot retrieves. As in the case of Internet search-engine robots, with potentially billions of web pages to download, it makes sense to re-retrieve content only if it has changed.

Some of these robots implement conditional HTTP requests,[*] comparing timestamps or entity tags to see if the last version that they retrieved has been updated. This is very similar to the way that an HTTP cache checks the validity of the local copy of a previously fetched resource. See Chapter 7 for more on how caches validate local copies of resources.

---

[*] "Conditional request headers" in Chapter 3 gives a complete listing of the conditional headers that a robot can implement.

# Response Handling

Because many robots are interested primarily in getting the content requested through simple GET methods, often they don't do much in the way of response handling. However, robots that use some features of HTTP (such as conditional requests), as well as those that want to better explore and interoperate with servers, need to be able to handle different types of HTTP responses.

## Status codes

In general, robots should be able to handle at least the common or expected status codes. All robots should understand HTTP status codes such as 200 OK and 404 Not Found. They also should be able to deal with status codes that they don't explicitly understand based on the general category of response. Table 3-2 in Chapter 3 gives a breakdown of the different status-code categories and their meanings.

It is important to note that some servers don't always return the appropriate error codes. Some servers even return 200 OK HTTP status codes with the text body of the message describing an error! It's hard to do much about this—it's just something for implementors to be aware of.

## Entities

Along with information embedded in the HTTP headers, robots can look for information in the entity itself. Meta HTML tags,* such as the meta http-equiv tag, are a means for content authors to embed additional information about resources. The http-equiv tag itself is a way for content authors to override certain headers that the server handling their content may serve:

```
<meta http-equiv="Refresh" content="1;URL=index.html">
```

This tag instructs the receiver to treat the document as if its HTTP response header contained a Refresh HTTP header with the value "1, URL=index.html".†

Some servers actually parse the contents of HTML pages prior to sending them and include http-equiv directives as headers; however, some do not. Robot implementors may want to scan the HEAD elements of HTML documents to look for http-equiv information. ‡

---

* "Robot META directives" lists additional meta directives that site administrators and content authors can use to control the behavior of robots and what they do with documents that have been retrieved.

† The Refresh HTTP header sometimes is used as a means to redirect users (or in this case, a robot) from one page to another.

‡ Meta tags must occur in the HEAD section of HTML documents, according to the HTML specification. However, they sometimes occur in other HTML document sections, as not all HTML documents adhere to the specification.

## User-Agent Targeting

Web administrators should keep in mind that many robots will visit their sites and therefore should expect requests from them. Many sites optimize content for various user agents, attempting to detect browser types to ensure that various site features are supported. By doing this, the sites serve error pages instead of content to robots. Performing a text search for the phrase "your browser does not support frames" on some search engines will yield a list of results for error pages that contain that phrase, when in fact the HTTP client was not a browser at all, but a robot.

Site administrators should plan a strategy for handling robot requests. For example, instead of limiting their content development to specific browser support, they can develop catch-all pages for non–feature rich browsers and robots. At a minimum, they should expect robots to visit their sites and not be caught off guard when they do.[*]

# Misbehaving Robots

There are many ways that wayward robots can cause mayhem. Here are a few mistakes robots can make, and the impact of their misdeeds:

*Runaway robots*
> Robots issue HTTP requests much faster than human web surfers, and they commonly run on fast computers with fast network links. If a robot contains a programming logic error, or gets caught in a cycle, it can throw intense load against a web server—quite possibly enough to overload the server and deny service to anyone else. All robot authors must take extreme care to design in safeguards to protect against runaway robots.

*Stale URLs*
> Some robots visit lists of URLs. These lists can be old. If a web site makes a big change in its content, robots may request large numbers of nonexistent URLs. This annoys some web site administrators, who don't like their error logs filling with access requests for nonexistent documents and don't like having their web server capacity reduced by the overhead of serving error pages.

*Long, wrong URLs*
> As a result of cycles and programming errors, robots may request large, nonsense URLs from web sites. If the URL is long enough, it may reduce the performance of the web server, clutter the web server access logs, and even cause fragile web servers to crash.

---

[*] "Excluding Robots" provides information for how site administrators can control the behavior of robots on their sites if there is content that should not be accessed by robots.

---

*Nosy robots**

Some robots may get URLs that point to private data and make that data easily accessible through Internet search engines and other applications. If the owner of the data didn't actively advertise the web pages, she may view the robotic publishing as a nuisance at best and an invasion of privacy at worst.

Usually this happens because a hyperlink to the "private" content that the robot followed already exists (i.e., the content isn't as secret as the owner thought it was, or the owner forgot to remove a preexisting hyperlink). Occasionally it happens when a robot is very zealous in trying to scavenge the documents on a site, perhaps by fetching the contents of a directory, even if no explicit hyperlink exists.

Robot implementors retrieving large amounts of data from the Web should be aware that their robots are likely to retrieve sensitive data at some point—data that the site implementor never intended to be accessible over the Internet. This sensitive data can include password files or even credit card information. Clearly, a mechanism to disregard content once this is pointed out (and remove it from any search index or archive) is important. Malicious search engine and archive users have been known to exploit the abilities of large-scale web crawlers to find content—some search engines, such as Google,[†] actually archive representations of the pages they have crawled, so even if content is removed, it can still be found and accessed for some time.

*Dynamic gateway access*

Robots don't always know what they are accessing. A robot may fetch a URL whose content comes from a gateway application. In this case, the data obtained may be special-purpose and may be expensive to compute. Many web site administrators don't like naïve robots requesting documents that come from gateways.

# Excluding Robots

The robot community understood the problems that robotic web site access could cause. In 1994, a simple, voluntary technique was proposed to keep robots out of where they don't belong and provide webmasters with a mechanism to better control their behavior. The standard was named the "Robots Exclusion Standard" but is often just called *robots.txt*, after the file where the access-control information is stored.

The idea of *robots.txt* is simple. Any web server can provide an optional file named *robots.txt* in the document root of the server. This file contains information about what robots can access what parts of the server. If a robot follows this voluntary

---

* Generally, if a resource is available over the public Internet, it is likely referenced somewhere. Few resources are truly private, with the web of links that exists on the Internet.

† See search results at *http://www.google.com*. A cached link, which is a copy of the page that the Google crawler retrieved and indexed, is available on most results.

standard, it will request the *robots.txt* file from the web site before accessing any other resource from that site. For example, the robot in Figure 9-6 wants to download *http://www.joes-hardware.com/specials/acetylene-torches.html* from Joe's Hardware. Before the robot can request the page, however, it needs to check the *robots.txt* file to see if it has permission to fetch this page. In this example, the *robots.txt* file does not block the robot, so the robot fetches the page.

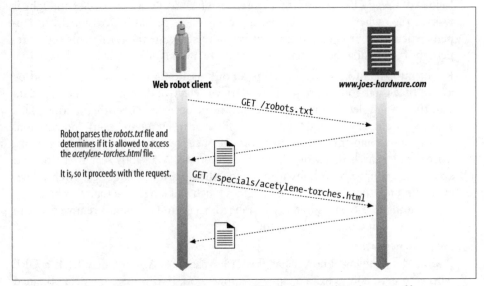

*Figure 9-6. Fetching robots.txt and verifying accessibility before crawling the target file*

## The Robots Exclusion Standard

The Robots Exclusion Standard is an ad hoc standard. At the time of this writing, no official standards body owns this standard, and vendors implement different subsets of the standard. Still, some ability to manage robots' access to web sites, even if imperfect, is better than none at all, and most major vendors and search-engine crawlers implement support for the exclusion standard.

There are three revisions of the Robots Exclusion Standard, though the naming of the versions is not well defined. We adopt the version numbering shown in Table 9-2.

*Table 9-2. Robots Exclusion Standard versions*

| Version | Title and description | Date |
|---------|----------------------|------|
| 0.0 | A Standard for Robot Exclusion—Martijn Koster's original *robots.txt* mechanism with Disallow directive | June 1994 |
| 1.0 | A Method for Web Robots Control—Martijn Koster's IETF draft with additional support for Allow | Nov. 1996 |
| 2.0 | An Extended Standard for Robot Exclusion—Sean Conner's extension including regex and timing information; not widely supported | Nov. 1996 |

Most robots today adopt the v0.0 or v1.0 standards. The v2.0 standard is much more complicated and hasn't been widely adopted. It may never be. We'll focus on the v1.0 standard here, because it is in wide use and is fully compatible with v0.0.

## Web Sites and robots.txt Files

Before visiting any URLs on a web site, a robot must retrieve and process the *robots.txt* file on the web site, if it is present.* There is a single *robots.txt* resource for the entire web site defined by the hostname and port number. If the site is virtually hosted, there can be a different *robots.txt* file for each virtual docroot, as with any other file.

Currently, there is no way to install "local" *robots.txt* files in individual subdirectories of a web site. The webmaster is responsible for creating an aggregate *robots.txt* file that describes the exclusion rules for all content on the web site.

### Fetching robots.txt

Robots fetch the *robots.txt* resource using the HTTP GET method, like any other file on the web server. The server returns the *robots.txt* file, if present, in a text/plain body. If the server responds with a 404 Not Found HTTP status code, the robot can assume that there are no robotic access restrictions and that it can request any file.

Robots should pass along identifying information in the From and User-Agent headers to help site administrators track robotic accesses and to provide contact information in the event that the site administrator needs to inquire or complain about the robot. Here's an example HTTP crawler request from a commercial web robot:

```
GET /robots.txt HTTP/1.0
Host: www.joes-hardware.com
User-Agent: Slurp/2.0
Date: Wed Oct 3 20:22:48 EST 2001
```

### Response codes

Many web sites do not have a *robots.txt* resource, but the robot doesn't know that. It must attempt to get the *robots.txt* resource from every site. The robot takes different actions depending on the result of the *robots.txt* retrieval:

- If the server responds with a success status (HTTP status code 2XX), the robot must parse the content and apply the exclusion rules to fetches from that site.
- If the server response indicates the resource does not exist (HTTP status code 404), the robot can assume that no exclusion rules are active and that access to the site is not restricted by *robots.txt*.

---

* Even though we say "*robots.txt* file," there is no reason that the *robots.txt* resource must strictly reside in a filesystem. For example, the *robots.txt* resource could be dynamically generated by a gateway application.

- If the server response indicates access restrictions (HTTP status code 401 or 403) the robot should regard access to the site as completely restricted.

- If the request attempt results in temporary failure (HTTP status code 503), the robot should defer visits to the site until the resource can be retrieved.

- If the server response indicates redirection (HTTP status code 3XX), the robot should follow the redirects until the resource is found.

## robots.txt File Format

The *robots.txt* file has a very simple, line-oriented syntax. There are three types of lines in a *robots.txt* file: blank lines, comment lines, and rule lines. Rule lines look like HTTP headers (*<Field>: <value>*) and are used for pattern matching. For example:

```
# this robots.txt file allows Slurp & Webcrawler to crawl
# the public parts of our site, but no other robots...

User-Agent: slurp
User-Agent: webcrawler
Disallow: /private

User-Agent: *
Disallow:
```

The lines in a *robots.txt* file are logically separated into "records." Each record describes a set of exclusion rules for a particular set of robots. This way, different exclusion rules can be applied to different robots.

Each record consists of a set of rule lines, terminated by a blank line or end-of-file character. A record starts with one or more User-Agent lines, specifying which robots are affected by this record, followed by Disallow and Allow lines that say what URLs these robots can access.[*]

The previous example shows a *robots.txt* file that allows the *Slurp* and *Webcrawler* robots to access any file except those files in the *private* subdirectory. The same file also prevents any other robots from accessing anything on the site.

Let's look at the User-Agent, Disallow, and Allow lines.

### The User-Agent line

Each robot's record starts with one or more User-Agent lines, of the form:

```
User-Agent: <robot-name>
```

or:

```
User-Agent: *
```

---

[*] For practical reasons, robot software should be robust and flexible with the end-of-line character. CR, LF, and CRLF should all be supported.

---

The robot name (chosen by the robot implementor) is sent in the User-Agent header of the robot's HTTP GET request.

When a robot processes a *robots.txt* file, it must obey the record with either:

- The first robot name that is a case-insensitive substring of the robot's name
- The first robot name that is "*"

If the robot can't find a User-Agent line that matches its name, and can't find a wild-carded "User-Agent: *" line, no record matches, and access is unlimited.

Because the robot name matches case-insensitive substrings, be careful about false matches. For example, "User-Agent: bot" matches all the robots named *Bot*, *Robot*, *Bottom-Feeder*, *Spambot*, and *Dont-Bother-Me*.

### The Disallow and Allow lines

The Disallow and Allow lines immediately follow the User-Agent lines of a robot exclusion record. They describe which URL paths are explicitly forbidden or explicitly allowed for the specified robots.

The robot must match the desired URL against *all* of the Disallow and Allow rules for the exclusion record, in order. The first match found is used. If no match is found, the URL is allowed.*

For an Allow/Disallow line to match a URL, the rule path must be a case-sensitive prefix of the URL path. For example, "Disallow: /tmp" matches all of these URLs:

```
http://www.joes-hardware.com/tmp
http://www.joes-hardware.com/tmp/
http://www.joes-hardware.com/tmp/pliers.html
http://www.joes-hardware.com/tmpspc/stuff.txt
```

### Disallow/Allow prefix matching

Here are a few more details about Disallow/Allow prefix matching:

- Disallow and Allow rules require case-sensitive prefix matches. The asterisk has no special meaning (unlike in User-Agent lines), but the universal wildcarding effect can be obtained from the empty string.
- Any "escaped" characters (%XX) in the rule path or the URL path are unescaped back into bytes before comparison (with the exception of %2F, the forward slash, which must match exactly).
- If the rule path is the empty string, it matches everything.

Table 9-3 lists several examples of matching between rule paths and URL paths.

---

* The *robots.txt* URL always is allowed and must not appear in the Allow/Disallow rules.

*Table 9-3. Robots.txt path matching examples*

| Rule path | URL path | Match? | Comments |
|-----------|----------|--------|----------|
| /tmp | /tmp | ✓ | Rule path == URL path |
| /tmp | /tmpfile.html | ✓ | Rule path is a prefix of URL path |
| /tmp | /tmp/a.html | ✓ | Rule path is a prefix of URL path |
| /tmp/ | /tmp | ✗ | /tmp/ is not a prefix of /tmp |
| | README.TXT | ✓ | Empty rule path matches everything |
| /~fred/hi.html | %7Efred/hi.html | ✓ | %7E is treated the same as ~ |
| /%7Efred/hi.html | /~fred/hi.html | ✓ | %7E is treated the same as ~ |
| /%7efred/hi.html | /%7Efred/hi.html | ✓ | Case isn't significant in escapes |
| /~fred/hi.html | ~fred%2Fhi.html | ✗ | %2F is slash, but slash is a special case that must match exactly |

Prefix matching usually works pretty well, but there are a few places where it is not expressive enough. If there are particular subdirectories for which you also want to disallow crawling, regardless of what the prefix of the path is, *robots.txt* provides no means for this. For example, you might want to avoid crawling of RCS version control subdirectories. Version 1.0 of the *robots.txt* scheme provides no way to support this, other than separately enumerating every path to every RCS subdirectory.

## Other robots.txt Wisdom

Here are some other rules with respect to parsing the *robots.txt* file:

- The *robots.txt* file may contain fields other than User-Agent, Disallow, and Allow, as the specification evolves. A robot should ignore any field it doesn't understand.

- For backward compatibility, breaking of lines is not allowed.

- Comments are allowed anywhere in the file; they consist of optional whitespace, followed by a comment character (#) followed by the comment, until the end-of-line character.

- Version 0.0 of the Robots Exclusion Standard didn't support the Allow line. Some robots implement only the Version 0.0 specification and ignore Allow lines. In this situation, a robot will behave conservatively, not retrieving URLs that are permitted.

## Caching and Expiration of robots.txt

If a robot had to refetch a *robots.txt* file before every file access, it would double the load on web servers, as well as making the robot less efficient. Instead, robots are expected to fetch the *robots.txt* file periodically and cache the results. The cached copy of *robots.txt* should be used by the robot until the *robots.txt* file expires. Standard HTTP cache-control mechanisms are used by both the origin server and robots to control the caching of the *robots.txt* file. Robots should take note of Cache-Control and Expires headers in the HTTP response.*

Many production crawlers today are not HTTP/1.1 clients; webmasters should note that those crawlers will not necessarily understand the caching directives provided for the *robots.txt* resource.

If no Cache-Control directives are present, the draft specification allows caching for seven days. But, in practice, this often is too long. Web server administrators who did not know about *robots.txt* often create one in response to a robotic visit, but if the lack of a *robots.txt* file is cached for a week, the newly created *robots.txt* file will appear to have no effect, and the site administrator will accuse the robot administrator of not adhering to the Robots Exclusion Standard.†

## Robot Exclusion Perl Code

A few publicly available Perl libraries exist to interact with *robots.txt* files. One example is the WWW::RobotsRules module available for the CPAN public Perl archive.

The parsed *robots.txt* file is kept in the WWW::RobotRules object, which provides methods to check if access to a given URL is prohibited. The same WWW::RobotRules object can parse multiple *robots.txt* files.

Here are the primary methods in the WWW::RobotRules API:

*Create RobotRules object*

```
$rules = WWW::RobotRules->new($robot_name);
```

*Load the robots.txt file*

```
$rules->parse($url, $content, $fresh_until);
```

*Check if a site URL is fetchable*

```
$can_fetch = $rules->allowed($url);
```

Here's a short Perl program that demonstrates the use of WWW::RobotRules:

```
require WWW::RobotRules;

# Create the RobotRules object, naming the robot "SuperRobot"
my $robotsrules = new WWW::RobotRules 'SuperRobot/1.0';
use LWP::Simple qw(get);

# Get and parse the robots.txt file for Joe's Hardware, accumulating the rules
$url = "http://www.joes-hardware.com/robots.txt";
my $robots_txt = get $url;
$robotsrules->parse($url, $robots_txt);
```

---

* See "Keeping Copies Fresh" in Chapter 7 for more on handling caching directives.

† Several large-scale web crawlers use the rule of refetching *robots.txt* daily when actively crawling the Web.

```
# Get and parse the robots.txt file for Mary's Antiques, accumulating the rules
$url = "http://www.marys-antiques.com/robots.txt";
my $robots_txt = get $url;
$robotsrules->parse($url, $robots_txt);

# Now RobotRules contains the set of robot exclusion rules for several
# different sites. It keeps them all separate. Now we can use RobotRules
# to test if a robot is allowed to access various URLs.
if ($robotsrules->allowed($some_target_url))
{
    $c = get $url;
    ...
}
```

The following is a hypothetical *robots.txt* file for *www.marys-antiques.com*:

```
##################################################################
# This is the robots.txt file for Mary's Antiques web site
##################################################################

# Keep Suzy's robot out of all the dynamic URLs because it doesn't
# understand them, and out of all the private data, except for the
# small section Mary has reserved on the site for Suzy.

User-Agent: Suzy-Spider
Disallow: /dynamic
Allow: /private/suzy-stuff
Disallow: /private

# The Furniture-Finder robot was specially designed to understand
# Mary's antique store's furniture inventory program, so let it
# crawl that resource, but keep it out of all the other dynamic
# resources and out of all the private data.

User-Agent: Furniture-Finder
Allow: /dynamic/check-inventory
Disallow: /dynamic
Disallow: /private

# Keep everyone else out of the dynamic gateways and private data.

User-Agent: *
Disallow: /dynamic
Disallow: /private
```

This *robots.txt* file contains a record for the robot called *SuzySpider*, a record for the robot called *FurnitureFinder*, and a default record for all other robots. Each record applies a different set of access policies to the different robots:

- The exclusion record for *SuzySpider* keeps the robot from crawling the store inventory gateway URLs that start with */dynamic* and out of the private user data, except for the section reserved for Suzy.

- The record for the *FurnitureFinder* robot permits the robot to crawl the furniture inventory gateway URL. Perhaps this robot understands the format and rules of Mary's gateway.

- All other robots are kept out of all the dynamic and private web pages, though they can crawl the remainder of the URLs.

Table 9-4 lists some examples for different robot accessibility to the Mary's Antiques web site.

*Table 9-4. Robot accessibility to the Mary's Antiques web site*

| URL | SuzySpider | FurnitureFinder | NosyBot |
| --- | --- | --- | --- |
| *http://www.marys-antiques.com/* | ✓ | ✓ | ✓ |
| *http://www.marys-antiques.com/index.html* | ✓ | ✓ | ✓ |
| *http://www.marys-antiques.com/private/payroll.xls* | ✗ | ✗ | ✗ |
| *http://www.marys-antiques.com/private/suzy-stuff/taxes.txt* | ✓ | ✗ | ✗ |
| *http://www.marys-antiques.com/dynamic/buy-stuff?id=3546* | ✗ | ✗ | ✗ |
| *http://www.marys-antiques.com/dynamic/check-inventory?kitchen* | ✗ | ✓ | ✗ |

# HTML Robot-Control META Tags

The *robots.txt* file allows a site administrator to exclude robots from some or all of a web site. One of the disadvantages of the *robots.txt* file is that it is owned by the web site administrator, not the author of the individual content.

HTML page authors have a more direct way of restricting robots from individual pages. They can add robot-control tags to the HTML documents directly. Robots that adhere to the robot-control HTML tags will still be able to fetch the documents, but if a robot exclusion tag is present, they will disregard the documents. For example, an Internet search-engine robot would not include the document in its search index. As with the *robots.txt* standard, participation is encouraged but not enforced.

Robot exclusion tags are implemented using HTML META tags, using the form:

```
<META NAME="ROBOTS" CONTENT=directive-list>
```

### Robot META directives

There are several types of robot META directives, and new directives are likely to be added over time and as search engines and their robots expand their activities and feature sets. The two most-often-used robot META directives are:

*NOINDEX*

Tells a robot not to process the page's content and to disregard the document (i.e., not include the content in any index or database).

```
<META NAME="ROBOTS" CONTENT="NOINDEX">
```

*NOFOLLOW*
> Tells a robot not to crawl any outgoing links from the page.
>
> ```
> <META NAME="ROBOTS" CONTENT="NOFOLLOW">
> ```

In addition to NOINDEX and NOFOLLOW, there are the opposite INDEX and FOLLOW directives, the NOARCHIVE directive, and the ALL and NONE directives. These robot META tag directives are summarized as follows:

*INDEX*
> Tells a robot that it may index the contents of the page.

*FOLLOW*
> Tells a robot that it may crawl any outgoing links in the page.

*NOARCHIVE*
> Tells a robot that it should not cache a local copy of the page.*

*ALL*
> Equivalent to INDEX, FOLLOW.

*NONE*
> Equivalent to NOINDEX, NOFOLLOW.

The robot META tags, like all HTML META tags, must appear in the HEAD section of an HTML page:

```
<html>
<head>
    <meta name="robots" content="noindex,nofollow">
    <title>...</title>
</head>
<body>
    ...
</body>
</html>
```

Note that the "robots" name of the tag and the content are case-insensitive.

You obviously should not specify conflicting or repeating directives, such as:

```
<meta name="robots" content="INDEX,NOINDEX,NOFOLLOW,FOLLOW,FOLLOW">
```

the behavior of which likely is undefined and certainly will vary from robot implementation to robot implementation.

### Search engine META tags

We just discussed robots META tags, used to control the crawling and indexing activity of web robots. All robots META tags contain the *name="robots"* attribute.

---

* This META tag was introduced by the folks who run the Google search engine as a way for webmasters to opt out of allowing Google to serve cached pages of their content. It also can be used with META NAME="googlebot".

Many other types of META tags are available, including those shown in Table 9-5. The DESCRIPTION and KEYWORDS META tags are useful for content-indexing search-engine robots.

*Table 9-5. Additional META tag directives*

| name= | content= | Description |
|---|---|---|
| DESCRIPTION | <text> | Allows an author to define a short text summary of the web page. Many search engines look at META DESCRIPTION tags, allowing page authors to specify appropriate short abstracts to describe their web pages. |
| | | `<meta name="description"`<br>`    content="Welcome to Mary's Antiques web site">` |
| KEYWORDS | <comma list> | Associates a comma-separated list of words that describe the web page, to assist in keyword searches. |
| | | `<meta name="keywords"`<br>`    content="antiques,mary,furniture,restoration">` |
| REVISIT-AFTER [a] | <no. days> | Instructs the robot or search engine that the page should be revisited, presumably because it is subject to change, after the specified number of days. |
| | | `<meta name="revisit-after" content="10 days">` |

[a] This directive is not likely to have wide support.

# Robot Etiquette

In 1993, Martijn Koster, a pioneer in the web robot community, wrote up a list of guidelines for authors of web robots. While some of the advice is dated, much of it still is quite useful. Martijn's original treatise, "Guidelines for Robot Writers," can be found at *http://www.robotstxt.org/wc/guidelines.html*.

Table 9-6 provides a modern update for robot designers and operators, based heavily on the spirit and content of the original list. Most of these guidelines are targeted at World Wide Web robots; however, they are applicable to smaller-scale crawlers too.

*Table 9-6. Guidelines for web robot operators*

| Guideline | Description |
|---|---|
| **(1) Identification** | |
| Identify Your Robot | Use the HTTP User-Agent field to tell web servers the name of your robot. This will help administrators understand what your robot is doing. Some robots also include a URL describing the purpose and policies of the robot in the User-Agent header. |
| Identify Your Machine | Make sure your robot runs from a machine with a DNS entry, so web sites can reverse-DNS the robot IP address into a hostname. This will help the administrator identify the organization responsible for the robot. |
| Identify a Contact | Use the HTTP From field to provide a contact email address. |

*Table 9-6. Guidelines for web robot operators (continued)*

| Guideline | Description |
| --- | --- |
| **(2) Operations** | |
| Be Alert | Your robot will generate questions and complaints. Some of this is caused by robots that run astray. You must be cautious and watchful that your robot is behaving correctly. If your robot runs around the clock, you need to be extra careful. You may need to have operations people monitoring the robot $24 \times 7$ until your robot is well seasoned. |
| Be Prepared | When you begin a major robotic journey, be sure to notify people at your organization. Your organization will want to watch for network bandwidth consumption and be ready for any public inquiries. |
| Monitor and Log | Your robot should be richly equipped with diagnostics and logging, so you can track progress, identify any robot traps, and sanity check that everything is working right. We cannot stress enough the importance of monitoring and logging a robot's behavior. Problems and complaints will arise, and having detailed logs of a crawler's behavior can help a robot operator backtrack to what has happened. This is important not only for debugging your errant web crawler but also for defending its behavior against unjustified complaints. |
| Learn and Adapt | Each crawl, you will learn new things. Adapt your robot so it improves each time and avoids the common pitfalls. |
| **(3) Limit Yourself** | |
| Filter on URL | If a URL looks like it refers to data that you don't understand or are not interested in, you might want to skip it. For example, URLs ending in ".Z", ".gz", ".tar", or ".zip" are likely to be compressed files or archives. URLs ending in ".exe" are likely to be programs. URLs ending in ".gif", ".tif", ".jpg" are likely to be images. Make sure you get what you are after. |
| Filter Dynamic URLs | Usually, robots don't want to crawl content from dynamic gateways. The robot won't know how to properly format and post queries to gateways, and the results are likely to be erratic or transient. If a URL contains "cgi" or has a "?", the robot may want to avoid crawling the URL. |
| Filter with Accept Headers | Your robot should use HTTP Accept headers to tell servers what kind of content it understands. |
| Adhere to *robots.txt* | Your robot should adhere to the *robots.txt* controls on the site. |
| Throttle Yourself | Your robot should count the number of accesses to each site and when they occurred, and use this information to ensure that it doesn't visit any site too frequently. When a robot accesses a site more frequently than every few minutes, administrators get suspicious. When a robot accesses a site every few seconds, some administrators get angry. When a robot hammers a site as fast as it can, shutting out all other traffic, administrators will be furious.<br><br>In general, you should limit your robot to a few requests per minute maximum, and ensure a few seconds between each request. You also should limit the total number of accesses to a site, to prevent loops. |
| **(4) Tolerate Loops and Dups and Other Problems** | |
| Handle All Return Codes | You must be prepared to handle all HTTP status codes, including redirects and errors. You should also log and monitor these codes. A large number of non-success results on a site should cause investigation. It may be that many URLs are stale, or the server refuses to serve documents to robots. |
| Canonicalize URLs | Try to remove common aliases by normalizing all URLs into a standard form. |
| Aggressively Avoid Cycles | Work very hard to detect and avoid cycles. Treat the process of operating a crawl as a feedback loop. The results of problems and their resolutions should be fed back into the next crawl, making your crawler better with each iteration. |

*Table 9-6. Guidelines for web robot operators (continued)*

| Guideline | Description |
|---|---|
| Monitor for Traps | Some types of cycles are intentional and malicious. These may be intentionally hard to detect. Monitor for large numbers of accesses to a site with strange URLs. These may be traps. |
| Maintain a Blacklist | When you find traps, cycles, broken sites, and sites that want your robot to stay away, add them to a blacklist, and don't visit them again. |
| **(5) Scalability** | |
| Understand Space | Work out the math in advance for how large a problem you are solving. You may be surprised how much memory your application will require to complete a robotic task, because of the huge scale of the Web. |
| Understand Bandwidth | Understand how much network bandwidth you have available and how much you will need to complete your robotic task in the required time. Monitor the actual usage of network bandwidth. You probably will find that the outgoing bandwidth (requests) is much smaller than the incoming bandwidth (responses). By monitoring network usage, you also may find the potential to better optimize your robot, allowing it to take better advantage of the network bandwidth by better usage of its TCP connections.[a] |
| Understand Time | Understand how long it should take for your robot to complete its task, and sanity check that the progress matches your estimate. If your robot is way off your estimate, there probably is a problem worth investigating. |
| Divide and Conquer | For large-scale crawls, you will likely need to apply more hardware to get the job done, either using big multiprocessor servers with multiple network cards, or using multiple smaller computers working in unison. |
| **(6) Reliability** | |
| Test Thoroughly | Test your robot thoroughly internally before unleashing it on the world. When you are ready to test off-site, run a few, small, maiden voyages first. Collect lots of results and analyze your performance and memory use, estimating how they will scale up to the larger problem. |
| Checkpoint | Any serious robot will need to save a snapshot of its progress, from which it can restart on failure. There will be failures: you will find software bugs, and hardware will fail. Large-scale robots can't start from scratch each time this happens. Design in a checkpoint/restart feature from the beginning. |
| Fault Resiliency | Anticipate failures, and design your robot to be able to keep making progress when they occur. |
| **(7) Public Relations** | |
| Be Prepared | Your robot probably will upset a number of people. Be prepared to respond quickly to their enquiries. Make a web page policy statement describing your robot, and include detailed instructions on how to create a *robots.txt* file. |
| Be Understanding | Some of the people who contact you about your robot will be well informed and supportive; others will be naïve. A few will be unusually angry. Some may well seem insane. It's generally unproductive to argue the importance of your robotic endeavor. Explain the Robots Exclusion Standard, and if they are still unhappy, remove the complainant URLs immediately from your crawl and add them to the blacklist. |
| Be Responsive | Most unhappy webmasters are just unclear about robots. If you respond immediately and professionally, 90% of the complaints will disappear quickly. On the other hand, if you wait several days before responding, while your robot continues to visit a site, expect to find a very vocal, angry opponent. |

[a] See Chapter 4 for more on optimizing TCP performance.

# Search Engines

The most widespread web robots are used by Internet search engines. Internet search engines allow users to find documents about any subject all around the world.

Many of the most popular sites on the Web today are search engines. They serve as a starting point for many web users and provide the invaluable service of helping users find the information in which they are interested.

Web crawlers feed Internet search engines, by retrieving the documents that exist on the Web and allowing the search engines to create indexes of what words appear in what documents, much like the index at the back of this book. Search engines are the leading source of web robots—let's take a quick look at how they work.

## Think Big

When the Web was in its infancy, search engines were relatively simple databases that helped users locate documents on the Web. Today, with the billions of pages accessible on the Web, search engines have become essential in helping Internet users find information. They also have become quite complex, as they have had to evolve to handle the sheer scale of the Web.

With billions of web pages and many millions of users looking for information, search engines have to deploy sophisticated crawlers to retrieve these billions of web pages, as well as sophisticated query engines to handle the query load that millions of users generate.

Think about the task of a production web crawler, having to issue billions of HTTP queries in order to retrieve the pages needed by the search index. If each request took half a second to complete (which is probably slow for some servers and fast for others[*]), that still takes (for 1 billion documents):

$$0.5 \text{ seconds} \times (1{,}000{,}000{,}000) / ((60 \text{ sec/day}) \times (60 \text{ min/hour}) \times (24 \text{ hour/day}))$$

which works out to roughly 5,700 days if the requests are made sequentially! Clearly, large-scale crawlers need to be more clever, parallelizing requests and using banks of machines to complete the task. However, because of its scale, trying to crawl the entire Web still is a daunting challenge.

## Modern Search Engine Architecture

Today's search engines build complicated local databases, called "full-text indexes," about the web pages around the world and what they contain. These indexes act as a sort of card catalog for all the documents on the Web.

---

[*] This depends on the resources of the server, the client robot, and the network between the two.

---

Search-engine crawlers gather up web pages and bring them home, adding them to the full-text index. At the same time, search-engine users issue queries against the full-text index through web search gateways such as HotBot (*http://www.hotbot.com*) or Google (*http://www.google.com*). Because the web pages are changing all the time, and because of the amount of time it can take to crawl a large chunk of the Web, the full-text index is at best a snapshot of the Web.

The high-level architecture of a modern search engine is shown in Figure 9-7.

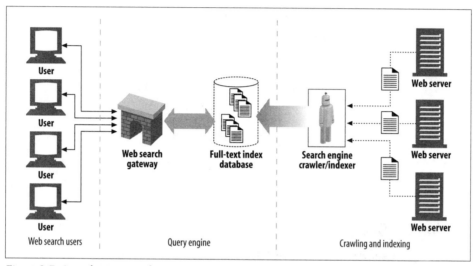

*Figure 9-7. A production search engine contains cooperating crawlers and query gateways*

## Full-Text Index

A full-text index is a database that takes a word and immediately tells you all the documents that contain that word. The documents themselves do not need to be scanned after the index is created.

Figure 9-8 shows three documents and the corresponding full-text index. The full-text index lists the documents containing each word.

For example:

- The word "a" is in documents A and B.
- The word "best" is in documents A and C.
- The word "drill" is in documents A and B.
- The word "routine" is in documents B and C.
- The word "the" is in all three documents, A, B, and C.

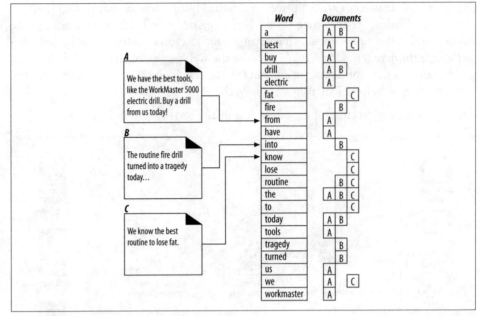

*Figure 9-8. Three documents and a full-text index*

## Posting the Query

When a user issues a query to a web search-engine gateway, she fills out an HTML form and her browser sends the form to the gateway, using an HTTP GET or POST request. The gateway program extracts the search query and converts the web UI query into the expression used to search the full-text index.[*]

Figure 9-9 shows a simple user query to the *www.joes-hardware.com* site. The user types "drills" into the search box form, and the browser translates this into a GET request with the query parameter as part of the URL.[†] The Joe's Hardware web server receives the query and hands it off to its search gateway application, which returns the resulting list of documents to the web server, which in turn formats those results into an HTML page for the user.

## Sorting and Presenting the Results

Once a search engine has used its index to determine the results of a query, the gateway application takes the results and cooks up a results page for the end user.

---

[*] The method for passing this query is dependent on the search solution being used.

[†] "Query Strings" in Chapter 2 discusses the common use of the query parameter in URLs.

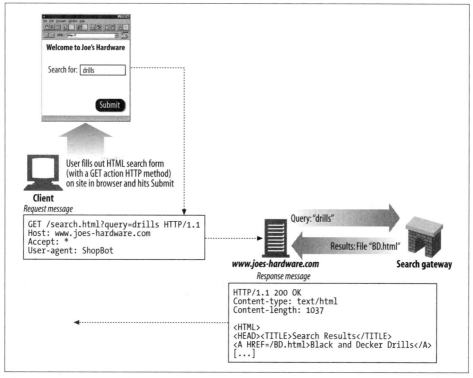

*Figure 9-9. Example search query request*

Since many web pages can contain any given word, search engines deploy clever algorithms to try to rank the results. For example, in Figure 9-8, the word "best" appears in multiple documents; search engines need to know the order in which they should present the list of result documents in order to present users with the most relevant results. This is called *relevancy ranking*—the process of scoring and ordering a list of search results.

To better aid this process, many of the larger search engines actually use census data collected during the crawl of the Web. For example, counting how many links point to a given page can help determine its popularity, and this information can be used to weight the order in which results are presented. The algorithms, tips from crawling, and other tricks used by search engines are some of their most guarded secrets.

## Spoofing

Since users often get frustrated when they do not see what they are looking for in the first few results of a search query, the order of search results can be important in finding a site. There is a lot of incentive for webmasters to attempt to get their sites listed near the top of the results sections for the words that they think best describe their sites, particularly if the sites are commercial and are relying on users to find them and use their services.

This desire for better listing has led to a lot of gaming of the search system and has created a constant tug-of-war between search-engine implementors and those seeking to get their sites listed prominently. Many webmasters list tons of keywords (some irrelevant) and deploy fake pages, or *spoofs*—even gateway applications that generate fake pages that may better trick the search engines' relevancy algorithms for particular words.

As a result of all this, search engine and robot implementors constantly have to tweak their relevancy algorithms to better catch these spoofs.

# For More Information

For more information on web clients, refer to:

*http://www.robotstxt.org/wc/robots.html*
  The Web Robots Pages—resources for robot developers, including the registry of Internet Robots.

*http://www.searchengineworld.com*
  Search Engine World—resources for search engines and robots.

*http://www.searchtools.com*
  Search Tools for Web Sites and Intranets—resources for search tools and robots.

*http://search.cpan.org/doc/ILYAZ/perl_ste/WWW/RobotRules.pm*
  RobotRules Perl source.

*http://www.conman.org/people/spc/robots2.html*
  An Extended Standard for Robot Exclusion.

*Managing Gigabytes: Compressing and Indexing Documents and Images*
  Witten, I., Moffat, A., and Bell, T., Morgan Kaufmann.

# CHAPTER 10

# HTTP-NG

As this book nears completion, HTTP is celebrating its tenth birthday. And it has been quite an accomplished decade for this Internet protocol. Today, HTTP moves the absolute majority of digital traffic around the world.

But as HTTP grows into its teenage years it faces a few challenges. In some ways, the pace of HTTP adoption has gotten ahead of its design. Today, people are using HTTP as a foundation for many diverse applications, over many different networking technologies.

This chapter outlines some of the trends and challenges for the future of HTTP, and a proposal for a next-generation architecture called HTTP-NG. While the working group for HTTP-NG has disbanded and its rapid adoption now appears unlikely, it nonetheless outlines some potential future directions of HTTP.

## HTTP's Growing Pains

HTTP originally was conceived as a simple technique for accessing linked multimedia content from distributed information servers. But, over the past decade, HTTP and its derivatives have taken on a much broader role.

HTTP/1.1 now provides tagging and fingerprinting to track document versions, methods to support document uploading and interactions with programmatic gateways, support for multilingual content, security and authentication, caching to reduce traffic, pipelining to reduce latency, persistent connections to reduce startup time and improve bandwidth, and range accesses to implement partial updates. Extensions and derivatives of HTTP have gone even further, supporting document publishing, application serving, arbitrary messaging, video streaming, and foundations for wireless multimedia access. HTTP is becoming a kind of "operating system" for distributed media applications.

The design of HTTP/1.1, while well considered, is beginning to show some strains as HTTP is used more and more as a unified substrate for complex remote operations. There are at least four areas where HTTP shows some growing pains:

*Complexity*
> HTTP is quite complex, and its features are interdependent. It is decidedly painful and error-prone to correctly implement HTTP software, because of the complex, interwoven requirements and the intermixing of connection management, message handling, and functional logic.

*Extensibility*
> HTTP is difficult to extend incrementally. There are many legacy HTTP applications that create incompatibilities for protocol extensions, because they contain no technology for autonomous functionality extensions.

*Performance*
> HTTP has performance inefficiencies. Many of these inefficiencies will become more serious with widespread adoption of high-latency, low-throughput wireless access technologies.

*Transport dependence*
> HTTP is designed around a TCP/IP network stack. While there are no restrictions against alternative substacks, there has been little work in this area. HTTP needs to provide better support for alternative substacks for it to be useful as a broader messaging platform in embedded and wireless applications.

# HTTP-NG Activity

In the summer of 1997, the World Wide Web Consortium launched a special project to investigate and propose a major new version of HTTP that would fix the problems related to complexity, extensibility, performance, and transport dependence. This new HTTP was called HTTP: The Next Generation (HTTP-NG).

A set of HTTP-NG proposals was presented at an IETF meeting in December 1998. These proposals outlined one possible major evolution of HTTP. This technology has not been widely implemented (and may never be), but HTTP-NG does represent the most serious effort toward extending the lineage of HTTP. Let's look at HTTP-NG in more detail.

# Modularize and Enhance

The theme of HTTP-NG can be captured in three words: "modularize and enhance." Instead of having connection management, message handling, server processing logic, and protocol methods all intermixed, the HTTP-NG working group proposed modularizing the protocol into three layers, illustrated in Figure 10-1:

---

- Layer 1, the *message transport layer*, focuses on delivering opaque messages between endpoints, independent of the function of the messages. The message transport layer supports various substacks (for example, stacks for wireless environments) and focuses on the problems of efficient message delivery and handling. The HTTP-NG project team proposed a protocol called *WebMUX* for this layer.

- Layer 2, the *remote invocation layer*, defines request/response functionality where clients can invoke operations on server resources. This layer is independent of message transport and of the precise semantics of the operations. It just provides a standard way of invoking any server operation. This layer attempts to provide an extensible, object-oriented framework more like CORBA, DCOM, and Java RMI than like the static, server-defined methods of HTTP/1.1. The HTTP-NG project team proposed the *Binary Wire Protocol* for this layer.

- Layer 3, the *web application layer*, provides most of the content-management logic. All of the HTTP/1.1 methods (GET, POST, PUT, etc.), as well as the HTTP/1.1 header parameters, are defined here. This layer also supports other services built on top of remote invocation, such as WebDAV.

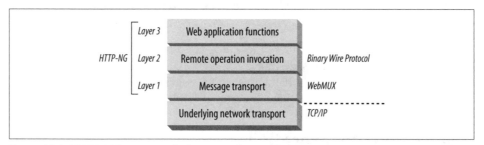

*Figure 10-1. HTTP-NG separates functions into layers*

Once the HTTP components are modularized, they can be enhanced to provide better performance and richer functionality.

# Distributed Objects

Much of the philosophy and functionality goals of HTTP-NG borrow heavily from structured, object-oriented, distributed-objects systems such as CORBA and DCOM. Distributed-objects systems can help with extensibility and feature functionality.

A community of researchers has been arguing for a convergence between HTTP and more sophisticated distributed-objects systems since 1996. For more information about the merits of a distributed-objects paradigm for the Web, check out the early paper from Xerox PARC entitled "Migrating the Web Toward Distributed Objects" (*ftp://ftp.parc.xerox.com/pub/ilu/misc/webilu.html*).

The ambitious philosophy of unifying the Web and distributed objects created resistance to HTTP-NG's adoption in some communities. Some past distributed-objects systems suffered from heavyweight implementation and formal complexity. The HTTP-NG project team attempted to address some of these concerns in the requirements.

# Layer 1: Messaging

Let's take a closer look at the three layers of HTTP-NG, starting with the lowest layer. The message transport layer is concerned with the efficient delivery of messages, independent of the meaning and purpose of the messages. The message transport layer provides an API for messaging, regardless of the actual underlying network stack.

This layer focuses on improving the performance of messaging, including:

- Pipelining and batching messages to reduce round-trip latency
- Reusing connections to reduce latency and improve delivered bandwidth
- Multiplexing multiple message streams in parallel, over the same connection, to optimize shared connections while preventing starvation of message streams
- Efficient message segmentation to make it easier to determine message boundaries

The HTTP-NG team invested much of its energy into the development of the Web-MUX protocol for layer 1 message transport. WebMUX is a high-performance message protocol that fragments and interleaves messages across a multiplexed TCP connection. We discuss WebMUX in a bit more detail later in this chapter.

# Layer 2: Remote Invocation

The middle layer of the HTTP-NG architecture supports remote method invocation. This layer provides a generic request/response framework where clients invoke operations on server resources. This layer does not concern itself with the implementation and semantics of the particular operations (caching, security, method logic, etc.); it is concerned only with the interface to allow clients to remotely invoke server operations.

Many remote method invocation standards already are available (CORBA, DCOM, and Java RMI, to name a few), and this layer is not intended to support every nifty feature of these systems. However, there is an explicit goal to extend the richness of HTTP RMI support from that provided by HTTP/1.1. In particular, there is a goal to provide more general remote procedure call support, in an extensible, object-oriented manner.

The HTTP-NG team proposed the Binary Wire Protocol for this layer. This protocol supports a high-performance, extensible technology for invoking well-described operations on a server and carrying back the results. We discuss the Binary Wire Protocol in a bit more detail later in this chapter.

---

# Layer 3: Web Application

The web application layer is where the semantics and application-specific logic are performed. The HTTP-NG working group shied away from the temptation to extend the HTTP application features, focusing instead on formal infrastructure.

The web application layer describes a system for providing application-specific services. These services are not monolithic; different APIs may be available for different applications. For example, the web application for HTTP/1.1 would constitute a different application from WebDAV, though they may share some common parts. The HTTP-NG architecture allows multiple applications to coexist at this level, sharing underlying facilities, and provides a mechanism for adding new applications.

The philosophy of the web application layer is to provide equivalent functionality for HTTP/1.1 and extension interfaces, while recasting them into a framework of extensible distributed objects. You can read more about the web application layer interfaces at *http://www.w3.org/Protocols/HTTP-NG/1998/08/draft-larner-nginterfaces-00.txt*.

# WebMUX

The HTTP-NG working group has invested much of its energy in the development of the WebMUX standard for message transport. WebMUX is a sophisticated, high-performance message system, where messages can be transported in parallel across a multiplexed TCP connection. Individual message streams, produced and consumed at different rates, can efficiently be packetized and multiplexed over a single or small number of TCP connections (see Figure 10-2).

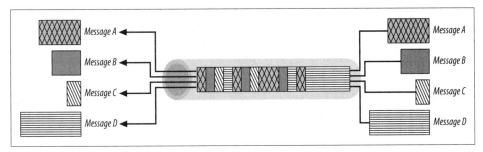

*Figure 10-2. WebMUX can multiplex multiple messages over a single connection*

Here are some of the significant goals of the WebMUX protocol:

- Simple design.
- High performance.
- Multiplexing—Multiple data streams (of arbitrary higher-level protocols) can be interleaved dynamically and efficiently over a single connection, without stalling data waiting for slow producers.

- Credit-based flow control—Data is produced and consumed at different rates, and senders and receivers have different amounts of memory and CPU resources available. WebMUX uses a "credit-based" flow-control scheme, where receivers preannounce interest in receiving data to prevent resource-scarcity deadlocks.
- Alignment preserving—Data alignment is preserved in the multiplexed stream so that binary data can be sent and processed efficiently.
- Rich functionality—The interface is rich enough to support a sockets API.

You can read more about the WebMUX Protocol at *http://www.w3.org/Protocols/MUX/WD-mux-980722.html*.

# Binary Wire Protocol

The HTTP-NG team proposed the Binary Wire Protocol to enhance how the next-generation HTTP protocol supports remote operations.

HTTP-NG defines "object types" and assigns each object type a list of methods. Each object type is assigned a URI, so its description and methods can be advertised. In this way, HTTP-NG is proposing a more extensible and object-oriented execution model than that provided with HTTP/1.1, where all methods were statically defined in the servers.

The Binary Wire Protocol carries operation-invocation requests from the client to the server and operation-result replies from the server to the client across a stateful connection. The stateful connection provides extra efficiency.

Request messages contain the operation, the target object, and optional data values. Reply messages carry back the termination status of the operation, the serial number of the matching request (allowing arbitrary ordering of parallel requests and responses), and optional return values. In addition to request and reply messages, this protocol defines several internal control messages used to improve the efficiency and robustness of the connection.

You can read more about the Binary Wire Protocol at *http://www.w3.org/Protocols/HTTP-NG/1998/08/draft-janssen-httpng-wire-00.txt*.

# Current Status

At the end of 1998, the HTTP-NG team concluded that it was too early to bring the HTTP-NG proposals to the IETF for standardization. There was concern that the industry and community had not yet fully adjusted to HTTP/1.1 and that the significant HTTP-NG rearchitecture to a distributed-objects paradigm would have been extremely disruptive without a clear transition plan.

Two proposals were made:

- Instead of attempting to promote the entire HTTP-NG rearchitecture in one step, it was proposed to focus on the WebMUX transport technology. But at the time of this writing, there hasn't been sufficient interest to establish a WebMUX working group.

- An effort was launched to investigate whether formal protocol types can be made flexible enough for use on the Web, perhaps using XML. This is especially important for a distributed-objects system that is extensible. This work is still in progress.

At the time of this writing, no major driving HTTP-NG effort is underway. But, with the ever-increasing use of HTTP, its growing use as a platform for diverse applications, and the growing adoption of wireless and consumer Internet technology, some of the techniques proposed in the HTTP-NG effort may prove significant in HTTP's teenage years.

# For More Information

For more information about HTTP-NG, please refer to the following detailed specifications and activity reports:

*http://www.w3.org/Protocols/HTTP-NG/*
  HTTP-NG Working Group (Proposed), W3C Consortium Web Site.

*http://www.w3.org/Protocols/MUX/WD-mux-980722.html*
  "The WebMUX Protocol," by J. Gettys and H. Nielsen.

*http://www.w3.org/Protocols/HTTP-NG/1998/08/draft-janssen-httpng-wire-00.txt*
  "Binary Wire Protocol for HTTP-NG," by B. Janssen.

*http://www.w3.org/Protocols/HTTP-NG/1998/08/draft-larner-nginterfaces-00.txt*
  "HTTP-NG Web Interfaces," by D. Larner.

*ftp://ftp.parc.xerox.com/pub/ilu/misc/webilu.html*
  "Migrating the Web Toward Distributed Objects," by D. Larner.

# PART III

# Identification, Authorization, and Security

The four chapters in Part III present a suite of techniques and technologies to track identity, enforce security, and control access to content:

- Chapter 11, *Client Identification and Cookies*, talks about techniques to identify users, so content can be personalized to the user audience.

- Chapter 12, *Basic Authentication*, highlights the basic mechanisms to verify user identity. This chapter also examines how HTTP authentication interfaces with databases.

- Chapter 13, *Digest Authentication*, explains digest authentication, a complex proposed enhancement to HTTP that provides significantly enhanced security.

- Chapter 14, *Secure HTTP*, is a detailed overview of Internet cryptography, digital certificates, and the Secure Sockets Layer (SSL).

# CHAPTER 11

# Client Identification and Cookies

Web servers may talk to thousands of different clients simultaneously. These servers often need to keep track of who they are talking to, rather than treating all requests as coming from anonymous clients. This chapter discusses some of the technologies that servers can use to identify who they are talking to.

## The Personal Touch

HTTP began its life as an anonymous, stateless, request/response protocol. A request came from a client, was processed by the server, and a response was sent back to the client. Little information was available to the web server to determine what user sent the request or to keep track of a sequence of requests from the visiting user.

Modern web sites want to provide a personal touch. They want to know more about users on the other ends of the connections and be able to keep track of those users as they browse. Popular online shopping sites like Amazon.com personalize their sites for you in several ways:

*Personal greetings*

Welcome messages and page contents are generated specially for the user, to make the shopping experience feel more personal.

*Targeted recommendations*

By learning about the interests of the customer, stores can suggest products that they believe the customer will appreciate. Stores can also run birthday specials near customers' birthdays and other significant days.

*Administrative information on file*

Online shoppers hate having to fill in cumbersome address and credit card forms over and over again. Some sites store these administrative details in a database. Once they identify you, they can use the administrative information on file, making the shopping experience much more convenient.

*Session tracking*

> HTTP transactions are stateless. Each request/response happens in isolation. Many web sites want to build up incremental state as you interact with the site (for example, filling an online shopping cart). To do this, web sites need a way to distinguish HTTP transactions from different users.

This chapter summarizes a few of the techniques used to identify users in HTTP. HTTP itself was not born with a rich set of identification features. The early web-site designers (practical folks that they were) built their own technologies to identify users. Each technique has its strengths and weaknesses. In this chapter, we'll discuss the following mechanisms to identify users:

- HTTP headers that carry information about user identity
- Client IP address tracking, to identify users by their IP addresses
- User login, using authentication to identify users
- Fat URLs, a technique for embedding identity in URLs
- Cookies, a powerful but efficient technique for maintaining persistent identity

# HTTP Headers

Table 11-1 shows the seven HTTP request headers that most commonly carry information about the user. We'll discuss the first three now; the last four headers are used for more advanced identification techniques that we'll discuss later.

*Table 11-1. HTTP headers carry clues about users*

| Header name | Header type | Description |
|---|---|---|
| From | Request | User's email address |
| User-Agent | Request | User's browser software |
| Referer | Request | Page user came from by following link |
| Authorization | Request | Username and password (discussed later) |
| Client-ip | Extension (Request) | Client's IP address (discussed later) |
| X-Forwarded-For | Extension (Request) | Client's IP address (discussed later) |
| Cookie | Extension (Request) | Server-generated ID label (discussed later) |

The From header contains the user's email address. Ideally, this would be a viable source of user identification, because each user would have a different email address. However, few browsers send From headers, due to worries of unscrupulous servers collecting email addresses and using them for junk mail distribution. In practice, From headers are sent by automated robots or spiders so that if something goes astray, a webmaster has someplace to send angry email complaints.

The User-Agent header tells the server information about the browser the user is using, including the name and version of the program, and often information about the operating system. This sometimes is useful for customizing content to interoperate well with particular browsers and their attributes, but that doesn't do much to help identify the particular user in any meaningful way. Here are two User-Agent headers, one sent by Netscape Navigator and the other by Microsoft Internet Explorer:

*Navigator 6.2*
```
User-Agent: Mozilla/5.0 (Windows; U; Windows NT 5.0; en-US; rv:0.9.4) Gecko/20011128
    Netscape6/6.2.1
```
*Internet Explorer 6.01*
```
User-Agent: Mozilla/4.0 (compatible; MSIE 6.0; Windows NT 5.0)
```

The Referer header provides the URL of the page the user is coming from. The Referer header alone does not directly identify the user, but it does tell what page the user previously visited. You can use this to better understand user browsing behavior and user interests. For example, if you arrive at a web server coming from a baseball site, the server may infer you are a baseball fan.

The From, User-Agent, and Referer headers are insufficient for dependable identification purposes. The remaining sections discuss more precise schemes to identify particular users.

# Client IP Address

Early web pioneers tried using the IP address of the client as a form of identification. This scheme works if each user has a distinct IP address, if the IP address seldom (if ever) changes, and if the web server can determine the client IP address for each request. While the client IP address typically is not present in the HTTP headers,[*] web servers can find the IP address of the other side of the TCP connection carrying the HTTP request. For example, on Unix systems, the *getpeername* function call returns the client IP address of the sending machine:

```
status = getpeername(tcp_connection_socket,...);
```

Unfortunately, using the client IP address to identify the user has numerous weaknesses that limit its effectiveness as a user-identification technology:

- Client IP addresses describe only the computer being used, not the user. If multiple users share the same computer, they will be indistinguishable.

- Many Internet service providers dynamically assign IP addresses to users when they log in. Each time they log in, they get a different address, so web servers can't assume that IP addresses will identify a user across login sessions.

---

[*] As we'll see later, some proxies do add a Client-ip header, but this is not part of the HTTP standard.

- To enhance security and manage scarce addresses, many users browse the Internet through Network Address Translation (NAT) firewalls. These NAT devices obscure the IP addresses of the real clients behind the firewall, converting the actual client IP address into a single, shared firewall IP address (and different port numbers).

- HTTP proxies and gateways typically open new TCP connections to the origin server. The web server will see the IP address of the proxy server instead of that of the client. Some proxies attempt to work around this problem by adding special Client-ip or X-Forwarded-For HTTP extension headers to preserve the original IP address (Figure 11-1). But not all proxies support this behavior.

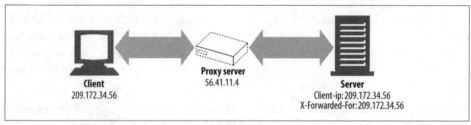

**Client**
209.172.34.56

**Proxy server**
56.41.11.4

**Server**
Client-ip: 209.172.34.56
X-Forwarded-For: 209.172.34.56

*Figure 11-1. Proxies can add extension headers to pass along the original client IP address*

Some web sites still use client IP addresses to keep track of the users between sessions, but not many. There are too many places where IP address targeting doesn't work well.

A few sites even use client IP addresses as a security feature, serving documents only to users from a particular IP address. While this may be adequate within the confines of an intranet, it breaks down in the Internet, primarily because of the ease with which IP addresses are spoofed (forged). The presence of intercepting proxies in the path also breaks this scheme. Chapter 14 discusses much stronger schemes for controlling access to privileged documents.

## User Login

Rather than passively trying to guess the identity of a user from his IP address, a web server can explicitly ask the user who he is by requiring him to authenticate (log in) with a username and password.

To help make web site logins easier, HTTP includes a built-in mechanism to pass username information to web sites, using the WWW-Authenticate and Authorization headers. Once logged in, the browsers continually send this login information with each request to the site, so the information is always available. We'll discuss this HTTP authentication in much more detail in Chapter 12, but let's take a quick look at it now.

If a server wants a user to register before providing access to the site, it can send back an HTTP 401 Login Required response code to the browser. The browser will then display a login dialog box and supply the information in the next request to the browser, using the Authorization header.* This is depicted in Figure 11-2.

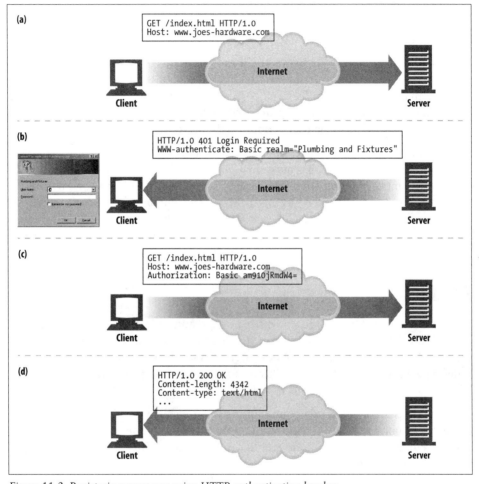

*Figure 11-2. Registering username using HTTP authentication headers*

Here's what's happening in this figure:

- In Figure 11-2a, a browser makes a request from the *www.joes-hardware.com* site.
- The site doesn't know the identity of the user, so in Figure 11-2b, the server requests a login by returning the 401 Login Required HTTP response code and

---

* To save users from having to log in for each request, most browsers will remember login information for a site and pass in the login information for each request to the site.

adds the WWW-Authenticate header. This causes the browser to pop up a login dialog box.

- Once the user enters a username and a password (to sanity check his identity), the browser repeats the original request. This time it adds an Authorization header, specifying the username and password. The username and password are scrambled, to hide them from casual or accidental network observers.[*]

- Now, the server is aware of the user's identity.

- For future requests, the browser will automatically issue the stored username and password when asked and will often even send it to the site when not asked. This makes it possible to log in once to a site and have your identity maintained through the session, by having the browser send the Authorization header as a token of your identity on each request to the server.

However, logging in to web sites is tedious. As Fred browses from site to site, he'll need to log in for each site. To make matters worse, it is likely that poor Fred will need to remember different usernames and passwords for different sites. His favorite username, "fred," will already have been chosen by someone else by the time he visits many sites, and some sites will have different rules about the length and composition of usernames and passwords. Pretty soon, Fred will give up on the Internet and go back to watching Oprah. The next section discusses a solution to this problem.

# Fat URLs

Some web sites keep track of user identity by generating special versions of each URL for each user. Typically, a real URL is extended by adding some state information to the start or end of the URL path. As the user browses the site, the web server dynamically generates hyperlinks that continue to maintain the state information in the URLs.

URLs modified to include user state information are called *fat URLs*. The following are some example fat URLs used in the Amazon.com e-commerce web site. Each URL is suffixed by a user-unique identification number (002-1145265-8016838, in this case) that helps track a user as she browses the store.

```
...
<a href="/exec/obidos/tg/browse/-/229220/ref=gr_gifts/002-1145265-8016838">All
    Gifts</a><br>
<a href="/exec/obidos/wishlist/ref=gr_pl1_/002-1145265-8016838">Wish List</a><br>
...
<a href="http://s1.amazon.com/exec/varzea/tg/armed-forces/-//ref=gr_af_/002-1145265-
    8016838">Salute Our Troops</a><br>
<a href="/exec/obidos/tg/browse/-/749188/ref=gr_p4_/002-1145265-8016838">Free
    Shipping</a><br>
```

---

[*] As we will see in Chapter 14, the HTTP basic authentication username and password can easily be unscrambled by anyone who wants to go through a minimal effort. More secure techniques will be discussed later.

```
<a href="/exec/obidos/tg/browse/-/468532/ref=gr_returns/002-1145265-8016838">Easy
   Returns</a>
...
```

You can use fat URLs to tie the independent HTTP transactions with a web server into a single "session" or "visit." The first time a user visits the web site, a unique ID is generated, it is added to the URL in a server-recognizable way, and the server redirects the client to this fat URL. Whenever the server gets a request for a fat URL, it can look up any incremental state associated with that user ID (shopping carts, profiles, etc.), and it rewrites all outgoing hyperlinks to make them fat, to maintain the user ID.

Fat URLs can be used to identify users as they browse a site. But this technology does have several serious problems. Some of these problems include:

*Ugly URLs*
> The fat URLs displayed in the browser are confusing for new users.

*Can't share URLs*
> The fat URLs contain state information about a particular user and session. If you mail that URL to someone else, you may inadvertently be sharing your accumulated personal information.

*Breaks caching*
> Generating user-specific versions of each URL means that there are no longer commonly accessed URLs to cache.

*Extra server load*
> The server needs to rewrite HTML pages to fatten the URLs.

*Escape hatches*
> It is too easy for a user to accidentally "escape" from the fat URL session by jumping to another site or by requesting a particular URL. Fat URLs work only if the user strictly follows the premodified links. If the user escapes, he may lose his progress (perhaps a filled shopping cart) and will have to start again.

*Not persistent across sessions*
> All information is lost when the user logs out, unless he bookmarks the particular fat URL.

# Cookies

Cookies are the best current way to identify users and allow persistent sessions. They don't suffer many of the problems of the previous techniques, but they often are used in conjunction with those techniques for extra value. Cookies were first developed by Netscape but now are supported by all major browsers.

Because cookies are important, and they define new HTTP headers, we're going to explore them in more detail than we did the previous techniques. The presence of cookies also impacts caching, and most caches and browsers disallow caching of any cookied content. The following sections present more details.

## Types of Cookies

You can classify cookies broadly into two types: session cookies and persistent cookies. A session cookie is a temporary cookie that keeps track of settings and preferences as a user navigates a site. A session cookie is deleted when the user exits the browser. Persistent cookies can live longer; they are stored on disk and survive browser exits and computer restarts. Persistent cookies often are used to retain a configuration profile or login name for a site that a user visits periodically.

The only difference between session cookies and persistent cookies is when they expire. As we will see later, a cookie is a session cookie if its Discard parameter is set, or if there is no Expires or Max-Age parameter indicating an extended expiration time.

## How Cookies Work

Cookies are like "Hello, My Name Is" stickers stuck onto users by servers. When a user visits a web site, the web site can read all the stickers attached to the user by that server.

The first time the user visits a web site, the web server doesn't know anything about the user (Figure 11-3a). The web server expects that this same user will return again, so it wants to "slap" a unique cookie onto the user so it can identify this user in the future. The cookie contains an arbitrary list of *name=value* information, and it is attached to the user using the Set-Cookie or Set-Cookie2 HTTP response (extension) headers.

Cookies can contain any information, but they often contain just a unique identification number, generated by the server for tracking purposes. For example, in Figure 11-3b, the server slaps onto the user a cookie that says id="34294". The server can use this number to look up database information that the server accumulates for its visitors (purchase history, address information, etc.).

However, cookies are not restricted to just ID numbers. Many web servers choose to keep information directly in the cookies. For example:

```
Cookie: name="Brian Totty"; phone="555-1212"
```

The browser remembers the cookie contents sent back from the server in Set-Cookie or Set-Cookie2 headers, storing the set of cookies in a browser cookie database (think of it like a suitcase with stickers from various countries on it). When the user returns to the same site in the future (Figure 11-3c), the browser will select those cookies slapped onto the user by that server and pass them back in a Cookie request header.

## Cookie Jar: Client-Side State

The basic idea of cookies is to let the browser accumulate a set of server-specific information, and provide this information back to the server each time you visit.

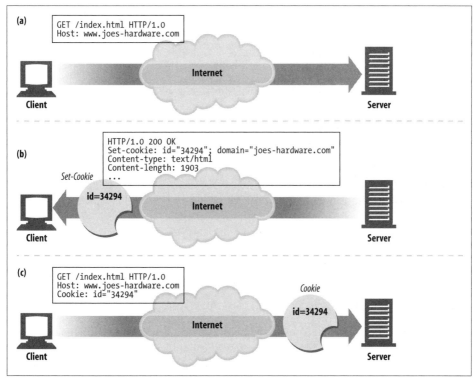

*Figure 11-3. Slapping a cookie onto a user*

Because the browser is responsible for storing the cookie information, this system is called *client-side state*. The official name for the cookie specification is the HTTP State Management Mechanism.

### Netscape Navigator cookies

Different browsers store cookies in different ways. Netscape Navigator stores cookies in a single text file called *cookies.txt*. For example:

```
# Netscape HTTP Cookie File
# http://www.netscape.com/newsref/std/cookie_spec.html
# This is a generated file!  Do not edit.
#
# domain                  allh   path     secure expires     name      value

www.fedex.com             FALSE  /        FALSE  1136109676  cc        /us/
.bankofamericaonline.com  TRUE   /        FALSE  1009789256  state     CA
.cnn.com                  TRUE   /        FALSE  1035069235  SelEdition www
secure.eepulse.net        FALSE  /eePulse FALSE  1007162968  cid       %FE%FF%002
www.reformamt.org         TRUE   /forum   FALSE  1033761379  LastVisit 1003520952
www.reformamt.org         TRUE   /forum   FALSE  1033761379  UserName  Guest
  ...
```

Each line of the text file represents a cookie. There are seven tab-separated fields:

*domain*
> The domain of the cookie

*allh*
> Whether all hosts in a domain get the cookie, or only the specific host named

*path*
> The path prefix in the domain associated with the cookie

*secure*
> Whether we should send this cookie only if we have an SSL connection

*expiration*
> The cookie expiration date in seconds since Jan 1, 1970 00:00:00 GMT

*name*
> The name of the cookie variable

*value*
> The value of the cookie variable

### Microsoft Internet Explorer cookies

Microsoft Internet Explorer stores cookies in individual text files in the cache directory. You can browse this directory to view the cookies, as shown in Figure 11-4. The format of the Internet Explorer cookie files is proprietary, but many of the fields are easily understood. Each cookie is stored one after the other in the file, and each cookie consists of multiple lines.

The first line of each cookie in the file contains the cookie variable name. The next line is the variable value. The third line contains the domain and path. The remaining lines are proprietary data, presumably including dates and other flags.

## Different Cookies for Different Sites

A browser can have hundreds or thousands of cookies in its internal cookie jar, but browsers don't send every cookie to every site. In fact, they typically send only two or three cookies to each site. Here's why:

- Moving all those cookie bytes would dramatically slow performance. Browsers would actually be moving more cookie bytes than real content bytes!

- Most of these cookies would just be unrecognizable gibberish for most sites, because they contain server-specific name/value pairs.

- Sending all cookies to all sites would create a potential privacy concern, with sites you don't trust getting information you intended only for another site.

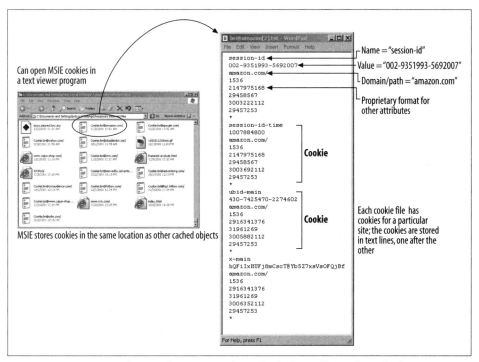

*Figure 11-4. Internet Explorer cookies are stored in individual text files in the cache directory*

In general, a browser sends to a server only those cookies that the server generated. Cookies generated by *joes-hardware.com* are sent to *joes-hardware.com* and not to *bobs-books.com* or *marys-movies.com*.

Many web sites contract with third-party vendors to manage advertisements. These advertisements are made to look like they are integral parts of the web site and do push persistent cookies. When the user goes to a different web site serviced by the same advertisement company, the persistent cookie set earlier is sent back again by the browser (because the domains match). A marketing company could use this technique, combined with the Referer header, to potentially build an exhaustive data set of user profiles and browsing habits. Modern browsers allow you to configure privacy settings to restrict third-party cookies.

### Cookie Domain attribute

A server generating a cookie can control which sites get to see that cookie by adding a Domain attribute to the Set-Cookie response header. For example, the following HTTP response header tells the browser to send the cookie user="mary17" to any site in the domain *.airtravelbargains.com*:

```
Set-cookie: user="mary17"; domain="airtravelbargains.com"
```

If the user visits *www.airtravelbargains.com*, *specials.airtravelbargains.com*, or any site ending in *.airtravelbargains.com*, the following Cookie header will be issued:

```
Cookie: user="mary17"
```

### Cookie Path attribute

The cookie specification even lets you associate cookies with *portions* of web sites. This is done using the Path attribute, which indicates the URL path prefix where each cookie is valid.

For example, one web server might be shared between two organizations, each having separate cookies. The site *www.airtravelbargains.com* might devote part of its web site to auto rentals—say, *http://www.airtravelbargains.com/autos/*—using a separate cookie to keep track of a user's preferred car size. A special auto-rental cookie might be generated like this:

```
Set-cookie: pref=compact; domain="airtravelbargains.com"; path=/autos/
```

If the user goes to *http://www.airtravelbargains.com/specials.html*, she will get only this cookie:

```
Cookie: user="mary17"
```

But if she goes to *http://www.airtravelbargains.com/autos/cheapo/index.html*, she will get both of these cookies:

```
Cookie: user="mary17"
Cookie: pref=compact
```

So, cookies are pieces of state, slapped onto the client by the servers, maintained by the clients, and sent back to only those sites that are appropriate. Let's look in more detail at the cookie technology and standards.

## Cookie Ingredients

There are two different versions of cookie specifications in use: Version 0 cookies (sometimes called "Netscape cookies"), and Version 1 ("RFC 2965") cookies. Version 1 cookies are a less widely used extension of Version 0 cookies.

Neither the Version 0 or Version 1 cookie specification is documented as part of the HTTP/1.1 specification. There are two primary adjunct documents that best describe the use of cookies, summarized in Table 11-2.

*Table 11-2. Cookie specifications*

| Title | Description | Location |
|-------|-------------|----------|
| Persistent Client State: HTTP Cookies | Original Netscape cookie standard | *http://home.netscape.com/newsref/ std/cookie_spec.html* |
| RFC 2965: HTTP State Management Mechanism | October 2000 cookie standard, obsoletes RFC 2109 | *http://www.ietf.org/rfc/rfc2965.txt* |

# Version 0 (Netscape) Cookies

The initial cookie specification was defined by Netscape. These "Version 0" cookies defined the Set-Cookie response header, the Cookie request header, and the fields available for controlling cookies. Version 0 cookies look like this:

```
Set-Cookie: name=value [; expires=date] [; path=path] [; domain=domain] [; secure]

Cookie: name1=value1 [; name2=value2] ...
```

## Version 0 Set-Cookie header

The Set-Cookie header has a mandatory cookie name and cookie value. It can be followed by optional cookie attributes, separated by semicolons. The Set-Cookie fields are described in Table 11-3.

*Table 11-3. Version 0 (Netscape) Set-Cookie attributes*

| Set-Cookie attribute | Description and examples |
| --- | --- |
| NAME=VALUE | Mandatory. Both NAME and VALUE are sequences of characters, excluding the semicolon, comma, equals sign, and whitespace, unless quoted in double quotes. The web server can create any NAME=VALUE association, which will be sent back to the web server on subsequent visits to the site. |
| | `Set-Cookie: customer=Mary` |
| Expires | Optional. This attribute specifies a date string that defines the valid lifetime of that cookie. Once the expiration date has been reached, the cookie will no longer be stored or given out. The date is formatted as: |
| | `Weekday, DD-Mon-YY HH:MM:SS GMT` |
| | The only legal time zone is GMT, and the separators between the elements of the date must be dashes. If Expires is not specified, the cookie will expire when the user's session ends. |
| | `Set-Cookie: foo=bar; expires=Wednesday, 09-Nov-99 23:12:40 GMT` |
| Domain | Optional. A browser sends the cookie only to server hostnames in the specified domain. This lets servers restrict cookies to only certain domains. A domain of "acme.com" would match hostnames "anvil.acme.com" and "shipping.crate.acme.com", but not "www.cnn.com". |
| | Only hosts within the specified domain can set a cookie for a domain, and domains must have at least two or three periods in them to prevent domains of the form ".com", ".edu", and "va.us". Any domain that falls within the fixed set of special top-level domains listed here requires only two periods. Any other domain requires at least three. The special top-level domains are: .com, .edu, .net, .org, .gov, .mil, .int, .biz, .info, .name, .museum, .coop, .aero, and .pro. |
| | If the domain is not specified, it defaults to the hostname of the server that generated the Set-Cookie response. |
| | `Set-Cookie: SHIPPING=FEDEX; domain="joes-hardware.com"` |
| Path | Optional. This attribute lets you assign cookies to particular documents on a server. If the Path attribute is a prefix of a URL path, a cookie can be attached. The path "/foo" matches "/foobar" and "/foo/bar.html". The path "/" matches everything in the domain. |
| | If the path is not specified, it is set to the path of the URL that generated the Set-Cookie response. |
| | `Set-Cookie: lastorder=00183; path=/orders` |
| Secure | Optional. If this attribute is included, a cookie will be sent only if HTTP is using an SSL secure connection. |
| | `Set-Cookie: private_id=519; secure` |

### Version 0 Cookie header

When a client sends requests, it includes all the unexpired cookies that match the domain, path, and secure filters to the site. All the cookies are combined into a Cookie header:

```
Cookie: session-id=002-1145265-8016838; session-id-time=1007884800
```

## Version 1 (RFC 2965) Cookies

An extended version of cookies is defined in RFC 2965 (previously RFC 2109). This Version 1 standard introduces the Set-Cookie2 and Cookie2 headers, but it also interoperates with the Version 0 system.

The RFC 2965 cookie standard is a bit more complicated than the original Netscape standard and is not yet completely supported. The major changes of RFC 2965 cookies are:

- Associate descriptive text with each cookie to explain its purpose
- Support forced destruction of cookies on browser exit, regardless of expiration
- Max-Age aging of cookies in relative seconds, instead of absolute dates
- Ability to control cookies by the URL port number, not just domain and path
- The Cookie header carries back the domain, port, and path filters (if any)
- Version number for interoperability
- $ prefix in Cookie header to distinguish additional keywords from usernames

The Version 1 cookie syntax is as follows:

```
set-cookie       =    "Set-Cookie2:" cookies
cookies          =    1#cookie
cookie           =    NAME "=" VALUE *(";" set-cookie-av)
NAME             =    attr
VALUE            =    value
set-cookie-av    =    "Comment" "=" value
                 |    "CommentURL" "=" <"> http_URL <">
                 |    "Discard"
                 |    "Domain" "=" value
                 |    "Max-Age" "=" value
                 |    "Path" "=" value
                 |    "Port" [ "=" <"> portlist <"> ]
                 |    "Secure"
                 |    "Version" "=" 1*DIGIT
portlist         =    1#portnum
portnum          =    1*DIGIT

cookie           =    "Cookie:" cookie-version 1*((";" | ",") cookie-value)
cookie-value     =    NAME "=" VALUE [";" path] [";" domain] [";" port]
cookie-version   =    "$Version" "=" value
NAME             =    attr
VALUE            =    value
```

```
path          =   "$Path" "=" value
domain        =   "$Domain" "=" value
port          =   "$Port" [ "=" <"> value <"> ]

cookie2 =         "Cookie2:" cookie-version
```

### Version 1 Set-Cookie2 header

More attributes are available in the Version 1 cookie standard than in the Netscape standard. Table 11-4 provides a quick summary of the attributes. Refer to RFC 2965 for more detailed explanation.

*Table 11-4. Version 1 (RFC 2965) Set-Cookie2 attributes*

| Set-Cookie2 attribute | Description and examples |
|---|---|
| NAME=VALUE | Mandatory. The web server can create any NAME=VALUE association, which will be sent back to the web server on subsequent visits to the site. The name must not begin with "$", because that character is reserved. |
| Version | Mandatory. The value of this attribute is an integer, corresponding to the version of the cookie specification. RFC 2965 is Version 1. `Set-Cookie2: Part="Rocket_Launcher_0001"; Version="1"` |
| Comment | Optional. This attribute documents how a server intends to use the cookie. The user can inspect this policy to decide whether to permit a session with this cookie. The value must be in UTF-8 encoding. |
| CommentURL | Optional. This attribute provides a URL pointer to detailed documentation about the purpose and policy for a cookie. The user can inspect this policy to decide whether to permit a session with this cookie. |
| Discard | Optional. If this attribute is present, it instructs the client to discard the cookie when the client program terminates. |
| Domain | Optional. A browser sends the cookie only to server hostnames in the specified domain. This lets servers restrict cookies to only certain domains. A domain of "acme.com" would match host-names "anvil.acme.com" and "shipping.crate.acme.com", but not "www.cnn.com". The rules for domain matching are basically the same as in Netscape cookies, but there are a few additional rules. Refer to RFC 2965 for details. |
| Max-Age | Optional. The value of this attribute is an integer that sets the lifetime of the cookie in seconds. Clients should calculate the age of the cookie according to the HTTP/1.1 age-calculation rules. When a cookie's age becomes greater than the Max-Age, the client should discard the cookie. A value of zero means the cookie with that name should be discarded immediately. |
| Path | Optional. This attribute lets you assign cookies to particular documents on a server. If the Path attribute is a prefix of a URL path, a cookie can be attached. The path "/foo" would match "/foobar" and "/foo/bar.html". The path "/" matches everything in the domain. If the path is not specified, it is set to the path of the URL that generated the Set-Cookie response. |
| Port | Optional. This attribute can stand alone as a keyword, or it can include a comma-separated list of ports to which a cookie may be applied. If there is a port list, the cookie can be served only to servers whose ports match a port in the list. If the Port keyword is provided in isolation, the cookie can be served only to the port number of the current responding server. `Set-Cookie2: foo="bar"; Version="1"; Port="80,81,8080"` `Set-Cookie2: foo="bar"; Version="1"; Port` |
| Secure | Optional. If this attribute is included, a cookie will be sent only if HTTP is using an SSL secure connection. |

### Version 1 Cookie header

Version 1 cookies carry back additional information about each delivered cookie, describing the filters each cookie passed. Each matching cookie must include any Domain, Port, or Path attributes from the corresponding Set-Cookie2 headers.

For example, assume the client has received these five Set-Cookie2 responses in the past from the *www.joes-hardware.com* web site:

```
Set-Cookie2: ID="29046"; Domain=".joes-hardware.com"
Set-Cookie2: color=blue
Set-Cookie2: support-pref="L2"; Domain="customer-care.joes-hardware.com"
Set-Cookie2: Coupon="hammer027"; Version="1"; Path="/tools"
Set-Cookie2: Coupon="handvac103"; Version="1"; Path="/tools/cordless"
```

If the client makes another request for path */tools/cordless/specials.html*, it will pass along a long Cookie2 header like this:

```
Cookie: $Version="1";
        ID="29046"; $Domain=".joes-hardware.com";
        color="blue";
        Coupon="hammer027"; $Path="/tools";
        Coupon="handvac103"; $Path="/tools/cordless"
```

Notice that all the matching cookies are delivered with their Set-Cookie2 filters, and the reserved keywords begin with a dollar sign ($).

### Version 1 Cookie2 header and version negotiation

The Cookie2 request header is used to negotiate interoperability between clients and servers that understand different versions of the cookie specification. The Cookie2 header advises the server that the user agent understands new-style cookies and provides the version of the cookie standard supported (it would have made more sense to call it Cookie-Version):

```
Cookie2: $Version="1"
```

If the server understands new-style cookies, it recognizes the Cookie2 header and should send Set-Cookie2 (rather than Set-Cookie) response headers. If a client gets both a Set-Cookie and a Set-Cookie2 header for the same cookie, it ignores the old Set-Cookie header.

If a client supports both Version 0 and Version 1 cookies but gets a Version 0 Set-Cookie header from the server, it should send cookies with the Version 0 Cookie header. However, the client also should send Cookie2: $Version="1" to give the server indication that it can upgrade.

## Cookies and Session Tracking

Cookies can be used to track users as they make multiple transactions to a web site. E-commerce web sites use session cookies to keep track of users' shopping carts as they browse. Let's take the example of the popular shopping site Amazon.com.

---

When you type *http://www.amazon.com* into your browser, you start a chain of transactions where the web server attaches identification information through a series of redirects, URL rewrites, and cookie setting.

Figure 11-5 shows a transaction sequence captured from an Amazon.com visit:

- Figure 11-5a—Browser requests Amazon.com root page for the first time.
- Figure 11-5b—Server redirects the client to a URL for the e-commerce software.
- Figure 11-5c—Client makes a request to the redirected URL.
- Figure 11-5d—Server slaps two session cookies on the response and redirects the user to another URL, so the client will request again with these cookies attached. This new URL is a fat URL, meaning that some state is embedded into the URL. If the client has cookies disabled, some basic identification can still be done as long as the user follows the Amazon.com-generated fat URL links and doesn't leave the site.
- Figure 11-5e—Client requests the new URL, but now passes the two attached cookies.
- Figure 11-5f—Server redirects to the *home.html* page and attaches two more cookies.
- Figure 11-5g—Client fetches the *home.html* page and passes all four cookies.
- Figure 11-5h—Server serves back the content.

## Cookies and Caching

You have to be careful when caching documents that are involved with cookie transactions. You don't want to assign one user some past user's cookie or, worse, show one user the contents of someone else's personalized document.

The rules for cookies and caching are not well established. Here are some guiding principles for dealing with caches:

*Mark documents uncacheable if they are*

The document owner knows best if a document is uncacheable. Explicitly mark documents uncacheable if they are—specifically, use Cache-Control: no-cache="Set-Cookie" if the document is cacheable except for the Set-Cookie header. The other, more general practice of using Cache-Control: public for documents that are cacheable promotes bandwidth savings in the Web.

*Be cautious about caching Set-Cookie headers*

If a response has a Set-Cookie header, you can cache the body (unless told otherwise), but you should be extra cautious about caching the Set-Cookie header. If you send the same Set-Cookie header to multiple users, you may be defeating user targeting.

Some caches delete the Set-Cookie header before storing a response in the cache, but that also can cause problems, because clients served from the cache will no

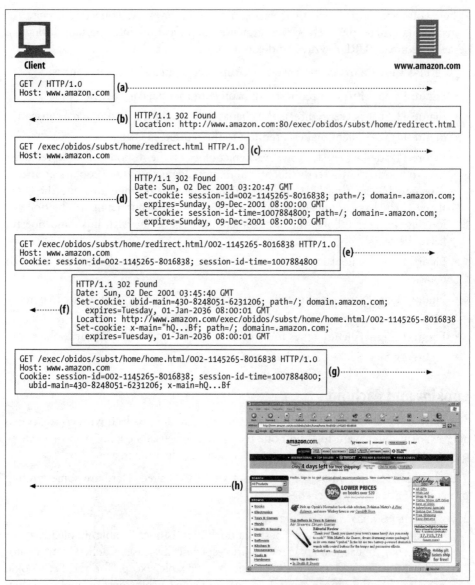

*Figure 11-5. The Amazon.com web site uses session cookies to track users*

longer get cookies slapped on them that they normally would without the cache. This situation can be improved by forcing the cache to revalidate every request with the origin server and merging any returned Set-Cookie headers with the client response. The origin server can dictate such revalidations by adding this header to the cached copy:

```
Cache-Control: must-revalidate, max-age=0
```

More conservative caches may refuse to cache any response that has a Set-Cookie header, even though the content may actually be cacheable. Some caches allow modes when Set-Cookied images are cached, but not text.

*Be cautious about requests with Cookie headers*

When a request arrives with a Cookie header, it provides a hint that the resulting content might be personalized. Personalized content must be flagged uncacheable, but some servers may erroneously not mark this content as uncacheable.

Conservative caches may choose not to cache any document that comes in response to a request with a Cookie header. And again, some caches allow modes when Cookied images are cached, but not text. The more accepted policy is to cache images with Cookie headers, with the expiration time set to zero, thus forcing a revalidate every time.

## Cookies, Security, and Privacy

Cookies themselves are not believed to be a tremendous security risk, because they can be disabled and because much of the tracking can be done through log analysis or other means. In fact, by providing a standardized, scrutinized method for retaining personal information in remote databases and using anonymous cookies as keys, the frequency of communication of sensitive data from client to server can be reduced.

Still, it is good to be cautious when dealing with privacy and user tracking, because there is always potential for abuse. The biggest misuse comes from third-party web sites using persistent cookies to track users. This practice, combined with IP addresses and information from the Referer header, has enabled these marketing companies to build fairly accurate user profiles and browsing patterns.

In spite of all the negative publicity, the conventional wisdom is that the session handling and transactional convenience of cookies outweighs most risks, if you use caution about who you provide personal information to and review sites' privacy policies.

The Computer Incident Advisory Capability (part of the U.S. Department of Energy) wrote an assessment of the overrepresented dangers of cookies in 1998. Here's an excerpt from that report:

```
CIAC I-034: Internet Cookies
(http://www.ciac.org/ciac/bulletins/i-034.shtml)

PROBLEM:

Cookies are short pieces of data used by web servers to help identify web users. The
popular concepts and rumors about what a cookie can do has reached almost mystical
proportions, frightening users and worrying their managers.
```

VULNERABILITY ASSESSMENT:

The vulnerability of systems to damage or snooping by using web browser cookies is essentially nonexistent. Cookies can only tell a web server if you have been there before and can pass short bits of information (such as a user number) from the web server back to itself the next time you visit. Most cookies last only until you quit your browser and then are destroyed. A second type of cookie known as a persistent cookie has an expiration date and is stored on your disk until that date. A persistent cookie can be used to track a user's browsing habits by identifying him whenever he returns to a site. Information about where you come from and what web pages you visit already exists in a web server's log files and could also be used to track users browsing habits, cookies just make it easier.

# For More Information

Here are a few more useful sources for additional information about cookies:

*Cookies*
Simon St.Laurent, McGraw-Hill.

*http://www.ietf.org/rfc/rfc2965.txt*
RFC 2965, "HTTP State Management Mechanism" (obsoletes RFC 2109).

*http://www.ietf.org/rfc/rfc2964.txt*
RFC 2964, "Use of HTTP State Management."

*http://home.netscape.com/newsref/std/cookie_spec.html*
This classic Netscape document, "Persistent Client State: HTTP Cookies," describes the original form of HTTP cookies that are still in common use today.

# CHAPTER 12

# Basic Authentication

Millions of people use the Web to perform private transactions and access private data. The Web makes it very easy to access this information, but easy isn't good enough. We need assurances about who can look at our sensitive data and who can perform our privileged transactions. Not all information is intended for the general public.

We need to feel comfortable that unauthorized users can't view our online travel profiles or publish documents onto our web sites without our consent. We need to make sure our most sensitive corporate-planning documents aren't available to unauthorized and potentially unscrupulous members of our organization. And we need to feel at ease that our personal web communications with our children, our spouses, and our secret loves all occur with a modicum of privacy.

Servers need a way to know who a user is. Once a server knows who the user is, it can decide which transactions and resources the user can access. Authentication means proving who you are; usually, you authenticate by providing a username and a secret password. HTTP provides a native facility for HTTP authentication. While it's certainly possible to "roll your own" authentication facility on top of HTTP forms and cookies, for many situations, HTTP's native authentication fits the bill nicely.

This chapter explains HTTP authentication and delves into the most common form of HTTP authentication, *basic authentication*. The next chapter explains a more powerful technique called *digest authentication*.

## Authentication

Authentication means showing some proof of your identity. When you show a photo ID, like a passport or a driver's license, you are showing some proof that you are who you claim to be. When you type a PIN number into an automatic teller machine, or type a secret password into a computer's dialog box, you also are proving that you are who you claim to be.

Now, none of these schemes are foolproof. Passwords can be guessed or overheard, and ID cards can be stolen or forged. But each piece of supporting evidence helps to build a reasonable trust that you are who you say you are.

## HTTP's Challenge/Response Authentication Framework

HTTP provides a native *challenge/response* framework to make it easy to authenticate users. HTTP's authentication model is sketched in Figure 12-1.

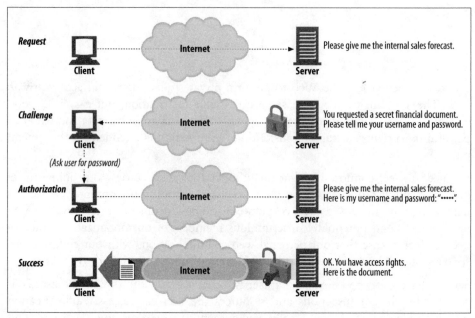

*Figure 12-1. Simplified challenge/response authentication*

Whenever a web application receives an HTTP request message, instead of acting on the request, the server can respond with an "authentication challenge," challenging the user to demonstrate who she is by providing some secret information.

The user needs to attach the secret credentials (username and password) when she repeats the request. If the credentials don't match, the server can challenge the client again or generate an error. If the credentials do match, the request completes normally.

## Authentication Protocols and Headers

HTTP provides an extensible framework for different authentication protocols, through a set of customizable control headers. The format and content of the headers listed in Table 12-1 vary depending on the authentication protocol. The authentication protocol also is specified in the HTTP authentication headers.

HTTP defines two official authentication protocols: basic authentication and digest authentication. In the future, people are free to devise new protocols that use HTTP's challenge/response framework. The rest of this chapter explains basic authentication. See Chapter 13 for details on digest authentication.

*Table 12-1. Four phases of authentication*

| Phase | Headers | Description | Method/Status |
|-------|---------|-------------|---------------|
| Request | | The first request has no authentication. | GET |
| Challenge | WWW-Authenticate | The server rejects the request with a 401 status, indicating that the user needs to provide his username and password. | 401 Unauthorized |
| | | Because the server might have different areas, each with its own password, the server describes the protection area in the WWW-Authenticate header. Also, the authentication algorithm is specified in the WWW-Authenticate header. | |
| Authorization | Authorization | The client retries the request, but this time attaching an Authorization header specifying the authentication algorithm, username, and password. | GET |
| Success | Authentication-Info | If the authorization credentials are correct, the server returns the document. Some authorization algorithms return some additional information about the authorization session in the optional Authentication-Info header. | 200 OK |

To make this concrete, let's take a look at Figure 12-2.

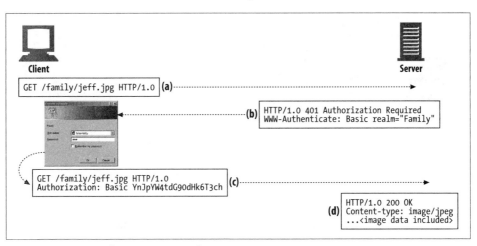

*Figure 12-2. Basic authentication example*

When a server challenges a user, it returns a 401 Unauthorized response and describes how and where to authenticate in the WWW-Authenticate header (Figure 12-2b).

When a client authorizes the server to proceed, it resends the request but attaches an encoded password and other authentication parameters in an Authorization header (Figure 12-2c).

When an authorized request is completed successfully, the server returns a normal status code (e.g., 200 OK) and, for advanced authentication algorithms, might attach additional information in an Authentication-Info header (Figure 12-2d).

## Security Realms

Before we discuss the details of basic authentication, we need to explain how HTTP allows servers to associate different access rights to different resources. You might have noticed that the WWW-Authenticate challenge in Figure 12-2b included a *realm* directive. Web servers group protected documents into *security realms*. Each security realm can have different sets of authorized users.

For example, suppose a web server has two security realms established: one for corporate financial information and another for personal family documents (see Figure 12-3). Different users will have different access to the realms. The CEO of your company probably should have access to the sales forecast, but you might not give her access to your family vacation photos!

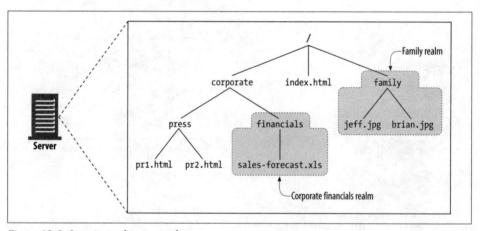

*Figure 12-3. Security realms in a web server*

Here's a hypothetical basic authentication challenge, with a realm specified:

```
HTTP/1.0 401 Unauthorized
WWW-Authenticate: Basic realm="Corporate Financials"
```

A realm should have a descriptive string name, like "Corporate Financials," to help the user understand which username and password to use. It may also be useful to list the server hostname in the realm name—for example, "executive-committee@big-company.com".

---

# Basic Authentication

Basic authentication is the most prevalent HTTP authentication protocol. Almost every major client and server implements basic authentication. Basic authentication was originally described in the HTTP/1.0 specification, but it has since been relocated into RFC 2617, which details HTTP authentication.

In basic authentication, a web server can refuse a transaction, challenging the client for a valid username and password. The server initiates the authentication challenge by returning a 401 status code instead of 200 and specifies the security realm being accessed with the WWW-Authenticate response header. When the browser receives the challenge, it opens a dialog box requesting the username and password for this realm. The username and password are sent back to the server in a slightly scrambled format inside an Authorization request header.

## Basic Authentication Example

Figure 12-2, earlier in this chapter, showed a detailed example of basic authentication:

- In Figure 12-2a, a user requests the personal family photo */family/jeff.jpg*.
- In Figure 12-2b, the server sends back a 401 Authorization Required password challenge for the personal family photo, along with the WWW-Authenticate header. The header requests basic authentication for the realm named *Family*.
- In Figure 12-2c, the browser receives the 401 challenge and pops open a dialog box asking for the username and password for the *Family* realm. When the user enters the username and password, the browser joins them with a colon, encodes them into a "scrambled" base-64 representation (discussed in the next section), and sends them back in the Authorization header.
- In Figure 12-2d, the server decodes the username and password, verifies that they are correct, and returns the requested document in an HTTP 200 OK message.

The HTTP basic authentication WWW-Authenticate and Authorization headers are summarized in Table 12-2.

*Table 12-2. Basic authentication headers*

| Challenge/Response | Header syntax and description |
|---|---|
| Challenge (server to client) | There may be different passwords for different parts of the site. The realm is a quoted string that names the set of documents being requested, so the user knows which password to use.<br><br>`WWW-Authenticate: Basic realm=`*`quoted-realm`* |
| Response (client to server) | The username and password are joined together by a colon (:) and then converted to base-64 encoding, making it a bit easier to include international characters in usernames and passwords and making it less likely that a cursory examination will yield usernames and passwords while watching network traffic.<br><br>`Authorization: Basic `*`base64-username-and-password`* |

Note that the basic authentication protocol does not make use of the Authentication-Info header we showed in Table 12-1.

## Base-64 Username/Password Encoding

HTTP basic authentication packs the username and password together (separated by a colon), and encodes them using the base-64 encoding method. If you don't know what base-64 encoding is, don't worry. You don't need to know much about it, and if you are curious, you can read all about it in Appendix E. In a nutshell, base-64 encoding takes a sequence of 8-bit bytes and breaks the sequence of bits into 6-bit chunks. Each 6-bit piece is used to pick a character in a special 64-character alphabet, consisting mostly of letters and numbers.

Figure 12-4 shows an example of using base-64 encoding for basic authentication. Here, the username is "brian-totty" and the password is "Ow!". The browser joins the username and password with a colon, yielding the packed string "brian-totty:Ow!". This string is then base 64–encoded into this mouthful: "YnJpYW4tdG90dHk6T3ch".

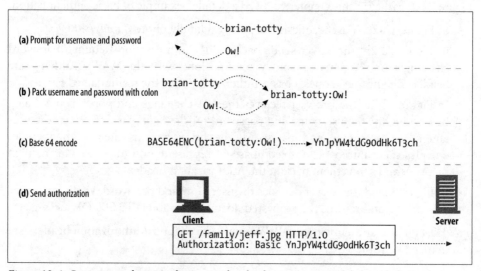

*Figure 12-4. Generating a basic Authorization header from username and password*

Base-64 encoding was invented to take strings of binary, text, and international character data (which caused problems on some systems) and convert them temporarily into a portable alphabet for transmission. The original strings could then be decoded on the remote end without fear of transmission corruption.

Base-64 encoding can be useful for usernames and passwords that contain international characters or other characters that are illegal in HTTP headers (such as quotation marks, colons, and carriage returns). Also, because base-64 encoding trivially scrambles the username and password, it can help prevent administrators from accidentally viewing usernames and passwords while administering servers and networks.

## Proxy Authentication

Authentication also can be done by intermediary proxy servers. Some organizations use proxy servers to authenticate users before letting them access servers, LANs, or wireless networks. Proxy servers can be a convenient way to provide unified access control across an organization's resources, because access policies can be centrally administered on the proxy server. The first step in this process is to establish the identity via *proxy authentication*.

The steps involved in proxy authentication are identical to that of web server identification. However, the headers and status codes are different. Table 12-3 contrasts the status codes and headers used in web server and proxy authentication.

*Table 12-3. Web server versus proxy authentication*

| Web server | Proxy server |
| --- | --- |
| Unauthorized status code: 401 | Unauthorized status code: 407 |
| WWW-Authenticate | Proxy-Authenticate |
| Authorization | Proxy-Authorization |
| Authentication-Info | Proxy-Authentication-Info |

# The Security Flaws of Basic Authentication

Basic authentication is simple and convenient, but it is not secure. It should only be used to prevent unintentional access from nonmalicious parties or used in combination with an encryption technology such as SSL.

Consider the following security flaws:

1. Basic authentication sends the username and password across the network in a form that can trivially be decoded. In effect, the secret password is sent in the clear, for anyone to read and capture. Base-64 encoding obscures the username and password, making it less likely that friendly parties will glean passwords by accidental network observation. However, given a base 64–encoded username and password, the decoding can be performed trivially by reversing the encoding process. Decoding can even be done in seconds, by hand, with pencil and paper! Base 64–encoded passwords are effectively sent "in the clear." Assume that motivated third parties will intercept usernames and passwords sent by basic authentication. If this is a concern, send all your HTTP transactions over SSL encrypted channels, or use a more secure authentication protocol, such as digest authentication.

2. Even if the secret password were encoded in a scheme that was more complicated to decode, a third party could still capture the garbled username and password and replay the garbled information to origin servers over and over again to gain access. No effort is made to prevent these replay attacks.

3. Even if basic authentication is used for noncritical applications, such as corporate intranet access control or personalized content, social behavior makes this dangerous. Many users, overwhelmed by a multitude of password-protected services, share usernames and passwords. A clever, malicious party may capture a username and password in the clear from a free Internet email site, for example, and find that the same username and password allow access to critical online banking sites!

4. Basic authentication offers no protection against proxies or intermediaries that act as middlemen, leaving authentication headers intact but modifying the rest of the message to dramatically change the nature of the transaction.

5. Basic authentication is vulnerable to spoofing by counterfeit servers. If a user can be led to believe that he is connecting to a valid host protected by basic authentication when, in fact, he is connecting to a hostile server or gateway, the attacker can request a password, store it for later use, and feign an error.

This all said, basic authentication still is useful for providing convenient personalization or access control to documents in a friendly environment, or where privacy is desired but not absolutely necessary. In this way, basic authentication is used to prevent accidental or casual access by curious users.*

For example, inside a corporation, product management may password-protect future product plans to limit premature distribution. Basic authentication makes it sufficiently inconvenient for friendly parties to access this data.† Likewise, you might password-protect personal photos or private web sites that aren't top-secret or don't contain valuable information, but really aren't anyone else's business either.

Basic authentication can be made secure by combining it with encrypted data transmission (such as SSL) to conceal the username and password from malicious individuals. This is a common technique.

We discuss secure encryption in Chapter 14. The next chapter explains a more sophisticated HTTP authentication protocol, digest authentication, that has stronger security properties than basic authentication.

---

* Be careful that the username/password in basic authentication is not the same as the password on your more secure systems, or malicious users can use them to break into your secure accounts!

† While not very secure, internal employees of the company usually are unmotivated to maliciously capture passwords. That said, corporate espionage does occur, and vengeful, disgruntled employees do exist, so it is wise to place any data that would be very harmful if maliciously acquired under a stronger security scheme.

# For More Information

For more information on basic authentication and LDAP, see:

*http://www.ietf.org/rfc/rfc2617.txt*
RFC 2617, "HTTP Authentication: Basic and Digest Access Authentication."

*http://www.ietf.org/rfc/rfc2616.txt*
RFC 2616 "Hypertext Transfer Protocol—HTTP/1.1."

# CHAPTER 13

# Digest Authentication

Basic authentication is convenient and flexible but completely insecure. Usernames and passwords are sent in the clear,* and there is no attempt to protect messages from tampering. The only way to use basic authentication securely is to use it in conjunction with SSL.

Digest authentication was developed as a compatible, more secure alternative to basic authentication. We devote this chapter to the theory and practice of digest authentication. Even though digest authentication is not yet in wide use, the concepts still are important for anyone implementing secure transactions.

## The Improvements of Digest Authentication

Digest authentication is an alternate HTTP authentication protocol that tries to fix the most serious flaws of basic authentication. In particular, digest authentication:

- Never sends secret passwords across the network in the clear
- Prevents unscrupulous individuals from capturing and replaying authentication handshakes
- Optionally can guard against tampering with message contents
- Guards against several other common forms of attacks

Digest authentication is not the most secure protocol possible.† Many needs for secure HTTP transactions cannot be met by digest authentication. For those needs, Transport Layer Security (TLS) and Secure HTTP (HTTPS) are more appropriate protocols.

---

\* Usernames and passwords are scrambled using a trivial base-64 encoding, which can be decoded easily. This protects against unintentional accidental viewing but offers no protection against malicious parties.

† For example, compared to public key–based mechanisms, digest authentication does not provide a strong authentication mechanism. Also, digest authentication offers no confidentiality protection beyond protecting the actual password—the rest of the request and response are available to eavesdroppers.

However, digest authentication is significantly stronger than basic authentication, which it was designed to replace. Digest authentication also is stronger than many popular schemes proposed for other Internet services, such as CRAM-MD5, which has been proposed for use with LDAP, POP, and IMAP.

To date, digest authentication has not been widely deployed. However, because of the security risks inherent to basic authentication, the HTTP architects counsel in RFC 2617 that "any service in present use that uses Basic should be switched to Digest as soon as practical."* It is not yet clear how successful this standard will become.

## Using Digests to Keep Passwords Secret

The motto of digest authentication is "never send the password across the network." Instead of sending the password, the client sends a "fingerprint" or "digest" of the password, which is an irreversible scrambling of the password. The client and the server both know the secret password, so the server can verify that the digest provided a correct match for the password. Given only the digest, a bad guy has no easy way to find what password it came from, other than going through every password in the universe, trying each one!†

Let's see how this works (this is a simplified version):

- In Figure 13-1a, the client requests a protected document.
- In Figure 13-1b, the server refuses to serve the document until the client authenticates its identity by proving it knows the password. The server issues a challenge to the client, asking for the username and a digested form of the password.
- In Figure 13-1c, the client proves that it knows the password by passing along the digest of the password. The server knows the passwords for all the users,‡ so it can verify that the user knows the password by comparing the client-supplied digest with the server's own internally computed digest. Another party would not easily be able to make up the right digest if it didn't know the password.
- In Figure 13-1d, the server compares the client-provided digest with the server's internally computed digest. If they match, it shows that the client knows the password (or made a really lucky guess!). The digest function can be set to generate so many digits that lucky guesses effectively are impossible. When the server verifies the match, the document is served to the client—all without ever sending the password over the network.

---

* There has been significant debate about the relevance of digest authentication, given the popularity and widespread adoption of SSL-encrypted HTTP. Time will tell if digest authentication gains the critical mass required.

† There are techniques, such as dictionary attacks, where common passwords are tried first. These cryptanalysis techniques can dramatically ease the process of cracking passwords.

‡ In fact, the server really needs to know only the digests of the passwords.

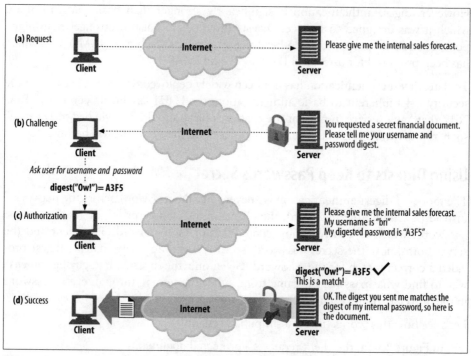

*Figure 13-1. Using digests for password-obscured authentication*

We'll discuss the particular headers used in digest authentication in more detail in Table 13-8.

## One-Way Digests

A digest is a "condensation of a body of information."[*] Digests act as one-way functions, typically converting an infinite number of possible input values into a finite range of condensations.[†] One popular digest function, MD5,[‡] converts any arbitrary sequence of bytes, of any length, into a 128-bit digest.

128 bits = $2^{128}$, or about 1,000,000,000,000,000,000,000,000,000,000,000,000,000 possible distinct condensations.

---

[*] Merriam-Webster dictionary, 1998.

[†] In theory, because we are converting an infinite number of input values into a finite number of output values, it is possible to have two distinct inputs map to the same digest. This is called a *collision*. In practice, the number of potential outputs is so large that the chance of a collision in real life is vanishingly small and, for the purpose of password matching, unimportant.

[‡] MD5 stands for "Message Digest #5," one in a series of digest algorithms. The Secure Hash Algorithm (SHA) is another popular digest function.

What is important about these digests is that if you don't know the secret password, you'll have an awfully hard time guessing the correct digest to send to the server. And likewise, if you have the digest, you'll have an awfully hard time figuring out which of the effectively infinite number of input values generated it.

The 128 bits of MD5 output often are written as 32 hexadecimal characters, each character representing 4 bits. Table 13-1 shows a few examples of MD5 digests of sample inputs. Notice how MD5 takes arbitrary inputs and yields a fixed-length digest output.

*Table 13-1. MD5 digest examples*

| Input | MD5 digest |
| --- | --- |
| "Hi" | C1A5298F939E87E8F962A5EDFC206918 |
| "bri:0w!" | BEAAA0E34EBDB072F8627C038AB211F8 |
| "3.1415926535897" | 475B977E19ECEE70835BC6DF46F4F6DE |
| "http://www.http-guide.com/index.htm" | C617C0C7D1D05F66F595E22A4B0EAAA5 |
| "WE hold these Truths to be self-evident, that all Men are created equal, that they are endowed by their Creator with certain unalienable Rights, that among these are Life, Liberty and the Pursuit of Happiness—That to secure these Rights, Governments are instituted among Men, deriving their just Powers from the Consent of the Governed, that whenever any Form of Government becomes destructive of these Ends, it is the Right of the People to alter or to abolish it, and to institute new Government, laying its Foundation on such Principles, and organizing its Powers in such Form, as to them shall seem most likely to effect their Safety and Happiness." | 66C4EF58DA7CB956BD04233FBB64E0A4 |

Digest functions sometimes are called cryptographic checksums, one-way hash functions, or fingerprint functions.

## Using Nonces to Prevent Replays

One-way digests save us from having to send passwords in the clear. We can just send a digest of the password instead, and rest assured that no malicious party can easily decode the original password from the digest.

Unfortunately, obscured passwords alone do not save us from danger, because a bad guy can capture the digest and replay it over and over again to the server, even though the bad guy doesn't know the password. The digest is just as good as the password.

To prevent such replay attacks, the server can pass along to the client a special token called a *nonce*,* which changes frequently (perhaps every millisecond, or for every

---

* The word nonce means "the present occasion" or "the time being." In a computer-security sense, the nonce captures a particular point in time and figures that into the security calculations.

authentication). The client appends this nonce token to the password before computing the digest.

Mixing the nonce in with the password causes the digest to change each time the nonce changes. This prevents replay attacks, because the recorded password digest is valid only for a particular nonce value, and without the secret password, the attacker cannot compute the correct digest.

Digest authentication requires the use of nonces, because a trivial replay weakness would make un-nonced digest authentication effectively as weak as basic authentication. Nonces are passed from server to client in the WWW-Authenticate challenge.

## The Digest Authentication Handshake

The HTTP digest authentication protocol is an enhanced version of authentication that uses headers similar to those used in basic authentication. Some new options are added to the traditional headers, and one new optional header, Authorization-Info, is added.

The simplified three-phase handshake of digest authentication is depicted in Figure 13-2.

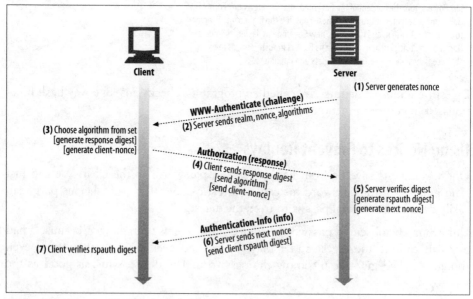

*Figure 13-2. Digest authentication handshake*

Here's what's happening in Figure 13-2:

- In Step 1, the server computes a nonce value. In Step 2, the server sends the nonce to the client in a WWW-Authenticate challenge message, along with a list of algorithms that the server supports.

- In Step 3, the client selects an algorithm and computes the digest of the secret password and the other data. In Step 4, it sends the digest back to the server in an Authorization message. If the client wants to authenticate the server, it can send a client nonce.

- In Step 5, the server receives the digest, chosen algorithm, and supporting data and computes the same digest that the client did. The server then compares the locally generated digest with the network-transmitted digest and validates that they match. If the client symmetrically challenged the server with a client nonce, a client digest is created. Additionally, the next nonce can be precomputed and handed to the client in advance, so the client can preemptively issue the right digest the next time.

Many of these pieces of information are optional and have defaults. To clarify things, Figure 13-3 compares the messages sent for basic authentication (Figure 13-3a–d) with a simple example of digest authentication (Figure 13-3e–h).

Now let's look a bit more closely at the internal workings of digest authentication.

# Digest Calculations

The heart of digest authentication is the one-way digest of the mix of public information, secret information, and a time-limited nonce value. Let's look now at how the digests are computed. The digest calculations generally are straightforward.* Sample source code is provided in Appendix F.

## Digest Algorithm Input Data

Digests are computed from three components:

- A pair of functions consisting of a one-way hash function H($d$) and digest KD($s,d$), where $s$ stands for secret and $d$ stands for data
- A chunk of data containing security information, including the secret password, called A1
- A chunk of data containing nonsecret attributes of the request message, called A2

The two pieces of data, A1 and A2, are processed by H and KD to yield a digest.

## The Algorithms H(d) and KD(s,d)

Digest authentication supports the selection of a variety of digest algorithms. The two algorithms suggested in RFC 2617 are MD5 and MD5-sess (where "sess" stands for session), and the algorithm defaults to MD5 if no other algorithm is specified.

---

* However, they are made a little more complicated for beginners by the optional compatibility modes of RFC 2617 and by the lack of background material in the specifications. We'll try to help...

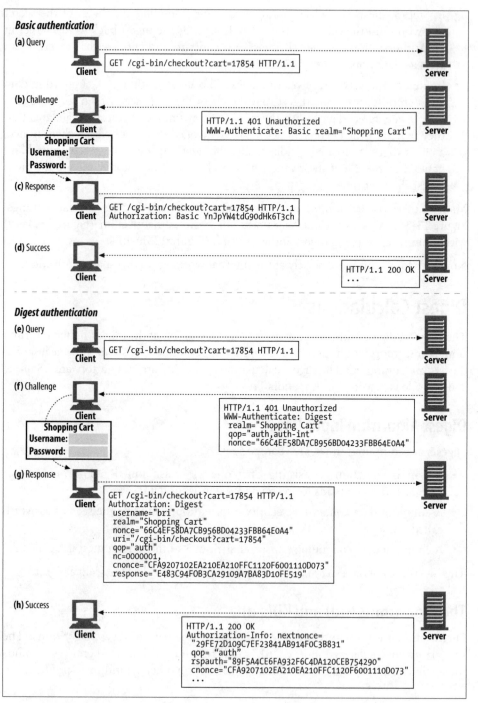

*Figure 13-3. Basic versus digest authentication syntax*

If either MD5 or MD5-sess is used, the H function computes the MD5 of the data, and the KD digest function computes the MD5 of the colon-joined secret and nonsecret data. In other words:

```
H(<data>) = MD5(<data>)
KD(<secret>,<data>) = H(concatenate(<secret>:<data>))
```

## The Security-Related Data (A1)

The chunk of data called A1 is a product of secret and protection information, such as the username, password, protection realm, and nonces. A1 pertains only to security information, not to the underlying message itself. A1 is used along with H, KD, and A2 to compute digests.

RFC 2617 defines two ways of computing A1, depending on the algorithm chosen:

*MD5*

> One-way hashes are run for every request; A1 is the colon-joined triple of username, realm, and secret password.

*MD5-sess*

> The hash function is run only once, on the first WWW-Authenticate handshake; the CPU-intensive hash of username, realm, and secret password is done once and prepended to the current nonce and client nonce (cnonce) values.

The definitions of A1 are shown in Table 13-2.

*Table 13-2. Definitions for A1 by algorithm*

| Algorithm | A1 |
| --- | --- |
| MD5 | A1 = <user>:<realm>:<password> |
| MD5-sess | A1 = MD5(<user>:<realm>:<password>):<nonce>:<cnonce> |

## The Message-Related Data (A2)

The chunk of data called A2 represents information about the message itself, such as the URL, request method, and message entity body. A2 is used to help protect against method, resource, or message tampering. A2 is used along with H, KD, and A1 to compute digests.

RFC 2617 defines two schemes for A2, depending on the quality of protection (qop) chosen:

- The first scheme involves only the HTTP request method and URL. This is used when qop="auth", which is the default case.

- The second scheme adds in the message entity body to provide a degree of message integrity checking. This is used when qop="auth-int".

The definitions of A2 are shown in Table 13-3.

*Table 13-3. Definitions for A2 by algorithm (request digests)*

| qop | A2 |
| --- | --- |
| undefined | `<request-method>:<uri-directive-value>` |
| auth | `<request-method>:<uri-directive-value>` |
| auth-int | `<request-method>:<uri-directive-value>:H(<request-entity-body>)` |

The *request-method* is the HTTP request method. The *uri-directive-value* is the request URI from the request line. This may be "*," an "absoluteURL," or an "abs_path," but it must agree with the request URI. In particular, it must be an absolute URL if the request URI is an absoluteURL.

## Overall Digest Algorithm

RFC 2617 defines two ways of computing digests, given H, KD, A1, and A2:

- The first way is intended to be compatible with the older specification RFC 2069, used when the qop option is missing. It computes the digest using the hash of the secret information and the nonced message data.

- The second way is the modern, preferred approach—it includes support for nonce counting and symmetric authentication. This approach is used whenever qop is "auth" or "auth-int". It adds nonce count, qop, and cnonce data to the digest.

The definitions for the resulting digest function are shown in Table 13-4. Notice the resulting digests use H, KD, A1, and A2.

*Table 13-4. Old and new digest algorithms*

| qop | Digest algorithm | Notes |
| --- | --- | --- |
| undefined | `KD(H(A1), <nonce>:H(A2))` | Deprecated |
| auth or auth-int | `KD(H(A1), <nonce>:<nc>:<cnonce>:<qop>:H(A2))` | Preferred |

It's a bit easy to get lost in all the layers of derivational encapsulation. This is one of the reasons that some readers have difficulty with RFC 2617. To try to make it a bit easier, Table 13-5 expands away the H and KD definitions, and leaves digests in terms of A1 and A2.

*Table 13-5. Unfolded digest algorithm cheat sheet*

| qop | Algorithm | Unfolded algorithm |
| --- | --- | --- |
| undefined | `<undefined>`<br>MD5<br>MD5-sess | `MD5(MD5(A1):<nonce>:MD5(A2))` |

*Table 13-5. Unfolded digest algorithm cheat sheet (continued)*

| qop | Algorithm | Unfolded algorithm |
| --- | --- | --- |
| auth | <undefined><br>MD5<br>MD5-sess | `MD5(MD5(A1):<nonce>:<nc>:<cnonce>:<qop>:MD5(A2))` |
| auth-int | <undefined><br>MD5<br>MD5-sess | `MD5(MD5(A1):<nonce>:<nc>:<cnonce>:<qop>:MD5(A2))` |

## Digest Authentication Session

The client response to a WWW-Authenticate challenge for a protection space starts an authentication session with that protection space (the realm combined with the canonical root of the server being accessed defines a "protection space").

The authentication session lasts until the client receives another WWW-Authenticate challenge from any server in the protection space. A client should remember the username, password, nonce, nonce count, and opaque values associated with an authentication session to use to construct the Authorization header in future requests within that protection space.

When the nonce expires, the server can choose to accept the old Authorization header information, even though the nonce value included may not be fresh. Alternatively, the server may return a 401 response with a new nonce value, causing the client to retry the request; by specifying "stale=true" with this response, the server tells the client to retry with the new nonce without prompting for a new username and password.

## Preemptive Authorization

In normal authentication, each request requires a request/challenge cycle before the transaction can be completed. This is depicted in Figure 13-4a.

This request/challenge cycle can be eliminated if the client knows in advance what the next nonce will be, so it can generate the correct Authorization header before the server asks for it. If the client can compute the Authorization header before it is requested, the client can preemptively issue the Authorization header to the server, without first going through a request/challenge. The performance impact is depicted in Figure 13-4b.

Preemptive authorization is trivial (and common) for basic authentication. Browsers commonly maintain client-side databases of usernames and passwords. Once a user authenticates with a site, the browser commonly sends the correct Authorization header for subsequent requests to that URL (see Chapter 12).

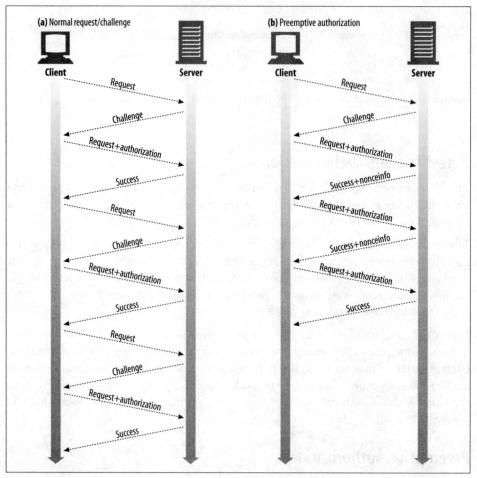

*Figure 13-4. Preemptive authorization reduces message count*

Preemptive authorization is a bit more complicated for digest authentication, because of the nonce technology intended to foil replay attacks. Because the server generates arbitrary nonces, there isn't always a way for the client to determine what Authorization header to send until it receives a challenge.

Digest authentication offers a few means for preemptive authorization while retaining many of the safety features. Here are three potential ways a client can obtain the correct nonce without waiting for a new WWW-Authenticate challenge:

- Server pre-sends the next nonce in the Authentication-Info success header.
- Server allows the same nonce to be reused for a small window of time.
- Both the client and server use a synchronized, predictable nonce-generation algorithm.

### Next nonce pregeneration

The next nonce value can be provided in advance to the client by the Authentication-Info success header. This header is sent along with the 200 OK response from a previous successful authentication.

```
Authentication-Info: nextnonce="<nonce-value>"
```

Given the next nonce, the client can preemptively issue an Authorization header.

While this preemptive authorization avoids a request/challenge cycle (speeding up the transaction), it also effectively nullifies the ability to pipeline multiple requests to the same server, because the next nonce value must be received before the next request can be issued. Because pipelining is expected to be a fundamental technology for latency avoidance, the performance penalty may be large.

### Limited nonce reuse

Instead of pregenerating a sequence of nonces, another approach is to allow limited reuse of nonces. For example, a server may allow a nonce to be reused 5 times, or for 10 seconds.

In this case, the client can freely issue requests with the Authorization header, and it can pipeline them, because the nonce is known in advance. When the nonce finally expires, the server is expected to send the client a 401 Unauthorized challenge, with the WWW-Authenticate: stale=true directive set:

```
WWW-Authenticate: Digest
    realm="<realm-value>"
    nonce="<nonce-value>"
    stale=true
```

Reusing nonces does reduce security, because it makes it easier for an attacker to succeed at replay attacks. Because the lifetime of nonce reuse is controllable, from strictly no reuse to potentially long reuse, trade-offs can be made between windows of vulnerability and performance.

Additionally, other features can be employed to make replay attacks more difficult, including incrementing counters and IP address tests. However, while making attacks more inconvenient, these techniques do not eliminate the vulnerability.

### Synchronized nonce generation

It is possible to employ time-synchronized nonce-generation algorithms, where both the client and the server can generate a sequence of identical nonces, based on a shared secret key, that a third party cannot easily predict (such as secure ID cards).

These algorithms are beyond the scope of the digest authentication specification.

## Nonce Selection

The contents of the nonce are opaque and implementation-dependent. However, the quality of performance, security, and convenience depends on a smart choice.

RFC 2617 suggests this hypothetical nonce formulation:

```
BASE64(time-stamp H(time-stamp ":" ETag ":" private-key))
```

where time-stamp is a server-generated time or other nonrepeating value, ETag is the value of the HTTP ETag header associated with the requested entity, and private-key is data known only to the server.

With a nonce of this form, a server will recalculate the hash portion after receiving the client authentication header and reject the request if it does not match the nonce from that header or if the time-stamp value is not recent enough. In this way, the server can limit the duration of the nonce's validity.

The inclusion of the ETag prevents a replay request for an updated version of the resource. (Note that including the IP address of the client in the nonce would appear to offer the server the ability to limit the reuse of the nonce to the same client that originally got it. However, that would break proxy farms, in which requests from a single user often go through different proxies. Also, IP address spoofing is not that hard.)

An implementation might choose not to accept a previously used nonce or digest, to protect against replay attacks. Or, an implementation might choose to use one-time nonces or digests for POST or PUT requests and time-stamps for GET requests.

Refer to "Security Considerations" for practical security considerations that affect nonce selection.

## Symmetric Authentication

RFC 2617 extends digest authentication to allow the client to authenticate the server. It does this by providing a client nonce value, to which the server generates a correct response digest based on correct knowledge of the shared secret information. The server then returns this digest to the client in the Authorization-Info header.

This symmetric authentication is standard as of RFC 2617. It is optional for backward compatibility with the older RFC 2069 standard, but, because it provides important security enhancements, all modern clients and servers are strongly recommended to implement all of RFC 2617's features. In particular, symmetric authentication is required to be performed whenever a qop directive is present and required not to be performed when the qop directive is missing.

The response digest is calculated like the request digest, except that the message body information (A2) is different, because there is no method in a response, and the message entity data is different. The methods of computation of A2 for request and response digests are compared in Tables 13-6 and 13-7.

*Table 13-6. Definitions for A2 by algorithm (request digests)*

| qop | A2 |
|---|---|
| undefined | `<request-method>:<uri-directive-value>` |
| auth | `<request-method>:<uri-directive-value>` |
| auth-int | `<request-method>:<uri-directive-value>:H(<request-entity-body>)` |

*Table 13-7. Definitions for A2 by algorithm (response digests)*

| qop | A2 |
|---|---|
| undefined | `:<uri-directive-value>` |
| auth | `:<uri-directive-value>` |
| auth-int | `:<uri-directive-value>:H(<response-entity-body>)` |

The cnonce value and nc value must be the ones for the client request to which this message is the response. The response auth, cnonce, and nonce count directives must be present if qop="auth" or qop="auth-int" is specified.

# Quality of Protection Enhancements

The qop field may be present in all three digest headers: WWW-Authenticate, Authorization, and Authentication-Info.

The qop field lets clients and servers negotiate for different types and qualities of protection. For example, some transactions may want to sanity check the integrity of message bodies, even if that slows down transmission significantly.

The server first exports a comma-separated list of qop options in the WWW-Authenticate header. The client then selects one of the options that it supports and that meets its needs and passes it back to the server in its Authorization qop field.

Use of qop is optional, but only for backward compatibility with the older RFC 2069 specification. The qop option should be supported by all modern digest implementations.

RFC 2617 defines two initial quality of protection values: "auth," indicating authentication, and "auth-int," indicating authentication with message integrity protection. Other qop options are expected in the future.

## Message Integrity Protection

If integrity protection is applied (qop="auth-int"), H (the entity body) is the hash of the entity body, not the message body. It is computed before any transfer encoding is applied by the sender and after it has been removed by the recipient. Note that this includes multipart boundaries and embedded headers in each part of any multipart content type.

## Digest Authentication Headers

Both the basic and digest authentication protocols contain an authorization challenge, carried by the WWW-Authenticate header, and an authorization response, carried by the Authorization header. Digest authentication adds an optional Authorization-Info header, which is sent after successful authentication, to complete a three-phase handshake and pass along the next nonce to use. The basic and digest authentication headers are shown in Table 13-8.

*Table 13-8. HTTP authentication headers*

| Phase | Basic | Digest |
|---|---|---|
| Challenge | WWW-Authenticate: Basic<br>    realm="<realm-value>" | WWW-Authenticate: Digest<br>    realm="<realm-value>"<br>    nonce="<nonce-value>"<br>    [domain="<list-of-URIs>"]<br>    [opaque="<opaque-token-value>"]<br>    [stale=<true-or-false>]<br>    [algorithm=<digest-algorithm>]<br>    [qop="<list-of-qop-values>"]<br>    [<extension-directive>] |
| Response | Authorization: Basic<br>    <base64(user:pass)> | Authorization: Digest<br>    username="<username>"<br>    realm="<realm-value>"<br>    nonce="<nonce-value>"<br>    uri=<request-uri><br>    response="<32-hex-digit-digest>"<br>    [algorithm=<digest-algorithm>]<br>    [opaque="<opaque-token-value>"]<br>    [cnonce="<nonce-value>"]<br>    [qop=<qop-value>]<br>    [nc=<8-hex-digit-nonce-count>]<br>    [<extension-directive>] |
| Info | n/a | Authentication-Info:<br>    nextnonce="<nonce-value>"<br>    [qop="<list-of-qop-values>"]<br>    [rspauth="<hex-digest>"]<br>    [cnonce="<nonce-value>"]<br>    [nc=<8-hex-digit-nonce-count>] |

The digest authentication headers are quite a bit more complicated. They are described in detail in Appendix F.

# Practical Considerations

There are several things you need to consider when working with digest authentication. This section discusses some of these issues.

## Multiple Challenges

A server can issue multiple challenges for a resource. For example, if a server does not know the capabilities of a client, it may provide both basic and digest authentication challenges. When faced with multiple challenges, the client must choose to answer with the strongest authentication mechanism that it supports.

User agents must take special care in parsing the WWW-Authenticate or Proxy-Authenticate header field value if it contains more than one challenge or if more than one WWW-Authenticate header field is provided, as a challenge may itself contain a comma-separated list of authentication parameters. Note that many browsers recognize only basic authentication and require that it be the first authentication mechanism presented.

There are obvious "weakest link" security concerns when providing a spectrum of authentication options. Servers should include basic authentication only if it is minimally acceptable, and administrators should caution users about the dangers of sharing the same password across systems when different levels of security are being employed.

## Error Handling

In digest authentication, if a directive or its value is improper, or if a required directive is missing, the proper response is 400 Bad Request.

If a request's digest does not match, a login failure should be logged. Repeated failures from a client may indicate an attacker attempting to guess passwords.

The authenticating server must assure that the resource designated by the "uri" directive is the same as the resource specified in the request line; if they are different, the server should return a 400 Bad Request error. (As this may be a symptom of an attack, server designers may want to consider logging such errors.) Duplicating information from the request URL in this field deals with the possibility that an intermediate proxy may alter the client's request line. This altered (but, presumably, semantically equivalent) request would not result in the same digest as that calculated by the client.

## Protection Spaces

The realm value, in combination with the canonical root URL of the server being accessed, defines the protection space.

Realms allow the protected resources on a server to be partitioned into a set of protection spaces, each with its own authentication scheme and/or authorization database. The realm value is a string, generally assigned by the origin server, which may have additional semantics specific to the authentication scheme. Note that there may be multiple challenges with the same authorization scheme but different realms.

The protection space determines the domain over which credentials can be automatically applied. If a prior request has been authorized, the same credentials may be reused for all other requests within that protection space for a period of time determined by the authentication scheme, parameters, and/or user preference. Unless otherwise defined by the authentication scheme, a single protection space cannot extend outside the scope of its server.

The specific calculation of protection space depends on the authentication mechanism:

- In basic authentication, clients assume that all paths at or below the request URI are within the same protection space as the current challenge. A client can preemptively authorize for resources in this space without waiting for another challenge from the server.

- In digest authentication, the challenge's WWW-Authenticate: domain field more precisely defines the protection space. The domain field is a quoted, space-separated list of URIs. All the URIs in the domain list, and all URIs logically beneath these prefixes, are assumed to be in the same protection space. If the domain field is missing or empty, all URIs on the challenging server are in the protection space.

## Rewriting URIs

Proxies may rewrite URIs in ways that change the URI syntax but not the actual resource being described. For example:

- Hostnames may be normalized or replaced with IP addresses.

- Embedded characters may be replaced with "%" escape forms.

- Additional attributes of a type that doesn't affect the resource fetched from the particular origin server may be appended or inserted into the URI.

Because URIs can be changed by proxies, and because digest authentication sanity checks the integrity of the URI value, the digest authentication will break if any of these changes are made. See "The Message-Related Data (A2)" for more information.

## Caches

When a shared cache receives a request containing an Authorization header and a response from relaying that request, it must not return that response as a reply to any other request, unless one of two Cache-Control directives was present in the response:

- If the original response included the "must-revalidate" Cache-Control directive, the cache may use the entity of that response in replying to a subsequent request. However, it must first revalidate it with the origin server, using the request headers from the new request, so the origin server can authenticate the new request.

- If the original response included the "public" Cache-Control directive, the response entity may be returned in reply to any subsequent request.

# Security Considerations

RFC 2617 does an admirable job of summarizing some of the security risks inherent in HTTP authentication schemes. This section describes some of these risks.

## Header Tampering

To provide a foolproof system against header tampering, you need either end-to-end encryption or a digital signature of the headers—preferably a combination of both! Digest authentication is focused on providing a tamper-proof authentication scheme, but it does not necessarily extend that protection to the data. The only headers that have some level of protection are WWW-Authenticate and Authorization.

## Replay Attacks

A replay attack, in the current context, is when someone uses a set of snooped authentication credentials from a given transaction for another transaction. While this problem is an issue with GET requests, it is vital that a foolproof method for avoiding replay attacks be available for POST and PUT requests. The ability to successfully replay previously used credentials while transporting form data could cause security nightmares.

Thus, in order for a server to accept "replayed" credentials, the nonce values must be repeated. One of the ways to mitigate this problem is to have the server generate a nonce containing a digest of the client's IP address, a time-stamp, the resource ETag, and a private server key (as recommended earlier). In such a scenario, the combination of an IP address and a short timeout value may provide a huge hurdle for the attacker.

However, this solution has a major drawback. As we discussed earlier, using the client's IP address in creating a nonce breaks transmission through proxy farms, in which requests from a single user may go through different proxies. Also, IP spoofing is not too difficult.

One way to completely avoid replay attacks is to use a unique nonce value for every transaction. In this implementation, for each transaction, the server issues a unique nonce along with a timeout value. The issued nonce value is valid only for the given transaction, and only for the duration of the timeout value. This accounting may increase the load on servers; however, the increase should be miniscule.

## Multiple Authentication Mechanisms

When a server supports multiple authentication schemes (such as basic and digest), it usually provides the choice in WWW-Authenticate headers. Because the client is not required to opt for the strongest authentication mechanism, the strength of the resulting authentication is only as good as that of the weakest of the authentication schemes.

The obvious ways to avoid this problem is to have the clients always choose the strongest authentication scheme available. If this is not practical (as most of us do use commercially available clients), the only other option is to use a proxy server to retain only the strongest authentication scheme. However, such an approach is feasible only in a domain in which all of the clients are known to be able to support the chosen authentication scheme—e.g., a corporate network.

## Dictionary Attacks

Dictionary attacks are typical password-guessing attacks. A malicious user can eavesdrop on a transaction and use a standard password-guessing program against nonce/response pairs. If the users are using relatively simple passwords and the servers are using simplistic nonces, it is quite possible to find a match. If there is no password aging policy, given enough time and the one-time cost of cracking the passwords, it is easy to collect enough passwords to do some real damage.

There really is no good way to solve this problem, other than using relatively complex passwords that are hard to crack and a good password aging policy.

## Hostile Proxies and Man-in-the-Middle Attacks

Much Internet traffic today goes through a proxy at one point or another. With the advent of redirection techniques and intercepting proxies, a user may not even realize that his request is going through a proxy. If one of those proxies is hostile or compromised, it could leave the client vulnerable to a man-in-the-middle attack.

Such an attack could be in the form of eavesdropping, or altering available authentication schemes by removing all of the offered choices and replacing them with the weakest authentication scheme (such as basic authentication).

One of the ways to compromise a trusted proxy is though its extension interfaces. Proxies sometimes provide sophisticated programming interfaces, and with such proxies it may be feasible to write an extension (i.e., plug-in) to intercept and modify the traffic. However, the data-center security and security offered by proxies themselves make the possibility of man-in-the-middle attacks via rogue plug-ins quite remote.

There is no good way to fix this problem. Possible solutions include clients providing visual cues regarding the authentication strength, configuring clients to always use the strongest possible authentication, etc., but even when using the strongest possible authentication scheme, clients still are vulnerable to eavesdropping. The only foolproof way to guard against these attacks is by using SSL.

# Chosen Plaintext Attacks

Clients using digest authentication use a nonce supplied by the server to generate the response. However, if there is a compromised or malicious proxy in the middle intercepting the traffic (or a malicious origin server), it can easily supply a nonce for response computation by the client. Using the known key for computing the response may make the cryptanalysis of the response easier. This is called a *chosen plaintext attack*. There are a few variants of chosen plaintext attacks:

*Precomputed dictionary attacks*
> This is a combination of a dictionary attack and a chosen plaintext attack. First, the attacking server generates a set of responses, using a predetermined nonce and common password variations, and creates a dictionary. Once a sizeable dictionary is available, the attacking server/proxy can complete the interdiction of the traffic and start sending predetermined nonces to the clients. When it gets a response from a client, the attacker searches the generated dictionary for matches. If a there is a match, the attacker has the password for that particular user.

*Batched brute-force attacks*
> The difference in a batched brute-force attack is in the computation of the password. Instead of trying to match a precomputed digest, a set of machines goes to work on enumerating all of the possible passwords for a given space. As the machines get faster, the brute-force attack becomes more and more viable.

In general, the threat posed by these attacks is easily countered. One way to prevent them is to configure clients to use the optional cnonce directive, so that the response is generated at the client's discretion, not using the nonce supplied by the server (which could be compromised by the attacker). This, combined with policies enforcing reasonably strong passwords and a good password aging mechanism, can mitigate the threat of chosen plaintext attacks completely.

# Storing Passwords

The digest authentication mechanism compares the user response to what is stored internally by the server—usually, usernames and H(A1) tuples, where H(A1) is derived from the digest of username, realm, and password.

Unlike with a traditional password file on a Unix box, if a digest authentication password file is compromised, all of the documents in the realm immediately are available to the attacker; there is no need for a decrypting step.

Some of the ways to mitigate this problem are to:

- Protect the password file as though it contained clear-text passwords.
- Make sure the realm name is unique among all the realms, so that if a password file is compromised, the damage is localized to a particular realm. A fully qualified realm name with host and domain included should satisfy this requirement.

While digest authentication provides a much more robust and secure solution than basic authentication, it still does not provide any protection for security of the content—a truly secure transaction is feasible only through SSL, which we describe in the next chapter.

## For More Information

For more information on authentication, see:

*http://www.ietf.org/rfc/rfc2617.txt*
  RFC 2617, "HTTP Authentication: Basic and Digest Access Authentication."

# CHAPTER 14

# Secure HTTP

The previous three chapters reviewed features of HTTP that help identify and authenticate users. These techniques work well in a friendly community, but they aren't strong enough to protect important transactions from a community of motivated and hostile adversaries.

This chapter presents a more complicated and aggressive technology to secure HTTP transactions from eavesdropping and tampering, using digital cryptography.

## Making HTTP Safe

People use web transactions for serious things. Without strong security, people wouldn't feel comfortable doing online shopping and banking. Without being able to restrict access, companies couldn't place important documents on web servers. The Web requires a secure form of HTTP.

The previous chapters talked about some lightweight ways of providing authentication (basic and digest authentication) and message integrity (digest qop="auth-int"). These schemes are good for many purposes, but they may not be strong enough for large purchases, bank transactions, or access to confidential data. For these more serious transactions, we combine HTTP with digital encryption technology.

A secure version of HTTP needs to be efficient, portable, easy to administer, and adaptable to the changing world. It also has to meet societal and governmental requirements. We need a technology for HTTP security that provides:

- Server authentication (clients know they're talking to the real server, not a phony)
- Client authentication (servers know they're talking to the real user, not a phony)
- Integrity (clients and servers are safe from their data being changed)
- Encryption (clients and servers talk privately without fear of eavesdropping)
- Efficiency (an algorithm fast enough for inexpensive clients and servers to use)
- Ubiquity (protocols are supported by virtually all clients and servers)

- Administrative scalability (instant secure communication for anyone, anywhere)
- Adaptability (supports the best known security methods of the day)
- Social viability (meets the cultural and political needs of the society)

## HTTPS

HTTPS is the most popular secure form of HTTP. It was pioneered by Netscape Communications Corporation and is supported by all major browsers and servers.

You can tell if a web page was accessed through HTTPS instead of HTTP, because the URL will start with the scheme *https://* instead of *http://* (some browsers also display iconic security cues, as shown in Figure 14-1).

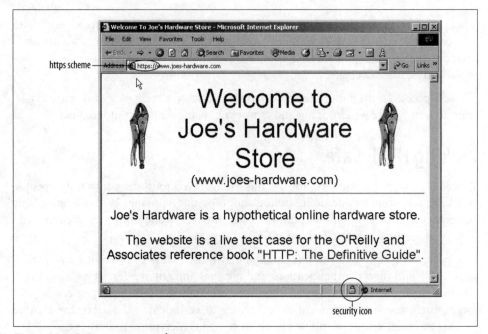

*Figure 14-1. Browsing secure web sites*

When using HTTPS, all the HTTP request and response data is encrypted before being sent across the network. HTTPS works by providing a transport-level cryptographic security layer—using either the Secure Sockets Layer (SSL) or its successor, Transport Layer Security (TLS)—underneath HTTP (Figure 14-2). Because SSL and TLS are so similar, in this book we use the term "SSL" loosely to represent both SSL and TLS.

Because most of the hard encoding and decoding work happens in the SSL libraries, web clients and servers don't need to change much of their protocol processing logic

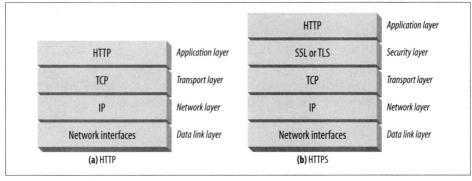

*Figure 14-2. HTTPS is HTTP layered over a security layer, layered over TCP*

to use secure HTTP. For the most part, they simply need to replace TCP input/output calls with SSL calls and add a few other calls to configure and manage the security information.

# Digital Cryptography

Before we talk in detail about HTTPS, we need to provide a little background about the cryptographic encoding techniques used by SSL and HTTPS. In the next few sections, we'll give a speedy primer of the essentials of digital cryptography. If you already are familiar with the technology and terminology of digital cryptography, feel free to jump ahead to "HTTPS: The Details."

In this digital cryptography primer, we'll talk about:

*Ciphers*
    Algorithms for encoding text to make it unreadable to voyeurs

*Keys*
    Numeric parameters that change the behavior of ciphers

*Symmetric-key cryptosystems*
    Algorithms that use the same key for encoding and decoding

*Asymmetric-key cryptosystems*
    Algorithms that use different keys for encoding and decoding

*Public-key cryptography*
    A system making it easy for millions of computers to send secret messages

*Digital signatures*
    Checksums that verify that a message has not been forged or tampered with

*Digital certificates*
    Identifying information, verified and signed by a trusted organization

## The Art and Science of Secret Coding

Cryptography is the art and science of encoding and decoding messages. People have used cryptographic methods to send secret messages for thousands of years. However, cryptography can do more than just encrypt messages to prevent reading by nosy folks; it also can be used to prevent tampering with messages. Cryptography even can be used to prove that you indeed authored a message or transaction, just like your handwritten signature on a check or an embossed wax seal on an envelope.

## Ciphers

Cryptography is based on secret codes called *ciphers*. A cipher is a coding scheme—a particular way to encode a message and an accompanying way to decode the secret later. The original message, before it is encoded, often is called *plaintext* or *cleartext*. The coded message, after the cipher is applied, often is called *ciphertext*. Figure 14-3 shows a simple example.

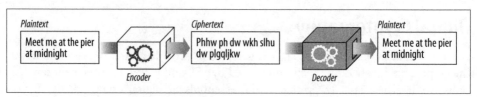

*Figure 14-3. Plaintext and ciphertext*

Ciphers have been used to generate secret messages for thousands of years. Legend has it that Julius Caesar used a three-character rotation cipher, where each character in the message is replaced with a character three alphabetic positions forward. In our modern alphabet, "A" would be replaced by "D," "B" would be replaced by "E," and so on.

For example, in Figure 14-4, the message "meet me at the pier at midnight" encodes into the ciphertext "phhw ph dw wkh slhu dw plgqljkw" using the rot3 (rotate by 3 characters) cipher.[*] The ciphertext can be decrypted back to the original plaintext message by applying the inverse coding, rotating −3 characters in the alphabet.

*Figure 14-4. Rotate-by-3 cipher example*

---

[*] For simplicity of example, we aren't rotating punctuation or whitespace, but you could.

## Cipher Machines

Ciphers began as relatively simple algorithms, because human beings needed to do the encoding and decoding themselves. Because the ciphers were simple, people could work the codes using pencil and paper and code books. However, it also was possible for clever people to "crack" the codes fairly easily.

As technology advanced, people started making machines that could quickly and accurately encode and decode messages using much more complicated ciphers. Instead of just doing simple rotations, these cipher machines could substitute characters, transpose the order of characters, and slice and dice messages to make codes much harder to crack.*

## Keyed Ciphers

Because code algorithms and machines could fall into enemy hands, most machines had dials that could be set to a large number of different values that changed how the cipher worked. Even if the machine was stolen, without the right dial settings (key values) the decoder wouldn't work.†

These cipher parameters were called *keys*. You needed to enter the right key into the cipher machine to get the decoding process to work correctly. Cipher keys make a single cipher machine act like a set of many virtual cipher machines, each of which behaves differently because they have different key values.

Figure 14-5 illustrates an example of keyed ciphers. The cipher algorithm is the trivial "rotate-by-N" cipher. The value of N is controlled by the key. The same input message, "meet me at the pier at midnight," passed through the same encoding machine, generates different outputs depending on the value of the key. Today, virtually all cipher algorithms use keys.

## Digital Ciphers

With the advent of digital computation, two major advances occurred:

- Complicated encoding and decoding algorithms became possible, freed from the speed and function limitations of mechanical machinery.

---

* Perhaps the most famous mechanical code machine was the World War II German Enigma code machine. Despite the complexity of the Enigma cipher, Alan Turing and colleagues were able to crack the Enigma codes in the early 1940s, using the earliest digital computers.

† In reality, having the logic of the machine in your possession can sometimes help you to crack the code, because the machine logic may point to patterns that you can exploit. Modern cryptographic algorithms usually are designed so that even if the algorithm is publicly known, it's difficult to come up with any patterns that will help evildoers crack the code. In fact, many of the strongest ciphers in common use have their source code available in the public domain, for all to see and study!

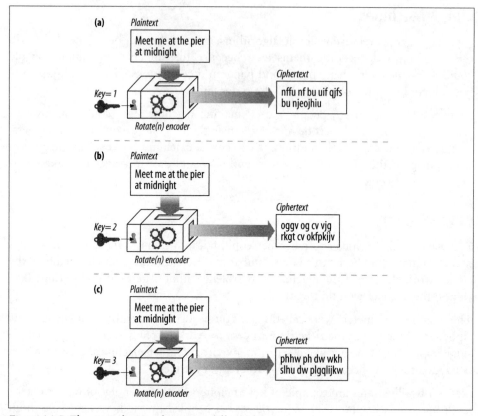

*Figure 14-5. The rotate-by-N cipher, using different keys*

- It became possible to support very large keys, so that a single cipher algorithm could yield trillions of virtual cipher algorithms, each differing by the value of the key. The longer the key, the more combinations of encodings are possible, and the harder it is to crack the code by randomly guessing keys.

Unlike physical metal keys or dial settings in mechanical devices, digital keys are just numbers. These digital key values are inputs to the encoding and decoding algorithms. The coding algorithms are functions that take a chunk of data and encode/decode it based on the algorithm and the value of the key.

Given a plaintext message called P, an encoding function called E, and a digital encoding key called e, you can generate a coded ciphertext message C (Figure 14-6). You can decode the ciphertext C back into the original plaintext P by using the decoder function D and the decoding key d. Of course, the decoding and encoding functions are inverses of each other; the decoding of the encoding of P gives back the original message P.

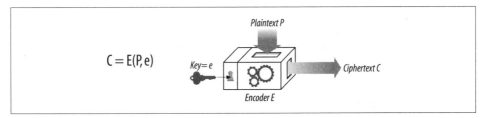

$$C = E(P, e)$$

Key = e

Plaintext P

Ciphertext C

Encoder E

*Figure 14-6. Plaintext is encoded with encoding key e, and decoded using decoding key d*

# Symmetric-Key Cryptography

Let's talk in more detail about how keys and ciphers work together. Many digital cipher algorithms are called *symmetric-key* ciphers, because they use the same key value for encoding as they do for decoding (e = d). Let's just call the key k.

In a symmetric key cipher, both a sender and a receiver need to have the same shared secret key, k, to communicate. The sender uses the shared secret key to encrypt the message and sends the resulting ciphertext to the receiver. The receiver takes the ciphertext and applies the decrypting function, along with the same shared secret key, to recover the original plaintext (Figure 14-7).

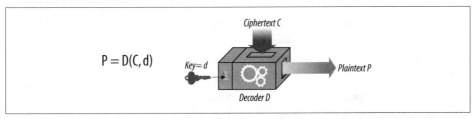

$$P = D(C, d)$$

Key = d

Ciphertext C

Plaintext P

Decoder D

*Figure 14-7. Symmetric-key cryptography algorithms use the same key for encoding and decoding*

Some popular symmetric-key cipher algorithms are DES, Triple-DES, RC2, and RC4.

## Key Length and Enumeration Attacks

It's very important that secret keys stay secret. In most cases, the encoding and decoding algorithms are public knowledge, so the key is the only thing that's secret!

A good cipher algorithm forces the enemy to try every single possible key value in the universe to crack the code. Trying all key values by brute force is called an *enumeration attack*. If there are only a few possible key values, a bad guy can go through all of them by brute force and eventually crack the code. But if there are a lot of possible key values, it might take the bad guy days, years, or even the lifetime of the universe to go through all the keys, looking for one that breaks the cipher.

The number of possible key values depends on the number of bits in the key and how many of the possible keys are valid. For symmetric-key ciphers, usually all of the key values are valid.* An 8-bit key would have only 256 possible keys, a 40-bit key would have $2^{40}$ possible keys (around one trillion keys), and a 128-bit key would generate around 340,000,000,000,000,000,000,000,000,000,000,000,000 possible keys.

For conventional symmetric-key ciphers, 40-bit keys are considered safe enough for small, noncritical transactions. However, they are breakable by today's high-speed workstations, which can now do billions of calculations per second.

In contrast, 128-bit keys are considered very strong for symmetric-key cryptography. In fact, long keys have such an impact on cryptographic security that the U.S. government has put export controls on cryptographic software that uses long keys, to prevent potentially antagonistic organizations from creating secret codes that the U. S. National Security Agency (NSA) would itself be unable to crack.

Bruce Schneier's excellent book, *Applied Cryptography* (John Wiley & Sons), includes a table describing the time it would take to crack a DES cipher by guessing all keys, using 1995 technology and economics.† Excerpts of this table are shown in Table 14-1.

*Table 14-1. Longer keys take more effort to crack (1995 data, from "Applied Cryptography")*

| Attack cost | 40-bit key | 56-bit key | 64-bit key | 80-bit key | 128-bit key |
|---|---|---|---|---|---|
| $100,000 | 2 secs | 35 hours | 1 year | 70,000 years | $10^{19}$ years |
| $1,000,000 | 200 msecs | 3.5 hours | 37 days | 7,000 years | $10^{18}$ years |
| $10,000,000 | 20 msecs | 21 mins | 4 days | 700 years | $10^{17}$ years |
| $100,000,000 | 2 msecs | 2 mins | 9 hours | 70 years | $10^{16}$ years |
| $1,000,000,000 | 200 usecs | 13 secs | 1 hour | 7 years | $10^{15}$ years |

Given the speed of 1995 microprocessors, an attacker willing to spend $100,000 in 1995 could break a 40-bit DES code in about 2 seconds. And computers in 2002 already are 20 times faster than they were in 1995. Unless the users change keys frequently, 40-bit keys are not safe against motivated opponents.

The DES standard key size of 56 bits is more secure. In 1995 economics, a $1 million assault still would take several hours to crack the code. But a person with access to supercomputers could crack the code by brute force in a matter of seconds. In

---

* There are ciphers where only some of the key values are valid. For example, in RSA, the best-known asymmetric-key cryptosystem, valid keys must be related to prime numbers in a certain way. Only a small number of the possible key values have this property.

† Computation speed has increased dramatically since 1995, and cost has been reduced. And the longer it takes you to read this book, the faster they'll become! However, the table still is relatively useful, even if the times are off by a factor of 5, 10, or more.

contrast, 128-bit DES keys, similar in size to Triple-DES keys, are believed to be effectively unbreakable by anyone, at any cost, using a brute-force attack.[*]

## Establishing Shared Keys

One disadvantage of symmetric-key ciphers is that both the sender and receiver have to have a shared secret key before they can talk to each other.

If you wanted to talk securely with Joe's Hardware store, perhaps to order some woodworking tools after watching a home-improvement program on public television, you'd have to establish a private secret key between you and *www.joes-hardware.com* before you could order anything securely. You'd need a way to generate the secret key and to remember it. Both you and Joe's Hardware, and every other Internet user, would have thousands of keys to generate and remember.

Say that Alice (A), Bob (B), and Chris (C) all wanted to talk to Joe's Hardware (J). A, B, and C each would need to establish their own secret keys with J. A would need key $k_{AJ}$, B would need key $k_{BJ}$, and C would need key $k_{CJ}$. Every pair of communicating parties needs its own private key. If there are N nodes, and each node has to talk securely with all the other N–1 nodes, there are roughly $N^2$ total secret keys: an administrative nightmare.

# Public-Key Cryptography

Instead of a single encoding/decoding key for every pair of hosts, public-key cryptography uses two asymmetric keys: one for encoding messages for a host, and another for decoding the host's messages. The encoding key is publicly known to the world (thus the name public-key cryptography), but only the host knows the private decoding key (see Figure 14-8). This makes key establishment much easier, because everyone can find the public key for a particular host. But the decoding key is kept secret, so only the recipient can decode messages sent to it.

Node X can take its encoding key $e_x$ and publish it publicly.[†] Now anyone wanting to send a message to node X can use the same, well-known public key. Because each host is assigned an encoding key, which everyone uses, public-key cryptography avoids the $N^2$ explosion of pairwise symmetric keys (see Figure 14-9).

---

[*] A large key does not mean that the cipher is foolproof, though! There may be an unnoticed flaw in the cipher algorithm or implementation that provides a weakness for an attacker to exploit. It's also possible that the attacker may have some information about how the keys are generated, so that he knows some keys are more likely than others, helping to focus a brute-force attack. Or a user might leave the secret key someplace where an attacker might be able to steal it.

[†] As we'll see later, most public-key lookup actually is done through digital certificates, but the details of how you find public keys don't matter much now—just know that they are publicly available somewhere.

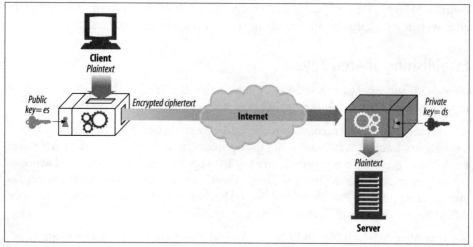

*Figure 14-8. Public-key cryptography is asymmetric, using different keys for encoding and decoding*

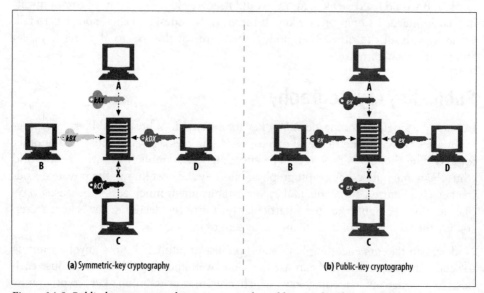

*Figure 14-9. Public-key cryptography assigns a single, public encoding key to each host*

Even though everyone can encode messages to X with the same key, no one other than X can decode the messages, because only X has the decoding private key $d^x$. Splitting the keys lets anyone encode a message but restricts the ability to decode messages to only the owner. This makes it easier for nodes to securely send messages to servers, because they can just look up the server's public key.

Public-key encryption technology makes it possible to deploy security protocols to every computer user around the world. Because of the great importance of making a standardized public-key technology suite, a massive Public-Key Infrastructure (PKI) standards initiative has been under way for well over a decade.

## RSA

The challenge of any public-key asymmetric cryptosystem is to make sure no bad guy can compute the secret, private key—even if he has all of the following clues:

- The public key (which anyone can get, because it's public)
- A piece of intercepted ciphertext (obtained by snooping the network)
- A message and its associated ciphertext (obtained by running the encoder on any text)

One popular public-key cryptosystem that meets all these needs is the RSA algorithm, invented at MIT and subsequently commercialized by RSA Data Security. Given a public key, an arbitrary piece of plaintext, the associated ciphertext from encoding the plaintext with the public key, the RSA algorithm itself, and even the source code of the RSA implementation, cracking the code to find the corresponding private key is believed to be as hard a problem as computing huge prime numbers—believed to be one of the hardest problems in all of computer science. So, if you can find a fast way of factoring large numbers into primes, not only can you break into Swiss bank accounts, but you can also win a Turing Award.

The details of RSA cryptography involve some tricky mathematics, so we won't go into them here. There are plenty of libraries available to let you perform the RSA algorithms without you needing a Ph.D. in number theory.

### Hybrid Cryptosystems and Session Keys

Asymmetric, public-key cryptography is nifty, because anyone can send secure messages to a public server, just by knowing its public key. Two nodes don't first have to negotiate a private key in order to communicate securely.

But public-key cryptography algorithms tend to be computationally slow. In practice, mixtures of both symmetric and asymmetric schemes are used. For example, it is common to use public-key cryptography to conveniently set up secure communication between nodes but then to use that secure channel to generate and communicate a temporary, random symmetric key to encrypt the rest of the data through faster, symmetric cryptography.

## Digital Signatures

So far, we've been talking about various kinds of keyed ciphers, using symmetric and asymmetric keys, to allow us to encrypt and decrypt secret messages.

In addition to encrypting and decrypting messages, cryptosystems can be used to *sign* messages, proving who wrote the message and proving the message hasn't been tampered with. This technique, called *digital signing*, is important for Internet security certificates, which we discuss in the next section.

## Signatures Are Cryptographic Checksums

Digital signatures are special cryptographic checksums attached to a message. They have two benefits:

- Signatures prove the author wrote the message. Because only the author has the author's top-secret private key,* only the author can compute these checksums. The checksum acts as a personal "signature" from the author.

- Signatures prevent message tampering. If a malicious assailant modified the message in-flight, the checksum would no longer match. And because the checksum involves the author's secret, private key, the intruder will not be able to fabricate a correct checksum for the tampered-with message.

Digital signatures often are generated using asymmetric, public-key technology. The author's private key is used as a kind of "thumbprint," because the private key is known only by the owner.

Figure 14-10 shows an example of how node A can send a message to node B and sign it:

- Node A distills the variable-length message into a fixed-sized digest.

- Node A applies a "signature" function to the digest that uses the user's private key as a parameter. Because only the user knows the private key, a correct signature function shows the signer is the owner. In Figure 14-10, we use the decoder function D as the signature function, because it involves the user's private key.†

- Once the signature is computed, node A appends it to the end of the message and sends both the message and the signature to node B.

- On receipt, if node B wants to make sure that node A really wrote the message, and that the message hasn't been tampered with, node B can check the signature. Node B takes the private-key scrambled signature and applies the inverse function using the public key. If the unpacked digest doesn't match node B's own version of the digest, either the message was tampered with in-flight, or the sender did not have node A's private key (and therefore was not node A).

---

\* This assumes the private key has not been stolen. Most private keys expire after a while. There also are "revocation lists" that keep track of stolen or compromised keys.

† With the RSA cryptosystem, the decoder function D is used as the signature function, because D already takes the private key as input. Note that the decoder function is just a function, so it can be used on any input. Also, in the RSA cryptosystem, the D and E functions work when applied in either order and cancel each other out. So, $E(D(stuff)) = stuff$, just as $D(E(stuff)) = stuff$.

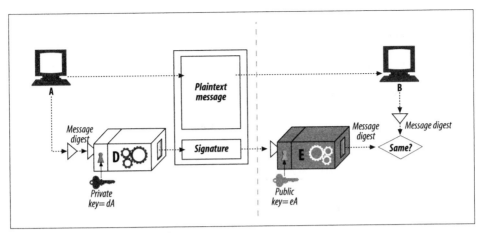

Figure 14-10. Unencrypted digital signature

# Digital Certificates

In this section, we talk about digital certificates, the "ID cards" of the Internet. Digital certificates (often called "certs," like the breath mints) contain information about a user or firm that has been vouched for by a trusted organization.

We all carry many forms of identification. Some IDs, such as passports and drivers' licenses, are trusted enough to prove one's identity in many situations. For example, a U.S. driver's license is sufficient proof of identity to let you board an airplane to New York for New Year's Eve, and it's sufficient proof of your age to let you drink intoxicating beverages with your friends when you get there.

More trusted forms of identification, such as passports, are signed and stamped by a government on special paper. They are harder to forge, so they inherently carry a higher level of trust. Some corporate badges and smart cards include electronics to help strengthen the identity of the carrier. Some top-secret government organizations even need to match up your fingerprints or retinal capillary patterns with your ID before trusting it!

Other forms of ID, such as business cards, are relatively easy to forge, so people trust this information less. They may be fine for professional interactions but probably are not enough proof of employment when you apply for a home loan.

## The Guts of a Certificate

Digital certificates also contain a set of information, all of which is digitally signed by an official "certificate authority." Basic digital certificates commonly contain basic things common to printed IDs, such as:

- Subject's name (person, server, organization, etc.)
- Expiration date

- Certificate issuer (who is vouching for the certificate)
- Digital signature from the certificate issuer

Additionally, digital certificates often contain the public key of the subject, as well as descriptive information about the subject and about the signature algorithm used. Anyone can create a digital certificate, but not everyone can get a well-respected signing authority to vouch for the certificate's information and sign the certificate with its private key. A typical certificate structure is shown in Figure 14-11.

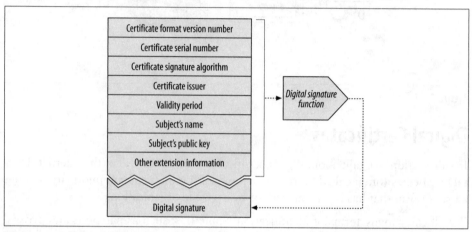

*Figure 14-11. Typical digital signature format*

## X.509 v3 Certificates

Unfortunately, there is no single, universal standard for digital certificates. There are many, subtly different styles of digital certificates, just as not all printed ID cards contain the same information in the same place. The good news is that most certificates in use today store their information in a standard form, called X.509 v3. X.509 v3 certificates provide a standard way of structuring certificate information into parseable fields. Different kinds of certificates have different field values, but most follow the X.509 v3 structure. The fields of an X.509 certificate are described in Table 14-2.

*Table 14-2. X.509 certificate fields*

| Field | Description |
| --- | --- |
| Version | The X.509 certificate version number for this certificate. Usually version 3 today. |
| Serial Number | A unique integer generated by the certification authority. Each certificate from a CA must have a unique serial number. |
| Signature Algorithm ID | The cryptographic algorithm used for the signature. For example, "MD2 digest with RSA encryption". |
| Certificate Issuer | The name for the organization that issued and signed this certificate, in X.500 format. |
| Validity Period | When this certificate is valid, defined by a start date and an end date. |

Table 14-2. X.509 certificate fields (continued)

| Field | Description |
|---|---|
| Subject's Name | The entity described in the certificate, such as a person or an organization. The subject name is in X.500 format. |
| Subject's Public Key Information | The public key for the certificate's subject, the algorithm used for the public key, and any additional parameters. |
| Issuer Unique ID (optional) | An optional unique identifier for the certificate issuer, to allow the potential reuse of the same issuer name. |
| Subject Unique ID (optional) | An optional unique identifier for the certificate subject, to allow the potential reuse of the same subject name. |
| Extensions | An optional set of extension fields (in version 3 and higher). Each extension field is flagged as critical or noncritical. Critical extensions are important and must be understood by the certificate user. If a certificate user doesn't recognize a critical extension field, it must reject the certificate. Common extension fields in use include:<br><br>*Basic Constraints*<br>   Subject's relationship to certification authority<br>*Certificate Policy*<br>   The policy under which the certificate is granted<br>*Key Usage*<br>   Restricts how the public key can be used |
| Certification Authority Signature | The certification authority's digital signature of all of the above fields, using the specified signing algorithm. |

There are several flavors of X.509-based certificates, including (among others) web server certificates, client email certificates, software code-signing certificates, and certificate authority certificates.

# Using Certificates to Authenticate Servers

When you establish a secure web transaction through HTTPS, modern browsers automatically fetch the digital certificate for the server being connected to. If the server does not have a certificate, the secure connection fails. The server certificate contains many fields, including:

- Name and hostname of the web site
- Public key of the web site
- Name of the signing authority
- Signature from the signing authority

When the browser receives the certificate, it checks the signing authority.* If it is a public, well-respected signing authority, the browser will already know its public key

---

\* Browsers and other Internet applications try hard to hide the details of most certificate management, to make browsing easier. But, when you are browsing through secure connections, all the major browsers allow you to personally examine the certificates of the sites to which you are talking, to be sure all is on the up-and-up.

(browsers ship with certificates of many signing authorities preinstalled), so it can verify the signature as we discussed in the previous section, "Digital Signatures." Figure 14-12 shows how a certificate's integrity is verified using its digital signature.

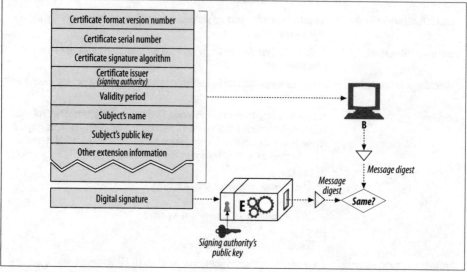

*Figure 14-12. Verifying that a signature is real*

If the signing authority is unknown, the browser isn't sure if it should trust the signing authority and usually displays a dialog box for the user to read and see if he trusts the signer. The signer might be the local IT department, or a software vendor.

# HTTPS: The Details

HTTPS is the most popular secure version of HTTP. It is widely implemented and available in all major commercial browsers and servers. HTTPS combines the HTTP protocol with a powerful set of symmetric, asymmetric, and certificate-based cryptographic techniques, making HTTPS very secure but also very flexible and easy to administer across the anarchy of the decentralized, global Internet.

HTTPS has accelerated the growth of Internet applications and has been a major force in the rapid growth of web-based electronic commerce. HTTPS also has been critical in the wide-area, secure administration of distributed web applications.

## HTTPS Overview

HTTPS is just HTTP sent over a secure transport layer. Instead of sending HTTP messages unencrypted to TCP and across the world-wide Internet (Figure 14-13a), HTTPS sends the HTTP messages first to a security layer that encrypts them before sending them to TCP (Figure 14-13b).

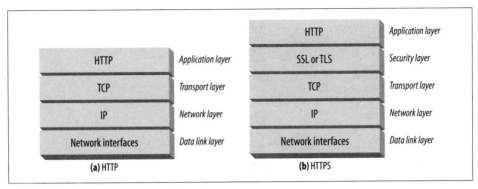

*Figure 14-13. HTTP transport-level security*

Today, the HTTP security layer is implemented by SSL and its modern replacement, TLS. We follow the common practice of using the term "SSL" to mean either SSL or TLS.

## HTTPS Schemes

Today, secure HTTP is optional. Thus, when making a request to a web server, we need a way to tell the web server to perform the secure protocol version of HTTP. This is done in the scheme of the URL.

In normal, nonsecure HTTP, the scheme prefix of the URL is *http*, as in:

> *http://www.joes-hardware.com/index.html*

In the secure HTTPS protocol, the scheme prefix of the URL is *https*, as in:

> *https://cajun-shop.securesites.com/Merchant2/merchant.mv?Store_Code=AGCGS*

When a client (such as a web browser) is asked to perform a transaction on a web resource, it examines the scheme of the URL:

- If the URL has an *http* scheme, the client opens a connection to the server on port 80 (by default) and sends it plain-old HTTP commands (Figure 14-14a).
- If the URL has an *https* scheme, the client opens a connection to the server on port 443 (by default) and then "handshakes" with the server, exchanging some SSL security parameters with the server in a binary format, followed by the encrypted HTTP commands (Figure 14-14b).

Because SSL traffic is a binary protocol, completely different from HTTP, the traffic is carried on different ports (SSL usually is carried over port 443). If both SSL and HTTP traffic arrived on port 80, most web servers would interpret binary SSL traffic as erroneous HTTP and close the connection. A more integrated layering of security services into HTTP would have eliminated the need for multiple destination ports, but this does not cause severe problems in practice.

Let's look a bit more closely at how SSL sets up connections with secure servers.

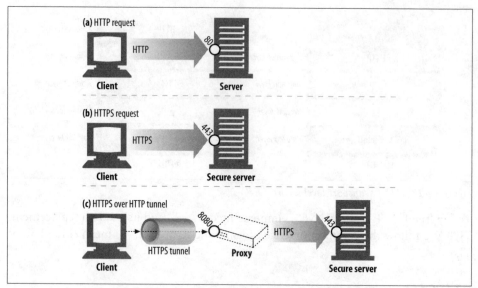

*Figure 14-14. HTTP and HTTPS port numbers*

## Secure Transport Setup

In unencrypted HTTP, a client opens a TCP connection to port 80 on a web server, sends a request message, receives a response message, and closes the connection. This sequence is sketched in Figure 14-15a.

The procedure is slightly more complicated in HTTPS, because of the SSL security layer. In HTTPS, the client first opens a connection to port 443 (the default port for secure HTTP) on the web server. Once the TCP connection is established, the client and server initialize the SSL layer, negotiating cryptography parameters and exchanging keys. When the handshake completes, the SSL initialization is done, and the client can send request messages to the security layer. These messages are encrypted before being sent to TCP. This procedure is depicted in Figure 14-15b.

## SSL Handshake

Before you can send encrypted HTTP messages, the client and server need to do an SSL handshake, where they:

- Exchange protocol version numbers
- Select a cipher that each side knows
- Authenticate the identity of each side
- Generate temporary session keys to encrypt the channel

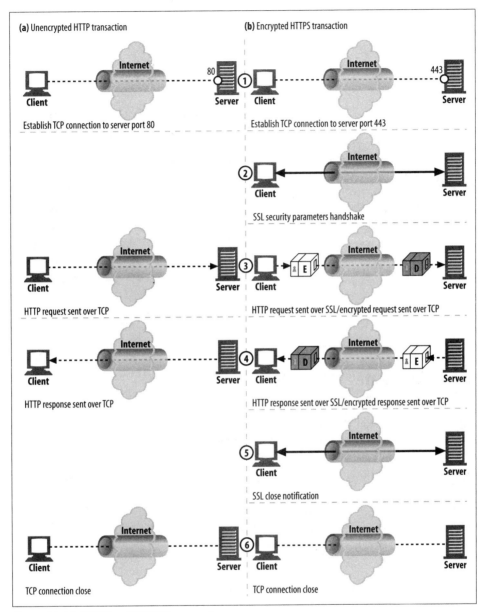

**(a)** Unencrypted HTTP transaction

Establish TCP connection to server port 80

HTTP request sent over TCP

HTTP response sent over TCP

TCP connection close

**(b)** Encrypted HTTPS transaction

① Establish TCP connection to server port 443

② SSL security parameters handshake

③ HTTP request sent over SSL/encrypted request sent over TCP

④ HTTP response sent over SSL/encrypted response sent over TCP

⑤ SSL close notification

⑥ TCP connection close

*Figure 14-15. HTTP and HTTPS transactions*

Before any encrypted HTTP data flies across the network, SSL already has sent a bunch of handshake data to establish the communication. The essence of the SSL handshake is shown in Figure 14-16.

This is a simplified version of the SSL handshake. Depending on how SSL is being used, the handshake can be more complicated, but this is the general idea.

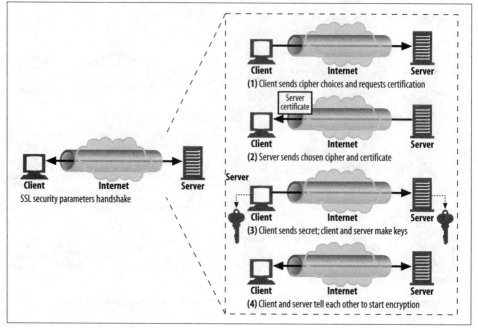

*Figure 14-16. SSL handshake (simplified)*

## Server Certificates

SSL supports mutual authentication, carrying server certificates to clients and carrying client certificates back to servers. But today, client certificates are not commonly used for browsing. Most users don't even possess personal client certificates.* A web server can demand a client certificate, but that seldom occurs in practice.†

On the other hand, secure HTTPS transactions always require server certificates. When you perform a secure transaction on a web server, such as posting your credit card information, you want to know that you are talking to the organization you think you are talking to. Server certificates, signed by a well-known authority, help you assess how much you trust the server before sending your credit card or personal information.

The server certificate is an X.509 v3–derived certificate showing the organization's name, address, server DNS domain name, and other information (see Figure 14-17). You and your client software can examine the certificate to make sure everything seems to be on the up-and-up.

---

* Client certificates are used for web browsing in some corporate settings, and client certificates are used for secure email. In the future, client certificates may become more common for web browsing, but today they've caught on very slowly.

† Some organizational intranets use client certificates to control employee access to information.

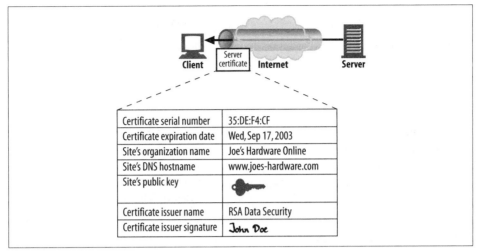

*Figure 14-17. HTTPS certificates are X.509 certificates with site information*

| | |
|---|---|
| Certificate serial number | 35:DE:F4:CF |
| Certificate expiration date | Wed, Sep 17, 2003 |
| Site's organization name | Joe's Hardware Online |
| Site's DNS hostname | www.joes-hardware.com |
| Site's public key | |
| Certificate issuer name | RSA Data Security |
| Certificate issuer signature | John Doe |

## Site Certificate Validation

SSL itself doesn't require you to examine the web server certificate, but most modern browsers do some simple sanity checks on certificates and provide you with the means to do more thorough checks. One algorithm for web server certificate validation, proposed by Netscape, forms the basis of most browser's validation techniques. The steps are:

*Date check*

First, the browser checks the certificate's start and end dates to ensure the certificate is still valid. If the certificate has expired or has not yet become active, the certificate validation fails and the browser displays an error.

*Signer trust check*

Every certificate is signed by some certificate authority (CA), who vouches for the server. There are different levels of certificate, each requiring different levels of background verification. For example, if you apply for an e-commerce server certificate, you usually need to provide legal proof of incorporation as a business.

Anyone can generate certificates, but some CAs are well-known organizations with well-understood procedures for verifying the identity and good business behavior of certificate applicants. For this reason, browsers ship with a list of signing authorities that are trusted. If a browser receives a certificate signed by some unknown (and possibly malicious) authority, the browser usually displays a warning. Browsers also may choose to accept any certificates with a valid signing path to a trusted CA. In other words, if a trusted CA signs a certificate for "Sam's Signing Shop" and Sam's Signing Shop signs a site certificate, the browser may accept the certificate as deriving from a valid CA path.

*Signature check*

> Once the signing authority is judged as trustworthy, the browser checks the certificate's integrity by applying the signing authority's public key to the signature and comparing it to the checksum.

*Site identity check*

> To prevent a server from copying someone else's certificate or intercepting their traffic, most browsers try to verify that the domain name in the certificate matches the domain name of the server they talked to. Server certificates usually contain a single domain name, but some CAs create certificates that contain lists of server names or wildcarded domain names, for clusters or farms of servers. If the hostname does not match the identity in the certificate, user-oriented clients must either notify the user or terminate the connection with a bad certificate error.

## Virtual Hosting and Certificates

It's sometimes tricky to deal with secure traffic on sites that are virtually hosted (multiple hostnames on a single server). Some popular web server programs support only a single certificate. If a user arrives for a virtual hostname that does not strictly match the certificate name, a warning box is displayed.

For example, consider the Louisiana-themed e-commerce site Cajun-Shop.com. The site's hosting provider provided the official name *cajun-shop.securesites.com*. When users go to *https://www.cajun-shop.com*, the official hostname listed in the server certificate (*\*.securesites.com*) does not match the virtual hostname the user browsed to (*www.cajun-shop.com*), and the warning in Figure 14-18 appears.

To prevent this problem, the owners of Cajun-Shop.com redirect all users to *cajun-shop.securesites.com* when they begin secure transactions. Cert management for virtually hosted sites can be a little tricky.

# A Real HTTPS Client

SSL is a complicated binary protocol. Unless you are a crypto expert, you shouldn't send raw SSL traffic directly. Thankfully, several commercial and open source libraries exist to make it easier to program SSL clients and servers.

## OpenSSL

OpenSSL is the most popular open source implementation of SSL and TLS. The OpenSSL Project is a collaborative volunteer effort to develop a robust, commercial-grade, full-featured toolkit implementing the SSL and TLS protocols, as well as a full-strength, general-purpose cryptography library. You can get information about OpenSSL, and download the software, from *http://www.openssl.org*.

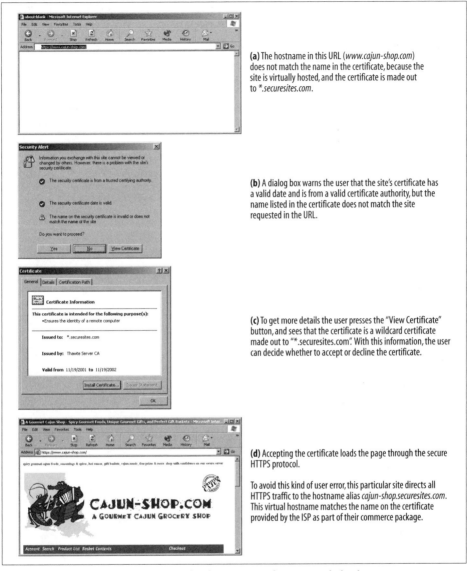

(a) The hostname in this URL (*www.cajun-shop.com*) does not match the name in the certificate, because the site is virtually hosted, and the certificate is made out to *\*.securesites.com*.

(b) A dialog box warns the user that the site's certificate has a valid date and is from a valid certificate authority, but the name listed in the certificate does not match the site requested in the URL.

(c) To get more details the user presses the "View Certificate" button, and sees that the certificate is a wildcard certificate made out to "*\*.securesites.com*". With this information, the user can decide whether to accept or decline the certificate.

(d) Accepting the certificate loads the page through the secure HTTPS protocol.

To avoid this kind of user error, this particular site directs all HTTPS traffic to the hostname alias *cajun-shop.securesites.com*. This virtual hostname matches the name on the certificate provided by the ISP as part of their commerce package.

*Figure 14-18. Certificate name mismatches bring up certificate error dialog boxes*

You might also hear of SSLeay (pronounced S-S-L-e-a-y). OpenSSL is the successor to the SSLeay library, and it has a very similar interface. SSLeay was originally developed by Eric A. Young (the "eay" of SSLeay).

## A Simple HTTPS Client

In this section, we'll use the OpenSSL package to write an extremely primitive HTTPS client. This client establishes an SSL connection with a server, prints out some identification information from the site server, sends an HTTP GET request across the secure channel, receives an HTTP response, and prints the response.

The C program shown below is an OpenSSL implementation of the trivial HTTPS client. To keep the program simple, error-handling and certificate-processing logic has not been included.

Because error handling has been removed from this example program, you should use it only for explanatory value. The software will crash or otherwise misbehave in normal error conditions.

```c
/***********************************************************************
 * https_client.c --- very simple HTTPS client with no error checking
 *      usage: https_client servername
 ***********************************************************************/

#include <stdio.h>
#include <memory.h>
#include <errno.h>
#include <sys/types.h>
#include <sys/socket.h>
#include <netinet/in.h>
#include <arpa/inet.h>
#include <netdb.h>

#include <openssl/crypto.h>
#include <openssl/x509.h>
#include <openssl/pem.h>
#include <openssl/ssl.h>
#include <openssl/err.h>

void main(int argc, char **argv)
{
    SSL *ssl;
    SSL_CTX *ctx;
    SSL_METHOD *client_method;
    X509 *server_cert;
    int sd,err;
    char *str,*hostname,outbuf[4096],inbuf[4096],host_header[512];
    struct hostent *host_entry;
    struct sockaddr_in server_socket_address;
    struct in_addr ip;

    /*========================================*/
    /* (1) initialize SSL library */
    /*========================================*/

    SSLeay_add_ssl_algorithms();
    client_method = SSLv2_client_method();
    SSL_load_error_strings();
    ctx = SSL_CTX_new(client_method);
```

```
printf("(1) SSL context initialized\n\n");

/*=============================================*/
/* (2) convert server hostname into IP address */
/*=============================================*/

hostname = argv[1];
host_entry = gethostbyname(hostname);
bcopy(host_entry->h_addr, &(ip.s_addr), host_entry->h_length);

printf("(2) '%s' has IP address '%s'\n\n", hostname, inet_ntoa(ip));

/*=============================================*/
/* (3) open a TCP connection to port 443 on server */
/*=============================================*/

sd = socket (AF_INET, SOCK_STREAM, 0);

memset(&server_socket_address, '\0', sizeof(server_socket_address));
server_socket_address.sin_family = AF_INET;
server_socket_address.sin_port = htons(443);
memcpy(&(server_socket_address.sin_addr.s_addr),
       host_entry->h_addr, host_entry->h_length);

err = connect(sd, (struct sockaddr*) &server_socket_address,
              sizeof(server_socket_address));
if (err < 0) { perror("can't connect to server port"); exit(1); }

printf("(3) TCP connection open to host '%s', port %d\n\n",
       hostname, server_socket_address.sin_port);

/*=============================================*/
/* (4) initiate the SSL handshake over the TCP connection */
/*=============================================*/

ssl = SSL_new(ctx);        /* create SSL stack endpoint */
SSL_set_fd(ssl, sd);       /* attach SSL stack to socket */
err = SSL_connect(ssl);    /* initiate SSL handshake */

printf("(4) SSL endpoint created & handshake completed\n\n");

/*=============================================*/
/* (5) print out the negotiated cipher chosen */
/*=============================================*/

printf("(5) SSL connected with cipher: %s\n\n", SSL_get_cipher(ssl));

/*=============================================*/
/* (6) print out the server's certificate */
/*=============================================*/

server_cert = SSL_get_peer_certificate(ssl);
```

```c
    printf("(6) server's certificate was received:\n\n");

    str = X509_NAME_oneline(X509_get_subject_name(server_cert), 0, 0);
    printf("    subject: %s\n", str);

    str = X509_NAME_oneline(X509_get_issuer_name(server_cert), 0, 0);
    printf("    issuer: %s\n\n", str);

    /* certificate verification would happen here */

    X509_free(server_cert);

    /*********************************************************/
    /* (7) handshake complete --- send HTTP request over SSL */
    /*********************************************************/

    sprintf(host_header,"Host: %s:443\r\n",hostname);
    strcpy(outbuf,"GET / HTTP/1.0\r\n");
    strcat(outbuf,host_header);
    strcat(outbuf,"Connection: close\r\n");
    strcat(outbuf,"\r\n");

    err = SSL_write(ssl, outbuf, strlen(outbuf));
    shutdown (sd, 1); /* send EOF to server */

    printf("(7) sent HTTP request over encrypted channel:\n\n%s\n",outbuf);

    /***************************************************/
    /* (8) read back HTTP response from the SSL stack */
    /***************************************************/

    err = SSL_read(ssl, inbuf, sizeof(inbuf) - 1);
    inbuf[err] = '\0';
    printf ("(8) got back %d bytes of HTTP response:\n\n%s\n",err,inbuf);

    /***************************************************/
    /* (9) all done, so close connection & clean up */
    /***************************************************/

    SSL_shutdown(ssl);
    close (sd);
    SSL_free (ssl);
    SSL_CTX_free (ctx);

    printf("(9) all done, cleaned up and closed connection\n\n");
}
```

This example compiles and runs on Sun Solaris, but it is illustrative of how SSL programs work on many OS platforms. This entire program, including all the encryption and key and certificate management, fits in a three-page C program, thanks to the powerful features provided by OpenSSL.

Let's walk through the program section by section:

- The top of the program includes support files needed to support TCP networking and SSL.
- Section 1 creates the local context that keeps track of the handshake parameters and other state about the SSL connection, by calling *SSL_CTX_new*.
- Section 2 converts the input hostname (provided as a command-line argument) to an IP address, using the Unix *gethostbyname* function. Other platforms may have other ways to provide this facility.
- Section 3 opens a TCP connection to port 443 on the server by creating a local socket, setting up the remote address information, and connecting to the remote server.
- Once the TCP connection is established, we attach the SSL layer to the TCP connection using *SSL_new* and *SSL_set_fd* and perform the SSL handshake with the server by calling *SSL_connect*. When section 4 is done, we have a functioning SSL channel established, with ciphers chosen and certificates exchanged.
- Section 5 prints out the value of the chosen bulk-encryption cipher.
- Section 6 prints out some of the information contained in the X.509 certificate sent back from the server, including information about the certificate holder and the organization that issued the certificate. The OpenSSL library doesn't do anything special with the information in the server certificate. A real SSL application, such as a web browser, would do some sanity checks on the certificate to make sure it is signed properly and came from the right host. We discussed what browsers do with server certificates in "Site Certificate Validation."
- At this point, our SSL connection is ready to use for secure data transfer. In section 7, we send the simple HTTP request "GET / HTTP/1.0" over the SSL channel using *SSL_write*, then close the outbound half of the connection.
- In section 8, we read the response back from the connection using *SSL_read*, and print it on the screen. Because the SSL layer takes care of all the encryption and decryption, we can just write and read normal HTTP commands.
- Finally, we clean up in section 9.

Refer to *http://www.openssl.org* for more information about the OpenSSL libraries.

## Executing Our Simple OpenSSL Client

The following shows the output of our simple HTTP client when pointed at a secure server. In this case, we pointed the client at the home page of the Morgan Stanley Online brokerage. Online trading companies make extensive use of HTTPS.

```
% https_client clients1.online.msdw.com
(1) SSL context initialized
```

(2) 'clients1.online.msdw.com' has IP address '63.151.15.11'

(3) TCP connection open to host 'clients1.online.msdw.com', port 443

(4) SSL endpoint created & handshake completed

(5) SSL connected with cipher: DES-CBC3-MD5

(6) server's certificate was received:

> subject: /C=US/ST=Utah/L=Salt Lake City/O=Morgan Stanley/OU=Online/CN=
> clients1.online.msdw.com
> issuer: /C=US/O=RSA Data Security, Inc./OU=Secure Server Certification
> Authority

(7) sent HTTP request over encrypted channel:

```
GET / HTTP/1.0
Host: clients1.online.msdw.com:443
Connection: close
```

(8) got back 615 bytes of HTTP response:

```
HTTP/1.1 302 Found
Date: Sat, 09 Mar 2002 09:43:42 GMT
Server: Stronghold/3.0 Apache/1.3.14 RedHat/3013c (Unix) mod_ssl/2.7.1 OpenSSL/0.9.6
Location: https://clients.online.msdw.com/cgi-bin/ICenter/home
Connection: close
Content-Type: text/html; charset=iso-8859-1

<!DOCTYPE HTML PUBLIC "-//IETF//DTD HTML 2.0//EN">
<HTML><HEAD>
<TITLE>302 Found</TITLE>
</HEAD><BODY>
<H1>Found</H1>
The document has moved <A HREF="https://clients.online.msdw.com/cgi-bin/ICenter/
home">here</A>.<P>
<HR>
<ADDRESS>Stronghold/3.0 Apache/1.3.14 RedHat/3013c Server at clients1.online.msdw.com
Port 443</ADDRESS>
</BODY></HTML>
```

(9) all done, cleaned up and closed connection

As soon as the first four sections are completed, the client has an open SSL connection. It can then inquire about the state of the connection and chosen parameters and can examine server certificates.

In this example, the client and server negotiated the DES-CBC3-MD5 bulk-encryption cipher. You also can see that the server site certificate belongs to the organization "Morgan Stanley" in "Salt Lake City, Utah, USA". The certificate was granted by RSA Data Security, and the hostname is "clients1.online.msdw.com," which matches our request.

Once the SSL channel is established and the client feels comfortable about the site certificate, it sends its HTTP request over the secure channel. In our example, the client sends a simple "GET / HTTP/1.0" HTTP request and receives back a 302 Redirect response, requesting that the user fetch a different URL.

# Tunneling Secure Traffic Through Proxies

Clients often use web proxy servers to access web servers on their behalf (proxies are discussed in Chapter 6). For example, many corporations place a proxy at the security perimeter of the corporate network and the public Internet (Figure 14-19). The proxy is the only device permitted by the firewall routers to exchange HTTP traffic, and it may employ virus checking or other content controls.

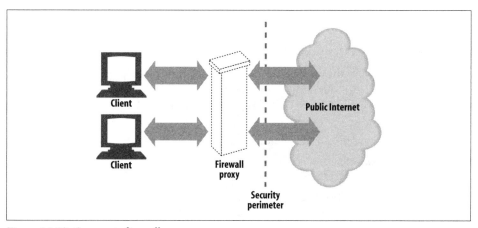

*Figure 14-19. Corporate firewall proxy*

But once the client starts encrypting the data to the server, using the server's public key, the proxy no longer has the ability to read the HTTP header! And if the proxy cannot read the HTTP header, it won't know where to forward the request (Figure 14-20).

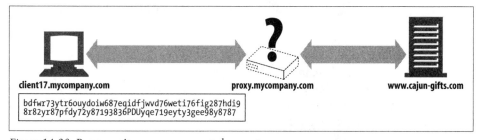

*Figure 14-20. Proxy can't proxy an encrypted request*

To make HTTPS work with proxies, a few modifications are needed to tell the proxy where to connect. One popular technique is the HTTPS SSL tunneling protocol.

Using the HTTPS tunneling protocol, the client first tells the proxy the secure host and port to which it wants to connect. It does this in plaintext, before encryption starts, so the proxy can read this information.

HTTP is used to send the plaintext endpoint information, using a new extension method called CONNECT. The CONNECT method tells the proxy to open a connection to the desired host and port number and, when that's done, to tunnel data directly between the client and server. The CONNECT method is a one-line text command that provides the hostname and port of the secure origin server, separated by a colon. The host:port is followed by a space and an HTTP version string followed by a CRLF. After that there is a series of zero or more HTTP request header lines, followed by an empty line. After the empty line, if the handshake to establish the connection was successful, SSL data transfer can begin. Here is an example:

```
CONNECT home.netscape.com:443 HTTP/1.0
User-agent: Mozilla/1.1N

<raw SSL-encrypted data would follow here...>
```

After the empty line in the request, the client will wait for a response from the proxy. The proxy will evaluate the request and make sure that it is valid and that the user is authorized to request such a connection. If everything is in order, the proxy will make a connection to the destination server and, if successful, send a 200 Connection Established response to the client.

```
HTTP/1.0 200 Connection established
Proxy-agent: Netscape-Proxy/1.1
```

For more information about secure tunnels and security proxies, refer back to "Tunnels" in Chapter 8.

# For More Information

Security and cryptography are hugely important and hugely complicated topics. If you'd like to learn more about HTTP security, digital cryptography, digital certificates, and the Public-Key Infrastructure, here are a few starting points.

## HTTP Security

*Web Security, Privacy & Commerce*
> Simson Garfinkel, O'Reilly & Associates, Inc. This is one of the best, most readable introductions to web security and the use of SSL/TLS and digital certificates.

*http://www.ietf.org/rfc/rfc2818.txt*
> RFC 2818, "HTTP Over TLS," specifies how to implement secure HTTP over Transport Layer Security (TLS), the modern successor to SSL.

*http://www.ietf.org/rfc/rfc2817.txt*

RFC 2817, "Upgrading to TLS Within HTTP/1.1," explains how to use the Upgrade mechanism in HTTP/1.1 to initiate TLS over an existing TCP connection. This allows unsecured and secured HTTP traffic to share the same well-known port (in this case, http: at 80 rather than https: at 443). It also enables virtual hosting, so a single HTTP+TLS server can disambiguate traffic intended for several hostnames at a single IP address.

## SSL and TLS

*http://www.ietf.org/rfc/rfc2246.txt*

RFC 2246, "The TLS Protocol Version 1.0," specifies Version 1.0 of the TLS protocol (the successor to SSL). TLS provides communications privacy over the Internet. The protocol allows client/server applications to communicate in a way that is designed to prevent eavesdropping, tampering, and message forgery.

*http://developer.netscape.com/docs/manuals/security/sslin/contents.htm*

"Introduction to SSL" introduces the Secure Sockets Layer (SSL) protocol. Originally developed by Netscape, SSL has been universally accepted on the World Wide Web for authenticated and encrypted communication between clients and servers.

*http://www.netscape.com/eng/ssl3/draft302.txt*

"The SSL Protocol Version 3.0" is Netscape's 1996 specification for SSL.

*http://developer.netscape.com/tech/security/ssl/howitworks.html*

"How SSL Works" is Netscape's introduction to key cryptography.

*http://www.openssl.org*

The OpenSSL Project is a collaborative effort to develop a robust, commercial-grade, full-featured, and open source toolkit implementing the Secure Sockets Layer (SSL v2/v3) and Transport Layer Security (TLS v1) protocols, as well as a full-strength, general-purpose cryptography library. The project is managed by a worldwide community of volunteers that use the Internet to communicate, plan, and develop the OpenSSL toolkit and its related documentation. OpenSSL is based on the excellent SSLeay library developed by Eric A. Young and Tim J. Hudson. The OpenSSL toolkit is licensed under an Apache-style licence, which basically means that you are free to get and use it for commercial and noncommercial purposes, subject to some simple license conditions.

## Public-Key Infrastructure

*http://www.ietf.org/html.charters/pkix-charter.html*

The IETF PKIX Working Group was established in 1995 with the intent of developing Internet standards needed to support an X.509-based Public-Key Infrastructure. This is a nice summary of that group's activities.

*http://www.ietf.org/rfc/rfc2459.txt*
> RFC 2459, "Internet X.509 Public Key Infrastructure Certificate and CRL Profile," contains details about X.509 v3 digital certificates.

## Digital Cryptography

*Applied Cryptography*
> Bruce Schneier, John Wiley & Sons. This is a classic book on cryptography for implementors.

*The Code Book: The Science of Secrecy from Ancient Egypt to Quantum Cryptography*
> Simon Singh, Anchor Books. This entertaining book is a cryptography primer. While it's not intended for technology experts, it is a lively historical tour of secret coding.

# Entities, Encodings, and Internationalization

Part IV is all about the entity bodies of HTTP messages and the content that the entity bodies ship around as cargo:

- Chapter 15, *Entities and Encodings*, describes the formats and syntax of HTTP content.

- Chapter 16, *Internationalization*, surveys the web standards that allow people to exchange content in different languages and different character sets, around the globe.

- Chapter 17, *Content Negotiation and Transcoding*, explains mechanisms for negotiating acceptable content.

# Entities and Encodings

HTTP ships billions of media objects of all kinds every day. Images, text, movies, software programs... you name it, HTTP ships it. HTTP also makes sure that its messages can be properly transported, identified, extracted, and processed. In particular, HTTP ensures that its cargo:

- Can be identified correctly (using Content-Type media formats and Content-Language headers) so browsers and other clients can process the content properly

- Can be unpacked properly (using Content-Length and Content-Encoding headers)

- Is fresh (using entity validators and cache-expiration controls)

- Meets the user's needs (based on content-negotiation Accept headers)

- Moves quickly and efficiently through the network (using range requests, delta encoding, and other data compression)

- Arrives complete and untampered with (using transfer encoding headers and Content-MD5 checksums)

To make all this happen, HTTP uses well-labeled entities to carry content.

This chapter discusses entities, their associated entity headers, and how they work to transport web cargo. We'll show how HTTP provides the essentials of content size, type, and encodings. We'll also explain some of the more complicated and powerful features of HTTP entities, including range requests, delta encoding, digests, and chunked encodings.

This chapter covers:

- The format and behavior of HTTP message entities as HTTP data containers

- How HTTP describes the size of entity bodies, and what HTTP requires in the way of sizing

- The entity headers used to describe the format, alphabet, and language of content, so clients can process it properly

- Reversible content encodings, used by senders to transform the content data format before sending to make it take up less space or be more secure

- Transfer encoding, which modifies how HTTP ships data to enhance the communication of some kinds of content, and chunked encoding, a transfer encoding that chops data into multiple pieces to deliver content of unknown length safely

- The assortment of tags, labels, times, and checksums that help clients get the latest version of requested content

- The validators that act like version numbers on content, so web applications can ensure they have fresh content, and the HTTP header fields designed to control object freshness

- Ranges, which are useful for continuing aborted downloads where they left off

- HTTP delta encoding extensions, which allow clients to request just those parts of a web page that actually have changed since a previously viewed revision

- Checksums of entity bodies, which are used to detect changes in entity content as it passes through proxies

## Messages Are Crates, Entities Are Cargo

If you think of HTTP messages as the crates of the Internet shipping system, then HTTP entities are the actual cargo of the messages. Figure 15-1 shows a simple entity, carried inside an HTTP response message.

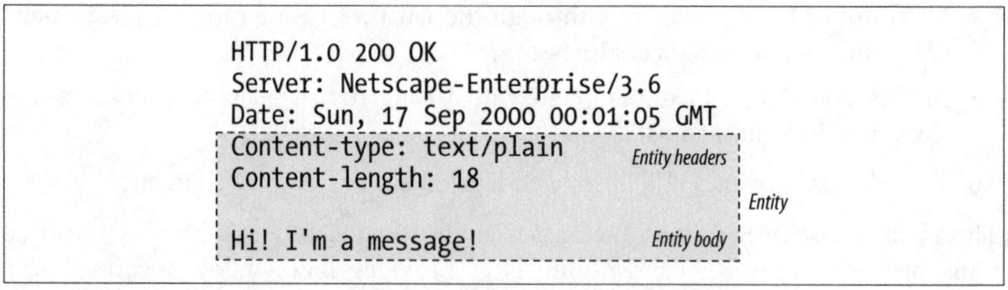

```
HTTP/1.0 200 OK
Server: Netscape-Enterprise/3.6
Date: Sun, 17 Sep 2000 00:01:05 GMT
Content-type: text/plain          Entity headers
Content-length: 18
                                                    Entity
Hi! I'm a message!                Entity body
```

Figure 15-1. Message entity is made up of entity headers and entity body

The entity headers indicate a plaintext document (Content-Type: text/plain) that is a mere 18 characters long (Content-Length: 18). As always, a blank line (CRLF) separates the header fields from the start of the body.

HTTP entity headers (covered in Chapter 3) describe the contents of an HTTP message. HTTP/1.1 defines 10 primary entity header fields:

Content-Type
    The kind of object carried by the entity.

Content-Length
    The length or size of the message being sent.

*Content-Language*
> The human language that best matches the object being sent.

*Content-Encoding*
> Any transformation (compression, etc.) performed on the object data.

*Content-Location*
> An alternate location for the object at the time of the request.

*Content-Range*
> If this is a partial entity, this header defines which pieces of the whole are included.

*Content-MD5*
> A checksum of the contents of the entity body.

*Last-Modified*
> The date on which this particular content was created or modified at the server.

*Expires*
> The date and time at which this entity data will become stale.

*Allow*
> What request methods are legal on this resource; e.g., GET and HEAD.

*ETag*
> A unique validator for this particular instance[*] of the document. The ETag header is not defined formally as an entity header, but it is an important header for many operations involving entities.

*Cache-Control*
> Directives on how this document can be cached. The Cache-Control header, like the ETag header, is not defined formally as an entity header.

## Entity Bodies

The entity body just contains the raw cargo.[†] Any other descriptive information is contained in the headers. Because the entity body cargo is just raw data, the entity headers are needed to describe the meaning of that data. For example, the Content-Type entity header tells us how to interpret the data (image, text, etc.), and the Content-Encoding entity header tells us if the data was compressed or otherwise recoded. We talk about all of this and more in upcoming sections.

The raw content begins immediately after the blank CRLF line that marks the end of the header fields. Whatever the content is—text or binary, document or image, compressed or uncompressed, English or French or Japanese—it is placed right after the CRLF.

---

[*] Instances are described later in this chapter, in the section "Time-Varying Instances."

[†] If there is a Content-Encoding header, the content already has been encoded by the content-encoding algorithm, and the first byte of the entity is the first byte of the encoded (e.g., compressed) cargo.

Figure 15-2 shows two examples of real HTTP messages, one carrying a text entity, the other carrying an image entity. The hexadecimal values show the exact contents of the message:

- In Figure 15-2a, the entity body begins at byte number 65, right after the end-of-headers CRLF. The entity body contains the ASCII characters for "Hi! I'm a message!"

- In Figure 15-2b, the entity body begins at byte number 67. The entity body contains the binary contents of the GIF image. GIF files begin with 6-byte version signature, a 16-bit width, and a 16-bit height. You can see all three of these directly in the entity body.

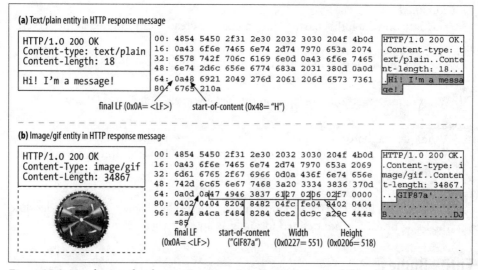

Figure 15-2. Hex dumps of real message content (raw message content follows blank CRLF)

# Content-Length: The Entity's Size

The Content-Length header indicates the size of the entity body in the message, in bytes. The size includes any content encodings (the Content-Length of a gzip-compressed text file will be the compressed size, not the original size).

The Content-Length header is mandatory for messages with entity bodies, unless the message is transported using chunked encoding. Content-Length is needed to detect premature message truncation when servers crash and to properly segment messages that share a persistent connection.

## Detecting Truncation

Older versions of HTTP used connection close to delimit the end of a message. But, without Content-Length, clients cannot distinguish between successful connection close at the end of a message and connection close due to a server crash in the middle of a message. Clients need Content-Length to detect message truncation.

Message truncation is especially severe for caching proxy servers. If a cache receives a truncated message and doesn't recognize the truncation, it may store the defective content and serve it many times. Caching proxy servers generally do not cache HTTP bodies that don't have an explicit Content-Length header, to reduce the risk of caching truncated messages.

## Incorrect Content-Length

An incorrect Content-Length can cause even more damage than a missing Content-Length. Because some early clients and servers had well-known bugs with respect to Content-Length calculations, some clients, servers, and proxies contain algorithms to try to detect and correct interactions with broken servers. HTTP/1.1 user agents officially are supposed to notify the user when an invalid length is received and detected.

## Content-Length and Persistent Connections

Content-Length is essential for persistent connections. If the response comes across a persistent connection, another HTTP response can immediately follow the current response. The Content-Length header lets the client know where one message ends and the next begins. Because the connection is persistent, the client cannot use connection close to identify the message's end. Without a Content-Length header, HTTP applications won't know where one entity body ends and the next message begins.

As we will see in "Transfer Encoding and Chunked Encoding," there is one situation where you can use persistent connections without having a Content-Length header: when you use *chunked encoding*. Chunked encoding sends the data in a series of chunks, each with a specified size. Even if the server does not know the size of the entire entity at the time the headers are generated (often because the entity is being generated dynamically), the server can use chunked encoding to transmit pieces of well-defined size.

## Content Encoding

HTTP lets you encode the contents of an entity body, perhaps to make it more secure or to compress it to take up less space (we explain compression in detail later in this chapter). If the body has been content-encoded, the Content-Length header specifies the length, in bytes, of the *encoded* body, *not* the length of the original, unencoded body.

Some HTTP applications have been known to get this wrong and to send the size of the data before the encoding, which causes serious errors, especially with persistent connections. Unfortunately, none of the headers described in the HTTP/1.1

specification can be used to send the length of the original, unencoded body, which makes it difficult for clients to verify the integrity of their unencoding processes.*

## Rules for Determining Entity Body Length

The following rules describe how to correctly determine the length and end of an entity body in several different circumstances. The rules should be applied in order; the first match applies.

1. If a particular HTTP message type is not allowed to have a body, ignore the Content-Length header for body calculations. The Content-Length headers are informational in this case and do not describe the actual body length. (Naïve HTTP applications can get in trouble if they assume Content-Length always means there is a body).

   The most important example is the HEAD response. The HEAD method requests that a server send the headers that would have been returned by an equivalent GET request, but no body. Because a GET response would send back a Content-Length header, so will the HEAD response—but unlike the GET response, the HEAD response will not have a body. 1XX, 204, and 304 responses also can have informational Content-Length headers but no entity body. Messages that forbid entity bodies must terminate at the first empty line after the headers, regardless of which entity header fields are present.

2. If a message contains a Transfer-Encoding header (other than the default HTTP "identity" encoding), the entity will be terminated by a special pattern called a "zero-byte chunk," unless the message is terminated first by closing the connection. We'll discuss transfer encodings and chunked encodings later in this chapter.

3. If a message has a Content-Length header (and the message type allows entity bodies), the Content-Length value contains the body length, unless there is a non-identity Transfer-Encoding header. If a message is received with both a Content-Length header field and a non-identity Transfer-Encoding header field, you must ignore the Content-Length, because the transfer encoding will change the way entity bodies are represented and transferred (and probably the number of bytes transmitted).

4. If the message uses the "multipart/byteranges" media type and the entity length is not otherwise specified (in the Content-Length header), each part of the multipart message will specify its own size. This multipart type is the only entity body type that self-delimits its own size, so this media type must not be sent unless the sender knows the recipient can parse it.†

---

* Even the Content-MD5 header, which can be used to send the 128-bit MD5 of the document, contains the MD5 of the encoded document. The Content-MD5 header is described later in this chapter.

† Because a Range header might be forwarded by a more primitive proxy that does not understand multipart/byteranges, the sender must delimit the message using methods 1, 3, or 5 in this section if it isn't sure the receiver understands the self-delimiting format.

5. If none of the above rules match, the entity ends when the connection closes. In practice, only servers can use connection close to indicate the end of a message. Clients can't close the connection to signal the end of client messages, because that would leave no way for the server to send back a response.[*]

# Entity Digests

Although HTTP typically is implemented over a reliable transport protocol such as TCP/IP, parts of messages may get modified in transit for a variety of reasons, such as noncompliant transcoding proxies or buggy intermediary proxies. To detect unintended (or undesired) modification of entity body data, the sender can generate a checksum of the data when the initial entity is generated, and the receiver can sanity check the checksum to catch any unintended entity modification.[†]

The Content-MD5 header is used by servers to send the result of running the MD5 algorithm on the entity body. Only the server where the response originates may compute and send the Content-MD5 header. Intermediate proxies and caches may not modify or add the header—that would violate the whole purpose of verifying end-to-end integrity. The Content-MD5 header contains the MD5 of the content after all content encodings have been applied to the entity body and before any transfer encodings have been applied to it. Clients seeking to verify the integrity of the message must first decode the transfer encodings, then compute the MD5 of the resulting unencoded entity body. As an example, if a document is compressed using the gzip algorithm, then sent with chunked encoding, the MD5 algorithm is run on the full gripped body.

In addition to checking message integrity, the MD5 can be used as a key into a hash table to quickly locate documents and reduce duplicate storage of content. Despite these possible uses, the Content-MD5 header is not sent often.

Extensions to HTTP have proposed other digest algorithms in IETF drafts. These extensions have proposed a new header, Want-Digest, that allows clients to specify the type of digest they expect with the response. Quality values can be used to suggest multiple digest algorithms and indicate preference.

---

[*] The client could do a half close of just its output connection, but many server applications aren't designed to handle this situation and will interpret a half close as the client disconnecting from the server. Connection management was never well specified in HTTP. See Chapter 4 for more details.

[†] This method, of course, is not immune to a malicious attack that replaces both the message body and digest header. It is intended only to detect unintentional modification. Other facilities, such as digest authentication, are needed to provide safeguards against malicious tampering.

# Media Type and Charset

The Content-Type header field describes the MIME type of the entity body.* The MIME type is a standardized name that describes the underlying type of media carried as cargo (HTML file, Microsoft Word document, MPEG video, etc.). Client applications use the MIME type to properly decipher and process the content.

The Content-Type values are standardized MIME types, registered with the Internet Assigned Numbers Authority (IANA). MIME types consist of a primary media type (e.g., text, image, audio), followed by a slash, followed by a subtype that further specifies the media type. Table 15-1 lists a few common MIME types for the Content-Type header. More MIME types are listed in Appendix D.

*Table 15-1. Common media types*

| Media type | Description |
| --- | --- |
| text/html | Entity body is an HTML document |
| text/plain | Entity body is a document in plain text |
| image/gif | Entity body is an image of type GIF |
| image/jpeg | Entity body is an image of type JPEG |
| audio/x-wav | Entity body contains WAV sound data |
| model/vrml | Entity body is a three-dimensional VRML model |
| application/vnd.ms-powerpoint | Entity body is a Microsoft PowerPoint presentation |
| multipart/byteranges | Entity body has multiple parts, each containing a different range (in bytes) of the full document |
| message/http | Entity body contains a complete HTTP message (see TRACE) |

It is important to note that the Content-Type header specifies the media type of the original entity body. If the entity has gone through content encoding, for example, the Content-Type header will still specify the entity body type *before* the encoding.

## Character Encodings for Text Media

The Content-Type header also supports optional parameters to further specify the content type. The "charset" parameter is the primary example, specifying the mechanism to convert bits from the entity into characters in a text file:

```
Content-Type: text/html; charset=iso-8859-4
```

We talk about character sets in detail in Chapter 16.

---

* In the case of the HEAD request, Content-Type shows the type that would have been sent if it was a GET request.

---

## Multipart Media Types

MIME "multipart" email messages contain multiple messages stuck together and sent as a single, complex message. Each component is self-contained, with its own set of headers describing its content; the different components are concatenated together and delimited by a string.

HTTP also supports multipart bodies; however, they typically are sent in only one of two situations: in fill-in form submissions and in range responses carrying pieces of a document.

## Multipart Form Submissions

When an HTTP fill-in form is submitted, variable-length text fields and uploaded objects are sent as separate parts of a multipart body, allowing forms to be filled out with values of different types and lengths. For example, you may choose to fill out a form that asks for your name and a description with your nickname and a small photo, while your friend may put down her full name and a long essay describing her passion for fixing Volkswagen buses.

HTTP sends such requests with a Content-Type: multipart/form-data header or a Content-Type: multipart/mixed header and a multipart body, like this:

```
Content-Type: multipart/form-data; boundary=[abcdefghijklmnopqrstuvwxyz]
```

where the boundary specifies the delimiter string between the different parts of the body.

The following example illustrates multipart/form-data encoding. Suppose we have this form:

```
<FORM action="http://server.com/cgi/handle"
      enctype="multipart/form-data"
      method="post">
<P>
What is your name? <INPUT type="text" name="submit-name"><BR>
What files are you sending? <INPUT type="file" name="files"><BR>
<INPUT type="submit" value="Send"> <INPUT type="reset">
</FORM>
```

If the user enters "Sally" in the text-input field and selects the text file "essayfile.txt," the user agent might send back the following data:

```
Content-Type: multipart/form-data; boundary=AaB03x
--AaB03x
Content-Disposition: form-data; name="submit-name"
Sally
--AaB03x
```

```
Content-Disposition: form-data; name="files"; filename="essayfile.txt"
Content-Type: text/plain
...contents of essayfile.txt...
--AaB03x--
```

If the user selected a second (image) file, "imagefile.gif," the user agent might construct the parts as follows:

```
Content-Type: multipart/form-data; boundary=AaB03x
--AaB03x
Content-Disposition: form-data; name="submit-name"
Sally
--AaB03x
Content-Disposition: form-data; name="files"
Content-Type: multipart/mixed; boundary=BbC04y
--BbC04y
Content-Disposition: file; filename="essayfile.txt"
Content-Type: text/plain
...contents of essayfile.txt...
--BbC04y
Content-Disposition: file; filename="imagefile.gif"
Content-Type: image/gif
Content-Transfer-Encoding: binary
...contents of imagefile.gif...
--BbC04y--
--AaB03x--
```

## Multipart Range Responses

HTTP responses to range requests also can be multipart. Such responses come with a Content-Type: multipart/byteranges header and a multipart body with the different ranges. Here is an example of a multipart response to a request for different ranges of a document:

```
HTTP/1.0 206 Partial content
Server: Microsoft-IIS/5.0
Date: Sun, 10 Dec 2000 19:11:20 GMT
Content-Location: http://www.joes-hardware.com/gettysburg.txt
Content-Type: multipart/x-byteranges; boundary=---[abcdefghijklmnopqrstuvwxyz]--
Last-Modified: Sat, 09 Dec 2000 00:38:47 GMT

--[abcdefghijklmnopqrstuvwxyz]--
Content-Type: text/plain
Content-Range: bytes 0-174/1441

Fourscore and seven years ago our fathers brough forth on this continent
a new nation, conceived in liberty and dedicated to the proposition that
all men are created equal.
--[abcdefghijklmnopqrstuvwxyz]--
Content-Type: text/plain
Content-Range: bytes 552-761/1441
```

```
But in a larger sense, we can not dedicate, we can not consecrate,
we can not hallow this ground. The brave men, living and dead who
struggled here have consecrated it far above our poor power to add
or detract.
--[abcdefghijklmnopqrstuvwxyz]--
Content-Type: text/plain
Content-Range: bytes 1344-1441/1441

and that government of the people, by the people, for the people shall
not perish from the earth.

--[abcdefghijklmnopqrstuvwxyz]--
```

Range requests are discussed in more detail later in this chapter.

# Content Encoding

HTTP applications sometimes want to encode content before sending it. For example, a server might compress a large HTML document before sending it to a client that is connected over a slow connection, to help lessen the time it takes to transmit the entity. A server might scramble or encrypt the contents in a way that prevents unauthorized third parties from viewing the contents of the document.

These types of encodings are applied to the content at the sender. Once the content is content-encoded, the encoded data is sent to the receiver in the entity body as usual.

## The Content-Encoding Process

The content-encoding process is:

1. A web server generates an original response message, with original Content-Type and Content-Length headers.

2. A content-encoding server (perhaps the origin server or a downstream proxy) creates an encoded message. The encoded message has the same Content-Type but (if, for example, the body is compressed) a different Content-Length. The content-encoding server adds a Content-Encoding header to the encoded message, so that a receiving application can decode it.

3. A receiving program gets the encoded message, decodes it, and obtains the original.

Figure 15-3 sketches a content-encoding example.

Here, an HTML page is encoded by a gzip content-encoding function, to produce a smaller, compressed body. The compressed body is sent across the network, flagged

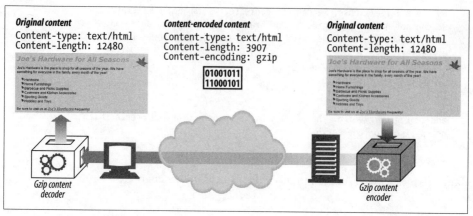

**Original content**
Content-type: text/html
Content-length: 12480

Joe's Hardware for All Seasons

Joe's Hardware is the place to shop for all seasons of the year. We have
something for everyone in the family, every month of the year!

► Hardware
► Home Furnishings
► Barbecue and Picnic Supplies
► Cookware and Kitchen Accessories
► Sporting Goods
► Hobbies and Toys

Be sure to visit us at *Joe's Hardware* frequently!

**Content-encoded content**
Content-type: text/html
Content-length: 3907
Content-encoding: gzip

01001011
11000101

**Original content**
Content-type: text/html
Content-length: 12480

Joe's Hardware for All Seasons

Joe's Hardware is the place to shop for all seasons of the year. We have
something for everyone in the family, every month of the year!

► Hardware
► Home Furnishings
► Barbecue and Picnic Supplies
► Cookware and Kitchen Accessories
► Sporting Goods
► Hobbies and Toys

Be sure to visit us at *Joe's Hardware* frequently!

Gzip content
decoder

Gzip content
encoder

*Figure 15-3. Content-encoding example*

with the gzip encoding. The receiving client decompresses the entity using the gzip
decoder.

This response snippet shows another example of an encoded response (a compressed image):

```
HTTP/1.1 200 OK
Date: Fri, 05 Nov 1999 22:35:15 GMT
Server: Apache/1.2.4
Content-Length: 6096
Content-Type: image/gif
Content-Encoding: gzip
[...]
```

Note that the Content-Type header can and should still be present in the message. It
describes the original format of the entity—information that may be necessary for
displaying the entity once it has been decoded. Remember that the Content-Length
header now represents the length of the *encoded* body.

## Content-Encoding Types

HTTP defines a few standard content-encoding types and allows for additional
encodings to be added as extension encodings. Encodings are standardized through
the IANA, which assigns a unique token to each content-encoding algorithm. The
Content-Encoding header uses these standardized token values to describe the algorithm used in the encoding.

Some of the common content-encoding tokens are listed in Table 15-2.

*Table 15-2. Content-encoding tokens*

| Content-encoding value | Description |
| --- | --- |
| gzip | Indicates that the GNU zip encoding was applied to the entity.[a] |
| compress | Indicates that the Unix file compression program has been run on the entity. |
| deflate | Indicates that the entity has been compressed into the zlib format.[b] |
| identity | Indicates that no encoding has been performed on the entity. When a Content-Encoding header is not present, this can be assumed. |

[a] RFC 1952 describes the gzip encoding.
[b] RFCs 1950 and 1951 describe the zlib format and deflate compression.

The gzip, compress, and deflate encodings are lossless compression algorithms used to reduce the size of transmitted messages without loss of information. Of these, gzip typically is the most effective compression algorithm and is the most widely used.

## Accept-Encoding Headers

Of course, we don't want servers encoding content in ways that the client can't decipher. To prevent servers from using encodings that the client doesn't support, the client passes along a list of supported content encodings in the Accept-Encoding request header. If the HTTP request does not contain an Accept-Encoding header, a server can assume that the client will accept any encoding (equivalent to passing Accept-Encoding: *).

Figure 15-4 shows an example of Accept-Encoding in an HTTP transaction.

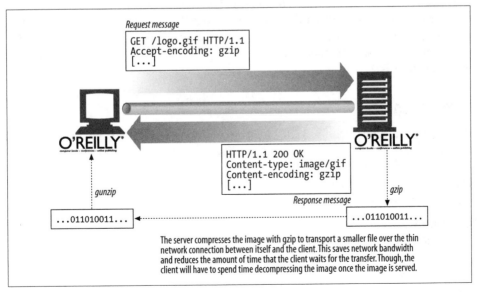

*Figure 15-4. Content encoding*

The Accept-Encoding field contains a comma-separated list of supported encodings. Here are a few examples:

```
Accept-Encoding: compress, gzip
Accept-Encoding:
Accept-Encoding: *
Accept-Encoding: compress;q=0.5, gzip;q=1.0
Accept-Encoding: gzip;q=1.0, identity; q=0.5, *;q=0
```

Clients can indicate preferred encodings by attaching Q (quality) values as parameters to each encoding. Q values can range from 0.0, indicating that the client does not want the associated encoding, to 1.0, indicating the preferred encoding. The token "*" means "anything else." The process of selecting which content encoding to apply is part of a more general process of deciding which content to send back to a client in a response. This process and the Content-Encoding and Accept-Encoding headers are discussed in more detail in Chapter 17.

The identity encoding token can be present only in the Accept-Encoding header and is used by clients to specify relative preference over other content-encoding algorithms.

# Transfer Encoding and Chunked Encoding

The previous section discussed *content* encodings—reversible transformations applied to the body of the message. Content encodings are tightly associated with the details of the particular content format. For example, you might compress a text file with gzip, but not a JPEG file, because JPEGs don't compress well with gzip.

This section discusses *transfer* encodings. Transfer encodings also are reversible transformations performed on the entity body, but they are applied for architectural reasons and are independent of the format of the content. You apply a transfer encoding to a message to change the way message data is transferred across the network (Figure 15-5).

## Safe Transport

Historically, transfer encodings exist in other protocols to provide "safe transport" of messages across a network. The concept of safe transport has a different focus for HTTP, where the transport infrastructure is standardized and more forgiving. In HTTP, there are only a few reasons why transporting message bodies can cause trouble. Two of these are:

*Unknown size*

Some gateway applications and content encoders are unable to determine the final size of a message body without generating the content first. Often, these servers would like to start sending the data before the size is known. Because

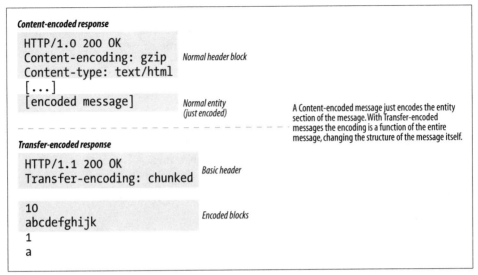

Figure 15-5. Content encodings versus transfer encodings

HTTP requires the Content-Length header to precede the data, some servers apply a transfer encoding to send the data with a special terminating footer that indicates the end of data.[*]

*Security*

You might use a transfer encoding to scramble the message content before sending it across a shared transport network. However, because of the popularity of transport layer security schemes like SSL, transfer-encoding security isn't very common.

## Transfer-Encoding Headers

There are just two defined headers to describe and control transfer encoding:

*Transfer-Encoding*

Tells the receiver what encoding has been performed on the message in order for it to be safely transported

*TE*

Used in the request header to tell the server what extension transfer encodings are okay to use[†]

---

[*] You could close the connection as a "poor man's" end-of-message signal, but this breaks persistent connections.

[†] The meaning of the TE header would be more intuitive if it were called the Accept-Transfer-Encoding header.

In the following example, the request uses the TE header to tell the server that it accepts the chunked encoding (which it must if it's an HTTP 1.1 application) and is willing to accept trailers on the end of chunk-encoded messages:

```
GET /new_products.html HTTP/1.1
Host: www.joes-hardware.com
User-Agent: Mozilla/4.61 [en] (WinNT; I)
TE: trailers, chunked
...
```

The response includes a Transfer-Encoding header to tell the receiver that the message has been transfer-encoded with the chunked encoding:

```
HTTP/1.1 200 OK
Transfer-Encoding: chunked
Server: Apache/3.0
...
```

After this initial header, the structure of the message will change.

All transfer-encoding values are case-insensitive. HTTP/1.1 uses transfer-encoding values in the TE header field and in the Transfer-Encoding header field. The latest HTTP specification defines only one transfer encoding, chunked encoding.

The TE header, like the Accept-Encoding header, can have Q values to describe preferred forms of transfer encoding. The HTTP/1.1 specification, however, forbids the association of a Q value of 0.0 to chunked encoding.

Future extensions to HTTP may drive the need for additional transfer encodings. If and when this happens, the chunked transfer encoding should always be applied on top of the extension transfer encodings. This guarantees that the data will get "tunneled" through HTTP/1.1 applications that understand chunked encoding but not other transfer encodings.

## Chunked Encoding

Chunked encoding breaks messages into chunks of known size. Each chunk is sent one after another, eliminating the need for the size of the full message to be known before it is sent.

Note that chunked encoding is a form of transfer encoding and therefore is an attribute of the message, not the body. Multipart encoding, described earlier in this chapter, is an attribute of the body and is completely separate from chunked encoding.

### Chunking and persistent connections

When the connection between the client and server is not persistent, clients do not need to know the size of the body they are reading—they expect to read the body until the server closes the connection.

With persistent connections, the size of the body must be known and sent in the Content-Length header before the body can be written. When content is dynamically created at a server, it may not be possible to know the length of the body before sending it.

Chunked encoding provides a solution for this dilemma, by allowing servers to send the body in chunks, specifying only the size of each chunk. As the body is dynamically generated, a server can buffer up a portion of it, send its size and the chunk, and then repeat the process until the full body has been sent. The server can signal the end of the body with a chunk of size 0 and still keep the connection open and ready for the next response.

Chunked encoding is fairly simple. Figure 15-6 shows the basic anatomy of a chunked message. It begins with an initial HTTP response header block, followed by a stream of chunks. Each chunk contains a length value and the data for that chunk. The length value is in hexadecimal form and is separated from the chunk data with a CRLF. The size of the chunk data is measured in bytes and includes neither the CRLF sequence between the length value and the data nor the CRLF sequence at the end of the chunk. The last chunk is special—it has a length of zero, which signifies "end of body."

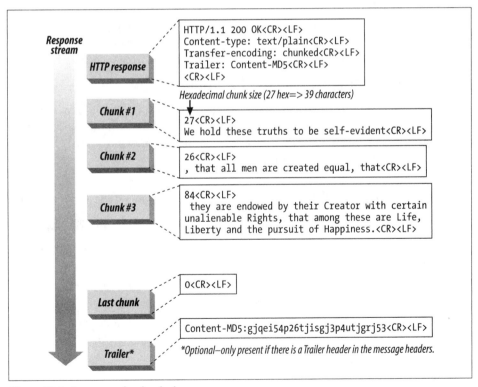

Figure 15-6. Anatomy of a chunked message

A client also may send chunked data to a server. Because the client does not know beforehand whether the server accepts chunked encoding (servers do not send TE headers in responses to clients), it must be prepared for the server to reject the chunked request with a 411 Length Required response.

### Trailers in chunked messages

A trailer can be added to a chunked message if the client's TE header indicates that it accepts trailers, or if the trailer is added by the server that created the original response and the contents of the trailer are optional metadata that it is not necessary for the client to understand and use (it is okay for the client to ignore and discard the contents of the trailer).[*]

The trailer can contain additional header fields whose values might not have been known at the start of the message (e.g., because the contents of the body had to be generated first). An example of a header that can be sent in the trailer is the Content-MD5 header—it would be difficult to calculate the MD5 of a document before the document has been generated. Figure 15-6 illustrates the use of trailers. The message headers contain a Trailer header listing the headers that will follow the chunked message. The last chunk is followed by the headers listed in the Trailer header.

Any of the HTTP headers can be sent as trailers, except for the Transfer-Encoding, Trailer, and Content-Length headers.

## Combining Content and Transfer Encodings

Content encoding and transfer encoding can be used simultaneously. For example, Figure 15-7 illustrates how a sender can compress an HTML file using a content encoding and send the data chunked using a transfer encoding. The process to "reconstruct" the body is reversed on the receiver.

## Transfer-Encoding Rules

When a transfer encoding is applied to a message body, a few rules must be followed:

- The set of transfer encodings must include "chunked." The only exception is if the message is terminated by closing the connection.

- When the chunked transfer encoding is used, it is required to be the last transfer encoding applied to the message body.

- The chunked transfer encoding must not be applied to a message body more than once.

---

[*] The Trailer header was added after the initial chunked encoding was added to drafts of the HTTP/1.1 specification, so some applications may not understand it (or understand trailers) even if they claim to be HTTP/1.1-compliant.

---

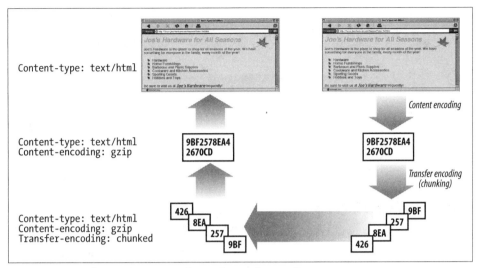

| Content-type: text/html | | |
|---|---|---|

| Content-type: text/html Content-encoding: gzip | 9BF2578EA4 2670CD | 9BF2578EA4 2670CD |
|---|---|---|

*Content encoding*

*Transfer encoding (chunking)*

| Content-type: text/html Content-encoding: gzip Transfer-encoding: chunked | 426 8EA 257 9BF | 9BF 257 8EA 426 |
|---|---|---|

*Figure 15-7. Combining content encoding with transfer encoding*

These rules allow the recipient to determine the transfer length of the message.

Transfer encodings are a relatively new feature of HTTP, introduced in Version 1.1. Servers that implement transfer encodings need to take special care not to send transfer-encoded messages to non-HTTP/1.1 applications. Likewise, if a server receives a transfer-encoded message that it can not understand, it should respond with the 501 Unimplemented status code. However, all HTTP/1.1 applications must at least support chunked encoding.

# Time-Varying Instances

Web objects are not static. The same URL can, over time, point to different versions of an object. Take the CNN home page as an example—going to "http://www.cnn.com" several times in a day is likely to result in a slightly different page being returned each time.

Think of the CNN home page as being an object and its different versions as being different *instances* of the object (see Figure 15-8). The client in the figure requests the same resource (URL) multiple times, but it gets different instances of the resource as it changes over time. At time (a) and (b) it has the same instance; at time (c) it has a different instance.

The HTTP protocol specifies operations for a class of requests and responses, called *instance manipulations*, that operate on instances of an object. The two main instance-manipulation methods are range requests and delta encoding. Both of these methods require clients to be able to identify the exact copy of the resource that they have (if any) and request new instances conditionally. These mechanisms are discussed later in this chapter.

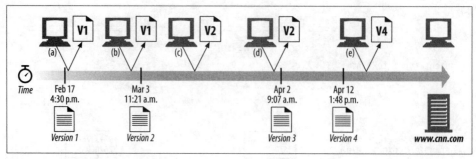

*Figure 15-8. Instances are "snapshots" of a resource in time*

## Validators and Freshness

Look back at Figure 15-8. The client does not initially have a copy of the resource, so it sends a request to the server asking for it. The server responds with Version 1 of the resource. The client can now cache this copy, but for how long?

Once the document has "expired" at the client (i.e., once the client can no longer consider its copy a valid copy), it must request a fresh copy from the server. If the document has not changed at the server, however, the client does not need to receive it again—it can just continue to use its cached copy.

This special request, called a *conditional request*, requires that the client tell the server which version it currently has, using a *validator*, and ask for a copy to be sent only if its current copy is no longer valid. Let's look at the three key concepts—freshness, validators, and conditionals—in more detail.

### Freshness

Servers are expected to give clients information about how long clients can cache their content and consider it fresh. Servers can provide this information using one of two headers: Expires and Cache-Control.

The Expires header specifies the exact date and time when the document "expires"—when it can no longer be considered fresh. The syntax for the Expires header is:

```
Expires: Sun Mar 18 23:59:59 GMT 2001
```

For a client and server to use the Expires header correctly, their clocks must be synchronized. This is not always easy, because neither may run a clock synchronization protocol such as the Network Time Protocol (NTP). A mechanism that defines expiration using relative time is more useful. The Cache-Control header can be used to specify the maximum age for a document in seconds—the total amount of time since the document left the server. Age is not dependent on clock synchronization and therefore is likely to yield more accurate results.

---

The Cache-Control header actually is very powerful. It can be used by both servers and clients to describe freshness using more directives than just specifying an age or expiration time. Table 15-3 lists some of the directives that can accompany the Cache-Control header.

*Table 15-3. Cache-Control header directives*

| Directive | Message type | Description |
|---|---|---|
| no-cache | Request | Do not return a cached copy of the document without first revalidating it with the server. |
| no-store | Request | Do not return a cached copy of the document. Do not store the response from the server. |
| max-age | Request | The document in the cache must not be older than the specified age. |
| max-stale | Request | The document may be stale based on the server-specified expiration information, but it must not have been expired for longer than the value in this directive. |
| min-fresh | Request | The document's age must not be more than its age plus the specified amount. In other words, the response must be fresh for at least the specified amount of time. |
| no-transform | Request | The document must not be transformed before being sent. |
| only-if-cached | Request | Send the document only if it is in the cache, without contacting the origin server. |
| public | Response | Response may be cached by any cache. |
| private | Response | Response may be cached such that it can be accessed only by a single client. |
| no-cache | Response | If the directive is accompanied by a list of header fields, the content may be cached and served to clients, but the listed header fields must first be removed. If no header fields are specified, the cached copy must not be served without revalidation with the server. |
| no-store | Response | Response must not be cached. |
| no-transform | Response | Response must not be modified in any way before being served. |
| must-revalidate | Response | Response must be revalidated with the server before being served. |
| proxy-revalidate | Response | Shared caches must revalidate the response with the origin server before serving. This directive can be ignored by private caches. |
| max-age | Response | Specifies the maximum length of time the document can be cached and still considered fresh. |
| s-max-age | Response | Specifies the maximum age of the document as it applies to shared caches (overriding the max-age directive, if one is present). This directive can be ignored by private caches. |

Caching and freshness were discussed in more detail in Chapter 7.

## Conditionals and Validators

When a cache's copy is requested, and it is no longer fresh, the cache needs to make sure it has a fresh copy. The cache can fetch the current copy from the origin server, but in many cases, the document on the server is still the same as the stale copy in the cache. We saw this in Figure 15-8b; the cached copy may have expired, but the server content still is the same as the cache content. If a cache always fetches a server's document, even if it's the same as the expired cache copy, the cache wastes network bandwidth, places unnecessary load on the cache and server, and slows everything down.

To fix this, HTTP provides a way for clients to request a copy *only if the resource has changed*, using special requests called *conditional requests*. Conditional requests are normal HTTP request messages, but they are performed only if a particular condition is true. For example, a cache might send the following conditional GET message to a server, asking it to send the file */announce.html* only if the file has been modified since June 29, 2002 (the date the cached document was last changed by the author):

```
GET /announce.html HTTP/1.0
If-Modified-Since: Sat, 29 Jun 2002, 14:30:00 GMT
```

Conditional requests are implemented by conditional headers that start with "If-". In the example above, the conditional header is If-Modified-Since. A conditional header allows a method to execute only if the condition is true. If the condition is not true, the server sends an HTTP error code back.

Each conditional works on a particular *validator*. A validator is a particular attribute of the document instance that is tested. Conceptually, you can think of the validator like the serial number, version number, or last change date of a document. A wise client in Figure 15-8b would send a conditional validation request to the server saying, "send me the resource only if it is no longer Version 1; I have Version 1." We discussed conditional cache revalidation in Chapter 7, but we'll study the details of entity validators more carefully in this chapter.

The If-Modified-Since conditional header tests the last-modified date of a document instance, so we say that the last-modified date is the validator. The If-None-Match conditional header tests the ETag value of a document, which is a special keyword or version-identifying tag associated with the entity. Last-Modified and ETag are the two primary validators used by HTTP. Table 15-4 lists four of the HTTP headers used for conditional requests. Next to each conditional header is the type of validator used with the header.

*Table 15-4. Conditional request types*

| Request type | Validator | Description |
| --- | --- | --- |
| If-Modified-Since | Last-Modified | Send a copy of the resource if the version that was last modified at the time in your previous Last-Modified response header is no longer the latest one. |
| If-Unmodified-Since | Last-Modified | Send a copy of the resource only if it is the same as the version that was last modified at the time in your previous Last-Modified response header. |
| If-Match | ETag | Send a copy of the resource if its entity tag is the same as that of the one in your previous ETag response header. |
| If-None-Match | ETag | Send a copy of the resource if its entity tag is different from that of the one in your previous ETag response header. |

HTTP groups validators into two classes: *weak validators* and *strong validators*. Weak validators may not always uniquely identify an instance of a resource; strong validators must. An example of a weak validator is the size of the object in bytes. The resource content might change even though the size remains the same, so a hypothetical byte-count validator only weakly indicates a change. A cryptographic checksum of the contents of the resource (such as MD5), however, is a strong validator; it changes when the document changes.

The last-modified time is considered a weak validator because, although it specifies the time at which the resource was last modified, it specifies that time to an accuracy of at most one second. Because a resource can change multiple times in a second, and because servers can serve thousands of requests per second, the last-modified date might not always reflect changes. The ETag header is considered a strong validator, because the server can place a distinct value in the ETag header every time a value changes. Version numbers and digest checksums are good candidates for the ETag header, but they can contain any arbitrary text. ETag headers are flexible; they take arbitrary text values ("tags"), and can be used to devise a variety of client and server validation strategies.

Clients and servers may sometimes want to adopt a looser version of entity-tag validation. For example, a server may want to make cosmetic changes to a large, popular cached document without triggering a mass transfer when caches revalidate. In this case, the server might advertise a "weak" entity tag by prefixing the tag with "W/". A weak entity tag should change only when the associated entity changes in a semantically significant way. A strong entity tag must change whenever the associated entity value changes in any way.

The following example shows how a client might revalidate with a server using a weak entity tag. The server would return a body only if the content changed in a meaningful way from Version 4.0 of the document:

```
GET /announce.html HTTP/1.1
If-None-Match: W/"v4.0"
```

In summary, when clients access the same resource more than once, they first need to determine whether their current copy still is fresh. If it is not, they must get the latest version from the server. To avoid receiving an identical copy in the event that the resource has not changed, clients can send conditional requests to the server, specifying validators that uniquely identify their current copies. Servers will then send a copy of the resource only if it is different from the client's copy. For more details on cache revalidation, please refer back to "Cache Processing Steps" in Chapter 7.

# Range Requests

We now understand how a client can ask a server to send it a resource only if the client's copy of the resource is no longer valid. HTTP goes further: it allows clients to actually request just part or a range of a document.

Imagine if you were three-fourths of the way through downloading the latest hot software across a slow modem link, and a network glitch interrupted your connection. You would have been waiting for a while for the download to complete, and now you would have to start all over again, hoping the same thing does not happen again.

With range requests, an HTTP client can resume downloading an entity by asking for the range or part of the entity it failed to get (provided that the object did not change at the origin server between the time the client first requested it and its subsequent range request). For example:

```
GET /bigfile.html HTTP/1.1
Host: www.joes-hardware.com
Range: bytes=4000-
User-Agent: Mozilla/4.61 [en] (WinNT; I)
...
```

In this example, the client is requesting the remainder of the document after the first 4,000 bytes (the end bytes do not have to be specified, because the size of the document may not be known to the requestor). Range requests of this form can be used for a failed request where the client received the first 4,000 bytes before the failure. The Range header also can be used to request multiple ranges (the ranges can be specified in any order and may overlap)—for example, imagine a client connecting to multiple servers simultaneously, requesting different ranges of the same document from different servers in order to speed up overall download time for the document. In the case where clients request multiple ranges in a single request, responses come back as a single entity, with a multipart body and a Content-Type: multipart/byteranges header.

Not all servers accept range requests, but many do. Servers can advertise to clients that they accept ranges by including the header Accept-Ranges in their responses. The value of this header is the unit of measure, usually bytes.* For example:

```
HTTP/1.1 200 OK
Date: Fri, 05 Nov 1999 22:35:15 GMT
Server: Apache/1.2.4
Accept-Ranges: bytes
...
```

Figure 15-9 shows an example of a set of HTTP transactions involving ranges.

Range headers are used extensively by popular peer-to-peer file-sharing client software to download different parts of multimedia files simultaneously, from different peers.

Note that range requests are a class of instance manipulations, because they are exchanges between a client and a server for a particular instance of an object. That is, a client's range request makes sense only if the client and server have the same version of a document.

---

* The HTTP/1.1 specification defines only the bytes token, but server and client implementors could come up with their own units to measure or chop up an entity.

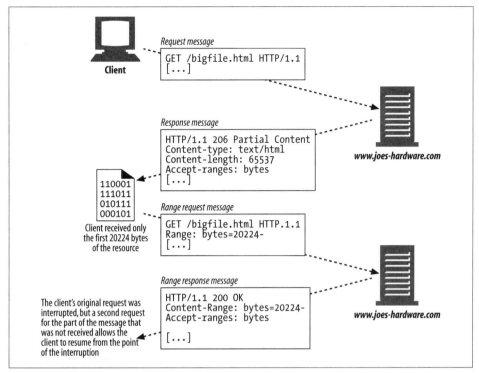

*Figure 15-9. Entity range request example*

# Delta Encoding

We have described different versions of a web page as different instances of a page. If a client has an expired copy of a page, it requests the latest instance of the page. If the server has a newer instance of the page, it will send it to the client, and it will send the full new instance of the page even if only a small portion of the page actually has changed.

Rather than sending it the entire new page, the client would get the page faster if the server sent just the changes to the client's copy of the page (provided that the number of changes is small). Delta encoding is an extension to the HTTP protocol that optimizes transfers by communicating changes instead of entire objects. Delta encoding is a type of instance manipulation, because it relies on clients and servers exchanging information about particular instances of an object. RFC 3229 describes delta encoding.

Figure 15-10 illustrates more clearly the mechanism of requesting, generating, receiving, and applying a delta-encoded document. The client has to tell the server which version of the page it has, that it is willing to accept a *delta* from the latest version of page, and which algorithms it knows for applying those deltas to its current version.

The server has to check if it has the client's version of the page and how to compute deltas from the latest version and the client's version (there are several algorithms for computing the difference between two objects). It then has to compute the delta, send it to the client, let the client know that it's sending a delta, and specify the new identifier for the latest version of the page (because this is the version that the client will end up with after it applies the delta to its old version).

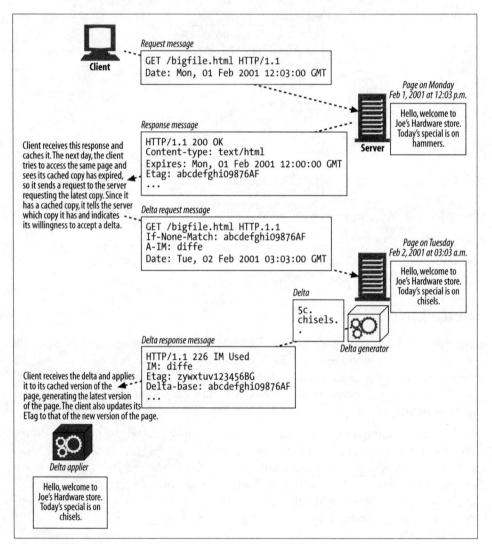

*Figure 15-10. Mechanics of delta-encoding*

The client uses the unique identifier for its version of the page (sent by the server in its previous response to the client in the ETag header) in an If-None-Match header. This is the client's way of telling the server, "if the latest version of the page you have does not have this same ETag, send me the latest version of the page." Just the If-None-Match header, then, would cause the server to send the client the full latest version of the page (if it was different from the client's version).

The client can tell the server, however, that it is willing to accept a delta of the page by also sending an A-IM header. A-IM is short for Accept-Instance-Manipulation ("Oh, by the way, I do accept some forms of instance manipulation, so if you apply one of those you will not have to send me the full document."). In the A-IM header, the client specifies the algorithms it knows how to apply in order to generate the latest version of a page given an old version and a delta. The server sends back the following: a special response code (226 IM Used) telling the client that it is sending it an instance manipulation of the requested object, not the full object itself; an IM (short for Instance-Manipulation) header, which specifies the algorithm used to compute the delta; the new ETag header; and a Delta-Base header, which specifies the ETag of the document used as the base for computing the delta (ideally, the same as the ETag in the client's If-None-Match request!). The headers used in delta encoding are summarized in Table 15-5.

*Table 15-5. Delta-encoding headers*

| Header | Description |
| --- | --- |
| ETag | Unique identifier for each instance of a document. Sent by the server in the response; used by clients in subsequent requests in If-Match and If-None-Match headers. |
| If-None-Match | Request header sent by the client, asking the server for a document if and only if the client's version of the document is different from the server's. |
| A-IM | Client request header indicating types of instance manipulations accepted. |
| IM | Server response header specifying the type of instance manipulation applied to the response. This header is sent when the response code is 226 IM Used. |
| Delta-Base | Server response header that specifies the ETag of the base document used for generating the delta (should be the same as the ETag in the client request's If-None-Match header). |

## Instance Manipulations, Delta Generators, and Delta Appliers

Clients can specify the types of instance manipulation they accept using the A-IM header. Servers specify the type of instance manipulation used in the IM header. Just what are the types of instance manipulation that are accepted, and what do they do? Table 15-6 lists some of the IANA registered types of instance manipulations.

*Table 15-6. IANA registered types of instance manipulations*

| Type | Description |
| --- | --- |
| vcdiff | Delta using the vcdiff algorithm[a] |
| diffe | Delta using the Unix *diff -e* command |
| gdiff | Delta using the gdiff algorithm[b] |

*Table 15-6. IANA registered types of instance manipulations (continued)*

| Type | Description |
|------|-------------|
| gzip | Compression using the gzip algorithm |
| deflate | Compression using the deflate algorithm |
| range | Used in a server response to indicate that the response is partial content as the result of a range selection |
| identity | Used in a client request's A-IM header to indicate that the client is willing to accept an identity instance manipulation |

[a] Internet draft *draft-korn-vcdiff-01* describes the vcdiff algorithm. This specification was approved by the IESG in early 2002 and should be released in RFC form shortly.

[b] *http://www.w3org/TR/NOTE-gdiff-19970901.html* describes the GDIFF algorithm.

A "delta generator" at the server, as in Figure 15-10, takes the base document and the latest instance of the document and computes the delta between the two using the algorithm specified by the client in the A-IM header. At the client side, a "delta applier" takes the delta and applies it to the base document to generate the latest instance of the document. For example, if the algorithm used to generate the delta is the Unix *diff -e* command, the client can apply the delta using the functionality of the Unix *ed* text editor, because *diff -e <file1> <file2>* generates the set of *ed* commands that will convert *<file1>* into *<file2>*. *ed* is a very simple editor with a few supported commands. In the example in Figure 15-10, *5c* says delete line 5 in the base document, and *chisels.<cr>.* says add "chisels.". That's it. More complicated instructions can be generated for bigger changes. The Unix *diff -e* algorithm does a line-by-line comparison of files. This obviously is okay for text files but breaks down for binary files. The vcdiff algorithm is more powerful, working even for non-text files and generally producing smaller deltas than *diff -e*.

The delta encoding specification defines the format of the A-IM and IM headers in detail. Suffice it to say that multiple instance manipulations can be specified in these headers (along with corresponding quality values). Documents can go through multiple instance manipulations before being returned to clients, in order to maximize compression. For example, deltas generated by the vcdiff algorithm may in turn be compressed using the gzip algorithm. The server response would then contain the header IM: vcdiff, gzip. The client would first gunzip the content, then apply the results of the delta to its base page in order to generate the final document.

Delta encoding can reduce transfer times, but it can be tricky to implement. Imagine a page that changes frequently and is accessed by many different people. A server supporting delta encoding must keep all the different copies of that page as it changes over time, in order to figure out what's changed between any requesting client's copy and the latest copy. (If the document changes frequently, as different clients request the document, they will get different instances of the document. When they make subsequent requests to the server, they will be requesting changes between their instance of the document and the latest instance of the document. To be able to send them just the changes, the server must keep copies of all the previous instances that the clients have.) In exchange for reduced latency in serving documents, servers need to increase disk space to keep old instances of documents around. The extra disk space necessary to do so may quickly negate the benefits from the smaller transfer amounts.

# For More Information

For more information on entities and encodings, see:

*http://www.ietf.org/rfc/rfc2616.txt*
> The HTTP/1.1 specification, RFC 2616, is the primary reference for entity body management and encodings.

*http://www.ietf.org/rfc/rfc3229.txt*
> RFC 3229, "Delta Encoding in HTTP," describes how delta encoding can be supported as an extension to HTTP/1.1.

*Introduction to Data Compression*
> Khalid Sayood, Morgan Kaufmann Publishers. This book explains some of the compression algorithms supported by HTTP content encodings.

*http://www.ietf.org/rfc/rfc1521.txt*
> RFC 1521, "Multipurpose Internet Mail Extensions, Part One: Mechanisms for Specifying and Describing the Format of Internet Message Bodies," describes the format of MIME bodies. This reference material is useful because HTTP borrows heavily from MIME. In particular, this document is designed to provide facilities to include multiple objects in a single message, to represent body text in character sets other than US-ASCII, to represent formatted multi-font text messages, and to represent nontextual material such as images and audio fragments.

*http://www.ietf.org/rfc/rfc2045.txt*
> RFC 2045, "Multipurpose Internet Mail Extensions, Part One: Format of Internet Message Bodies," specifies the various headers used to describe the structure of MIME messages, many of which are similar or identical to HTTP.

*http://www.ietf.org/rfc/rfc1864.txt*
> RFC 1864, "The Content-MD5 Header Field," provides some historical detail about the behavior and intended use of the Content-MD5 header field in MIME content as a message integrity check.

*http://www.ietf.org/rfc/rfc3230.txt*
> RFC 3230, "Instance Digests in HTTP," describes improvements to HTTP entity-digest handling that fix weaknesses present in the Content-MD5 formulation.

# CHAPTER 16

# Internationalization

Every day, billions of people write documents in hundreds of languages. To live up to the vision of a truly world-wide Web, HTTP needs to support the transport and processing of international documents, in many languages and alphabets.

This chapter covers two primary internationalization issues for the Web: *character set encodings* and *language tags*. HTTP applications use character set encodings to request and display text in different alphabets, and they use language tags to describe and restrict content to languages the user understands. We finish with a brief chat about multilingual URIs and dates.

This chapter:

- Explains how HTTP interacts with schemes and standards for multilingual alphabets
- Gives a rapid overview of the terminology, technology, and standards to help HTTP programmers do things right (readers familiar with character encodings can skip this section)
- Explains the standard naming system for languages, and how standardized language tags describe and select content
- Outlines rules and cautions for international URIs
- Briefly discusses rules for dates and other internationalization issues

## HTTP Support for International Content

HTTP messages can carry content in any language, just as it can carry images, movies, or any other kind of media. To HTTP, the entity body is just a box of bits.

To support international content, servers need to tell clients about the alphabet and languages of each document, so the client can properly unpack the document bits into characters and properly process and present the content to the user.

Servers tell clients about a document's alphabet and language with the HTTP Content-Type charset parameter and Content-Language headers. These headers describe what's in the entity body's "box of bits," how to convert the contents into the proper characters that can be displayed onscreen, and what spoken language the words represent.

At the same time, the client needs to tell the server which languages the user understands and which alphabetic coding algorithms the browser has installed. The client sends Accept-Charset and Accept-Language headers to tell the server which character set encoding algorithms and languages the client understands, and which of them are preferred.

The following HTTP Accept headers might be sent by a French speaker who prefers his native language (but speaks some English in a pinch) and who uses a browser that supports the iso-8859-1 West European charset encoding and the UTF-8 Unicode charset encoding:

```
Accept-Language: fr, en;q=0.8
Accept-Charset: iso-8859-1, utf-8
```

The parameter "q=0.8" is a *quality factor*, giving lower priority to English (0.8) than to French (1.0 by default).

# Character Sets and HTTP

So, let's jump right into the most important (and confusing) aspects of web internationalization—international alphabetic scripts and their character set encodings.

Web character set standards can be pretty confusing. Lots of people get frustrated when they first try to write international web software, because of complex and inconsistent terminology, standards documents that you have to pay to read, and unfamiliarity with foreign languages. This section and the next section should make it easier for you to use character sets with HTTP.

## Charset Is a Character-to-Bits Encoding

The HTTP charset values tell you how to convert from entity content bits into characters in a particular alphabet. Each charset tag names an algorithm to translate bits to characters (and vice versa). The charset tags are standardized in the MIME character set registry, maintained by the IANA (see *http://www.iana.org/assignments/character-sets*). Appendix H summarizes many of them.

The following Content-Type header tells the receiver that the content is an HTML file, and the charset parameter tells the receiver to use the iso-8859-6 Arabic character set decoding scheme to decode the content bits into characters:

```
Content-Type: text/html; charset=iso-8859-6
```

The iso-8859-6 encoding scheme maps 8-bit values into both the Latin and Arabic alphabets, including numerals, punctuation and other symbols.* For example, in Figure 16-1, the highlighted bit pattern has code value 225, which (under iso-8859-6) maps into the Arabic letter "FEH" (a sound like the English letter "F").

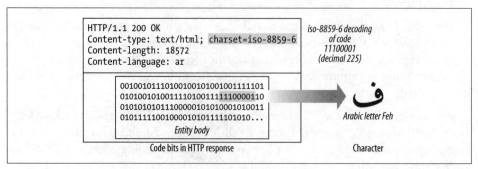

*Figure 16-1. The charset parameter tells the client how to go from bits to characters*

Some character encodings (e.g., UTF-8 and iso-2022-jp) are more complicated, *variable-length* codes, where the number of bits per character varies. This type of coding lets you use extra bits to support alphabets with large numbers of characters (such as Chinese and Japanese), while using fewer bits to support standard Latin characters.

## How Character Sets and Encodings Work

Let's see what character sets and encodings really do.

We want to convert from bits in a document into characters that we can display onscreen. But because there are many different alphabets, and many different ways of encoding characters into bits (each with advantages and disadvantages), we need a standard way to describe and apply the bits-to-character decoding algorithm.

Bits-to-character conversions happen in two steps, as shown in Figure 16-2:

- In Figure 16-2a, bits from a document are converted into a character code that identifies a particular numbered character in a particular coded character set. In the example, the decoded character code is numbered 225.

- In Figure 16-2b, the character code is used to select a particular element of the coded character set. In iso-8859-6, the value 225 corresponds to "ARABIC LETTER FEH." The algorithms used in Steps a and b are determined from the MIME charset tag.

A key goal of internationalized character systems is the isolation of the semantics (letters) from the presentation (graphical presentation forms). HTTP concerns itself

---

* Unlike Chinese and Japanese, Arabic has only 28 characters. Eight bits provides 256 unique values, which gives plenty of room for Latin characters, Arabic characters, and other useful symbols.

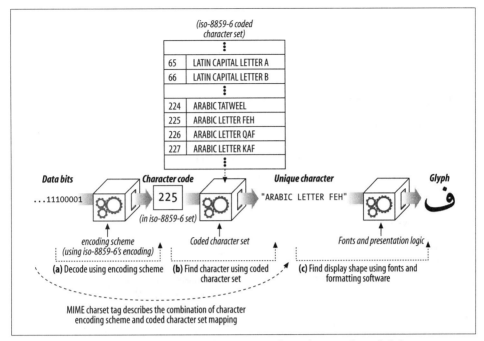

*Figure 16-2. HTTP "charset" combines a character encoding scheme and a coded character set*

only with transporting the character data and the associated language and charset labels. The presentation of the character shapes is handled by the user's graphics display software (browser, operating system, fonts), as shown in Figure 16-2c.

## The Wrong Charset Gives the Wrong Characters

If the client uses the wrong charset parameter, the client will display strange, bogus characters. Let's say a browser got the value 225 (binary 11100001) from the body:

- If the browser thinks the body is encoded with iso-8859-1 Western European character codes, it will show a lowercase Latin "a" with acute accent:

$$á$$

- If the browser is using iso-8859-6 Arabic codes, it will show "FEH":

- If the browser is using iso-8859-7 Greek, it will show a small "Alpha":

- If the browser is using iso-8859-8 Hebrew codes, it will show "BET":

## Standardized MIME Charset Values

The combination of a particular character encoding and a particular coded character set is called a *MIME charset*. HTTP uses standardized MIME charset tags in the Content-Type and Accept-Charset headers. MIME charset values are registered with the IANA.[*] Table 16-1 lists a few MIME charset encoding schemes used by documents and browsers. A more complete list is provided in Appendix H.

*Table 16-1. MIME charset encoding tags*

| MIME charset value | Description |
| --- | --- |
| us-ascii | The famous character encoding standardized in 1968 as ANSI_X3.4-1968. It is also named ASCII, but the "US" prefix is preferred because of several international variants in ISO 646 that modify selected characters. US-ASCII maps 7-bit values into 128 characters. The high bit is unused. |
| iso-8859-1 | iso-8859-1 is an 8-bit extension to ASCII to support Western European languages. It uses the high bit to include many West European characters, while leaving the ASCII codes (0–127) intact. Also called iso-latin-1, or nicknamed "Latin1." |
| iso-8859-2 | Extends ASCII to include characters for Central and Eastern European languages, including Czech, Polish, and Romanian. Also called iso-latin-2. |
| iso-8859-5 | Extends ASCII to include Cyrillic characters, for languages including Russian, Serbian, and Bulgarian. |
| iso-8859-6 | Extends ASCII to include Arabic characters. Because the shapes of Arabic characters change depending on their position in a word, Arabic requires a display engine that analyzes the context and generates the correct shape for each character. |
| iso-8859-7 | Extends ASCII to include modern Greek characters. Formerly known as ELOT-928 or ECMA-118:1986. |
| iso-8859-8 | Extends ASCII to include Hebrew and Yiddish characters. |
| iso-8859-15 | Updates iso-8859-1, replacing some less-needed punctuation and fraction symbols with forgotten French and Finnish letters and replacing the international currency sign with the symbol for the new Euro currency. This character set is nicknamed "Latin0" and may one day replace iso-8859-1 as the preferred default character set in Europe. |
| iso-2022-jp | iso-2022-jp is a widely used encoding for Japanese email and web content. It is a variable-length encoding scheme that supports ASCII characters with single bytes but uses three-character modal escape sequences to shift into three different Japanese character sets. |
| euc-jp | euc-jp is an ISO 2022–compliant variable-length encoding that uses explicit bit patterns to identify each character, without requiring modes and escape sequences. It uses 1-byte, 2-byte, and 3-byte sequences of characters to identify characters in multiple Japanese character sets. |
| Shift_JIS | This encoding was originally developed by Microsoft and sometimes is called SJIS or MS Kanji. It is a bit complicated, for reasons of historic compatibility, and it cannot map all characters, but it still is common. |

[*] See *http://www.iana.org/numbers.htm* for the list of registered charset values.

*Table 16-1. MIME charset encoding tags (continued)*

| MIME charset value | Description |
|---|---|
| koi8-r | KOI8-R is a popular 8-bit Internet character set encoding for Russian, defined in IETF RFC 1489. The initials are transliterations of the acronym for "Code for Information Exchange, 8 bit, Russian." |
| utf-8 | UTF-8 is a common variable-length character encoding scheme for representing UCS (Unicode), which is the Universal Character Set of the world's characters. UTF-8 uses a variable-length encoding for character code values, representing each character by from one to six bytes. One of the primary features of UTF-8 is backward compatibility with ordinary 7-bit ASCII text. |
| windows-1252 | Microsoft calls its coded character sets "code pages." Windows code page 1252 (a.k.a. "CP1252" or "WinLatin1") is an extension of iso-8859-1. |

## Content-Type Charset Header and META Tags

Web servers send the client the MIME charset tag in the Content-Type header, using the charset parameter:

```
Content-Type: text/html; charset=iso-2022-jp
```

If no charset is explicitly listed, the receiver may try to infer the character set from the document contents. For HTML content, character sets might be found in <META HTTP-EQUIV="Content-Type"> tags that describe the charset.

Example 16-1 shows how HTML META tags set the charset to the Japanese encoding iso-2022-jp. If the document is not HTML, or there is no META Content-Type tag, software may attempt to infer the character encoding by scanning the actual text for common patterns indicative of languages and encodings.

*Example 16-1. Character encoding can be specified in HTML META tags*

```
<HEAD>
    <META HTTP-EQUIV="Content-Type" CONTENT="text/html; charset=iso-2022-jp">
    <META LANG="jp">
    <TITLE>A Japanese Document</TITLE>
</HEAD>
<BODY>
 ...
```

If a client cannot infer a character encoding, it assumes iso-8859-1.

## The Accept-Charset Header

There are thousands of defined character encoding and decoding methods, developed over the past several decades. Most clients do not support all the various character coding and mapping systems.

HTTP clients can tell servers precisely which character systems they support, using the Accept-Charset request header. The Accept-Charset header value provides a list of character encoding schemes that the client supports. For example, the following HTTP request header indicates that a client accepts the Western European iso-8859-1 character system as well as the UTF-8 variable-length Unicode compatibility system. A server is free to return content in either of these character encoding schemes.

```
Accept-Charset: iso-8859-1, utf-8
```

Note that there is no Content-Charset response header to match the Accept-Charset request header. The response character set is carried back from the server by the charset parameter of the Content-Type response header, to be compatible with MIME. It's too bad this isn't symmetric, but all the information still is there.

# Multilingual Character Encoding Primer

The previous section described how the HTTP Accept-Charset header and the Content-Type charset parameter carry character-encoding information from the client and server. HTTP programmers who do a lot of work with international applications and content need to have a deeper understanding of multilingual character systems to understand technical specifications and properly implement software.

It isn't easy to learn multilingual character systems—the terminology is complex and inconsistent, you often have to pay to read the standards documents, and you may be unfamiliar with the other languages with which you're working. This section is an overview of character systems and standards. If you are already comfortable with character encodings, or are not interested in this detail, feel free to jump ahead to "Language Tags and HTTP."

## Character Set Terminology

Here are eight terms about electronic character systems that you should know:

*Character*
    An alphabetic letter, numeral, punctuation mark, ideogram (as in Chinese), symbol, or other textual "atom" of writing. The Universal Character Set (UCS) initiative, known informally as Unicode,* has developed a standardized set of textual names for many characters in many languages, which often are used to conveniently and uniquely name characters.†

*Glyph*
    A stroke pattern or unique graphical shape that describes a character. A character may have multiple glyphs if it can be written different ways (see Figure 16-3).

*Coded character*
    A unique number assigned to a character so that we can work with it.

*Coding space*
    A range of integers that we plan to use as character code values.

---

\* Unicode is a commercial consortium based on UCS that drives commercial products.
† The names look like "LATIN CAPITAL LETTER S" and "ARABIC LETTER QAF."

*Code width*

The number of bits in each (fixed-size) character code.

*Character repertoire*

A particular working set of characters (a subset of all the characters in the world).

*Coded character set*

A set of coded characters that takes a character repertoire (a selection of characters from around the world) and assigns each character a code from a coding space. In other words, it maps numeric character codes to real characters.

*Character encoding scheme*

An algorithm to encode numeric character codes into a sequence of content bits (and to decode them back). Character encoding schemes can be used to reduce the amount of data required to identify characters (compression), work around transmission restrictions, and unify overlapping coded character sets.

## Charset Is Poorly Named

Technically, the MIME charset tag (used in the Content-Type charset parameter and the Accept-Charset header) doesn't specify a character set at all. The MIME charset value names a total algorithm for mapping data bits to codes to unique characters. It combines the two separate concepts of *character encoding scheme* and *coded character set* (see Figure 16-2).

This terminology is sloppy and confusing, because there already are published standards for character encoding schemes and for coded character sets.* Here's what the HTTP/1.1 authors say about their use of terminology (in RFC 2616):

> The term "character set" is used in this document to refer to a method ... to convert a sequence of octets into a sequence of characters... Note: This use of the term "character set" is more commonly referred to as a "character encoding." However, since HTTP and MIME share the same registry, it's important that the terminology also be shared.

The IETF also adopts nonstandard terminology in RFC 2277:

> This document uses the term "charset" to mean a set of rules for mapping from a sequence of octets to a sequence of characters, such as the combination of a coded character set and a character encoding scheme; this is also what is used as an identifier in MIME "charset=" parameters, and registered in the IANA charset registry. (Note that this is NOT a term used by other standards bodies, such as ISO).

So, be careful when reading standards documents, so you know exactly what's being defined. Now that we've got the terminology sorted out, let's look a bit more closely at characters, glyphs, character sets, and character encodings.

---

* Worse, the MIME charset tag often co-opts the name of a particular coded character set or encoding scheme. For example, iso-8859-1 is a coded character set (it assigns numeric codes to a set of 256 European characters), but MIME uses the charset value "iso-8859-1" to mean an 8-bit identity encoding of the coded character set. This imprecise terminology isn't fatal, but when reading standards documents, be clear on the assumptions.

## Characters

Characters are the most basic building blocks of writing. A character represents an alphabetic letter, numeral, punctuation mark, ideogram (as in Chinese), mathematical symbol, or other basic unit of writing.

Characters are independent of font and style. Figure 16-3 shows several variants of the same character, called "LATIN SMALL LETTER A." A native reader of Western European languages would immediately recognize all five of these shapes as the same character, even though the stroke patterns and styles are quite different.

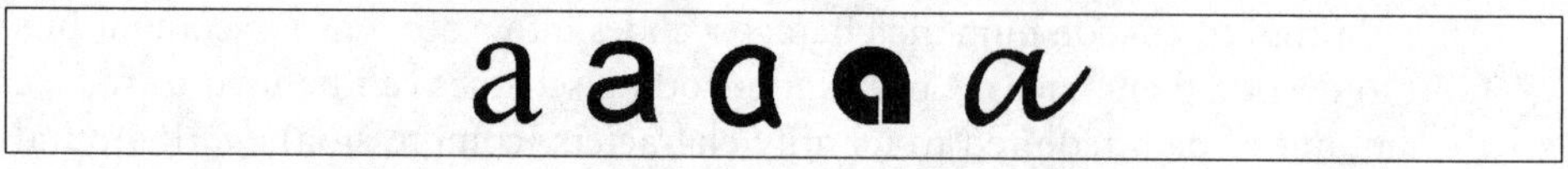

aaaɑα

*Figure 16-3. One character can have many different written forms*

Many writing systems also have different stroke shapes for a single character, depending on the position of the character in the word. For example, the four strokes in Figure 16-4 all represent the character "ARABIC LETTER AIN."[*] Figure 16-4a shows how "AIN" is written as a standalone character. Figure 16-4d shows "AIN" at the beginning of a word, Figure 16-4c shows "AIN" in the middle of a word, and Figure 16-4b shows "AIN" at the end of a word.[†]

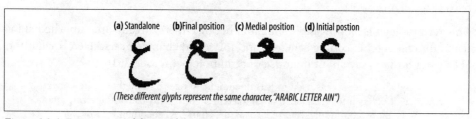

*(These different glyphs represent the same character, "ARABIC LETTER AIN")*

*Figure 16-4. Four positional forms of the single character "ARABIC LETTER AIN"*

## Glyphs, Ligatures, and Presentation Forms

Don't confuse characters with glyphs. Characters are the unique, abstract "atoms" of language. Glyphs are the particular ways you draw each character. Each character has many different glyphs, depending on the artistic style and script.[‡]

Also, don't confuse characters with presentation forms. To make writing look nicer, many handwritten scripts and typefaces let you join adjacent characters into pretty *ligatures*, in which the two characters smoothly connect. English-speaking

---

[*] The sound "AIN" is pronounced something like "ayine," but toward the back of the throat.

[†] Note that Arabic words are written from right to left.

[‡] Many people use the term "glyph" to mean the final rendered bitmap image, but technically a glyph is the inherent shape of a character, independent of font and minor artistic style. This distinction isn't very easy to apply, or useful for our purposes.

typesetters often join "F" and "I" into an "FI ligature" (see Figure 16-5a–b), and Arabic writers often join the "LAM" and "ALIF" characters into an attractive ligature (Figure 16-5c–d).

(a) Without FI ligature    (b) With FI ligature    (c) Without LA ligature    (d) With LA ligature

*Figure 16-5. Ligatures are stylistic presentation forms of adjacent characters, not new characters*

Here's the general rule: if the meaning of the text changes when you replace one glyph with another, the glyphs are different characters. Otherwise, they are the same characters, with a different stylistic presentation.[*]

## Coded Character Sets

Coded character sets, defined in RFCs 2277 and 2130, map integers to characters. Coded character sets often are implemented as arrays,[†] indexed by code number (see Figure 16-6). The array elements are characters.[‡]

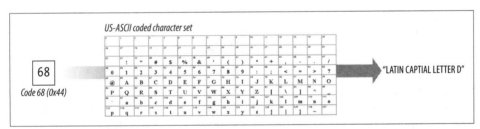

*Figure 16-6. Coded character sets can be thought of as arrays that map numeric codes to characters*

Let's look at a few important coded character set standards, including the historic US-ASCII character set, the iso-8859 extensions to ASCII, the Japanese JIS X 0201 character set, and the Universal Character Set (Unicode).

### US-ASCII: The mother of all character sets

ASCII is the most famous coded character set, standardized back in 1968 as ANSI standard X3.4 "American Standard Code for Information Interchange." ASCII uses

---

* The division between semantics and presentation isn't always clear. For ease of implementation, some presentation variants of the same characters have been assigned distinct characters, but the goal is to avoid this.

† The arrays can be multidimensional, so different bits of the code number index different axes of the array.

‡ Figure 16-6 uses a grid to represent a coded character set. Each element of the grid contains a character image. These images are symbolic. The presence of an image "D" is shorthand for the character "LATIN CAPITAL LETTER D," not for any particular graphical glyph.

only the code values 0–127, so only 7 bits are required to cover the code space. The preferred name for ASCII is "US-ASCII," to distinguish it from international variants of the 7-bit character set.

HTTP messages (headers, URIs, etc.) use US-ASCII.

### iso-8859

The iso-8859 character set standards are 8-bit supersets of US-ASCII that use the high bit to add characters for international writing. The additional space provided by the extra bit (128 extra codes) isn't large enough to hold even all of the European characters (not to mention Asian characters), so iso-8859 provides customized character sets for different regions:

| | |
|---|---|
| iso-8859-1 | Western European languages (e.g., English, French) |
| iso-8859-2 | Central and Eastern European languages (e.g., Czech, Polish) |
| iso-8859-3 | Southern European languages |
| iso-8859-4 | Northern European languages (e.g., Latvian, Lithuanian, Greenlandic) |
| iso-8859-5 | Cyrillic (e.g., Bulgarian, Russian, Serbian) |
| iso-8859-6 | Arabic |
| iso-8859-7 | Greek |
| iso-8859-8 | Hebrew |
| iso-8859-9 | Turkish |
| iso-8859-10 | Nordic languages (e.g., Icelandic, Inuit) |
| iso-8859-15 | Modification to iso-8859-1 that includes the new Euro currency character |

iso-8859-1, also known as Latin1, is the default character set for HTML. It can be used to represent text in most Western European languages. There has been some discussion of replacing iso-8859-1 with iso-8859-15 as the default HTTP coded character set, because it includes the new Euro currency symbol. However, because of the widespread adoption of iso-8859-1, it's unlikely that a widespread change to iso-8859-15 will be adopted for quite some time.

### JIS X 0201

JIS X 0201 is an extremely minimal character set that extends ASCII with Japanese half width katakana characters. The half-width katakana characters were originally used in the Japanese telegraph system. JIS X 0201 is often called "JIS Roman." JIS is an acronym for "Japanese Industrial Standard."

### JIS X 0208 and JIS X 0212

Japanese includes thousands of characters from several writing systems. While it is possible to limp by (painfully) using the 63 basic phonetic katakana characters in JIS X 0201, a much more complete character set is required for practical use.

The JIS X 0208 character set was the first multi-byte Japanese character set; it defined 6,879 coded characters, most of which are Chinese-based kanji. The JIS X 0212 character set adds an additional 6,067 characters.

## UCS

The Universal Character Set (UCS) is a worldwide standards effort to combine all of the world's characters into a single coded character set. UCS is defined by ISO 10646. Unicode is a commercial consortium that tracks the UCS standards. UCS has coding space for millions of characters, although the basic set consists of only about 50,000 characters.

## Character Encoding Schemes

Character encoding schemes pack character code numbers into content bits and unpack them back into character codes at the other end (Figure 16-7). There are three broad classes of character encoding schemes:

*Fixed width*
> Fixed-width encodings represent each coded character with a fixed number of bits. They are fast to process but can waste space.

*Variable width (nonmodal)*
> Variable-width encodings use different numbers of bits for different character code numbers. They can reduce the number of bits required for common characters, and they retain compatibility with legacy 8-bit character sets while allowing the use of multiple bytes for international characters.

*Variable width (modal)*
> Modal encodings use special "escape" patterns to shift between different modes. For example, a modal encoding can be used to switch between multiple, overlapping character sets in the middle of text. Modal encodings are complicated to process, but they can efficiently support complicated writing systems.

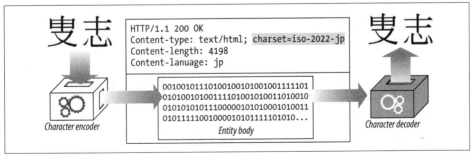

*Figure 16-7. Character encoding scheme encodes character codes into bits and back again*

Let's look at a few common encoding schemes.

## 8-bit

The 8-bit fixed-width identity encoding simply encodes each character code with its corresponding 8-bit value. It supports only character sets with a code range of 256 characters. The iso-8859 family of character sets uses the 8-bit identity encoding.

## UTF-8

UTF-8 is a popular character encoding scheme designed for UCS (UTF stands for "UCS Transformation Format"). UTF-8 uses a nonmodal, variable-length encoding for the character code values, where the leading bits of the first byte tell the length of the encoded character in bytes, and any subsequent byte contains six bits of code value (see Table 16-2).

If the first encoded byte has a high bit of 0, the length is just 1 byte, and the remaining 7 bits contain the character code. This has the nice result of ASCII compatibility (but not iso-8859 compatibility, because iso-8859 uses the high bit).

*Table 16-2. UTF-8 variable-width, nonmodal encoding*

| Character code bits | Byte 1 | Byte 2 | Byte 3 | Byte 4 | Byte 5 | Byte 6 |
|---|---|---|---|---|---|---|
| 0–7 | 0ccccccc | - | - | - | - | - |
| 8–11 | 110ccccc | 10cccccc | - | - | - | - |
| 12–16 | 1110cccc | 10cccccc | 10cccccc | - | - | - |
| 17–21 | 11110ccc | 10cccccc | 10cccccc | 10cccccc | - | - |
| 22–26 | 111110cc | 10cccccc | 10cccccc | 10cccccc | 10cccccc | - |
| 27–31 | 1111110c | 10cccccc | 10cccccc | 10cccccc | 10cccccc | 10cccccc |

For example, character code 90 (ASCII "Z") would be encoded as 1 byte (01011010), while code 5073 (13-bit binary value 1001111010001) would be encoded into 3 bytes:

```
11100001 10001111 10010001
```

## iso-2022-jp

iso-2022-jp is a widely used encoding for Japanese Internet documents. iso-2022-jp is a variable-length, modal encoding, with all values less than 128 to prevent problems with non–8-bit-clean software.

The encoding context always is set to one of four predefined character sets.[*] Special "escape sequences" shift from one set to another. iso-2022-jp initially uses the US-ASCII character set, but it can switch to the JIS X 0201 (JIS-Roman) character set or the much larger JIS X 0208-1978 and JIS X 0208-1983 character sets using 3-byte escape sequences.

---

[*] The iso-2022-jp encoding is tightly bound to these four character sets, whereas some other encodings are independent of the particular character set.

The escape sequences are shown in Table 16-3. In practice, Japanese text begins with "ESC $ @" or "ESC $ B" and ends with "ESC ( B" or "ESC ( J".

*Table 16-3. iso-2022-jp character set switching escape sequences*

| Escape sequence | Resulting coded character set | Bytes per code |
|---|---|---|
| ESC ( B | US-ASCII | 1 |
| ESC ( J | JIS X 0201-1976 (JIS Roman) | 1 |
| ESC $ @ | JIS X 0208-1978 | 2 |
| ESC $ B | JIS X 0208-1983 | 2 |

When in the US-ASCII or JIS-Roman modes, a single byte is used per character. When using the larger JIS X 0208 character set, two bytes are used per character code. The encoding restricts the bytes sent to be between 33 and 126.*

## euc-jp

euc-jp is another popular Japanese encoding. EUC stands for "Extended Unix Code," first developed to support Asian characters on Unix operating systems.

Like iso-2022-jp, the euc-jp encoding is a variable-length encoding that allows the use of several standard Japanese character sets. But unlike iso-2022-jp, the euc-jp encoding is not modal. There are no escape sequences to shift between modes.

euc-jp supports four coded character sets: JIS X 0201 (JIS-Roman, ASCII with a few Japanese substitutions), JIS X 0208, half-width katakana (63 characters used in the original Japanese telegraph system), and JIS X 0212.

One byte is used to encode JIS Roman (ASCII compatible), two bytes are used for JIS X 0208 and half-width katakana, and three bytes are used for JIS X 0212. The coding is a bit wasteful but is simple to process.

The encoding patterns are outlined in Table 16-4.

*Table 16-4. euc-jp encoding values*

| Which byte | Encoding values |
|---|---|
| JIS X 0201 (94 coded characters) | |
| 1st byte | 33–126 |
| JIS X 0208 (6879 coded characters) | |
| 1st byte | 161–254 |
| 2nd byte | 161–254 |

---

\* Though the bytes can have only 94 values (between 33 and 126), this is sufficient to cover all the characters in the JIS X 0208 character sets, because the character sets are organized into a 94 × 94 grid of code values, enough to cover all JIS X 0208 character codes.

*Table 16-4. euc-jp encoding values (continued)*

| Which byte | Encoding values |
|---|---|
| Half-width katakana (63 coded characters) | |
| 1st byte | 142 |
| 2nd byte | 161–223 |
| JIS X 0212 (6067 coded characters) | |
| 1st byte | 143 |
| 2nd byte | 161–254 |
| 3rd byte | 161–254 |

This wraps up our survey of character sets and encodings. The next section explains language tags and how HTTP uses language tags to target content to audiences. Please refer to Appendix H for a detailed listing of standardized character sets.

# Language Tags and HTTP

Language tags are short, standardized strings that name spoken languages.

We need standardized names, or some people will tag French documents as "French," others will use "Français," others still might use "France," and lazy people might just use "Fra" or "F." Standardized language tags avoid this confusion.

There are language tags for English (en), German (de), Korean (ko), and many other languages. Language tags can describe regional variants and dialects of languages, such as Brazilian Portuguese (pt-BR), U.S. English (en-US), and Hunan Chinese (zh-xiang). There is even a standard language tag for Klingon (i-klingon)!

## The Content-Language Header

The Content-Language entity header field describes the target audience languages for the entity. If the content is intended primarily for a French audience, the Content-Language header field would contain:

```
Content-Language: fr
```

The Content-Language header isn't limited to text documents. Audio clips, movies, and applications might all be intended for a particular language audience. Any media type that is targeted to particular language audiences can have a Content-Language header. In Figure 16-8, the audio file is tagged for a Navajo audience.

If the content is intended for multiple audiences, you can list multiple languages. As suggested in the HTTP specification, a rendition of the "Treaty of Waitangi," presented simultaneously in the original Maori and English versions, would call for:

```
Content-Language: mi, en
```

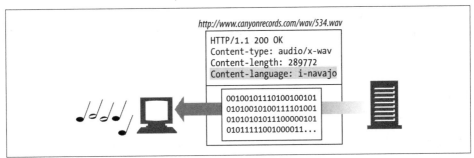

*Figure 16-8. Content-Language header marks a "Rain Song" audio clip for Navajo speakers*

However, just because multiple languages are present within an entity does not mean that it is intended for multiple linguistic audiences. A beginner's language primer, such as "A First Lesson in Latin," which clearly is intended to be used by an English-literate audience, would properly include only "en".

## The Accept-Language Header

Most of us know at least one language. HTTP lets us pass our language restrictions and preferences along to web servers. If the web server has multiple versions of a resource, in different languages, it can give us content in our preferred language.*

Here, a client requests Spanish content:

```
Accept-Language: es
```

You can place multiple language tags in the Accept-Language header to enumerate all supported languages and the order of preference (left to right). Here, the client prefers English but will accept Swiss German (de-CH) or other variants of German (de):

```
Accept-Language: en, de-CH, de
```

Clients use Accept-Language and Accept-Charset to request content they can understand. We'll see how this works in more detail in Chapter 17.

## Types of Language Tags

Language tags have a standardized syntax, documented in RFC 3066, "Tags for the Identification of Languages." Language tags can be used to represent:

- General language classes (as in "es" for Spanish)
- Country-specific languages (as in "en-GB" for English in Great Britain)
- Dialects of languages (as in "no-bok" for Norwegian "Book Language")

---

* Servers also can use the Accept-Language header to generate dynamic content in the language of the user or to select images or target language-appropriate merchandising promotions.

- Regional languages (as in "sgn-US-MA" for Martha's Vineyard sign language)
- Standardized nonvariant languages (e.g., "i-navajo")
- Nonstandard languages (e.g., "x-snowboarder-slang"[*])

## Subtags

Language tags have one or more parts, separated by hyphens, called *subtags*:

- The first subtag called the *primary subtag*. The values are standardized.
- The second subtag is optional and follows its own naming standard.
- Any trailing subtags are unregistered.

The primary subtag contains only letters (A–Z). Subsequent subtags can contain letters or numbers, up to eight characters in length. An example is shown in Figure 16-9.

*Figure 16-9. Language tags are separated into subtags*

## Capitalization

All tags are case-insensitive—the tags "en" and "eN" are equivalent. However, lowercasing conventionally is used to represent general languages, while uppercasing is used to signify particular countries. For example, "fr" means all languages classified as French, while "FR" signifies the country France.[†]

## IANA Language Tag Registrations

The values of the first and second language subtags are defined by various standards documents and their maintaining organizations. The IANA[‡] administers the list of standard language tags, using the rules outlined in RFC 3066.

If a language tag is composed of standard country and language values, the tag doesn't have to be specially registered. Only those language tags that can't be composed out of the standard country and language values need to be registered specially with the

---

[*] Describes the unique dialect spoken by "shredders."

[†] This convention is recommended by ISO standard 3166.

[‡] See *http://www.iana.org* and RFC 2860.

IANA.* The following sections outline the RFC 3066 standards for the first and second subtags.

## First Subtag: Namespace

The first subtag usually is a standardized *language* token, chosen from the ISO 639 set of language standards. But it also can be the letter "i" to identify IANA-registered names, or "x" for private, extension names. Here are the rules:

If the first subtag has:

- Two characters, it is a language code from the ISO 639† and 639-1 standards
- Three characters, it is a language code listed in the ISO 639-2‡ standard and extensions
- The letter "i," the language tag is explicitly IANA-registered
- The letter "x," the language tag is a private, nonstandard, extension subtag

The ISO 639 and 639-2 names are summarized in Appendix G. A few examples are shown here in Table 16-5.

*Table 16-5. Sample ISO 639 and 639-2 language codes*

| Language | ISO 639 | ISO 639-2 |
|----------|---------|-----------|
| Arabic | ar | ara |
| Chinese | zh | chi/zho |
| Dutch | nl | dut/nla |
| English | en | eng |
| French | fr | fra/fre |
| German | de | deu/ger |
| Greek (Modern) | el | ell/gre |
| Hebrew | he | heb |
| Italian | it | ita |
| Japanese | ja | jpn |
| Korean | ko | kor |
| Norwegian | no | nor |
| Russian | ru | rus |
| Spanish | es | esl/spa |

* At the time of writing, only 21 language tags have been explicitly registered with the IANA, including Cantonese ("zh-yue"), New Norwegian ("no-nyn"), Luxembourgish ("i-lux"), and Klingon ("i-klingon"). The hundreds of remaining spoken languages in use on the Internet have been composed from standard components.

† See ISO standard 639, "Codes for the representation of names of languages."

‡ See ISO 639-2, "Codes for the representation of names of languages—Part 2: Alpha-3 code."

*Table 16-5. Sample ISO 639 and 639-2 language codes (continued)*

| Language | ISO 639 | ISO 639-2 |
|----------|---------|-----------|
| Swedish | sv | sve/swe |
| Turkish | tr | tur |

## Second Subtag: Namespace

The second subtag usually is a standardized *country* token, chosen from the ISO 3166 set of country code and region standards. But it may also be another string, which you may register with the IANA. Here are the rules:

If the second subtag has:

- Two characters, it's a country/region defined by ISO 3166[*]
- Three to eight characters, it may be registered with the IANA
- One character, it is illegal

Some of the ISO 3166 country codes are shown in Table 16-6. The complete list of country codes can be found in Appendix G.

*Table 16-6. Sample ISO 3166 country codes*

| Country | Code |
|---------|------|
| Brazil | BR |
| Canada | CA |
| China | CN |
| France | FR |
| Germany | DE |
| Holy See (Vatican City State) | VA |
| Hong Kong | HK |
| India | IN |
| Italy | IT |
| Japan | JP |
| Lebanon | LB |
| Mexico | MX |
| Pakistan | PK |
| Russian Federation | RU |
| United Kingdom | GB |
| United States | US |

[*] The country codes AA, QM–QZ, XA–XZ and ZZ are reserved by ISO 3166 as user-assigned codes. These must not be used to form language tags.

## Remaining Subtags: Namespace

There are no rules for the third and following subtags, apart from being up to eight characters (letters and digits).

## Configuring Language Preferences

You can configure language preferences in your browser profile.

Netscape Navigator lets you set language preferences through Edit → Preferences... → Languages..., and Microsoft Internet Explorer lets you set languages through Tools → Internet Options... → Languages.

## Language Tag Reference Tables

Appendix G contains convenient reference tables for language tags:

- IANA-registered language tags are shown in Table G-1.
- ISO 639 language codes are shown in Table G-2.
- ISO 3166 country codes are shown in Table G-3.

# Internationalized URIs

Today, URIs don't provide much support for internationalization. With a few (poorly defined) exceptions, today's URIs are comprised of a subset of US-ASCII characters. There are efforts underway that might let us include a richer set of characters in the hostnames and paths of URLs, but right now, these standards have not been widely accepted or deployed. Let's review today's practice.

## Global Transcribability Versus Meaningful Characters

The URI designers wanted everyone around the world to be able to share URIs with each other—by email, by phone, by billboard, even over the radio. And they wanted URIs to be easy to use and remember. These two goals are in conflict.

To make it easy for folks around the globe to enter, manipulate, and share URIs, the designers chose a very limited set of common characters for URIs (basic Latin alphabet letters, digits, and a few special characters). This small repertoire of characters is supported by most software and keyboards around the world.

Unfortunately, by restricting the character set, the URI designers made it much harder for people around the globe to create URIs that are easy to use and remember. The majority of world citizens don't even recognize the Latin alphabet, making it nearly impossible to remember URIs as abstract patterns.

The URI authors felt it was more important to ensure transcribability and sharability of resource identifiers than to have them consist of the most meaningful characters. So we have URIs that (today) essentially consist of a restricted subset of ASCII characters.

## URI Character Repertoire

The subset of US-ASCII characters permitted in URIs can be divided into *reserved*, *unreserved*, and *escape* character classes. The unreserved character classes can be used generally within any component of URIs that allow them. The reserved characters have special meanings in many URIs, so they shouldn't be used in general. See Table 16-7 for a list of the unreserved, reserved, and escape characters.

*Table 16-7. URI character syntax*

| Character class | Character repertoire |
| --- | --- |
| Unreserved | [A-Za-z0-9] \| "-" \| "_" \| "." \| "!" \| "~" \| "*" \| "'" \| "(" \| ")" |
| Reserved | ";" \| "/" \| "?" \| ":" \| "@" \| "&" \| "=" \| "+" \| "$" \| "," |
| Escape | "%" <HEX> <HEX> |

## Escaping and Unescaping

URI "escapes" provide a way to safely insert reserved characters and other unsupported characters (such as spaces) inside URIs. An escape is a three-character sequence, consisting of a percent character (%) followed by two hexadecimal digit characters. The two hex digits represent the code for a US-ASCII character.

For example, to insert a space (ASCII 32) in a URL, you could use the escape "%20", because 20 is the hexadecimal representation of 32. Similarly, if you wanted to include a percent sign and have it not be treated as an escape, you could enter "%25", where 25 is the hexadecimal value of the ASCII code for percent.

Figure 16-10 shows how the conceptual characters for a URI are turned into code bytes for the characters, in the current character set. When the URI is needed for processing, the escapes are undone, yielding the underlying ASCII code bytes.

Internally, HTTP applications should transport and forward URIs with the escapes in place. HTTP applications should unescape the URIs only when the data is needed. And, more importantly, the applications should ensure that no URI ever is unescaped twice, because percent signs that might have been encoded in an escape will themselves be unescaped, leading to loss of data.

## Escaping International Characters

Note that escape values should be in the range of US-ASCII codes (0–127). Some applications attempt to use escape values to represent iso-8859-1 extended characters (128–255)—for example, web servers might erroneously use escapes to code

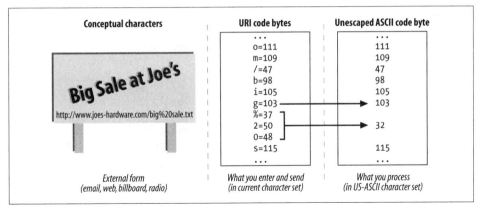

*Figure 16-10. URI characters are transported as escaped code bytes but processed unescaped*

filenames that contain international characters. This is incorrect and may cause problems with some applications.

For example, the filename *Sven Ölssen.html* (containing an umlaut) might be encoded by a web server as *Sven%20%D6lssen.html*. It's fine to encode the space with %20, but is technically illegal to encode the Ö with %D6, because the code D6 (decimal 214) falls outside the range of ASCII. ASCII defines only codes up to 0x7F (decimal 127).

## Modal Switches in URIs

Some URIs also use sequences of ASCII characters to represent characters in other character sets. For example, iso-2022-jp encoding might be used to insert "ESC ( J" to shift into JIS-Roman and "ESC ( B" to shift back to ASCII. This works in some local circumstances, but the behavior is not well defined, and there is no standardized scheme to identify the particular encoding used for the URL. As the authors of RFC 2396 say:

> For original character sequences that contain non-ASCII characters, however, the situation is more difficult. Internet protocols that transmit octet sequences intended to represent character sequences are expected to provide some way of identifying the charset used, if there might be more than one [RFC2277].

> However, there is currently no provision within the generic URI syntax to accomplish this identification. An individual URI scheme may require a single charset, define a default charset, or provide a way to indicate the charset used. It is expected that a systematic treatment of character encoding within URI will be developed as a future modification of this specification.

Currently, URIs are not very international-friendly. The goal of URI portability outweighed the goal of language flexibility. There are efforts currently underway to internationalize URIs, but in the near term, HTTP applications should stick with ASCII. It's been around since 1968, so it can't be all that bad.

# Other Considerations

This section discusses a few other things you should keep in mind when writing international HTTP applications.

## Headers and Out-of-Spec Data

HTTP headers must consist of characters from the US-ASCII character set. However, not all clients and servers implement this correctly, so you may on occasion receive illegal characters with code values larger than 127.

Many HTTP applications use operating-system and library routines for processing characters (for example, the Unix ctype character classification library). Not all of these libraries support character codes outside of the ASCII range (0–127).

In some circumstances (generally, with older implementations), these libraries may return improper results or crash the application when given non-ASCII characters. Carefully read the documentation for your character classification libraries before using them to process HTTP messages, in case the messages contain illegal data.

## Dates

The HTTP specification clearly defines the legal GMT date formats, but be aware that not all web servers and clients follow the rules. For example, we have seen web servers send invalid HTTP Date headers with months expressed in local languages.

HTTP applications should attempt to be tolerant of out-of-spec dates, and not crash on receipt, but they may not always be able to interpret all dates sent. If the date is not parseable, servers should treat it conservatively.

## Domain Names

DNS doesn't currently support international characters in domain names. There are standards efforts under way to support multilingual domain names, but they have not yet been widely deployed.

# For More Information

The very success of the World Wide Web means that HTTP applications will continue to exchange more and more content in different languages and character sets. For more information on the important but slightly complex topic of multilingual multimedia, please refer to the following sources.

## Appendixes

- IANA-registered charset tags are listed in Table H-1.
- IANA-registered language tags are shown in Table G-1.
- ISO 639 language codes are shown in Table G-2.
- ISO 3166 country codes are shown in Table G-3.

## Internet Internationalization

*http://www.w3.org/International/*
  "Making the WWW Truly World Wide"—the W3C Internationalization and Localization web site.

*http://www.ietf.org/rfc/rfc2396.txt*
  RFC 2396, "Uniform Resource Identifiers (URI): Generic Syntax," is the defining document of URIs. This document includes sections describing character set restrictions for international URIs.

*CJKV Information Processing*
  Ken Lunde, O'Reilly & Associates, Inc. CJKV is the bible of Asian electronic character processing. Asian character sets are varied and complex, but this book provides an excellent introduction to the standards technologies for large character sets.

*http://www.ietf.org/rfc/rfc2277.txt*
  RFC 2277, "IETF Policy on Character Sets and Languages," documents the current policies being applied by the Internet Engineering Steering Group (IESG) toward the standardization efforts in the Internet Engineering Task Force (IETF) in order to help Internet protocols interchange data in multiple languages and characters.

## International Standards

*http://www.iana.org/numbers.htm*
  The Internet Assigned Numbers Authority (IANA) contains repositories of registered names and numbers. The "Protocol Numbers and Assignments Directory" contains records of registered character sets for use on the Internet. Because much work on international communications falls under the domain of the ISO, and not the Internet community, the IANA listings are not exhaustive.

*http://www.ietf.org/rfc/rfc3066.txt*
  RFC 3066, "Tags for the Identification of Languages," describes language tags, their values, and how to construct them.

*"Codes for the representation of names of languages"*
> ISO 639:1988 (E/F), The International Organization for Standardization, first edition.

*"Codes for the representation of names of languages—Part 2: Alpha-3 code"*
> ISO 639-2:1998, Joint Working Group of ISO TC46/SC4 and ISO TC37/SC2, first edition.

*"Codes for the representation of names of countries"*
> ISO 3166:1988 (E/F), The International Organization for Standardization, third edition.

# CHAPTER 17

# Content Negotiation and Transcoding

Often, a single URL may need to correspond to different resources. Take the case of a web site that wants to offer its content in multiple languages. If a site such as Joe's Hardware has both French- and English-speaking users, it might want to offer its web site in both languages. However, if this is the case, when one of Joe's customers requests "http://www.joes-hardware.com," which version should the server send? French or English?

Ideally, the server will send the English version to an English speaker and the French version to a French speaker—a user could go to Joe's Hardware's home page and get content in the language he speaks. Fortunately, HTTP provides *content-negotiation* methods that allow clients and servers to make just such determinations. Using these methods, a single URL can correspond to different resources (e.g., a French and English version of the same web page). These different versions are called *variants*.

Servers also can make other types of decisions about what content is best to send to a client for a particular URL. In some cases, servers even can automatically generate customized pages—for instance, a server can convert an HTML page into a WML page for your handheld device. These kinds of dynamic content transformations are called *transcodings*. They are done in response to content negotiation between HTTP clients and servers.

In this chapter, we will discuss content negotiation and how web applications go about their content-negotiation duties.

## Content-Negotiation Techniques

There are three distinct methods for deciding which page at a server is the right one for a client: present the choice to the client, decide automatically at the server, or ask an intermediary to select. These three techniques are called client-driven negotiation, server-driven negotiation, and transparent negotiation, respectively (see Table 17-1).

In this chapter, we will look at the mechanics of each technique as well as their advantages and disadvantages.

*Table 17-1. Summary of content-negotiation techniques*

| Technique | How it works | Advantages | Drawbacks |
|---|---|---|---|
| Client-driven | Client makes a request, server sends list of choices to client, client chooses. | Easiest to implement at server side. Client can make best choice. | Adds latency: at least two requests are needed to get the correct content. |
| Server-driven | Server examines client's request headers and decides what version to serve. | Quicker than client-driven negotiation. HTTP provides a q-value mechanism to allow servers to make approximate matches and a Vary header for servers to tell downstream devices how to evaluate requests. | If the decision is not obvious (headers don't match up), the server must guess. |
| Transparent | An intermediate device (usually a proxy cache) does the request negotiation on the client's behalf. | Offloads the negotiation from the web server. Quicker than client-driven negotiation. | No formal specifications for how to do transparent negotiation. |

# Client-Driven Negotiation

The easiest thing for a server to do when it receives a client request is to send back a response listing the available pages and let the client decide which one it wants to see. This, of course, is the easiest to implement at the server and is likely to result in the best copy being selected (provided that the list has enough information to allow the client to pick the right copy). The disadvantage is that two requests are needed for each page—one to get the list and a second to get the selected copy. This is a slow and tedious process, and it's likely to become annoying to the client.

Mechanically, there are actually two ways for servers to present the choices to the client for selection: by sending back an HTML document with links to the different versions of the page and descriptions of each of the versions, or by sending back an HTTP/1.1 response with the 300 Multiple Choices response code. The client browser may receive this response and display a page with the links, as in the first method, or it may pop up a dialog window asking the user to make a selection. In any case, the decision is made manually at the client side by the browser user.

In addition to the increased latency and annoyance of multiple requests per page, this method has another drawback: it requires multiple URLs—one for the main page and one for each specific page. So, if the original request was for *www.joes-hardware.com*, Joe's server may respond with a page that has links to *www.joes-hardware.com/english* and *www.joes-hardware.com/french*. Should clients now bookmark the original main page or the selected ones? Should they tell their friends about the great web site at *www.joes-hardware.com* or tell only their English-speaking friends about the web site at *www.joes-hardware.com/english*?

# Server-Driven Negotiation

Client-driven negotiation has several drawbacks, as discussed in the previous section. Most of these drawbacks center around the increased communication between the client and server to decide on the best page in response to a request. One way to reduce this extra communication is to let the server decide which page to send back—but to do this, the client must send enough information about its preferences to allow the server to make an informed decision. The server gets this information from the client's request headers.

There are two mechanisms that HTTP servers use to evaluate the proper response to send to a client:

- Examining the set of content-negotiation headers. The server looks at the client's Accept headers and tries to match them with corresponding response headers.
- Varying on other (non–content-negotiation) headers. For example, the server could send responses based on the client's User-Agent header.

These two mechanisms are explained in more detail in the following sections.

## Content-Negotiation Headers

Clients may send their preference information using the set of HTTP headers listed in Table 17-2.

*Table 17-2. Accept headers*

| Header | Description |
| --- | --- |
| Accept | Used to tell the server what media types are okay to send |
| Accept-Language | Used to tell the server what languages are okay to send |
| Accept-Charset | Used to tell the server what charsets are okay to send |
| Accept-Encoding | Used to tell the server what encodings are okay to send |

Notice how similar these headers are to the entity headers discussed in Chapter 15. However, there is a clear distinction between the purposes of the two types of headers. As mentioned in Chapter 15, entity headers are like shipping labels—they specify attributes of the message body that are necessary during the transfer of messages from the server to the client. Content-negotiation headers, on the other hand, are used by clients and servers to exchange preference information and to help choose between different versions of a document, so that the one most closely matching the client's preferences is served.

Servers match clients' Accept headers with the corresponding entity headers, listed in Table 17-3.

*Table 17-3. Accept and matching document headers*

| Accept header | Entity header |
|---|---|
| Accept | Content-Type |
| Accept-Language | Content-Language |
| Accept-Charset | Content-Type |
| Accept-Encoding | Content-Encoding |

Note that because HTTP is a stateless protocol (meaning that servers do not keep track of client preferences across requests), clients must send their preference information with every request.

If both clients sent Accept-Language header information specifying the language in which they were interested, the server could decide which copy of *www.joes-hardware.com* to send back to each client. Letting the server automatically pick which document to send back reduces the latency associated with the back-and-forth communication required by the client-driven model.

However, say that one of the clients prefers Spanish. Which version of the page should the server send back? English or French? The server has just two choices: either guess, or fall back on the client-driven model and ask the client to choose. However, if the Spaniard happens to understand some English, he might choose the English page—it wouldn't be ideal, but it would do. In this case, the Spaniard needs the ability to pass on more information about his preferences, conveying that he does have minimal knowledge of English and that, in a pinch, English will suffice.

Fortunately, HTTP does provide a mechanism for letting clients like our Spaniard give richer descriptions of their preferences, using *quality values* ("q values" for short).

## Content-Negotiation Header Quality Values

The HTTP protocol defines quality values to allow clients to list multiple choices for each category of preference and associate an order of preference with each choice. For example, clients can send an Accept-Language header of the form:

```
Accept-Language: en;q=0.5, fr;q=0.0, nl;q=1.0, tr;q=0.0
```

Where the q values can range from 0.0 to 1.0 (with 0.0 being the lowest preference and 1.0 being the highest). The header above, then, says that the client prefers to receive a Dutch (nl) version of the document, but an English (en) version will do. Under no circumstances does the client want a French (fr) or Turkish (tr) version, though. Note that the order in which the preferences are listed is not important; only the q values associated with them are.

Occasionally, the server may not have any documents that match any of the client's preferences. In this case, the server may change or transcode the document to match the client's preferences. This mechanism is discussed later in this chapter.

# Varying on Other Headers

Servers also can attempt to match up responses with other client request headers, such as User-Agent. Servers may know that old versions of a browser do not support JavaScript, for example, and may therefore send back a version of the page that does not contain JavaScript.

In this case, there is no q-value mechanism to look for approximate "best" matches. The server either looks for an exact match or simply serves whatever it has (depending on the implementation of the server).

Because caches must attempt to serve correct "best" versions of cached documents, the HTTP protocol defines a Vary header that the server sends in responses; the Vary header tells caches (and clients, and any downstream proxies) which headers the server is using to determine the best version of the response to send. The Vary header is discussed in more detail later in this chapter.

# Content Negotiation on Apache

Here is an overview of how the Apache web server supports content negotiation. It is up to the web site content provider—Joe, for example—to provide different versions of Joe's index page. Joe must put all his index page files in the appropriate directory on the Apache server corresponding to his web site. There are two ways to enable content negotiation:

- In the web site directory, create a *type-map file* for each URI in the web site that has variants. The type-map file lists all the variants and the content-negotiation headers to which they correspond.
- Enable the MultiViews directive, which causes Apache to create type-map files for the directory automatically.

### Using type-map files

The Apache server needs to know what type-map files look like. To configure this, set a handler in the server configuration file that specifies the file suffix for type-map files. For example:

```
AddHandler type-map .var
```

This line indicates that files with the extension *.var* are type-map files.

Here is a sample type-map file:

```
URI: joes-hardware.html

URI: joes-hardware.en.html
Content-type: text/html
Content-language: en
```

```
URI: joes-hardware.fr.de.html
Content-type: text/html;charset=iso-8859-2
Content-language: fr, de
```

From this type-map file, the Apache server knows to send *joes-hardware.en.html* to clients requesting English and *joes-hardware.fr.de.html* to clients requesting French. Quality values also are supported; see the Apache server documentation.

### Using MultiViews

To use MultiViews, you must enable it for the directory containing the web site, using an Options directive in the appropriate section of the *access.conf* file (*<Directory>*, *<Location>*, or *<Files>*).

If MultiViews is enabled and a browser requests a resource named *joes-hardware*, the server looks for all files with "joes-hardware" in the name and creates a type-map file for them. Based on the names, the server guesses the appropriate content-negotiation headers to which the files correspond. For example, a French-language version of *joes-hardware* should contain *.fr*.

## Server-Side Extensions

Another way to implement content negotiation at the server is by server-side extensions, such as Microsoft's Active Server Pages (ASP). See Chapter 8 for an overview of server-side extensions.

# Transparent Negotiation

Transparent negotiation seeks to move the load of server-driven negotiation away from the server, while minimizing message exchanges with the client by having an intermediary proxy negotiate on behalf of the client. The proxy is assumed to have knowledge of the client's expectations and be capable of performing the negotiations on its behalf (the proxy has received the client's expectations in the request for content). To support transparent content negotiation, the server must be able to tell proxies what request headers the server examines to determine the best match for the client's request. The HTTP/1.1 specification does not define any mechanisms for transparent negotiation, but it does define the Vary header. Servers send Vary headers in their responses to tell intermediaries what request headers they use for content negotiation.

Caching proxies can store different copies of documents accessed via a single URL. If servers communicate their decision-making processes to caches, the caches can negotiate with clients on behalf of the servers. Caches also are great places to transcode content, because a general-purpose transcoder deployed in a cache can transcode content from any server, not just one. Transcoding of content at a cache is illustrated in Figure 17-3 and discussed in more detail later in the chapter.

---

# Caching and Alternates

Caching of content assumes that the content can be reused later. However, caches must employ much of the decision-making logic that servers do when sending back a response, to ensure that they send back the correct cached response to a client request.

The previous section described the Accept headers sent by clients and the corresponding entity headers that servers match them up against in order to choose the best response to each request. Caches must use these same headers to decide which cached response to send back.

Figure 17-1 illustrates both a correct and incorrect sequence of operations involving a cache. The first request results in the cache forwarding the request to the server and storing the response. The second response is looked up by the cache, and a document matching the URL is found. This document, however, is in French, and the requestor wants a Spanish document. If the cache just sends back the French document to the requestor, it will be behaving incorrectly.

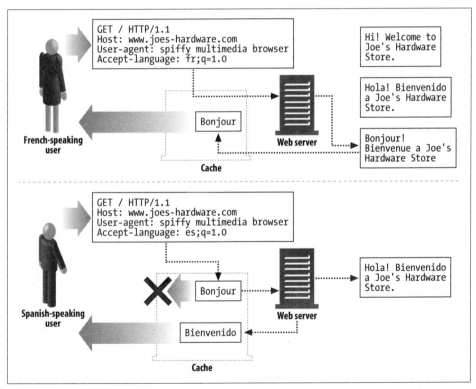

*Figure 17-1. Caches use content-negotiation headers to send back correct responses to clients*

The cache must therefore forward the second request to the server as well, and store both the response and an "alternate" response for that URL. The cache now has two different documents for the same URL, just as the server does. These different versions are called *variants* or *alternates*. Content negotiation can be thought of as the process of selecting, from the variants, the best match for a client request.

## The Vary Header

Here's a typical set of request and response headers from a browser and server:

```
GET http://www.joes-hardware.com/ HTTP/1.0
Proxy-Connection: Keep-Alive
User-Agent: Mozilla/4.73 [en] (WinNT; U)
Host: www.joes-hardware.com
Accept: image/gif, image/x-xbitmap, image/jpeg, image/pjpeg, image/png, */*
Accept-Encoding: gzip
Accept-Language: en, pdf
Accept-Charset: iso-8859-1, *, utf-8

HTTP/1.1 200 OK
Date: Sun, 10 Dec 2000 22:13:40 GMT
Server: Apache/1.3.12 OpenSSL/0.9.5a (Unix) FrontPage/4.0.4.3
Last-Modified: Fri, 05 May 2000 04:42:52 GMT
Etag: "1b7ddf-48-3912514c"
Accept-Ranges: Bytes
Content-Length: 72
Connection: close
Content-Type: text/html
```

What happens, however, if the server's decision was based on headers other than the Accept headers, such as the User-Agent header? This is not as radical as it may sound. Servers may know that old versions of a browser do not support JavaScript, for example, and may therefore send back a version of the page that does not have JavaScript in it. If servers are using other headers to make their decisions about which pages to send back, caches must know what those headers are, so that they can perform parallel logic in choosing which cached page to send back.

The HTTP Vary response header lists all of the client request headers that the server considers to select the document or generate custom content (in addition to the regular content-negotiation headers). For example, if the served document depends on the User-Agent header, the Vary header must include "User-Agent".

When a new request arrives, the cache finds the best match using the content-negotiation headers. Before it can serve this document to the client, however, it must see whether the server sent a Vary header in the cached response. If a Vary header is present, the header values for the headers in the new request must match the header values in the old, cached request. Because servers may vary their responses based on client request headers, caches must store both the client request headers and the corresponding server response headers with each cached variant, in order to implement transparent negotiation. This is illustrated in Figure 17-2.

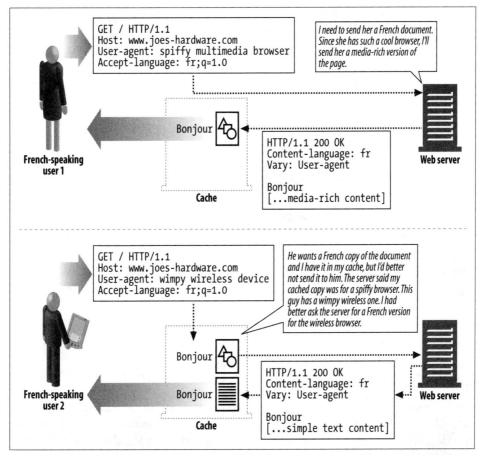

*Figure 17-2. If servers vary on specific request headers, caches must match those request headers in addition to the regular content-negotiation headers before sending back cached responses*

If a server's Vary header looked like this, the huge number of different User-Agent and Cookie values could generate many variants:

```
Vary: User-Agent, Cookie
```

A cache would have to store each document version corresponding to each variant. When the cache does a lookup, it first does content matching with the content-negotiation headers, then matches the request's variant with cached variants. If there is no match, the cache fetches the document from the origin server.

# Transcoding

We have discussed in some detail the mechanism by which clients and servers can choose between a set of documents for a URL and send the one that best matches the client's needs. These mechanisms rely on the presence of documents that match the client's needs—whether they match the needs perfectly or not so well.

What happens, however, when a server does not have a document that matches the client's needs at all? The server may have to respond with an error, but theoretically, the server may be able to transform one of its existing documents into something that the client can use. This option is called *transcoding*.

Table 17-4 lists some hypothetical transcodings.

*Table 17-4. Hypothetical transcodings*

| Before | After |
|---|---|
| HTML document | WML document |
| High-resolution image | Low-resolution image |
| Image in 64K colors | Black-and-white image |
| Complex page with frames | Simple text page without frames or images |
| HTML page with Java applets | HTML page without Java applets |
| Page with ads | Page with ads removed |

There are three categories of transcoding: format conversion, information synthesis, and content injection.

## Format Conversion

*Format conversion* is the transformation of data from one format to another to make it viewable by a client. A wireless device seeking to access a document typically viewed by a desktop client may be able do so with an HTML-to-WML conversion. A client accessing a web page over a slow link that is not very interested in high-resolution images may be able to view an image-rich page more easily if the images are reduced in size and resolution by converting them from color to black and white and shrinking them.

Format conversion is driven by the content-negotiation headers listed in Table 17-2, although it may also be driven by the User-Agent header. Note that content transformation or transcoding is different from content encoding or transfer encoding, in that the latter two typically are used for more efficient or safe transport of content, whereas the former is used to make content viewable on the access device.

## Information Synthesis

The extraction of key pieces of information from a document—known as *information synthesis*—can be a useful transcoding process. A simple example of this is the generation of an outline of a document based on section headings, or the removal of advertisements and logos from a page.

More sophisticated technologies that categorize pages based on keywords in content also are useful in summarizing the essence of a document. This technology often is used by automatic web page–classification systems, such as web-page directories at portal sites.

## Content Injection

The two categories of transcodings described so far typically reduce the amount of content in web documents, but there is another category of transformations that increases the amount of content: *content-injection* transcodings. Examples of content-injection transcodings are automatic ad generators and user-tracking systems.

Imagine the appeal (and offence) of an ad-insertion transcoder that automatically adds advertisements to each HTML page as it goes by. Transcoding of this type has to be dynamic—it must be done on the fly in order to be effective in adding ads that currently are relevant or somehow have been targeted for a particular user. User-tracking systems also can be built to add content to pages dynamically, for the purpose of collecting statistics about how the page is viewed and how clients surf the Web.

## Transcoding Versus Static Pregeneration

An alternative to transcodings is to build different copies of web pages at the web server—for example, one with HTML, one with WML, one with high-resolution images, one with low-resolution images, one with multimedia content, and one without. This, however, is not a very practical technique, for many reasons: any small change in a page requires multiple pages to be modified, more space is necessary to store all the different versions of each page, and it's harder to catalog pages and program web servers to serve the right ones. Some transcodings, such as ad insertion (especially targeted ad insertion), cannot be done statically—the ad inserted will depend upon the user requesting the page.

An on-the-fly transformation of a single root page can be an easier solution than static pregeneration. It can come, however, at the cost of increased latency in serving the content. Some of this computation can, however, be done by a third party, thereby offloading the computation from the web server—the transformation can be done by an external agent at a proxy or cache. Figure 17-3 illustrates transcoding at a proxy cache.

# Next Steps

The story of content negotiation does not end with the Accept and Content headers, for a couple of reasons:

- Content negotiation in HTTP incurs some performance limits. Searching through many variants for appropriate content, or trying to "guess" the best match, can

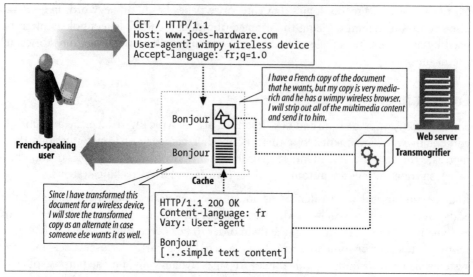

*Figure 17-3. Content transformation or transcoding at a proxy cache*

be costly. Are there ways to streamline and focus the content-negotiation proto-col? RFCs 2295 and 2296 attempt to address this question for transparent HTTP content negotiation.

- HTTP is not the only protocol that needs to do content negotiation. Streaming media and fax are two other examples where client and server need to discuss the best answer to the client's request. Can a general content-negotiation proto-col be developed on top of TCP/IP application protocols? The Content Negotia-tion Working Group was formed to tackle this question. The group is now closed, but it contributed several RFCs. See the next section for a link to the group's web site.

## For More Information

The following Internet drafts and online documentation can give you more details about content negotiation:

*http://www.ietf.org/rfc/rfc2616.txt*

RFC 2616, "Hypertext Transfer Protocol—HTTP/1.1," is the official specifica-tion for HTTP/1.1, the current version of the HTTP protocol. The specification is a well-written, well-organized, detailed reference for HTTP, but it isn't ideal for readers who want to learn the underlying concepts and motivations of HTTP or the differences between theory and practice. We hope that this book fills in the underlying concepts, so you can make better use of the specification.

*http://search.ietf.org/rfc/rfc2295.txt*

RFC 2295, "Transparent Content Negotiation in HTTP," is a memo describing a transparent content-negotiation protocol on top of HTTP. The status of this memo remains experimental.

*http://search.ietf.org/rfc/rfc2296.txt*

RFC 2296, "HTTP Remote Variant Selection Algorithm—RVSA 1.0," is a memo describing an algorithm for the transparent selection of the "best" content for a particular HTTP request. The status of this memo remains experimental.

*http://search.ietf.org/rfc/rfc2936.txt*

RFC 2936, "HTTP MIME Type Handler Detection," is a memo describing an approach for determining the actual MIME type handlers that a browser supports. This approach can help if the Accept header is not specific enough.

*http://www.imc.org/ietf-medfree/index.htm*

This is a link to the Content Negotiation (CONNEG) Working Group, which looked into transparent content negotiation for HTTP, fax, and print. This group is now closed.

# Content Publishing and Distribution

Part V talks all about the technology for publishing and disseminating web content:

- Chapter 18, *Web Hosting*, discusses the ways people deploy servers in modern web hosting environments, HTTP support for virtual web hosting, and how to replicate content across geographically distant servers.

- Chapter 19, *Publishing Systems*, discusses the technologies for creating web content and installing it onto web servers.

- Chapter 20, *Redirection and Load Balancing*, surveys the tools and techniques for distributing incoming web traffic among a collection of servers.

- Chapter 21, *Logging and Usage Tracking*, covers log formats and common questions.

# CHAPTER 18

# Web Hosting

When you place resources on a public web server, you make them available to the Internet community. These resources can be as simple as text files or images, or as complicated as real-time driving maps or e-commerce shopping gateways. It's critical that this rich variety of resources, owned by different organizations, can be conveniently published to web sites and placed on web servers that offer good performance at a fair price.

The collective duties of storing, brokering, and administering content resources is called *web hosting*. Hosting is one of the primary functions of a web server. You need a server to hold, serve, log access to, and administer your content. If you don't want to manage the required hardware and software yourself, you need a hosting service, or *hoster*. Hosters rent you serving and web-site administration services and provide various degrees of security, reporting, and ease of use. Hosters typically pool web sites on heavy-duty web servers for cost-efficiency, reliability, and performance.

This chapter explains some of the most important features of web hosting services and how they interact with HTTP applications. In particular, this chapter covers:

- How different web sites can be "virtually hosted" on the same server, and how this affects HTTP
- How to make web sites more reliable under heavy traffic
- How to make web sites load faster

## Hosting Services

In the early days of the World Wide Web, individual organizations purchased their own computer hardware, built their own computer rooms, acquired their own network connections, and managed their own web server software.

As the Web quickly became mainstream, everyone wanted a web site, but few people had the skills or time to build air-conditioned server rooms, register domain names, or purchase network bandwidth. To save the day, many new businesses emerged, offering professionally managed web hosting services. Many levels of service are available, from physical facilities management (providing space, air conditioning, and wiring) to full-service web hosting, where all the customer does is provide the content.

This chapter focuses on what the hosting web server provides. Much of what makes a web site work—as well as, for example, its ability to support different languages and its ability to do secure e-commerce transactions—depends on what capabilities the hosting web server supports.

## A Simple Example: Dedicated Hosting

Suppose that Joe's Hardware Online and Mary's Antique Auction both want fairly high-volume web sites. Irene's ISP has racks and racks full of identical, high-performance web servers that it can lease to Joe and Mary, instead of having Joe and Mary purchase their own servers and maintain the server software.

In Figure 18-1, both Joe and Mary sign up for the *dedicated web hosting* service offered by Irene's ISP. Joe leases a dedicated web server that is purchased and maintained by Irene's ISP. Mary gets a different dedicated server from Irene's ISP. Irene's ISP gets to buy server hardware in volume and can select hardware that is reliable, time-tested, and low-cost. If either Joe's Hardware Online or Mary's Antique Auction grows in popularity, Irene's ISP can offer Joe or Mary additional servers immediately.

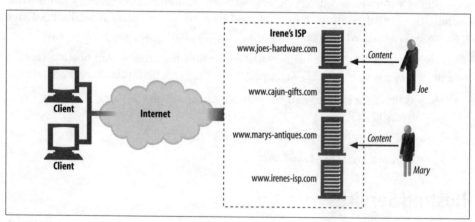

*Figure 18-1. Outsourced dedicated hosting*

In this example, browsers send HTTP requests for *www.joes-hardware.com* to the IP address of Joe's server and requests for *www.marys-antiques.com* to the (different) IP address of Mary's server.

# Virtual Hosting

Many folks want to have a web presence but don't have high-traffic web sites. For these people, providing a dedicated web server may be a waste, because they're paying many hundreds of dollars a month to lease a server that is mostly idle!

Many web hosters offer lower-cost web hosting services by sharing one computer between several customers. This is called *shared hosting* or *virtual hosting*. Each web site appears to be hosted by a different server, but they really are hosted on the same physical server. From the end user's perspective, virtually hosted web sites should be indistinguishable from sites hosted on separate dedicated servers.

For cost efficiency, space, and management reasons, a virtual hosting company wants to host tens, hundreds, or thousands of web sites on the same server—but this does not necessarily mean that 1,000 web sites are served from only one PC. Hosters can create banks of replicated servers (called *server farms*) and spread the load across the farm of servers. Because each server in the farm is a clone of the others, and hosts many virtual web sites, administration is much easier. (We'll talk more about server farms in Chapter 20.)

When Joe and Mary started their businesses, they might have chosen virtual hosting to save money until their traffic levels made a dedicated server worthwhile (see Figure 18-2).

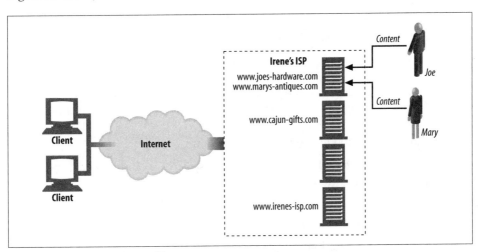

*Figure 18-2. Outsourced virtual hosting*

## Virtual Server Request Lacks Host Information

Unfortunately, there is a design flaw in HTTP/1.0 that makes virtual hosters pull their hair out. The HTTP/1.0 specification didn't give any means for shared web servers to identify which of the virtual web sites they're hosting is being accessed.

Recall that HTTP/1.0 requests send only the path component of the URL in the request message. If you try to get *http://www.joes-hardware.com/index.html*, the browser connects to the server *www.joes-hardware.com*, but the HTTP/1.0 request says "GET /index.html", with no further mention of the hostname. If the server is virtually hosting multiple sites, this isn't enough information to figure out what virtual web site is being accessed. For example, in Figure 18-3:

- If client A tries to access *http://www.joes-hardware.com/index.html*, the request "GET /index.html" will be sent to the shared web server.

- If client B tries to access *http://www.marys-antiques.com/index.html*, the identical request "GET /index.html" will be sent to the shared web server.

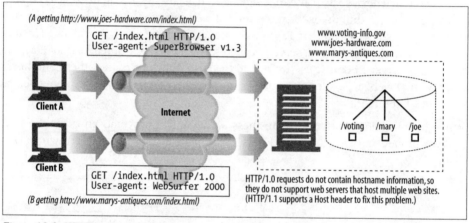

*Figure 18-3. HTTP/1.0 server requests don't contain hostname information*

As far as the web server is concerned, there is not enough information to determine which web site is being accessed! The two requests look the same, even though they are for totally different documents (from different web sites). The problem is that the web site host information has been stripped from the request.

As we saw in Chapter 6, HTTP surrogates (reverse proxies) and intercepting proxies also need site-specifying information.

## Making Virtual Hosting Work

The missing host information was an oversight in the original HTTP specification, which mistakenly assumed that each web server would host exactly one web site. HTTP's designers didn't provide support for virtually hosted, shared servers. For this reason, the hostname information in the URL was viewed as redundant and stripped away; only the path component was required to be sent.

Because the early specifications did not make provisions for virtual hosting, web hosters needed to develop workarounds and conventions to support shared virtual hosting. The problem could have been solved simply by requiring all HTTP request messages to send the full URL instead of just the path component. HTTP/1.1 does require servers to handle full URLs in the request lines of HTTP messages, but it will be a long time before all legacy applications are upgraded to this specification. In the meantime, four techniques have emerged:

*Virtual hosting by URL path*
Adding a special path component to the URL so the server can determine the site.

*Virtual hosting by port number*
Assigning a different port number to each site, so requests are handled by separate instances of the web server.

*Virtual hosting by IP address*
Dedicating different IP addresses for different virtual sites and binding all the IP addresses to a single machine. This allows the web server to identify the site name by IP address.

*Virtual hosting by Host header*
Many web hosters pressured the HTTP designers to solve this problem. Enhanced versions of HTTP/1.0 and the official version of HTTP/1.1 define a Host request header that carries the site name. The web server can identify the virtual site from the Host header.

Let's take a closer look at each technique.

## Virtual hosting by URL path

You can use brute force to isolate virtual sites on a shared server by assigning them different URL paths. For example, you could give each logical web site a special path prefix:

- Joe's Hardware store could be *http://www.joes-hardware.com/joe/index.html*.
- Mary's Antiques store could be *http://www.marys-antiques.com/mary/index.html*.

When the requests arrive at the server, the hostname information is not present in the request, but the server can tell them apart based on the path:

- The request for Joe's hardware is "GET /joe/index.html".
- The request for Mary's antiques is "GET /mary/index.html".

This is not a good solution. The "/joe" and "/mary" prefixes are redundant and confusing (we already mentioned "joe" in the hostname). Worse, the common convention of specifying *http://www.joes-hardware.com* or *http://www.joes-hardware.com/ index.html* for the home page won't work.

In general, URL-based virtual hosting is a poor solution and seldom is used.

## Virtual hosting by port number

Instead of changing the pathname, Joe and Mary could each be assigned a different port number on the web server. Instead of port 80, for example, Joe could get 82 and

Mary could have 83. But this solution has the same problem: an end user would expect to find the resources without having to specify a nonstandard port in the URL.

## Virtual hosting by IP address

A much better approach (in common use) is virtual IP addressing. Here, each virtual web site gets one or more unique IP addresses. The IP addresses for all of the virtual web sites are attached to the same shared server. The server can look up the destination IP address of the HTTP connection and use that to determine what web site the client thinks it is connected to.

Say a hoster assigned the IP address 209.172.34.3 to *www.joes-hardware.com*, assigned 209.172.34.4 to *www.marys-antiques.com*, and tied both IP addresses to the same physical server machine. The web server could then use the destination IP address to identify which virtual site is being requested, as shown in Figure 18-4:

- Client A fetches *http://www.joes-hardware.com/index.html*.
- Client A finds the IP address for *www.joes-hardware.com*, getting 209.172.34.3.
- Client A opens a TCP connection to the shared web server at 209.172.34.3.
- Client A sends the request "GET /index.html HTTP/1.0".
- Before the web server serves a response, it notes the actual destination IP address (209.172.34.3), determines that this is a virtual IP address for Joe's web site, and fulfills the request from the */joe* subdirectory. The page */joe/index.html* is returned.

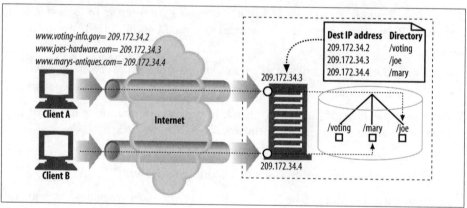

*Figure 18-4. Virtual IP hosting*

Similarly, if client B asks for *http://www.marys-antiques.com/index.html*:

- Client B finds the IP address for *www.marys-antiques.com*, getting 209.172.34.4.
- Client B opens a TCP connection to the web server at 209.172.34.4.
- Client B sends the request "GET /index.html HTTP/1.0".
- The web server determines that 209.172.34.4 is Mary's web site and fulfills the request from the */mary* subdirectory, returning the document */mary/index.html*.

Virtual IP hosting works, but it causes some difficulties, especially for large hosters:

- Computer systems usually have a limit on how many virtual IP addresses can be bound to a machine. Hosters that want hundreds or thousands of virtual sites to be hosted on a shared server may be out of luck.

- IP addresses are a scarce commodity. Hosters with many virtual sites might not be able to obtain enough virtual IP addresses for the hosted web sites.

- The IP address shortage is made worse when hosters replicate their servers for additional capacity. Different virtual IP addresses may be needed on each replicated server, depending on the load-balancing architecture, so the number of IP addresses needed can multiply by the number of replicated servers.

Despite the address consumption problems with virtual IP hosting, it is used widely.

### Virtual hosting by Host header

To avoid excessive address consumption and virtual IP limits, we'd like to share the same IP address among virtual sites, but still be able to tell the sites apart. But as we've seen, because most browsers send just the path component of the URL to servers, the critical virtual hostname information is lost.

To solve this problem, browser and server implementors extended HTTP to provide the original hostname to servers. But browsers couldn't just send a full URL, because that would break many servers that expected to receive only a path component. Instead, the hostname (and port) is passed in a Host extension header in all requests.

In Figure 18-5, client A and client B both send Host headers that carry the original hostname being accessed. When the server gets the request for *index.html*, it can use the Host header to decide which resources to use.

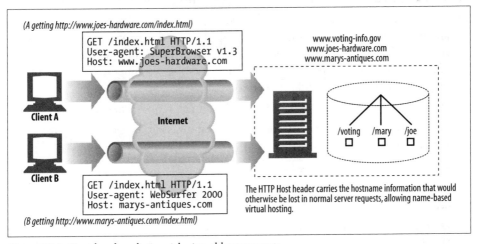

Figure 18-5. Host headers distinguish virtual host requests

Host headers were first introduced with HTTP/1.0+, a vendor-extended superset of HTTP/1.0. Host headers are required for HTTP/1.1 compliance. Host headers are supported by most modern browsers and servers, but there are still a few clients and servers (and robots) that don't support them.

## HTTP/1.1 Host Headers

The Host header is an HTTP/1.1 request header, defined in RFC 2068. Virtual servers are so common that most HTTP clients, even if they are not HTTP/1.1-compliant, implement the Host header.

### Syntax and usage

The Host header specifies the Internet host and port number for the resource being requested, as obtained from the original URL:

```
Host = "Host" ":" host [ ":" port ]
```

In particular:

- If the Host header does not contain a port, the default port for the scheme is assumed.
- If the URL contains an IP address, the Host header should contain the same address.
- If the URL contains a hostname, the Host header must contain the same name.
- If the URL contains a hostname, the Host header should *not* contain the IP address equivalent to the URL's hostname, because this will break virtually hosted servers, which layer multiple virtual sites over a single IP address.
- If the URL contains a hostname, the Host header should not contain another alias for this hostname, because this also will break virtually hosted servers.
- If the client is using an explicit proxy server, the client must include the name and port of the *origin* server in the Host header, *not* the proxy server. In the past, several web clients had bugs where the outgoing Host header was set to the hostname of the proxy, when the client's proxy setting was enabled. This incorrect behavior causes proxies and origin servers to misbehave.
- Web clients must include a Host header field in all request messages.
- Web proxies must add Host headers to request messages before forwarding them.
- HTTP/1.1 web servers must respond with a 400 status code to any HTTP/1.1 request message that lacks a Host header field.

Here is a sample HTTP request message used to fetch the home page of *www.joes-hardware.com*, along with the required Host header field:

```
GET http://www.joes-hardware.com/index.html HTTP/1.0
Connection: Keep-Alive
User-Agent: Mozilla/4.51 [en] (X11; U; IRIX 6.2 IP22)
```

```
Accept: image/gif, image/x-xbitmap, image/jpeg, image/pjpeg, image/png, */*
Accept-Encoding: gzip
Accept-Language: en
Host: www.joes-hardware.com
```

### Missing Host headers

A small percentage of old browsers in use do not send Host headers. If a virtual hosting server is using Host headers to determine which web site to serve, and no Host header is present, it probably will either direct the user to a default web page (such as the web page of the ISP) or return an error page suggesting that the user upgrade her browser.

### Interpreting Host headers

An origin server that isn't virtually hosted, and doesn't allow resources to differ by the requested host, may ignore the Host header field value. But any origin server that does differentiate resources based on the host must use the following rules for determining the requested resource on an HTTP/1.1 request:

1. If the URL in the HTTP request message is absolute (i.e., contains a scheme and host component), the value in the Host header is ignored in favor of the URL.

2. If the URL in the HTTP request message doesn't have a host, and the request contains a Host header, the value of the host/port is obtained from the Host header.

3. If no valid host can be determined through Steps 1 or 2, a 400 Bad Response response is returned to the client.

### Host headers and proxies

Some browser versions send incorrect Host headers, especially when configured to use proxies. For example, when configured to use a proxy, some older versions of Apple and PointCast clients mistakenly sent the name of the proxy instead of the origin server in the Host header.

# Making Web Sites Reliable

There are several times during which web sites commonly break:

- Server downtime
- Traffic spikes: suddenly everyone wants to see a particular news broadcast or rush to a sale. Sudden spikes can overload a web server, slowing it down or stopping it completely.
- Network outages or losses

This section presents some ways of anticipating and dealing with these common problems.

## Mirrored Server Farms

A server farm is a bank of identically configured web servers that can cover for each other. The content on each server in the farm can be mirrored, so that if one has a problem, another can fill in.

Often, mirrored servers follow a hierarchical relationship. One server might act as the "content authority"—the server that contains the original content (perhaps a server to which the content authors post). This server is called the *master origin server*. The mirrored servers that receive content from the master origin server are called *replica origin servers*. One simple way to deploy a server farm is to use a network switch to distribute requests to the servers. The IP address for each of the web sites hosted on the servers is the IP address of the switch.

In the mirrored server farm shown in Figure 18-6, the master origin server is responsible for sending content to the replica origin servers. To the outside world, the IP address for this content is the IP address of the switch. The switch is responsible for sending requests to the servers.

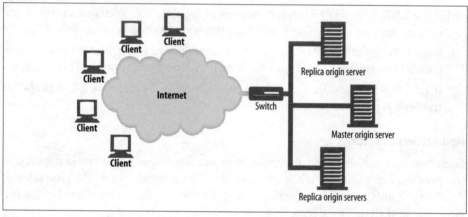

*Figure 18-6. Mirrored server farm*

Mirrored web servers can contain copies of the exact same content at different locations. Figure 18-7 illustrates four mirrored servers, with a master server in Chicago and replicas in New York, Miami, and Little Rock. The master server serves clients in the Chicago area and also has the job of propagating its content to the replica servers.

In the Figure 18-7 scenario, there are a couple of ways that client requests would be directed to a particular server:

*HTTP redirection*
    The URL for the content could resolve to the IP address of the master server, which could then send redirects to replica servers.

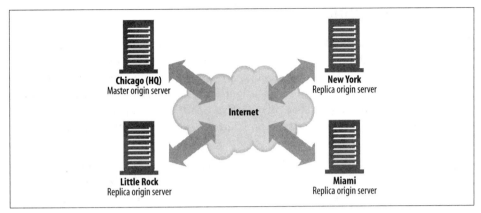

*Figure 18-7. Dispersed mirrored servers*

*DNS redirection*

The URL for the content could resolve to four IP addresses, and the DNS server could choose the IP address that it sends to clients.

See Chapter 20 for more details.

## Content Distribution Networks

A *content distribution network* (CDN) is simply a network whose purpose is the distribution of specific content. The nodes of the network can be web servers, surrogates, or proxy caches.

## Surrogate Caches in CDNs

Surrogate caches can be used in place of replica origin servers in Figures 18-6 and 18-7. Surrogates, also known as reverse proxies, receive server requests for content just as mirrored web servers do. They receive server requests on behalf of a specific set of origin servers (this is possible because of the way IP addresses for content are advertised; there usually is a working relationship between origin server and surrogate, and surrogates expect to receive requests aimed at specific origin servers).

The difference between a surrogate and a mirrored server is that surrogates typically are demand-driven. They do not store entire copies of the origin server content; they store whatever content their clients request. The way content is distributed in their caches depends on the requests that they receive; the origin server does not have the responsibility to update their content. For easy access to "hot" content (content that is in high demand), some surrogates have "prefetching" features that enable them to pull content in advance of user requests.

An added complexity in CDNs with surrogates is the possibility of cache hierarchies.

## Proxy Caches in CDNs

Proxy caches also can be deployed in configurations similar to those in Figures 18-6 and 18-7. Unlike surrogates, traditional proxy caches can receive requests aimed at any web servers (there need not be any working relationship or IP address agreement between a proxy cache and an origin server). As with surrogates, however, proxy cache content typically is demand-driven and is not expected to be an exact duplicate of the origin server content. Some proxy caches also can be preloaded with hot content.

Demand-driven proxy caches can be deployed in other kinds of configurations—in particular, interception configurations, where a layer-2 or -3 device (switch or router) intercepts web traffic and sends it to a proxy cache (see Figure 18-8).

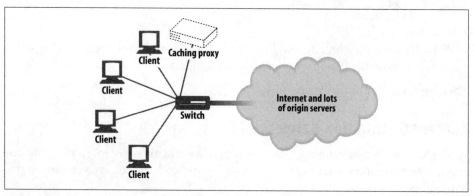

*Figure 18-8. Client requests intercepted by a switch and sent to a proxy*

An interception configuration depends on being able to set up the network between clients and servers so that all of the appropriate HTTP requests are physically channeled to the cache. (See Chapter 20). The content is distributed in the cache according to the requests it receives.

# Making Web Sites Fast

Many of the technologies mentioned in the previous section also help web sites load faster. Server farms and distributed proxy caches or surrogate servers distribute network traffic, avoiding congestion. Distributing the content brings it closer to end users, so that the travel time from server to client is lower. The key to speed of resource access is how requests and responses are directed from client to server and back across the Internet. See Chapter 20 for details on redirection methods.

Another approach to speeding up web sites is encoding the content for fast transportation. This can mean, for example, compressing the content, assuming that the receiving client can uncompress it. See Chapter 15 for details.

# For More Information

See Part III, *Identification, Authorization, and Security*, for details on how to make web sites secure. The following Internet drafts and documentation can give you more details about web hosting and content distribution:

*http://www.ietf.org/rfc/rfc3040.txt*
> RFC 3040, "Internet Web Replication and Caching Taxonomy," is a reference for the vocabulary of web replication and caching applications.

*http://search.ietf.org/internet-drafts/draft-ietf-cdi-request-routing-reqs-00.txt*
> "Request-Routing Requirements for Content Internetworking."

*Apache: The Definitive Guide*
> Ben Laurie and Peter Laurie, O'Reilly & Associates, Inc. This book describes how to run the open source Apache web server.

# CHAPTER 19
# Publishing Systems

How do you create web pages and get them onto a web server? In the dark ages of the Web (let's say, 1995), you might have hand-crafted your HTML in a text editor and manually uploaded the content to the web server using FTP. This procedure was painful, difficult to coordinate with coworkers, and not particularly secure.

Modern-day publishing tools make it much more convenient to create, publish, and manage web content. Today, you can interactively edit web content as you'll see it on the screen and publish that content to servers with a single click, while being notified of any files that have changed.

Many of the tools that support remote publishing of content use extensions to the HTTP protocol. In this chapter, we explain two important technologies for web-content publishing based on HTTP: FrontPage and DAV.

## FrontPage Server Extensions for Publishing Support

FrontPage (commonly referred to as FP) is a versatile web authoring and publishing toolkit provided by Microsoft Corp. The original idea for FrontPage (FrontPage 1.0) was conceived in 1994, at Vermeer Technologies, Inc., and was dubbed the first product to combine web site management and creation into a single, unified tool. Microsoft purchased Vermeer and shipped FrontPage 1.1 in 1996. The latest version, FrontPage Version 2002, is the sixth version in the line and a core part of the Microsoft Office suite.

### FrontPage Server Extensions

As part of the "publish anywhere" strategy, Microsoft released a set of server-side software called FrontPage Server Extensions (FPSE). These server-side components integrate with the web server and provide the necessary translation between the web site and the client running FrontPage (and other clients that support these extensions).

Our primary interest lies in the publishing protocol between the FP clients and FPSE. This protocol provides an example of designing extensions to the core services available in HTTP without changing HTTP semantics.

The FrontPage publishing protocol implements an RPC layer on top of the HTTP POST request. This allows the FrontPage client to send commands to the server to update documents on the web site, perform searches, collaborate amongst the web authors, etc. Figure 19-1 gives an overview of the communication.

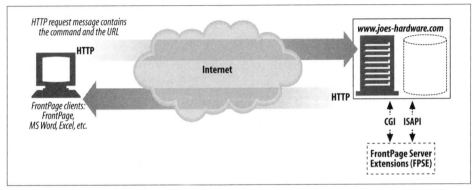

*Figure 19-1. FrontPage publishing architecture*

The web server sees POST requests addressed to the FPSE (implemented as a set of CGI programs, in the case of a non-Microsoft IIS server) and directs those requests accordingly. As long as intervening firewalls and proxy servers are configured to allow the POST method, FrontPage can continue communicating with the server.

## FrontPage Vocabulary

Before we dive deeper into the RPC layer defined by FPSE, it may help to establish the common vocabulary:

*Virtual server*
> One of the multiple web sites running on the same server, each with a unique domain name and IP address. In essence, a virtual server allows a single web server to host multiple web sites, each of which appears to a browser as being hosted by its own web server. A web server that supports virtual servers is called a *multi-hosting* web server. A machine that is configured with multiple IP addresses is called a *multi-homed* server (for more details, please refer to "Virtual Hosting" in Chapter 18).

*Root web*
> The default, top-level content directory of a web server, or, in a multi-hosting environment, the top-level content directory of a virtual web server. To access the root web, it is enough to specify the URL of the server without specifying a page name. There can be only one root web per web server.

*Subweb*

A named subdirectory of the root web or another subweb that is a complete FPSE extended web. A subweb can be a complete independent entity with the ability to specify its own administration and authoring permissions. In addition, subwebs may provide scoping for methods such as searches.

# The FrontPage RPC Protocol

The FrontPage client and FPSE communicate using a proprietary RPC protocol. This protocol is layered on top of HTTP POST by embedding the RPC methods and their associated variables in the body of the POST request.

To start the process, the client needs to determine the location and the name of the target programs on the server (the part of the FPSE package that can execute the POST request). It then issues a special GET request (see Figure 19-2).

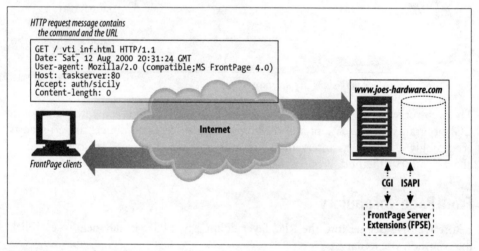

*Figure 19-2. Initial request*

When the file is returned, the FrontPage client reads the response and finds the values associated with FPShtmlScriptUrl, FPAuthorScriptUrl, and FPAdminScriptUrl. Typically, this may look like:

```
FPShtmlScriptUrl="_vti_bin/_vti_rpc/shtml.dll"
FPAuthorScriptUrl="_vti_bin/_vti_aut/author.dll"
FPAdminScriptUrl="_vti_bin/_vti_adm/admin.dll"
```

FPShtmlScriptUrl tells the client where to POST requests for "browse time" commands (e.g., getting the version of FPSE) to be executed.

FPAuthorScriptUrl tells the client where to POST requests for "authoring time" commands to be executed. Similarly, FPAdminScriptUrl tells FrontPage where to POST requests for administrative actions.

Now that we know where the various programs are located, we are ready to send a request.

### Request

The body of the POST request contains the RPC command, in the form of "method=<command>" and any required parameters. For example, consider the RPC message requesting a list of documents, as follows:

```
POST /_vti_bin/_vti_aut/author.dll HTTP/1.1
Date:  Sat, 12 Aug 2000 20:32:54 GMT
User-Agent: MSFrontPage/4.0
.........................................

<BODY>
method=list+documents%3a4%2e0%2e2%2e3717&service%5fname=&listHiddenDocs=false&listExp
lorerDocs=false&listRecurse=false&listFiles=true&listFolders=true&listLinkInfo=true&l
istIncludeParent=true&listDerived=false
&listBorders=false&listChildWebs=true&initialUrl=&folderList=%5b%3bTW%7c12+Aug+2000+2
0%3a33%3a04+%2d0000%5d
```

The body of the POST command contains the RPC command being sent to the FPSE. As with CGI programs, the spaces in the method are encoded as plus sign (+) characters. All other nonalphanumeric characters in the method are encoded using *%XX* format, where the *XX* stands for the ASCII representation of the character. Using this notation, a more readable version of the body would look like the following:

```
method=list+documents:4.0.1.3717
&service_name=
&listHiddenDocs=false
&listExplorerDocs=false
.....
```

Some of the elements listed are:

*service_name*
> The URL of the web site on which the method should act. Must be an existing folder or one level below an existing folder.

*listHiddenDocs*
> Shows the hidden documents in a web if its value is "true". The "hidden" documents are designated by URLs with path components starting with "_".

*listExploreDocs*
> If the value is "true", lists the task lists.

### Response

Most RPC protocol methods have return values. Most common return values are for successful methods and errors. Some methods also have a third subsection, "Sample Return Code." FrontPage properly interprets the codes to provide accurate feedback to the user.

Continuing with our example, the FPSE processes the "list+documents" request and returns the necessary information. A sample response follows:

```
HTTP/1.1 200 OK
Server: Microsoft-IIS/5.0
Date: Sat, 12 Aug 2000 22:49:50 GMT
Content-type: application/x-vermeer-rpc
X-FrontPage-User-Name: IUSER_MINSTAR

<html><head><title>RPC packet</title></head>
<body>
<p>method=list documents: 4.0.2.3717
<p>document_list=
<ul>
    <li>document_name=help.gif
<\ul>
```

As you can see from the response, a formatted list of documents available on the web server is returned to the FP client. You can find the complete list of commands and responses at the Microsoft web site.

## FrontPage Security Model

Any publishing system directly accessing web server content needs to be very conscious of the security implications of its actions. For the most part, FPSE depends on the web server to provide the security.

The FPSE security model defines three kinds of users: administrators, authors, and browsers, with administrators having complete control. All permissions are cumulative; i.e., all administrators may author and browse the FrontPage web. Similarly, all authors have browsing permissions.

The list of administrators, authors, and browsers is defined for a given FPSE extended web. All of the subwebs may inherit the permissions from the root web or set their own. For non-IIS web servers, all the FPSE programs are required to be stored in directories marked "executable" (the same restriction as for any other CGI program). *Fpsrvadm*, the FrontPage server administrator utility, may be used for this purpose. On IIS servers, the integrated Windows security model prevails.

On non-IIS servers, web server access-control mechanisms specify the users who are allowed to access a given program. On Apache and NCSA web servers, the file is named *.htaccess*; on Netscape servers, it is named *.nsconfig*. The access file associates users, groups, and IP addresses with various levels of permissions: GET (read), POST (execute), etc. For example, for a user to be an author on an Apache web server, the *.htaccess* file should permit that user to POST to *author.exe*. These access-specification files often are defined on a per-directory basis, providing greater flexibility in defining the permissions.

On IIS servers, the permissions are checked against the ACLs for a given root or subroot. When IIS gets a request, it first logs on and impersonates the user, then sends the request to one of the three extension dynamic link libraries (DLLs). The DLL checks the impersonation credentials against the ACL defined for the destination folder. If the check is successful, the requested operation is executed by the extension DLL. Otherwise, a "permission denied" message is sent back to the client. Given the tight integration of Windows security with IIS, the User Manager may be used to define fine-grained control.

In spite of this elaborate security model, enabling FPSE has gained notoriety as a nontrivial security risk. In most cases, this is due to sloppy practices adopted by web site administrators. However, the earlier versions of FPSE did have severe security loopholes and thus contributed to the general perception of security risk. This problem also was exacerbated by the arcane practices needed to fully implement a tight security model.

# WebDAV and Collaborative Authoring

Web Distributed Authoring and Versioning (WebDAV) adds an extra dimension to web publishing—collaboration. Currently, the most common practice of collaboration is decidedly low-tech: predominantly email, sometimes combined with distributed fileshares. This practice has proven to be very inconvenient and error-prone, with little or no control over the process. Consider an example of launching a multinational, multilingual web site for an automobile manufacturer. It's easy to see the need for a robust system with secure, reliable publishing primitives, along with collaboration primitives such as locking and versioning.

WebDAV (published as RFC 2518) is focused on extending HTTP to provide a suitable platform for collaborative authoring. It currently is an IETF effort with support from various vendors, including Adobe, Apple, IBM, Microsoft, Netscape, Novell, Oracle, and Xerox.

## WebDAV Methods

WebDAV defines a set of new HTTP methods and modifies the operational scope of a few other HTTP methods. The new methods added by WebDAV are:

*PROPFIND*
Retrieves the properties of a resource.

*PROPPATCH*
Sets one or more properties on one or many resources.

*MKCOL*
Creates collections.

*COPY*

Copies a resource or a collection of resources from a given source to a given destination. The destination need not be on the same machine.

*MOVE*

Moves a resource or a collection of resources from a given source to a given destination. The destination need not be on the same machine.

*LOCK*

Locks a resource or multiple resources.

*UNLOCK*

Unlocks a previously locked resource.

HTTP methods modified by WebDAV are DELETE, PUT, and OPTIONS. Both the new and the modified methods are discussed in detail later in this chapter.

## WebDAV and XML

WebDAV's methods generally require a great deal of information to be associated with both requests and responses. HTTP usually communicates this information in message headers. However, transporting necessary information in headers alone imposes some limitations, including the difficulties of selective application of header information to multiple resources in a request, to represent hierarchy, etc.

To solve this problem, WebDAV embraces the Extensible Markup Language (XML), a meta-markup language that provides a format for describing structured data. XML provides WebDAV with:

- A method of formatting instructions describing how data is to be handled
- A method of formatting complex responses from the server
- A method of communicating customized information about the collections and resources handled
- A flexible vehicle for the data itself
- A robust solution for most of the internationalization issues

Traditionally, the schema definition for XML documents is kept in a Document Type Definition (DTD) file that is referenced within the XML document itself. Therefore, when trying to interpret an XML document, the DOCTYPE definition entity gives the name of the DTD file associated with the XML document in question.

WebDAV defines an explicit XML namespace, "DAV:". Without going into many details, an XML namespace is a collection of names of elements or attributes. The namespace qualifies the embedded names uniquely across the domain, thus avoiding any name collisions.

The complete XML schema is defined in the WebDAV specification, RFC 2518. The presence of a predefined schema allows the parsing software to make assumptions on the XML schema without having to read in DTD files and interpret them correctly.

---

# WebDAV Headers

WebDAV does introduce several HTTP headers to augment the functionality of the new methods. This section provides a brief overview; see RFC 2518 for more information. The new headers are:

*DAV*

> Used to communicate the WebDAV capabilities of the server. All resources supported by WebDAV are required to return this header in the response to the OPTIONS request. See "The OPTIONS method" for more details.
>
> ```
> DAV = "DAV" ":" "1" ["," "2"] ["," 1#extend]
> ```

*Depth*

> The crucial element for extending WebDAV to grouped resources with multiple levels of hierarchy (for more detailed explanation about collections, please refer to "Collections and Namespace Management").
>
> ```
> Depth = "Depth" ":" ("0" | "1" | "infinity")
> ```
>
> Let's look at a simple example. Consider a directory *DIR_A* with files *file_1.html* and *file_2.html*. If a method uses Depth: 0, the method applies to the *DIR_A* directory alone, and Depth: 1 applies to the *DIR_A* directory and its files, *file_1.html* and *file_2.html*.
>
> The Depth header modifies many WebDAV-defined methods. Some of the methods that use the Depth header are LOCK, COPY, and MOVE.

*Destination*

> Defined to assist the COPY or MOVE methods in identifying the destination URI.
>
> ```
> Destination = "Destination" ":" absoluteURI
> ```

*If*

> The only defined state token is a lock token (see "The LOCK Method"). The If header defines a set of conditionals; if they all evaluate to false, the request will fail. Methods such as COPY and PUT conditionalize the applicability by specifying preconditions in the If header. In practice, the most common precondition to be satisfied is the prior acquisition of a lock.
>
> ```
> If = "If" ":" (1*No-tag-list | 1*Tagged-list)
>     No-tag-list = List
>     Tagged-list = Resource 1*List
>     Resource = Coded-URL
>     List = "(" 1*(["Not"](State-token | "[" entity-tag "]")) ")"
>     State-token = Coded-URL
>     Coded-URL = "<" absoluteURI ">"
> ```

*Lock-Token*

> Used by the UNLOCK method to specify the lock that needs to be removed. A response to a LOCK method also has a Lock-Token header, carrying the necessary information about the lock token.
>
> ```
> Lock-Token = "Lock-Token" ":" Coded-URL
> ```

*Overwrite*

> Used by the COPY and MOVE methods to designate whether the destination should be overwritten. See the discussion of the COPY and MOVE methods later in this chapter for more details.

```
Overwrite = "Overwrite" ":" ("T" | "F")
```

*Timeout*

> A request header used by a client to specify a desired lock timeout value. For more information, refer to the section "Lock refreshes and the Timeout header."

```
TimeOut = "Timeout" ":" 1#TimeType
TimeType = ("Second-" DAVTimeOutVal | "Infinite" | Other)
DAVTimeOutVal = 1*digit
Other = "Extend" field-value
```

Now that we have sketched the intent and implementation of WebDAV, let's look more closely at the functions provided.

## WebDAV Locking and Overwrite Prevention

By definition, collaboration requires more than one person working on a given document. The inherent problem associated with collaboration is illustrated in Figure 19-3.

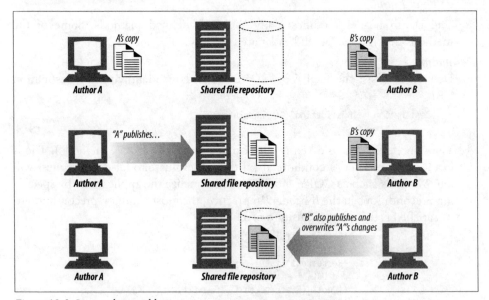

*Figure 19-3. Lost update problem*

In this example, authors A and B are jointly writing a specification. A and B independently make a set of changes to the document. A pushes the updated document to the repository, and at a later point, B posts her own version of the document into the repository. Unfortunately, because B never knew about A's changes, she never merged her version with A's version, resulting in A's work being lost.

To ameliorate the problem, WebDAV supports the concept of locking. Locking alone will not fully solve the problem. Versioning and messaging support are needed to complete the solution.

WebDAV supports two types of locks:

- Exclusive write locking of a resource or a collection
- Shared write locking of a resource or a collection

An *exclusive* write lock guarantees write privileges only to the lock owner. This type of locking completely eliminates potential conflicts. A *shared* write lock allows a group of people to work on a given document. This type of locking works well in an environment where all the authors are aware of each other's activities. WebDAV provides a property discovery mechanism, via PROPFIND, to determine the support for locking and the types of locks supported.

WebDAV has two new methods to support locking: LOCK and UNLOCK.

To accomplish locking, there needs to be a mechanism for identifying the author. WebDAV requires digest authentication (discussed in Chapter 13).

When a lock is granted, the server returns a token that is unique across the domain to the client. The specification refers to this as the opaquelocktoken lock token URI scheme. When the client subsequently wants to perform a write, it connects to the server and completes the digest authentication sequence. Once the authentication is complete, the WebDAV client presents the lock token, along with the PUT request. Thus, the combination of the correct user and the lock token is required to complete the write.

## The LOCK Method

A powerful feature of WebDAV is its ability to lock multiple resources with a single LOCK request. WebDAV locking does not require the client to stay connected to the server.

For example, here's a simple LOCK request:

```
LOCK /ch-publish.fm HTTP/1.1
Host: minstar
Content-Type: text/xml
User-Agent: Mozilla/4.0 (compatible; MSIE 5.0; Windows NT)
Content-Length: 201

<?xml version="1.0"?>
<a:lockinfo xmlns:a="DAV:">
    <a:lockscope><a:exclusive/></a:lockscope>
    <a:locktype><a:write/></a:locktype>
    <a:owner><a:href>AuthorA</a:href></a:owner>
</a:lockinfo>
```

The XML being submitted has the <lockinfo> element as its base element. Within the <lockinfo> structure, there are three subelements:

*<locktype>*

Indicates the type of lock. Currently there is only one, "write."

*<lockscope>*

Indicates whether this is an exclusive lock or a shared lock.

*<owner>*

Field is set with the person who holds the current lock.

Here's a successful response to our LOCK request:

```
HTTP/1.1 200 OK
Server: Microsoft-IIS/5.0
Date: Fri, 10 May 2002 20:56:18 GMT
Content-Type: text/xml
Content-Length: 419

<?xml version="1.0"?>
<a:prop xmlns:a="DAV:">
<a:lockdiscovery><a:activelock>
<a:locktype><a:write/></a:locktype>
<a:lockscope><a:exclusive/></a:lockscope>
<a:owner xmlns:a="DAV:"><a:href>AutherA</a:href></a:owner>
<a:locktoken><a:href>opaquelocktoken:*****</a:href></a:locktoken>
<a:depth>0</a:depth>
<a:timeout>Second-180</a:timeout>
</a:activelock></a:lockdiscovery>
</a:prop>
```

The <lockdiscovery> element acts as a container for information about the lock. Embedded in the <lockdiscovery> element is an <activelock> subelement that holds the information sent with the request (<locktype>, <lockscope>, and <owner>). In addition, <activelock> has the following subelements:

*<locktoken>*

Uniquely identifies the lock in a URI scheme called opaquelocktoken. Given the stateless nature of HTTP, this token is used to identify the ownership of the lock in future requests.

*<depth>*

Mirrors the value of the Depth header.

*<timeout>*

Indicates the timeout associated with the lock. In the above response (Figure 19-3), the timeout value is 180 seconds.

### The opaquelocktoken scheme

The opaquelocktoken scheme is designed to provide a unique token across all resources for all times. To guarantee uniqueness, the WebDAV specification mandates the use of the universal unique identifier (UUID) mechanism, as described in ISO-11578.

When it comes to actual implementation, there is some leeway. The server has the choice of generating a UUID for each LOCK request, or generating a single UUID and maintaining the uniqueness by appending extra characters at the end. For performance considerations, the latter choice is better. However, if the server chooses to implement the latter choice, it is required to guarantee that none of the added extensions will ever be reused.

### The <lockdiscovery> XML element

The <lockdiscovery> XML element provides a mechanism for active lock discovery. If others try to lock the file while a lock is in place, they will receive a <lockdiscovery> XML element that indicates the current owner. The <lockdiscovery> element lists all outstanding locks along with their properties.

### Lock refreshes and the Timeout header

To refresh a lock, a client needs to resubmit a lock request with the lock token in the If header. The timeout value returned may be different from the earlier timeout values.

Instead of accepting the timeout value given by the server, a client may indicate the timeout value required in the LOCK request. This is done through the Timeout header. The syntax of the Timeout header allows the client to specify a few options in a comma-separated list. For example:

```
Timeout : Infinite, Second-86400
```

The server is not obligated to honor either of the options. However, it is required to provide the lock expiration time in the <timeout> XML element. In all cases, lock timeout is only a guideline and is not necessarily binding on the server. The administrator may do a manual reset, or some other extraordinary event may cause the server to reset the lock. The clients should avoid taking lengthy locks.

In spite of these primitives, we may not completely solve the "lost update problem" illustrated in Figure 19-3. To completely solve it, a cooperative event system with a versioning control is needed.

## The UNLOCK Method

The UNLOCK method removes a lock on a resource, as follows:

```
UNLOCK /ch-publish.fm HTTP/1.1
Host: minstar.inktomi.com
User-Agent: Mozilla/4.0 (compatible; MSIE 5.0; Windows NT)
Lock-Token:
opaquelocktoken:*********

HTTP/1.1 204 OK
Server: Microsoft-IIS/5.0
Date: Fri, 10 May 2002 20:56:18 GMT
```

As with most resource management requests, WebDAV has two requirements for UNLOCK to succeed: prior completion of a successful digest authentication sequence, and matching the lock token that is sent in the Lock-Token header.

If the unlock is successful, a 204 No Content status code is returned to client. Table 19-1 summarizes the possible status codes with the LOCK and UNLOCK methods.

*Table 19-1. Status codes for LOCK and UNLOCK methods*

| Status code | Defined by | Method | Effect |
| --- | --- | --- | --- |
| 200 OK | HTTP | LOCK | Indicates successful locking. |
| 201 Created | HTTP | LOCK | Indicates that a lock on a nonexistent resource succeeded by creating the resource. |
| 204 No Content | HTTP | UNLOCK | Indicates successful unlocking. |
| 207 Multi-Status | WebDAV | LOCK | The request was for locking multiple resources. Not all status codes returned were the same. Hence, they are all encapsulated in a 207 response. |
| 403 Forbidden | HTTP | LOCK | Indicates that the client does not have permission to lock the resource. |
| 412 Precondition Failed | HTTP | LOCK | Either the XML sent with the LOCK command indicated a condition to be satisfied and the server failed to complete the required condition, or the lock token could not be enforced. |
| 422 Unprocessable Property | WebDAV | LOCK | Inapplicable semantics—an example may be specifying a non-zero Depth for a resource that is not a collection. |
| 423 Locked | WebDAV | LOCK | Already locked. |
| 424 Failed Dependency | WebDAV | UNLOCK | UNLOCK specifies other actions and their success as a condition for the unlocking. This error is returned if the dependency fails to complete. |

## Properties and META Data

Properties describe information about the resource, including the author's name, modification date, content rating, etc. META tags in HTML do provide a mechanism to embed this information as part of the content; however, many resources (such as any binary data) have no capability for embedding META data.

A distributed collaborative system such as WebDAV adds more complexity to the property requirement. For example, consider an author property: when a document gets edited, this property needs to be updated to reflect the new authors. WebDAV terms such dynamically modifiable properties "live" properties. The more permanent, static properties, such as Content-Type, are termed "dead" properties.

To support discovery and modification of properties, WebDAV extends HTTP to include two new methods, PROPFIND and PROPPATCH. Examples and corresponding XML elements are described in the following sections.

# The PROPFIND Method

The PROPFIND (property find) method is used for retrieving the properties of a given file or a group of files (also known as a "collection"). PROPFIND supports three types of operations:

- Request all properties and their values.
- Request a selected set of properties and values.
- Request all property names.

Here's the scenario where all the properties and their values are requested:

```
PROPFIND /ch-publish.fm HTTP/1.1
Host: minstar.inktomi.com
User-Agent: Mozilla/4.0 (compatible; MSIE 5.0; Windows NT)
Depth: 0
Cache-Control: no-cache
Connection: Keep-Alive
Content-Length: 0
```

The <propfind> request element specifies the properties to be returned from a PROPFIND method. The following list summarizes a few XML elements that are used with PROPFIND requests:

*<allprop>*
Requires all property names and values to be returned. To request all properties and their values, a WebDAV client may either send an <allprop> XML subelement as part of the <propfind> element, or submit a request with no body.

*<propname>*
Specifies the set of property names to be returned.

*<prop>*
A subelement of the <propfind> element. Specifies a specific property whose value is to be returned. For example: "<a:prop> <a:owner />..... </a:prop>".

Here's a response to a sample PROPFIND request:

```
HTTP/1.1 207 Multi-Status
Server: Microsoft-IIS/5.0
..........

<?xml version="1.0"?>
<a:multistatusxmlns:b="urn:uuid:*******/" xmlns:c="xml:" xmlns:a="DAV:">
<a:response>
  <a:href>http://minstar/ch-publish.fm </a:href>
  <a:propstat>
    <a:status>HTTP/1.1 200OK</a:status>
    <a:prop>
      <a:getcontentlength b:dt="int">1155</a:getcontentlength>
      ......................
      ......................
```

```
        <a:ishidden b:dt="boolean">0</a:ishidden>
        <a:iscollection b:dt="boolean">0</a:iscollection>
      </a:prop>
    </a:propstat>
  </a:response></a:multistatus>
```

In this example, the server responds with a 207 Multi-Status code. WebDAV uses the 207 response for PROPFIND and a few other WebDAV methods that act simultaneously on multiple resources and potentially have different responses for each resource.

A few XML elements in the response need to be defined:

*<multistatus>*
  A container for multiple responses.

*<href>*
  Identifies the resource's URI.

*<status>*
  Contains the HTTP status code for the particular request.

*<propstat>*
  Groups one <status> element and one <prop> element. The <prop> element may contain one or more property name/value pairs for the given resource.

In the sample response listed above, the response is for one URI, *http://minstar/ch-publish.fm*. The <propstat> element embeds one <status> element and one <prop> element. For this URI, the server returned a 200 OK response, as defined by the <status> element. The <prop> element has several subelements; only some are listed in the example.

One instant application of PROPFIND is the support for directory listing. Given the expressability of a PROPFIND request, one single call can retrieve the entire hierarchy of the collection with all the properties of individual entities.

## The PROPPATCH Method

The PROPPATCH method provides an atomic mechanism to set or remove multiple properties on a given resource. The atomicity will guarantee that either all of the requests are successful or none of them made it.

The base XML element for the PROPPATCH method is <propertyupdate>. It acts as a container for all the properties that need updating. The XML elements <set> and <remove> are used to specify the operation:

*<set>*
  Specifies the property values to be set. The <set> contains one or more <prop> subelements, which in turn contains the name/value pairs of the properties to be set for the resource. If the property already exists, the value is replaced.

*<remove>*

Specifies the properties that are to be removed. Unlike with <set>, only the names of the properties are listed in the <prop> container.

This trivial example sets and removes the "owner" property:

```
<d:propertyupdate xmlns:d="DAV:" xmlns:o="http://name-space/scheme/">
  <d:set>
    <d:prop>
      <o:owner>Author A</o:owner>
    </d:prop>
  </d:set>

  <d:remove>
    <d:prop>
      <o:owner/>
    </d:prop>
  </d:remove>
</d:propertyupdate>
```

The response to PROPPATCH requests is very similar to that for PROPFIND requests. For more information, refer to RFC 2518.

Table 19-2 summarizes the status codes for the PROPFIND and PROPPATCH methods.

*Table 19-2. Status codes for PROPFIND and PROPPATCH methods*

| Status code | Defined by | Methods | Effect |
|---|---|---|---|
| 200 OK | HTTP | PROPFIND, PROPPATCH | Command success. |
| 207 Multi-Status | WEBDAV | PROPFIND, PROPPATCH | When acting on one or more resources (or a collection), the status for each object is encapsulated into one 207 response. This is a typical success response. |
| 401 Unauthorized | HTTP | PROPATCH | Requires authorization to complete the property modification operation. |
| 403 Forbidden | HTTP | PROPFIND, PROPPATCH | For PROPFIND, the client is not allowed to access the property. For PROPPATCH, the client may not change the property. |
| 404 Not Found | HTTP | PROPFIND | No such property. |
| 409 Conflict | HTTP | PROPPATCH | Conflict of update semantics—for example, trying to update a read-only property. |
| 423 Locked | WebDAV | PROPPATCH | Destination resource is locked and there is no lock token or the lock token does not match. |
| 507 Insufficient Storage | WebDAV | PROPPATCH | Not enough space for registering the modified property. |

## Collections and Namespace Management

A collection refers to a logical or physical grouping of resources in a predefined hierachy. A classic example of a collection is a directory. Like directories in a filesystem, collections act as containers of other resources, including other collections (equivalent to directories on the filesystem).

WebDAV uses the XML namespace mechanism. Unlike traditional namespaces, XML namespace partitions allow for precise structural control while preventing any namespace collisions.

WebDAV provides five methods for manipulating the namespace: DELETE, MKCOL, COPY, MOVE, and PROPFIND. PROPFIND was discussed previously in this chapter, but let's talk about the other methods.

## The MKCOL Method

The MKCOL method allows clients to create a collection at the indicated URL on the server. At first sight, it may seem rather redundant to define an entire new method just for creating a collection. Overlaying on top of a PUT or POST method seems like a perfect alternative. The designers of the WebDAV protocol did consider these alternatives and still chose to define a new method. Some of the reasons behind that decision are:

- To have a PUT or a POST create a collection, the client needs to send some extra "semantic glue" along with the request. While this certainly is feasible, defining an ad hoc protocol may become tedious and error-prone.

- Most of the access-control mechanisms are based on the type of methods—only a few are allowed to create and delete resources in the repository. If we overload other methods, these access-control mechanisms will not work.

For example, a request might be:

```
MKCOL /publishing HTTP/1.1
Host: minstar
Content-Length: 0
Connection: Keep-Alive
```

And the response might be:

```
HTTP/1.1 201 Created
Server: Microsoft-IIS/5.0
Date: Fri, 10 May 2002 23:20:36 GMT
Location: http://minstar/publishing/
Content-Length: 0
```

Let us examine a few pathological cases:

- Suppose the collection already exists. If a MKCOL /colA request is made and colA already exists (i.e., namespace conflict), the request will fail with a 405 Method Not Allowed status code.

- If there are no write permissions, the MKCOL request will fail with a 403 Forbidden status code.

- If a request such as MKCOL /colA/colB is made and colA does not exist, the request will fail with a 409 Conflict status code.

Once the file or collection is created, we can delete it with the DELETE method.

## The DELETE Method

We already saw the DELETE method in Chapter 3. WebDAV extends the semantics to cover collections.

If we need to delete a directory, the Depth header is needed. If the Depth header is not specified, the DELETE method assumes the Depth header to be set to infinity—that is, all the files in the directory and any subdirectories thereof are deleted. The response also has a Content-Location header identifying the collection that just got deleted. The request might read:

```
DELETE /publishing HTTP/1.0
Host: minstar
```

And the response might read:

```
HTTP/1.1 200 OK
Server: Microsoft-IIS/5.0
Date: Tue, 14 May 2002 16:41:44 GMT
Content-Location: http://minstar/publishing/
Content-Type: text/xml
Content-Length: 0
```

When removing collections, there always is a chance that a file in the collection is locked by someone else and can't be deleted. In such a case, the collection itself can't be deleted, and the server replies with a 207 Multi-Status status code. The request might read:

```
DELETE /publishing HTTP/1.0
Host: minstar
```

And the response might read:

```
HTTP/1.1 207 Multi-Status
Server: Microsoft-IIS/5.0
Content-Location: http://minstar/publishing/
..............
<?xml version="1.0"?>
<a:multistatus xmlns:a="DAV:">
<a:response>
<a:href>http://minstar/index3/ch-publish.fm</a:href>
<a:status> HTTP/1.1 423 Locked </a:status>
</a:response>
</a:multistatus>
```

In this transaction, the <status> XML element contains the status code 423 Locked, indicating that the resource *ch-publish.fm* is locked by another user.

# The COPY and MOVE Methods

As with MKCOL, there are alternatives to defining new methods for COPY and MOVE operations. One such alternative for the COPY method is to do a GET request on the source, thus downloading the resource, and then to upload it back to the server with a PUT request. A similar scenario could be envisioned for MOVE (with the additional DELETE operation). However, this process does not scale well—consider all the issues involved in managing a COPY or MOVE operation on a multilevel collection.

Both the COPY and MOVE methods use the request URL as the source and the contents of the Destination HTTP header as the target. The MOVE method performs some additional work beyond that of the COPY method: it copies the source URL to the destination, checks the integrity of the newly created URI, and then deletes the source. The request might read:

```
{COPY,MOVE} /publishing HTTP/1.1
Destination: http://minstar/pub-new
Depth: infinity
Overwrite: T
Host: minstar
```

And the response might read:

```
HTTP/1.1 201 Created
Server: Microsoft-IIS/5.0
Date: Wed, 15 May 2002 18:29:53 GMT
Location: http://minstar.inktomi.com/pub-new/
Content-Type: text/xml
Content-Length: 0
```

When acting on a collection, the behavior of COPY or MOVE is affected by the Depth header. In the absence of the Depth header, infinity is assumed (i.e., by default, the entire structure of the source directory will be copied or moved). If the Depth is set to zero, the method is applied just to the resource. If we are doing a copy or a move of a collection, only a collection with properties identical to those of the source is created at the destination—no internal members of the collection are copied or moved.

For obvious reasons, only a Depth value of infinity is allowed with the MOVE method.

## Overwrite header effect

The COPY and MOVE methods also may use the Overwrite header. The Overwrite header can be set to either T or F. If it's set to T and the destination exists, a DELETE with a Depth value of infinity is performed on the destination resource before a COPY or MOVE operation. If the Overwrite flag is set to F and the destination resource exists, the operation will fail.

## COPY/MOVE of properties

When a collection or an element is copied, all of its properties are copied by default. However, a request may contain an optional XML body that supplies additional information for the operation. You can specify that all properties must be copied successfully for the operation to succeed, or define which properties must be copied for the operation to succeed.

A couple of pathological cases to consider are:

- Suppose COPY or MOVE is applied to the output of a CGI program or other script that generates content. To preserve the semantics, if a file generated by a CGI script is to be copied or moved, WebDAV provides "src" and "link" XML elements that point to the location of the program that generated the page.

- The COPY and MOVE methods may not be able to completely duplicate all of the live properties. For example, consider a CGI program. If it is copied away from the *cgi-bin* directory, it may no longer be executed. The current specification of WebDAV makes COPY and MOVE a "best effort" solution, copying all the static properties and the appropriate live properties.

## Locked resources and COPY/MOVE

If a resource currently is locked, both COPY and MOVE are prohibited from moving or duplicating the lock at the destination. In both cases, if the destination is to be created under an existing collection with its own lock, the duplicated or moved resource is added to the lock. Consider the following example:

```
COPY /publishing HTTP/1.1
Destination: http://minstar/archived/publishing-old
```

Let's assume that */publishing* and */archived* already are under two different locks, lock1 and lock2. When the COPY operation completes, */publishing* continues to be under the scope of lock1, while, by virtue of moving into a collection that's already locked by lock2, *publishing-old* gets added to lock2. If the operation was a MOVE, just *publishing-old* gets added to lock2.

Table 19-3 lists most of the possible status codes for the MKCOL, DELETE, COPY, and MOVE methods.

*Table 19-3. Status codes for the MKCOL, DELETE, COPY, and MOVE methods*

| Status code | Defined by | Methods | Effect |
| --- | --- | --- | --- |
| 102 Processing | WebDAV | MOVE, COPY | If the request takes longer than 20 seconds, the server sends this status code to keep clients from timing out. This usually is seen with a COPY or MOVE of a large collection. |
| 201 Created | HTTP | MKCOL, COPY, MOVE | For MKCOL, a collection has been created. For COPY and MOVE, a resource/collection was copied or moved successfully. |

| Status code | Defined by | Methods | Effect |
|---|---|---|---|
| 204 No Content | HTTP | DELETE, COPY, MOVE | For DELETE, a standard success response. For COPY and MOVE, the resource was copied over successfully or moved to replace an existing entity. |
| 207 Multi-Status | WebDAV | MKCOL, COPY, MOVE | For MKCOL, a typical success response. For COPY and MOVE, if an error is associated with a resource other than the request URI, the server returns a 207 response with the XML body detailing the error. |
| 403 Forbidden | HTTP | MKCOL, COPY, MOVE | For MKCOL, the server does not allow creation of a collection at the specified location. For COPY and MOVE, the source and destination are the same. |
| 409 Conflict | HTTP | MKCOL, COPY, MOVE | In all cases, the methods are trying to create a collection or a resource when an intermediate collection does not exist—for example, trying to create colA/colB when colA does not exist. |
| 412 Precondition Failed | HTTP | COPY, MOVE | Either the Overwrite header is set to F and the destination exists, or the XML body specifies a certain requirement (such as keeping the "liveness" property) and the COPY or MOVE methods are not able to retain the property. |
| 415 Unsupported Media Type | HTTP | MKCOL | The server does not support or understand the creation of the request entity type. |
| 422 Unprocessable Entity | WebDAV | MKCOL | The server does not understand the XML body sent with the request. |
| 423 Locked | WebDAV | DELETE, COPY, MOVE | The source or the destination resource is locked, or the lock token supplied with the method does not match. |
| 502 Bad Gateway | HTTP | COPY, MOVE | The destination is on a different server and permissions are missing. |
| 507 Insufficient Storage | WebDAV | MKCOL COPY | There is not enough free space to create the resource. |

# Enhanced HTTP/1.1 Methods

WebDAV modifies the semantics of the HTTP methods DELETE, PUT, and OPTIONS. Semantics for the GET and HEAD methods remain unchanged. Operations performed by POST always are defined by the specific server implementation, and WebDAV does not modify any of the POST semantics. We already covered the DELETE method, in "Collections and Namespace Management." We'll discuss the PUT and OPTIONS methods here.

### The PUT method

Though PUT is not defined by WebDAV, it is the only way for an author to transport the content to a shared site. We discussed the general functionality of PUT in Chapter 3. WebDAV modifies its behavior to support locking.

Consider the following example:

```
PUT /ch-publish.fm HTTP/1.1
Accept: */*
If:<http://minstar/index.htm>(<opaquelocktoken:*******>)
User-Agent: DAV Client (C)
Host: minstar.inktomi.com
Connection: Keep-Alive
Cache-Control: no-cache
Content-Length: 1155
```

To support locking, WebDAV adds an If header to the PUT request. In the above transaction, the semantics of the If header state that if the lock token specified with the If header matches the lock on the resource (in this case, *ch-publish.fm*), the PUT operation should be performed. The If header also is used with a few other methods, such as PROPPATCH, DELETE, MOVE, LOCK, UNLOCK, etc.

### The OPTIONS method

We discussed OPTIONS in Chapter 3. This usually is the first request a WebDAV-enabled client makes. Using the OPTIONS method, the client tries to establish the capability of the WebDAV server. Consider a transaction in which the request reads:

```
OPTIONS /ch-publish.fm HTTP/1.1
Accept: */*
Host: minstar.inktomi.com
```

And the response reads:

```
HTTP/1.1 200 OK
Server: Microsoft-IIS/5.0
MS-Author-Via: DAV
DASL: <DAV:sql>
DAV: 1, 2
Public: OPTIONS, TRACE, GET, HEAD, DELETE, PUT, POST, COPY, MOVE, MKCOL,PROPFIND,
PROPPATCH, LOCK, UNLOCK, SEARCH
Allow: OPTIONS, TRACE, GET, HEAD, DELETE, PUT, COPY, MOVE, PROPFIND,PROPPATCH,
SEARCH, LOCK, UNLOCK
```

There are several interesting headers in the response to the OPTIONS method. A slightly out-of-order examination follows:

- The DAV header carries the information about DAV compliance classes. There are two classes of compliance:

  *Class 1 compliance*
  Requires the server to comply with all MUST requirements in all sections of RFC 2518. If the resource complies only at the Class 1 level, it will send 1 with the DAV header.

  *Class 2 compliance*
  Meets all the Class 1 requirements and adds support for the LOCK method. Along with LOCK, Class 2 compliance requires support for the Timeout and

Lock-Token headers and the <supportedlock> and <lockdiscovery> XML elements. A value of 2 in the DAV header indicates Class 2 compliance.

In the above example, the DAV header indicates both Class 1 and Class 2 compliance.

- The Public header lists all methods supported by this particular server.
- The Allow header usually contains a subset of the Public header methods. It lists only those methods that are allowed on this particular resource (*ch-publish.fm*).
- The DASL header provides the type of query grammar used in the SEARCH method. In this case, it is sql. More details about the DASL header are provided at *http://www.webdav.org*.

## Version Management in WebDAV

It may be ironic, given the "V" in "DAV," but versioning is a feature that did not make the first cut. In a multi-author, collaborative environment, version management is critical. In fact, to completely fix the lost update problem (illustrated in Figure 19-3), locking and versioning are essential. Some of the common features associated with versioning are the ability to store and access previous document versions and the ability to manage the change history and any associated annotations detailing the changes.

Versioning was added to WebDAV in RFC 3253.

## Future of WebDAV

WebDAV is well supported today. Working implementations of clients include IE 5.x and above, Windows Explorer, and Microsoft Office. On the server side, implementations include IIS5.x and above, Apache with mod_dav, and many others. Both Windows XP and Mac OS 10.x provide support for WebDAV out of the box; thus, any applications written to run on these operating systems are WebDAV-enabled natively.

## For More Information

For more information, refer to:

*http://officeupdate.microsoft.com/frontpage/wpp/serk/*

Microsoft FrontPage 2000 Server Extensions Resource Kit.

*http://www.ietf.org/rfc/rfc2518.txt?number=2518*

"HTTP Extensions for Distributed Authoring—WEBDAV," by Y. Goland, J. Whitehead, A. Faizi, S. Carter, and D. Jensen.

*http://www.ietf.org/rfc/rfc3253.txt?number=3253*

"Versioning Extensions to WebDAV," by G. Clemm, J. Amsden, T. Ellison, C. Kaler, and J. Whitehead.

*http://www.ics.uci.edu/pub/ietf/webdav/intro/webdav_intro.pdf*

"WEBDAV: IETF Standard for Collaborative Authoring on the Web," by J. Whitehead and M. Wiggins.

*http://www.ics.uci.edu/~ejw/http-future/whitehead/http_pos_paper.html*

"Lessons from WebDAV for the Next Generation Web Infrastructure," by J. Whitehead.

*http://www.microsoft.com/msj/0699/dav/davtop.htm*

"Distributed Authoring and Versioning Extensions for HTTP Enable Team Authoring," by L. Braginski and M. Powell.

*http://www.webdav.org/dasl/protocol/draft-dasl-protocol-00.html*

"DAV Searching & Locating," by S. Reddy, D. Lowry, S. Reddy, R. Henderson, J. Davis, and A. Babich.

# CHAPTER 20
# Redirection and Load Balancing

HTTP does not walk the Web alone. The data in an HTTP message is governed by many protocols on its journey. HTTP cares only about the endpoints of the journey—the sender and the receiver—but in a world with mirrored servers, web proxies, and caches, the destination of an HTTP message is not necessarily straightforward.

This chapter is about redirection technologies—network tools, techniques, and protocols that determine the final destination of an HTTP message. Redirection technologies usually determine whether the message ends up at a proxy, a cache, or a particular web server in a server farm. Redirection technologies may send your messages to places a client didn't explicitly request.

In this chapter, we'll take a look at the following redirection techniques, how they work, and what their load-balancing capabilities are (if any):

- HTTP redirection
- DNS redirection
- Anycast routing
- Policy routing
- IP MAC forwarding
- IP address forwarding
- The Web Cache Coordination Protocol (WCCP)
- The Intercache Communication Protocol (ICP)
- The Hyper Text Caching Protocol (HTCP)
- The Network Element Control Protocol (NECP)
- The Cache Array Routing Protocol (CARP)
- The Web Proxy Autodiscovery Protocol (WPAD)

# Why Redirect?

Redirection is a fact of life in the modern Web because HTTP applications always want to do three things:

- Perform HTTP transactions reliably
- Minimize delay
- Conserve network bandwidth

For these reasons, web content often is distributed in multiple locations. This is done for reliability, so that if one location fails, another is available; it is done to lower response times, because if clients can access a nearer resource, they receive their requested content faster; and it's done to lower network congestion, by spreading out target servers. You can think of redirection as a set of techniques that help to find the "best" distributed content.

The subject of load balancing is included because redirection and load balancing coexist. Most redirection deployments include some form of load balancing; that is, they are capable of spreading incoming message load among a set of servers. Conversely, any form of load balancing involves redirection, because incoming messages must somehow be somehow among the servers sharing the load.

# Where to Redirect

Servers, proxies, caches, and gateways all appear to clients as servers, in the sense that a client sends them an HTTP request, and they process it. Many redirection techniques work for servers, proxies, caches, and gateways because of their common, server-like traits. Other redirection techniques are specially designed for a particular class of endpoint and are not generally applicable. We'll see general techniques and specialized techniques in later sections of this chapter.

Web servers handle requests on a per-IP basis. Distributing requests to duplicate servers means that each request for a specific URL should be sent to an optimal web server (the one nearest to the client, or the least-loaded one, or some other optimization). Redirecting to a server is like sending all drivers in search of gasoline to the nearest gas station.

Proxies tend to handle requests on a per-protocol basis. Ideally, all HTTP traffic in the neighborhood of a proxy should go through the proxy. For instance, if a proxy cache is near various clients, all requests ideally will flow through the proxy cache, because the cache will store popular documents and serve them directly, avoiding longer and more expensive trips to the origin servers. Redirecting to a proxy is like siphoning off traffic on a main access road (no matter where it is headed) to a local shortcut.

# Overview of Redirection Protocols

The goal of redirection is to send HTTP messages to available web servers as quickly as possible. The direction that an HTTP message takes on its way through the Internet is affected by the HTTP applications and routing devices it passes from, through, and toward. For example:

- The browser application that creates the client's message could be configured to send it to a proxy server.
- DNS resolvers choose the IP address that is used for addressing the message. This IP address can be different for different clients in different geographical locations.
- As the message passes through networks, it is divided into addressed packets; switches and routers examine the TCP/IP addressing on the packets and make decisions about routing the packets on that basis.
- Web servers can bounce requests back to different web servers with HTTP redirects.

Browser configuration, DNS, TCP/IP routing, and HTTP all provide mechanisms for redirecting messages. Notice that some methods, such as browser configuration, make sense only for redirecting traffic to proxies, while others, such as DNS redirection, can be used to send traffic to any server.

Table 20-1 summarizes the redirection methods used to redirect messages to servers, each of which is discussed later in this chapter.

*Table 20-1. General redirection methods*

| Mechanism | How it works | Basis for rerouting | Limitations |
|---|---|---|---|
| HTTP redirection | Initial HTTP request goes to a first web server that chooses a "best" web server to serve the content. The first web server sends the client an HTTP redirect to the chosen server. The client resends the request to the chosen server. | Many options, from round-robin load balancing, to minimizing latency, to choosing the shortest path. | Can be slow—every transaction involves the extra redirect step. Also, the first server must be able to handle the request load. |
| DNS redirection | DNS server decides which IP address, among several, to return for the hostname in the URL. | Many options, from round-robin load balancing, to minimizing latency, to choosing the shortest path. | Need to configure DNS server. |
| Anycast addressing | Several servers use the same IP address. Each server masquerades as a backbone router. The other routers send packets addressed to the shared IP to the nearest server (believing they are sending packets to the nearest router). | Routers use built-in shortest-path routing capabilities. | Need to own/configure routers. Risks address conflicts. Established TCP connections can break if routing changes and packets associated with a connection get sent to different servers. |

*Table 20-1. General redirection methods (continued)*

| Mechanism | How it works | Basis for rerouting | Limitations |
|---|---|---|---|
| IP MAC forwarding | A network element such as a switch or router reads a packet's destination address; if the packet should be redirected, the switch gives the packet the destination MAC address of a server or proxy. | Save bandwidth and improve QOS. Load balance. | Server or proxy must be one hop away. |
| IP address forwarding | Layer-4 switch evaluates a packet's destination port and changes the IP address of a redirect packet to that of a proxy or mirrored server. | Save bandwidth and improve QOS. Load balance. | IP address of the client can be lost to the server/proxy. |

Table 20-2 summarizes the redirection methods used to redirect messages to proxy servers.

*Table 20-2. Proxy and cache redirection techniques*

| Mechanism | How it works | Basis for rerouting | Limitations |
|---|---|---|---|
| Explicit browser configuration | Web browser is configured to send HTTP messages to a nearby proxy, usually a cache. The configuration can be done by the end user or by a service that manages the browser. | Save bandwidth and improve QOS. Load balance. | Depends on ability to configure the browser. |
| Proxy auto-configuration (PAC) | Web browser retrieves a PAC file from a configuration server. The PAC file tells the browser what proxy to use for each URL. | Save bandwidth and improve QOS. Load balance. | Browser must be configured to query the configuration server. |
| Web Proxy Autodiscovery Protocol (WPAD) | Web browser asks a configuration server for the URL of a PAC file. Unlike PAC alone, the browser does not have to be configured with a specific configuration server. | The configuration server bases the URL on information in client HTTP request headers. Load balance. | Only a few browsers support WPAD. |
| Web Cache Coordination Protocol (WCCP) | Router evaluates a packet's destination address and encapsulates redirect packets with the IP address of a proxy or mirrored server. Works with many existing routers. Packet can be encapsulated, so the client's IP address is not lost. | Save bandwidth and improve QOS. Load balance. | Must use routers that support WCCP. Some topological limitations. |
| Internet Cache Protocol (ICP) | A proxy cache can query a group of sibling caches for requested content. Also supports cache hierarchies. | Obtaining content from a sibling or parent cache is faster than applying to the origin server. | False cache hits can arise because only the URL is used to request content. |
| Cache Array Routing Protocol (CARP) | A proxy cache hashing protocol. Allows a cache to forward a request to a parent cache. Unlike with ICP, the content on the caches is disjoint, and the group of caches acts as a single large cache. | Obtaining content from a nearby peer cache is faster than applying to the origin server. | CARP cannot support sibling relationships. All CARP clients must agree on the configuration; otherwise, different clients will send the same URI to different parents, reducing hit ratios. |

Table 20-2. Proxy and cache redirection techniques (continued)

| Mechanism | How it works | Basis for rerouting | Limitations |
|-----------|--------------|---------------------|-------------|
| Hyper Text Caching Protocol (HTCP) | Participating proxy caches can query a group of sibling caches for requested content. Supports HTTP 1.0 and 1.1 headers to fine-tune cache queries. | Obtaining content from a sibling or parent cache is faster than applying to the origin server. | |

# General Redirection Methods

In this section, we will delve deeper into the various redirection methods that are commonly used for both servers and proxies. These techniques can be used to redirect traffic to a different (presumably more optimal) server or to vector traffic through a proxy. Specifically, we'll cover HTTP redirection, DNS redirection, anycast addressing, IP MAC forwarding, and IP address forwarding.

## HTTP Redirection

Web servers can send short redirect messages back to clients, telling them to try someplace else. Some web sites use HTTP redirection as a simple form of load balancing; the server that handles the redirect (the redirecting server) finds the least-loaded content server available and redirects the browser to that server. For widely distributed web sites, determining the "best" available server gets more complicated, taking into account not only the servers' load but the Internet distance between the browser and the server. One advantage of HTTP redirection over some other forms of redirection is that the redirecting server knows the client's IP address; in theory, it may be able to make a more informed choice.

Here's how HTTP redirection works. In Figure 20-1a, Alice sends a request to *www.joes-hardware.com*:

```
GET /hammers.html HTTP/1.0
Host: www.joes-hardware.com
User-Agent: Mozilla/4.51 [en] (X11; U; IRIX 6.2 IP22)
```

In Figure 20-1b, instead of sending back a web page body with HTTP status code 200, the server sends back a redirect message with status code 302:

```
HTTP/1.0 302 Redirect
Server: Stronghold/2.4.2 Apache/1.3.6
Location: http://161.58.228.45/hammers.html
```

Now, in Figure 20-1c, the browser resends the request using the redirected URL, this time to host 161.58.228.45:

```
GET /hammers.html HTTP/1.0
Host: 161.58.228.45
User-Agent: Mozilla/4.51 [en] (X11; U; IRIX 6.2 IP22)
```

Another client could get redirected to a different server. In Figure 20-1d–f, Bob's request gets redirected to 161.58.228.46.

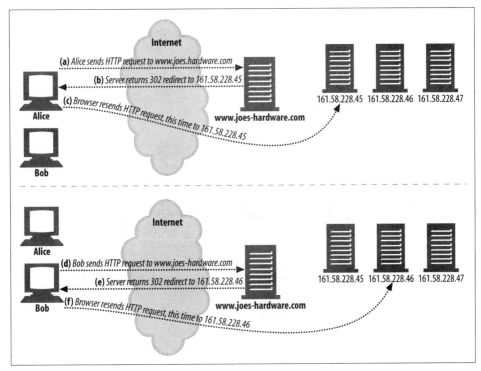

*Figure 20-1. HTTP redirection*

HTTP redirection can vector requests across servers, but it has several disadvantages:

- A significant amount of processing power is required from the original server to determine which server to redirect to. Sometimes almost as much server horse-power is required to issue the redirect as would be to serve up the page itself.
- User delays are increased, because two round trips are required to access pages.
- If the redirecting server is broken, the site will be broken.

Because of these weaknesses, HTTP redirection usually is used in combination with some of the other redirection techniques.

## DNS Redirection

Every time a client tries to access Joe's Hardware's web site, the domain name *www.joes-hardware.com* must be resolved to an IP address. The DNS resolver may be the client's own operating system, a DNS server in the client's network, or a more remote DNS server. DNS allows several IP addresses to be associated to a single domain, and DNS resolvers can be configured or programmed to return varying IP addresses. The basis on which the resolver returns the IP address can run from the simple (round robin) to the complex (such as checking the load on several servers and returning the IP address of the least-loaded server).

In Figure 20-2, Joe runs four servers for *www.joes-hardware.com*. The DNS server has to decide which of four IP addresses to return for *www.joes-hardware.com*. The easiest DNS decision algorithm is a simple round robin.

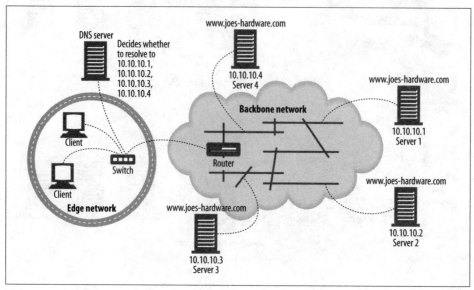

*Figure 20-2. DNS-based redirection*

For a run-through of the DNS resolution process, see the DNS reference listed at the end of this chapter.

### DNS round robin

One of the most common redirection techniques also is one of the simplest. DNS round robin uses a feature of DNS hostname resolution to balance load across a farm of web servers. It is a pure load-balancing strategy, and it does not take into account any factors about the location of the client relative to the server or the current stress on the server.

Let's look at what CNN.com really does. In early May of 2000, we used the *nslookup* Unix tool to find the IP addresses associated with CNN.com. Example 20-1 shows the results.*

*Example 20-1. IP addresses for www.cnn.com*

```
% nslookup www.cnn.com
Name:   cnn.com
```

---

* DNS results as of May 7, 2000 and resolved from Northern California. The particular values likely will change over time, and some DNS systems return different values based on client location.

*Example 20-1. IP addresses for www.cnn.com (continued)*

```
Addresses:  207.25.71.5, 207.25.71.6, 207.25.71.7, 207.25.71.8
            207.25.71.9, 207.25.71.12, 207.25.71.20, 207.25.71.22, 207.25.71.23
            207.25.71.24, 207.25.71.25, 207.25.71.26, 207.25.71.27, 207.25.71.28
            207.25.71.29, 207.25.71.30, 207.25.71.82, 207.25.71.199, 207.25.71.245
            207.25.71.246
Aliases:  www.cnn.com
```

The web site *www.cnn.com* actually is a farm of 20 distinct IP addresses! Each IP address might typically translate to a different physical server.

### Multiple addresses and round-robin address rotation

Most DNS clients just use the first address of the multi-address set. To balance load, most DNS servers rotate the addresses each time a lookup is done. This address rotation often is called *DNS round robin*.

For example, three consecutive DNS lookups of *www.cnn.com* might return rotated lists of IP addresses like those shown in Example 20-2.

*Example 20-2. Rotating DNS address lists*

```
% nslookup www.cnn.com
Name:    cnn.com
Addresses:  207.25.71.5, 207.25.71.6, 207.25.71.7, 207.25.71.8
            207.25.71.9, 207.25.71.12, 207.25.71.20, 207.25.71.22, 207.25.71.23
            207.25.71.24, 207.25.71.25, 207.25.71.26, 207.25.71.27, 207.25.71.28
            207.25.71.29, 207.25.71.30, 207.25.71.82, 207.25.71.199, 207.25.71.245
            207.25.71.246

% nslookup www.cnn.com
Name:    cnn.com
Addresses:  207.25.71.6, 207.25.71.7, 207.25.71.8, 207.25.71.9
            207.25.71.12, 207.25.71.20, 207.25.71.22, 207.25.71.23, 207.25.71.24
            207.25.71.25, 207.25.71.26, 207.25.71.27, 207.25.71.28, 207.25.71.29
            207.25.71.30, 207.25.71.82, 207.25.71.199, 207.25.71.245, 207.25.71.246
            207.25.71.5

% nslookup www.cnn.com
Name:    cnn.com
Addresses:  207.25.71.7, 207.25.71.8, 207.25.71.9, 207.25.71.12
            207.25.71.20, 207.25.71.22, 207.25.71.23, 207.25.71.24, 207.25.71.25
            207.25.71.26, 207.25.71.27, 207.25.71.28, 207.25.71.29, 207.25.71.30
            207.25.71.82, 207.25.71.199, 207.25.71.245, 207.25.71.246, 207.25.71.5
            207.25.71.6
```

In Example 20-2:

- The first address of the first DNS lookup is 207.25.71.5.
- The first address of the second DNS lookup is 207.25.71.6.
- The first address of the third DNS lookup is 207.25.71.7.

### DNS round robin for load balancing

Because most DNS clients just use the first address, the DNS rotation serves to balance load among servers. If DNS did not rotate the addresses, most clients would always send load to the first client.

Figure 20-3 shows how DNS round-robin rotation acts to balance load:

- When Alice tries to connect to *www.cnn.com*, she looks up the IP address using DNS and gets back 207.25.71.5 as the first IP address. Alice connects to the web server 207.25.71.5 in Figure 20-3c.

- When Bob subsequently tries to connect to *www.cnn.com*, he also looks up the IP address using DNS, but he gets back a different result because the address list has been rotated one position, based on Alice's previous request. Bob gets back 207.25.71.6 as the first IP address, and he connects to this server in Figure 20-3f.

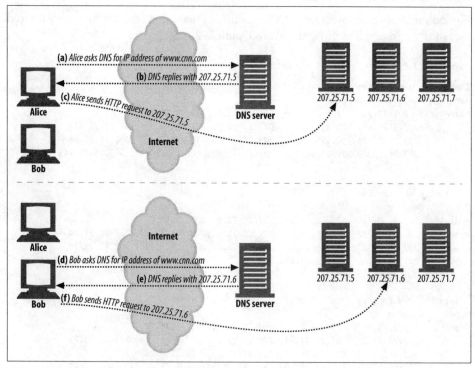

*Figure 20-3. DNS round robin load balances across servers in a server farm*

### The impact of DNS caching

DNS address rotation spreads the load around, because each DNS lookup to a server gets a different ordering of server addresses. However, this load balancing isn't perfect, because the results of the DNS lookup may be memorized and reused by applications, operating systems, and some primitive child DNS servers. Many web browsers perform a DNS lookup for a host but then use the same address over and over again, to eliminate the cost of DNS lookups and because some servers prefer to keep talking to the same client. Furthermore, many operating systems perform the DNS lookup automatically, and cache the result, but don't rotate the addresses. Consequently, DNS round robin generally doesn't balance the load of a single client—one client typically will be stuck to one server for a long period of time.

But, even though DNS doesn't deal out the transactions of a single client across server replicas, it does a decent job of spreading the aggregate load of multiple clients. As long as there is a modestly large number of clients with similar demand, the load will be relatively well distributed across servers.

### Other DNS-based redirection algorithms

We've already discussed how DNS rotates address lists with each request. However, some enhanced DNS servers use other techniques for choosing the order of the addresses:

*Load-balancing algorithms*
> Some DNS servers keep track of the load on the web servers and place the least-loaded web servers at the front of the list.

*Proximity-routing algorithms*
> DNS servers can attempt to direct users to nearby web servers, when the farm of web servers is geographically dispersed.

*Fault-masking algorithms*
> DNS servers can monitor the health of the network and route requests away from service interruptions or other faults.

Typically, the DNS server that runs sophisticated server-tracking algorithms is an authoritative server that is under the control of the content provider (see Figure 20-4).

Several distributed hosting services use this DNS redirection model. One drawback of the model for services that look for nearby servers is that the only information that the authoritative DNS server uses to make its decision is the IP address of the local DNS server, not the IP address of the client.

## Anycast Addressing

In anycast addressing, several geographically dispersed web servers have the exact same IP address and rely on the "shortest-path" routing capabilities of backbone routers to send client requests to the server nearest to the client. One way this method can work is for each web server to advertise itself as a router to a neighboring backbone router. The web server talks to its neighboring backbone router using a router communication protocol. When the backbone router receives packets aimed at the anycast address, it looks (as it usually would) for the nearest "router" that

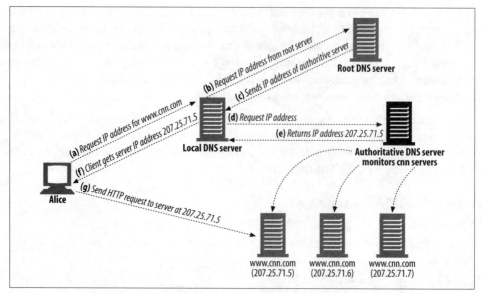

*Figure 20-4. DNS request involving authoritative server*

accepts that IP address. Because the server will have advertised itself as a router for that address, the backbone router will send the server the packet.

In Figure 20-5, three servers front the same IP address, 10.10.10.1. The Los Angeles (LA) server advertises this address to the LA router, the New York (NY) server advertises the same address to the NY router, and so on. The servers communicate with the routers using a router protocol. The routers automatically route client requests aimed at 10.10.10.1 to the nearest server that advertises the address. In Figure 20-5, a request for the IP address 10.10.10.1 will be routed to server 3.

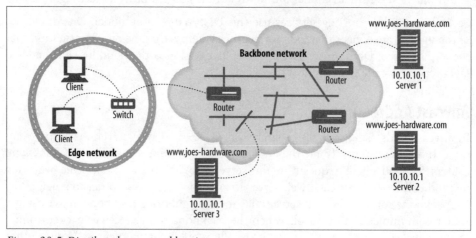

*Figure 20-5. Distributed anycast addressing*

Anycast addressing is still an experimental technique. For distributed anycast to work, the servers must "speak router language" and the routers must be able to handle possible address conflicts, because Internet addressing basically assumes one server for one address. (If done improperly, this can lead to serious problems known as "route leaks.") Distributed anycast is an emerging technology and might be a solution for content providers who control their own backbone networks.

## IP MAC Forwarding

In Ethernet networks, HTTP messages are sent in the form of addressed data packets. Each packet has a layer-4 address, consisting of the source and destination IP address and TCP port numbers; this is the address to which layer 4–aware devices pay attention. Each packet also has a layer-2 address, the Media Access Control (MAC) address, to which layer-2 devices (commonly switches and hubs) pay attention. The job of layer-2 devices is to receive packets with particular incoming MAC addresses and forward them to particular outgoing MAC addresses.

In Figure 20-6, for example, the switch is programmed to send all traffic from MAC address "MAC3" to MAC address "MAC4."

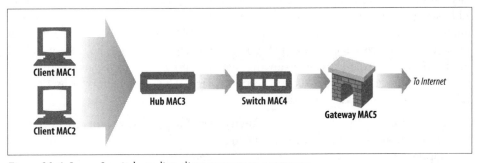

*Figure 20-6. Layer-2 switch sending client requests to a gateway*

A layer 4–aware switch is able to examine the layer-4 addressing (IP addresses and TCP port numbers) and make routing decisions based on this information. For example, a layer-4 switch could send all port 80–destined web traffic to a proxy. In Figure 20-7, the switch is programmed to send all port 80 traffic from MAC3 to MAC6 (a proxy cache). All other MAC3 traffic goes to MAC5.

Typically, if the requested HTTP content is in the cache and is fresh, the proxy cache serves it; otherwise, the proxy cache sends an HTTP request to the origin server for the content, on the client's behalf. The switch sends port 80 requests from the proxy (MAC6) to the Internet gateway (MAC5).

Layer-4 switches that support MAC forwarding usually can forward requests to several proxy caches and balance the load among them. Likewise, HTTP traffic also can be forwarded to alternate HTTP servers.

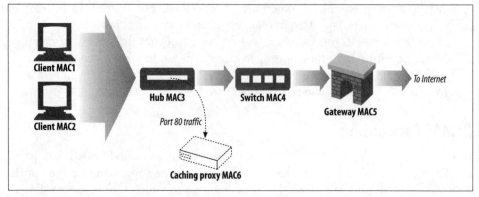

*Figure 20-7. MAC forwarding using a layer-4 switch*

Because MAC address forwarding is point-to-point only, the server or proxy has to be located one hop away from the switch.

## IP Address Forwarding

In IP address forwarding, a switch or other layer 4–aware device examines TCP/IP addressing on incoming packets and routes packets accordingly by changing the destination IP address, instead of the destination MAC address. An advantage over MAC forwarding is that the destination server need not be one hop away; it just needs to be located upstream from the switch, and the usual layer-3 end-to-end Internet routing gets the packet to the right place. This type of forwarding also is called Network Address Translation (NAT).

There is a catch, however: routing symmetry. The switch that accepts the incoming TCP connection from the client is managing that connection; the switch must send the response back to the client on that TCP connection. Therefore, any response from the destination server or proxy must return to the switch (see Figure 20-8).

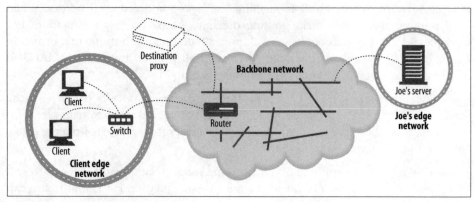

*Figure 20-8. A switch doing IP forwarding to a caching proxy or mirrored web server*

Two ways to control the return path of the response are:

- Change the source IP address of the packet to the IP address of the switch. That way, regardless of the network configuration between the switch and server, the response packet goes to the switch. This is called *full NAT*, where the IP forwarding device translates both destination and source IP addresses. Figure 20-9 shows the effect of full NAT on a TCP/IP datagram. The consequence is that the client IP address is unknown to the web server, which might want it for authentication or billing purposes, for example.

- If the source IP address remains the client's IP address, make sure (from a hardware perspective) that no routes exist directly from server to client (bypassing the switch). This sometimes is called *half NAT*. The advantage here is that the server obtains the client IP address, but the disadvantage is the requirement of some control of the entire network between client and server.

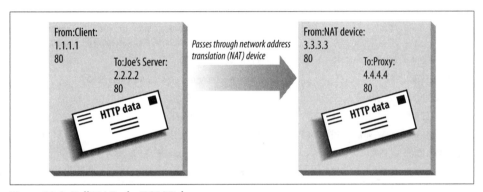

*Figure 20-9. Full NAT of a TCP/IP datagram*

## Network Element Control Protocol

The Network Element Control Protocol (NECP) allows network elements (NEs)—devices such as routers and switches that forward IP packets—to talk with server elements (SEs)—devices such as web servers and proxy caches that serve application layer requests. NECP does not explicitly support load balancing; it only offers a way for an SE to send an NE load-balancing information so that the NE can load balance as it sees fit. Like WCCP, NECP offers several ways to forward packets: MAC forwarding, GRE encapsulation, and NAT.

NECP supports the idea of exceptions. The SE can decide that it cannot service particular source IP addresses, and send those addresses to the NE. The NE can then forward requests from those IP addresses to the origin server.

### Messages

The NECP messages are described in Table 20-3.

*Table 20-3. NECP messages*

| Message | Who sends it | Meaning |
| --- | --- | --- |
| NECP_NOOP | | No operation—do nothing. |
| NECP_INIT | SE | SE initiates communication with NE. SE sends this message to NE after opening TCP connection with NE. SE must know which NE port to connect to. |
| NECP_INIT_ACK | NE | Acknowledges NECP_INIT. |
| NECP_KEEPALIVE | NE or SE | Asks if peer is alive. |
| NECP_KEEPALIVE_ACK | NE or SE | Answers keep-alive message. |
| NECP_START | SE | SE says "I am here and ready to accept network traffic." Can specify a port. |
| NECP_START_ACK | NE | Acknowledges NECP_START. |
| NECP_STOP | SE | SE tells NE "stop sending me traffic." |
| NECP_STOP_ACK | NE | NE acknowledges stop. |
| NECP_EXCEPTION_ADD | SE | SE says to add one or more exceptions to NE's list. Exceptions can be based on source IP, destination IP, protocol (above IP), or port. |
| NECP_EXCEPTION_ADD_ACK | NE | Confirms EXCEPTION_ADD. |
| NECP_EXCEPTION_DEL | SE | Asks NE to delete one or more exceptions from its list. |
| NECP_EXCEPTION_DEL_ACK | NE | Confirms EXCEPTION_DEL. |
| NECP_EXCEPTION_RESET | SE | Asks NE to delete entire exception list. |
| NECP_EXCEPTION_RESET_ACK | NE | Confirms EXCEPTION_RESET. |
| NECP_EXCEPTION_QUERY | SE | Queries NE's entire exception list. |
| NECP_EXCEPTION_RESP | NE | Responds to exception query. |

# Proxy Redirection Methods

So far, we have talked about general redirection methods. Content also may need to be accessed through various proxies (potentially for security reasons), or there might be a proxy cache in the network that a client should take advantage of (because it likely will be much faster to retrieve the cached content than it would be to go directly to the origin server).

But how do clients such as web browsers know to go to a proxy? There are three ways to determine this: by explicit browser configuration, by dynamic automatic configuration, and by transparent interception. We will discuss these three techniques in this section.

A proxy can, in turn, redirect client requests to a different proxy. For example, a proxy cache that does not have the content in its cache may choose to redirect the client to another cache. As this results in the response coming from a location different from the one from which the client requested the resource, we also will discuss several protocols used for peer proxy-cache redirection: the Internet Cache Protocol (ICP), the Cache Array Routing Protocol (CARP), and the Hyper Text Caching Protocol (HTCP).

# Explicit Browser Configuration

Most browsers can be configured to contact a proxy server for content—there is a pull-down menu where the user can enter the proxy's name or IP address and port number. The browser then contacts the proxy for all requests. Rather than relying on users to correctly configure their browsers to use proxies, some service providers require users to download preconfigured browsers. These browsers know the address of the proxy to contact.

Explicit browser configuration has two main disadvantages:

- Browsers configured to use proxies do not contact the origin server even if the proxy is not responding. If the proxy is down or if the browser is incorrectly configured, the user experiences connectivity problems.
- It is difficult to make changes in network architecture and propagate those changes to all end users. If a service provider wants to add more proxies or take some out of service, browser users have to change their proxy settings.

# Proxy Auto-configuration

Explicit configuration of browsers to contact specific proxies can restrict changes in network architecture, because it depends on users to intervene and reconfigure their browsers. An automatic configuration methodology that allows browsers to dynamically configure themselves to contact the correct proxy server solves this problem. Such a methodology exists; it is called the Proxy Auto-configuration (PAC) protocol. PAC was defined by Netscape and is supported by the Netscape Navigator and Microsoft Internet Explorer browsers.

The basic idea behind PAC is to have browsers retrieve a special file, called the PAC file, which specifies the proxy to contact for each URL. The browser must be configured to contact a specific server for the PAC file. The browser then fetches the PAC file every time it is restarted.

The PAC file is a JavaScript file, which must define the function:

```
function FindProxyForURL(url, host)
```

Browsers call this function for every requested URL, as follows:

```
return_value = FindProxyForURL(url_of_request, host_in_url);
```

where the return value is a string specifying where the browser should request this URL. The return value can be a list of the names of proxies to contact (for example, "PROXY proxy1.domain.com; PROXY proxy2.domain.com") or the string "DIRECT", which means that the browser should go directly to the origin server, bypassing any proxies.

The sequence of operations that illustrate the request for and response to a browser's request for the PAC file are illustrated in Figure 20-10. In this example, the server sends back a PAC file with a JavaScript program. The JavaScript program has a function called "FindProxyForURL" that tells the browser to contact the origin server directly if the host in the requested URL is in the "netscape.com" domain, and to go to "proxy1.joes-cache.com" for all other requests. The browser calls this function for each URL it requests and connects according to the results returned by the function.

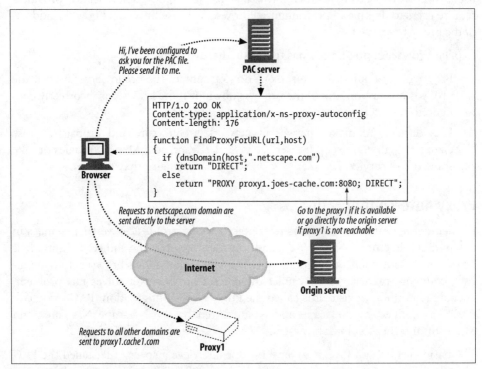

*Figure 20-10. Proxy auto-configuration*

The PAC protocol is quite powerful: the JavaScript program can ask the browser to choose a proxy based on any of a number of parameters related to the hostname, such as the DNS address and subnet, and even the day of week or time of day. PAC allows browsers automatically to contact the right proxy with changes in network architecture, as long as the PAC file is updated at the server to reflect changes to the proxy locations. The main drawback with PAC is that the browser must be configured to know which server to fetch the PAC file from, so it is not a completely automatic configuration system. WPAD, discussed in the next section, addresses this problem.

PAC, like preconfigured browsers, is used by some major ISPs today.

## Web Proxy Autodiscovery Protocol

The Web Proxy Autodiscovery Protocol (WPAD) aims to provide a way for web browsers to find and use nearby proxies, without requiring the end user to manually configure a proxy setting and without relying on transparent traffic interception. The general problem of defining a web proxy autodiscovery protocol is complicated by the existence of many discovery protocols to choose from and the differences in proxy-use configurations in different browsers.

This section contains an abbreviated and slightly reorganized version of the WPAD Internet draft. The draft currently is being developed as part of the Web Intermediaries Working Group of the IETF.

### PAC file autodiscovery

WPAD enables HTTP clients to locate a PAC file and use the PAC file to discover the name of an appropriate proxy server. WPAD does not directly determine the name of the proxy server, because that would circumvent the additional capabilities provided by PAC files (load balancing, request routing to an array of servers, automated failover to backup proxy servers, and so on).

As shown in Figure 20-11, the WPAD protocol discovers a PAC file URL, also known as a *configuration URL* (CURL). The PAC file executes a JavaScript program that returns the address of an appropriate proxy server.

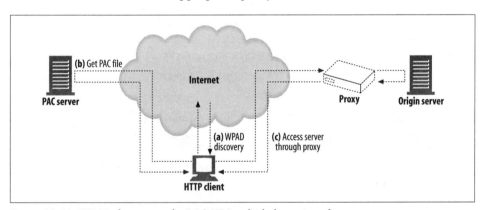

*Figure 20-11. WPAD determines the PAC URL, which determines the proxy server*

An HTTP client that implements the WPAD protocol:

- Uses WPAD to find the PAC file CURL
- Fetches the PAC file (a.k.a. configuration file, or CFILE) corresponding to the CURL
- Executes the PAC file to determine the proxy server
- Sends HTTP requests to the proxy server returned by the PAC file

### WPAD algorithm

WPAD uses a series of resource-discovery techniques to determine the proper PAC file CURL. Multiple discovery techniques are specified, because not all organizations can use all techniques. WPAD clients attempt each technique, one by one, until they succeed in obtaining a CURL.

The current WPAD specification defines the following techniques, in order:

- DHCP (Dynamic Host Configuration Protocol)
- SLP (Service Location Protocol)
- DNS well-known hostnames
- DNS SRV records
- DNS service URLs in TXT records

Of these five mechanisms, only the DHCP and DNS well-known hostname techniques are required for WPAD clients. We present more details in subsequent sections.

The WPAD client sends a series of resource-discovery requests, using the discovery mechanisms mentioned above, in order. Clients attempt only mechanisms that they support. Whenever a discovery attempt succeeds, the client uses the information obtained to construct a PAC CURL.

If a PAC file is retrieved successfully at that CURL, the process completes. If not, the client resumes where it left off in the predefined series of resource-discovery requests. If, after trying all discovery mechanisms, no PAC file is retrieved, the WPAD protocol fails and the client is configured to use no proxy server.

The client tries DHCP first, followed by SLP. If no PAC file is retrieved, the client moves on to the DNS-based mechanisms.

The client cycles through the DNS SRV, well-known hostnames, and DNS TXT record methods multiple times. Each time, the DNS query QNAME is made less and less specific. In this manner, the client can locate the most specific configuration information possible, but still can fall back on less specific information. Every DNS lookup has the QNAME prefixed with "wpad" to indicate the resource type being requested.

Consider a client with hostname *johns-desktop.development.foo.com*. This is the sequence of discovery attempts a complete WPAD client would perform:

- DHCP
- SLP
- DNS A lookup on "QNAME=wpad.development.foo.com"
- DNS SRV lookup on "QNAME=wpad.development.foo.com"
- DNS TXT lookup on "QNAME=wpad.development.foo.com"
- DNS A lookup on "QNAME=wpad.foo.com"
- DNS SRV lookup on "QNAME=wpad.foo.com"
- DNS TXT lookup on "QNAME=wpad.foo.com"

Refer to the WPAD specification to get detailed pseudocode that addresses the entire sequence of operations. The following sections discuss the two required mechanisms, DHCP and DNS A lookup. For more details about the reminder of the CURL discovery methods, refer to the WPAD specification.

### CURL discovery using DHCP

For this mechanism to work, the CURLs must be stored on DHCP servers that WPAD clients can query. The WPAD client obtains the CURL by sending a DHCP query to a DHCP server. The CURL is contained in DHCP option code 252 (if the DHCP server is configured with this information). All WPAD client implementations are required to support DHCP. The DHCP protocol is detailed in RFC 2131. See RFC 2132 for a list of existing DHCP options.

If the WPAD client already has conducted DHCP queries during its initialization, the DHCP server might already have supplied that value. If the value is not available through a client OS API, the client sends a DHCPINFORM message to query the DHCP server to obtain the value.

The DHCP option code 252 for WPAD is of type STRING and is of arbitrary size. This string contains a URL that points to an appropriate PAC file. For example:

```
"http://server.domain/proxyconfig.pac"
```

### DNS A record lookup

For this mechanism to work, the IP addresses of suitable proxy servers must be stored on DNS servers that the WPAD clients can query. The WPAD client obtains the CURL by sending an A record lookup to a DNS server. The result of a successful lookup contains an IP address for an appropriate proxy server.

WPAD client implementations are required to support this mechanism. This should be straightforward, as only basic DNS lookup of A records is required. See RFC 2219 for a description of using well-known DNS aliases for resource discovery. For WPAD, the specification uses "well known alias" of "wpad" for web proxy autodiscovery.

The client performs the following DNS lookup:

```
QNAME=wpad.TGTDOM., QCLASS=IN, QTYPE=A
```

A successful lookup contains an IP address from which the WPAD client constructs the CURL.

### Retrieving the PAC file

Once a candidate CURL is created, the WPAD client usually makes a GET request to the CURL. When making requests, WPAD clients are required to send Accept headers with appropriate CFILE format information that they are capable of handling. For example:

```
Accept: application/x-ns-proxy-autoconfig
```

In addition, if the CURL results in a redirect, the clients are required to follow the redirect to its final destination.

## When to execute WPAD

The web proxy autodiscovery process is required to occur at least as frequently as one of the following:

- Upon startup of the web client—WPAD is performed only for the start of the first instance. Subsequent instances inherit the settings.
- Whenever there is an indication from the networking stack that the IP address of the client host has changed.

A web client can use either option, depending on what makes sense in its environment. In addition, the client must attempt a discovery cycle upon expiration of a previously downloaded PAC file in accordance with HTTP expiration. It's important that the client obey the timeouts and rerun the WPAD process when the PAC file expires.

Optionally, the client also may implement rerunning the WPAD process on failure of the currently configured proxy if the PAC file does not provide an alternative.

Whenever the client decides to invalidate the current PAC file, it must rerun the entire WPAD protocol to ensure it discovers the currently correct CURL. Specifically, there is no provision in the protocol to do an If-Modified-Since conditional fetch of the PAC file.

A number of network round trips might be required during the WPAD protocol broadcast and/or multicast communications. The WPAD protocol should not be invoked at a more frequent rate than specified above (such as per-URL retrieval).

## WPAD spoofing

The IE 5 implementation of WPAD enabled web clients to detect proxy settings automatically, without user intervention. The algorithm used by WPAD prepends the hostname "wpad" to the fully qualified domain name and progressively removes subdomains until it either finds a WPAD server answering the hostname or reaches the third-level domain. For instance, web clients in the domain *a.b.microsoft.com* would query *wpad.a.b.microsoft*, *wpad.b.microsoft.com*, then *wpad.microsoft.com*.

This exposed a security hole, because in international usage (and certain other configurations), the third-level domain may not be trusted. A malicious user could set up a WPAD server and serve proxy configuration commands of her choice. Subsequent versions of IE (5.01 and later) rectified the problem.

## Timeouts

WPAD goes through multiple levels of discovery, and clients must make sure that each phase is time-bound. When possible, limiting each phase to 10 seconds is considered reasonable, but implementors may choose a different value that is more appropriate to their network properties. For example, a device implementation, operating over a wireless network, might use a much larger timeout to account for low bandwidth or high latency.

### Administrator considerations

Administrators should configure at least one of the DHCP or DNS A record lookup methods in their environments, as those are the only two that all compatible clients are required to implement. Beyond that, configuring to support mechanisms earlier in the search order will improve client startup time.

One of the major motivations for this protocol structure was to support client location of nearby proxy servers. In many environments, there are several proxy servers (workgroup, corporate gateway, ISP, backbone).

There are a number of possible points at which "nearness" decisions can be made in the WPAD framework:

- DHCP servers for different subnets can return different answers. They also can base decisions on the client cipaddr field or the client identifier option.
- DNS servers can be configured to return different SRV/A/TXT resource records (RRs) for different domain suffixes (for example, QNAMEs *wpad.marketing.bigcorp.com* and *wpad.development.bigcorp.com*).
- The web server handling the CURL request can make decisions based on the User-Agent header, Accept header, client IP address/subnet/hostname, topological distribution of nearby proxy servers, etc. This can occur inside a CGI executable created to handle the CURL. As mentioned earlier, it even can be a proxy server handling the CURL requests and making these decisions.
- The PAC file may be expressive enough to select from a set of alternatives at runtime on the client. CARP is based on this premise for an array of caches. It is not inconceivable that the PAC file could compute some network distance or fitness metrics to a set of candidate proxy servers and then select the "closest" or "most responsive" server.

# Cache Redirection Methods

We've discussed techniques to redirect traffic to general servers and specialized techniques to vector traffic to proxies and gateways. This final section will explain some of the more sophisticated redirection techniques used for caching proxy servers. These techniques are more complex than the previously discussed protocols because they try to be reliable, high-performance, and content-aware—dispatching requests to locations likely to have particular pieces of content.

# WCCP Redirection

Cisco Systems developed the Web Cache Coordination Protocol (WCCP) to enable routers to redirect web traffic to proxy caches. WCCP governs communication between routers and caches so that routers can verify caches (make sure they are up and running), load balance among caches, and send specific types of traffic to specific caches. WCCP Version 2 (WCCP2) is an open protocol. We'll discuss WCCP2 here.

## How WCCP redirection works

Here's a brief overview of how WCCP redirection works for HTTP (WCCP redirects other protocols similarly):

- Start with a network containing WCCP-enabled routers and caches that can communicate with one another.

- A set of routers and their target caches form a WCCP service group. The configuration of the service group specifies what traffic is sent where, how traffic is sent, and how load should be balanced among the caches in the service group.

- If the service group is configured to redirect HTTP traffic, routers in the service group send HTTP requests to caches in the service group.

- When an HTTP request arrives at a router in the service group, the router chooses one of the caches in the service group to serve the request (based on either a hash on the request's IP address or a mask/value set pairing scheme).

- The router sends the request packets to the cache, either by encapsulating the packets with the cache's IP address or by IP MAC forwarding.

- If the cache cannot serve the request, the packets are returned to the router for normal forwarding.

- The members of the service group exchange heartbeat messages with one another, continually verifying one another's availability.

## WCCP2 messages

There are four WCCP2 messages, described in Table 20-4.

*Table 20-4. WCCP2 messages*

| Message name | Who sends it | Information carried |
|---|---|---|
| WCCP2_HERE_I_AM | Cache to router | These messages tell routers that caches are available to receive traffic. The messages contain all of the cache's service group information. As soon as a cache joins a service group, it sends these messages to all routers in the group. These messages negotiate with routers sending WCCP2_I_SEE_YOU messages. |
| WCCP2_I_SEE_YOU | Router to cache | These messages respond to WCCP2_HERE_I_AM messages. They are used to negotiate the packet forwarding method, assignment method (who is the designated cache), packet return method, and security. |

*Table 20-4. WCCP2 messages (continued)*

| Message name | Who sends it | Information carried |
|---|---|---|
| WCCP2_REDIRECT_ASSIGN | Designated cache to router | These messages make assignments for load balancing; they send bucket information for hash table load balancing or mask/value set pair information for mask/value load balancing. |
| WCCP2_REMOVAL_QUERY | Router to cache that has not sent WCCP2_HERE_I_AM messages for 2.5 × HERE_I_AM_T seconds | If a router does not receive WCCP2_HERE_I_AM messages regularly, the router sends this message to see if the cache should be removed from the service group. The proper response from a cache is three identical WCCP2_HERE_I_AM messages, separated by HERE_I_AM_T/10 seconds. |

The WCCP2_HERE_I_AM message format is:

```
WCCP Message Header
Security Info Component
Service Info Component
Web-cache Identity Info Component
Web-cache View Info Component
Capability Info Component (optional)
Command Extension Component (optional)
```

The WCCP2_I_SEE_YOU message format is:

```
WCCP Message Header
Security Info Component
Service Info Component
Router Identity Info Component
Router View Info Component
Capability Info Component (optional)
Command Extension Component (optional)
```

The WCCP2_REDIRECT_ASSIGN message format is:

```
WCCP Message Header
Security Info Component
Service Info Component
Assignment Info Component, or Alternate Assignment Component
```

The WCCP2_REMOVAL_QUERY message format is:

```
WCCP Message Header
Security Info Component
Service Info Component
Router Query Info Component
```

### Message components

Each WCCP2 message consists of a header and components. The WCCP header information contains the message type (Here I Am, I See You, Assignment, or Removal Query), WCCP version, and message length (not including the length of the header).

The components each begin with a four-octet header describing the component type and length. The component length does not include the length of the component header. The message components are described in Table 20-5.

*Table 20-5. WCCP2 message components*

| Component | Description |
|---|---|
| Security Info | Contains the security option and security implementation. The security option can be:<br><br>WCCP2_NO_SECURITY (0)<br>WCCP2_MD5_SECURITY (1)<br><br>If the option is no security, the security implementation field does not exist. If the option is MD5, the security implementation field is a 16-octet field containing the message checksum and Service Group password. The password can be no more than eight octets. |
| Service Info | Describes the service group. The service type ID can have two values:<br><br>WCCP2_SERVICE_STANDARD (0)<br>WCCP2_SERVICE_DYNAMIC (1)<br><br>If the service type is standard, the service is a well-known service, defined entirely by service ID. HTTP is an example of a well-known service. If the service type is dynamic, the following settings define the service: priority, protocol, service flags (which determine hashing), and port. |
| Router Identity Info | Contains the router IP address and ID, and lists (by IP address) all of the web caches with which the router intends to communicate. |
| Web Cache Identity Info | Contains the web cache IP address and redirection hash table mapping. |
| Router View Info | Contains the router's view of the service group (identities of the routers and caches). |
| Web Cache View Info | Contains the web cache's view of the service group. |
| Assignment Info | Shows the assignment of a web cache to a particular hashing bucket. |
| Router Query Info | Contains the router's IP address, address of the web cache being queried, and ID of the last router in the service group that received a Here I Am message from the web cache. |
| Capabilities Info | Used by routers to advertise supported packet forwarding, load balancing, and packet return methods; used by web caches to let routers know what method the web cache prefers. |
| Alternate Assignment | Contains hash table assignment information for load balancing. |
| Assignment Map | Contains mask/value set elements for service group. |
| Command Extension | Used by web caches to tell routers they are shutting down; used by routers to acknowledge a cache shutdown. |

### Service groups

A *service group* consists of a set of WCCP-enabled routers and caches that exchange WCCP messages. The routers send web traffic to the caches in the service group. The configuration of the service group determines how traffic is distributed to caches in the service group. The routers and caches exchange service group configuration information in Here I Am and I See You messages.

### GRE packet encapsulation

Routers that support WCCP redirect HTTP packets to a particular server by encapsulating them with the server's IP address. The packet encapsulation also contains an IP header proto field that indicates Generic Router Encapsulation (GRE). The existence of the proto field tells the receiving proxy that it has an encapsulated packet.

Because the packet is encapsulated, the client IP address is not lost. Figure 20-12 illustrates GRE packet encapsulation.

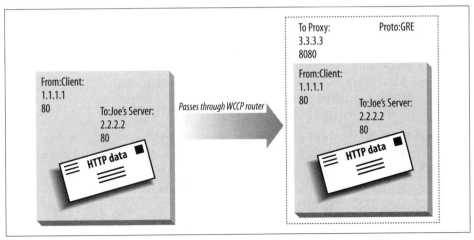

*Figure 20-12. How a WCCP router changes an HTTP packet's destination IP address*

### WCCP load balancing

In addition to routing, WCCP routers can balance load among several receiving servers. WCCP routers and their receiving servers exchange *heartbeat messages* to let one another know they are up and running. If a particular receiving server stops sending heartbeat messages, the WCCP router sends request traffic directly to the Internet, instead of redirecting it to that node. When the node returns to service, the WCCP router begins receiving heartbeat messages again and resumes sending request traffic to the node.

# Internet Cache Protocol

The Internet Cache Protocol (ICP) allows caches to look for content hits in sibling caches. If a cache does not have the content requested in an HTTP message, it can find out if the content is in a nearby sibling cache and, if so, retrieve the content from there, hopefully avoiding a more costly query to an origin server. ICP can be thought of as a cache clustering protocol. It is a redirection protocol in the sense that the final destination of an HTTP request message can be determined by a series of ICP queries.

ICP is an object discovery protocol. It asks nearby caches, all at the same time, if any of them have a particular URL in their caches. The nearby caches send back a short message saying "HIT" if they have that URL or "MISS" if they don't. The cache is then free to open an HTTP connection to a neighbor cache that has the object.

ICP is simple and lightweight. ICP messages are 32-bit packed structures in network byte order, making them easy to parse. They are carried in UDP datagrams for efficiency. UDP is an unreliable Internet protocol, which means that the data can get destroyed in transit, so programs that speak ICP need to have timeouts to detect lost datagrams.

Here is a brief description of the parts of an ICP message:

*Opcode*

> The opcode is an 8-bit value that describes the meaning of the ICP message. Basic opcodes are ICP_OP_QUERY request messages and ICP_OP_HIT and ICP_OP_MISS response messages.

*Version*

> The 8-bit version number describes the version number of the ICP protocol. The version of ICP used by Squid, documented in Internet RFC 2186, is Version 2.

*Message length*

> The total size in bytes of the ICP message. Because there are only 16 bits, the ICP message size cannot be larger than 16,383 bytes. URLs usually are shorter than 16 KB; if they're longer than that, many web applications will not process them.

*Request number*

> ICP-enabled caches use the request number to keep track of multiple simultaneous requests and replies. An ICP reply message always must contain the same request number as the ICP request message that triggered the reply.

*Options*

> The 32-bit ICP options field is a bit vector containing flags that modify ICP behavior. ICPv2 defines two flags, both of which modify ICP_OP_QUERY requests. The ICP_FLAG_HIT_OBJ flag enables and disables the return of document data in ICP responses. The ICP_FLAG_SRC_RTT flag requests an estimate of the round-trip time to the origin server, as measured by a sibling cache.

*Option data*

> The 32-bit option data is reserved for optional features. ICPv2 uses the low 16 bits of the option data to hold an optional round-trip time estimate from the sibling to the origin server.

*Sender host address*

> A historic field carrying the 32-bit IP address of the message sender; not used in practice.

*Payload*

> The contents of the payload vary depending on the message type. For ICP_OP_QUERY, the payload is a 4-byte original requester host address followed by a NUL-terminated URL. For ICP_OP_HIT_OBJ, the payload is a NUL-terminated URL followed by a 16 bit object size, followed by the object data.

For more information about ICP, refer to informational RFCs 2186 and 2187. Excellent ICP and peering references also are available from the U.S. National Laboratory for Applied Network Research (*http://www.nlanr.net/Squid/*).

# Cache Array Routing Protocol

Proxy servers greatly reduce traffic to the Internet by intercepting requests from individual users and serving cached copies of the requested web objects. However, as the number of users grows, a high volume of traffic can overload the proxy servers themselves.

One solution to this problem is to use multiple proxy servers to distribute the load to a collection of servers. The Cache Array Routing Protocol (CARP) is a standard proposed by Microsoft Corporation and Netscape Communication Corporation to administer a collection of proxy servers such that an array of proxy servers appears to clients as one logical cache.

CARP is an alternative to ICP. Both CARP and ICP allow administrators to improve performance by using multiple proxy servers. This section discusses how CARP differs from ICP, the advantages and disadvantages of using CARP over ICP, and the technical details of how the CARP protocol is implemented.

Upon a cache miss in ICP, the proxy server queries neighboring caches using an ICP message format to determine the availability of the web object. The neighboring caches respond with either a "HIT" or a "MISS," and the requesting proxy server uses these responses to select the most appropriate location from which to retrieve the object. If the ICP proxy servers were arranged in a hierarchical fashion, a miss would be elevated to the parent. Figure 20-13 diagrammatically shows how hits and misses are resolved using ICP.

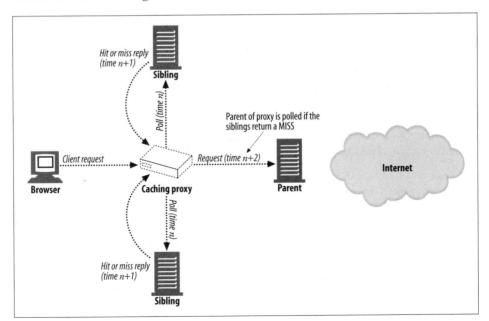

*Figure 20-13. ICP queries*

Note that each of the proxy servers, connected together using the ICP protocol, is a standalone cache server with redundant mirrors of content, meaning that duplicate entries of web objects across proxy servers is possible. In contrast, the collection of servers connected using CARP operates as a single, large server with each component server containing only a fraction of the total cached documents. By applying a hash function to the URL of a web object, CARP maps web objects to a specific proxy server. Because each web object has a unique home, we can determine the location of the object by a single lookup, rather than polling each of the proxy servers configured in the collection. Figure 20-14 summarizes the CARP approach.

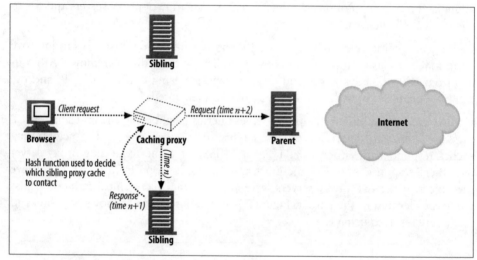

Figure 20-14. CARP redirection

Although Figure 20-14 shows the caching proxy as being the intermediary between clients and proxy servers that distributes the load to the various proxy servers, it is possible for this function to be served by the clients themselves. Commercial browsers such as Internet Explorer and Netscape Navigator can be configured to compute the hash function in the form of a plug-in that determines the proxy server to which the request should be sent.

Deterministic resolution of the proxy server in CARP means that it isn't necessary to send queries to all the neighbors, which means that this method requires fewer inter-cache messages to be sent out. As more proxy servers are added to the configuration, the collective cache system will scale fairly well. However, a disadvantage of CARP is that if one of the proxy servers becomes unavailable, the hash function needs to be modified to reflect this change, and the contents of the proxy servers must be reshuffled across the existing proxy servers. This can be expensive if the proxy server crashes often. In contrast, redundant content in ICP proxy servers means that reshuffling is not required. Another potential problem is that, because CARP is a new protocol, existing proxy servers running only the ICP protocol may not be included readily in a CARP collection.

Having described the difference between CARP and ICP, let us now describe CARP in a little more detail. The CARP redirection method involves the following tasks:

- Keep a table of participating proxy servers. These proxy servers are polled periodically to see which ones are still active.
- For each participating proxy server, compute a hash function. The value returned by the hash function takes into account the amount of load this proxy can handle.
- Define a separate hash function that returns a number based on the URL of the requested web object.
- Take the sum of the hash function of the URL and the hash function of the proxy servers to get an array of numbers. The maximum value of these numbers determines the proxy server to use for the URL. Because the computed values are deterministic, subsequent requests for the same web object will be forwarded to the same proxy server.

These four chores can either be carried out on the browser, in a plug-in, or be computed on an intermediate server.

For each collection of proxy servers, create a table listing all of the servers in the collection. Each entry in the table should contain information about load factors, time-to-live (TTL) countdown values, and global parameters such as how often members should be polled. The load factor indicates how much load that machine can handle, which depends on the CPU speed and hard drive capacity of that machine. The table can be maintained remotely via an RPC interface. Once the fields in the tables have been updated by RPC, they can be made available or published to downstream clients and proxies. This publication is done in HTTP, allowing any client or proxy server to consume the table information without introducing another inter-proxy protocol. Clients and proxy servers simply use a well-known URL to retrieve the table.

The hash function used must ensure that the web objects are statistically distributed across the participating proxy servers. The load factor of the proxy server should be used to determine the statistic probability of a web object being assigned to that proxy.

In summary, the CARP protocol allows a group of proxy servers to be viewed as single collective cache, instead of a group of cooperating but separate caches (as in ICP). A deterministic request resolution path finds the home of a specific web object within a single hop. This eliminates the inter-proxy traffic that often is generated to find the web object in a group of proxy servers in ICP. CARP also avoids duplicate copies of web objects being stored on different proxy servers, which has the advantage that the cache system collectively has a larger capacity for storing web objects but also has the disadvantage that a failure in any one proxy requires reshuffling some of the cache contents to existing proxies.

# Hyper Text Caching Protocol

Earlier, we discussed ICP, a protocol that allows proxy caches to query siblings about the presence of documents. ICP, however, was designed with HTTP/0.9 in mind and therefore allows caches to send just the URL when querying a sibling about the presence of a resource. Versions 1.0 and 1.1 of HTTP introduced many new request headers that, along with the URL, are used to make decisions about document matching, so simply sending the URL in a request may not result in accurate responses.

The Hyper Text Caching Protocol (HTCP) reduces the probability of false hits by allowing siblings to query each other for the presence of documents using the URL and all of the request and response headers. Further, HTCP allows sibling caches to monitor and request the addition and deletion of selected documents in each other's caches and to make changes in the caching policies of each other's cached documents.

Figure 20-13, which illustrates an ICP transaction, also can be used to illustrate an HTCP transaction—HTCP is just another object discovery protocol. If a nearby cache has the document, the requesting cache can open an HTTP connection to the cache to get a copy of the document. The difference between an ICP and an HTCP transaction is in the level of detail in the requests and responses.

The structure of HTCP messages is illustrated in Figure 20-15. The Header portion includes the message length and message versions. The Data portion starts with the data length and includes opcodes, response codes, and some flags and IDs, and it terminates with the actual data. An optional Authentication section may follow the Data section.

Details of the message fields are as follows:

*Header*
> The Header section consists of a 32-bit message length, an 8-bit major protocol version, and an 8-bit minor protocol version. The message length includes all of the header, data, and authentication sizes.

*Data*
> The Data section contains the HTCP message and has the structure illustrated in Figure 20-15. The data components are described in Table 20-6.

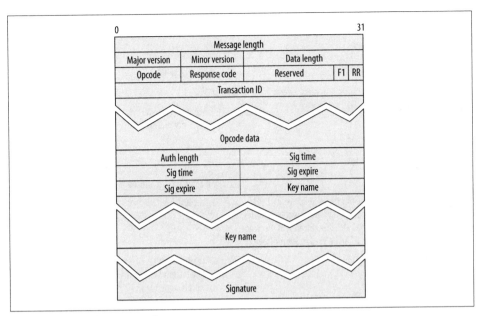

Figure 20-15. HTCP message format

Table 20-6. HTCP data components

| Component | Description |
|---|---|
| Data length | A 16-bit value of the number of bytes in the Data section including the length of the Length field itself. |
| Opcode | The 4-bit operation code for the HTCP transaction. The full list of opcodes is provided in Table 20-7. |
| Response code | A 4-bit key indicating the success or failure of the transaction. The possible values are:<br><br>• 0—Authentication was not used, but is needed<br>• 1—Authentication was used, but is not satisfactory<br>• 2—Unimplemented opcode<br>• 3—Major version not supported<br>• 4—Minor version not supported<br>• 5—Inappropriate, disallowed, or undesirable opcode |
| F1 | F1 is overloaded—if the message is a request, F1 is a 1-bit flag set by the requestor indicating that it needs a response (F1=1); if the message is a response, F1 is a 1-bit flag indicating whether the response is to be interpreted as a response to the overall message (F1=1) or just as a response to the Opcode data fields (F1=0). |
| RR | A 1-bit flag indicating that the message is a request (RR=0) or a response (RR=1). |
| Transaction ID | A 32-bit value that, combined with the requestor's network address, uniquely identifies the HTCP transaction. |
| Opcode data | Opcode data is opcode-dependent. See Table 20-7. |

Table 20-7 lists the HTCP opcodes and their corresponding data types.

*Table 20-7. HTCP opcodes*

| Opcode | Value | Description | Response codes | Opcode data |
|---|---|---|---|---|
| NOP | 0 | Essentially a "ping" operation. | Always 0 | None |
| TST | 1 | | 0 if entity is present, 1 if entity is not present | Contains the URL and request headers in the request and just response headers in the response |
| MON | 2 | | 0 if accepted, 1 if refused | |
| SET | 3 | The SET message allows caches to request changes in caching policies. See Table 20-9 for a list of the headers that can be used in SET messages. | 0 if accepted, 1 if ignored | |
| CLR | 4 | | 0 if I had it, but it's now gone; 1 if I had it, but I am keeping it; and 2 if I didn't have it | |

## HTCP Authentication

The authentication portion of the HTCP message is optional. Its structure is illustrated in Figure 20-15, and its components are described inTable 20-8.

*Table 20-8. HTCP authentication components*

| Component | Description |
|---|---|
| Auth length | The 16-bit number of bytes in the Authentication section of the message, including the length of the Length field itself. |
| Sig time | A 32-bit number representing the number of seconds since 00:00:00 Jan 1, 1970 GMT at the time that the signature is generated. |
| Sig expire | A 32-bit number representing the number of seconds since 00:00:00 Jan 1, 1970 GMT when the signature will expire. |
| Key name | A string that specifies the name of the shared secret. The Key section has two parts: the 16-bit length in bytes of the string that follows, followed by the stream of uninterrupted bytes of the string. |
| Signature | The HMAC-MD5 digest with a B value of 64 (representing the source and destination IP addresses and ports), the major and minor HTCP versions of the message, the Sig time and Sig expires values, the full HTCP data, and the key. The Signature also has two parts: the 16-bit length in bytes of the string, followed by the string. |

## Setting Caching Policies

The SET message allows caches to request changes in the caching policies of cached documents. The headers that can be used in SET messages are described in Table 20-9.

*Table 20-9. List of Cache headers for modifying caching policies*

| Header | Description |
|--------|-------------|
| Cache-Vary | The requestor has learned that the content varies on a set of headers different from the set in the response Vary header. This header overrides the response Vary header. |
| Cache-Location | The list of proxy caches that also may have copies of this object. |
| Cache-Policy | The requestor has learned the caching policies for this object in more detail than is specified in the response headers. Possible values are: "no-cache," meaning that the response is not cacheable but may be shareable among simultaneous requestors; "no-share," meaning that the object is not shareable; and "no-cache-cookie," meaning that the content may change as a result of cookies and caching therefore is not advised. |
| Cache-Flags | The requestor has modified the object's caching policies and the object may have to be treated specially and not necessarily in accordance with the object's actual policies. |
| Cache-Expiry | The actual expiration time for the document as learned by the requestor. |
| Cache-MD5 | The requestor-computed MD5 checksum of the object, which may be different from the value in the Content-MD5 header, or may be supplied because the object does not have a Content-MD5 header. |
| Cache-to-Origin | The requestor-measured round-trip time to an origin server. The format of the values in this header is *<origin server name or ip> <average round-trip time in seconds> <number of samples> <number of router hops between requestor and origin server>*. |

By allowing request and response headers to be sent in query messages to sibling caches, HTCP can decrease the false-hit rate in cache queries. By further allowing sibling caches to exchange policy information with each other, HTCP can improve sibling caches' ability to cooperate with each other.

# For More Information

For more information, consult the following references:

*DNS and Bind*
Cricket Liu, Paul Albitz, and Mike Loukides, O'Reilly & Associates, Inc.

*http://www.wrec.org/Drafts/draft-cooper-webi-wpad-00.txt*
"Web Proxy Auto-Discovery Protocol."

*http://home.netscape.com/eng/mozilla/2.0/relnotes/demo/proxy-live.html*
"Navigator Proxy Auto-Config File Format."

*http://www.ietf.org/rfc/rfc2186.txt*
IETF RFC 2186, "Intercache Communication Protocol (ICP) Version 2," by D. Wessels and K. Claffy.

*http://icp.ircache.net/carp.txt*
"Cache Array Routing Protocol v1.0."

*http://www.ietf.org/rfc/rfc2756.txt*
IETF RFC 2756, "Hyper Text Caching Protocol (HTCP/0.0)," by P. Vixie and D. Wessels.

*http://www.ietf.org/internet-drafts/draft-wilson-wrec-wccp-v2-00.txt*
    *draft-wilson-wrec-wccp-v2-01.txt*, "Web Cache Communication Protocol V2.0,"
    by M. Cieslak, D. Forster, G. Tiwana, and R. Wilson.

*http://www.ietf.org/rfc/rfc2131.txt?number=2131*
    "Dynamic Host Configuration Protocol."

*http://www.ietf.org/rfc/rfc2132.txt?number=2132*
    "DHCP Options and BOOTP Vendor Extensions."

*http://www.ietf.org/rfc/rfc2608.txt?number=2608*
    "Service Location Protocol, Version 2."

*http://www.ietf.org/rfc/rfc2219.txt?number=2219*
    "Use of DNS Aliases for Network Services."

# CHAPTER 21

# Logging and Usage Tracking

Almost all servers and proxies log summaries of the HTTP transactions they process. This is done for a variety of reasons: usage tracking, security, billing, error detection, and so on. In this chapter, we take a brief tour of logging, examining what information about HTTP transactions typically is logged and what some of the common log formats contain.

## What to Log?

For the most part, logging is done for two reasons: to look for problems on the server or proxy (e.g., which requests are failing), and to generate statistics about how web sites are accessed. Statistics are useful for marketing, billing, and capacity planning (for instance, determining the need for additional servers or bandwidth).

You could log all of the headers in an HTTP transaction, but for servers and proxies that process millions of transactions per day, the sheer bulk of all of that data quickly would get out of hand. You also would end up logging a lot of information that you don't really care about and may never even look at.

Typically, just the basics of a transaction are logged. A few examples of commonly logged fields are:

- HTTP method
- HTTP version of client and server
- URL of the requested resource
- HTTP status code of the response
- Size of the request and response messages (including any entity bodies)
- Timestamp of when the transaction occurred
- Referer and User-Agent header values

The HTTP method and URL tell what the request was trying to do—for example, GETting a resource or POSTing an order form. The URL can be used to track popularity of pages on the web site.

The version strings give hints about the client and server, which are useful in debugging strange or unexpected interactions between clients and servers. For example, if requests are failing at a higher-than-expected rate, the version information may point to a new release of a browser that is unable to interact with the server.

The HTTP status code tells what happened to the request: whether it was successful, the authorization attempt failed, the resource was found, etc. (See "Status Codes" in Chapter 3 for a list of HTTP status codes.)

The size of the request/response and the timestamp are used mainly for accounting purposes; i.e., to track how many bytes flowed into, out of, or through the application. The timestamp also can be used to correlate observed problems with the requests that were being made at the time.

# Log Formats

Several log formats have become standard, and we'll discuss some of the most common formats in this section. Most commercial and open source HTTP applications support logging in one or more of these common formats. Many of these applications also support the ability of administrators to configure log formats and create their own custom formats.

One of the main benefits of supporting (for applications) and using (for administrators) these more standard formats rests in the ability to leverage the tools that have been built to process and generate basic statistics from these logs. Many open source and commercial packages exist to crunch logs for reporting purposes, and by utilizing standard formats, applications and their administrators can plug into these resources.

## Common Log Format

One of the most common log formats in use today is called, appropriately, the Common Log Format. Originally defined by NCSA, many servers use this log format as a default. Most commercial and open source servers can be configured to use this format, and many commercial and freeware tools exist to help parse common log files. Table 21-1 lists, in order, the fields of the Common Log Format.

*Table 21-1. Common Log Format fields*

| Field | Description |
|-------|-------------|
| remotehost | The hostname or IP address of the requestor's machine (IP if the server was not configured to perform reverse DNS or cannot look up the requestor's hostname) |
| username | If an *ident* lookup was performed, the requestor's authenticated username[a] |

*Table 21-1. Common Log Format fields (continued)*

| Field | Description |
| --- | --- |
| auth-username | If authentication was performed, the username with which the requestor authenticated |
| timestamp | The date and time of the request |
| request-line | The exact text of the HTTP request line, "GET /index.html HTTP/1.1" |
| response-code | The HTTP status code that was returned in the response |
| response-size | The Content-Length of the response entity—if no entity was returned in the response, a zero is logged |

[a] RFC 931 describes the *ident* lookup used in this authentication. The *ident* protocol was discussed in Chapter 5.

Example 21-1 lists a few examples of Common Log Format entries.

*Example 21-1. Common Log Format*
```
209.1.32.44 - - [03/Oct/1999:14:16:00 -0400] "GET / HTTP/1.0" 200 1024
http-guide.com - dg [03/Oct/1999:14:16:32 -0400] "GET / HTTP/1.0" 200 477
http-guide.com - dg [03/Oct/1999:14:16:32 -0400] "GET /foo HTTP/1.0" 404 0
```

In these examples, the fields are assigned as follows:

| Field | Entry 1 | Entry 2 | Entry 2 |
| --- | --- | --- | --- |
| remotehost | 209.1.32.44 | http-guide.com | http-guide.com |
| username | <empty> | <empty> | <empty> |
| auth-username | <empty> | dg | dg |
| timestamp | 03/Oct/1999:14:16:00 -0400 | 03/Oct/1999:14:16:32 -0400 | 03/Oct/1999:14:16:32 -0400 |
| request-line | GET / HTTP/1.0 | GET / HTTP/1.0 | GET /foo HTTP/1.0 |
| response-code | 200 | 200 | 404 |
| response-size | 1024 | 477 | 0 |

Note that the *remotehost* field can be either a hostname, as in *http-guide.com*, or an IP address, such as 209.1.32.44.

The dashes in the second (username) and third (auth-username) fields indicate that the fields are empty. This indicates that either an *ident* lookup did not occur (second field empty) or authentication was not performed (third field empty).

## Combined Log Format

Another commonly used log format is the Combined Log Format. This format is supported by servers such as Apache. The Combined Log Format is very similar to the Common Log Format; in fact, it mirrors it exactly, with the addition of two fields (listed in Table 21-2). The User-Agent field is useful in noting which HTTP client applications are making the logged requests, while the Referer field provides more detail about where the requestor found this URL.

*Table 21-2. Additional Combined Log Format fields*

| Field | Description |
| --- | --- |
| Referer | The contents of the Referer HTTP header |
| User-Agent | The contents of the User-Agent HTTP header |

Example 21-2 gives an example of a Combined Log Format entry.

*Example 21-2. Combined Log Format*

```
209.1.32.44 - - [03/Oct/1999:14:16:00 -0400] "GET / HTTP/1.0" 200 1024 "http://www.joes-
hardware.com/"  "5.0: Mozilla/4.0 (compatible; MSIE 5.0; Windows 98)"
```

In Example 21-2, the Referer and User-Agent fields are assigned as follows:

| Field | Value |
| --- | --- |
| Referer | http://www.joes-hardware.com/ |
| User-Agent | 5.0: Mozilla/4.0 (compatible; MSIE 5.0; Windows 98) |

The first seven fields of the example Combined Log Format entry in Example 21-2 are exactly as they would be in the Common Log Format (see the first entry in Example 21-1). The two new fields, Referer and User-Agent, are tacked onto the end of the log entry.

## Netscape Extended Log Format

When Netscape entered into the commercial HTTP application space, it defined for its servers many log formats that have been adopted by other HTTP application developers. Netscape's formats derive from the NCSA Common Log Format, but they extend that format to incorporate fields relevant to HTTP applications such as proxies and web caches.

The first seven fields in the Netscape Extended Log Format are identical to those in the Common Log Format (see Table 21-1). Table 21-3 lists, in order, the new fields that the Netscape Extended Log Format introduces.

*Table 21-3. Additional Netscape Extended Log Format fields*

| Field | Description |
| --- | --- |
| proxy-response-code | If the transaction went through a proxy, the HTTP response code from the server to the proxy |
| proxy-response-size | If the transaction went through a proxy, the Content-Length of the server's response entity sent to the proxy |
| client-request-size | The Content-Length of any body or entity in the client's request to the proxy |
| proxy-request-size | If the transaction went through a proxy, the Content-Length of any body or entity in the proxy's request to the server |
| client-request-hdr-size | The length, in bytes, of the client's request headers |

*Table 21-3. Additional Netscape Extended Log Format fields (continued)*

| Field | Description |
|---|---|
| proxy-response-hdr-size | If the transaction went through a proxy, the length, in bytes, of the proxy's response headers that were sent to the requestor |
| proxy-request-hdr-size | If the transaction went through a proxy, the length, in bytes, of the proxy's request headers that were sent to the server |
| server-response-hdr-size | The length, in bytes, of the server's response headers |
| proxy-timestamp | If the transaction went through a proxy, the elapsed time for the request and response to travel through the proxy, in seconds |

Example 21-3 gives an example of a Netscape Extended Log Format entry.

*Example 21-3. Netscape Extended Log Format*

```
209.1.32.44 - - [03/Oct/1999:14:16:00-0400] "GET / HTTP/1.0" 200 1024 200 1024 0 0 215 260
279 254 3
```

In this example, the extended fields are assigned as follows:

| Field | Value |
|---|---|
| proxy-response-code | 200 |
| proxy-response-size | 1024 |
| client-request-size | 0 |
| proxy-request-size | 0 |
| client-request-hdr-size | 215 |
| proxy-response-hdr-size | 260 |
| proxy-request-hdr-size | 279 |
| server-response-hdr-size | 254 |
| proxy-timestamp | 3 |

The first seven fields of the example Netscape Extended Log Format entry in Example 21-3 mirror the entries in the Common Log Format example (see the first entry in Example 21-1).

## Netscape Extended 2 Log Format

Another Netscape log format, the Netscape Extended 2 Log Format, takes the Extended Log Format and adds further information relevant to HTTP proxy and web caching applications. These extra fields help paint a better picture of the interactions between an HTTP client and an HTTP proxy application.

The Netscape Extended 2 Log Format derives from the Netscape Extended Log Format, and its initial fields are identical to those listed in Table 21-3 (it also extends the Common Log Format fields listed in Table 21-1).

Table 21-4 lists, in order, the additional fields of the Netscape Extended 2 Log Format.

*Table 21-4. Additional Netscape Extended 2 Log Format fields*

| Field | Description |
|-------|-------------|
| route | The route that the proxy used to make the request for the client (see Table 21-5) |
| client-finish-status-code | The client finish status code; specifies whether the client request to the proxy completed successfully (FIN) or was interrupted (INTR) |
| proxy-finish-status-code | The proxy finish status code; specifies whether the proxy request to the server completed successfully (FIN) or was interrupted (INTR) |
| cache-result-code | The cache result code; tells how the cache responded to the request[a] |

[a] Table 21-7 lists the Netscape cache result codes.

Example 21-4 gives an example of a Netscape Extended 2 Log Format entry.

*Example 21-4. Netscape Extended 2 Log Format*

```
209.1.32.44 - - [03/Oct/1999:14:16:00-0400] "GET / HTTP/1.0" 200 1024 200 1024 0 0 215 260
279 254 3 DIRECT FIN FIN WRITTEN
```

The extended fields in this example are assigned as follows:

| Field | Value |
|-------|-------|
| route | DIRECT |
| client-finish-status-code | FIN |
| proxy-finish-status-code | FIN |
| cache-result-code | WRITTEN |

The first 16 fields in the Netscape Extended 2 Log Format entry in Example 21-4 mirror the entries in the Netscape Extended Log Format example (see Example 21-3).

Table 21-5 lists the valid Netscape route codes.

*Table 21-5. Netscape route codes*

| Value | Description |
|-------|-------------|
| DIRECT | The resource was fetched directly from the server. |
| PROXY(host:port) | The resource was fetched through the proxy "host." |
| SOCKS(socks:port) | The resource was fetched through the SOCKS server "host." |

Table 21-6 lists the valid Netscape finish codes.

*Table 21-6. Netscape finish status codes*

| Value | Description |
|-------|-------------|
| - | The request never even started. |
| FIN | The request was completed successfully. |

*Table 21-6. Netscape finish status codes (continued)*

| Value | Description |
|---|---|
| INTR | The request was interrupted by the client or ended by a proxy/server. |
| TIMEOUT | The request was timed out by the proxy/server. |

Table 21-7 lists the valid Netscape cache codes.[*]

*Table 21-7. Netscape cache codes*

| Code | Description |
|---|---|
| - | The resource was uncacheable. |
| WRITTEN | The resource was written into the cache. |
| REFRESHED | The resource was cached and it was refreshed. |
| NO-CHECK | The cached resource was returned; no freshness check was done. |
| UP-TO-DATE | The cached resource was returned; a freshness check was done. |
| HOST-NOT-AVAILABLE | The cached resource was returned; no freshness check was done because the remote server was not available. |
| CL-MISMATCH | The resource was not written to the cache; the write was aborted because the Content-Length did not match the resource size. |
| ERROR | The resource was not written to the cache due to some error; for example, a timeout occurred or the client aborted the transaction. |

Netscape applications, like many other HTTP applications, have other log formats too, including a Flexible Log Format and a means for administrators to output custom log fields. These formats allow administrators greater control and the ability to customize their logs by choosing which parts of the HTTP transaction (headers, status, sizes, etc.) to report in their logs.

The ability for administrators to configure custom formats was added because it is difficult to predict what information administrators will be interested in getting from their logs. Many other proxies and servers also have the ability to emit custom logs.

## Squid Proxy Log Format

The Squid proxy cache (*http://www.squid-cache.org*) is a venerable part of the Web. Its roots trace back to one of the early web proxy cache projects (*ftp://ftp.cs.colorado.edu/pub/techreports/schwartz/Harvest.Conf.ps.Z*). Squid is an open source project that has been extended and enhanced by the open source community over the years. Many tools have been written to help administer the Squid application, including tools to help process, audit, and mine its logs. Many subsequent proxy caches adopted the Squid format for their own logs so that they could leverage these tools.

---

[*] Chapter 7 discusses HTTP caching in detail.

The format of a Squid log entry is fairly simple. Its fields are summarized in Table 21-8.

*Table 21-8. Squid Log Format fields*

| Field | Description |
|---|---|
| timestamp | The timestamp when the request arrived, in seconds since January 1, 1970 GMT. |
| time-elapsed | The elapsed time for request and response to travel through the proxy, in milliseconds. |
| host-ip | The IP address of the client's (requestor's) host machine. |
| result-code/status | The result field is a Squid-ism that tells what action the proxy took during this request[a]; the code field is the HTTP response code that the proxy sent to the client. |
| size | The length of the proxy's response to the client, including HTTP response headers and body, in bytes. |
| method | The HTTP method of the client's request. |
| url | The URL in the client's request.[b] |
| rfc931-ident[c] | The client's authenticated username.[d] |
| hierarchy/from | Like the route field in Netscape formats, the hierarchy field tells what route the proxy used to make the request for the client.[e] The from field tells the name of the server that the proxy used to make the request. |
| content-type | The Content-Type of the proxy response entity. |

[a] Table 21-9 lists the various result codes and their meanings.

[b] Recall from Chapter 2 that proxies often log the entire requested URL, so if a username and password component are in the URL, a proxy can inadvertently record this information.

[c] The rfc931-ident, hierarchy/from, and content-type fields were added in Squid 1.1. Previous versions did not have these fields.

[d] RFC 931 describes the *ident* lookup used in this authentication.

[e] *http://squid.nlanr.net/Doc/FAQ/FAQ-6.html#ss6.6* lists all of the valid Squid hierarchy codes.

Example 21-5 gives an example of a Squid Log Format entry.

*Example 21-5. Squid Log Format*

```
99823414 3001 209.1.32.44 TCP_MISS/200 4087 GET http://www.joes-hardware.com - DIRECT/
proxy.com text/html
```

The fields are assigned as follows:

| Field | Value |
|---|---|
| timestamp | 99823414 |
| time-elapsed | 3001 |
| host-ip | 209.1.32.44 |
| action-code | TCP_MISS |
| status | 200 |
| size | 4087 |
| method | GET |
| URL | http://www.joes-hardware.com |

| Field | Value |
|---|---|
| RFC 931 ident | - |
| hierarchy | DIRECT[a] |
| from | proxy.com |
| content-type | text/html |

[a] The DIRECT Squid hierarchy value is the same as the DIRECT route value in Netscape log formats.

Table 21-9 lists the various Squid result codes.[*]

*Table 21-9. Squid result codes*

| Action | Description |
|---|---|
| TCP_HIT | A valid copy of the resource was served out of the cache. |
| TCP_MISS | The resource was not in the cache. |
| TCP_REFRESH_HIT | The resource was in the cache but needed to be checked for freshness. The proxy revalidated the resource with the server and found that the in-cache copy was indeed still fresh. |
| TCP_REF_FAIL_HIT | The resource was in the cache but needed to be checked for freshness. However, the revalidation failed (perhaps the proxy could not connect to the server), so the "stale" resource was returned. |
| TCP_REFRESH_MISS | The resource was in the cache but needed to be checked for freshness. Upon checking with the server, the proxy learned that the resource in the cache was out of date and received a new version. |
| TCP_CLIENT_REFRESH_MISS | The requestor sent a Pragma: no-cache or similar Cache-Control directive, so the proxy was forced to fetch the resource. |
| TCP_IMS_HIT | The requestor issued a conditional request, which was validated against the cached copy of the resource. |
| TCP_SWAPFAIL_MISS | The proxy thought the resource was in the cache but for some reason could not access it. |
| TCP_NEGATIVE_HIT | A cached response was returned, but the response was a negatively cached response. Squid supports the notion of caching errors for resources—for example, caching a 404 Not Found response—so if multiple requests go through the proxy-cache for an invalid resource, the error is served from the proxy cache. |
| TCP_MEM_HIT | A valid copy of the resource was served out of the cache, and the resource was in the proxy cache's memory (as opposed to having to access the disk to retrieve the cached resource). |
| TCP_DENIED | The request for this resource was denied, probably because the requestor does not have permission to make requests for this resource. |
| TCP_OFFLINE_HIT | The requested resource was retrieved from the cache during its *offline* mode. Resources are not validated when Squid (or another proxy using this format) is in offline mode. |
| UDP_* | The UDP_* codes indicate that requests were received through the UDP interface to the proxy. HTTP normally uses the TCP transport protocol, so these requests are not using the HTTP protocol.[a] |

---

[*] Several of these action codes deal more with the internals of the Squid proxy cache, so not all of them are used by other proxies that implement the Squid Log Format.

*Table 21-9. Squid result codes (continued)*

| Action | Description |
| --- | --- |
| UDP_HIT | A valid copy of the resource was served out of the cache. |
| UDP_MISS | The resource was not in the cache. |
| UDP_DENIED | The request for this resource was denied, probably because the requestor does not have permission to make requests for this resource. |
| UDP_INVALID | The request that the proxy received was invalid. |
| UDP_MISS_NOFETCH | Used by Squid during specific operation modes or in the cache of frequent failures. A cache miss was returned and the resource was not fetched. |
| NONE | Logged sometimes with errors. |
| TCP_CLIENT_REFRESH | See TCP_CLIENT_REFRESH_MISS. |
| TCP_SWAPFAIL | See TCP_SWAPFAIL_MISS. |
| UDP_RELOADING | See UDP_MISS_NOFETCH. |

a  Squid has its own protocol for making these requests: ICP. This protocol is used for cache-to-cache requests. See *http://www.squid-cache.org* for more information.

# Hit Metering

Origin servers often keep detailed logs for billing purposes. Content providers need to know how often URLs are accessed, advertisers want to know how often their ads are shown, and web authors want to know how popular their content is. Logging works well for tracking these things when clients visit web servers directly.

However, caches stand between clients and servers and prevent many accesses from reaching servers (the very purpose of caches).[*] Because caches handle many HTTP requests and satisfy them without visiting the origin server, the server has no record that a client accessed its content, creating omissions in log files.

Missing log data makes content providers resort to *cache busting* for their most important pages. Cache busting refers to a content producer intentionally making certain content uncacheable, so all requests for this content must go to the origin server.[†] This allows the origin server to log the access. Defeating caching might yield better logs, but it slows down requests and increases load on the origin server and network.

Because proxy caches (and some clients) keep their own logs, if servers could get access to these logs—or at least have a crude way to determine how often their content is served by a proxy cache—cache busting could be avoided. The proposed Hit Metering protocol, an extension to HTTP, suggests a solution to this problem. The Hit Metering protocol requires caches to periodically report cache access statistics to origin servers.

---

[*] Recall that virtually every browser has a cache.

[†] Chapter 7 describes how HTTP responses can be marked as uncacheable.

RFC 2227 defines the Hit Metering protocol in detail. This section provides a brief tour of the proposal.

## Overview

The Hit Metering protocol defines an extension to HTTP that provides a few basic facilities that caches and servers can implement to share access information and to regulate how many times cached resources can be used.

Hit Metering is, by design, not a complete solution to the problem caches pose for logging access, but it does provide a basic means for obtaining metrics that servers want to track. The Hit Metering protocol has not been widely implemented or deployed (and may never be). That said, a cooperative scheme like Hit Metering holds some promise of providing accurate access statistics while retaining caching performance gains. Hopefully, that will be motivation to implement the Hit Metering protocol instead of marking content uncacheable.

## The Meter Header

The Hit Metering extension proposes the addition of a new header, Meter, that caches and servers can use to pass to each other directives about usage and reporting, much like the Cache-Control header allows caching directives to be exchanged.

Table 21-10 defines the various directives and who can pass them in the Meter header.

*Table 21-10. Hit Metering directives*

| Directive | Abbreviation | Who | Description |
| --- | --- | --- | --- |
| will-report-and-limit | w | Cache | The cache is capable of reporting usage and obeying any usage limits the server specifies. |
| wont-report | x | Cache | The cache is able to obey usage limits but won't report usage. |
| wont-limit | y | Cache | The cache is able to report usage but won't limit usage. |
| count | c | Cache | The reporting directive, specified as "uses/reuses" integers—for example, ":count=2/4".[a] |
| max-uses | u | Server | Allows the server to specify the maximum number of times a response can be used by a cache—for example, "max-uses=100". |
| max-reuses | r | Server | Allows the server to specify the maximum number of times a response can be reused by a cache—for example, "max-reuses=100". |
| do-report | d | Server | The server requires proxies to send usage reports. |
| dont-report | e | Server | The server does not want usage reports. |
| timeout | t | Server | Allows the server to specify a timeout on the metering of a resource. The cache should send a report at or before the specified timeout, plus or minus 1 minute. The timeout is specified in minutes—for example, "timeout=60". |
| wont-ask | n | Server | The server does not want any metering information. |

[a] Hit Metering defines a *use* as satisfying a request with the response, whereas a *reuse* is revalidating a client request.

Figure 21-1 shows an example of Hit Metering in action. The first part of the transaction is just a normal HTTP transaction between a client and proxy cache, but in the proxy request, note the insertion of the Meter header and the response from the server. Here, the proxy is informing the server that it is capable of doing Hit Metering, and the server in turn is asking the proxy to report its hit counts.

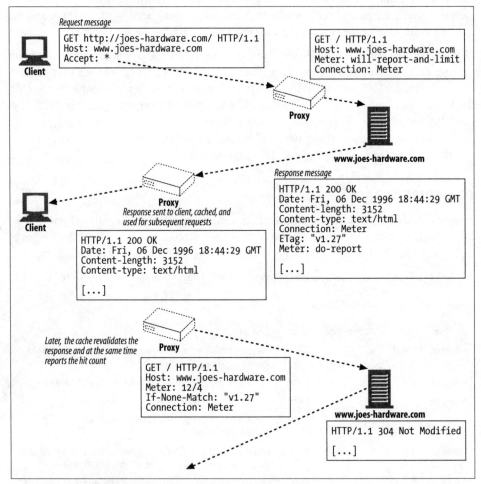

*Figure 21-1. Hit Metering example*

The request completes as it normally would, from the client's perspective, and the proxy begins tracking hits to that resource on behalf of the server. Later, the proxy tries to revalidate the resource with the server. The proxy embeds the metered information it has been tracking in the conditional request to the server.

# A Word on Privacy

Because logging really is an administrative function that servers and proxies perform, the whole operation is transparent to users. Often, they may not even be aware that their HTTP transactions are being logged—in fact, many users probably do not even know that they are using the HTTP protocol when accessing content on the Web.

Web application developers and administrators need to be aware of the implications of tracking a user's HTTP transactions. Much can be gleaned about a user based on the information he retrieves. This information obviously can be put to bad use—discrimination, harassment, blackmail, etc. Web servers and proxies that log must be vigilant in protecting the privacy of their end users.

Sometimes, such as in work environments, tracking a user's usage to make sure he is not goofing off may be appropriate, but administrators also should make public the fact that people's transactions are being monitored.

In short, logging is a very useful tool for the administrator and developer—just be aware of the privacy infringements that logs can have without the permission or knowledge of the users whose actions are being logged.

# For More Information

For more information on logging, refer to:

*http://httpd.apache.org/docs/logs.html*
  "Apache HTTP Server: Log Files." Apache HTTP Server Project web site.

*http://www.squid-cache.org/Doc/FAQ/FAQ-6.html*
  "Squid Log Files." Squid Proxy Cache web site.

*http://www.w3.org/Daemon/User/Config/Logging.html#common-logfile-format*
  "Logging Control in W3C httpd."

*http://www.w3.org/TR/WD-logfile.html*
  "Extended Log File Format."

*http://www.ietf.org/rfc/rfc2227.txt*
  RFC 2227, "Simple Hit-Metering and Usage-Limiting for HTTP," by J. Mogul and P. Leach.

# PART VI

# Appendixes

This collection of appendixes contains useful reference tables, background information, and tutorials on a variety of topics relevant to HTTP architecture and implementation:

- Appendix A, *URI Schemes*
- Appendix B, *HTTP Status Codes*
- Appendix C, *HTTP Header Reference*
- Appendix D, *MIME Types*
- Appendix E, *Base-64 Encoding*
- Appendix F, *Digest Authentication*
- Appendix G, *Language Tags*
- Appendix H, *MIME Charset Registry*

# URI Schemes

Many URI schemes have been defined, but few are in common use. Generally speaking, those URI schemes with associated RFCs are in more common use, though there are a few schemes that have been developed by leading software corporations (notably Netscape and Microsoft), but not formalized, that also are in wide use.

The W3C maintains a list of URI schemes, which you can view at:

*http://www.w3.org/Addressing/schemes.html*

The IANA also maintains a list of URL schemes, at:

*http://www.iana.org/assignments/uri-schemes*

Table A-1 informally describes some of the schemes that have been proposed and those that are in active use. Note that many of the approximately 90 schemes in the table are not widely used, and many are extinct.

*Table A-1. URI schemes from the W3C registry*

| Scheme | Description | RFCs |
|--------|-------------|------|
| about | Netscape scheme to explore aspects of the browser. For example: about by itself is the same as choosing "About Communicator" from the Navigator Help menu, about:cache displays disk-cache statistics, and about:plugins displays information about configured plug-ins. Other browsers, such as Microsoft Internet Explorer, also use this scheme. | |
| acap | Application Configuration Access Protocol. | 2244 |
| afp | For file-sharing services using the Apple Filing Protocol (AFP) protocol, defined as part of the expired IETF *draft-ietf-svrloc-afp-service-01.txt*. | |
| afs | Reserved for future use by the Andrew File System. | |
| callto | Initiates a Microsoft NetMeeting conference session, such as: *callto: ws3.joes-hardware.com/joe@joes-hardware.com* | |
| chttp | The CHTTP caching protocol defined by Real Networks. RealPlayer does not cache all items streamed by HTTP. Instead, you designate files to cache by using *chttp://* instead of *http://* in the file's URL. When RealPlayer reads a CHTTP URL in a SMIL file, it first checks its disk cache for the file. If the file isn't present, it requests the file through HTTP, storing the file in its cache. | |

| Scheme | Description | RFCs |
|--------|-------------|------|
| cid | The use of [MIME] within email to convey web pages and their associated images requires a URL scheme to permit the HTML to refer to the images or other data included in the message. The Content-ID URL, "cid:", serves that purpose. | 2392 2111 |
| clsid | Allows Microsoft OLE/COM (Component Object Model) classes to be referenced. Used to insert active objects into web pages. | |
| data | Allows inclusion of small, constant data items as "immediate" data. This URL encodes the text/plain string "A brief note": <br> *data:A%20brief%20note* | 2397 |
| date | Proposal for scheme to support dates, as in *date:1999-03-04T20:42:08.* | |
| dav | To ensure correct interoperation based on this specification, the IANA must reserve the URI namespaces starting with "DAV:" and with "opaquelocktoken:" for use by this specification, its revisions, and related WebDAV specifications. | 2518 |
| dns | Used by REBOL software. <br> See *http://www.rebol.com/users/valurl.html.* | |
| eid | The external ID (eid) scheme provides a mechanism by which the local application can reference data that has been obtained by other, non-URL scheme means. The scheme is intended to provide a general escape mechanism to allow access to information for applications that are too specialized to justify their own schemes. There is some controversy about this URI. <br> See *http://www.ics.uci.edu/pub/ietf/uri/draft-finseth-url-00.txt.* | |
| fax | The "fax" scheme describes a connection to a terminal that can handle telefaxes (facsimile machines). | 2806 |
| file | Designates files accessible on a particular host computer. A hostname can be included, but the scheme is unusual in that it does not specify an Internet protocol or access method for such files; as such, its utility in network protocols between hosts is limited. | 1738 |
| finger | The finger URL has the form: <br> *finger://host[:port][/<request>]* <br> The <request> must conform with the RFC 1288 request format. <br> See *http://www.ics.uci.edu/pub/ietf/uri/draft-ietf-uri-url-finger-03.txt.* | |
| freenet | URIs for information in the Freenet distributed information system. <br> See *http://freenet.sourceforge.net.* | |
| ftp | File Transfer Protocol scheme. | 1738 |
| gopher | The archaic gopher protocol. | 1738 |
| gsm-sms | URIs for the GSM mobile phone short message service. | |
| h323, h324 | Multimedia conferencing URI schemes. <br> See *http://www.ics.uci.edu/pub/ietf/uri/draft-cordell-sg16-conv-url-00.txt.* | |
| hdl | The Handle System is a comprehensive system for assigning, managing, and resolving persistent identifiers, known as "handles," for digital objects and other resources on the Internet. Handles can be used as URNs. <br> See *http://www.handle.net.* | |
| hnews | HNEWS is an HTTP-tunneling variant of the NNTP news protocol. The syntax of hnews URLs is designed to be compatible with the current common usage of the news URL scheme. <br> See *http://www.ics.uci.edu/pub/ietf/uri/draft-stockwell-hnews-url-00.txt.* | |

| Scheme | Description | RFCs |
|---|---|---|
| http | The HTTP protocol. Read this book for more information. | 2616 |
| https | HTTP over SSL. | |
| | See *http://sitesearch.netscape.com/eng/ssl3/draft302.txt*. | |
| iioploc | CORBA extensions. The Interoperable Name Service defines one URL-format object reference, iioploc, that can be typed into a program to reach defined services at remote locations, including the Naming Service. For example, this iioploc identifier: | |
| |     *iioploc://www.omg.org/NameService* | |
| | would resolve to the CORBA Naming Service running on the machine whose IP address corresponded to the domain name *www.omg.org*. | |
| | See *http://www.omg.org*. | |
| ilu | The Inter-Language Unification (ILU) system is a multilingual object interface system. The object interfaces provided by ILU hide implementation distinctions between different languages, different address spaces, and different operating system types. ILU can be used to build multilingual object-oriented libraries ("class libraries") with well-specified, language-independent interfaces. It also can be used to implement distributed systems. | |
| | See *ftp://parcftp.parc.xerox.com/pub/ilu/ilu.html*. | |
| imap | The IMAP URL scheme is used to designate IMAP servers, mailboxes, messages, MIME bodies [MIME], and search programs on Internet hosts accessible using the IMAP protocol. | 2192 |
| IOR | CORBA interoperable object reference. | |
| | See *http://www.omg.org*. | |
| irc | The irc URL scheme is used to refer to either Internet Relay Chat (IRC) servers or individual entities (channels or people) on IRC servers. | |
| | See *http://www.w3.org/Addressing/draft-mirashi-url-irc-01.txt*. | |
| isbn | Proposed scheme for ISBN book references. | |
| | See *http://lists.w3.org/Archives/Public/www-talk/1991NovDec/0008.html*. | |
| java | Identifies Java classes. | |
| javascript | The Netscape browser processes javascript URLs, evaluates the expression after the colon (:), if there is one, and loads a page containing the string value of the expression, unless it is undefined. | |
| jdbc | Used in the Java SQL API. | |
| ldap | Allows Internet clients direct access to the LDAP protocol. | 2255 |
| lid | The Local Identifier (lid:) scheme. | |
| | See *draft-blackketter-lid-00*. | |
| lifn | A Location-Independent File Name (LIFN) for the Bulk File Distribution distributed storage system developed at UTK. | |
| livescript | Old name for JavaScript. | |
| lrq | See h323. | |
| mailto | The mailto URL scheme is used to designate the Internet mailing address of an individual or service. | 2368 |
| mailserver | Old proposal from 1994–1995 to let an entire message be encoded in a URL, so that (for example) the URL can automatically send email to a mail server for subscribing to a mailing list. | |

| Scheme | Description | RFCs |
|---|---|---|
| md5 | MD5 is a cryptographic checksum. | |
| mid | The mid scheme uses (a part of) the message-id of an email message to refer to a specific message. | 2392 2111 |
| mocha | See javascript. | |
| modem | The modem scheme describes a connection to a terminal that can handle incoming data calls. | 2806 |
| mms, mmst, mmsu | Scheme for Microsoft Media Server (MMS) to stream Active Streaming Format (ASF) files. To force UDP transport, use the mmsu scheme. To force TCP transport, use mmst. | |
| news | The news URL scheme is used to refer to either news groups or individual articles of USENET news. A news URL takes one of two forms: *news:<newsgroup-name>* or *news:<message-id>*. | 1738 1036 |
| nfs | Used to refer to files and directories on NFS servers. | 2224 |
| nntp | An alternative method of referencing news articles, useful for specifying news articles from NNTP servers. An nntp URL looks like: <br><br>    *nntp://<host>:<port>/<newsgroup-name>/<article-num>* <br><br> Note that while nntp URLs specify a unique location for the article resource, most NNTP servers currently on the Internet are configured to allow access only from local clients, and thus nntp URLs do not designate globally accessible resources. Hence, the news form of URL is preferred as a way of identifying news articles. | 1738 977 |
| opaquelocktoken | A WebDAV lock token, represented as a URI, that identifies a particular lock. A lock token is returned by every successful LOCK operation in the lockdiscovery property in the response body and also can be found through lock discovery on a resource. See RFC 2518. | |
| path | The path scheme defines a uniformly hierarchical namespace where a path URN is a sequence of components and an optional opaque string. <br><br> See *http://www.hypernews.org/~liberte/www/path.html*. | |
| phone | Used in "URLs for Telephony"; replaced with tel: in RFC 2806. | |
| pop | The POP URL designates a POP email server, and optionally a port number, authentication mechanism, authentication ID, and/or authorization ID. | 2384 |
| pnm | Real Networks's streaming protocol. | |
| pop3 | The POP3 URL scheme allows a URL to specify a POP3 server, allowing other protocols to use a general "URL to be used for mail access" in place of an explicit reference to POP3. Defined in expired *draft-earhart-url-pop3-00.txt*. | |
| printer | Abstract URLs for use with the Service Location standard. <br><br> See *draft-ietf-srvloc-printer-scheme-02.txt*. | |
| prospero | Names resources to be accessed via the Prospero Directory Service. | 1738 |
| res | Microsoft scheme that specifies a resource to be obtained from a module. Consists of a string or numerical resource type, and a string or numerical ID. | |
| rtsp | Real-time streaming protocol that is the basis for Real Networks's modern streaming control protocols. | 2326 |
| rvp | URLs for the RVP rendezvous protocol, used to notify the arrival of users on a computer network. <br><br> See *draft-calsyn-rvp-01*. | |

| Scheme | Description | RFCs |
|--------|-------------|------|
| rwhois | RWhois is an Internet directory access protocol, defined in RFC 1714 and RFC 2167. The RWhois URL gives clients direct access to rwhois. <br><br> See *http://www.rwhois.net/rwhois/docs/*. | |
| rx | An architecture to allow remote graphical applications to display data inside web pages. <br><br> See *http://www.w3.org/People/danield/papers/mobgui/*. | |
| sdp | Session Description Protocol (SDP) URLs. See RFC 2327. | |
| service | The service scheme is used to provide access information for arbitrary network services. These URLs provide an extensible framework for client-based network software to obtain configuration information required to make use of network services. | 2609 |
| sip | The sip* family of schemes are used to establish multimedia conferences using the Session Initiation Protocol (SIP). | 2543 |
| shttp | S-HTTP is a superset of HTTP designed to secure HTTP connections and provide a wide variety of mechanisms to provide for confidentiality, authentication, and integrity. It has not been widely deployed, and it has mostly been supplanted with HTTPS SSL-encrypted HTTP. <br><br> See *http://www.homeport.org/~adam/shttp.html*. | |
| snews | SSL-encrypted news. | |
| STANF | Old proposal for stable network filenames. Related to URNs. <br><br> See *http://web3.w3.org/Addressing/#STANF*. | |
| t120 | See h323. | |
| tel | URL to place a call using the telephone network. | 2806 |
| telephone | Used in previous drafts of tel. | |
| telnet | Designates interactive services that may be accessed by the Telnet protocol. A telnet URL takes the form: <br><br> *telnet://<user>:<password>@<host>:<port>/* | 1738 |
| tip | Supports TIP atomic Internet transactions. | 2371 <br> 2372 |
| tn3270 | Reserved, as per *ftp://ftp.isi.edu/in-notes/iana/assignments/url-schemes*. | |
| tv | The TV URL names a particular television broadcast channel. | 2838 |
| uuid | Universally unique identifiers (UUIDs) contain no information about location. They also are known as globally unique identifiers (GUIDs). They are persistent over time, like URNs, and consist of a 128-bit unique ID. UUID URIs are useful in situations where a unique identifier is required that cannot or should not be tied to a particular physical root namespace (such as a DNS name). <br><br> See *draft-kindel-uuid-uri-00.txt*. | |
| urn | Persistent, location-independent, URNs. | 2141 |
| vemmi | Allows versatile multimedia interface (VEMMI) client software and VEMMI terminals to connect to VEMMI-compliant services. VEMMI is an international standard for online multimedia services. | 2122 |
| videotex | Allows videotex client software or terminals to connect to videotex services compliant with the ITU-T and ETSI videotex standards. <br><br> See *http://www.ics.uci.edu/pub/ietf/uri/draft-mavrakis-videotex-url-spec-01.txt*. | |

*Table A-1. URI schemes from the W3C registry (continued)*

| Scheme | Description | RFCs |
|---|---|---|
| view-source | Netscape Navigator source viewers. These view-source URLs display HTML that was generated with JavaScript. | |
| wais | The wide area information service—an early form of search engine. | 1738 |
| whois++ | URLs for the WHOIS++ simple Internet directory protocol.<br>See *http://martinh.net/wip/whois-url.txt*. | 1835 |
| whodp | The Widely Hosted Object Data Protocol (WhoDP) exists to communicate the current location and state of large numbers of dynamic, relocatable objects. A WhoDP program "subscribes" to locate and receive information about an object and "publishes" to control the location and visible state of an object.<br>See *draft-mohr-whodp-00.txt*. | |
| z39.50r, z39.50s | Z39.50 session and retrieval URLs. Z39.50 is an information retrieval protocol that does not fit neatly into a retrieval model designed primarily around the stateless fetch of data. Instead, it models a general user inquiry as a session-oriented, multi-step task, any step of which may be suspended temporarily while the server requests additional parameters from the client before continuing. | 2056 |

# HTTP Status Codes

This appendix is a quick reference of HTTP status codes and their meanings.

## Status Code Classifications

HTTP status codes are segmented into five classes, shown in Table B-1.

*Table B-1. Status code classifications*

| Overall range | Defined range | Category |
|---|---|---|
| 100–199 | 100–101 | Informational |
| 200–299 | 200–206 | Successful |
| 300–399 | 300–305 | Redirection |
| 400–499 | 400–415 | Client error |
| 500–599 | 500–505 | Server error |

## Status Codes

Table B-2 is a quick reference for all the status codes defined in the HTTP/1.1 specification, providing a brief summary of each. "Status Codes" in Chapter 3 goes into more detailed descriptions of these status codes and their uses.

*Table B-2. Status codes*

| Status code | Reason phrase | Meaning |
|---|---|---|
| 100 | Continue | An initial part of the request was received, and the client should continue. |
| 101 | Switching Protocols | The server is changing protocols, as specified by the client, to one listed in the Upgrade header. |
| 200 | OK | The request is okay. |
| 201 | Created | The resource was created (for requests that create server objects). |

*Table B-2. Status codes (continued)*

| Status code | Reason phrase | Meaning |
| --- | --- | --- |
| 202 | Accepted | The request was accepted, but the server has not yet performed any action with it. |
| 203 | Non-Authoritative Information | The transaction was okay, except the information contained in the entity headers was not from the origin server, but from a copy of the resource. |
| 204 | No Content | The response message contains headers and a status line, but no entity body. |
| 205 | Reset Content | Another code primarily for browsers; basically means that the browser should clear any HTML form elements on the current page. |
| 206 | Partial Content | A partial request was successful. |
| 300 | Multiple Choices | A client has requested a URL that actually refers to multiple resources. This code is returned along with a list of options; the user can then select which one he wants. |
| 301 | Moved Permanently | The requested URL has been moved. The response should contain a Location URL indicating where the resource now resides. |
| 302 | Found | Like the 301 status code, but the move is temporary. The client should use the URL given in the Location header to locate the resource temporarily. |
| 303 | See Other | Tells the client that the resource should be fetched using a different URL. This new URL is in the Location header of the response message. |
| 304 | Not Modified | Clients can make their requests conditional by the request headers they include. This code indicates that the resource has not changed. |
| 305 | Use Proxy | The resource must be accessed through a proxy, the location of the proxy is given in the Location header. |
| 306 | (Unused) | This status code currently is not used. |
| 307 | Temporary Redirect | Like the 301 status code; however, the client should use the URL given in the Location header to locate the resource temporarily. |
| 400 | Bad Request | Tells the client that it sent a malformed request. |
| 401 | Unauthorized | Returned along with appropriate headers that ask the client to authenticate itself before it can gain access to the resource. |
| 402 | Payment Required | Currently this status code is not used, but it has been set aside for future use. |
| 403 | Forbidden | The request was refused by the server. |
| 404 | Not Found | The server cannot find the requested URL. |
| 405 | Method Not Allowed | A request was made with a method that is not supported for the requested URL. The Allow header should be included in the response to tell the client what methods are allowed on the requested resource. |
| 406 | Not Acceptable | Clients can specify parameters about what types of entities they are willing to accept. This code is used when the server has no resource matching the URL that is acceptable for the client. |
| 407 | Proxy Authentication Required | Like the 401 status code, but used for proxy servers that require authentication for a resource. |

*Table B-2. Status codes (continued)*

| Status code | Reason phrase | Meaning |
|---|---|---|
| 408 | Request Timeout | If a client takes too long to complete its request, a server can send back this status code and close down the connection. |
| 409 | Conflict | The request is causing some conflict on a resource. |
| 410 | Gone | Like the 404 status code, except that the server once held the resource. |
| 411 | Length Required | Servers use this code when they require a Content-Length header in the request message. The server will not accept requests for the resource without the Content-Length header. |
| 412 | Precondition Failed | If a client makes a conditional request and one of the conditions fails, this response code is returned. |
| 413 | Request Entity Too Large | The client sent an entity body that is larger than the server can or wants to process. |
| 414 | Request URI Too Long | The client sent a request with a request URL that is larger than what the server can or wants to process. |
| 415 | Unsupported Media Type | The client sent an entity of a content type that the server does not understand or support. |
| 416 | Requested Range Not Satisfiable | The request message requested a range of a given resource, and that range either was invalid or could not be met. |
| 417 | Expectation Failed | The request contained an expectation in the Expect request header that could not be satisfied by the server. |
| 500 | Internal Server Error | The server encountered an error that prevented it from servicing the request. |
| 501 | Not Implemented | The client made a request that is beyond the server's capabilities. |
| 502 | Bad Gateway | A server acting as a proxy or gateway encountered a bogus response from the next link in the request response chain. |
| 503 | Service Unavailable | The server cannot currently service the request but will be able to in the future. |
| 504 | Gateway Timeout | Similar to the 408 status code, except that the response is coming from a gateway or proxy that has timed out waiting for a response to its request from another server. |
| 505 | HTTP Version Not Supported | The server received a request in a version of the protocol that it can't or won't support. |

## APPENDIX C

# HTTP Header Reference

It's almost amusing to remember that the first version of HTTP, 0.9, had no headers. While this certainly had its down sides, its fun to marvel in its simplistic elegance.

Well, back to reality. Today there are a horde of HTTP headers, many part of the specification and still others that are extensions to it. This appendix provides some background on these official and extension headers. It also acts as an index for the various headers in this book, pointing out where their concepts and features are discussed in the running text. Most of these headers are simple up-front; it's the interactions with each other and other features of HTTP where things get hairy. This appendix provides a bit of background for the headers listed and directs you to the sections of the book where they are discussed at length.

The headers listed in this appendix are drawn from the HTTP specifications, related documents, and our own experience poking around with HTTP messages and the various servers and clients on the Internet.

This list is far from exhaustive. There are many other extension headers floating around on the Web, not to mention those potentially used in private intranets. Nonetheless, we have attempted to make this list as complete as possible. See RFC 2616 for the current version of the HTTP/1.1 specification and a list of official headers and their specification descriptions.

## Accept

The Accept header is used by clients to let servers know what media types are *acceptable*. The value of the Accept header field is a list of media types that the client can use. For instance, your web browser cannot display every type of multimedia object on the Web. By including an Accept header in your requests, your browser can save you from downloading a video or other type of object that you can't use.

The Accept header field also may include a list of quality values (q values) that tell the server which media type is preferred, in case the server has multiple versions of the media type. See Chapter 17 for a complete discussion of content negotiation and q values.

| Type | Request header |
|---|---|
| Notes | "*" is a special value that is used to wildcard media types. For example, "*/*" represents all types, and "image/*" represents all image types. |
| Examples | Accept: text/*, image/* |
| | Accept: text/*, image/gif, image/jpeg;q=1 |

## Accept-Charset

The Accept-Charset header is used by clients to tell servers what character sets are acceptable or preferred. The value of this request header is a list of character sets and possibly quality values for the listed character sets. The quality values let the server know which character set is preferred, in case the server has the document in multiple acceptable character sets. See Chapter 17 for a complete discussion of content negotiation and q values.

| Type | Request header |
|---|---|
| Notes | As with the Accept header, "*" is a special character. If present, it represents all character sets, except those that also are mentioned explicitly in the value. If it's not present, any charset not in the value field has a default q value of zero, with the exception of the iso-latin-1 charset, which gets a default of 1. |
| Basic Syntax | Accept-Charset: 1# ((charset \| "*") [";" "q" "=" qvalue]) |
| Example | Accept-Charset: iso-latin-1 |

## Accept-Encoding

The Accept-Encoding header is used by clients to tell servers what encodings are acceptable. If the content the server is holding is encoded (perhaps compressed), this request header lets the server know whether the client will accept it. Chapter 17 contains a complete description of the Accept-Encoding header.

| Type | Request header |
|---|---|
| Basic Syntax | Accept-Encoding: 1# ((content-coding \| "*") [";" "q" "=" qvalue]) |
| Examples* | Accept-Encoding: |
| | Accept-Encoding: gzip |
| | Accept-Encoding: compress;q=0.5, gzip;q=1 |

---

* The empty Accept-Encoding example is not a typo. It refers to the identity encoding—that is, the unencoded content. If the Accept-Encoding header is present and empty, only the unencoded content is acceptable.

# Accept-Language

The Accept-Language request header functions like the other Accept headers, allowing clients to inform the server about what languages (e.g., the natural language for content) are acceptable or preferred. Chapter 17 contains a complete description of the Accept-Language header.

| | |
|---|---|
| **Type** | Request header |
| **Basic Syntax** | Accept-Language: 1# (language-range [";" "q" "=" qvalue])<br>language-range = ((1*8ALPHA * ("-" 1*8ALPHA)) \| "*") |
| **Examples** | Accept-Language: en<br>Accept-Language: en;q=0.7, en-gb;q=0.5 |

# Accept-Ranges

The Accept-Ranges header differs from the other Accept headers—it is a response header used by servers to tell clients whether they accept requests for ranges of a resource. The value of this header tells what type of ranges, if any, the server accepts for a given resource.

A client can attempt to make a range request on a resource without having received this header. If the server does not support range requests for that resource, it can respond with an appropriate status code* and the Accept-Ranges value "none". Servers might want to send the "none" value for normal requests to discourage clients from making range requests in the future.

Chapter 17 contains a complete description of the Accept-Ranges header.

| | |
|---|---|
| **Type** | Response header |
| **Basic Syntax** | Accept-Ranges: 1# range-unit \| none |
| **Examples** | Accept-Ranges: none<br>Accept-Ranges: bytes |

# Age

The Age header tells the receiver how old a response is. It is the sender's best guess as to how long ago the response was generated by or revalidated with the origin server. The value of the header is the sender's guess, a delta in seconds. See Chapter 7 for more on the Age header.

| | |
|---|---|
| **Type** | Response header |
| **Notes** | HTTP/1.1 caches must include an Age header in every response they send. |

---

* For example, status code 416 (see "400–499: Client Error Status Codes" in Chapter 3).

| Basic Syntax | Age: delta-seconds |
|---|---|
| Example | Age: 60 |

## Allow

The Allow header is used to inform clients what HTTP methods are supported on a particular resource.

| Type | Response header |
|---|---|
| Notes | An HTTP/1.1 server sending a 405 Method Not Allowed response must include an Allow header.* |
| Basic Syntax | Allow: #Method |
| Example | Allow: GET, HEAD |

## Authorization

The Authorization header is sent by a client to authenticate itself with a server. A client will include this header in its request after receiving a 401 Authentication Required response from a server. The value of this header depends on the authentication scheme in use. See Chapter 14 for a detailed discussion of the Authorization header.

| Type | Response header |
|---|---|
| Basic Syntax | Authorization: authentication-scheme #authentication-param |
| Example | Authorization: Basic YnJpYW4tdG90dHk6T3ch |

## Cache-Control

The Cache-Control header is used to pass information about how an object can be cached. This header is one of the more complex headers introduced in HTTP/1.1. Its value is a caching directive, giving caches special instructions about an object's cacheability.

In Chapter 7, we discuss caching in general as well as the specific details about this header.

| Type | General header |
|---|---|
| Example | Cache-Control: no-cache |

---

* See "Status Codes" in Chapter 3 for more on the 405 status code.

# Client-ip

The Client-ip header is an extension header used by some older clients and some proxies to transmit the IP address of the machine on which the client is running.

**Type**             Extension request header

**Notes**            Implementors should be aware that the information provided in the value of this header is not secure.

**Basic Syntax**     Client-ip: ip-address

**Example**          Client-ip: 209.1.33.49

# Connection

The Connection header is a somewhat overloaded header that can lead to a bit of confusion. This header was used in HTTP/1.0 clients that were extended with keep-alive connections for control information.* In HTTP/1.1, the older semantics are mostly recognized, but the header has taken on a new function.

In HTTP/1.1, the Connection header's value is a list of tokens that correspond to header names. Applications receiving an HTTP/1.1 message with a Connection header are supposed to parse the list and remove any of the headers in the message that are in the Connection header list. This is mainly for proxies, allowing a server or other proxy to specify hop-by-hop headers that should not be passed along.

One special token value is "close". This token means that the connection is going to be closed after the response is completed. HTTP/1.1 applications that do not support persistent connections need to insert the Connection header with the "close" token in all requests and responses.

**Type**             General header

**Notes**            While RFC 2616 does not specifically mention keep-alive as a connection token, some browsers (including those sending HTTP/1.1 as their versions) use it in making requests.

**Basic Syntax**     Connection: 1# (connection-token)

**Examples**         Connection: close

---

* See Chapter 4 for more on keep-alive and persistent connections.

## Content-Base

The Content-Base header provides a way for a server to specify a base URL for resolving URLs found in the entity body of a response.* The value of the Content-Base header is an absolute URL that can be used to resolve relative URLs found inside the entity.

| | |
|---|---|
| **Type** | Entity header |
| **Notes** | This header is not defined in RFC 2616; it was previously defined in RFC 2068, an earlier draft of the HTTP/1.1 specification, and has since been removed from the official specification. |
| **Basic Syntax** | Content-Base: absoluteURL |
| **Example** | Content-Base: http://www.joes-hardware.com/ |

## Content-Encoding

The Content-Encoding header is used to specify whether any encodings have been performed on the object. By encoding the content, a server can compress it before sending the response. The value of the Content-Encoding header tells the client what type or types of encoding have been performed on the object. With that information, the client can then decode the message.

Sometimes more than one encoding is applied to an entity, in which case the encodings must be listed in the order in which they were performed.

| | |
|---|---|
| **Type** | Entity header |
| **Basic Syntax** | Content-Encoding: 1# content-coding |
| **Examples** | Content-Encoding: gzip |
| | Content-Encoding: compress, gzip |

## Content-Language

The Content-Language header tells the client the natural language that should be understood in order to understand the object. For instance, a document written in French would have a Content-Language value indicating French. If this header is not present in the response, the object is intended for all audiences. Multiple languages in the header's value indicate that the object is suitable for audiences of each language listed.

One caveat about this header is that the header's value may just represent the natural language of the intended audience of this object, not all or any of the languages contained

---

* See Chapter 2 for more on base URLs.

in the object. Also, this header is not limited to text or written data objects; images, video, and other media types can be tagged with their intended audiences' natural languages.

| | |
|---|---|
| **Type** | Entity header |
| **Basic Syntax** | Content-Language: 1# language-tag |
| **Examples** | Content-Language: en |
| | Content-Language: en, fr |

## Content-Length

The Content-Length header gives the length or size of the entity body. If the header is in a response message to a HEAD HTTP request, the value of the header indicates the size that the entity body would have been had it been sent.

| | |
|---|---|
| **Type** | Entity header |
| **Basic Syntax** | Content-Length: 1*DIGIT |
| **Example** | Content-Length: 2417 |

## Content-Location

The Content-Location header is included in an HTTP message to give the URL corresponding to the entity in the message. For objects that may have multiple URLs, a response message can include a Content-Location header indicating the URL of the object used to generate the response. The Content-Location can be different from the requested URL. This generally is used by servers that are directing or redirecting a client to a new URL.

If the URL is relative, it should be interpreted relative to the Content-Base header. If the Content-Base header is not present, the URL used in the request should be used.

| | |
|---|---|
| **Type** | Entity header |
| **Basic Syntax** | Content-Location: (absoluteURL | relativeURL) |
| **Example** | Content-Location: http://www.joes-hardware.com/index.html |

## Content-MD5

The Content-MD5 header is used by servers to provide a message-integrity check for the message body. Only an origin server or requesting client should insert a Content-MD5 header in the message. The value of the header is an MD5 digest[*] of the (potentially encoded) message body.

The value of this header allows for an end-to-end check on the data, useful for detecting unintentional modifications to the data in transit. It is not intended to be used for security purposes.

RFC 1864 defines this header in more detail.

| | |
|---|---|
| **Type** | Entity header |
| **Notes** | The MD5 digest value is a base-64 (see Appendix E) or 128-bit MD5 digest, as defined in RFC 1864. |
| **Basic Syntax** | Content-MD5: md5-digest |
| **Example** | Content-MD5: Q2h1Y2sgSW51ZwDIAXR5IQ== |

## Content-Range

The Content-Range header is sent as the result of a request that transmitted a range of a document. It provides the location (range) within the original entity that this entity represents. It also gives the length of the entire entity.

If an "*" is present in the value instead of the length of the entire entity, this means that the length was not known when the response was sent.

See Chapter 15 for more on the Content-Range header.

| | |
|---|---|
| **Type** | Entity header |
| **Notes** | Servers responding with the 206 Partial Content response code must not include a Content-Range header with an "*" as the length. |
| **Example** | Content-Range: bytes 500-999 / 5400 |

## Content-Type

The Content-Type header tells the media type of the object in the message.

| | |
|---|---|
| **Type** | Entity header |
| **Basic Syntax** | Content-Type: media-type |
| **Example** | Content-Type: text/html; charset=iso-latin-1 |

---

[*] The MD5 digest is defined in RFC 1864.

## Cookie

The Cookie header is an extension header used for client identification and tracking. Chapter 11 talks about the Cookie header and its use in detail (also see "Set-Cookie").

| | |
|---|---|
| **Type** | Extension request header |
| **Example** | Cookie: ink=IUOK164y59BC708378908CFF89OE5573998A115 |

## Cookie2

The Cookie2 header is an extension header used for client identification and tracking. Cookie2 is used to identify what version of cookies a requestor understands. It is defined in greater detail in RFC 2965.

Chapter 11 talks about the Cookie2 header and its use in detail.

| | |
|---|---|
| **Type** | Extension request header |
| **Example** | Cookie2: $version="1" |

## Date

The Date header gives the date and time at which the message was created. This header is required in servers' responses because the time and date at which the server believes the message was created can be used by caches in evaluating the freshness of a response. For clients, this header is completely optional, although it's good form to include it.

**Type**　　　　General header

**Basic Syntax**　Date: HTTP-date

**Examples**　　Date: Tue, 3 Oct 1997 02:15:31 GMT

HTTP has a few specific date formats. This one is defined in RFC 822 and is the preferred format for HTTP/1.1 messages. However, in earlier specifications of HTTP, the date format was not spelled out as well, so server and client implementors have used other formats, which need to be supported for the sake of legacy. You will run into date formats like the one specified in RFC 850, as well as dates in the format produced by the *asctime()* system call. Here they are for the date represented above:

```
Date: Tuesday, 03-Oct-97 02:15:31 GMT      RFC 850 format
Date: Tue Oct 3 02:15:31 1997              asctime() format
```

The *asctime()* format is looked down on because it is in local time and it does not specify its time zone (e.g., GMT). In general, the date header should be in GMT; however, robust applications should handle dates that either do not specify the time zone or include Date values in non-GMT time.

# ETag

The ETag header provides the *entity tag* for the entity contained in the message. An entity tag is basically a way of identifying a resource.

Entity tags and their relationship to resources are discussed in detail in Chapter 15.

| | |
|---|---|
| **Type** | Entity header |
| **Basic Syntax** | ETag: entity-tag |
| **Examples** | ETag: "11e92a-457b-31345aa" |
| | ETag: W/"11e92a-457b-3134b5aa" |

# Expect

The Expect header is used by clients to let servers know that they expect certain behavior. This header currently is closely tied to the response code 100 Continue (see "100–199: Informational Status Codes" in Chapter 3).

If a server does not understand the Expect header's value, it should respond with a status code of 417 Expectation Failed.

| | |
|---|---|
| **Type** | Request header |
| **Basic Syntax** | Expect: 1# ("100-continue" \| expectation-extension) |
| **Example** | Expect: 100-continue |

# Expires

The Expires header gives a date and time at which the response is no longer valid. This allows clients such as your browser to cache a copy and not have to ask the server if it is still valid until after this time has expired.

Chapter 7 discusses how the Expires header is used—in particular, how it relates to caches and having to revalidate responses with the origin server.

| | |
|---|---|
| **Type** | Entity header |
| **Basic Syntax** | Expires: HTTP-date |
| **Example** | Expires: Thu, 03 Oct 1997 17:15:00 GMT |

# From

The From header says who the request is coming from. The format is just a valid Internet email address (specified in RFC 1123) for the user of the client.

There are potential privacy issues with using/populating this header. Client implementors should be careful to inform their users and give them a choice before including this header in a request message. Given the potential for abuse by people collecting email addresses for unsolicited mail messages, woe to the implementor who broadcasts this header unannounced and has to answer to angry users.

| | |
|---|---|
| **Type** | Request header |
| **Basic Syntax** | From: mailbox |
| **Example** | From: slurp@inktomi.com |

## Host

The Host header is used by clients to provide the server with the Internet hostname and port number of the machine from which the client wants to make a request. The hostname and port are those from the URL the client was requesting.

The Host header allows servers to differentiate different relative URLs based on the hostname, giving the server the ability to host several different hostnames on the same machine (i.e., the same IP address).

| | |
|---|---|
| **Type** | Request header |
| **Notes** | HTTP/1.1 clients must include a Host header in all requests. All HTTP/1.1 servers must respond with the 400 Bad Request status code to HTTP/1.1 clients that do not provide a Host header. |
| **Basic Syntax** | Host: host [":" port] |
| **Example** | Host: www.hotbot.com:80 |

## If-Modified-Since

The If-Modified-Since request header is used to make conditional requests. A client can use the GET method to request a resource from a server, having the response hinge on whether the resource has been modified since the client last requested it.

If the object has not been modified, the server will respond with a 304 Not Modified response, instead of with the resource. If the object has been modified, the server will respond as if it was a non-conditional GET request. Chapter 7 discusses conditional requests in detail.

| | |
|---|---|
| **Type** | Request header |
| **Basic Syntax** | If-Modified-Since: HTTP-date |
| **Example** | If-Modified-Since: Thu, 03 Oct 1997 17:15:00 GMT |

# If-Match

Like the If-Modified-Since header, the If-Match header can be used to make a request conditional. Instead of a date, the If-Match request uses an entity tag. The server compares the entity tag in the If-Match header with the current entity tag of the resource and returns the object if the tags match.

The server should use the If-Match value of "*" to match any entity tag it has for a resource; "*" will always match, unless the server no longer has the resource.

This header is useful for updating resources that a client or cache already has. The resource is returned only if it has changed—that is, if the previously requested object's entity tag does not match the entity tag of the current version on the server. Chapter 7 discusses conditional requests in detail.

| | |
|---|---|
| **Type** | Request header |
| **Basic Syntax** | If-Match: ("*" \| 1# entity-tag) |
| **Example** | If-Match: "11e92a-457b-31345aa" |

# If-None-Match

The If-None-Match header, like all the If headers, can be used to make a request conditional. The client supplies the server with a list of entity tags, and the server compares those tags against the entity tags it has for the resource, returning the resource only if none match.

This allows a cache to update resources only if they have changed. Using the If-None-Match header, a cache can use a single request to both invalidate the entities it has and receive the new entity in the response. Chapter 7 discusses conditional requests in detail.

| | |
|---|---|
| **Type** | Request header |
| **Basic Syntax** | If-None-Match: ("*" \| 1# entity-tag) |
| **Example** | If-None-Match: "11e92a-457b-31345aa" |

# If-Range

The If-Range header, like all the If headers, can be used to make a request conditional. It is used when an application has a copy of a range of a resource, to revalidate the range or get the complete resource if the range is no longer valid. Chapter 7 discusses conditional requests in detail.

| | |
|---|---|
| **Type** | Request header |
| **Basic Syntax** | If-Range: (HTTP-date \| entity-tag) |

**Examples**      If-Range: Tue, 3 Oct 1997 02:15:31 GMT
                  If-Range: "11e92a-457b-3134b5aa"

## If-Unmodified-Since

The If-Unmodified-Since header is the twin of the If-Modified-Since header. Including it in a request makes the request conditional. The server should look at the date value of the header and return the object only if it has not been modified since the date provided. Chapter 7 discusses conditional requests in detail.

**Type**          Request header

**Basic Syntax**  If-Unmodified-Since: HTTP-date

**Example**       If-Unmodified-Since: Thu, 03 Oct 1997 17:15:00 GMT

## Last-Modified

The Last-Modified header tries to provide information about the last time this entity was changed. This could mean a lot of things. For example, resources typically are files on a server, so the Last-Modified value could be the last-modified time provided by the server's filesystem. On the other hand, for dynamically created resources such as those created by scripts, the Last-Modified value could be the time the response was created.

Servers need to be careful that the Last-Modified time is not in the future. HTTP/1.1 servers should reset the Last-Modified time if it is later than the value that would be sent in the Date header.

**Type**          Entity header

**Basic Syntax**  Last-Modified: HTTP-date

**Example**       Last-Modified: Thu, 03 Oct 1997 17:15:00 GMT

## Location

The Location header is used by servers to direct clients to the location of a resource that either was moved since the client last requested it or was created in response to the request.

**Type**          Response header

**Basic Syntax**  Location: absoluteURL

**Example**       Location: http://www.hotbot.com

## Max-Forwards

This header is used only with the TRACE method, to limit the number of proxies or other intermediaries that a request goes through. Its value is an integer. Each application that receives a TRACE request with this header should decrement the value before it forwards the request along.

If the value is zero when the application receives the request, it should send back a 200 OK response to the request, with an entity body containing the original request. If the Max-Forwards header is missing from a TRACE request, assume that there is no maximum number of forwards.

For other HTTP methods, this header should be ignored. See "Methods" in Chapter 3 for more on the TRACE method.

**Type**          Request header

**Basic Syntax**  Max-Forwards: 1*DIGIT

**Example**       Max-Forwards: 5


## MIME-Version

MIME is HTTP's cousin. While they are radically different, some HTTP servers do construct messages that are valid under the MIME specification. When this is the case, the MIME-Version header can be supplied by the server.

This header has never been part of the official specification, although it is mentioned in the HTTP/1.0 specification. Many older servers send messages with this header, however, those messages often are not valid MIME messages, making this header both confusing and impossible to trust.

**Type**          Extension general header

**Basic Syntax**  MIME-Version: DIGIT "." DIGIT

**Example**       MIME-Version: 1.0


## Pragma

The Pragma header is used to pass directions along with the message. These directions could be almost anything, but often they are used to control caching behavior. Proxies and gateways must not remove the Pragma header, because it could be intended for all applications that receive the message.

The most common form of Pragma, Pragma: no-cache, is a request header that forces caches to request or revalidate the document from the origin server even when a fresh copy is available in the cache. It is sent by browsers when users click on the Reload/Refresh button. Many servers send Pragma: no-cache as a response header (as an equivalent to

Cache-Control: no-cache), but despite its common use, this behavior is technically undefinded. Not all applications support Pragma response headers.

Chapter 7 discusses the Pragma header and how it is used by HTTP/1.0 applications to control caches.

| | |
|---|---|
| **Type** | Request header |
| **Basic Syntax** | Pragma: 1# pragma-directive* |
| **Example** | Pragma: no-cache |

## Proxy-Authenticate

The Proxy-Authenticate header functions like the WWW-Authenticate header. It is used by proxies to challenge an application sending a request to authenticate itself. The full details of this challenge/response, and other security mechanisms of HTTP, are discussed in detail in Chapter 14.

If an HTTP/1.1 proxy server is sending a 407 Proxy Authentication Required response, it must include the Proxy-Authenticate header.

Proxies and gateways must be careful in interpreting all the Proxy headers. They generally are hop-by-hop headers, applying only to the current connection. For instance, the Proxy-Authenticate header requests authentication for the current connection.

| | |
|---|---|
| **Type** | Response header |
| **Basic Syntax** | Proxy-Authenticate: challenge |
| **Example** | Proxy-Authenticate: Basic realm="Super Secret Corporate Financial Documents" |

## Proxy-Authorization

The Proxy-Authorization header functions like the Authorization header. It is used by client applications to respond to Proxy-Authenticate challenges. See Chapter 14 for more on how the challenge/response security mechanism works.

| | |
|---|---|
| **Type** | Request header |
| **Basic Syntax** | Proxy-Authorization: credentials |
| **Example** | Proxy-Authorization: Basic YnJpYW4tdG90dHk6T3ch |

---

* The only specification-defined Pragma directive is "no-cache"; however, you may run into other Pragma headers that have been defined as extensions to the specification.

## Proxy-Connection

The Proxy-Connection header was meant to have similar semantics to the HTTP/1.0 Connection header. It was to be used between clients and proxies to specify options about the connections (chiefly keep-alive connections).* It is not a standard header and is viewed as an ad hoc header by the standards committee. However, it is widely used by browsers and proxies.

Browser implementors created the Proxy-Connection header to solve the problem of a client sending an HTTP/1.0 Connection header that gets blindly forwarded by a dumb proxy. A server receiving the blindly forwarded Connection header could confuse the capabilities of the client connection with those of the proxy connection.

The Proxy-Connection header is sent instead of the Connection header when the client knows that it is going through a proxy. Because servers don't recognize the Proxy-Connection header, they ignore it, allowing dumb proxies that blindly forward the header to do so without causing harm.

The problem with this solution occurs if there is more than one proxy in the path of the client to the server. If the first one blindly forwards the header to the second, which understands it, the second proxy can suffer from the same confusion the server did with the Connection header.

This is the problem that the HTTP working group had with this solution—they saw it as a hack that solved the case of a single proxy, but not the bigger problem. Nonetheless, it does handle some of the more common cases, and because older versions of both Netscape Navigator and Microsoft Internet Explorer implement it, proxy implementors need to deal with it. See Chapter 4 for more information.

| | |
|---|---|
| **Type** | General header |
| **Basic Syntax** | Proxy-Connection: 1# (connection-token) |
| **Example** | Proxy-Connection: close |

## Public

The Public header allows a server to tell a client what methods it supports. These methods can be used in future requests by the client. Proxies need to be careful when they receive a response from a server with the Public header. The header indicates the capabilities of the server, not the proxy, so the proxy needs to either edit the list of methods in the header or remove the header before it sends the response to the client.

| | |
|---|---|
| **Type** | Response header |

---

* See Chapter 4 for more on keep-alive and persistent connections.

| **Notes** | This header is not defined in RFC 2616. It was previously defined in RFC 2068, an earlier draft of the HTTP/1.1 specification, but it has since been removed from the official specification. |
|---|---|
| **Basic Syntax** | Public: 1# HTTP-method |
| **Example** | Public: OPTIONS, GET, HEAD, TRACE, POST |

## Range

The Range header is used in requests for parts or ranges of an entity. Its value indicates the range of the entity that is included in the message.

Requests for ranges of a document allow for more efficient requests of large objects (by requesting them in segments) or for recovery from failed transfers (allowing a client to request the range of the resource that did not make it). Range requests and the headers that make the requests possible are discussed in detail in Chapter 15.

| **Type** | Entity header |
|---|---|
| **Example** | Range: bytes=500-1500 |

## Referer

The Referer header is inserted into client requests to let the server know where the client got the URL from. This is a voluntary effort, for the server's benefit; it allows the server to better log the requests or perform other tasks. The misspelling of "Referer" hearkens back to the early days of HTTP, to the frustration of English-speaking copyeditors throughout the world.

What your browser does is fairly simple. If you get home page A and click on a link to go to home page B, your browser will insert a Referer header in the request with value A. Referer headers are inserted by your browser only when you click on links; requests for URLs you type in yourself will not contain a Referer header.

Because some pages are private, there are some privacy concerns with this header. While some of this is unwarranted paranoia, this header does allow web servers and their administrators to see where you came from, potentially allowing them to better track your surfing. As a result, the HTTP/1.1 specification recommends that application writers allow the user to decide whether this header is transmitted.

| **Type** | Request header |
|---|---|
| **Basic Syntax** | Referer: (absoluteURL \| relativeURL) |
| **Example** | Referer: http://www.inktomi.com/index.html |

# Retry-After

Servers can use the Retry-After header to tell a client when to retry its request for a resource. It is used with the 503 Service Unavailable status code to give the client a specific date and time (or number of seconds) at which it should retry its request.

A server can also use this header when it is redirecting clients to resources, giving the client a time to wait before making a request on the resource to which it is redirected.* This can be very useful to servers that are creating dynamic resources, allowing the server to redirect the client to the newly created resource but giving time for the resource to be created.

| | |
|---|---|
| **Type** | Response header |
| **Basic Syntax** | Retry-After: (HTTP-date \| delta-seconds) |
| **Examples** | Retry-After: Tue, 3 Oct 1997 02:15:31 GMT |
| | Retry-After: 120 |

# Server

The Server header is akin to the User-Agent header; it provides a way for servers to identify themselves to clients. Its value is the server name and an optional comment about the server.

Because the Server header identifies the server product and can contain additional comments about the product, its format is somewhat free-form. If you are writing software that depends on how a server identifies itself, you should experiment with the server software to see what it sends back, because these tokens vary from product to product and release to release.

As with the User-Agent header, don't be surprised if an older proxy or gateway inserts what amounts to a Via header in the Server header itself.

| | |
|---|---|
| **Type** | Response header |
| **Basic Syntax** | Server: 1* (product \| comment) |
| **Examples** | Server: Microsoft-Internet-Information-Server/1.0 |
| | Server: websitepro/1.1f (s/n wpo-07d0) |
| | Server: apache/1.2b6 via proxy gateway CERN-HTTPD/3.0 libwww/2.13 |

# Set-Cookie

The Set-Cookie header is the partner to the Cookie header; in Chapter 11, we discuss the use of this header in detail.

---

* See "Redirection status codes and reason phrases" in Chapter 3 for more on server redirect responses.

| Type | Extension response header |
|------|----------------------------|
| **Basic Syntax** | Set-Cookie: command |
| **Examples** | Set-Cookie: lastorder=00183; path=/orders |
|  | Set-Cookie: private_id=519; secure |

## Set-Cookie2

The Set-Cookie2 header is an extension of the Set-Cookie header; in Chapter 11, we discuss the use of this header in detail.

| Type | Extension response header |
|------|----------------------------|
| **Basic Syntax** | Set-Cookie2: command |
| **Examples** | Set-Cookie2: ID="29046"; Domain=".joes-hardware.com" |
|  | Set-Cookie2: color=blue |

## TE

The poorly named TE header functions like the Accept-Encoding header, but for transfer encodings (it could have been named Accept-Transfer-Encoding, but it wasn't). The TE header also can be used to indicate whether a client can handle headers in the trailer of a response that has been through the chunked encoding. See Chapter 15 for more on the TE header, chunked encoding, and trailers.

| Type | Request header |
|------|----------------|
| **Notes** | If the value is empty, only the chunked transfer encoding is acceptable. The special token "trailers" indicates that trailer headers are acceptable in a chunked response. |
| **Basic Syntax** | TE: # (transfer-codings) |
|  | transfer-codings= "trailers" \| (transfer-extension [accept-params]) |
| **Examples** | TE: |
|  | TE: chunked |

## Trailer

The Trailer header is used to indicate which headers are present in the trailer of a message. Chapter 15 discusses chunked encodings and trailers in detail.

| Type | General header |
|------|----------------|

| **Basic Syntax** | Trailer: 1#field-name |
|---|---|
| **Example** | Trailer: Content-Length |

# Title

The Title header is a non-specification header that is supposed to give the title of the entity. This header was part of an early HTTP/1.0 extension and was used primarily for HTML pages, which have clear title markers that servers can use. Because many, if not most, media types on the Web do not have such an easy way to extract a title, this header has limited usefulness. As a result, it never made it into the official specification, though some older servers on the Net still send it faithfully.

| **Type** | Response header |
|---|---|
| **Notes** | The Title header is not defined in RFC 2616. It was originally defined in the HTTP/1.0 draft definition (*http://www.w3.org/Protocols/HTTP/HTTP2.html*) but has since been removed from the official specification. |
| **Basic Syntax** | Title: document-title |
| **Example** | Title: CNN Interactive |

# Transfer-Encoding

If some encoding had to be performed to transfer the HTTP message body safely, the message will contain the Transfer-Encoding header. Its value is a list of the encodings that were performed on the message body. If multiple encodings were performed, they are listed in order.

The Transfer-Encoding header differs from the Content-Encoding header because the transfer encoding is an encoding that was performed by a server or other intermediary application to transfer the message.

Transfer encodings are discussed in Chapter 15.

| **Type** | General header |
|---|---|
| **Basic Syntax** | Transfer-Encoding: 1# transfer-coding |
| **Example** | Transfer-Encoding: chunked |

# UA-(CPU, Disp, OS, Color, Pixels)

These User-Agent headers are nonstandard and no longer common. They provide information about the client machine that could allow for better content selection by a server. For instance, if a server knew that a user's machine had only an 8-bit color display, the server could select images that were optimized for that type of display.

With any header that gives information about the client that otherwise would be unavailable, there are some security concerns (see Chapter 14 for more information).

| | |
|---|---|
| **Type** | Extension request headers |
| **Notes** | These headers are not defined in RFC 2616, and their use is frowned upon. |
| **Basic Syntax** | "UA" "-" ("CPU" \| "Disp" \| "OS" \| "Color" \| "Pixels") ":" machine-value <br> machine-value = (cpu \| screensize \| os-name \| display-color-depth) |
| **Examples** | UA-CPU: x86 *CPU of client's machine* <br> UA-Disp: 640, 480, 8 *Size and color depth of client's display* <br> UA-OS: Windows 95 *Operating system of client machine* <br> UA-Color: color8 *Color depth of client's display* <br> UA-Pixels: 640x480 *Size of client's display* |

## Upgrade

The Upgrade header provides the sender of a message with a means of broadcasting the desire to use another, perhaps completely different, protocol. For instance, an HTTP/1.1 client could send an HTTP/1.0 request to a server and include an Upgrade header with the value "HTTP/1.1", allowing the client to test the waters and see whether the server speaks HTTP/1.1.

If the server is capable, it can send an appropriate response letting the client know that it is okay to use the new protocol. This provides an efficient way to move to other protocols. Most servers currently are only HTTP/1.0-compliant, and this strategy allows a client to avoid confusing a server with too many HTTP/1.1 headers until it determines whether the server is indeed capable of speaking HTTP/1.1.

When a server sends a 101 Switching Protocols response, it must include this header.

| | |
|---|---|
| **Type** | General header |
| **Basic Syntax** | Upgrade: 1# protocol |
| **Example** | Upgrade: HTTP/2.0 |

## User-Agent

The User-Agent header is used by client applications to identify themselves, much like the Server header for servers. Its value is the product name and possibly a comment describing the client application.

This header's format is somewhat free-form. Its value varies from client product to product and release to release. This header sometimes even contains information about the machine on which the client is running.

As with the Server header, don't be surprised if older proxy or gateway applications insert what amounts to a Via header in the User-Agent header itself.

**Type;**        Request header

**Basic Syntax**        User-Agent: 1* (product | comment)

**Example**        User-Agent: Mozilla/4.0 (compatible; MSIE 5.5; Windows NT 5.0)

## Vary

The Vary header is used by servers to inform clients what headers from a client's request will be used in server-side negotiation.* Its value is a list of headers that the server looks at to determine what to send the client as a response.

An example of this would be a server that sends special HTML pages based on your web browser's features. A server sending these special pages for a URL would include a Vary header that indicated that it looked at the User-Agent header of the request to determine what to send as a response.

The Vary header also is used by caching proxies; see Chapter 7 for more on how the Vary header relates to cached HTTP responses.

**Type**        Response header

**Basic Syntax**        Vary: ("*" | 1# field-name)

**Example**        Vary: User-Agent

## Via

The Via header is used to trace messages as they pass through proxies and gateways. It is an informational header that can be used to see what applications are handling requests and responses.

When a message passes through an HTTP application on its way to a client or a server, that application can use the Via header to tag the message as having gone *via* it. This is an HTTP/1.1 header; many older applications insert a Via-like string in the User-Agent or Server headers of requests and responses.

If the message passes through multiple in-between applications, each one should tack on its Via string. The Via header must be inserted by HTTP/1.1 proxies and gateways.

* See Chapter 17 for more on content negotiation.

| Type | General header |
|------|----------------|
| Basic Syntax* | Via: 1# (received-protocol received-by [comment]) |
| Example | Via: 1.1 joes-hardware.com (Joes-Server/1.0) |

The above says that the message passed through the Joes Server Version 1.0 software running on the machine *joes-hardware.com*. Joe's Server was speaking HTTP 1.1. The Via header should be formatted like this:

```
HTTP-Version machine-hostname (Application-Name-Version)
```

## Warning

The Warning header is used to give a little more information about what happened during a request. It provides the server with a way to send additional information that is not in the status code or reason phrase. Several warning codes are defined in the HTTP/1.1 specification:

*101 Response Is Stale*
When a response message is known to be stale—for instance, if the origin server is unavailable for revalidation—this warning must be included.

*111 Revalidation Failed*
If a cache attempts to revalidate a response with an origin server and the revalidation fails because the cache cannot reach the origin server, this warning must be included in the response to the client.

*112 Disconnected Operation*
An informative warning; should be used if a cache's connectivity to the network is removed.

*113 Heuristic Expiration*
Caches must include this warning if their freshness heuristic is greater than 24 hours and they are returning a response with an age greater than 24 hours.

*199 Miscellaneous Warning*
Systems receiving this warning must not take any automated response; the message may and probably should contain a body with additional information for the user.

*214 Transformation Applied*
Must be added by any intermediate application, such as a proxy, if the application performs any transformation that changes the content encoding of the response.

*299 Miscellaneous Persistent Warning*
Systems receiving this warning must not take any automated reaction; the error may contain a body with more information for the user.

* See the HTTP/1.1 specification for the complete Via header syntax.

| **Type** | Response header |
|---|---|
| **Basic Syntax** | Warning: 1# warning-value |
| **Example** | Warning: 113 |

## WWW-Authenticate

The WWW-Authenticate header is used in 401 Unauthorized responses to issue a challenge authentication scheme to the client. Chapter 14 discusses the WWW-Authenticate header and its use in HTTP's basic challenge/response authentication system.

| **Type** | Response header |
|---|---|
| **Basic Syntax** | WWW-Authenticate: 1# challenge |
| **Example** | WWW-Authenticate: Basic realm="Your Private Travel Profile" |

## X-Cache

The X headers are all extension headers. The X-Cache header is used by Squid to inform a client whether a resource is available.

| **Type** | Extension response header |
|---|---|
| **Example** | X-Cache: HIT |

## X-Forwarded-For

This header is used by many proxy servers (e.g., Squid) to note whom a request has been forwarded for. Like the Client-ip header mentioned earlier, this request header notes the address from which the request originates.

| **Type** | Extension request header |
|---|---|
| **Basic Syntax** | X-Forwarded-For: addr |
| **Example** | X-Forwarded-For: 64.95.76.161 |

## X-Pad

This header is used to overcome a bug related to response header length in some browsers; it pads the response message headers with extra bytes to work around the bug.

| Type | Extension general header |
|------|--------------------------|
| **Basic Syntax** | X-Pad: pad-text |
| **Example** | X-Pad: bogosity |

## X-Serial-Number

The X-Serial-Number header is an extension header. It was used by some older HTTP applications to insert the serial number of the licensed software in the HTTP message.

Its use has pretty much died out, but it is listed here as an example of the X headers that are out there.

| Type | Extension general header |
|------|--------------------------|
| **Basic Syntax** | X-Serial-Number: serialno |
| **Example** | X-Serial-Number: 010014056 |

# MIME Types

MIME media types (MIME types, for short) are standardized names that describe the contents of a message entity body (e.g., text/html, image/jpeg). This appendix explains how MIME types work, how to register new ones, and where to go for more information.

In addition, this appendix contains 10 convenient tables, detailing hundreds of MIME types, gathered from many sources around the globe. This may be the most detailed tabular listing of MIME types ever compiled. We hope these tables are useful to you.

In this appendix, we will:

- Outline the primary reference material, in "Background."
- Explain the structure of MIME types, in "MIME Type Structure."
- Show you how to register MIME types, in "MIME Type IANA Registration."
- Make it easier for you to look up MIME types.

The following MIME type tables are included in this appendix:

- application/*—Table D-3
- audio/*—Table D-4
- chemical/*—Table D-5
- image/*—Table D-6
- message/*—Table D-7
- model/*—Table D-8
- multipart/*—Table D-9
- text/*—Table D-10
- video/*—Table D-11
- Other—Table D-12

# Background

MIME types originally were developed for multimedia email (MIME stands for Multipurpose Internet Mail Extensions), but they have been reused for HTTP and several other protocols that need to describe the format and purpose of data objects.

MIME is defined by five primary documents:

*RFC 2045, "MIME: Format of Internet Message Bodies"*
Describes the overall MIME message structure, and introduces the Content-Type header, borrowed by HTTP

*RFC 2046, "MIME: Media Types"*
Introduces MIME types and their structure

*RFC 2047, "MIME: Message Header Extensions for Non-ASCII Text"*
Defines ways to include non-ASCII characters in headers

*RFC 2048, "MIME: Registration Procedures"*
Defines how to register MIME values with the Internet Assigned Numbers Authority (IANA)

*RFC 2049, "MIME: Conformance Criteria and Examples"*
Details rules for compliance, and provides examples

For the purposes of HTTP, we are most interested in RFC 2046 (Media Types) and RFC 2048 (Registration Procedures).

# MIME Type Structure

Each MIME media type consists of a type, a subtype, and a list of optional parameters. The type and subtype are separated by a slash, and the optional parameters begin with a semicolon, if they are present. In HTTP, MIME media types are widely used in Content-Type and Accept headers. Here are a few examples:

```
Content-Type: video/quicktime
Content-Type: text/html; charset="iso-8859-6"
Content-Type: multipart/mixed; boundary=gc0p4Jq0M2Yt08j34c0p
Accept: image/gif
```

## Discrete Types

MIME types can directly describe the object type, or they can describe collections or packages of other object types. If a MIME type describes an object type directly, it is a *discrete type*. These include text files, videos, and application-specific file formats.

## Composite Types

If a MIME type describes a collection or encapsulation of other content, the MIME type is called a *composite type*. A composite type describes the format of the enclosing package. When the enclosing package is opened, each enclosed object will have its own type.

## Multipart Types

Multipart media types are composite types. A multipart object consists of multiple component types. Here's an example of multipart/mixed content, where each component has its own MIME type:

```
Content-Type: multipart/mixed; boundary=unique-boundary-1

--unique-boundary-1
Content-type: text/plain; charset=US-ASCII

Hi there, I'm some boring ASCII text...

--unique-boundary-1
Content-Type: multipart/parallel; boundary=unique-boundary-2

--unique-boundary-2
Content-Type: audio/basic

    ... 8000 Hz single-channel mu-law-format
        audio data goes here ...

--unique-boundary-2
Content-Type: image/jpeg

    ... image data goes here ...

--unique-boundary-2--

--unique-boundary-1
Content-type: text/enriched

This is <bold><italic>enriched.</italic></bold>
<smaller>as defined in RFC 1896</smaller>

Isn't it <bigger><bigger>cool?</bigger></bigger>

--unique-boundary-1
Content-Type: message/rfc822

From: (mailbox in US-ASCII)
To: (address in US-ASCII)
Subject: (subject in US-ASCII)
Content-Type: Text/plain; charset=ISO-8859-1
Content-Transfer-Encoding: Quoted-printable

    ... Additional text in ISO-8859-1 goes here ...

--unique-boundary-1--
```

## Syntax

As we stated earlier, MIME types consist of a primary type, a subtype, and an optional list of parameters.

The primary type can be a predefined type, an IETF-defined extension token, or an experimental token (beginning with "x-"). Some common primary types are described in Table D-1.

*Table D-1. Common primary MIME types*

| Type | Description |
|------|-------------|
| application | Application-specific content format (discrete type) |
| audio | Audio format (discrete type) |
| chemical | Chemical data set (discrete IETF extension type) |
| image | Image format (discrete type) |
| message | Message format (composite type) |
| model | 3-D model format (discrete IETF extension type) |
| multipart | Collection of multiple objects (composite type) |
| text | Text format (discrete type) |
| video | Video movie format (discrete type) |

Subtypes can be primary types (as in "text/text"), IANA-registered subtypes, or experimental extension tokens (beginning with "x-").

Types and subtypes are made up of a subset of US-ASCII characters. Spaces and certain reserved grouping and punctuation characters, called "tspecials," are control characters and are forbidden from type and subtype names.

The grammar from RFC 2046 is shown below:

```
TYPE := "application" | "audio" | "image" | "message" | "multipart" |
        "text" | "video" | IETF-TOKEN | X-TOKEN
SUBTYPE := IANA-SUBTOKEN | IETF-TOKEN | X-TOKEN

IETF-TOKEN := <extension token with RFC and registered with IANA>
IANA-SUBTOKEN := <extension token registered with IANA>
X-TOKEN := <"X-" or "x-" prefix, followed by any token>

PARAMETER := TOKEN "=" VALUE
VALUE := TOKEN / QUOTED-STRING
TOKEN := 1*<any (US-ASCII) CHAR except SPACE, CTLs, or TSPECIALS>
TSPECIALS :=  "(" | ")" | "<" | ">" | "@" |
              "," | ";" | ":" | "\" | <"> |
              "/" | "[" | "]" | "?" | "="
```

# MIME Type IANA Registration

The MIME media type registration process is described in RFC 2048. The goal of the registration process is to make it easy to register new media types but also to provide some sanity checking to make sure the new types are well thought out.

## Registration Trees

MIME type tokens are split into four classes, called "registration trees," each with its own registration rules. The four trees—IETF, vendor, personal, and experimental—are described in Table D-2.

*Table D-2. Four MIME media type registration trees*

| Registration tree | Example | Description |
|---|---|---|
| IETF | text/html<br>(HTML text) | The IETF tree is intended for types that are of general significance to the Internet community. New IETF tree media types require approval by the Internet Engineering Steering Group (IESG) and an accompanying standards-track RFC.<br>IETF tree types have no periods (.) in tokens. |
| Vendor<br>(vnd.) | image/vnd.fpx<br>(Kodak FlashPix image) | The vendor tree is intended for media types used by commercially available products. Public review of new vendor types is encouraged but not required.<br>Vendor tree types begin with "vnd.". |
| Personal/Vanity<br>(prs.) | image/prs.btif<br>(internal check-management format used by Nations Bank) | Private, personal, or vanity media types can be registered in the personal tree. These media types will not be distributed commercially.<br>Personal tree types begin with "prs.". |
| Experimental<br>(x- or x.) | application/x-tar<br>(Unix tar archive) | The experimental tree is for unregistered or experimental media types. Because it's relatively simple to register a new vendor or personal media type, software should not be distributed widely using x- types.<br>Experimental tree types begin with "x." or "x-". |

## Registration Process

Read RFC 2048 carefully for the details of MIME media type registration.

The basic registration process is not a formal standards process; it's just an administrative procedure intended to sanity check new types with the community, and record them in a registry, without much delay. The process follows the following steps:

1. Present the media type to the community for review.

   Send a proposed media type registration to the *ietf-types@iana.org* mailing list for a two-week review period. The public posting solicits feedback about the choice of name, interoperability, and security implications. The "x-" prefix specified in RFC 2045 can be used until registration is complete.

2. IESG approval (for IETF tree only).

   If the media type is being registered in the IETF tree, it must be submitted to the IESG for approval and must have an accompanying standards-track RFC.

3. IANA registration.

   As soon as the media type meets the approval requirements, the author can submit the registration request to the IANA, using the email template in Example D-1 and mailing the information to *ietf-types@iana.org*. The IANA will register the media type and make the media type application available to the community at *http://www.isi.edu/in-notes/iana/assignments/media-types/*.

## Registration Rules

The IANA will register media types in the IETF tree only in response to a communication from the IESG stating that a given registration has been approved.

Vendor and personal types will be registered by the IANA automatically and without any formal review as long as the following minimal conditions are met:

1. Media types must function as actual media formats. Types that act like transfer encodings or character sets may not be registered as media types.

2. All media types must have proper type and subtype names. All type names must be defined by standards-track RFCs. All subtype names must be unique, must conform to the MIME grammar for such names, and must contain the proper tree prefixes.

3. Personal tree types must provide a format specification or a pointer to one.

4. Any security considerations given must not be obviously bogus. Everyone who is developing Internet software needs to do his part to prevent security holes.

## Registration Template

The actual IANA registration is done via email. You complete a registration form using the template shown in Example D-1, and mail it to *ietf-types@iana.org*.*

*Example D-1. IANA MIME registration email template*

```
To: ietf-types@iana.org
Subject: Registration of MIME media type XXX/YYY

MIME media type name:
```

---

* The lightly structured nature of the form makes the submitted information fine for human consumption but difficult for machine processing. This is one reason why it is difficult to find a readable, well-organized summary of MIME types, and the reason we created the tables that end this appendix.

*Example D-1. IANA MIME registration email template (continued)*

```
MIME subtype name:

Required parameters:

Optional parameters:

Encoding considerations:

Security considerations:

Interoperability considerations:

Published specification:

Applications which use this media type:

Additional information:

    Magic number(s):
    File extension(s):
    Macintosh File Type Code(s):

Person & email address to contact for further information:

Intended usage:

(One of COMMON, LIMITED USE or OBSOLETE)

Author/Change controller:

(Any other information that the author deems interesting may be added below this line.)
```

## MIME Media Type Registry

The submitted forms are accessible from the IANA web site (*http://www.iana.org*). At the time of writing, the actual database of MIME media types is stored on an ISI web server, at *http://www.isi.edu/in-notes/iana/assignments/media-types/*.

The media types are stored in a directory tree, structured by primary type and subtype, with one leaf file per media type. Each file contains the email submission. Unfortunately, each person completes the registration template slightly differently, so the quality and format of information varies across submissions. (In the tables in this appendix, we tried to fill in the holes omitted by registrants.)

# MIME Type Tables

This section summarizes hundreds of MIME types in 10 tables. Each table lists the MIME media types within a particular primary type (image, text, etc.).

The information is gathered from many sources, including the IANA media type registry, the Apache *mime.types* file, and assorted Internet web pages. We spent several days refining the data, plugging holes, and including descriptive summaries from cross-references to make the data more useful.

This may well be the most detailed tabular listing of MIME types ever compiled. We hope you find it handy!

## application/*

Table D-3 describes many of the application-specific MIME media types.

*Table D-3. "Application" MIME types*

| MIME type | Description | Extension | Contact and reference |
|---|---|---|---|
| application/activemessage | Supports the Active Mail groupware system. | | "Active Mail: A Framework for Integrated Groupware Applications" in *Readings in Groupware and Computer-Supported Cooperative Work*, Ronald M. Baecker, ed., Morgan Kaufmann, ISBN 1558602410 |
| application/andrew-inset | Supports the creation of multimedia content with the Andrew toolkit. | ez | *Multimedia Applications Development with the Andrew Toolkit*, Nathaniel S. Borenstein, Prentice Hall, ASIN 0130366331<br><br>*nsb@bellcore.com* |
| application/applefile | Permits MIME-based transmission of data with Apple/Macintosh-specific information, while allowing general access to nonspecific user data. | | RFC 1740 |
| application/atomicmail | ATOMICMAIL was an experimental research project at Bellcore, designed for including programs in electronic mail messages that are executed when mail is read. ATOMICMAIL is rapidly becoming obsolete in favor of safe-tcl. | | "ATOMICMAIL Language Reference Manual," Nathaniel S. Borenstein, Bellcore Technical Memorandum TM ARH-018429 |
| application/batch-SMTP | Defines a MIME content type suitable for tunneling an ESMTP mail transaction through any MIME-capable transport. | | RFC 2442 |
| application/beep+xml | Supports the interaction protocol called BEEP. BEEP permits simultaneous and independent exchanges of MIME messages between peers, where the messages usually are XML-structured text. | | RFC 3080 |

| MIME type | Description | Extension | Contact and reference |
|---|---|---|---|
| application/cals-1840 | Supports MIME email exchanges of U.S. Department of Defense digital data that was previously exchanged by tapem, as defined by MIL-STD-1840. | | RFC 1895 |
| application/commonground | Common Ground is an electronic document exchange and distribution program that lets users create documents that anyone can view, search, and print, without requiring that they have the creating applications or fonts on their systems. | | Nick Gault<br>No Hands Software<br>*ngault@nohands.com* |
| application/cybercash | Supports credit card payment through the CyberCash protocol. When a user starts payment, a message is sent by the merchant to the customer as the body of a message of MIME type application/cybercash. | | RFC 1898 |
| application/dca-rft | IBM Document Content Architecture. | | "IBM Document Content Architecture/Revisable Form Text Reference," document number SC23-0758-1, International Business Machines |
| application/dec-dx | DEC Document Transfer Format. | | "Digital Document Transmission (DX) Technical Notebook," document number EJ29141-86, Digital Equipment Corporation |
| application/dvcs | Supports the protocols used by a Data Validation and Certification Server (DVCS), which acts as a trusted third party in a public-key security infrastructure. | | RFC 3029 |
| application/EDI-Consent | Supports bilateral trading via electronic data interchange (EDI), using nonstandard specifications. | | *http://www.isi.edu/in-notes/iana/assignments/media-types/application/EDI-Consent* |
| application/EDI-X12 | Supports bilateral trading via electronic data interchange (EDI), using the ASC X12 EDI specifications. | | *http://www.isi.edu/in-notes/iana/assignments/media-types/application/EDI-X12* |
| application/EDIFACT | Supports bilateral trading via electronic data interchange (EDI), using the EDIFACT specifications. | | *http://www.isi.edu/in-notes/iana/assignments/media-types/application/EDIFACT* |
| application/eshop | Unknown. | | Steve Katz<br>System Architecture Shop<br>*steve_katz@eshop.com* |
| application/font-tdpfr | Defines a Portable Font Resource (PFR) that contains a set of glyph shapes, each associated with a character code. | | RFC 3073 |

| MIME type | Description | Extension | Contact and reference |
|---|---|---|---|
| application/http | Used to enclose a pipeline of one or more HTTP request or response messages (not intermixed). | | RFC 2616 |
| application/hyperstudio | Supports transfer of HyperStudio educational hypermedia files. | stk | *http://www.hyperstudio.com* |
| application/iges | A commonly used format for CAD model interchange. | | "ANS/US PRO/IPO-100" U.S. Product Data Association 2722 Merrilee Drive, Suite 200 Fairfax, VA 22031-4499 |
| application/index application/index.cmd application/index.obj application/index.response application/index.vnd | Support the Common Indexing Protocol (CIP). CIP is an evolution of the Whois++ directory service, used to pass indexing information from server to server in order to redirect and replicate queries through a distributed database system. | | RFC 2652, and RFCs 2651, 1913, and 1914 |
| application/iotp | Supports Internet Open Trading Protocol (IOTP) messages over HTTP. | | RFC 2935 |
| application/ipp | Supports Internet Printing Protocol (IPP) over HTTP. | | RFC 2910 |
| application/mac-binhex40 | Encodes a string of 8-bit bytes into a string of 7-bit bytes, which is safer for some applications (though not quite as safe as the 6-bit base-64 encoding). | hqx | RFC 1341 |
| application/mac-compactpro | From Apache *mime.types*. | cpt | |
| application/macwriteii | Claris MacWrite II. | | |
| application/marc | MARC objects are Machine-Readable Cataloging records—standards for the representation and communication of bibliographic and related information. | mrc | RFC 2220 |
| application/mathematica application/mathematica-old | Supports Mathematica and MathReader numerical analysis software. | nb, ma, mb | *The Mathematica Book*, Stephen Wolfram, Cambridge University Press, ISBN 0521643147 |
| application/msword | Microsoft Word MIME type. | doc | |
| application/news-message-id | | | RFCs 822 (message IDs), 1036 (application to news), and 977 (NNTP) |
| application/news-transmission | Allows transmission of news articles by email or other transport. | | RFC 1036 |
| application/ocsp-request | Supports the Online Certificate Status Protocol (OCSP), which provides a way to check on the validity of a digital certificate without requiring local certificate revocation lists. | orq | RFC 2560 |

| MIME type | Description | Extension | Contact and reference |
|---|---|---|---|
| application/ocsp-response | Same as above. | ors | RFC 2560 |
| application/octet-stream | Unclassified binary data. | bin, dms, lha, lzh, exe, class | RFC 1341 |
| application/oda | Used for information encoded according to the Office Document Architecture (ODA) standards, using the Office Document Interchange Format (ODIF) representation format. The Content-Type line also should specify an attribute/value pair that indicates the document application profile (DAP), as in:<br><br>Content-Type: application/oda; profile=Q112 | oda | RFC 1341<br><br>ISO 8613; "Information Processing: Text and Office System; Office Document Architecture (ODA) and Interchange Format (ODIF)," Part 1-8, 1989 |
| application/parityfec | Forward error correction parity encoding for RTP data streams. | | RFC 3009 |
| application/pdf | Adode PDF files. | pdf | See *Portable Document Format Reference Manual*, Adobe Systems, Inc., Addison Wesley, ISBN 0201626284 |
| application/pgp-encrypted | PGP encrypted data. | | RFC 2015 |
| application/pgp-keys | PGP public-key blocks. | | RFC 2015 |
| application/pgp-signature | PGP cryptographic signature. | | RFC 2015 |
| application/pkcs10 | Public Key Crypto System #10—the application/pkcs10 body type *must* be used to transfer a PKCS #10 certification request. | p10 | RFC 2311 |
| application/pkcs7-mime | Public Key Crypto System #7—this type is used to carry PKCS #7 objects of several types including envelopedData and signedData. | p7m | RFC 2311 |
| application/pkcs7-signature | Public Key Crypto System #7—this type always contains a single PKCS #7 object of type signedData. | p7s | RFC 2311 |
| application/pkix-cert | Transports X.509 certificates. | cer | RFC 2585 |
| application/pkix-crl | Transports X.509 certificate revocation lists. | crl | RFC 2585 |
| application/pkixcmp | Message format used by X.509 Public Key Infrastructure Certificate Management Protocols. | pki | RFC 2510 |
| application/postscript | An Adobe PostScript graphics file (program). | ai, ps, eps | RFC 2046 |
| application/prs.alvestrand.titrax-sheet | "TimeTracker" program by Harald T. Alvestrand. | | *http://domen.uninett.no/~hta/titrax/* |

| MIME type | Description | Extension | Contact and reference |
|---|---|---|---|
| application/prs.cww | CU-Writer for Windows. | cw, cww | Dr. Somchai Prasitjutrakul<br>*somchaip@chulkn.car.chula.ac.th* |
| application/prs.nprend | Unknown. | rnd, rct | John M. Doggett<br>*jdoggett@tiac.net* |
| application/remote-printing | Contains meta information used when remote printing, for the printer cover sheet. | | RFC 1486<br>Marshall T. Rose<br>*mrose@dbc.mtview.ca.us* |
| application/riscos | Acorn RISC OS binaries. | | *RISC OS Programmer's Reference Manuals*, Acorn Computers, Ltd., ISBN1852501103 |
| application/sdp | SDP is intended for describing live multimedia sessions for the purposes of session announcement, session invitation, and other forms of multimedia session initiation. | | RFC 2327<br>Henning Schulzrinne<br>*hgs@cs.columbia.edu* |
| application/set-payment<br>application/set-payment-initiation<br>application/set-registration<br>application/set-registration-initiation | Supports the SET secure electronic transaction payment protocol. | | *http://www.visa.com*<br>*http://www.mastercard.com* |
| application/sgml-open-catalog | Intended for use with systems that support the SGML Open TR9401:1995 "Entity Management" specification. | | SGML Open<br>910 Beaver Grade Road, #3008<br>Coraopolis, PA 15109<br>*info@sgmlopen.org* |
| application/sieve | Sieve mail filtering script. | | RFC 3028 |
| application/slate | The BBN/Slate document format is published as part of the standard documentation set distributed with the BBN/Slate product. | | BBN/Slate Product Mgr<br>BBN Systems and Technologies<br>10 Moulton Street<br>Cambridge, MA 02138 |
| application/smil | The Synchronized Multimedia Integration Language (SMIL) integrates a set of independent multimedia objects into a synchronized multimedia presentation. | smi, smil | *http://www.w3.org/AudioVideo/* |
| application/tve-trigger | Supports embedded URLs in enhanced television receivers. | | "SMPTE: Declarative Data Essence, Content Level 1," produced by the Society of Motion Picture and Television Engineers<br>*http://www.smpte.org* |
| application/vemmi | Enhanced videotex standard. | | RFC 2122 |
| application/vnd.3M.Post-it-Notes | Used by the "Post-it® Notes for Internet Designers" Internet control/plug-in. | pwn | *http://www.3M.com/psnotes/* |

| MIME type | Description | Extension | Contact and reference |
|---|---|---|---|
| application/vnd.accpac.simply.aso | Simply Accounting v7.0 and higher. Files of this type conform to Open Financial Exchange v1.02 specifications. | aso | *http://www.ofx.net* |
| application/vnd.accpac.simply.imp | Used by Simply Accounting v7.0 and higher, to import its own data. | imp | *http://www.ofx.net* |
| application/vnd.acucobol | ACUCOBOL-GT Runtime. | | Dovid Lubin *dovid@acucobol.com* |
| application/vnd.aether.imp | Supports airtime-efficient Instant Message communications between an Instant Messaging service, such as AOL Instant Messenger, Yahoo! Messenger, or MSN Messenger, and a special set of Instant Messaging client software on a wireless device. | | Wireless Instant Messaging Protocol (IMP) specification available from Aether Systems by license |
| application/vnd.anser-web-certificate-issue-initiation | Trigger for web browsers to launch the ANSER-WEB Terminal Client. | cii | Hiroyoshi Mori *mori@mm.rd.nttdata.co.jp* |
| application/vnd.anser-web-funds-transfer-initiation | Same as above. | fti | Same as above |
| application/vnd.audiograph | AudioGraph. | aep | Horia Cristian *H.C.Slusanschi@massey.ac.nz* |
| application/vnd.bmi | BMI graphics format by CADAM Systems. | bmi | Tadashi Gotoh *tgotoh@cadamsystems.co.jp* |
| application/vnd.businessobjects | BusinessObjects 4.0 and higher. | rep | |
| application/vnd.canon-cpdl application/vnd.canon-lips | Supports Canon, Inc. office imaging products. | | Shin Muto *shinmuto@pure.cpdc.canon.co.jp* |
| application/vnd.claymore | Claymore.exe. | cla | Ray Simpson *ray@cnation.com* |
| application/vnd.commerce-battelle | Supports a generic mechanism for delimiting smart card–based information, for digital commerce, identification, authentication, and exchange of smart card–based card holder information. | ica, icf, icd, icc, ic0, ic1, ic2, ic3, ic4, ic5, ic6, ic7, ic8 | David C. Applebaum *applebau@131.167.52.15* |
| application/vnd.commonspace | Allows for proper transmission of CommonSpace™ documents via MIME-based processes. CommonSpace is published by Sixth Floor Media, part of the Houghton-Mifflin Company. | csp, cst | Ravinder Chandhok *chandhok@within.com* |
| application/vnd.contact.cmsg | Used for CONTACT software's CIM DATABASE. | cdbcmsg | Frank Patz *fp@contact.de* *http://www.contact.de* |

| MIME type | Description | Extension | Contact and reference |
|-----------|-------------|-----------|----------------------|
| application/vnd.cosmocaller | Allows for files containing connection parameters to be downloaded from web sites, invokes the CosmoCaller application to interpret the parameters, and initiates connections with the CosmoCallACD server. | cmc | Steve Dellutri *sdellutri@cosmocom.com* |
| application/vnd.ctc-posml | Continuum Technology's PosML. | pml | Bayard Kohlhepp *bayardk@ctcexchange.com* |
| application/vnd.cups-postscript application/vnd.cups-raster application/vnd.cups-raw | Supports Common UNIX Printing System (CUPS) servers and clients. | | *http://www.cups.org* |
| application/vnd.cybank | Proprietary data type for Cybank data. | | Nor Helmee B. Abd. Halim *helmee@cybank.net* *http://www.cybank.net* |
| application/vnd.dna | DNA is intended to easily Web-enable any 32-bit Windows application. | dna | Meredith Searcy *msearcy@newmoon.com* |
| application/vnd.dpgraph | Used by DPGraph 2000 and Math-Ware Cyclone. | dpg, mwc, dpgraph | David Parker *http://www.davidparker.com* |
| application/vnd.dxr | Digital Xpress Reports by PSI Technologies. | dxr | Michael Duffy *miked@psiaustin.com* |
| application/vnd.ecdis-update | Supports ECDIS applications. | | *http://www.sevencs.com* |
| application/vnd.ecowin.chart application/vnd.ecowin. filerequest application/vnd.ecowin. fileupdate application/vnd.ecowin.series application/vnd.ecowin. seriesrequest application/vnd.ecowin. seriesupdate | EcoWin. | mag | Thomas Olsson *thomas@vinga.se* |
| application/vnd.enliven | Supports delivery of Enliven interactive multimedia. | nml | Paul Santinelli *psantinelli@narrative.com* |
| application/vnd.epson.esf | Proprietary content for Seiko Epson QUASS Stream Player. | esf | Shoji Hoshina *Hoshina.Shoji@exc.epson.co.jp* |
| application/vnd.epson.msf | Proprietary content for Seiko Epson QUASS Stream Player. | msf | Same as above |
| application/vnd.epson. quickanime | Proprietary content for Seiko Epson QuickAnime Player. | qam | Yu Gu *guyu@rd.oda.epson.co.jp* |
| application/vnd.epson.salt | Proprietary content for Seiko Epson SimpleAnimeLite Player. | slt | Yasuhito Nagatomo *naga@rd.oda.epson.co.jp* |
| application/vnd.epson.ssf | Proprietary content for Seiko Epson QUASS Stream Player. | ssf | Shoji Hoshina *Hoshina.Shoji@exc.epson.co.jp* |

| MIME type | Description | Extension | Contact and reference |
|---|---|---|---|
| application/vnd.ericsson.quickcall | Phone Doubler Quick Call. | qcall, qca | Paul Tidwell<br>*paul.tidwell@ericsson.com*<br>*http://www.ericsson.com* |
| application/vnd.eudora.data | Eudora Version 4.3 and later. | | Pete Resnick<br>*presnick@qualcomm.com* |
| application/vnd.fdf | Adobe Forms Data Format. | | "Forms Data Format," Technical Note 5173, Adobe Systems |
| application/vnd.ffsns | Used for application communication with FirstFloor's Smart Delivery. | | Mary Holstege<br>*holstege@firstfloor.com* |
| application/vnd.FloGraphIt | NpGraphIt. | gph | |
| application/vnd.framemaker | Adobe FrameMaker files. | fm, mif, book | *http://www.adobe.com* |
| application/vnd.fsc.weblaunch | Supports Friendly Software Corporation's golf simulation software. | fsc | Derek Smith<br>*derek@friendlysoftware.com* |
| application/vnd.fujitsu.oasys<br>application/vnd.fujitsu.oasys2 | Supports Fujitsu's OASYS software. | oas | Nobukazu Togashi<br>*togashi@ai.cs.fujitsu.co.jp* |
| application/vnd.fujitsu.oasys2 | Supports Fujitsu's OASYS V2 software. | oa2 | Same as above |
| application/vnd.fujitsu.oasys3 | Support's Fujitsu's OASYS V5 software. | oa3 | Seiji Okudaira<br>*okudaira@candy.paso.fujitsu.co.jp* |
| application/vnd.fujitsu.oasysgp | Supports Fujitsu's OASYS GraphPro software. | fg5 | Masahiko Sugimoto<br>*sugimoto@sz.sel.fujitsu.co.jp* |
| application/vnd.fujitsu.oasysprs | Support's Fujitsu's OASYS Presentation software. | bh2 | Masumi Ogita<br>*ogita@oa.tfl.fujitsu.co.jp* |
| application/vnd.fujixerox.ddd | Supports Fuji Xerox's EDMICS 2000 and DocuFile. | ddd | Masanori Onda<br>*Masanori.Onda@fujixerox.co.jp* |
| application/vnd.fujixerox.docuworks | Supports Fuji Xerox's DocuWorks Desk and DocuWorks Viewer software. | xdw | Yasuo Taguchi<br>*yasuo.taguchi@fujixerox.co.jp* |
| application/vnd.fujixerox.docuworks.binder | Supports Fuji Xerox's DocuWorks Desk and DocuWorks Viewer software. | xbd | Same as above. |
| application/vnd.fut-misnet | Unknown. | | Jaan Pruulmann<br>*jaan@fut.ee* |
| application/vnd.grafeq | Lets users of GrafEq exchange GrafEq documents through the Web and email. | gqf, gqs | *http://www.peda.com* |
| application/vnd.groove-account | Groove is a peer-to-peer communication system implementing a virtual space for small group interaction. | gac | Todd Joseph<br>*todd_joseph@groove.net* |
| application/vnd.groove-identity-message | Same as above. | gim | Same as above |
| application/vnd.groove-injector | Same as above. | grv | Same as above |
| application/vnd.groove-tool-message | Same as above. | gtm | Same as above |

| MIME type | Description | Extension | Contact and reference |
|---|---|---|---|
| application/vnd.groove-tool-template | Same as above. | tpl | Same as above |
| application/vnd.groove-vcard | Same as above. | vcg | Same as above |
| application/vnd.hhe.lesson-player | Supports the LessonPlayer and Pre-sentationEditor software. | les | Randy Jones<br>Harcourt E-Learning<br>*randy_jones@archipelago.com* |
| application/vnd.hp-HPGL | HPGL files. | | *The HP-GL/2 and HP RTL Reference Guide*, Addison Wesley, ISBN 0201310147 |
| application/vnd.hp-hpid | Supports Hewlett-Packard's Instant Delivery Software. | hpi, hpid | *http://www.instant-delivery.com* |
| application/vnd.hp-hps | Supports Hewlett-Packard's Web-PrintSmart software. | hps | *http://www.hp.com/go/webprintsmart_mimetype_specs/* |
| application/vnd.hp-PCL<br>application/vnd.hp-PCLXL | PCL printer files. | pcl | "PCL-PJL Technical Reference Manual Documentation Package," HP Part No. 5012-0330 |
| application/vnd.httphone | HTTPhone asynchronous voice over IP system. | | Franck LeFevre<br>*franck@k1info.com* |
| application/vnd.hzn-3d-crossword | Used to encode crossword puzzles by Horizon, A Glimpse of Tomorrow. | x3d | James Minnis<br>*james_minnis@glimpse-of-tomorrow.com* |
| application/vnd.ibm.afplinedata | Print Services Facility (PSF), AFP Conversion and Indexing Facility (ACIF). | | Roger Buis<br>*buis@us.ibm.com* |
| application/vnd.ibm.MiniPay | MiniPay authentication and payment software. | mpy | Amir Herzberg<br>*amirh@vnet.ibm.com* |
| application/vnd.ibm.modcap | Mixed Object Document Content. | list3820, listafp, afp, pseg3820 | Reinhard Hohensee<br>*rhohensee@vnet.ibm.com*<br>"Mixed Object Document Content Architecture Reference," IBM publication SC31-6802 |
| application/vnd.informix-visionary | Informix Visionary. | vis | Christopher Gales<br>*christopher.gales@informix.com* |
| application/vnd.intercon.formnet | Supports Intercon Associates FormNet software. | xpw, xpx | Thomas A. Gurak<br>*assoc@intercon.roc.servtech.com* |
| application/vnd.intertrust.digibox<br>application/vnd.intertrust.nncp | Supports InterTrust architecture for secure electronic commerce and digital rights management. | | InterTrust Technologies<br>460 Oakmead Parkway<br>Sunnyvale, CA 94086 USA<br>*info@intertrust.com*<br>*http://www.intertrust.com* |
| application/vnd.intu.qbo | Intended for use only with Quick-Books 6.0 (Canada). | qbo | Greg Scratchley<br>*greg_scratchley@intuit.com*<br>Format of these files discussed in the Open Financial Exchange specs, available from *http://www.ofx.net* |

| MIME type | Description | Extension | Contact and reference |
|---|---|---|---|
| application/vnd.intu.qfx | Intended for use only with Quicken 99 and following versions. | qfx | Same as above |
| application/vnd.is-xpr | Express by Infoseek. | xpr | Satish Natarajan *satish@infoseek.com* |
| application/vnd.japannet-directory-service application/vnd.japannet-jpnstore-wakeup application/vnd.japannet-payment-wakeup application/vnd.japannet-registration application/vnd.japannet-registration-wakeup application/vnd.japannet-setstore-wakeup application/vnd.japannet-verification application/vnd.japannet-verification-wakeup | Supports Mitsubishi Electric's Japan-Net security, authentication, and payment sofwtare. | | Jun Yoshitake *yositake@iss.isl.melco.co.jp* |
| application/vnd.koan | Supports the automatic playback of Koan music files over the Internet, by helper applications such as SSEYO Koan Netscape Plugin. | skp, skd, skm, skt | Peter Cole *pcole@sseyod.demon.co.uk* |
| application/vnd.lotus-1-2-3 | Lotus 1-2-3 and Lotus approach. | 123, wk1, wk3, wk4 | Paul Wattenberger *Paul_Wattenberger@lotus.com* |
| application/vnd.lotus-approach | Lotus Approach. | apr, vew | Same as above |
| application/vnd.lotus-freelance | Lotus Freelance. | prz, pre | Same as above |
| application/vnd.lotus-notes | Lotus Notes. | nsf, ntf, ndl, ns4, ns3, ns2, nsh, nsg | Michael Laramie *laramiem@btv.ibm.com* |
| application/vnd.lotus-organizer | Lotus Organizer. | or3, or2, org | Paul Wattenberger *Paul_Wattenberger@lotus.com* |
| application/vnd.lotus-screencam | Lotus ScreenCam. | scm | Same as above |
| application/vnd.lotus-wordpro | Lotus Word Pro. | lwp, sam | Same as above |
| application/vnd.mcd | Micro CADAM CAD software. | mcd | Tadashi Gotoh *tgotoh@cadamsystems.co.jp* *http://www.cadamsystems.co.jp* |

| MIME type | Description | Extension | Contact and reference |
|---|---|---|---|
| application/vnd. mediastation.cdkey | Supports Media Station's CDKey remote CDROM communications protocol. | cdkey | Henry Flurry *henryf@mediastation.com* |
| application/vnd.meridian-slingshot | Slingshot by Meridian Data. | | Eric Wedel Meridian Data, Inc. 5615 Scotts Valley Drive Scotts Valley, CA 95066 *ewedel@meridian-data.com* |
| application/vnd.mif | FrameMaker interchange format. | mif | *ftp://ftp.frame.com/pub/techsup/ techinfo/dos/mif4.zip* Mike Wexler Adobe Systems, Inc 333 W. San Carlos St. San Jose, CA 95110 USA *mwexler@adobe.com* |
| application/vnd.minisoft-hp3000-save | NetMail 3000 save format. | | Minisoft, Inc. *support@minisoft.com* *ftp://ftp.3k.com/DOC/ms92-save-format.txt* |
| application/vnd.mitsubishi. misty-guard.trustweb | Supports Mitsubishi Electric's Trustweb software. | | Manabu Tanaka *mtana@iss.isl.melco.co.jp* |
| application/vnd.Mobius.DAF | Supports Mobius Management Systems software. | daf | Celso Rodriguez *crodrigu@mobius.com* Greg Chrzczon *gchrzczo@mobius.com* |
| application/vnd.Mobius.DIS | Same as above. | dis | Same as above |
| application/vnd.Mobius.MBK | Same as above. | mbk | Same as above |
| application/vnd.Mobius.MQY | Same as above. | mqy | Same as above |
| application/vnd.Mobius.MSL | Same as above. | msl | Same as above |
| application/vnd.Mobius.PLC | Same as above. | plc | Same as above |
| application/vnd.Mobius.TXF | Same as above. | txf | Same as above |
| application/vnd.motorola. flexsuite | FLEXsuite™ is a collection of wireless messaging protocols. This type is used by the network gateways of wireless messaging service providers as well as wireless OSs and applications. | | Mark Patton Motorola Personal Networks Group *fmp014@email.mot.com* FLEXsuite™ specification available from Motorola under appropriate licensing agreement |
| application/vnd.motorola. flexsuite.adsi | FLEXsuite™ is a collection of wireless messaging protocols. This type provides a wireless-friendly format for enabling various data-encryption solutions. | | Same as above |

| MIME type | Description | Extension | Contact and reference |
|---|---|---|---|
| application/vnd.motorola. flexsuite.fis | FLEXsuite™ is a collection of wireless messaging protocols. This type is a wireless-friendly format for the efficient delivery of structured information (e.g., news, stocks, weather) to a wireless device. | | Same as above |
| application/vnd.motorola. flexsuite.gotap | FLEXsuite™ is a collection of wireless messaging protocols. This type provides a common wireless-friendly format for the programming of wireless device attributes via over-the-air messages. | | Same as above |
| application/vnd.motorola. flexsuite.kmr | FLEXsuite™ is a collection of wireless messaging protocols. This type provides a wireless-friendly format for encryption key management. | | Same as above |
| application/vnd.motorola. flexsuite.ttc | FLEXsuite™ is a collection of wireless messaging protocols. This type supports a wireless-friendly format for the efficient delivery of text using token text compression. | | Same as above |
| application/vnd.motorola. flexsuite.wem | FLEXsuite™ is a collection of wireless messaging protocols. This type provides a wireless-friendly format for the communication of Internet email to wireless devices. | | Same as above |
| application/vnd.mozilla. xul+xml | Supports the Mozilla Internet application suite. | xul | Dan Rosen2 *dr@netscape.com* |
| application/vnd.ms-artgalry | Supports Microsoft's Art Gallery. | cil | *deansl@microsoft.com* |
| application/vnd.ms-asf | ASF is a multimedia file format whose contents are designed to be streamed across a network to support distributed multimedia applications. ASF content may include any combination of any media type (e.g., audio, video, images, URLs, HTML content, MIDI, 2-D and 3-D modeling, scripts, and objects of various types). | asf | Eric Fleischman *ericf@microsoft.com* *http://www.microsoft.com/ mind/0997/netshow/netshow.asp* |
| application/vnd.ms-excel | Microsoft Excel spreadsheet. | xls | Sukvinder S. Gill *sukvg@microsoft.com* |
| application/vnd.ms-lrm | Microsoft proprietary. | lrm | Eric Ledoux *ericle@microsoft.com* |
| application/vnd.ms-powerpoint | Microsoft PowerPoint presentation. | ppt | Sukvinder S. Gill *sukvg@microsoft.com* |
| application/vnd.ms-project | Microsoft Project file. | mpp | Same as above |

| MIME type | Description | Extension | Contact and reference |
|---|---|---|---|
| application/vnd.ms-tnef | Identifies an attachment that in general would be processable only by a MAPI-aware application. This type is an encapsulated format of rich MAPI properties, such as Rich Text and Icon information, that may otherwise be degraded by the messaging transport. | | Same as above |
| application/vnd.ms-works | Microsoft Works software. | | Same as above |
| application/vnd.mseq | MSEQ is a compact multimedia format suitable for wireless devices. | mseq | Gwenael Le Bodic *Gwenael.le_bodic@alcatel.fr* *http://www.3gpp.org* |
| application/vnd.msign | Used by applications implementing the msign protocol, which requests signatures from mobile devices. | | Malte Borcherding *Malte.Borcherding@brokat.com* |
| application/vnd.music-niff | NIFF music files. | | Cindy Grande *72723.1272@compuserve.com* *ftp://blackbox.cartah.washington.edu/pub/NIFF/NIFF6A.TXT* |
| application/vnd.musician | MUSICIAN scoring language/encoding conceived and developed by Renai-Science Corporation. | mus | Robert G. Adams *gadams@renaiscience.com* |
| application/vnd.netfpx | Intended for dynamic retrieval of multiresolution image information, as used by Hewlett-Packard Company Imaging for Internet. | fpx | Andy Mutz *andy_mutz@hp.com* |
| application/vnd.noblenet-directory | Supports the NobleNet Directory software, purchased by RogueWave. | nnd | *http://www.noblenet.com* |
| application/vnd.noblenet-sealer | Supports the NobleNet Sealer software, purchased by RogueWave. | nns | *http://www.noblenet.com* |
| application/vnd.noblenet-web | Supports the NobleNet Web software, purchased by RogueWave. | nnw | *http://www.noblenet.com* |
| application/vnd.novadigm.EDM | Supports Novadigm's RADIA and EDM products. | edm | Phil Burgard *pburgard@novadigm.com* |
| application/vnd.novadigm.EDX | Same as above. | edx | Same as above |
| application/vnd.novadigm.EXT | Same as above. | ext | Same as above |
| application/vnd.osa.netdeploy | Supports the Open Software Associates netDeploy application deployment software. | ndc | Steve Klos *stevek@osa.com* *http://www.osa.com* |
| application/vnd.palm | Used by PalmOS system software and applications—this new type, "application/vnd.palm," replaces the old type "application/x-pilot." | prc, pdb, pqa, oprc | Gavin Peacock *gpeacock@palm.com* |

| MIME type | Description | Extension | Contact and reference |
|---|---|---|---|
| application/vnd.pg.format | Proprietary Proctor & Gamble Standard Reporting System. | str | April Gandert<br>TN152<br>Procter & Gamble Way<br>Cincinnati, Ohio 45202<br>(513) 983-4249 |
| application/vnd.pg.osasli | Proprietary Proctor & Gamble Standard Reporting System. | ei6 | Same as above |
| application/vnd.powerbuilder6<br>application/vnd.powerbuilder6-s<br>application/vnd.powerbuilder7<br>application/vnd.powerbuilder7-s<br>application/vnd.powerbuilder75<br>application/vnd.powerbuilder75-s | Used only by Sybase PowerBuilder release 6, 7, and 7.5 runtime environments, nonsecure and secure. | pbd | Reed Shilts<br>*reed.shilts@sybase.com* |
| application/vnd.previewsystems.box | Preview Systems ZipLock/VBox product. | box,<br>vbox | Roman Smolgovsky<br>*romans@previewsystems.com*<br>*http://www.previewsystems.com* |
| application/vnd.publishare-delta-tree | Used by Capella Computers' PubliShare runtime environment. | qps | Oren Ben-Kiki<br>*publishare-delta-tree@capella.co.il* |
| application/vnd.rapid | Emultek's rapid packaged applications. | zrp | Itay Szekely<br>*etay@emultek.co.il* |
| application/vnd.s3sms | Integrates the transfer mechanisms of the Sonera SmartTrust products into the Internet infrastructure. | | Lauri Tarkkala<br>*Lauri.Tarkkala@sonera.com*<br>*http://www.smarttrust.com* |
| application/vnd.seemail | Supports the transmission of SeeMail files. SeeMail is an application that captures video and sound and uses bitwise compression to compress and archive the two pieces into one file. | see | Steven Webb<br>*steve@wynde.com*<br>*http://www.realmediainc.com* |
| application/vnd.shana.informed.formdata | Shana e-forms data formats. | ifm | Guy Selzler<br>Shana Corporation<br>*gselzler@shana.com* |
| application/vnd.shana.informed.formtemp | Shana e-forms data formats. | itp | Same as above |
| application/vnd.shana.informed.interchange | Shana e-forms data formats. | iif, iif1 | Same as above |
| application/vnd.shana.informed.package | Shana e-forms data formats. | ipk, ipkg | Same as above |
| application/vnd.street-stream | Proprietary to Street Technologies. | | Glenn Levitt<br>Street Technologies<br>*streetd1@ix.netcom.com* |

| MIME type | Description | Extension | Contact and reference |
|---|---|---|---|
| application/vnd.svd | Dateware Electronics SVD files. | | Scott Becker<br>*dataware@compumedia.com* |
| application/vnd.swiftview-ics | Supports SwiftView®. | | Randy Prakken<br>*tech@ndg.com*<br>*http://www.ndg.com/svm.htm* |
| application/vnd.triscape.mxs | Supports Triscape Map Explorer. | mxs | Steven Simonoff<br>*scs@triscape.com* |
| application/vnd.trueapp | True BASIC files. | tra | J. Scott Hepler<br>*scott@truebasic.com* |
| application/vnd.truedoc | Proprietary to Bitstream, Inc. | | Brad Chase<br>*brad_chase@bitstream.com* |
| application/vnd.ufdl | UWI's UFDL files. | ufdl, ufd,<br>frm | Dave Manning<br>*dmanning@uwi.com*<br>*http://www.uwi.com/* |
| application/vnd.uplanet.alert<br>application/vnd.uplanet.<br>alert-wbxml<br>application/vnd.uplanet.<br>bearer-choi-wbxml<br>application/vnd.uplanet.<br>bearer-choice<br>application/vnd.uplanet.<br>cacheop<br>application/vnd.uplanet.<br>cacheop-wbxml<br>application/vnd.uplanet.<br>channel<br>application/vnd.uplanet.<br>channel-wbxml<br>application/vnd.uplanet.list<br>application/vnd.uplanet.list-<br>wbxml<br>application/vnd.uplanet.<br>listcmd<br>application/vnd.uplanet.<br>listcmd-wbxml<br>application/vnd.uplanet.<br>signal | Formats used by Unwired Planet (now<br>Openwave) UP browser micro-<br>browser for mobile devices. | | *iana-registrar@uplanet.com*<br>*http://www.openwave.com* |
| application/vnd.vcx | VirtualCatalog. | vcx | Taisuke Sugimoto<br>*sugimototi@noanet.nttdata.co.jp* |
| application/vnd.vectorworks | VectorWorks graphics files. | mcd | Paul C. Pharr<br>*pharr@diehlgraphsoft.com* |
| application/vnd.vidsoft.<br>vidconference | VidConference format. | vsc | Robert Hess<br>*hess@vidsoft.de* |
| application/vnd.visio | Visio files. | vsd, vst,<br>vsw, vss | Troy Sandal<br>*troys@visio.com* |

| MIME type | Description | Extension | Contact and reference |
|---|---|---|---|
| application/vnd.vividence. scriptfile | Vividence files. | vsf, vtd, vd | Mark Risher *markr@vividence.com* |
| application/vnd.wap.sic | WAP Service Indication format. | sic, wbxml | WAP Forum Ltd *http://www.wapforum.org* |
| application/vnd.wap.slc | WAP Service Loading format. Anything that conforms to the Service Loading specification, available at *http://www.wapforum.org*. | slc, wbxml | Same as above |
| application/vnd.wap.wbxml | WAP WBXML binary XML format for wireless devices. | wbxml | Same as above "WAP Binary XML Content Format—WBXML version 1.1" |
| application/vnd.wap.wmlc | WAP WML format for wireless devices. | wmlc, wbxml | Same as above |
| application/vnd.wap. wmlscriptc | WAP WMLScript format. | wmlsc | Same as above |
| application/vnd.webturbo | WebTurbo format. | wtb | Yaser Rehem Sapient Corporation *yrehem@sapient.com* |
| application/vnd.wrq-hp3000-labelled | Supports HP3000 formats. | | *support@wrq.com* *support@3k.com* |
| application/vnd.wt.stf | Supports Worldtalk software. | stf | Bill Wohler *wohler@worldtalk.com* |
| application/vnd.xara | Xara files are saved by CorelXARA, an object-oriented vector graphics package written by Xara Limited (and marketed by Corel). | xar | David Matthewman *david@xara.com* *http://www.xara.com* |
| application/vnd.xfdl | UWI's XFDL files. | xfdl, xfd, frm | Dave Manning *dmanning@uwi.com* *http://www.uwi.com* |
| application/vnd.yellowriver-custom-menu | Supports the Yellow River Custom-Menu plug-in, which provides customized browser drop-down menus. | cmp | *yellowriversw@yahoo.com* |
| application/whoispp-query | Defines Whois++ protocol queries within MIME. | | RFC 2957 |
| application/whoispp-response | Defines Whois++ protocol responses within MIME. | | RFC 2958 |
| application/wita | Wang Information Transfer Architecture. | | Document number 715-0050A, Wang Laboratories *campbell@redsox.bsw.com* |
| application/wordperfect5.1 | WordPerfect documents. | | |
| application/x400-bp | Carries any X.400 body part for which there is no registered IANA mapping. | | RFC 1494 |

| MIME type | Description | Extension | Contact and reference |
|---|---|---|---|
| application/x-bcpio | Old-style binary CPIO archives. | bcpio | |
| application/x-cdlink | Allows integration of CD-ROM media within web pages. | vcd | *http://www.cdlink.com* |
| application/x-chess-pgm | From Apache *mime.types*. | pgn | |
| application/x-compress | Binary data from Unix compress. | z | |
| application/x-cpio | CPIO archive file. | cpio | |
| application/x-csh | CSH scripts. | csh | |
| application/x-director | Macromedia director files. | dcr, dir, dxr | |
| application/x-dvi | TeX DVI files. | dvi | |
| application/x-futuresplash | From Apache *mime.types*. | spl | |
| application/x-gtar | GNU tar archives. | gtar | |
| application/x-gzip | GZIP compressed data. | gz | |
| application/x-hdf | From Apache *mime.types*. | hdf | |
| application/x-javascript | JavaScript files. | js | |
| application/x-koan | Supports the automatic playback of Koan music files over the Internet, by helper applications such as SSEYO Koan Netscape Plugin. | skp, skd, skt, skm | |
| application/x-latex | LaTeX files. | latex | |
| application/x-netcdf | NETCDF files. | nc, cdf | |
| application/x-sh | SH scripts. | sh | |
| application/x-shar | SHAR archives. | shar | |
| application/x-shockwave-flash | Macromedia Flash files. | swf | |
| application/x-stuffit | StuffIt archives. | sit | |
| application/x-sv4cpio | Unix SysV R4 CPIO archives. | sv4cpio | |
| application/x-sv4crc | Unix SysV R4 CPIO w/CRC archives. | sv4crc | |
| application/x-tar | TAR archives. | tar | |
| application/x-tcl | TCL scripts. | tcl | |
| application/x-tex | TeX files. | tex | |
| application/x-texinfo | TeX info files. | texinfo, texi | |
| application/x-troff | TROFF files. | t, tr, roff | |
| application/x-troff-man | TROFF Unix manpages. | man | |
| application/x-troff-me | TROFF+me files. | me | |
| application/x-troff-ms | TROFF+ms files | ms | |

| MIME type | Description | Extension | Contact and reference |
|---|---|---|---|
| application/x-ustar | The extended tar interchange format. | ustar | See the IEEE 1003.1(1990) specifications |
| application/x-wais-source | WAIS source structure. | src | |
| application/xml | Extensible Markup Language format file (use text/xml if you want the file treated as plain text by browsers, etc.). | xml, dtd | RFC 2376 |
| application/zip | PKWARE zip archives. | zip | |

# audio/*

Table D-4 summarizes audio content types.

Table D-4. *"Audio" MIME types*

| MIME type | Description | Extension | Contact and reference |
|---|---|---|---|
| audio/32kadpcm | 8 kHz ADPCM audio encoding. | | RFC 2421 |
| audio/basic | Audio encoded with 8-kHz monaural 8-bit ISDN u-law PCM. | au, snd | RFC 1341 |
| audio/G.772.1 | G.722.1 compresses 50Hz–7kHz audio signals into 24 kbit/s or 32 kbit/s. It may be used for speech, music, and other types of audio. | | RFC 3047 |
| audio/L16 | Audio/L16 is based on L16, described in RFC 1890. L16 denotes uncompressed audio data, using 16-bit signed representation. | | RFC 2586 |
| audio/MP4A-LATM | MPEG-4 audio. | | RFC 3016 |
| audio/midi | MIDI music files. | mid, midi, kar | |
| audio/mpeg | MPEG encoded audio files. | mpga, mp2, mp3 | RFC 3003 |
| audio/parityfec | Parity-based forward error correction for RTP audio. | | RFC 3009 |
| audio/prs.sid | Commodore 64 SID audio files. | sid, psid | *http://www.geocities.com/ SiliconValley/Lakes/5147/sidplay/ docs.html#fileformats* |
| audio/telephone-event | Logical telephone event. | | RFC 2833 |
| audio/tone | Telephonic sound pattern. | | RFC 2833 |
| audio/vnd.cns.anp1 | Supports voice and unified messaging application features available on the Access NP network services platform from Comverse Network Systems. | | Ann McLaughlin Comverse Network Systems *amclaughlin@comversens.com* |

| MIME type | Description | Extension | Contact and reference |
|---|---|---|---|
| audio/vnd.cns.inf1 | Supports voice and unified messaging application features available on the TRILOGUE Infinity network services platform from Comverse Network Systems. | | Same as above |
| audio/vnd.digital-winds | Digital Winds music is never-ending, reproducible, and interactive MIDI music in very small packages (<3K). | eol | Armands Strazds *armands.strazds@medienhaus-bremen.de* |
| audio/vnd.everad.plj | Proprietary EverAD audio encoding. | plj | Tomer Weisberg *tomer@everad.com* |
| audio/vnd.lucent.voice | Voice messaging including Lucent Technologies' Intuity™ AUDIX® Multimedia Messaging System and the Lucent Voice Player. | lvp | Frederick Block *rickblock@lucent.com* *http://www.lucent.com/lvp/* |
| audio/vnd.nortel.vbk | Proprietary Nortel Networks Voice Block audio encoding. | vbk | Glenn Parsons *Glenn.Parsons@NortelNetworks.com* |
| audio/vnd.nuera.ecelp4800 | Proprietary Nuera Communications audio and speech encoding, available in Nuera voice-over-IP gateways, terminals, application servers, and as a media service for various host platforms and OSs. | ecelp4800 | Michael Fox *mfox@nuera.com* |
| audio/vnd.nuera.ecelp7470 | Same as above. | ecelp7470 | Same as above |
| audio/vnd.nuera.ecelp9600 | Same as above. | ecelp9600 | Same as above |
| audio/vnd.octel.sbc | Variable-rate encoding averaging 18 kbps used for voice messaging in Lucent Technologies' Sierra™, Overture™, and IMA™ platforms. | | Jeff Bouis *jbouis@lucent.com* |
| audio/vnd.qcelp | Qualcomm audio encoding. | qcp | Andy Dejaco *adejaco@qualcomm.com* |
| audio/vnd.rhetorex.32kadpcm | 32-kbps Rhetorex™ ADPCM audio encoding used in voice messaging products such as Lucent Technologies's CallPerformer™, Unified Messenger™, and other products. | | Jeff Bouis *jbouis@lucent.com* |
| audio/vnd.vmx.cvsd | Audio encoding used in voice messaging products including Lucent Technologies' Overture200™, Overture 300™, and VMX 300™ product lines. | | Same as above |
| audio/x-aiff | AIFF audio file format. | aif, aiff, aifc | |
| audio/x-pn-realaudio | RealAudio metafile format by Real Networks (formerly Progressive Networks). | ram, rm | |
| audio/x-pn-realaudio-plugin | From Apache *mime.types*. | rpm | |

| MIME type | Description | Extension | Contact and reference |
|-----------|-------------|-----------|----------------------|
| audio/x-realaudio | RealAudio audio format by Real Networks (formerly Progressive Networks). | ra | |
| audio/x-wav | WAV audio files. | wav | |

# chemical/*

Much of the information in Table D-5 was obtained courtesy of the "Chemical MIME Home Page" (*http://www.ch.ic.ac.uk/chemime/*).

*Table D-5. "Chemical" MIME types*

| MIME type | Description | Extension | Contact and reference |
|-----------|-------------|-----------|----------------------|
| chemical/x-alchemy | Alchemy format | alc | *http://www.camsoft.com* |
| chemical/x-cache-csf | | csf | |
| chemical/x-cactvs-binary | CACTVS binary format | cbin | *http://cactvs.cit.nih.gov* |
| chemical/x-cactvs-ascii | CACTVS ASCII format | cascii | *http://cactvs.cit.nih.gov* |
| chemical/x-cactvs-table | CACTVS table format | ctab | *http://cactvs.cit.nih.gov* |
| chemical/x-cdx | ChemDraw eXchange file | cdx | *http://www.camsoft.com* |
| chemical/x-cerius | MSI Cerius II format | cer | *http://www.msi.com* |
| chemical/x-chemdraw | ChemDraw file | chm | *http://www.camsoft.com* |
| chemical/x-cif | Crystallographic Interchange Format | cif | *http://www.bernstein-plus-sons.com/software/rasmol/*<br>*http://ndbserver.rutgers.edu/NDB/mmcif/examples/index.html* |
| chemical/x-mmcif | MacroMolecular CIF | mcif | Same as above |
| chemical/x-chem3d | Chem3D format | c3d | *http://www.camsoft.com* |
| chemical/x-cmdf | CrystalMaker Data Format | cmdf | *http://www.crystalmaker.co.uk* |
| chemical/x-compass | Compass program of the Takahashi | cpa | |
| chemical/x-crossfire | Crossfire file | bsd | |
| chemical/x-cml | Chemical Markup Language | cml | *http://www.xml-cml.org* |
| chemical/x-csml | Chemical Style Markup Language | csml, csm | *http://www.mdli.com* |
| chemical/x-ctx | Gasteiger group CTX file format | ctx | |
| chemical/x-cxf | | cxf | |
| chemical/x-daylight-smiles | Smiles format | smi | *http://www.daylight.com/dayhtml/smiles/index.html* |
| chemical/x-embl-dl-nucleotide | EMBL nucleotide format | emb | *http://mercury.ebi.ac.uk* |
| chemical/x-galactic-spc | SPC format for spectral and chromatographic data | spc | *http://www.galactic.com/galactic/Data/spcvue.htm* |

| MIME type | Description | Extension | Contact and reference |
|---|---|---|---|
| chemical/x-gamess-input | GAMESS Input format | inp, gam | *http://www.msg.ameslab.gov/ GAMESS/Graphics/ MacMolPlt.shtml* |
| chemical/x-gaussian-input | Gaussian Input format | gau | *http://www.mdli.com* |
| chemical/x-gaussian-checkpoint | Gaussian Checkpoint format | fch, fchk | *http://products.camsoft.com* |
| chemical/x-gaussian-cube | Gaussian Cube (Wavefunction) format | cub | *http://www.mdli.com* |
| chemical/x-gcg8-sequence | | gcg | |
| chemical/x-genbank | ToGenBank format | gen | |
| chemical/x-isostar | IsoStar Library of intermolecular interactions | istr, ist | *http://www.ccdc.cam.ac.uk* |
| chemical/x-jcamp-dx | JCAMP Spectroscopic Data Exchange format | jdx, dx | *http://www.mdli.com* |
| chemical/x-jjc-review-surface | Re_View3 Orbital Contour files | rv3 | *http://www.brunel.ac.uk/depts/ chem/ch241s/re_view/rv3.htm* |
| chemical/x-jjc-review-xyz | Re_View3 Animation files | xyb | *http://www.brunel.ac.uk/depts/ chem/ch241s/re_view/rv3.htm* |
| chemical/x-jjc-review-vib | Re_View3 Vibration files | rv2, vib | *http://www.brunel.ac.uk/depts/ chem/ch241s/re_view/rv3.htm* |
| chemical/x-kinemage | Kinetic (Protein Structure) Images | kin | *http://www.faseb.org/protein/ kinemages/MageSoftware.html* |
| chemical/x-macmolecule | MacMolecule file format | mcm | |
| chemical/x-macromodel-input | MacroModel Molecular Mechanics | mmd, mmod | *http://www.columbia.edu/cu/ chemistry/* |
| chemical/x-mdl-molfile | MDL Molfile | mol | *http://www.mdli.com* |
| chemical/x-mdl-rdfile | Reaction data file | rd | *http://www.mdli.com* |
| chemical/x-mdl-rxnfile | MDL Reaction format | rxn | *http://www.mdli.com* |
| chemical/x-mdl-sdfile | MDL Structure data file | sd | *http://www.mdli.com* |
| chemical/x-mdl-tgf | MDL Transportable Graphics Format | tgf | *http://www.mdli.com* |
| chemical/x-mif | | mif | |
| chemical/x-mol2 | Portable representation of a SYBYL molecule | mol2 | *http://www.tripos.com* |
| chemical/x-molconn-Z | Molconn-Z format | b | *http://www.eslc.vabiotech.com/ molconn/molconnz.html* |
| chemical/x-mopac-input | MOPAC Input format | mop | *http://www.mdli.com* |
| chemical/x-mopac-graph | MOPAC Graph format | gpt | *http://products.camsoft.com* |
| chemical/x-ncbi-asn1 | | asn (old form) | |
| chemical/x-ncbi-asn1-binary | | val | |
| chemical/x-pdb | Protein DataBank pdb | pdb | *http://www.mdli.com* |

| MIME type | Description | Extension | Contact and reference |
|---|---|---|---|
| chemical/x-swissprot | SWISS-PROT protein sequence database | sw | *http://www.expasy.ch/spdbv/text/ download.htm* |
| chemical/x-vamas-iso14976 | Versailles Agreement on Materials and Standards | vms | *http://www.acolyte.co.uk/JISO/* |
| chemical/x-vmd | Visual Molecular Dynamics | vmd | *http://www.ks.uiuc.edu/Research/ vmd/* |
| chemical/x-xtel | Xtelplot file format | xtel | *http://www.recipnet.indiana.edu/ graphics/xtelplot/xtelplot.htm* |
| chemical/x-xyz | Co-ordinate Animation format | xyz | *http://www.mdli.com* |

# image/*

Table D-6 summarizes some of the image types commonly exchanged by email and HTTP.

Table D-6. "Image" MIME types

| MIME type | Description | Extension | Contact and reference |
|---|---|---|---|
| image/bmp | Windows BMP image format. | bmp | |
| image/cgm | Computer Graphics Metafile (CGM) is an International Standard for the portable storage and transfer of 2-D illustrations. | | Alan Francis A.H.Francis@open.ac.uk See ISO 8632:1992, IS 8632:1992 Amendment 1 (1994), and IS 8632: 1992 Amendment 2 (1995) |
| image/g3fax | G3 Facsimile byte streams. | | RFC 1494 |
| image/gif | Compuserve GIF images. | gif | RFC 1341 |
| image/ief | | ief | RFC 1314 |
| image/jpeg | JPEG images. | jpeg, jpg, jpe, jfif | JPEG Draft Standard ISO 10918-1 CD |
| image/naplps | North American Presentation Layer Protocol Syntax (NAPLPS) images. | | ANSI X3.110-1983 CSA T500-1983 |
| image/png | Portable Network Graphics (PNG) images. | png | Internet draft *draft-boutell-png-spec-04.txt*, "Png (Portable Network Graphics) Specification Version 1.0" |
| image/prs.btif | Format used by Nations Bank for BTIF image viewing of checks and other applications. | btif, btf | Arthur Rubin *arthurr@crt.com* |
| image/prs.pti | PTI encoded images. | pti | Juern Laun *juern.laun@gmx.de http://server.hvzgymn.wn.schule-bw.de/pti/* |
| image/tiff | TIFF images. | tiff, tif | RFC 2302 |

| MIME type | Description | Extension | Contact and reference |
|---|---|---|---|
| image/vnd.cns.inf2 | Supports application features available on the TRILOGUE Infinity network services platform from Comverse Network Systems. | | Ann McLaughlin Comverse Network Systems *amclaughlin@comversens.com* |
| image/vnd.dxf | DXF vector CAD files. | dxf | |
| image/vnd.fastbidsheet | A FastBid Sheet contains a raster or vector image that represents an engineering or architectural drawing. | fbs | Scott Becker *scottb@bxwa.com* |
| image/vnd.fpx | Kodak FlashPix images. | fpx | Chris Wing *format_change_request@kodak. com* *http://www.kodak.com* |
| image/vnd.fst | Image format from FAST Search and Transfer. | fst | Arild Fuldseth *Arild.Fuldseth@fast.no* |
| image/vnd.fujixerox.edmics-mmr | Fuji Xerox EDMICS MMR image format. | mmr | Masanori Onda *Masanori.Onda@fujixerox.co.jp* |
| image/vnd.fujixerox.edmics-rlc | Fuji Xerox EDMICS RLC image format. | rlc | Same as above |
| image/vnd.mix | MIX files contain binary data in streams that are used to represent images and related information. They are used by Microsoft PhotDraw and PictureIt software. | | Saveen Reddy2 *saveenr@microsoft.com* |
| image/vnd.net-fpx | Kodak FlashPix images. | | Chris Wing *format_change_request@kodak. com* *http://www.kodak.com* |
| image/vnd.wap.wbmp | From Apache *mime.types*. | wbmp | |
| image/vnd.xiff | Extended Image Format used by Pagis software. | xif | Steve Martin *smartin@xis.xerox.com* |
| image/x-cmu-raster | From Apache *mime.types*. | ras | |
| image/x-portable-anymap | PBM generic images. | pnm | Jeff Poskanzer *http://www.acme.com/software/ pbmplus/* |
| image/x-portable-bitmap | PBM bitmap images. | pbm | Same as above |
| image/x-portable-graymap | PBM grayscale images. | pgm | Same as above |
| image/x-portable-pixmap | PBM color images. | ppm | Same as above |
| image/x-rgb | Silicon Graphics's RGB images. | rgb | |
| image/x-xbitmap | X-Window System bitmap images. | xbm | |
| image/x-xpixmap | X-Window System color images. | xpm | |
| image/x-xwindowdump | X-Window System screen capture images. | xwd | |

# message/*

Messages are composite types used to communicate data objects (through email, HTTP, or other transport protocols). Table D-7 describes the common MIME message types.

*Table D-7. "Message" MIME types*

| MIME type | Description | Extension | Contact and reference |
|-----------|-------------|-----------|----------------------|
| message/delivery-status | | | |
| message/disposition-notification | | | RFC 2298 |
| message/external-body | | | RFC 1341 |
| message/http | | | RFC 2616 |
| message/news | Defines a way to transmit news articles via email for human reading—message/rfc822 is not sufficient because news headers have semantics beyond those defined by RFC 822. | | RFC 1036 |
| message/partial | Permits the fragmented transmission of bodies that are thought to be too large to be sent directly by email. | | RFC 1341 |
| message/rfc822 | A complete email message. | | RFC 1341 |
| message/s-http | Secure HTTP messages, an alternative to HTTP over SSL. | | RFC 2660 |

# model/*

The model MIME type is an IETF-registered extension type. It represents mathematical models of physical worlds, for computer-aided design, and 3-D graphics. Table D-8 describes some of the model formats.

*Table D-8. "Model" MIME types*

| MIME type | Description | Extension | Contact and reference |
|-----------|-------------|-----------|----------------------|
| model/iges | The Initial Graphics Exchange Specification (IGES) defines a neutral data format that allows for the digital exchange of information between computer-aided design (CAD) systems. | igs, iges | RFC 2077 |
| model/mesh | | msh, mesh, silo | RFC 2077 |
| model/vnd.dwf | DWF CAD files. | dwf | Jason Pratt *jason.pratt@autodesk.com* |
| model/vnd.flatland.3dml | Supports 3DML models supported by Flatland products. | 3dml, 3dm | Michael Powers *pow@flatland.com* *http://www.flatland.com* |

| MIME type | Description | Extension | Contact and reference |
|-----------|-------------|-----------|-----------------------|
| model/vnd.gdl<br>model/vnd.gs-gdl | The Geometric Description Language (GDL) is a parametric object definition language for ArchiCAD by Graphisoft. | gdl, gsm, win, dor, lmp, rsm, msm, ism | Attila Babits<br>*ababits@graphisoft.hu*<br>*http://www.graphisoft.com* |
| model/vnd.gtw | Gen-Trix models. | gtw | Yutaka Ozaki<br>*yutaka_ozaki@gen.co.jp* |
| model/vnd.mts | MTS model format by Virtue. | mts | Boris Rabinovitch<br>*boris@virtue3d.com* |
| model/vnd.parasolid.trans-mit.binary | Binary Parasolid modeling file. | x_b | *http://www.ugsolutions.com/products/parasolid/* |
| model/vnd.parasolid.trans-mit.text | Text Parasolid modeling file. | x_t | *http://www.ugsolutions.com/products/parasolid/* |
| model/vnd.vtu | VTU model format by Virtue. | vtu | Boris Rabinovitch<br>*boris@virtue3d.com* |
| model/vrml | Virtual Reality Markup Language format files. | wrl, vrml | RFC 2077 |

# multipart/*

Multipart MIME types are composite objects that contain other objects. The subtype describes the implementation of the multipart packaging and how to process the components. Multipart media types are summarized in Table D-9.

*Table D-9. "Multipart" MIME types*

| MIME type | Description | Extension | Contact and reference |
|-----------|-------------|-----------|-----------------------|
| multipart/alternative | The content consists of a list of alternative representations, each with its own Content-Type. The client can select the best supported component. | | RFC 1341 |
| multipart/appledouble | Apple Macintosh files contain "resource forks" and other desktop data that describes the actual file contents. This multipart content sends the Apple metadata in one part and the actual content in another part. | | *http://www.isi.edu/in-notes/iana/assignments/media-types/multipart/appledouble* |
| multipart/byteranges | When an HTTP message includes the content of multiple ranges, these are transmitted in a "multipart/byteranges" object. This media type includes two or more parts, separated by MIME boundaries, each with its own Content-Type and Content-Range fields. | | RFC 2068 |

| MIME type | Description | Extension | Contact and reference |
|---|---|---|---|
| multipart/digest | Contains a collection of individual email messages, in an easy-to-read form. | | RFC 1341 |
| multipart/encrypted | Uses two parts to support crypto-graphically encrypted content. The first part contains the control infor-mation necessary to decrypt the data in the second body part and is labeled according to the value of the protocol parameter. The second part contains the encrypted data in type applica-tion/octet-stream. | | RFC 1847 |
| multipart/form-data | Used to bundle up a set of values as the result of a user filling out a form. | | RFC 2388 |
| multipart/header-set | Separates user data from arbitrary descriptive metadata. | | *http://www.isi.edu/in-notes/iana/ assignments/media-types/ multipart/header-set* |
| multipart/mixed | A collection of objects. | | RFC 1341 |
| multipart/parallel | Syntactically identical to multipart/ mixed, but all of the parts are intended to be presented simultaneously, on systems capable of doing so. | | RFC 1341 |
| multipart/related | Intended for compound objects con-sisting of several interrelated body parts. The relationships between the body parts distinguish them from other object types. These relation-ships often are represented by links internal to the object's components that reference the other components. | | RFC 2387 |
| multipart/report | Defines a general container type for electronic mail reports of any kind. | | RFC 1892 |
| multipart/signed | Uses two parts to support crypto-graphically signed content. The first part is the content, including its MIME headers. The second part contains the information necessary to verify the digital signature. | | RFC 1847 |
| multipart/voice-message | Provides a mechanism for packaging a voice message into one container that is tagged as VPIM v2–compliant. | | RFCs 2421 and 2423 |

# text/*

Text media types contain characters and potential formatting information. Table D-10 summarizes text MIME types.

*Table D-10. "Text" MIME types*

| MIME type | Description | Extension | Contact and reference |
|---|---|---|---|
| text/calendar | Supports the iCalendar calendaring and scheduling standard. | | RFC 2445 |
| text/css | Cascading Style Sheets. | css | RFC 2318 |
| text/directory | Holds record data from a directory database, such as LDAP. | | RFC 2425 |
| text/enriched | Simple formatted text, supporting fonts, colors, and spacing. SGML-like tags are used to begin and end formatting. | | RFC 1896 |
| text/html | HTML file. | html, htm | RFC 2854 |
| text/parityfec | Forward error correction for text streamed in an RTP stream. | | RFC 3009 |
| text/plain | Plain old text. | asc, txt | |
| text/prs.lines.tag | Supports tagged forms, as used for email registration. | tag, dsc | John Lines *john@paladin.demon.co.uk http://www.paladin.demon.co.uk/ tag-types/* |
| text/rfc822-headers | Used to bundle a set of email headers, such as when sending mail failure reports. | | RFC 1892 |
| text/richtext | Older form of enriched text. See text/enriched. | rtx | RFC 1341 |
| text/rtf | The Rich Text Format (RTF) is a method of encoding formatted text and graphics for transfer between applications. The format is widely supported by word-processing applications on the MS-DOS, Windows, OS/2, and Macintosh platforms. | rtf | |
| text/sgml | SGML markup files. | sgml, sgm | RFC 1874 |
| text/t140 | Supports standardized T.140 text, as used in synchronized RTP multimedia. | | RFC 2793 |
| text/tab-separated-values | TSV is a popular method of data interchange among databases and spreadsheets and word processors. It consists of a set of lines, with fields separated by tab characters. | tsv | *http://www.isi.edu/in-notes/iana/ assignments/media-types/text/tab-separated-values* |
| text/uri-list | Simple, commented lists of URLs and URNs used by URN resolvers, and any other applications that need to communicate bulk URI lists. | uris, uri | RFC 2483 |

| MIME type | Description | Extension | Contact and reference |
|-----------|-------------|-----------|----------------------|
| text/vnd.abc | ABC files are a human-readable format for musical scores. | abc | *http://www.gre.ac.uk/ ~c.walshaw/abc/* <br><br> *http://home1.swipnet.se/ ~w-11382/abcbnf.htm* |
| text/vnd.curl | Provides a set of content definition languages interpreted by the CURL runtime plug-in. | curl | Tim Hodge <br> *thodge@curl.com* |
| text/vnd.DMClientScript | CommonDM Client Script files are used as hyperlinks to non-http sites (such as BYOND, IRC, or telnet) accessed by the Dream Seeker client application. | dms | Dan Bradley <br> *dan@dantom.com* <br> *http://www.byond.com/code/ref/* |
| text/vnd.fly | Fly is a text preprocessor that uses a simple syntax to create an interface between databases and web pages. | fly | John-Mark Gurney <br> *jmg@flyidea.com* <br> *http://www.flyidea.com* |
| text/vnd.fmi.flexstor | For use in the SUVDAMA and UVRAPPF projects. | flx | *http://www.ozone.fmi.fi/ SUVDAMA/* <br><br> *http://www.ozone.fmi.fi/UVRAPPF/* |
| text/vnd.in3d.3dml | For In3D Player. | 3dml, 3dm | Michael Powers <br> *powers@insideout.net* |
| text/vnd.in3d.spot | For In3D Player. | spot, spo | Same as above |
| text/vnd.IPTC.NewsML | NewsML format specified by the International Press Telecommunications Council (IPTC). | xml | David Allen <br> *m_director_iptc@dial.pipex.com* <br> *http://www.iptc.org* |
| text/vnd.IPTC.NITF | NITF format specified by the IPTC. | xml | Same as above <br> *http://www.nitf.org* |
| text/vnd.latex-z | Supports LaTeX documents containing Z notation. Z notation (pronounced "zed"), is based on Zermelo-Fraenkel set theory and first order predicate logic, and it is useful for describing computer systems. | | *http://www.comlab.ox.ac.uk/ archive/z/* |
| text/vnd.motorola.reflex | Provides a common method for submitting simple text messages from ReFLEX™ wireless devices. | | Mark Patton <br> *fmp014@email.mot.com* <br><br> Part of the FLEXsuite™ of Enabling Protocols specification available from Motorola under the licensing agreement |
| text/vnd.ms-mediapackage | This type is intended to be handled by the Microsoft application programs MStore.exe and 7 storDB.exe. | mpf | Jan Nelson <br> *jann@microsoft.com* |

| MIME type | Description | Extension | Contact and reference |
|---|---|---|---|
| text/vnd.wap.si | Service Indication (SI) objects contain a message describing an event and a URI describing where to load the corresponding service. | si, xml | WAP Forum Ltd<br>*http://www.wapforum.org* |
| text/vnd.wap.sl | The Service Loading (SL) content type provides a means to convey a URI to a user agent in a mobile client. The client itself automatically loads the content indicated by that URI and executes it in the addressed user agent without user intervention when appropriate. | sl, xml | Same as above |
| text/vnd.wap.wml | Wireless Markup Language (WML) is a markup language, based on XML, that defines content and user interface for narrow-band devices, including cellular phones and pagers. | wml | Same as above |
| text/vnd.wap.wmlscript | WMLScript is an evolution of JavaScript for wireless devices. | wmls | Same as above |
| text/x-setext | From Apache *mime.types*. | etx | |
| text/xml | Extensible Markup Language format file (use application/xml if you want the browser to save to file when downloaded). | xml | RFC 2376 |

# video/*

Table D-11 lists some popular video movie formats. Note that some video formats are classified as application types.

*Table D-11. "Video" MIME types*

| MIME type | Description | Extension | Contact and reference |
|---|---|---|---|
| video/MP4V-ES | MPEG-4 video payload, as carried by RTP. | | RFC 3016 |
| video/mpeg | Video encoded per the ISO 11172 CD MPEG standard. | mpeg, mpg, mpe | RFC 1341 |
| video/parityfec | Forward error correcting video format for data carried through RTP streams. | | RFC 3009 |
| video/pointer | Transporting pointer position information for presentations. | | RFC 2862 |
| video/quicktime | Apple Quicktime video format. | qt, mov | *http://www.apple.com* |
| video/vnd.fvt | Video format from FAST Search & Transfer. | fvt | Arild Fuldseth<br>*Arild.Fuldseth@fast.no* |

| MIME type | Description | Extension | Contact and reference |
|-----------|-------------|-----------|----------------------|
| video/vnd.motorola.video<br>video/vnd.motorola.videop | Proprietary formats used by products from Motorola ISG. | | Tom McGinty<br>Motorola ISG<br>*tmcginty@dma.isg.mot* |
| video/vnd.mpegurl | This media type consists of a series of URLs of MPEG Video files. | mxu | Heiko Recktenwald<br>*uzs106@uni-bonn.de* |
| | | | "Power and Responsibility: Conversations with Contributors," Guy van Belle, et al., LMJ 9 (1999), 127– 133, 129 (MIT Press) |
| video/vnd.nokia.interleaved-multimedia | Used in Nokia 9210 Communicator video player and related tools. | nim | Petteri Kangaslampi<br>*petteri.kangaslampi@nokia.com* |
| video/x-msvideo | Microsoft AVI movies. | avi | *http://www.microsoft.com* |
| video/x-sgi-movie | Silicon Graphics's movie format. | movie | *http://www.sgi.com* |

# Experimental Types

The set of primary types supports most content types. Table D-12 lists one experimental type, for conferencing software, that is configured in some web servers.

Table D-12. Extension MIME types

| MIME type | Description | Extension | Contact and reference |
|-----------|-------------|-----------|----------------------|
| x-conference/x-cooltalk | Collaboration tool from Netscape | ice | |

# APPENDIX E

# Base-64 Encoding

Base-64 encoding is used by HTTP, for basic and digest authentication, and by several HTTP extensions. This appendix explains base-64 encoding and provides conversion tables and pointers to Perl software to help you correctly use base-64 encoding in HTTP software.

## Base-64 Encoding Makes Binary Data Safe

The base-64 encoding converts a series of arbitrary bytes into a longer sequence of common text characters that are all legal header field values. Base-64 encoding lets us take user input or binary data, pack it into a safe format, and ship it as HTTP header field values without fear of them containing colons, newlines, or binary values that would break HTTP parsers.

Base-64 encoding was developed as part of the MIME multimedia electronic mail standard, so MIME could transport rich text and arbitrary binary data between different legacy email gateways.* Base-64 encoding is similar in spirit, but more efficient in space, to the uuencode and BinHex standards for textifying binary data. Section 6.8 of MIME RFC 2045 details the base-64 algorithm.

## Eight Bits to Six Bits

Base-64 encoding takes a sequence of 8-bit bytes, breaks the sequence into 6-bit pieces, and assigns each 6-bit piece to one of 64 characters comprising the base-64 alphabet. The 64 possible output characters are common and safe to place in HTTP header fields. The 64 characters include upper- and lowercase letters, numbers, +,

---

* Some mail gateways would silently strip many "non-printing" characters with ASCII values between 0 and 31. Other programs would interpret some bytes as flow control characters or other special control characters, or convert carriage returns to line feeds and the like. Some programs would experience fatal errors upon receiving international characters with a value above 127 because the software was not "8-bit clean."

and /. The special character = also is used. The base-64 alphabet is shown in Table E-1.

Note that because the base-64 encoding uses 8-bit characters to represent 6 bits of information, base 64–encoded strings are about 33% larger than the original values.

*Table E-1. Base-64 alphabet*

| | | | | | | | | | | | | | | | |
|---|---|---|---|---|---|---|---|---|---|---|---|---|---|---|---|
| 0 | A | 8 | I | 16 | Q | 24 | Y | 32 | g | 40 | o | 48 | w | 56 | 4 |
| 1 | B | 9 | J | 17 | R | 25 | Z | 33 | h | 41 | p | 49 | x | 57 | 5 |
| 2 | C | 10 | K | 18 | S | 26 | a | 34 | i | 42 | q | 50 | y | 58 | 6 |
| 3 | D | 11 | L | 19 | T | 27 | b | 35 | j | 43 | r | 51 | z | 59 | 7 |
| 4 | E | 12 | M | 20 | U | 28 | c | 36 | k | 44 | s | 52 | 0 | 60 | 8 |
| 5 | F | 13 | N | 21 | V | 29 | d | 37 | l | 45 | t | 53 | 1 | 61 | 9 |
| 6 | G | 14 | O | 22 | W | 30 | e | 38 | m | 46 | u | 54 | 2 | 62 | + |
| 7 | H | 15 | P | 23 | X | 31 | f | 39 | n | 47 | v | 55 | 3 | 63 | / |

Figure E-1 shows a simple example of base-64 encoding. Here, the three-character input value "Ow!" is base 64–encoded, resulting in the four-character base 64–encoded value "T3ch". It works like this:

1. The string "Ow!" is broken into 3 8-bit bytes (0x4F, 0x77, 0x21).
2. The 3 bytes create the 24-bit binary value 010011110111011100100001.
3. These bits are segmented into the 6-bit sequences 010011, 110111, 01110, 100001.
4. Each of these 6-bit values represents a number from 0 to 63, corresponding to one of 64 characters in the base-64 alphabet. The resulting base 64–encoded string is the 4-character string "T3ch", which can then be sent across the wire as "safe" 8-bit characters, because only the most portable characters are used (letters, numbers, etc.).

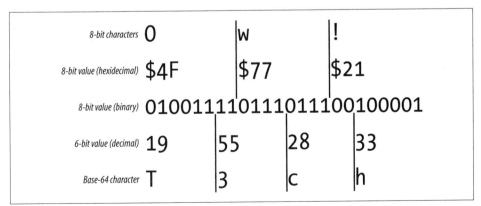

*Figure E-1. Base-64 encoding example*

# Base-64 Padding

Base-64 encoding takes a sequence of 8-bit bytes and segments the bit stream into 6-bit chunks. It is unlikely that the sequence of bits will divide evenly into 6-bit pieces. When the bit sequence does not divide evenly into 6-bit pieces, the bit sequence is padded with zero bits at the end to make the length of the bit sequence a multiple of 24 (the least common multiple of 6 and 8 bits).

When encoding the padded bit string, any group of 6 bits that is completely padding (containing no bits from the original data) is represented by a special 65th symbol: "=". If a group of 6 bits is partially padded, the padding bits are set to zero.

Table E-2 shows examples of padding. The initial input string "a:a" is 3 bytes long, or 24 bits. 24 is a multiple of 6 and 8, so no padding is required. The resulting base 64–encoded string is "YTph".

*Table E-2. Base-64 padding examples*

| Input data | Binary sequence (padding noted as "x") | Encoded data |
|---|---|---|
| a:a | 011000 010011 101001 100001 | YTph |
| a:aa | 011000 010011 101001 100001 011000 01xxxx xxxxxx xxxxxx | YTphYQ== |
| a:aaa | 011000 010011 101001 100001 011000 010110 0001xx xxxxxx | YTphYWE= |
| a:aaaa | 011000 010011 101001 100001 011000 010110 000101 100001 | YTphYWFh |

However, when another character is added, the input string grows to 32 bits long. The next smallest multiple of 6 and 8 is 48 bits, so 16 bits of padding are added. The first 4 bits of padding are mixed with data bits. The resulting 6-bit group, 01xxxx, is treated as 010000, 16 decimal, or base-64 encoding Q. The remaining two 6-bit groups are all padding and are represented by "=".

# Perl Implementation

MIME::Base64 is a Perl module for base-64 encoding and decoding. You can read about this module at *http://www.perldoc.com/perl5.6.1/lib/MIME/Base64.html*.

You can encode and decode strings using the MIME::Base64 encode_base64 and decode_base64 methods:

```
use MIME::Base64;

$encoded = encode_base64('Aladdin:open sesame');
$decoded = decode_base64($encoded);
```

# For More Information

For more information on base-64 encoding, see:

*http://www.ietf.org/rfc/rfc2045.txt*
> Section 6.8 of RFC 2045, "MIME Part 1: Format of Internet Message Bodies," provides an official specification of base-64 encoding.

*http://www.perldoc.com/perl5.6.1/lib/MIME/Base64.html*
> This web site contains documentation for the MIME::Base64 Perl module that provides encoding and decoding of base-64 strings.

# Digest Authentication

This appendix contains supporting data and source code for implementing HTTP digest authentication facilities.

## Digest WWW-Authenticate Directives

WWW-Authenticate directives are described in Table F-1, paraphrased from the descriptions in RFC 2617. As always, refer to the official specifications for the most up-to-date details.

*Table F-1. Digest WWW-Authenticate header directives (from RFC 2617)*

| Directive | Description |
|---|---|
| realm | A string to be displayed to users so they know which username and password to use. This string should contain at least the name of the host performing the authentication and might additionally indicate the collection of users who might have access. An example might be "registered_users@gotham.news.com". |
| nonce | A server-specified data string that should be uniquely generated each time a 401 response is made. It is recommended that this string be base-64 or hexadecimal data. Specifically, because the string is passed in the header lines as a quoted string, the double-quote character is not allowed. |
| | The contents of the nonce are implementation-dependent. The quality of the implementation depends on a good choice. A nonce might, for example, be constructed as the base-64 encoding of: |
| | `time-stamp H(time-stamp ":" ETag ":" private-key)` |
| | where *time-stamp* is a server-generated time or other nonrepeating value, *ETag* is the value of the HTTP ETag header associated with the requested entity, and *private-key* is data known only to the server. With a nonce of this form, a server would recalculate the hash portion after receiving the client Authentication header and reject the request if it did not match the nonce from that header or if the time-stamp value is not recent enough. In this way, the server can limit the time of the nonce's validity. The inclusion of the ETag prevents a replay request for an updated version of the resource. (Note: including the IP address of the client in the nonce appears to offer the server the ability to limit the reuse of the nonce to the same client that originally got it. However, that would break proxy farms, where requests from a single user often go through different proxies in the farm. Also, IP address spoofing is not that hard.) |
| | An implementation might choose not to accept a previously used nonce or a previously used digest, to protect against replay attacks, or it might choose to use one-time nonces or digests for POST or PUT requests and time-stamps for GET requests. |

*Table F-1. Digest WWW-Authenticate header directives (from RFC 2617) (continued)*

| Directive | Description |
|---|---|
| domain | A quoted, space-separated list of URIs (as specified in RFC 2396, "Uniform Resource Identifiers: Generic Syntax") that define the protection space. If a URI is an abs_path, it is relative to the canonical root URL of .the server being accessed. An absolute URI in this list may refer to a different server than the one being accessed. |
| | The client can use this list to determine the set of URIs for which the same authentication information may be sent: any URI that has a URI in this list as a prefix (after both have been made absolute) may be assumed to be in the same protection space. |
| | If this directive is omitted or its value is empty, the client should assume that the protection space consists of all URIs on the responding server. |
| | This directive is not meaningful in Proxy-Authenticate headers, for which the protection space is always the entire proxy; if present, it should be ignored. |
| opaque | A string of data, specified by the server, that should be returned by the client unchanged in the Authorization header of subsequent requests with URIs in the same protection space. It is recommended that this string be base-64 or hexadecimal data. |
| stale | A flag indicating that the previous request from the client was rejected because the nonce value was stale. If stale is TRUE (case-insensitive), the client may want to retry the request with a new encrypted response, without reprompting the user for a new username and password. The server should set stale to TRUE only if it receives a request for which the nonce is invalid but has a valid digest (indicating that the client knows the correct username/password). If stale is FALSE, or anything other than TRUE, or the stale directive is not present, the username and/or password are invalid, and new values must be obtained. |
| algorithm | A string indicating a pair of algorithms used to produce the digest and a checksum. If this is not present, it is assumed to be "MD5". If the algorithm is not understood, the challenge should be ignored (and a different one used, if there is more than one). |
| | In this document, the string obtained by applying the digest algorithm to the data "data" with secret "secret" will be denoted by "KD(secret, data)", and the string obtained by applying the checksum algorithm to the data "data" will be denoted "H(data)". The notation "unq(X)" means the value of the quoted string "X" without the surrounding quotes. |
| | For the MD5 and MD5-sess algorithms: |
| | ```
H(data) = MD5(data)
HD(secret, data) = H(concat(secret, ":", data))
``` |
| | I.e., the digest is the MD5 of the secret concatenated with a colon concatenated with the data. The MD5-sess algorithm is intended to allow efficient third-party authentication servers. |
| qop | This directive is optional but is made so only for backward compatibility with RFC 2069 [6]; it should be used by all implementations compliant with this version of the digest scheme. |
| | If present, it is a quoted string of one or more tokens indicating the "quality of protection" values supported by the server. The value "auth" indicates authentication; the value "auth-int" indicates authentication with integrity protection. Unrecognized options must be ignored. |
| <extension> | This directive allows for future extensions. Any unrecognized directives must be ignored. |

# Digest Authorization Directives

Each of the Authorization directives is described in Table F-2, paraphrased from the descriptions in RFC 2617. Refer to the official specifications for the most up-to-date details.
```

*Table F-2. Digest Authorization header directives (from RFC 2617)*

| Directive | Description |
|---|---|
| username | The user's name in the specified realm. |
| realm | The realm passed to the client in the WWW-Authenticate header. |
| nonce | The same nonce passed to the client in the WWW-Authenticate header. |
| uri | The URI from the request URI of the request line; duplicated because proxies are allowed to change the request line in transit, and we may need the original URI for proper digest verification calculations. |
| response | This is the actual digest—the whole point of digest authentication! The response is a string of 32 hexadecimal digits, computed by a negotiated digest algorithm, which proves that the user knows the password. |
| algorithm | A string indicating a pair of algorithms used to produce the digest and a checksum. If this is not present, it is assumed to be "MD5". |
| opaque | A string of data, specified by the server in a WWW-Authenticate header, that should be returned by the client unchanged in the Authorization header of subsequent requests with URIs in the same protection space. |
| cnonce | This must be specified if a qop directive is sent and must not be specified if the server did not send a qop directive in the WWW-Authenticate header field. |
| | The cnonce value is an opaque quoted string value provided by the client and used by both client and server to avoid chosen plaintext attacks, to provide mutual authentication, and to provide some message-integrity protection. |
| | See the descriptions of the response-digest and request-digest calculations later in this appendix. |
| qop | Indicates what "quality of protection" the client has applied to the message. If present, its value must be one of the alternatives the server indicated it supports in the WWW-Authenticate header. These values affect the computation of the request digest. |
| | This is a single token, not a quoted list of alternatives, as in WWW-Authenticate. |
| | This directive is optional, to preserve backward compatibility with a minimal implementation of RFC 2069, but it should be used if the server indicated that qop is supported by providing a qop directive in the WWW-Authenticate header field. |
| nc | This must be specified if a qop directive is sent and must not be specified if the server did not send a qop directive in the WWW-Authenticate header field. |
| | The value is the hexadecimal count of the number of requests (including the current request) that the client has sent with the nonce value in this request. For example, in the first request sent in response to a given nonce value, the client sends nc="00000001". |
| | The purpose of this directive is to allow the server to detect request replays by maintaining its own copy of this count—if the same nc value is seen twice, the request is a replay. |
| <extension> | This directive allows for future extensions. Any unrecognized directive must be ignored. |

# Digest Authentication-Info Directives

Each of the Authentication-Info directives is described in Table F-3, paraphrased from the descriptions in RFC 2617. Refer to the official specifications for the most up-to-date details.

*Table F-3. Digest Authentication-Info header directives (from RFC 2617)*

| Directive | Description |
|---|---|
| nextnonce | The value of the nextnonce directive is the nonce the server wants the client to use for a future authentication response. The server may send the Authentication-Info header with a nextnonce field as a means of implementing one-time or otherwise changing nonces. If the nextnonce field is present the client should use it when constructing the Authorization header for its next request. Failure of the client to do so may result in a reauthentication request from the server with "stale=TRUE". |
| | Server implementations should carefully consider the performance implications of the use of this mechanism; pipelined requests will not be possible if every response includes a nextnonce directive that must be used on the next request received by the server. Consideration should be given to the performance versus security trade-offs of allowing an old nonce value to be used for a limited time to permit request pipelining. Use of the nonce count can retain most of the security advantages of a new server nonce without the deleterious effects on pipelining. |
| qop | Indicates the "quality of protection" options applied to the response by the server. The value "auth" indicates authentication; the value "auth-int" indicates authentication with integrity protection. The server should use the same value for the qop directive in the response as was sent by the client in the corresponding request. |
| rspauth | The optional response digest in the "response auth" directive supports mutual authentication—the server proves that it knows the user's secret, and, with qop="auth-int", it also provides limited integrity protection of the response. The "response-digest" value is calculated as for the "request-digest" in the Authorization header, except that if qop="auth" or qop is not specified in the Authorization header for the request, A2 is:<br><br>`A2 = ":" digest-uri-value`<br><br>and if qop="auth-int", A2 is:<br><br>`A2 = ":" digest-uri-value ":" H(entity-body)`<br><br>where *digest-uri-value* is the value of the uri directive on the Authorization header in the request. The cnonce and nc values must be the same as the ones in the client request to which this message is a response. The rspauth directive must be present if qop="auth" or qop="auth-int" is specified. |
| cnonce | The cnonce value must be the same as the one in the client request to which this message is a response. The cnonce directive must be present if qop="auth" or qop="auth-int" is specified. |
| nc | The nc value must be the same as the one in the client request to which this message is a response. The nc directive must be present if qop="auth" or qop="auth-int" is specified. |
| <extension> | This directive allows for future extensions. Any unrecognized directive must be ignored. |

# Reference Code

The following code implements the calculations of H(A1), H(A2), request-digest, and response-digest, from RFC 2617. It uses the MD5 implementation from RFC 1321.

## File "digcalc.h"

```
#define HASHLEN 16
typedef char HASH[HASHLEN];
#define HASHHEXLEN 32
typedef char HASHHEX[HASHHEXLEN+1];
#define IN
```

```
#define OUT
/* calculate H(A1) as per HTTP Digest spec */
void DigestCalcHA1(
    IN char * pszAlg,
    IN char * pszUserName,
    IN char * pszRealm,
    IN char * pszPassword,
    IN char * pszNonce,
    IN char * pszCNonce,
    OUT HASHHEX SessionKey
    );

/* calculate request-digest/response-digest as per HTTP Digest spec */
void DigestCalcResponse(
    IN HASHHEX HA1,           /* H(A1) */
    IN char * pszNonce,       /* nonce from server */
    IN char * pszNonceCount,  /* 8 hex digits */
    IN char * pszCNonce,      /* client nonce */
    IN char * pszQop,         /* qop-value: "", "auth", "auth-int" */
    IN char * pszMethod,      /* method from the request */
    IN char * pszDigestUri,   /* requested URL */
    IN HASHHEX HEntity,       /* H(entity body) if qop="auth-int" */
    OUT HASHHEX Response      /* request-digest or response-digest */
    );
```

## File "digcalc.c"

```
#include <global.h>
#include <md5.h>
#include <string.h>
#include "digcalc.h"

void CvtHex(
    IN HASH Bin,
    OUT HASHHEX Hex
    )
{
    unsigned short i;
    unsigned char j;
    for (i = 0; i < HASHLEN; i++) {
        j = (Bin[i] >> 4) & 0xf;
        if (j <= 9)
            Hex[i*2] = (j + '0');
         else
            Hex[i*2] = (j + 'a' - 10);
        j = Bin[i] & 0xf;
        if (j <= 9)
            Hex[i*2+1] = (j + '0');
         else
            Hex[i*2+1] = (j + 'a' - 10);
    };
    Hex[HASHHEXLEN] = '\0';
};
```

```
/* calculate H(A1) as per spec */
void DigestCalcHA1(
    IN char * pszAlg,
    IN char * pszUserName,
    IN char * pszRealm,
    IN char * pszPassword,
    IN char * pszNonce,
    IN char * pszCNonce,
    OUT HASHHEX SessionKey
    )
{
    MD5_CTX Md5Ctx;
    HASH HA1;
    MD5Init(&Md5Ctx);
    MD5Update(&Md5Ctx, pszUserName, strlen(pszUserName));
    MD5Update(&Md5Ctx, ":", 1);
    MD5Update(&Md5Ctx, pszRealm, strlen(pszRealm));
    MD5Update(&Md5Ctx, ":", 1);
    MD5Update(&Md5Ctx, pszPassword, strlen(pszPassword));
    MD5Final(HA1, &Md5Ctx);
    if (stricmp(pszAlg, "md5-sess") == 0) {
          MD5Init(&Md5Ctx);
          MD5Update(&Md5Ctx, HA1, HASHLEN);
          MD5Update(&Md5Ctx, ":", 1);
          MD5Update(&Md5Ctx, pszNonce, strlen(pszNonce));
          MD5Update(&Md5Ctx, ":", 1);
          MD5Update(&Md5Ctx, pszCNonce, strlen(pszCNonce));
          MD5Final(HA1, &Md5Ctx);
    };
    CvtHex(HA1, SessionKey);
};
/* calculate request-digest/response-digest as per HTTP Digest spec */
void DigestCalcResponse(
    IN HASHHEX HA1,           /* H(A1) */
    IN char * pszNonce,       /* nonce from server */
    IN char * pszNonceCount,  /* 8 hex digits */
    IN char * pszCNonce,      /* client nonce */
    IN char * pszQop,         /* qop-value: "", "auth", "auth-int" */
    IN char * pszMethod,      /* method from the request */
    IN char * pszDigestUri,   /* requested URL */
    IN HASHHEX HEntity,       /* H(entity body) if qop="auth-int" */
    OUT HASHHEX Response      /* request-digest or response-digest */
    )
{
    MD5_CTX Md5Ctx;
    HASH HA2;
    HASH RespHash;
     HASHHEX HA2Hex;
    // calculate H(A2)
    MD5Init(&Md5Ctx);
    MD5Update(&Md5Ctx, pszMethod, strlen(pszMethod));
    MD5Update(&Md5Ctx, ":", 1);
    MD5Update(&Md5Ctx, pszDigestUri, strlen(pszDigestUri));
    if (stricmp(pszQop, "auth-int") == 0) {
```

```
        MD5Update(&Md5Ctx, ":", 1);
        MD5Update(&Md5Ctx, HEntity, HASHHEXLEN);
    };
    MD5Final(HA2, &Md5Ctx);
     CvtHex(HA2, HA2Hex);
    // calculate response
    MD5Init(&Md5Ctx);
    MD5Update(&Md5Ctx, HA1, HASHHEXLEN);
    MD5Update(&Md5Ctx, ":", 1);
    MD5Update(&Md5Ctx, pszNonce, strlen(pszNonce));
    MD5Update(&Md5Ctx, ":", 1);
    if (*pszQop) {
        MD5Update(&Md5Ctx, pszNonceCount, strlen(pszNonceCount));
        MD5Update(&Md5Ctx, ":", 1);
        MD5Update(&Md5Ctx, pszCNonce, strlen(pszCNonce));
        MD5Update(&Md5Ctx, ":", 1);
        MD5Update(&Md5Ctx, pszQop, strlen(pszQop));
        MD5Update(&Md5Ctx, ":", 1);
    };
    MD5Update(&Md5Ctx, HA2Hex, HASHHEXLEN);
    MD5Final(RespHash, &Md5Ctx);
    CvtHex(RespHash, Response);
};
```

## File "digtest.c"

```
#include <stdio.h>
#include "digcalc.h"

void main(int argc, char ** argv) {
    char * pszNonce = "dcd98b7102dd2f0e8b11d0f600bfb0c093";
    char * pszCNonce = "0a4f113b";
    char * pszUser = "Mufasa";
    char * pszRealm = "testrealm@host.com";
    char * pszPass = "Circle Of Life";
    char * pszAlg = "md5";
    char szNonceCount[9] = "00000001";
    char * pszMethod = "GET";
    char * pszQop = "auth";
    char * pszURI = "/dir/index.html";
    HASHHEX HA1;
    HASHHEX HA2 = "";
    HASHHEX Response;
    DigestCalcHA1(pszAlg, pszUser, pszRealm, pszPass,
        pszNonce, pszCNonce, HA1);
    DigestCalcResponse(HA1, pszNonce, szNonceCount, pszCNonce, pszQop,
        pszMethod, pszURI, HA2, Response);
    printf("Response = %s\n", Response);
};
```

# Language Tags

Language tags are short, standardized strings that name spoken languages—for example, "fr" (French) and "en-GB" (Great Britain English). Each tag has one or more parts, separated by hyphens, called *subtags*. Language tags were described in detail in the section "Language Tags and HTTP" in Chapter 16.

This appendix summarizes the rules, standardized tags, and registration information for language tags. It contains the following reference material:

- Rules for the first (primary) subtag are summarized in "First Subtag Rules."
- Rules for the second subtag are summarized in "Second Subtag Rules."
- IANA-registered language tags are shown in Table G-1.
- ISO 639 language codes are shown in Table G-2.
- ISO 3166 country codes are shown in Table G-3.

## First Subtag Rules

If the first subtag is:

- Two characters long, it's a language code from the ISO 639[*] and 639-1 standards
- Three characters long, it's a language code listed in the ISO 639-2[†] standard
- The letter "i," the language tag is explicitly IANA-registered
- The letter "x," the language tag is a private, nonstandard, extension subtag

The ISO 639 and 639-2 names are summarized in Table G-2.

---

[*] See ISO standard 639, "Codes for the representation of names of languages."
[†] See ISO 639-2, "Codes for the representation of names of languages—Part 2: Alpha-3 code."

# Second Subtag Rules

If the second subtag is:

- Two characters long, it's a country/region defined by ISO 3166*
- Three to eight characters long, it may be registered with the IANA
- One character long, it is illegal

The ISO 3166 country codes are summarized in Table G-3.

# IANA-Registered Language Tags

*Table G-1. Language tags*

| IANA language tag | Description |
|---|---|
| i-bnn | Bunun |
| i-default | Default language context |
| i-hak | Hakka |
| i-klingon | Klingon |
| i-lux | Luxembourgish |
| i-mingo | Mingo |
| i-navajo | Navajo |
| i-pwn | Paiwan |
| i-tao | Tao |
| i-tay | Tayal |
| i-tsu | Tsou |
| no-bok | Norwegian "Book language" |
| no-nyn | Norwegian "New Norwegian" |
| zh-gan | Kan or Gan |
| zh-guoyu | Mandarin or Standard Chinese |
| zh-hakka | Hakka |
| zh-min | Min, Fuzhou, Hokkien, Amoy, or Taiwanese |
| zh-wuu | Shanghaiese or Wu |
| zh-xiang | Xiang or Hunanese |
| zh-yue | Cantonese |

---

* The country codes AA, QM–QZ, XA–XZ and ZZ are reserved by ISO 3166 as user-assigned codes. These must not be used to form language tags.

# ISO 639 Language Codes

*Table G-2. ISO 639 and 639-2 language codes*

| Language | ISO 639 | ISO 639-2 |
|---|---|---|
| Abkhazian | ab | abk |
| Achinese | | ace |
| Acoli | | ach |
| Adangme | | ada |
| Afar | aa | aar |
| Afrihili | | afh |
| Afrikaans | af | afr |
| Afro-Asiatic (Other) | | afa |
| Akan | | aka |
| Akkadian | | akk |
| Albanian | sq | alb/sqi |
| Aleut | | ale |
| Algonquian languages | | alg |
| Altaic (Other) | | tut |
| Amharic | am | amh |
| Apache languages | | apa |
| Arabic | ar | ara |
| Aramaic | | arc |
| Arapaho | | arp |
| Araucanian | | arn |
| Arawak | | arw |
| Armenian | hy | arm/hye |
| Artificial (Other) | | art |
| Assamese | as | asm |
| Athapascan languages | | ath |
| Austronesian (Other) | | map |
| Avaric | | ava |
| Avestan | | ave |
| Awadhi | | awa |
| Aymara | ay | aym |
| Azerbaijani | az | aze |
| Aztec | | nah |
| Balinese | | ban |
| Baltic (Other) | | bat |

| Language | ISO 639 | ISO 639-2 |
|---|---|---|
| Baluchi | | bal |
| Bambara | | bam |
| Bamileke languages | | bai |
| Banda | | bad |
| Bantu (Other) | | bnt |
| Basa | | bas |
| Bashkir | ba | bak |
| Basque | eu | baq/eus |
| Beja | | bej |
| Bemba | | bem |
| Bengali | bn | ben |
| Berber (Other) | | ber |
| Bhojpuri | | bho |
| Bihari | bh | bih |
| Bikol | | bik |
| Bini | | bin |
| Bislama | bi | bis |
| Braj | | bra |
| Breton | be | bre |
| Buginese | | bug |
| Bulgarian | bg | bul |
| Buriat | | bua |
| Burmese | my | bur/mya |
| Byelorussian | be | bel |
| Caddo | | cad |
| Carib | | car |
| Catalan | ca | cat |
| Caucasian (Other) | | cau |
| Cebuano | | ceb |
| Celtic (Other) | | cel |
| Central American Indian (Other) | | cai |
| Chagatai | | chg |
| Chamorro | | cha |
| Chechen | | che |
| Cherokee | | chr |
| Cheyenne | | chy |

| Language | ISO 639 | ISO 639-2 |
|---|---|---|
| Chibcha | | chb |
| Chinese | zh | chi/zho |
| Chinook jargon | | chn |
| Choctaw | | cho |
| Church Slavic | | chu |
| Chuvash | | chv |
| Coptic | | cop |
| Cornish | | cor |
| Corsican | co | cos |
| Cree | | cre |
| Creek | | mus |
| Creoles and Pidgins (Other) | | crp |
| Creoles and Pidgins, English-based (Other) | | cpe |
| Creoles and Pidgins, French-based (Other) | | cpf |
| Creoles and Pidgins, Portuguese-based (Other) | | cpp |
| Cushitic (Other) | | cus |
| Croatian | hr | |
| Czech | cs | ces/cze |
| Dakota | | dak |
| Danish | da | dan |
| Delaware | | del |
| Dinka | | din |
| Divehi | | div |
| Dogri | | doi |
| Dravidian (Other) | | dra |
| Duala | | dua |
| Dutch | nl | dut/nla |
| Dutch, Middle (ca. 1050-1350) | | dum |
| Dyula | | dyu |
| Dzongkha | dz | dzo |
| Efik | | efi |
| Egyptian (Ancient) | | egy |
| Ekajuk | | eka |
| Elamite | | elx |
| English | en | eng |
| English, Middle (ca. 1100-1500) | | enm |

*Table G-2. ISO 639 and 639-2 language codes (continued)*

| Language | ISO 639 | ISO 639-2 |
|---|---|---|
| English, Old (ca. 450-1100) | | ang |
| Eskimo (Other) | | esk |
| Esperanto | eo | epo |
| Estonian | et | est |
| Ewe | | ewe |
| Ewondo | | ewo |
| Fang | | fan |
| Fanti | | fat |
| Faroese | fo | fao |
| Fijian | fj | fij |
| Finnish | fi | fin |
| Finno-Ugrian (Other) | | fiu |
| Fon | | fon |
| French | fr | fra/fre |
| French, Middle (ca. 1400-1600) | | frm |
| French, Old (842- ca. 1400) | | fro |
| Frisian | fy | fry |
| Fulah | | ful |
| Ga | | gaa |
| Gaelic (Scots) | | gae/gdh |
| Gallegan | gl | glg |
| Ganda | | lug |
| Gayo | | gay |
| Geez | | gez |
| Georgian | ka | geo/kat |
| German | de | deu/ger |
| German, Middle High (ca. 1050-1500) | | gmh |
| German, Old High (ca. 750-1050) | | goh |
| Germanic (Other) | | gem |
| Gilbertese | | gil |
| Gondi | | gon |
| Gothic | | got |
| Grebo | | grb |
| Greek, Ancient (to 1453) | | grc |
| Greek, Modern (1453-) | el | ell/gre |
| Greenlandic | kl | kal |

*Table G-2. ISO 639 and 639-2 language codes (continued)*

| Language | ISO 639 | ISO 639-2 |
|---|---|---|
| Guarani | gn | grn |
| Gujarati | gu | guj |
| Haida | | hai |
| Hausa | ha | hau |
| Hawaiian | | haw |
| Hebrew | he | heb |
| Herero | | her |
| Hiligaynon | | hil |
| Himachali | | him |
| Hindi | hi | hin |
| Hiri Motu | | hmo |
| Hungarian | hu | hun |
| Hupa | | hup |
| Iban | | iba |
| Icelandic | is | ice/isl |
| Igbo | | ibo |
| Ijo | | ijo |
| Iloko | | ilo |
| Indic (Other) | | inc |
| Indo-European (Other) | | ine |
| Indonesian | id | ind |
| Interlingua (IALA) | ia | ina |
| Interlingue | ie | ine |
| Inuktitut | iu | iku |
| Inupiak | ik | ipk |
| Iranian (Other) | | ira |
| Irish | ga | gai/iri |
| Irish, Old (to 900) | | sga |
| Irish, Middle (900 - 1200) | | mga |
| Iroquoian languages | | iro |
| Italian | it | ita |
| Japanese | ja | jpn |
| Javanese | jv/jw | jav/jaw |
| Judeo-Arabic | | jrb |
| Judeo-Persian | | jpr |
| Kabyle | | kab |

*Table G-2. ISO 639 and 639-2 language codes (continued)*

| Language | ISO 639 | ISO 639-2 |
|---|---|---|
| Kachin | | kac |
| Kamba | | kam |
| Kannada | kn | kan |
| Kanuri | | kau |
| Kara-Kalpak | | kaa |
| Karen | | kar |
| Kashmiri | ks | kas |
| Kawi | | kaw |
| Kazakh | kk | kaz |
| Khasi | | kha |
| Khmer | km | khm |
| Khoisan (Other) | | khi |
| Khotanese | | kho |
| Kikuyu | | kik |
| Kinyarwanda | rw | kin |
| Kirghiz | ky | kir |
| Komi | | kom |
| Kongo | | kon |
| Konkani | | kok |
| Korean | ko | kor |
| Kpelle | | kpe |
| Kru | | kro |
| Kuanyama | | kua |
| Kumyk | | kum |
| Kurdish | ku | kur |
| Kurukh | | kru |
| Kusaie | | kus |
| Kutenai | | kut |
| Ladino | | lad |
| Lahnda | | lah |
| Lamba | | lam |
| Langue d'Oc (post-1500) | oc | oci |
| Lao | lo | lao |
| Latin | la | lat |
| Latvian | lv | lav |
| Letzeburgesch | | ltz |

| Language | ISO 639 | ISO 639-2 |
|---|---|---|
| Lezghian | | lez |
| Lingala | ln | lin |
| Lithuanian | lt | lit |
| Lozi | | loz |
| Luba-Katanga | | lub |
| Luiseno | | lui |
| Lunda | | lun |
| Luo (Kenya and Tanzania) | | luo |
| Macedonian | mk | mac/mak |
| Madurese | | mad |
| Magahi | | mag |
| Maithili | | mai |
| Makasar | | mak |
| Malagasy | mg | mlg |
| Malay | ms | may/msa |
| Malayalam | | mal |
| Maltese | ml | mlt |
| Mandingo | | man |
| Manipuri | | mni |
| Manobo languages | | mno |
| Manx | | max |
| Maori | mi | mao/mri |
| Marathi | mr | mar |
| Mari | | chm |
| Marshall | | mah |
| Marwari | | mwr |
| Masai | | mas |
| Mayan languages | | myn |
| Mende | | men |
| Micmac | | mic |
| Minangkabau | | min |
| Miscellaneous (Other) | | mis |
| Mohawk | | moh |
| Moldavian | mo | mol |
| Mon-Kmer (Other) | | mkh |
| Mongo | | lol |

| Language | ISO 639 | ISO 639-2 |
|---|---|---|
| Mongolian | mn | mon |
| Mossi | | mos |
| Multiple languages | | mul |
| Munda languages | | mun |
| Nauru | na | nau |
| Navajo | | nav |
| Ndebele, North | | nde |
| Ndebele, South | | nbl |
| Ndongo | | ndo |
| Nepali | ne | nep |
| Newari | | new |
| Niger-Kordofanian (Other) | | nic |
| Nilo-Saharan (Other) | | ssa |
| Niuean | | niu |
| Norse, Old | | non |
| North American Indian (Other) | | nai |
| Norwegian | no | nor |
| Norwegian (Nynorsk) | | nno |
| Nubian languages | | nub |
| Nyamwezi | | nym |
| Nyanja | | nya |
| Nyankole | | nyn |
| Nyoro | | nyo |
| Nzima | | nzi |
| Ojibwa | | oji |
| Oriya | or | ori |
| Oromo | om | orm |
| Osage | | osa |
| Ossetic | | oss |
| Otomian languages | | oto |
| Pahlavi | | pal |
| Palauan | | pau |
| Pali | | pli |
| Pampanga | | pam |
| Pangasinan | | pag |
| Panjabi | pa | pan |

| Language | ISO 639 | ISO 639-2 |
|---|---|---|
| Papiamento | | pap |
| Papuan-Australian (Other) | | paa |
| Persian | fa | fas/per |
| Persian, Old (ca 600 - 400 B.C.) | | peo |
| Phoenician | | phn |
| Polish | pl | pol |
| Ponape | | pon |
| Portuguese | pt | por |
| Prakrit languages | | pra |
| Provencal, Old (to 1500) | | pro |
| Pushto | ps | pus |
| Quechua | qu | que |
| Rhaeto-Romance | rm | roh |
| Rajasthani | | raj |
| Rarotongan | | rar |
| Romance (Other) | | roa |
| Romanian | ro | ron/rum |
| Romany | | rom |
| Rundi | rn | run |
| Russian | ru | rus |
| Salishan languages | | sal |
| Samaritan Aramaic | | sam |
| Sami languages | | smi |
| Samoan | sm | smo |
| Sandawe | | sad |
| Sango | sg | sag |
| Sanskrit | sa | san |
| Sardinian | | srd |
| Scots | | sco |
| Selkup | | sel |
| Semitic (Other) | | sem |
| Serbian | sr | |
| Serbo-Croatian | sh | scr |
| Serer | | srr |
| Shan | | shn |
| Shona | sn | sna |

*Table G-2. ISO 639 and 639-2 language codes (continued)*

| Language | ISO 639 | ISO 639-2 |
|---|---|---|
| Sidamo | | sid |
| Siksika | | bla |
| Sindhi | sd | snd |
| Singhalese | si | sin |
| Sino-Tibetan (Other) | | sit |
| Siouan languages | | sio |
| Slavic (Other) | | sla |
| Siswant | ss | ssw |
| Slovak | sk | slk/slo |
| Slovenian | sl | slv |
| Sogdian | | sog |
| Somali | so | som |
| Songhai | | son |
| Sorbian languages | | wen |
| Sotho, Northern | | nso |
| Sotho, Southern | st | sot |
| South American Indian (Other) | | sai |
| Spanish | es | esl/spa |
| Sukuma | | suk |
| Sumerian | | sux |
| Sudanese | su | sun |
| Susu | | sus |
| Swahili | sw | swa |
| Swazi | | ssw |
| Swedish | sv | sve/swe |
| Syriac | | syr |
| Tagalog | tl | tgl |
| Tahitian | | tah |
| Tajik | tg | tgk |
| Tamashek | | tmh |
| Tamil | ta | tam |
| Tatar | tt | tat |
| Telugu | te | tel |
| Tereno | | ter |
| Thai | th | tha |
| Tibetan | bo | bod/tib |

| Language | ISO 639 | ISO 639-2 |
|---|---|---|
| Tigre | | tig |
| Tigrinya | ti | tir |
| Timne | | tem |
| Tivi | | tiv |
| Tlingit | | tli |
| Tonga (Nyasa) | to | tog |
| Tonga (Tonga Islands) | | ton |
| Truk | | tru |
| Tsimshian | | tsi |
| Tsonga | ts | tso |
| Tswana | tn | tsn |
| Tumbuka | | tum |
| Turkish | tr | tur |
| Turkish, Ottoman (1500–1928) | | ota |
| Turkmen | tk | tuk |
| Tuvinian | | tyv |
| Twi | tw | twi |
| Ugaritic | | uga |
| Uighur | ug | uig |
| Ukrainian | uk | ukr |
| Umbundu | | umb |
| Undetermined | | und |
| Urdu | ur | urd |
| Uzbek | uz | uzb |
| Vai | | vai |
| Venda | | ven |
| Vietnamese | vi | vie |
| Volapük | vo | vol |
| Votic | | vot |
| Wakashan languages | | wak |
| Walamo | | wal |
| Waray | | war |
| Washo | | was |
| Welsh | cy | cym/wel |
| Wolof | wo | wol |
| Xhosa | xh | xho |

*Table G-2. ISO 639 and 639-2 language codes (continued)*

| Language | ISO 639 | ISO 639-2 |
|----------|---------|-----------|
| Yakut | | sah |
| Yao | | yao |
| Yap | | yap |
| Yiddish | yi | yid |
| Yoruba | yo | yor |
| Zapotec | | zap |
| Zenaga | | zen |
| Zhuang | za | zha |
| Zulu | zu | zul |
| Zuni | | zun |

# ISO 3166 Country Codes

*Table G-3. ISO 3166 country codes*

| Country | Code |
|---------|------|
| Afghanistan | AF |
| Albania | AL |
| Algeria | DZ |
| American Samoa | AS |
| Andorra | AD |
| Angola | AO |
| Anguilla | AI |
| Antarctica | AQ |
| Antigua and Barbuda | AG |
| Argentina | AR |
| Armenia | AM |
| Aruba | AW |
| Australia | AU |
| Austria | AT |
| Azerbaijan | AZ |
| Bahamas | BS |
| Bahrain | BH |
| Bangladesh | BD |
| Barbados | BB |
| Belarus | BY |
| Belgium | BE |

*Table G-3. ISO 3166 country codes (continued)*

| Country | Code |
|---|---|
| Belize | BZ |
| Benin | BJ |
| Bermuda | BM |
| Bhutan | BT |
| Bolivia | BO |
| Bosnia and Herzegovina | BA |
| Botswana | BW |
| Bouvet Island | BV |
| Brazil | BR |
| British Indian Ocean Territory | IO |
| Brunei Darussalam | BN |
| Bulgaria | BG |
| Burkina Faso | BF |
| Burundi | BI |
| Cambodia | KH |
| Cameroon | CM |
| Canada | CA |
| Cape Verde | CV |
| Cayman Islands | KY |
| Central African Republic | CF |
| Chad | TD |
| Chile | CL |
| China | CN |
| Christmas Island | CX |
| Cocos (Keeling) Islands | CC |
| Colombia | CO |
| Comoros | KM |
| Congo | CG |
| Congo (Democratic Republic of the) | CD |
| Cook Islands | CK |
| Costa Rica | CR |
| Cote D'Ivoire | CI |
| Croatia | HR |
| Cuba | CU |
| Cyprus | CY |
| Czech Republic | CZ |

*Table G-3. ISO 3166 country codes (continued)*

| Country | Code |
|---|---|
| Denmark | DK |
| Djibouti | DJ |
| Dominica | DM |
| Dominican Republic | DO |
| East Timor | TP |
| Ecuador | EC |
| Egypt | EG |
| El Salvador | SV |
| Equatorial Guinea | GQ |
| Eritrea | ER |
| Estonia | EE |
| Ethiopia | ET |
| Falkland Islands (Malvinas) | FK |
| Faroe Islands | FO |
| Fiji | FJ |
| Finland | FI |
| France | FR |
| French Guiana | GF |
| French Polynesia | PF |
| French Southern Territories | TF |
| Gabon | GA |
| Gambia | GM |
| Georgia | GE |
| Germany | DE |
| Ghana | GH |
| Gibraltar | GI |
| Greece | GR |
| Greenland | GL |
| Grenada | GD |
| Guadeloupe | GP |
| Guam | GU |
| Guatemala | GT |
| Guinea | GN |
| Guinea-Bissau | GW |
| Guyana | GY |
| Haiti | HT |

*Table G-3. ISO 3166 country codes (continued)*

| Country | Code |
| --- | --- |
| Heard Island and Mcdonald Islands | HM |
| Holy See (Vatican City State) | VA |
| Honduras | HN |
| Hong Kong | HK |
| Hungary | HU |
| Iceland | IS |
| India | IN |
| Indonesia | ID |
| Iran (Islamic Republic of) | IR |
| Iraq | IQ |
| Ireland | IE |
| Israel | IL |
| Italy | IT |
| Jamaica | JM |
| Japan | JP |
| Jordan | JO |
| Kazakstan | KZ |
| Kenya | KE |
| Kiribati | KI |
| Korea (Democratic People's Republic of) | KP |
| Korea (Republic of) | KR |
| Kuwait | KW |
| Kyrgyzstan | KG |
| Lao People's Democratic Republic | LA |
| Latvia | LV |
| Lebanon | LB |
| Lesotho | LS |
| Liberia | LR |
| Libyan Arab Jamahiriya | LY |
| Liechtenstein | LI |
| Lithuania | LT |
| Luxembourg | LU |
| Macau | MO |
| Macedonia (The Former Yugoslav Republic of) | MK |
| Madagascar | MG |
| Malawi | MW |

*Table G-3. ISO 3166 country codes (continued)*

| Country | Code |
| --- | --- |
| Malaysia | MY |
| Maldives | MV |
| Mali | ML |
| Malta | MT |
| Marshall Islands | MH |
| Martinique | MQ |
| Mauritania | MR |
| Mauritius | MU |
| Mayotte | YT |
| Mexico | MX |
| Micronesia (Federated States of) | FM |
| Moldova (Republic of) | MD |
| Monaco | MC |
| Mongolia | MN |
| Montserrat | MS |
| Morocco | MA |
| Mozambique | MZ |
| Myanmar | MM |
| Namibia | NA |
| Nauru | NR |
| Nepal | NP |
| Netherlands | NL |
| Netherlands Antilles | AN |
| New Caledonia | NC |
| New Zealand | NZ |
| Nicaragua | NI |
| Niger | NE |
| Nigeria | NG |
| Niue | NU |
| Norfolk Island | NF |
| Northern Mariana Islands | MP |
| Norway | NO |
| Oman | OM |
| Pakistan | PK |
| Palau | PW |
| Palestinian Territory (Occupied) | PS |
| Panama | PA |

| Country | Code |
|---|---|
| Papua New Guinea | PG |
| Paraguay | PY |
| Peru | PE |
| Philippines | PH |
| Pitcairn | PN |
| Poland | PL |
| Portugal | PT |
| Puerto Rico | PR |
| Qatar | QA |
| Reunion | RE |
| Romania | RO |
| Russian Federation | RU |
| Rwanda | RW |
| Saint Helena | SH |
| Saint Kitts and Nevis | KN |
| Saint Lucia | LC |
| Saint Pierre and Miquelon | PM |
| Saint Vincent and the Grenadines | VC |
| Samoa | WS |
| San Marino | SM |
| Sao Tome and Principe | ST |
| Saudi Arabia | SA |
| Senegal | SN |
| Seychelles | SC |
| Sierra Leone | SL |
| Singapore | SG |
| Slovakia | SK |
| Slovenia | SI |
| Solomon Islands | SB |
| Somalia | SO |
| South Africa | ZA |
| South Georgia and the South Sandwich Islands | GS |
| Spain | ES |
| Sri Lanka | LK |
| Sudan | SD |
| Suriname | SR |
| Svalbard and Jan Mayen | SJ |

| Country | Code |
|---|---|
| Swaziland | SZ |
| Sweden | SE |
| Switzerland | CH |
| Syrian Arab Republic | SY |
| Taiwan, Province of China | TW |
| Tajikistan | TJ |
| Tanzania (United Republic of) | TZ |
| Thailand | TH |
| Togo | TG |
| Tokelau | TK |
| Tonga | TO |
| Trinidad and Tobago | TT |
| Tunisia | TN |
| Turkey | TR |
| Turkmenistan | TM |
| Turks and Caicos Islands | TC |
| Tuvalu | TV |
| Uganda | UG |
| Ukraine | UA |
| United Arab Emirates | AE |
| United Kingdom | GB |
| United States | US |
| United States Minor Outlying Islands | UM |
| Uruguay | UY |
| Uzbekistan | UZ |
| Vanuatu | VU |
| Venezuela | VE |
| Viet NAM | VN |
| Virgin Islands (British) | VG |
| Virgin ISLANDS (U.S.) | VI |
| Wallis and Futuna | WF |
| Western Sahara | EH |
| Yemen | YE |
| Yugoslavia | YU |
| Zambia | ZM |

# Language Administrative Organizations

ISO 639 defines a maintenance agency for additions to and changes in the list of languages in ISO 639. This agency is:

International Information Centre for Terminology (Infoterm)
P.O. Box 130
A-1021 Wien
Austria

Phone: +43 1 26 75 35 Ext. 312
Fax: +43 1 216 32 72

ISO 639-2 defines a maintenance agency for additions to and changes in the list of languages in ISO 639-2. This agency is:

Library of Congress
Network Development and MARC Standards Office
Washington, D.C. 20540
USA

Phone: +1 202 707 6237
Fax: +1 202 707 0115
URL: *http://www.loc.gov/standards/iso639/*

The maintenance agency for ISO 3166 (country codes) is:

ISO 3166 Maintenance Agency Secretariat
c/o DIN Deutsches Institut fuer Normung
Burggrafenstrasse 6
Postfach 1107
D-10787 Berlin
Germany

Phone: +49 30 26 01 320
Fax: +49 30 26 01 231
URL: *http://www.din.de/gremien/nas/nabd/iso3166ma/*

# APPENDIX H

# MIME Charset Registry

This appendix describes the MIME charset registry maintained by the Internet Assigned Numbers Authority (IANA). A formatted table of charsets from the registry is provided in Table H-1.

## MIME Charset Registry

MIME charset tags are registered with the IANA (*http://www.iana.org/numbers.htm*). The charset registry is a flat-file text database of records. Each record contains a charset name, reference citations, a unique MIB number, a source description, and a list of aliases. A name or alias may be flagged "preferred MIME name."

Here is the record for US-ASCII:

```
Name: ANSI_X3.4-1968                              [RFC1345, KXS2]^
MIBenum: 3
Source: ECMA registry
Alias: iso-ir-6
Alias: ANSI_X3.4-1986
Alias: ISO_646.irv:1991
Alias: ASCII
Alias: ISO646-US
Alias: US-ASCII (preferred MIME name)
Alias: us
Alias: IBM367
Alias: cp367
Alias: csASCII
```

The procedure for registering a charset with the IANA is documented in RFC 2978 (*http://www.ietf.org/rfc/rfc2978.txt*).

# Preferred MIME Names

Of the 235 charsets registered at the time of this writing, only 20 include "preferred MIME names"—common charsets used by email and web applications. These are:

| | | |
|---|---|---|
| Big5 | EUC-JP | EUC-KR |
| GB2312 | ISO-2022-JP | ISO-2022-JP-2 |
| ISO-2022-KR | ISO-8859-1 | ISO-8859-2 |
| ISO-8859-3 | ISO-8859-4 | ISO-8859-5 |
| ISO-8859-6 | ISO-8859-7 | ISO-8859-8 |
| ISO-8859-9 | ISO-8859-10 | KOI8-R |
| Shift-JIS | US-ASCII | |

# Registered Charsets

Table H-1 lists the contents of the charset registry as of March 2001. Refer directly to *http://www.iana.org* for more information about the contents of this table.

*Table H-1. IANA MIME charset tags*

| Charset tag | Aliases | Description | References |
|---|---|---|---|
| US-ASCII | ANSI_X3.4-1968, iso-ir-6, ANSI_X3.4-1986, ISO_646.irv:1991, ASCII, ISO646-US, us, IBM367, cp367, csASCII | ECMA registry | RFC1345, KXS2 |
| ISO-10646-UTF-1 | csISO10646UTF1 | Universal Transfer Format (1)—this is the multibyte encoding that subsets ASCII-7; it does not have byte-ordering issues | |
| ISO_646.basic:1983 | ref, csISO646basic1983 | ECMA registry | RFC1345, KXS2 |
| INVARIANT | csINVARIANT | | RFC1345, KXS2 |
| ISO_646.irv:1983 | iso-ir-2, irv, csISO2IntlRefVersion | ECMA registry | RFC1345, KXS2 |
| BS_4730 | iso-ir-4, ISO646-GB, gb, uk, csISO4UnitedKingdom | ECMA registry | RFC1345, KXS2 |
| NATS-SEFI | iso-ir-8-1, csNATSSEFI | ECMA registry | RFC1345, KXS2 |
| NATS-SEFI-ADD | iso-ir-8-2, csNATSSEFIADD | ECMA registry | RFC1345, KXS2 |
| NATS-DANO | iso-ir-9-1, csNATSDANO | ECMA registry | RFC1345, KXS2 |
| NATS-DANO-ADD | iso-ir-9-2, csNATSDANOADD | ECMA registry | RFC1345, KXS2 |

| Charset tag | Aliases | Description | References |
|---|---|---|---|
| SEN_850200_B | iso-ir-10, FI, ISO646-FI, ISO646-SE, se, csISO10Swedish | ECMA registry | RFC1345, KXS2 |
| SEN_850200_C | iso-ir-11, ISO646-SE2, se2, csISO11SwedishForNames | ECMA registry | RFC1345, KXS2 |
| KS_C_5601-1987 | iso-ir-149, KS_C_5601-1989, KSC_5601, korean, csKSC56011987 | ECMA registry | RFC1345, KXS2 |
| ISO-2022-KR | csISO2022KR | RFC 1557 (see also KS_C_5601-1987) | RFC1557, Choi |
| EUC-KR | csEUCKR | RFC 1557 (see also KS_C_5861-1992) | RFC1557, Choi |
| ISO-2022-JP | csISO2022JP | RFC 1468 (see also RFC 2237) | RFC1468, Murai |
| ISO-2022-JP-2 | csISO2022JP2 | RFC 1554 | RFC1554, Ohta |
| ISO-2022-CN | | RFC 1922 | RFC1922 |
| ISO-2022-CN-EXT | | RFC 1922 | RFC1922 |
| JIS_C6220-1969-jp | JIS_C6220-1969, iso-ir-13, katakana, x0201-7, csISO13JISC6220jp | ECMA registry | RFC1345, KXS2 |
| JIS_C6220-1969-ro | iso-ir-14, jp, ISO646-JP, csISO14JISC6220ro | ECMA registry | RFC1345, KXS2 |
| IT | iso-ir-15, ISO646-IT, csISO15Italian | ECMA registry | RFC1345, KXS2 |
| PT | iso-ir-16, ISO646-PT, csISO16Portuguese | ECMA registry | RFC1345, KXS2 |
| ES | iso-ir-17, ISO646-ES, csISO17Spanish | ECMA registry | RFC1345, KXS2 |
| greek7-old | iso-ir-18, csISO18Greek7Old | ECMA registry | RFC1345, KXS2 |
| latin-greek | iso-ir-19, csISO19LatinGreek | ECMA registry | RFC1345, KXS2 |
| DIN_66003 | iso-ir-21, de, ISO646-DE, csISO21German | ECMA registry | RFC1345, KXS2 |
| NF_Z_62-010_(1973) | iso-ir-25, ISO646-FR1, csISO25French | ECMA registry | RFC1345, KXS2 |
| Latin-greek-1 | iso-ir-27, csISO27LatinGreek1 | ECMA registry | RFC1345, KXS2 |
| ISO_5427 | iso-ir-37, csISO5427Cyrillic | ECMA registry | RFC1345, KXS2 |
| JIS_C6226-1978 | iso-ir-42, csISO42JISC62261978 | ECMA registry | RFC1345, KXS2 |
| BS_viewdata | iso-ir-47, csISO47BSViewdata | ECMA registry | RFC1345, KXS2 |
| INIS | iso-ir-49, csISO49INIS | ECMA registry | RFC1345, KXS2 |
| INIS-8 | iso-ir-50, csISO50INIS8 | ECMA registry | RFC1345, KXS2 |
| INIS-cyrillic | iso-ir-51, csISO51INISCyrillic | ECMA registry | RFC1345, KXS2 |

| Charset tag | Aliases | Description | References |
|---|---|---|---|
| ISO_5427:1981 | iso-ir-54, ISO5427Cyrillic1981 | ECMA registry | RFC1345, KXS2 |
| ISO_5428:1980 | iso-ir-55, csISO5428Greek | ECMA registry | RFC1345, KXS2 |
| GB_1988-80 | iso-ir-57, cn, ISO646-CN, csISO57GB1988 | ECMA registry | RFC1345, K5, KXS2 |
| GB_2312-80 | iso-ir-58, chinese, csISO58GB231280 | ECMA registry | RFC1345, KXS2 |
| NS_4551-1 | iso-ir-60, ISO646-NO, no, csISO60DanishNorwegian, csISO60Norwegian1 | ECMA registry | RFC1345, KXS2 |
| NS_4551-2 | ISO646-NO2, iso-ir-61, no2, csISO61Norwegian2 | ECMA registry | RFC1345, KXS2 |
| NF_Z_62-010 | iso-ir-69, ISO646-FR, fr, csISO69French | ECMA registry | RFC1345, KXS2 |
| videotex-suppl | iso-ir-70, csISO70VideotexSupp1 | ECMA registry | RFC1345, KXS2 |
| PT2 | iso-ir-84, ISO646-PT2, csISO84Portuguese2 | ECMA registry | RFC1345, KXS2 |
| ES2 | iso-ir-85, ISO646-ES2, csISO85Spanish2 | ECMA registry | RFC1345, KXS2 |
| MSZ_7795.3 | iso-ir-86, ISO646-HU, hu, csISO86Hungarian | ECMA registry | RFC1345, KXS2 |
| JIS_C6226-1983 | iso-ir-87, x0208, JIS_X0208-1983, csISO87JISX0208 | ECMA registry | RFC1345, KXS2 |
| greek7 | iso-ir-88, csISO88Greek7 | ECMA registry | RFC1345, KXS2 |
| ASMO_449 | ISO_9036, arabic7, iso-ir-89, csISO89ASMO449 | ECMA registry | RFC1345, KXS2 |
| iso-ir-90 | csISO90 | ECMA registry | RFC1345, KXS2 |
| JIS_C6229-1984-a | iso-ir-91, jp-ocr-a, csISO91JISC62291984a | ECMA registry | RFC1345, KXS2 |
| JIS_C6229-1984-b | iso-ir-92, ISO646-JP-OCR-B, jp-ocr-b, csISO92JISC62991984b | ECMA registry | RFC1345, KXS2 |
| JIS_C6229-1984-b-add | iso-ir-93, jp-ocr-b-add, csISO93JIS62291984badd | ECMA registry | RFC1345, KXS2 |
| JIS_C6229-1984-hand | iso-ir-94, jp-ocr-hand, csISO94JIS62291984hand | ECMA registry | RFC1345, KXS2 |
| JIS_C6229-1984-hand-add | iso-ir-95, jp-ocr-hand-add, csISO95JIS62291984handadd | ECMA registry | RFC1345, KXS2 |
| JIS_C6229-1984-kana | iso-ir-96, csISO96JISC62291984kana | ECMA registry | RFC1345, KXS2 |

| Charset tag | Aliases | Description | References |
|---|---|---|---|
| ISO_2033-1983 | iso-ir-98, e13b, csISO2033 | ECMA registry | RFC1345, KXS2 |
| ANSI_X3.110-1983 | iso-ir-99, CSA_T500-1983, NAPLPS, csISO99NAPLPS | ECMA registry | RFC1345, KXS2 |
| ISO-8859-1 | ISO_8859-1:1987, iso-ir-100, ISO_8859-1, latin1, l1, IBM819, CP819, csISOLatin1 | ECMA registry | RFC1345, KXS2 |
| ISO-8859-2 | ISO_8859-2:1987, iso-ir-101, ISO_8859-2, latin2, l2, csISOLatin2 | ECMA registry | RFC1345, KXS2 |
| T.61-7bit | iso-ir-102, csISO102T617bit | ECMA registry | RFC1345, KXS2 |
| T.61-8bit | T.61, iso-ir-103, csISO103T618bit | ECMA registry | RFC1345, KXS2 |
| ISO-8859-3 | ISO_8859-3:1988, iso-ir-109, ISO_8859-3, latin3, l3, csISOLatin3 | ECMA registry | RFC1345, KXS2 |
| ISO-8859-4 | ISO_8859-4:1988, iso-ir-110, ISO_8859-4, latin4, l4, csISOLatin4 | ECMA registry | RFC1345, KXS2 |
| ECMA-cyrillic | iso-ir-111, csISO111ECMACyrillic | ECMA registry | RFC1345, KXS2 |
| CSA_Z243.4-1985-1 | iso-ir-121, ISO646-CA, csa7-1, ca, csISO121Canadian1 | ECMA registry | RFC1345, KXS2 |
| CSA_Z243.4-1985-2 | iso-ir-122, ISO646-CA2, csa7-2, csISO122Canadian2 | ECMA registry | RFC1345, KXS2 |
| CSA_Z243.4-1985-gr | iso-ir-123, csISO123CSAZ24341985gr | ECMA registry | RFC1345, KXS2 |
| ISO-8859-6 | ISO_8859-6:1987, iso-ir-127, ISO_8859-6, ECMA-114, ASMO-708, arabic, csISOLatinArabic | ECMA registry | RFC1345, KXS2 |
| ISO_8859-6-E | csISO88596E | RFC 1556 | RFC1556, IANA |
| ISO_8859-6-I | csISO88596I | RFC 1556 | RFC1556, IANA |
| ISO-8859-7 | ISO_8859-7:1987, iso-ir-126, ISO_8859-7, ELOT_928, ECMA-118, greek, greek8, csISOLatinGreek | ECMA registry | RFC1947, RFC1345, KXS2 |
| T.101-G2 | iso-ir-128, csISO128T101G2 | ECMA registry | RFC1345, KXS2 |
| ISO-8859-8 | ISO_8859-8:1988, iso-ir-138, ISO_8859-8, hebrew, csISOLatinHebrew | ECMA registry | RFC1345, KXS2 |
| ISO_8859-8-E | csISO88598E | RFC 1556 | RFC1556, Nussbacher |

| Charset tag | Aliases | Description | References |
|---|---|---|---|
| ISO_8859-8-I | csISO88598I | RFC 1556 | RFC1556, Nussbacher |
| CSN_369103 | iso-ir-139, csISO139CSN369103 | ECMA registry | RFC1345, KXS2 |
| JUS_I.B1.002 | iso-ir-141, ISO646-YU, js, yu, csISO141JUSIB1002 | ECMA registry | RFC1345, KXS2 |
| ISO_6937-2-add | iso-ir-142, csISOTextComm | ECMA registry and ISO 6937-2:1983 | RFC1345, KXS2 |
| IEC_P27-1 | iso-ir-143, csISO143IECP271 | ECMA registry | RFC1345, KXS2 |
| ISO-8859-5 | ISO_8859-5:1988, iso-ir-144, ISO_8859-5, cyrillic, csISOLatinCyrillic | ECMA registry | RFC1345, KXS2 |
| JUS_I.B1.003-serb | iso-ir-146, serbian, csISO146Serbian | ECMA registry | RFC1345, KXS2 |
| JUS_I.B1.003-mac | macedonian, iso-ir-147, csISO147Macedonian | ECMA registry | RFC1345, KXS2 |
| ISO-8859-9 | ISO_8859-9:1989, iso-ir-148, ISO_8859-9, latin5, l5, csISOLatin5 | ECMA registry | RFC1345, KXS2 |
| greek-ccitt | iso-ir-150, csISO150, csISO150GreekCCITT | ECMA registry | RFC1345, KXS2 |
| NC_NC00-10:81 | cuba, iso-ir-151, ISO646-CU, csISO151Cuba | ECMA registry | RFC1345, KXS2 |
| ISO_6937-2-25 | iso-ir-152, csISO6937Add | ECMA registry | RFC1345, KXS2 |
| GOST_19768-74 | ST_SEV_358-88, iso-ir-153, csISO153GOST1976874 | ECMA registry | RFC1345, KXS2 |
| ISO_8859-supp | iso-ir-154, latin1-2-5, csISO8859Supp | ECMA registry | RFC1345, KXS2 |
| ISO_10367-box | iso-ir-155, csISO10367Box | ECMA registry | RFC1345, KXS2 |
| ISO-8859-10 | iso-ir-157, l6, ISO_8859-10:1992, csISOLatin6, latin6 | ECMA registry | RFC1345, KXS2 |
| latin-lap | lap, iso-ir-158, csISO158Lap | ECMA registry | RFC1345, KXS2 |
| JIS_X0212-1990 | x0212, iso-ir-159, csISO159JISX02121990 | ECMA registry | RFC1345, KXS2 |
| DS_2089 | DS2089, ISO646-DK, dk, csISO646Danish | Danish Standard, DS 2089, February 1974 | RFC1345, KXS2 |
| us-dk | csUSDK | | RFC1345, KXS2 |
| dk-us | csDKUS | | RFC1345, KXS2 |
| JIS_X0201 | X0201, csHalfWidthKatakana | JIS X 0201-1976—1 byte only; this is equivalent to JIS/Roman (similar to ASCII) plus 8-bit half-width katakana | RFC1345, KXS2 |

| Charset tag | Aliases | Description | References |
|---|---|---|---|
| KSC5636 | ISO646-KR, csKSC5636 | | RFC1345, KXS2 |
| ISO-10646-UCS-2 | csUnicode | The 2-octet Basic Multilingual Plane, a.k.a. Unicode—this needs to specify network byte order; the standard does not specify it (it is a 16-bit integer space) | |
| ISO-10646-UCS-4 | csUCS4 | The full code space (same comment about byte order; these are 31-bit numbers) | |
| DEC-MCS | dec, csDECMCS | VAX/VMS User's Manual, Order Number: AI-Y517A-TE, April 1986 | RFC1345, KXS2 |
| hp-roman8 | roman8, r8, csHPRoman8 | LaserJet IIP Printer User's Manual, HP part no 33471-90901, Hewlett-Packard, June 1989 | HP-PCL5, RFC1345, KXS2 |
| macintosh | mac, csMacintosh | The Unicode Standard v1.0, ISBN 0201567881, Oct 1991 | RFC1345, KXS2 |
| IBM037 | cp037, ebcdic-cp-us, ebcdic-cp-ca, ebcdic-cp-wt, ebcdic-cp-nl, csIBM037 | IBM NLS RM Vol2 SE09-8002-01, March 1990 | RFC1345, KXS2 |
| IBM038 | EBCDIC-INT, cp038, csIBM038 | IBM 3174 Character Set Ref, GA27-3831-02, March 1990 | RFC1345, KXS2 |
| IBM273 | CP273, csIBM273 | IBM NLS RM Vol2 SE09-8002-01, March 1990 | RFC1345, KXS2 |
| IBM274 | EBCDIC-BE, CP274, csIBM274 | IBM 3174 Character Set Ref, GA27-3831-02, March 1990 | RFC1345, KXS2 |
| IBM275 | EBCDIC-BR, cp275, csIBM275 | IBM NLS RM Vol2 SE09-8002-01, March 1990 | RFC1345, KXS2 |
| IBM277 | EBCDIC-CP-DK, EBCDIC-CP-NO, csIBM277 | IBM NLS RM Vol2 SE09-8002-01, March 1990 | RFC1345, KXS2 |
| IBM278 | CP278, ebcdic-cp-fi, ebcdic-cp-se, csIBM278 | IBM NLS RM Vol2 SE09-8002-01, March 1990 | RFC1345, KXS2 |
| IBM280 | CP280, ebcdic-cp-it, csIBM280 | IBM NLS RM Vol2 SE09-8002-01, March 1990 | RFC1345, KXS2 |
| IBM281 | EBCDIC-JP-E, cp281, csIBM281 | IBM 3174 Character Set Ref, GA27-3831-02, March 1990 | RFC1345, KXS2 |
| IBM284 | CP284, ebcdic-cp-es, csIBM284 | IBM NLS RM Vol2 SE09-8002-01, March 1990 | RFC1345, KXS2 |
| IBM285 | CP285, ebcdic-cp-gb, csIBM285 | IBM NLS RM Vol2 SE09-8002-01, March 1990 | RFC1345, KXS2 |
| IBM290 | cp290, EBCDIC-JP-kana, csIBM290 | IBM 3174 Character Set Ref, GA27-3831-02, March 1990 | RFC1345, KXS2 |
| IBM297 | cp297, ebcdic-cp-fr, csIBM297 | IBM NLS RM Vol2 SE09-8002-01, March 1990 | RFC1345, KXS2 |

| Charset tag | Aliases | Description | References |
|---|---|---|---|
| IBM420 | cp420, ebcdic-cp-ar1, csIBM420 | IBM NLS RM Vol2 SE09-8002-01, March 1990, IBM NLS RM p 11-11 | RFC1345, KXS2 |
| IBM423 | cp423, ebcdic-cp-gr, csIBM423 | IBM NLS RM Vol2 SE09-8002-01, March 1990 | RFC1345, KXS2 |
| IBM424 | cp424, ebcdic-cp-he, csIBM424 | IBM NLS RM Vol2 SE09-8002-01, March 1990 | RFC1345, KXS2 |
| IBM437 | cp437, 437, csPC8CodePage437 | IBM NLS RM Vol2 SE09-8002-01, March 1990 | RFC1345, KXS2 |
| IBM500 | CP500, ebcdic-cp-be, ebcdic-cp-ch, csIBM500 | IBM NLS RM Vol2 SE09-8002-01, March 1990 | RFC1345, KXS2 |
| IBM775 | cp775, csPC775Baltic | HP PCL 5 Comparison Guide (P/N 5021-0329) pp B-13, 1996 | HP-PCL5 |
| IBM850 | cp850, 850, csPC850Multilingual | IBM NLS RM Vol2 SE09-8002-01, March 1990 | RFC1345, KXS2 |
| IBM851 | cp851, 851, csIBM851 | IBM NLS RM Vol2 SE09-8002-01, March 1990 | RFC1345, KXS2 |
| IBM852 | cp852, 852, csPCp852 | IBM NLS RM Vol2 SE09-8002-01, March 1990 | RFC1345, KXS2 |
| IBM855 | cp855, 855, csIBM855 | IBM NLS RM Vol2 SE09-8002-01, March 1990 | RFC1345, KXS2 |
| IBM857 | cp857, 857, csIBM857 | IBM NLS RM Vol2 SE09-8002-01, March 1990 | RFC1345, KXS2 |
| IBM860 | cp860, 860, csIBM860 | IBM NLS RM Vol2 SE09-8002-01, March 1990 | RFC1345, KXS2 |
| IBM861 | cp861, 861, cp-is, csIBM861 | IBM NLS RM Vol2 SE09-8002-01, March 1990 | RFC1345, KXS2 |
| IBM862 | cp862, 862, csPC862LatinHebrew | IBM NLS RM Vol2 SE09-8002-01, March 1990 | RFC1345, KXS2 |
| IBM863 | cp863, 863, csIBM863 | IBM keyboard layouts and code pages, PN 07G4586, June 1991 | RFC1345, KXS2 |
| IBM864 | cp864, csIBM864 | IBM keyboard layouts and code pages, PN 07G4586, June 1991 | RFC1345, KXS2 |
| IBM865 | cp865, 865, csIBM865 | IBM DOS 3.3 Ref (Abridged), 94X9575, Feb 1987 | RFC1345, KXS2 |
| IBM866 | cp866, 866, csIBM866 | IBM NLDG Vol2 SE09-8002-03, August 1994 | Pond |
| IBM868 | CP868, cp-ar, csIBM868 | IBM NLS RM Vol2 SE09-8002-01, March 1990 | RFC1345, KXS2 |
| IBM869 | cp869, 869, cp-gr, csIBM869 | IBM keyboard layouts and code pages, PN 07G4586, June 1991 | RFC1345, KXS2 |
| IBM870 | CP870, ebcdic-cp-roece, ebcdic-cp-yu, csIBM870 | IBM NLS RM Vol2 SE09-8002-01, March 1990 | RFC1345, KXS2 |

| Charset tag | Aliases | Description | References |
|---|---|---|---|
| IBM871 | CP871, ebcdic-cp-is, csIBM871 | IBM NLS RM Vol2 SE09-8002-01, March 1990 | RFC1345, KXS2 |
| IBM880 | cp880, EBCDIC-Cyrillic, csIBM880 | IBM NLS RM Vol2 SE09-8002-01, March 1990 | RFC1345, KXS2 |
| IBM891 | cp891, csIBM891 | IBM NLS RM Vol2 SE09-8002-01, March 1990 | RFC1345, KXS2 |
| IBM903 | cp903, csIBM903 | IBM NLS RM Vol2 SE09-8002-01, March 1990 | RFC1345, KXS2 |
| IBM904 | cp904, 904, csIBBM904 | IBM NLS RM Vol2 SE09-8002-01, March 1990 | RFC1345, KXS2 |
| IBM905 | CP905, ebcdic-cp-tr, csIBM905 | IBM 3174 Character Set Ref, GA27-3831-02, March 1990 | RFC1345, KXS2 |
| IBM918 | CP918, ebcdic-cp-ar2, csIBM918 | IBM NLS RM Vol2 SE09-8002-01, March 1990 | RFC1345, KXS2 |
| IBM1026 | CP1026, csIBM1026 | IBM NLS RM Vol2 SE09-8002-01, March 1990 | RFC1345, KXS2 |
| EBCDIC-AT-DE | csIBMEBCDICATDE | IBM 3270 Char Set Ref Ch 10, GA27-2837-9, April 1987 | RFC1345, KXS2 |
| EBCDIC-AT-DE-A | csEBCDICATDEA | IBM 3270 Char Set Ref Ch 10, GA27-2837-9, April 1987 | RFC1345, KXS2 |
| EBCDIC-CA-FR | csEBCDICCAFR | IBM 3270 Char Set Ref Ch 10, GA27-2837-9, April 1987 | RFC1345, KXS2 |
| EBCDIC-DK-NO | csEBCDICDKNO | IBM 3270 Char Set Ref Ch 10, GA27-2837-9, April 1987 | RFC1345, KXS2 |
| EBCDIC-DK-NO-A | csEBCDICDKNOA | IBM 3270 Char Set Ref Ch 10, GA27-2837-9, April 1987 | RFC1345, KXS2 |
| EBCDIC-FI-SE | csEBCDICFISE | IBM 3270 Char Set Ref Ch 10, GA27-2837-9, April 1987 | RFC1345, KXS2 |
| EBCDIC-FI-SE-A | csEBCDICFISEA | IBM 3270 Char Set Ref Ch 10, GA27-2837-9, April 1987 | RFC1345, KXS2 |
| EBCDIC-FR | csEBCDICFR | IBM 3270 Char Set Ref Ch 10, GA27-2837-9, April 1987 | RFC1345, KXS2 |
| EBCDIC-IT | csEBCDICIT | IBM 3270 Char Set Ref Ch 10, GA27-2837-9, April 1987 | RFC1345, KXS2 |
| EBCDIC-PT | | IBM 3270 Char Set Ref Ch 10, GA27-2837-9, April 1987 | RFC1345, KXS2 |
| EBCDIC-ES | csEBCDICES | IBM 3270 Char Set Ref Ch 10, GA27-2837-9, April 1987 | RFC1345, KXS2 |
| EBCDIC-ES-A | csEBCDICESA | IBM 3270 Char Set Ref Ch 10, GA27-2837-9, April 1987 | RFC1345, KXS2 |

*Table H-1. IANA MIME charset tags (continued)*

| Charset tag | Aliases | Description | References |
|---|---|---|---|
| EBCDIC-ES-S | csEBCDICESS | IBM 3270 Char Set Ref Ch 10, GA27-2837-9, April 1987 | RFC1345, KXS2 |
| EBCDIC-UK | csEBCDICUK | IBM 3270 Char Set Ref Ch 10, GA27-2837-9, April 1987 | RFC1345, KXS2 |
| EBCDIC-US | csEBCDICUS | IBM 3270 Char Set Ref Ch 10, GA27-2837-9, April 1987 | RFC1345, KXS2 |
| UNKNOWN-8BIT | csUnknown8BiT | | RFC1428 |
| MNEMONIC | csMnemonic | RFC 1345, also known as "mnemonic+ascii+38" | RFC1345, KXS2 |
| MNEM | csMnem | RFC 1345, also known as "mnemonic+ascii+8200" | RFC1345, KXS2 |
| VISCII | csVISCII | RFC 1456 | RFC1456 |
| VIQR | csVIQR | RFC 1456 | RFC1456 |
| KOI8-R | csKOI8R | RFC 1489, based on GOST-19768-74, ISO-6937/8, INIS-Cyrillic, ISO-5427 | RFC1489 |
| KOI8-U | | RFC 2319 | RFC2319 |
| IBM00858 | CCSID00858, CP00858, PC-Multilingual-850+euro | IBM (see .../assignments/character-set-info/IBM00858) [Mahdi] | |
| IBM00924 | CCSID00924, CP00924, ebcdic-Latin9--euro | IBM (see .../assignments/character-set-info/IBM00924) [Mahdi] | |
| IBM01140 | CCSID01140, CP01140, ebcdic-us-37+euro | IBM (see .../assignments/character-set-info/IBM01140) [Mahdi] | |
| IBM01141 | CCSID01141, CP01141, ebcdic-de-273+euro | IBM (see .../assignments/character-set-info/IBM01141) [Mahdi] | |
| IBM01142 | CCSID01142, CP01142, ebcdic-dk-277+euro, ebcdic-no-277+euro | IBM (see .../assignments/character-set-info/IBM01142) [Mahdi] | |
| IBM01143 | CCSID01143, CP01143, ebcdic-fi-278+euro, ebcdic-se-278+euro | IBM (see .../assignments/character-set-info/IBM01143) [Mahdi] | |
| IBM01144 | CCSID01144, CP01144, ebcdic-it-280+euro | IBM (see .../assignments/character-set-info/IBM01144) [Mahdi] | |
| IBM01145 | CCSID01145, CP01145, ebcdic-es-284+euro | IBM (see .../assignments/character-set-info/IBM01145) [Mahdi] | |
| IBM01146 | CCSID01146, CP01146, ebcdic-gb-285+euro | IBM (see .../assignments/character-set-info/IBM01146) [Mahdi] | |
| IBM01147 | CCSID01147, CP01147, ebcdic-fr-297+euro | IBM (see .../assignments/character-set-info/IBM01147) [Mahdi] | |
| IBM01148 | CCSID01148, CP01148, ebcdic-international-500+euro | IBM (see .../assignments/character-set-info/IBM01148) [Mahdi] | |

| Charset tag | Aliases | Description | References |
|---|---|---|---|
| IBM01149 | CCSID01149, CP01149, ebcdic-is-871+euro | IBM (see .../assignments/character-set-info/IBM01149) [Mahdi] | |
| Big5-HKSCS | None | See (.../assignments/character-set-info/Big5-HKSCS) [Yick] | |
| UNICODE-1-1 | csUnicode11 | RFC 1641 | RFC1641 |
| SCSU | None | SCSU (see .../assignments/character-set-info/SCSU) [Scherer] | |
| UTF-7 | None | RFC 2152 | RFC2152 |
| UTF-16BE | None | RFC 2781 | RFC2781 |
| UTF-16LE | None | RFC 2781 | RFC2781 |
| UTF-16 | None | RFC 2781 | RFC2781 |
| UNICODE-1-1-UTF-7 | csUnicode11UTF7 | RFC 1642 | RFC1642 |
| UTF-8 | | RFC 2279 | RFC2279 |
| iso-8859-13 | | ISO (see ...assignments/character-set-info/iso-8859-13)[Tumasonis] | |
| iso-8859-14 | iso-ir-199, ISO_8859-14:1998, ISO_8859-14, latin8, iso-celtic, l8 | ISO (see ...assignments/character-set-info/iso-8859-14) [Simonsen] | |
| ISO-8859-15 | ISO_8859-15 | ISO | |
| JIS_Encoding | csJISEncoding | JIS X 0202-1991; uses ISO 2022 escape sequences to shift code sets, as documented in JIS X 0202-1991 | |
| Shift_JIS | MS_Kanji, csShiftJIS | This charset is an extension of csHalfWidthKatakana—it adds graphic characters in JIS X 0208. The CCSs areJIS X0201:1997 and JIS X0208:1997. The complete definition is shown in Appendix 1 of JISX0208:1997. This charset can be used for the top-level media type "text". | |
| EUC-JP | Extended_UNIX_Code_Packed_Format_for_Japanese, csEUCPkdFmtJapanese | Standardized by OSF, UNIX International, and UNIX Systems Laboratories Pacific. Uses ISO 2022 rules to select code set. code set 0: US-ASCII (a single 7-bit byte set); code set 1: JIS X0208-1990 (a double 8-bit byte set) restricted to A0–FF in both bytes; code set 2: half-width katakana (a single 7-bit byte set) requiring SS2 as the character prefix; code set 3: JIS X0212-1990 (a double 7-bit byte set) restricted to A0–FF in both bytes requiring SS3 as the character prefix. | |

| Charset tag | Aliases | Description | References |
|---|---|---|---|
| Extended_UNIX_Code_ Fixed_Width_for_ Japanese | csEUCFixWidJapanese | Used in Japan. Each character is 2 octets. code set 0: US-ASCII (a single 7-bit byte set), 1st byte = 00, 2nd byte = 20−7E; code set 1: JIS X0208-1990 (a double 7-bit byte set) restricted to A0−FF in both bytes; code set 2: half-width katakana (a single 7-bit byte set), 1st byte = 00, 2nd byte = A0−FF; code set 3: JIS X0212-1990 (a double 7-bit byte set) restricted to A0−FF in the first byte and 21−7E in the second byte. | |
| ISO-10646-UCS-Basic | csUnicodeASCII | ASCII subset of Unicode. Basic Latin = collection 1. See ISO 10646, Appendix A. | |
| ISO-10646-Unicode-Latin1 | csUnicodeLatin1, ISO-10646 | ISO Latin-1 subset of Unicode. Basic Latin and Latin-1. Supplement = collections 1 and 2. See ISO 10646, Appendix A, and RFC 1815. | |
| ISO-10646-J-1 | | ISO 10646 Japanese. See RFC 1815. | |
| ISO-Unicode-IBM-1261 | csUnicodeIBM1261 | IBM Latin-2, -3, -5, Extended Presentation Set, GCSGID: 1261 | |
| ISO-Unicode-IBM-1268 | csUnidoceIBM1268 | IBM Latin-4 Extended Presentation Set, GCSGID: 1268 | |
| ISO-Unicode-IBM-1276 | csUnicodeIBM1276 | IBM Cyrillic Greek Extended Presentation Set, GCSGID: 1276 | |
| ISO-Unicode-IBM-1264 | csUnicodeIBM1264 | IBM Arabic Presentation Set, GCSGID: 1264 | |
| ISO-Unicode-IBM-1265 | csUnicodeIBM1265 | IBM Hebrew Presentation Set, GCSGID: 1265 | |
| ISO-8859-1-Windows-3.0-Latin-1 | csWindows30Latin1 | Extended ISO 8859-1 Latin-1 for Windows 3.0. PCL Symbol Set ID: 9U. | HP-PCL5 |
| ISO-8859-1-Windows-3.1-Latin-1 | csWindows31Latin1 | Extended ISO 8859-1 Latin-1 for Windows 3.1. PCL Symbol Set ID: 19U. | HP-PCL5 |
| ISO-8859-2-Windows-Latin-2 | csWindows31Latin2 | Extended ISO 8859-2. Latin-2 for Windows 3.1. PCL Symbol Set ID: 9E. | HP-PCL5 |
| ISO-8859-9-Windows-Latin-5 | csWindows31Latin5 | Extended ISO 8859-9. Latin-5 for Windows 3.1. PCL Symbol Set ID: 5T. | HP-PCL5 |
| Adobe-Standard-Encoding | csAdobeStandardEncoding | PostScript Language Reference Manual. PCL Symbol Set ID: 10J. | Adobe |
| Ventura-US | csVenturaUS | Ventura US-ASCII plus characters typically used in publishing, such as pilcrow, copyright, registered, trademark, section, dagger, and double dagger in the range A0 (hex) to FF (hex). PCL Symbol Set ID: 14J. | HP-PCL5 |

| Charset tag | Aliases | Description | References |
|---|---|---|---|
| Ventura-International | csVenturaInternational | Ventura International. ASCII plus coded characters similar to Roman8. PCL Symbol Set ID: 13J. | HP-PCL5 |
| PC8-Danish-Norwegian | csPC8DanishNorwegian | PC Danish Norwegian 8-bit PC set for Danish Norwegian. PCL Symbol Set ID: 11U. | HP-PCL5 |
| PC8-Turkish | csPC8Turkish | PC Latin Turkish. PCL Symbol Set ID: 9T. | HP-PCL5 |
| IBM-Symbols | csIBMSymbols | Presentation Set, CPGID: 259 | IBM-CIDT |
| IBM-Thai | csIBMThai | Presentation Set, CPGID: 838 | IBM-CIDT |
| HP-Legal | csHPLegal | PCL 5 Comparison Guide, Hewlett-Packard, HP part number 5961-0510, October 1992. PCL Symbol Set ID: 1U. | HP-PCL5 |
| HP-Pi-font | csHPPiFont | PCL 5 Comparison Guide, Hewlett-Packard, HP part number 5961-0510, October 1992. PCL Symbol Set ID: 15U. | HP-PCL5 |
| HP-Math8 | csHPMath8 | PCL 5 Comparison Guide, Hewlett-Packard, HP part number 5961-0510, October 1992. PCL Symbol Set ID: 8M. | HP-PCL5 |
| Adobe-Symbol-Encoding | csHPPSMath | PostScript Language Reference Manual. PCL Symbol Set ID: 5M. | Adobe |
| HP-DeskTop | csHPDesktop | PCL 5 Comparison Guide, Hewlett-Packard, HP part number 5961-0510, October 1992. PCL Symbol Set ID: 7J. | HP-PCL5 |
| Ventura-Math | csVenturaMath | PCL 5 Comparison Guide, Hewlett-Packard, HP part number 5961-0510, October 1992. PCL Symbol Set ID: 6M. | HP-PCL5 |
| Microsoft-Publishing | csMicrosoftPublishing | PCL 5 Comparison Guide, Hewlett-Packard, HP part number 5961-0510, October 1992. PCL Symbol Set ID: 6J. | HP-PCL5 |
| Windows-31J | csWindows31J | Windows Japanese. A further extension of Shift_JIS to include NEC special characters (Row 13), NEC selection of IBM extensions (Rows 89 to 92), and IBM extensions (Rows 115 to 119). The CCSs are JIS X0201:1997, JIS X0208:1997, and these extensions. This charset can be used for the top-level media type "text", but it is of limited or specialized use (see RFC 2278). PCL Symbol Set ID: 19K. | |
| GB2312 | csGB2312 | Chinese for People's Republic of China (PRC) mixed 1-byte, 2-byte set: 20–7E = 1-byte ASCII; A1–FE = 2-byte PRC Kanji. See GB 2312-80. PCL Symbol Set ID: 18C. | |

*Table H-1. IANA MIME charset tags (continued)*

| Charset tag | Aliases | Description | References |
|---|---|---|---|
| Big5 | csBig5 | Chinese for Taiwan Multibyte set. PCL Symbol Set id: 18T. | |
| windows-1250 | | Microsoft (see .../character-set-info/windows-1250) [Lazhintseva] | |
| windows-1251 | | Microsoft (see .../character-set-info/windows-1251) [Lazhintseva] | |
| windows-1252 | | Microsoft (see .../character-set-info/windows-1252) [Wendt] | |
| windows-1253 | | Microsoft (see .../character-set-info/windows-1253) [Lazhintseva] | |
| windows-1254 | | Microsoft (see .../character-set-info/windows-1254) [Lazhintseva] | |
| windows-1255 | | Microsoft (see .../character-set-info/windows-1255) [Lazhintseva] | |
| windows-1256 | | Microsoft (see .../character-set-info/windows-1256) [Lazhintseva] | |
| windows-1257 | | Microsoft (see .../character-set-info/windows-1257) [Lazhintseva] | |
| windows-1258 | | Microsoft (see .../character-set-info/windows-1258) [Lazhintseva] | |
| TIS-620 | | Thai Industrial Standards Institute (TISI) | [Tantsetthi] |
| HZ-GB-2312 | | RFC 1842, RFC 1843 [RFC1842, RFC1843] | |

# Index

## Symbols

: (colon), use in headers, 47
= (equals sign), base-64 encoding, 572
/~ (slash-tilde), 122

## Numbers

8-bit identity encoding, 382
100 Continue status code, 59, 60
100-199 status codes, 59–60, 505
200-299 status codes, 61, 505
300-399 status codes, 61–64, 506
400-499 status codes, 65–66, 506
500-599 status codes, 66, 507
2MSL (maximum segment lifetime), 85

## A

absolute URLs, 30
Accept headers, 69, 508
    robots and, 225
Accept-Charset headers, 371, 375, 509
    MIME charset encoding tags and, 374
Accept-Encoding headers, 509
Accept-Instance-Manipulation headers, 367
Accept-Language headers, 371, 385, 510
    content negotiation and, 398
Accept-Ranges headers, 510
access controls, 124
    proxy authentication, 156
access proxies, 137
advertising, hit counts and caches, 194–196
age and freshness lifetime, 188
Age headers, 510
agents, 19

algorithms
    aging and freshness, 187–194
    document age calculation, 189–194
    instance-manipulation algorithms, 367
    LM-Factor, 184
    message digest algorithms, 291–294
        symmetric authentication, 298
    Nagle's algorithm, 84
    redirection, enhanced DNS-based, 457
    resource-discovery algorithm
        (WPAD), 143, 465
    RSA, 317
aliases (URLs), 219
Allow headers, 159, 511
<allprop> element, 437
anonymizers, 136
anycast addressing, 457
Apache web servers, 110
    content negotiation, 399
        MultiViews directive, 400
        type-map files, 399
    DirectoryIndex configuration
        directive, 123
    document root, setting, 121
    HostnameLookups configuration
        directive, 115
    HTTP headers, control of, 186
    IdentityCheck configuration
        directive, 116
    magic typing, 126
APIs (application programming
        interfaces), 203
    server extensions, 205
    web services and, 205

We'd like to hear your suggestions for improving our indexes. Send email to *index@oreilly.com*.

multiprocess, multithreaded web
servers, 118
Multipurpose Internet Mail Extensions (see
MIME; MIME types)
<multistatus> element, 438
MultiViews directive, 400
must-revalidate response headers, 183

# N

Nagle's algorithm, 84
namespace management, 439–444
methods used for, 440
status codes, 443
namespaces, 388
language subtags, 387–389
XML, 430
NAT (Network Address Translation), 460
NECP (Network Element Control
Protocol), 461
negotiation headers, 71
Netscape Extended 2 Log Format, 487–489
Netscape Extended Log Format, 486
Netscape Navigator
cookies
storage, 265
Version 0, 269
language preference configuration, 389
Network Address Translation (NAT), 460
network bottlenecks, 161
Network Element Control Protocol
(NECP), 461
network exchange proxies, 137
news scheme, 39
no-cache response headers, 182
nonces, 289–298
next nonce pregeneration, 297
reuse, 297
selection, 298
time-synchronized generation, 297
no-store response headers, 182
.nsconfig, 428

# O

object types, HTTP-NG, 252
one-way digests, 288
one-way hashes, 291
functions, 289
opaquelocktoken scheme, 433, 434
OpenSSL, 328–335
example client, 329–335

OPTIONS method, 57, 445
requests, 159
response headers to, 445
origin servers, 420
outbound messages, 43
outbound proxies, 138
Overwrite headers, 432, 442

# P

PAC files, 142
autodiscovery, 465
PAC (Proxy Auto-Configuration)
protocol, 142, 463
parallel connections, 88–90
impression of speed, 90
loading speed, 88
open connection limits, 90
persistent connections vs., 91
parameters component, URLs, 28
parent and child relationships, 138
parent caches, 169
password component, URLs, 27
passwords
digest authentication password file,
risks, 305
digest authentication, security, 287
path component, URLs, 28
Perl code for interaction with robots.txt
files, 235
Perl web server, 111
persistent connections, 90–99
Content-Length headers and, 345
keep-alive connections
(HTTP/1.0+), 91–96
parallel connections vs., 91
restrictions and rules, 98
persistent uniform resource locators
(PURLs), 40
pipelined connections, 99
plaintext, security and, 310
port component, URLS, 27
port exhaustion, 85
port numbers, 13, 77
default values, 13
virtual hosting and, 415
POST method, 55
POST requests, FrontPage and, 425
Pragma headers, 68, 182, 521
Pragma: no-cache headers, 182
precompiled dictionary attacks, 305

# R

# About the Authors

**David Gourley** is the Chief Technology Officer of Endeca, where he leads the research and development of Endeca's products. Endeca develops Internet and intranet information-access solutions that provide new ways to navigate and explore enterprise data. Prior to working at Endeca, David was a member of the founding engineering team at Inktomi, where he helped develop Inktomi's Internet search database and was a key developer of Inktomi's web caching products.

David earned a B.A. in Computer Science from the University of California at Berkeley, and he holds several patents in web technologies.

**Brian Totty** was most recently the Vice President of R&D at Inktomi Corporation (a company he helped found in 1996), where he led research and development of web caching, streaming media, and Internet search technologies. Formerly, he was a scientist at Silicon Graphics, where he designed and optimized software for high-performance networking and supercomputing systems. Before that, he held an engineering position at Apple Computer's Advanced Technology Group.

Brian holds a Ph.D. in Computer Science from the University of Illinois at Urbana-Champaign and a B.S. degree in Computer Science and Electrical Engineering from MIT, where he received the Organick award for computer systems research. He also has developed and taught award-winning courses on Internet technology for the University of California Extension system.

**Marjorie Sayer** writes about network caching software at Inktomi Corporation. After earning M.A. and Ph.C. degrees in Mathematics at the University of California at Berkeley, she worked on mathematics curriculum reform. Since 1990 she has written about energy resource management, parallel systems software, telephony, and networking.

**Sailu Reddy** currently leads the development of embedded performance-enhancing HTTP proxies at Inktomi Corporation. Sailu has been developing complex software systems for 12 years and has been deeply involved in web infrastructure research and development since 1995. He was a core engineer of Netscape's first web server and web proxy products and of several following generations. His technical experience includes HTTP applications, data compression techniques, database engines, and collaboration management. Sailu earned an M.S. in Information Systems from the University of Arizona and holds several patents in web technologies.

**Anshu Aggarwal** is a Director of Engineering at Inktomi Corporation. He leads the protocol-processing engineering teams for Inktomi's web caching products, and he has been involved in the design of web technologies at Inktomi since 1997. Anshu holds M.S. and Ph.D. degrees in Computer Science from the University of Colorado at Boulder, specializing in memory-consistent techniques for distributed multiprocessor machines. He also holds M.S. and B.S. degrees in Electrical Engineering. Anshu is the author of several technical papers and holds two patents.

# Colophon

Our look is the result of reader comments, our own experimentation, and feedback from distribution channels. Distinctive covers complement our distinctive approach to technical topics, breathing personality and life into potentially dry subjects.

The animal on the cover of *HTTP: The Definitive Guide* is a thirteen-lined ground squirrel (*Spermophilus tridecemlineatus*), common to central North America. True to its name, the thirteen-lined ground squirrel has thirteen stripes with rows of light spots that run the length of its back. Its color pattern blends into its surroundings, protecting it from predators. Thirteen-lined ground squirrels are members of the squirrel family, which includes chipmunks, ground squirrels, tree squirrels, prairie dogs, and woodchucks. They are similar in size to the eastern chipmunk but smaller than the common gray squirrel, averaging about 11 inches in length (including a 5–6 inch tail).

Thirteen-lined ground squirrels go into hibernation in October and emerge in late March or early April. Each female usually produces one litter of 7–10 young each May. The young leave the burrows at four to five weeks of age and are fully grown at six weeks. Ground squirrels prefer open areas with short grass and well-drained sandy or loamy soils for burrows, and they avoid wooded areas—mowed lawns, golf courses, and parks are common habitats.

Ground squirrels can cause problems when they create burrows, dig up newly planted seeds, and damage vegetable gardens. However, they are important prey to several predators, including badgers, coyotes, hawks, weasels, and various snakes, and they benefit humans directly by feeding on many harmful weeds, weed seeds, and insects.

Rachel Wheeler was the production editor and copyeditor for *HTTP: The Definitive Guide*. Leanne Soylemez, Sarah Sherman, and Mary Anne Weeks Mayo provided quality control, and Derek Di Matteo and Brian Sawyer provided production assistance. John Bickelhaupt wrote the index.

Ellie Volckhausen designed the cover of this book, based on a series design by Edie Freedman. The cover image is an original illustration created by Lorrie LeJeune. Emma Colby produced the cover layout with QuarkXPress 4.1 using Adobe's ITC Garamond font.

David Futato and Melanie Wang designed the interior layout, based on a series design by David Futato. Joe Wizda prepared the files for production in FrameMaker 5.5.6. The text font is Linotype Birka; the heading font is Adobe Myriad Condensed; and the code font is LucasFont's TheSans Mono Condensed. The illustrations that appear in the book were produced by Robert Romano and Jessamyn Read using Macromedia FreeHand 9 and Adobe Photoshop 6. This colophon was written by Rachel Wheeler.